*Revolution and War*

A volume in the series

CORNELL STUDIES IN SECURITY AFFAIRS

*edited by* Robert J. Art, Robert Jervis, *and* Stephen M. Walt

A complete list of titles in the series appears at the end of this book.

# Revolution and War

STEPHEN M. WALT

*Cornell University Press*

ITHACA AND LONDON

First published 1996 by Cornell University Press


Printed in the United States of America


♾ The paper in this book meets the minimum requirements of the American National Standard for Information Sciences— Permanence of Paper for Printed Library Materials, ANSI Z39.48–1984.


Library of Congress Cataloging-in-Publication Data

Walt, Stephen M.
    Revolution and war / Stephen M. Walt.
        p.   cm. — (Cornell studies in security affairs)
    Includes bibliographical references and index.
    ISBN 0-8014-3205-7 (alk. paper). — ISBN 0-8014-8297-6 (pk. : alk. paper)
    1. World politics.   2. Revolutions—History.   3. War.   4. Revolutions—Philosophy.   5. Politics and war.   I. Title.   II. Series.
D21.3.W27   1996
303.6'4  dc20                                                      95-45006

# Contents

[v]

# *Preface*

Revolution and war are among the most dramatic and important events in political life, yet few of the countless works on either topic devote much attention to the relationship between them. Students of revolution generally focus on the causes of revolution or its domestic consequences, examining its international aspects only insofar as they shaped the origins or course of the revolution itself. Students of international politics, by contrast, tend to take the state for granted and spend little time on those moments in history where one state structure dissolves and a new one arises in its place. With a few notable exceptions, therefore, the literatures on revolution and war do not overlap. Indeed, the two fields do not even engage in much of a dialogue.

This book is an attempt to bridge the gap. Specifically, I seek to explain why revolutions intensify the security competition between states and sharply increase the risk of war. I do so by examining the international consequences of the French, Russian, Iranian, American, Mexican, Turkish, and Chinese revolutions, drawing both on the theoretical and empirical literature on revolutions and on several important ideas from international relations theory.

My interest in this subject stems in part from a broader interest in U.S. foreign policy. Throughout the Cold War, the United States repeatedly sought to prevent revolutionary movements from coming to power and often tried to overthrow them when they did. U.S. relations with most revolutionary states were predictably poor, even when these states were neither Marxist nor pro-Soviet. The U.S. experience was hardly unique: revolutions have been equally troublesome for others. By exploring how and why revolutions lead to war, therefore, I hope to provide practical guidance for national leaders who face an unexpected revolutionary upheaval.

The perspective I adopt is based on the familiar realist paradigm. I assume that states exist in an anarchic environment, which leads them to place a very high value on security. In contrast to neorealist *balance-of-power* theory, however, my focus is not limited to the distribution of aggregate power. I also examine the ways that domestic politics and ideology shape how national leaders evaluate their security environment and how they choose among alternative courses of action. As we shall see, one cannot understand the international effects of a mass revolution by focusing solely on the balance of power or the constraining effects of international anarchy. Nor can these factors explain why revolutionary states adopt particular policies, why other states regard them as especially dangerous, or why revolutionary regimes are unwilling to abandon cherished international objectives even when their pursuit entails high costs. The balance of power is not irrelevant, but it is neither the sole nor the most important factor in explaining how revolutions affect international politics.

Revolutions, I argue, intensify security competition and increase the probability of war by altering each side's perceptions of the *balance of threats*. In addition to affecting the balance of power, a revolution also fosters malign perceptions of intent and a perverse combination of insecurity and overconfidence, based primarily on the possibility that revolution will spread to other countries. Although war does not occur in every case, strong pressures for war are always present and, invariably, the level of security competition increases significantly.

Much of this book takes the form of detailed narrative history. I found I could neither understand nor explain these events without exploring them in some depth. Its length also reflects my own fascination with the events I was investigating—and if a great revolution is not fascinating, what is?—as well as my belief that valid empirical tests require a sophisticated understanding of the historical record. As the evolutionary biologist Stephen Jay Gould reminds us, "Theories must sink a huge anchor in details."

Revolutions are highly partisan events, and scholarship on them often reflects these political biases. To compensate, I have tried to document my claims as extensively as possible, relying upon multiple sources and the most widely accepted historical accounts. A number of these works, such as T. C. W. Blanning's superb *Origins of the French Revolutionary Wars* and E. H. Carr's masterful *History of Soviet Russia*, both guided my interpretation of particular cases and shaped my thinking on the broader subject of revolution and war.

Like most scholarly endeavors, this book took longer than I expected. Yet I never found the subject boring; indeed, had I been less captivated by the drama of the events I was investigating, the book surely would have been finished more quickly. There is much that I still find puzzling about these events and much that I will never fully comprehend. In the end, this volume is simply my best effort to add to our evolving understanding of the phenomena of revolution and war.

I am grateful to the many scholars who have offered advice and criticism on some or all of the manuscript. In particular, I thank Said Amir Arjomand, George Breslauer, Richard Cottam, Thomas Christensen, Steve David, Michael Desch, Jim Fearon, Markus Fischer, Gregory Gause, Alexander George, Charles Glaser, Avery Goldstein, Judith Goldstein, Jack Goldstone, Louisa Bertch Green, Robert Johnson, Friedrich Katz, David Laitin, Colin Lucas, Bernard Manin, Andrew Moravcsik, Norman Nie, Kenneth Oye, M. J. Peterson, John Padgett, R. K. Ramazani, Paul Schroeder, Jack Snyder, George Steinmetz, Ronald Suny, Sidney Tarrow, Stephen Van Evera, John Waterbury, Dali Yang, and Marvin Zonis. I am especially indebted to John Mearsheimer, whose comments were extremely helpful despite his basic disagreement with my argument. I am also grateful to various research assistants who helped me along the way, especially Elizabeth Boyd, James Marquardt, Lisa Moses, Julie Alig, and David Edelstein.

Portions of the book were presented at seminars at the Center for Science and International Affairs and the John M. Olin Institute for Strategic Studies, both at Harvard University, and at the University of Michigan, the Brookings Institution, the Carnegie Endowment for International Peace, the Department of Political Science at the Massachusetts Institute of Technology, the Department of Sociology at Northwestern University, and the Workshop on Comparative Politics and Historical Sociology at the University of Chicago. I am grateful for these opportunities to try out my ideas, and I thank the participants at these meetings for many helpful comments. Their suggestions added to my labors, but they also made this a better book.

This project would not have been possible without generous grants from the John D. and Catherine T. MacArthur Foundation, the Carnegie Endowment for International Peace, the U.S. Institute of Peace, and the Division of Social Sciences at the University of Chicago. I did the initial work as a resident associate at the Carnegie Endowment and as a guest scholar in the Foreign Policy Studies Program at the Brookings Institution, and I thank the heads of these two institutions, Thomas Hughes and John D. Steinbruner, for providing supportive and stimulating environments in which to work.

An earlier and somewhat different version of my central argument was published as "Revolution and War" in volume 44 of *World Politics* (April 1992). I am grateful to Johns Hopkins University Press for permission to adapt the material here. I also express my thanks to Roger Haydon of Cornell University Press, who answered my various inquiries with his usual combination of sympathy and wit.

I dedicate this book to my wife, Rebecca Stone, to whom I owe just about everything.

STEPHEN M. WALT

*Chicago, Illinois*

*Revolution and War*

# [1]

## *Introduction*

Like professional revolutionaries, social scientists seldom clearly understand quite what they are doing. But, again like professional revolutionaries, they do sometimes attain a relatively clear grasp of the implications of what they have already done; and sometimes at least, this constitutes a marked improvement on the achievements of their immediate predecessors.

—John Dunn

In this book I examine the international impact of revolutionary change, focusing primarily on the relationship between revolution and war. My chief objective is to explain why revolutions increase the intensity of security competition between states and thereby create a high probability of war. Because war does not occur in every case, my second objective is to clarify why certain revolutions lead to all-out war while others stop at the brink.

Although major revolutions are relatively rare, this subject is worth studying for at least two reasons. First, revolutions are more than just critical events in the history of individual nations; they are usually watershed events in international politics. Revolutions cause sudden shifts in the balance of power, alter the pattern of international alignments, cast doubt on existing agreements and diplomatic norms, and provide inviting opportunities for other states to improve their positions. They also demonstrate that novel ways of organizing social and political life are possible and often inspire sympathizers in other countries. Thus, although revolutions by definition occur within a single country, their impact is rarely confined to one state alone.[1]

Indeed, revolutions usually disrupt the international system in important ways. According to one quantitative study, for example, states that undergo a "revolutionary" regime change are nearly twice as likely to be involved in war as are states that emerge from an "evolutionary" political process.[2] And

---

[1] Elbaki Hermassi, "Toward a Comparative Study of Revolutions," *Comparative Studies in Society and History* 18, no. 2 (1976).

[2] Zeev Maoz, "Joining the Club of Nations: Political Development and International Conflict, 1816–1876," *International Studies Quarterly* 33, no. 2 (1989); and also see Jonathan R. Adelman, *Revolution, Armies, and War: A Political History* (Boulder, Colo.: Lynne Rienner, 1985), 3–6.

as the cases presented in this volume will show, revolutions invariably trigger intense policy debates in other countries. These disputes, typically divided between advocates of accommodation and advocates of intervention against the new regime, are strikingly similar, whether it is the European response to the French or Bolshevik revolutions or the U.S. reaction to the revolutions in Mexico, Russia, China, Cuba, Nicaragua, or Iran. Yet despite the obvious relevance of this problem for policy makers, little effort has been made to assemble hypotheses and evidence that might resolve (or at least advance) the debate.

The need for a more informed debate is also apparent from the poor track record of U.S. policy in this area. Fear of revolution played a major role in shaping U.S. foreign policy throughout the Cold War, but U.S. responses to revolutionary change during this period were rarely very successful.[3] Although the United States occasionally made modest efforts to reach a modus vivendi with new revolutionary governments (generally in the latter stages of the revolutionary process), it usually regarded these groups with suspicion, if not outright hostility, having sought to prevent them from gaining power in the first place and still hoping to remove them from power after they obtained it. Not surprisingly, U.S. relations with most revolutionary regimes have been quite poor.[4] Hard-liners blame these failures on ill-advised efforts at appeasement, while moderates attribute the problem primarily to exaggerated U.S. hostility. Although U.S. policy makers did achieve their objectives in a few cases (such as the overthrow of the New Jewel Movement in Grenada in 1983), it is hard to view U.S. policy as a success story.[5]

The foreign policies of most revolutionary states have been equally unsuccessful. Many of these regimes were suspicious of the West in general

---

[3] See Robert Pastor, "Preempting Revolutions: The Boundaries of U.S. Influence," *International Security* 15, no. 4 (1991) and *Condemned to Repetition: The United States and Nicaragua* (Princeton: Princeton University Press, 1987); Gary Sick, *All Fall Down: America's Tragic Encounter with Iran* (New York: Random House, 1985); and Robert Packenham, *Liberal America and the Third World: Political Development Ideas in Foreign Aid and Social Science* (Princeton: Princeton University Press, 1973), esp. 140–42.

[4] As the Mexican, Russian, and Turkish cases will show, this problem predates the Cold War.

[5] For examples of these contending views, see W. Anthony Lake, "Wrestling with Third World Radical Regimes: Theory and Practice," in *U.S. Foreign Policy and the Third World: Agenda 1985–86*, ed. John W. Sewell, Richard E. Feinberg, and Valeriana Kallab (New Brunswick, N.J.: Transaction Books, 1985); Richard E. Feinberg and Kenneth A. Oye, "After the Fall: U.S. Policy toward Radical Regimes," *World Policy Journal* 1, no. 1 (1983); Cole Blasier, *The Hovering Giant: U.S. Responses to Revolutionary Change in Latin America* (Pittsburgh: University of Pittsburgh Press, 1976); Walter LaFeber, *Inevitable Revolutions: The United States in Central America* (New York: W. W. Norton, 1984); W. Scott Thompson, "Choosing to Win," *Foreign Policy* no. 43 (summer 1981); and Douglas J. Macdonald, *Adventures in Chaos: American Intervention for Reform in the Third World* (Cambridge: Harvard University Press, 1992).

[2]

and the United States in particular, but most sought to avoid an immediate military confrontation. Often, however, they were unable to do so, suggesting that policy makers on both sides did not fully understand the problems they would encounter when dealing with each other, which in turn points to the need for more informed policy guidance. Providing that guidance is a major goal of this book.

In addition to these practical benefits, examining the international consequences of revolutions should yield important theoretical insights as well. In particular, exploring the connection between revolution and war can illuminate both the strengths and weaknesses of realism and help us identify which strands of realism are most useful.[6] For example, the "neorealist" version of realism developed by Kenneth Waltz focuses on the constraining effects of the international system (defined in terms of the distribution of power) and downplays the impact of domestic politics, ideology, and other unit-level factors.[7] Revolutions are a distinctly unit-level phenomenon, however. The obvious question is whether the constraining effects of anarchy will be more powerful than the unit-level forces unleashed by a revolutionary upheaval. For neorealists, the answer is straightforward: because international politics is regarded as a realm in which security takes precedence over other goals, Waltz predicts that revolutionary states will moderate their radical ambitions in order to avoid being isolated or punished by the self-interested actions of others. In other words, they will be "socialized" by the system.[8]

Neorealism also implies that revolutions will affect a state's foreign policy primarily through their influence on the balance of power. When a revolution occurs, both the new regime and the other major powers are forced to recalculate the available possibilities and adjust their foreign policies to take account of these shifts. By altering the distribution of power in the system, a revolution can yield far-reaching effects on the conduct of the new regime and the behavior of other states.

---

[6] Stephen Van Evera identifies four main strands of realism in his *Causes of War,* vol. 1: *The Structure of Power and the Roots of War* (Ithaca: Cornell University Press, forthcoming), chap. 1. For other discussions of the basic features of the realist paradigm, see my "Alliances, Threats, and U.S. Grand Strategy: A Reply to Kaufman and Labs," *Security Studies* 1, no. 2 (1992), 473–74 n. 1, and Robert O. Keohane, "Theory of World Politics: Structural Realism and Beyond," in *Neorealism and Its Critics,* ed. Robert O. Keohane (New York: Columbia University Press, 1986).

[7] Kenneth N. Waltz, *Theory of International Politics* (Reading, Mass.: Addison-Wesley, 1979).

[8] Waltz acknowledges that state behavior is affected by system-level and unit-level factors but believes the system-level to be more important. In his words, "state behavior varies more with differences of power than with differences in ideology, in internal structure of property relations, or in governmental form. In self-help systems, the pressures of competition weigh more heavily than ideological preferences or internal political pressures." See his "Reflections on *Theory of International Politics:* A Response to My Critics," in Keohane, *Neorealism and Its Critics,* 329; and *Theory of International Politics,* 127–28.

As we shall see, neorealism provides a useful "first cut" at understanding how revolutions affect international politics. Like any theory, however, it also leaves important gaps. To explain the link between revolution and war, for example, one could argue that increased power would make a revolutionary state more aggressive, while declining power would tempt others to exploit its vulnerability. But the opposite logic is equally persuasive: increased power might enhance the new regime's security and obviate the need to expand, while declining power would reduce the threat that others face and thus their inclination to use force. By itself, therefore, a shift in the balance of power cannot explain decisions for war.[9]

In addition, although it correctly emphasizes that security is the highest aim of states, neorealism does not tell us how a specific state will choose to pursue this goal. As a result, it offers limited practical guidance to leaders who must grapple with a revolutionary upheaval. The knowledge that revolutionary states will eventually moderate their conduct may be comforting, but it is of little value for those who are forced to deal with the new regime's ambitions in the here and now. Will other states be better off by isolating the new regime, befriending it, or overthrowing it? Will a revolutionary state be more secure if it tempers its revolutionary objectives so as not to provoke opposition from others or if it tries to sponsor revolutions elsewhere as a means of undermining potential enemies and creating new allies?

We can answer these puzzles by recognizing that revolutions affect more than just the aggregate distribution of power. They also alter perceptions of intent and beliefs about the relative strength of offense and defense. Beliefs about the intentions of other states and their specific capacity to do harm will exert a powerful influence on the foreign policy of the revolutionary state, and the responses of other states will be similarly affected by their perceptions of the new regime. To understand the international consequences of revolutions, in short, we must move beyond the relatively spare world of neorealist theory and incorporate unit-level factors as well.

Finally, examining the foreign policies of revolutionary states may also shed some light on the merits of critical theory as an approach to international politics. Despite the important differences among critical theorists, they all emphasize the role of language and social processes in shaping actors' goals, purposes, and self-understandings, and they focus on how discourse, norms, and identities affect the behavior of actors within a social setting.[10] Revolution should be an especially interesting phenomenon from

---

[9] See Robert Gilpin, "Theories of Hegemonic War," in *The Origins and Prevention of Major Wars*, ed. Robert I. Rotberg and Theodore K. Rabb (Cambridge: Cambridge University Press, 1989), 26; and Jack S. Levy, "Declining Power and the Preventive Motivation for War," *World Politics* 40, no. 1 (1987).

[10] This summary of the critical theory perspective on international relations is based on, among others, Mark Hoffman, "Critical Theory and the Inter-Paradigm Debate,"

this perspective, because state identities are rapidly and radically transformed by such events. If actors' identities and purposes are powerful determinants of behavior, then the ideas and values embodied in a revolution should have an especially strong influence on the behavior of the new regime. Thus, where neorealism predicts continuity (within a certain range), critical theory predicts dramatic and enduring change (despite the presence of external constraints). In broad terms, studying revolutions may help us assess the relative merits of these two perspectives as well.

The central question that informs my work here is whether revolutions encourage states to view the external environment in ways that intensify their security competition and make war appear to be a more attractive option. In the pages that follow, I argue that this is precisely what they do. First, revolutions usually exert dramatic effects on a state's overall capabilities, especially its ability to fight. Even if the revolutionary state is not regarded as dangerous, foreign states may still be tempted to intervene to improve their own positions or to prevent other powers from doing the same thing. As neorealism suggests, therefore, revolutions foster conflict by creating seemingly inviting windows of opportunity.

Second, revolutions often bring to power movements that are strongly opposed to the policies of the old regime, and whose motivating ideologies portray their opponents in harsh and uncompromising terms. As a result, revolutions create severe conflicts of interest between the new regime and other powers, especially the allies of the old regime. In addition, new regimes are prone to exaggerate the degree to which others are hostile. Other states will usually react negatively, thereby creating an atmosphere of intense suspicion and increased insecurity.

Third, in some cases, the possibility of the revolution spreading may scare other states even more while making the new regime overly optimistic. At the same time, the chaos and confusion that are an inevitable part of the revolutionary process may encourage other states to assume that the new state can be defeated easily, which will make them more willing to use force against it. The belief that the revolution will be both easy to export and easy to overthrow creates an especially intense security dilemma and increases the danger of war.

---

*Millennium* 16, no. 2 (1987); Richard K. Ashley, "The Geopolitics of Geopolitical Space: Toward a Critical Social Theory of International Politics," *Alternatives* 12, no. 4 (1987), and "Untying the Sovereign State: A Double Reading of the Anarchy Problematique," *Millennium* 17, no. 2 (1988); Alexander Wendt, "The Agent-Structure Problem in International Relations Theory," *International Organization* 41, no. 3 (1987), and "Anarchy Is What States Make of It: The Social Construction of Power Politics," *International Organization* 46, no. 2 (1993); James Der Derian and Michael Shapiro, eds., *International/Intertextual Relations* (Lexington, Mass: Lexington Books, 1989); and John Gerard Ruggie, "Territoriality and Beyond," *International Organization* 47, no. 1 (1993).

These problems are all compounded by the enormous uncertainty that accompanies a revolution. Measuring the balance of power is more difficult after a revolution (especially if the new regime is based on novel principles), so the danger of miscalculation rises. Estimating intentions is harder as well, with both sides prone to rely on ideology in order to predict how others will behave. Revolutions also disrupt the normal channels of communication and evaluation between states at precisely the time when accurate information is most needed, further increasing the chances of a spiral of suspicion.

In short, revolutions exert far-reaching effects on states' estimates of the threats they face, and they encourage both the revolutionary state and the onlookers to view the use of force as an effective way to deal with the problem. Each side will see the other as a threat, but neither can estimate the real danger accurately. For all of these reasons, revolutions exacerbate the security competition between states and increase the likelihood of war.

This argument does not imply either that revolutions are a unique cause of security competition and war or that none of the dynamics that drive revolutionary states toward war apply to nonrevolutionary states as well. Indeed, several of the causal links outlined in the next chapter are drawn from more general propositions in international relations theory. Rather, I argue that revolutions are a powerful proximate cause of these familiar phenomena and that they are especially destabilizing because they tend to trigger several causes of conflict simultaneously. As a result, competition and war are particularly likely in the aftermath of a revolutionary upheaval.

## THE LITERATURE

Despite its practical importance and theoretical potential, the topic of the relationship between revolution and international politics is surprisingly under-studied. Although the literature on revolution is enormous, virtually all of it focuses either on the *causes* of revolution or on the *domestic* consequences of revolutionary change.[11] There are also valuable case studies on

[11] The vast literature on revolution defies easy summation. Useful surveys include Peter Calvert, *Revolution and Counter-Revolution* (Minneapolis: University of Minnesota Press, 1992); Charles Tilly, "Revolutions and Collective Violence," in *Handbook of Political Science*, vol. 3: *Macropolitical Theory*, ed. Nelson W. Polsby and Fred I. Greenstein (Reading, Mass.: Addison-Wesley, 1976); Jack A. Goldstone, "Theories of Revolution: The Third Generation," *World Politics* 32, no. 2 (1980); Rod Aya, *Rethinking Revolutions and Collective Violence: Studies in Concept, Theory, and Method* (Amsterdam: Het Spinhuis, 1990); Mark N. Hagopian, *The Phenomenon of Revolution* (New York: Dodd Mead, 1974); Ekkart Zimmermann, *Political Violence, Crises, and Revolutions: Theories and Research* (Cambridge, Mass.: Schenkman, 1983); and James B. Rule, *Theories of Civil Violence* (Berkeley: University of California Press, 1988). An insightful historical introduction is Charles Tilly, *European Revolutions: 1492–1992* (Oxford: Basil Blackwell, 1993); a useful bibliography is Robert Blackey, *Revolutions and Revolutionists: A Comprehensive Guide to the Literature* (Santa Barbara, Calif.: ABC-Clio, 1982).

[6]

individual revolutionary states, but very few works address either the general subject of revolutionary foreign policy or the specific connection between revolution and war.

Three exceptions to the above claim are worth noting, although none lays out a fully articulated theory of the relationship. In *Revolution and International System*, Kyung-Won Kim analyzes the French Revolution from a "systemic" perspective, based on concepts drawn from the writings of Raymond Aron. He draws a number of plausible conclusions (for example, that "heterogeneous" ideologies fuel misperception and thus encourage conflict), but the book's value is limited by its focus on a single case. Peter Calvert's *Revolution and International Politics* is more comprehensive and offers a number of interesting insights, but he does not develop a coherent theory and presents only anecdotal support for his claims.[12] Finally, David Armstrong's *Revolution and World Order* offers a more detailed and explicitly comparative analysis of relations between revolutionary states and "normal" powers, based on many of the same cases examined in the present book. His focus is different from mine, however; drawing on the concept of "international society" expounded by Hedley Bull and others, Armstrong's "essential aim is to elucidate the interaction between revolutions and revolutionary ideas . . . and the established norms and processes of international society." For him, a revolutionary state is one that stands "for a fundamental change in the principles on the basis of which states conduct their relations with each other." This definition is almost tautological, however—a state is revolutionary if it pursues "revolutionary" objectives—and Armstrong does not present a theory explaining why revolutions make conflict more likely or more intense.[13]

Apart from the works just noted, efforts to explain the foreign policies of revolutionary states have been relatively unsystematic or else confined to a single case. Our *theoretical* understanding of revolution and war thus consists largely of untested "folk theories." At the risk of oversimplifying a diverse body of scholarship, we may group the alternative explanations into three broad families, whose focus, respectively, is on revolutionary ideology, domestic politics, and the revolutionary personality.

---

[12] Kim, *Revolution and International System: A Study in the Breakdown of International Stability* (New York: New York University Press, 1970); Calvert, *Revolution and International Politics* (New York: St. Martin's, 1984). The diffuse nature of Calvert's work is also due to his extremely broad definition of revolution, which includes any "forcible overthrow of a government or regime." For Calvert, a coup d'état that reshuffles a military regime is just as "revolutionary" as a mass upheaval that destroys the existing social structure and erects a new one in its place.

[13] Armstrong is admirably candid on this point and admits that his study "is not tightly organized around a systematic set of theoretical propositions"; David Armstrong, *Revolution and World Order: The Revolutionary State in International Society* (Oxford: Clarendon Press, 1993), 3, 11.

## Revolutionary Ideology

One popular approach views revolutionary foreign policy as a direct result of the ideology of the revolutionary movement. The logic of this perspective is straightforward: revolutionary states cause war by deliberately trying to export their ideological principles to other countries. They do this because the movement's core beliefs prescribe such efforts, contrary to the usual norms of sovereignty and nonintervention.

Not surprisingly, this interpretation of revolutionary foreign policy is especially popular among the revolutionary state's opponents. During the French Revolution, for example, Edmund Burke argued that England "was at war with an armed doctrine," just as U.S. leaders blamed the expansionist thrust of Soviet foreign policy on the revolutionary ideology of Marxism-Leninism. President Ronald Reagan told the United Nations General Assembly in 1986, "Marxist-Leninist regimes tend to wage war as readily against their neighbors as they routinely do against their own people."[14] In much the same way, several examinations of Iranian foreign policy have attributed its bellicose nature to the expansionist strands of the Ayatollah Khomeini's Shiite theology.[15]

Despite its popularity, however, this approach is an unsatisfying explanation for war. It is wholly one-sided: war is seen as a direct result of the revolutionary regime's aggressive beliefs (and presumably aggressive conduct). Empirical support for this view is at best mixed, however, as revolutionary states frequently behave with restraint and are as often the victims as the initiators of aggression. As we shall see, French foreign policy was fairly passive from 1789 to 1792; it was Poland that began the Russo-Polish war of 1920, and the Soviet Union generally avoided significant conflicts or international commitments until the eve of World War II. Iraq started the war with revolutionary Iran, Somalia attacked Ethiopia, and Chinese intervention in Korea was a reluctant response to the U.S. advance to the Yalu River

[14] See Edmund Burke, "First Letter on a Regicide Peace," in *The Works of the Rt. Hon. Edmund Burke* (Boston: Little, Brown, 1869), 5:250. On Western appraisals of Soviet conduct, see "X" [George F. Kennan], "The Sources of Soviet Conduct," *Foreign Affairs* 25, no. 4 (1947); Nathan C. Leites, *A Study of Bolshevism* (Glencoe, Ill.: Free Press, 1953); and "U.S. Objectives and Programs for National Security" (NSC–68), in *Containment: Documents on American Policy and Strategy, 1945–1950*, ed. Thomas H. Etzold and John Lewis Gaddis (New York: Columbia University Press, 1978), 386–96. Reagan also argued "it was difficult [for Americans] to understand the [Soviet] ideological premise that force is an acceptable way to expand a political system." See "Text of President Reagan's United Nations Speech," *Washington Post*, 25 October 1985, A23; and "Transcript of Reagan's Speech to the U.N. General Assembly," *New York Times* 23 September 1986, A10.

[15] See R. K. Ramazani, *Revolutionary Iran: Challenge and Response in the Middle East* (Baltimore: Johns Hopkins University Press, 1986) 19–26, and Marvin Zonis and Daniel Brumberg, *Khomeini, the Islamic Republic of Iran, and the Arab World* (Cambridge: Center for Middle East Studies, Harvard University, 1987).

rather than an enthusiastic act of political evangelism. Were ideology always a direct and sufficient cause of conflict, these revolutionary states would have been the aggressors rather than the victims.

In addition, revolutionary ideologies rarely specify the precise tactics to follow to achieve the movement's general goals; indeed, they often stress the need for tactical flexibility.[16] Either war or peace can thus be justified on ideological grounds. Moreover, because official ideologies change relatively slowly, they cannot account for shifts in the revolutionary state's foreign policy as it learns from experience or adapts to conditions.

As we shall see, ideology does play an important role in determining both how revolutionary states behave and how their actions are perceived by others. By itself, however, it does not adequately explain the connection between revolution and war.

### Domestic Politics

A second approach to understanding revolutionary foreign policy draws on the familiar linkage between domestic instability and international conflict.[17] In this view, conflicts within the revolutionary state are believed to encourage aggressive behavior toward others: the greater the divisions within the revolutionary state (either within the elite or between the government and the population at large), the more hostile its foreign policy.

This hypothesis usually takes one of two distinct forms. One version focuses on elite conflict: contending factions within the revolutionary movement promote conflicts with other states in order to secure greater power for themselves. A second version argues that revolutionary leaders seek conflicts with other states in order to rally popular support, justify internal repression, and provide a scapegoat in case domestic problems persist. Thus, the radicals in France used the threat of a vast "aristocratic conspiracy" to justify suppression of the clergy and nobility, just as Castro in Cuba and the Sandinistas in Nicaragua used conflict with the United States to justify the repression of domestic opponents and to excuse their own policy mistakes.[18] In each case, an external enemy was used to solidify the regime's internal position and account for internal failures.

[16] See Nathan C. Leites, *The Operational Code of the Politburo* (New York: McGraw-Hill, 1951), 32–35; and Tang Tsou and Morton H. Halperin, "Mao Tse-tung's Revolutionary Strategy and Peking's International Behavior," *American Political Science Review* 59, no. 1 (1965), 89–90.

[17] For a summary and critique of these theories, see Jack S. Levy, "Domestic Politics and War," in Rotberg and Rabb, *Origins and Prevention of Major Wars*, 79–100, and "The Causes of Wars: A Review of Theories and Evidence," in *Behavior, Society, and Nuclear War*, vol. 1, ed. Philip E. Tetlock et al. (New York: Oxford University Press, 1989), 262–73.

[18] Dennis Gilbert, *Sandinistas: The Party and the Revolution* (Cambridge, Mass.: Basil Blackwell, 1988), 94–95, 119, 183.

Both forms of the hypothesis share the tenet that revolutionary foreign policy is determined largely by domestic politics. Despite its intuitive appeal, however, there are at least two problems with this approach as an explanation for conflict and war. As with ideology-centered explanations, this type also assumes the revolutionary state to be the principal aggressor. But a state that has just undergone a revolution is rarely ready for war, and it would be foolhardy indeed for a victorious revolutionary movement to risk its newly won position in a test of strength with a powerful neighbor. Revolutionary leaders may use tensions with other states to cement their hold on power, but we would expect them to focus primarily on internal problems and to avoid a direct clash of arms.[19] Nor does this approach explain why other states respond to these provocations in ways that strengthen extreme factions and heighten the danger of war. It takes two to quarrel, and theories focusing solely on domestic politics deal with only one side of the story.

The empirical record supports this assessment. Revolutionary states often seek at least cordial relations with potentially threatening regimes, if only to buy time until they can secure their internal positions. Thus, Robert Pastor argues, the Sandinistas sought a modus vivendi with the United States after gaining power in Nicaragua, a goal that Castro had recommended to them and one that many U.S. leaders endorsed. Nevertheless, Nicaragua and the United States quickly entered a spiral of hostility that eventually led to the *contra* war.[20] Domestic politics clearly affects the foreign policies of revolutionary states, but it cannot adequately explain the relationship between revolution and war.[21]

## The Revolutionary Personality

A third approach focuses on the personality traits of revolutionary leaders.[22] Its proponents argue that the leaders of revolutions tend to be self-confident, ruthless individuals who have risen to power precisely because such personal traits are valuable assets in a revolutionary situation. These traits

[19] Lenin told the Tenth Party Congress in March 1921, "For a long time we are condemned merely to heal wounds." Quoted in William Henry Chamberlin, *The Bolshevik Revolution, 1917–1921* (1935; reprint, Princeton: Princeton University Press, 1987), 2:446.

[20] Pastor, *Condemned to Repetition*, esp. 191.

[21] Not surprisingly, efforts to test the hypotheses linking domestic conflict with involvement in war have been inconclusive. See Levy, "Causes of Wars," 273–74.

[22] Works in this genre include E. Victor Wolfenstein, *The Revolutionary Personality: Lenin, Trotsky, Gandhi* (Princeton: Princeton University Press, 1971); Bruce Mazlish, *The Revolutionary Ascetic: Evolution of a Political Type* (New York: Basic Books, 1976); Robert Jay Lifton, *Revolutionary Immortality: Mao Tse-tung and the Chinese Cultural Revolution* (New York: Vintage Books, 1968); and Mostafa Rejai and Kay Phillips, *World Revolutionary Leaders* (New Brunswick, N.J.: Rutgers University Press, 1983). For summaries, see Thomas H. Greene, *Comparative Revolutionary Movements: The Search for Theory and Justice*, 2d ed. (Englewood Cliffs, N.J.: Prentice-Hall, 1984), chap. 4; and Hagopian, *Phenomenon of Revolution*, 318–33.

allegedly make these individuals difficult to deter and prone to reckless or aggressive foreign policies, because they are attracted to violence, convinced of their own infallibility, and driven to perform new acts of revolutionary heroism.[23]

This approach is perhaps most evident in biographies and other popular accounts; to date, most scholarship on the "revolutionary personality" has ignored issues of foreign policy.[24] Given the inability of this approach to explain war, this omission is perhaps not surprising. The main difficulty is the lack of a strong theoretical connection between personality traits and foreign policy preferences. Even if we knew that a leader possessed a "revolutionary personality" (whatever that may be), we would be able to deduce very little about that person's choices when facing a specific decision for war or peace. For example, although Maximilien Robespierre fit the classic profile of a revolutionary leader, he opposed the French declaration of war in 1792. Moreover, members of the same revolutionary elite often disagree about foreign policy, as Lenin and the Politburo did about the Treaty of Brest-Litvosk or the conduct of the war with Poland, or as Iran's leaders did over the export of Islamic fundamentalism versus the benefits of improving ties with the West.[25]

In addition, the popular stereotype of revolutionary leaders is inconsistent: the same leaders are sometimes portrayed as simultaneously both irrational and fanatical, on one hand, and disciplined, calculating, and crafty, on the other. Thus, this approach seems especially limited as an explanation for why revolutionary states are so prone to war.

Each of these three perspectives provides some insight into the behavior of revolutionary states and their relations with other powers. Nonetheless, they all err in focusing exclusively on the revolutionary state rather than on the larger setting in which foreign policy is made: war is seen as following more or less directly from the characteristics of the revolutionary regime.

[23] Robert C. Tucker suggests that the organizational milieu of revolutionary and extremist organizations is "favorable for the emergence in leadership positions of individuals of a type that may be called the 'warfare personality.' " *The Soviet Political Mind* (New York: W. W. Norton, 1971), 40–46; and see also Chamberlin, *Russian Revolution*, 1:44; Henry Kissinger, "Domestic Structure and Foreign Policy," in his *American Foreign Policy,* expanded ed. (New York: W. W. Norton, 1974), 39–41; John H. Kautsky, "Revolutionary and Managerial Elites in Modernizing Regimes," *Comparative Politics* 1, no. 4 (1969); and Patrick M. Morgan, *Deterrence: A Conceptual Analysis* (Beverly Hills, Calif.: Sage, 1977), 162.
[24] An exception is Arthur Schlesinger's explanation of the Cold War as due in part to Stalin's paranoid personality: "Origins of the Cold War," *Foreign Affairs* 46, no. 1 (1967), 46–50. For a recent version of this argument, see John Lewis Gaddis, "The Tragedy of Cold War History," *Diplomatic History* 17, no. 1 (1993), 4–7.
[25] See Georges Michon, *Robespierre et la guerre révolutionnaire, 1791–1792* (Paris: Marcel Rivière, 1937), 51–55; Louis Fischer, *The Life of Lenin* (New York: Harper Colophon, 1964), 220–22, 392–93; and David Menashri, *Iran: A Decade of War and Revolution* (New York: Holmes and Meier, 1990), 151–52, 379–82, 395–96.

But decisions to go to war are not made in a vacuum. War is ultimately a response to problems that arise between two or more states. Understanding revolution and war thus requires an *international-political* perspective: instead of focusing primarily on the revolutionary state itself, we should consider how revolutions will affect the relationship *between* that state and the other members of the system. A systemic approach is needed, therefore, particularly if we want to understand why revolutions often lead both sides to regard the other as a threat and to favor the use of force. Before I turn to the task of providing such an approach, however, a brief discussion of research design is in order.

## RESEARCH METHODS AND PROCEDURES

I define a "revolution" as the destruction of an existing state by members of its own society, followed by the creation of a new political order.[26]

A revolution is more than just a rearrangement of the administrative apparatus or the replacement of one set of rulers by other members of the old elite. Instead, a revolution creates a fundamentally new state based on different values, myths, social classes, political institutions, and conceptions of the political community. By shaping national identities and setting the parameters of subsequent political activity, a revolution establishes the basic nature of a polity.[27]

Revolutions may be divided into two basic types: first, mass revolutions (or "revolutions from below"), and second, elite revolutions (or "revolutions from above"). In a mass revolution, the old regime is swept away in an explosion of political participation by individuals or groups that were marginalized or excluded under the old order. In an elite revolution, by contrast, the old regime is challenged and eventually replaced by a movement whose leaders were

[26] The term "state," as used here, refers to the administrative and coercive agencies possessing legitimate authority over a particular territorial area. For similar conceptions of revolution, see Franz Borkenau, "State and Revolution in the Paris Commune, the Russian Civil War, and the Spanish Civil War," *Sociological Review* 29, no. 1 (1937); John M. Dunn, *Modern Revolutions: An Introduction to the Analysis of a Political Phenomenon* (Cambridge: Cambridge University Press, 1972), xi; Samuel P. Huntington, *Political Order in Changing Societies* (New Haven: Yale University Press, 1968), 264–65; and George Pettee, "The Process of Revolution," in *Why Revolution? Theories and Analyses*, ed. Clifford T. Paynton and Robert Blackey (Cambridge, Mass.: Schenkman, 1971), 34–35. For alternative definitions and the historical evolution of the term, see Eugene Kamenka, "The Concept of a Political Revolution," in *Nomos VIII: Revolution*, ed. Carl J. Friedrich (New York: Atherton, 1966), 122–35; Stanislaw Andrewski, *Wars, Revolutions, Dictatorships* (London: Frank Cass, 1992), chap. 2; and Peter C. Sederberg, *Fires Within: Political Violence and Revolutionary Change* (New York: HarperCollins, 1994), 54–55.
[27] See Robert Jervis, *Perception and Misperception in International Politics* (Princeton: Princeton University Press, 1976), 262–66.

themselves part of the old regime—normally military and civil bureaucrats who become convinced that the old order can no longer defend vital national interests.[28] As discussed at greater length in chapter 2, elite revolutions tend to be less violent and entail less extensive social transformations than mass revolutions and their international consequences are usually less dangerous.

In this book I will examine principally mass revolutions, although I have also included one clear case of an elite revolution for purposes of comparison. This focus is appropriate both because mass revolutions are more common and because their international effects are usually more worrisome. In order to derive the greatest practical benefit from our results, it makes sense to concentrate on the category of events that is both most frequent and most likely to cause trouble.

The definition of revolution used here excludes both simple coups d'état (where one elite faction replaces another) and pure national liberation movements (where a colonized group establishes an independent state by expelling a foreign ruler).[29] It also excludes most civil wars, unless the victorious faction eventually imposes a new political order on its society. Because the definition I am using is fairly restrictive, the universe of cases is small. It is much smaller, for example, than those resulting from the definitions of Peter Calvert or Zeev Maoz, who conceive of revolution as any violent regime change and whose universe of cases numbers well over a hundred.[30] On the other hand, it is slightly broader than the definition used by Theda Skocpol, for whom revolutions are "rapid, basic transformations of a society's state and class structures . . . accomplished and in part carried through by class-based revolts from below."[31] If we adopt the definition

---

[28] See Ellen Kay Trimberger, *Revolution from Above: Military Bureaucrats and Development in Japan, Turkey, Egypt, and Peru* (New Brunswick, N.J.: Transaction Books, 1978).

[29] Owing to the similarities between national liberation movements and revolutionary organizations, successful wars of national liberation and successful revolutions are likely to generate similar international effects. I include the American Revolution (which can also be thought of as a national liberation movement) because it had far-reaching social effects and because contemporaries saw it as presenting a new model for social and political life.

[30] Peter Calvert defines "revolution" as "a change in government at a clearly defined point in time by the use of armed force," and Maoz defines "revolutionary regime change" as "a violent domestic struggle (of magnitudes ranging from a brief coup d'état to an all-out civil war) resulting in a change of government over a relatively short time interval." *A Study of Revolution* (Oxford: Clarendon Press, 1970), 4 and app. A; and see Maoz, "Joining the Club of Nations," 205.

[31] The first sentence of Theda Skocpol's book proclaims, "Social revolutions have been rare but momentous events in world history," and she notes that "this conception of social revolution . . . identifies a *complex* object of explanation of which there have been relatively few historical instances." She offers a list of additional cases in her conclusion (Mexico, Yugoslavia, Bolivia, Vietnam, Algeria, Mozambique, Guinea-Bissau, and Ethiopia), but some of these examples may not fit her own definition. Skocpol, *States and Social Revolutions: A Comparative Analysis of France, Russia, and China* (Cambridge: Cambridge University Press, 1979), 3–5, 287; and see Tilly, *From Mobilization to Revolution*, 193; and Aya, *Rethinking Revolutions and Collective Violence*, 70.

above, however, the potential universe of revolutions includes the English, French, American, Russian, Mexican, Turkish, Chinese, Cuban, Ethiopian, Nicaraguan, and Iranian revolutions. This list is not exhaustive—even for the modern era alone—but I believe it is sufficiently representative of a larger universe so that the inclusion of other cases would not undermine my fundamental results.[32]

The bulk of this book consists of seven case studies. In chapters 3, 4 and 5, I examine the French, Russian, and Iranian revolutions, while chapter 6 contains shorter studies of the American, Mexican, Turkish, and Chinese revolutions. These cases were chosen with several aims in mind. First, although the precise nature of the revolutionary process differs from case to case, all seven are widely recognized as revolutionary events (the French, Russian, Iranian, Chinese, and Mexican revolutions were all mass revolutions, the Turkish was an elite revolution, and the American somewhere in between). Picking relatively uncontroversial examples of revolution may reduce controversy over whether the cases chosen were appropriate for testing the theory.

Second, the timing, geographic location, and ideological orientation of each case varies considerably from the others. The French and American revolutions were based on liberal principles (at least initially), the Russian and Chinese revolutions brought Marxist movements to power, the Iranian rested on a radical interpretation of Twelver Shiism, and the Turkish and Mexican were shaped by nationalist ideologies. Moreover, the states' international positions and immediate prior histories were distinct as well. By applying the theory to a diverse set of revolutions rather than a set of very similar cases, we can gain greater confidence in its range.[33]

Third, although each of these revolutions led to greater security competition between the new regime and several other powers (and sometimes *between* other powers as well), open warfare occurred in only four of them. By comparing these four with the cases where war was avoided, we can try to discern why war follows some revolutions but not others.[34]

Finally, each of these cases constitutes a critical event in modern world history. Both contemporaries and subsequent historians have regarded them as having far-reaching implications; other things being equal, we prefer to study significant events rather than trivial ones. There is also a large

[32] Needless to say, this claim could be challenged by future research.

[33] Adam Przeworski and Henry Teune term this approach a "most similar systems" design; see *The Logic of Comparative Social Inquiry* (New York: John Wiley, 1970), 34–39.

[34] This is essentially Mill's "Method of Difference": one compares cases where the outcomes were different in order to identify the causal factor that accounts for the change. See John Stuart Mill, "Two Methods of Comparison," in *Comparative Perspectives: Theories and Methods*, ed. Amitai Etzioni and Frederic L. Dubow (Boston: Little, Brown, 1970).

secondary literature on these seven revolutions, which facilitates the researcher's task considerably.

Taken together, these cases permit three basic comparisons.[35] In order to demonstrate that revolutions do increase the level of security competition, I first compare the foreign relations of each country before and after its revolution. This procedure in effect uses the old regime as a control case in order to isolate the independent impact of the revolution on foreign policy. The old regime is an ideal candidate for comparison, insofar as it shares many characteristics (such as size, geographic location, population, etc.) with the revolutionary state. If one can show that the revolution altered the country's foreign policy or international position—and especially the level of security competition—one can plausibly infer that the revolution was at least partly responsible for the change. To do this, I ask whether, other things being equal, the level of security competition would have been higher or lower had the old regime survived. If the answer is "lower," then the revolution probably exerted an independent causal effect.[36]

To test the specific theory that explains *why* revolutions exert this effect, I next "process trace" the relationship between each revolutionary state and its main foreign interlocutors for at least ten years after the revolution. This method is especially appropriate because the universe of cases is too small for a statistical analysis and the number of independent variables too large for a rigorous application of John Stuart Mill's "method of difference." This technique is also appropriate because my theory focuses on the ways revolutions shape the perceptions of the relevant actors. Process tracing allows the analyst

[35] Basic works on case study methodology include Arend Lijphart, "Comparative Politics and the Comparative Method," *American Political Science Review* 65, no. 4 (1971); Alexander L. George, "Case Studies and Theory Development: The Method of Structured, Focussed Comparison," in *Diplomacy: New Approaches in History, Theory and Policy*, ed. Paul Gordon Lauren (New York: Free Press, 1979); Alexander L. George and Timothy J. McKeown, "Case Studies and Theories of Organizational Decisionmaking," in *Advances in Information Processing in Organizations*, ed. Robert F. Coulam and Richard A. Smith, vol. 2 (Greenwich, Conn.: JAI Press, 1985); Harry G. Eckstein, "Case Study and Theory in Political Science," in Polsby and Greenstein, *Handbook of Political Science*, vol. 7: *Strategies of Inquiry*; David Collier, "The Comparative Method," in *Political Science: The State of the Discipline*, ed. Ada W. Finifter (Washington, D.C.: American Political Science Association, 1993); and Gary King, Robert O. Keohane, and Sidney Verba, *Designing Social Inquiry: Scientific Inference in Qualitative Research* (Princeton: Princeton University Press, 1994).

[36] Such an inference gains strength if our case selection allows us to control for potentially omitted variables, which might be correlated with both the independent and dependent variables. For example, defeat in war might be correlated with the occurrence of revolution and with subsequent increases in security competition, which could lead us to overstate the impact of the former on the latter. But if the level of security competition increases whether the revolution was preceded by military defeat or not, then the inference that revolution has an independent causal effect becomes more credible. This particular possibility is not a problem here; although the Turkish and Russian revolutions followed major military defeats, the French, American, Mexican, and Iranian ones did not.

to "get inside" the case (where one may find multiple opportunities to test the theory's predictions) and to evaluate the separate causal links that connect the explanatory variables with the predicted outcomes.[37]

Finally, to explain why only some revolutions lead to war, I compare the French, Russian, Iranian, and Chinese revolutions against the American, Mexican, and Turkish cases. Although the results are not definitive, this comparison suggests that the absence of open warfare was due to the relatively high level of defense dominance that characterized the latter three revolutions. Not only was the danger of contagion either nonexistent or greatly muted (in part because these revolutions were not seen as especially infectious) but each of these revolutions occurred in geopolitical circumstances that discouraged the use of force. Thus, although each regime faced intense crises on one or more occasions, they all managed to avoid the final plunge into war.

Two caveats should be noted before we proceed. First, inferences about the causal effects of a revolution may be biased if there is a reciprocal relationship between the domestic and international effects of revolution. We are more likely to regard a revolution as significant if it has large international repercussions, but these same repercussions may have a powerful impact on internal developments as well. Had France avoided war in 1792, for example, Louis XVI might have kept his throne (and his head) and the more radical aspects of the revolution been averted. If this had occurred, what we now regard as the "French Revolution" might be viewed as an important but not "revolutionary" event and would not be included in this book. In other words, because the dependent variable (war) may affect the scope and importance of a revolution, thereby shaping its prominence in our historical accounts, there is the danger that our universe of revolutions is slanted in favor of the argument I am advancing here.[38] Although the observable evidence is quite strong, it thus ought to be regarded with some caution.

Second, in this book I focus on the direct diplomatic and strategic consequences of revolution, especially the relationship between revolution and

[37] On "process tracing," see George and McKeown, "Case Studies and Theory Development," 34–41; Stephen Van Evera, "What Are Case Studies? How Should They Be Performed?" memorandum, Massachusetts Institute of Technology, 1993; Bruce Russett, "International Behavior Research: Case Studies and Cumulation," in his *Power and Community in World Politics* (San Francisco: W. H. Freeman, 1974), 17–18: and Charles Ragin and David Zaret, "Theory and Method in Comparative Research: Two Strategies," *Social Forces* 61, no. 3 (1983), 748. Even advocates of statistical approaches concede that many theories can be tested only through a relatively small number of case studies, because the amount of research needed to obtain valid measures of key variables "precludes, for all practical purposes, the examination of many randomly selected cases." See Barbara Geddes, "How the Cases You Choose Affect the Answers You Get: Selection Bias in Comparative Politics," *Political Analysis* 2 (1990), 141–43.

[38] This is an example of "endogeneity bias." See King, Keohane, and Verba, *Designing Social Inquiry*, 185–96.

[16]

war, and I do not devote much attention to their long-term, indirect impact on culture, norms, or notions of political legitimacy. Thus, although I do consider whether revolutionary states are able to export their revolution to other societies, I address the question of whether other states were undermined by contagion (or subversion) rather than whether a revolution affected other societies through a more gradual spread of norms or beliefs. The latter question is obviously important, but it is not a central part of this study.[39]

The remainder of this book is organized as follows. Chapter 2 presents my theoretical argument in detail and lays out the explanatory propositions that I evaluate in the rest of the book. Chapters 3, 4, and 5 are case studies of the French, Bolshevik, and Iranian revolutions, covering roughly a ten-year period from the fall of each old regime. In chapter 6 I briefly analyze four additional cases—the American, Mexican, Turkish, and Chinese revolutions—which I use to refine my central argument and to consider why some revolutions do *not* lead to war. Finally, chapter 7 summarizes the results of the historical cases, describes their theoretical and practical implications, and highlights their future relevance, stressing in particular the recent transformation of the former Soviet empire.

[39] Works that address these issues include Joseph Klaits and Michael H. Haltzel, eds., *The Global Ramifications of the French Revolution* (Cambridge: Cambridge University Press, 1994); Geoffrey Best, ed., *The Permanent Revolution: The French Revolution and Its Legacy* (Chicago: University of Chicago Press, 1988); Keith Baker, Colin Lucas, François Furet, and Mona Ozouf, eds., *The French Revolution and the Creation of Modern Political Culture*, 4 vols. (New York: Pergamon, 1987–94); and E. H. Carr, *The Soviet Impact on the Western World* (New York: Macmillan, 1947).

# [2]

## A Theory of
## Revolution and War

"Without a revolutionary theory there can be no revolutionary movement."
—V. I. Lenin

Why do revolutions intensify security competition among states and
markedly increase the danger of war? My explanation is laid out in three
steps. I begin by setting aside the subject of revolution to consider how states
interact in the international system, focusing on those factors that account for
security competition and war. To this end, I offer a simple theory of international politics, which I call balance-of-threat theory. I then analyze the revolutionary process in some detail, in order to identify how revolutions affect
the states in which they occur. Next, I bring these two lines of analysis together and show how revolutions affect international politics. Specifically,
revolutions alter the main elements of threat identified by balance-of-threat
theory, thereby encouraging states to favor the use of force. I conclude with
specific predictions and set the stage for the subsequent case studies.

### BALANCE-OF-THREAT THEORY

Like all realist theories, balance-of-threat theory begins by recognizing
that states dwell in an anarchic environment in which no agency or institution exists to protect them from each other. Security is thus the highest aim
of states, and foreign policy decisions will be strongly influenced by how
national leaders perceive the external environment and by how different
strategies are expected to affect their relative positions.[1]

---

[1] See my *Origins of Alliances* (Ithaca: Cornell University Press, 1987), and "Testing Theories
of Alliance Formation: The Case of Southwest Asia," *International Organization* 42, no. 2
(1988), and "Alliances, Threats, and U.S. Grand Strategy: A Reply to Kaufman and Labs," *Security Studies* 1, no. 3 (1992).

Where neorealist balance-of-power theory predicts that states will respond primarily to changes in the distribution of capabilities, however, balance-of-threat theory argues that states are actually more sensitive to *threats*, which are a function of several different components. The first is *aggregate power:* other things being equal, the greater a state's total resources (such as population, industrial and military capability, raw material endowment, etc.), the greater the threat it can pose to others. The level of threat is also affected by *perceptions of intent:* if a state is believed to be unusually aggressive, potential victims will be more willing to use force to reduce its power, to moderate its aggressive aims, or to eliminate it entirely. Finally, the level of threat is also affected by the *offense-defense balance:* states will be less secure when it is easy for them to harm one another and when the means for doing so are easy to acquire. Furthermore, incentives to use force increase when the offense has the advantage, because the expected cost to the attacker will decline and the expected benefits of aggression will increase. Offensive power is usually defined in terms of specific military capabilities (that is, whether the present state of military technology favors attacking or defending), but political factors can be equally important. In particular, the ability to undermine a foreign government through propaganda or subversion can be an especially potent form of offensive power, because it allows one state to "conquer" others at little or no cost to itself. In general, the greater a state's offensive power is, the greater the threat it will pose to others and the greater their incentive to try to contain or reduce the danger.[2]

By incorporating the other factors that will shape a state's estimates of its level of security, balance-of-threat theory provides a more complete and accurate account of the forces that influence state behavior.[3] The question, therefore, is whether revolutions affect the balance of threats in ways that increase the intensity of international conflict and raise the danger of war. To begin to answer that question, let us consider the nature of the revolutionary process in a bit more detail.

## THE REVOLUTIONARY PROCESS

The main object of revolutionary struggle is control of the state.[4] A revolutionary *situation* exists when control of the government becomes "the ob-

---

[2] See George Quester, *Offense and Defense in the International System* (New York: Wiley, 1977); Robert Jervis, "Cooperation under the Security Dilemma," *World Politics* 30, no. 2 (1978); Stephen Van Evera, *Causes of War*, vol. 1: *The Structure of Power and the Roots of War* (Ithaca: Cornell University Press, forthcoming).

[3] In earlier presentations of balance-of-threat theory, I included geographic proximity as another element of threat. Because a state's geographic location is not affected by a revolution, I have omitted it from this discussion, although I would expect states to be more sensitive to revolutions near their own borders than to ones at a distance.

[4] Lenin once remarked, "The key question of every revolution is undoubtedly the question

ject of effective, competing, mutually exclusive claims on the part of two or more distinct polities." A revolutionary *outcome* occurs when the challengers are able to defeat the old regime and erect a new and fundamentally different political order.[5]

The specific process by which a revolution occurs will vary, but nearly all revolutions exhibit certain common features. First, revolutions become possible when the administrative and coercive capacities of the state have been weakened by a combination of internal and external challenges.[6] Second, revolutions feature an explosion of political activity. In a mass revolution, this activity is conducted by individuals who were marginalized or excluded under the old regime. In an elite revolution, the movement is led by dissident members of the old regime (usually military bureaucrats) who become convinced that a revolution is necessary to protect the nation from foreign domination and whose positions grant them access to capabilities (such as the armed forces) that are needed to challenge the old regime.[7] In either type, this explosion of participation takes the form of illegal methods and activities, because the institutions and principles of the old regime offer no legitimate outlet for them.[8] Third, revolutions alter the language of political discourse and foster the development of new symbols and social customs.[9] Fourth, revolutions also alter the principles by which leaders are chosen. In most cases, the new rulers will be drawn from groups that were formerly barred from power while excluding prominent members of the old regime. Thus, revolutions inevitably involve a redefinition of the political community.

Finally, revolutions are usually characterized by violence. Force is often needed in order to oust the old regime, and even when it collapses without

---

of state power. Which class holds power decides everything." *Selected Works* (Moscow: Progress Publishers, 1970–71), 2:276.

[5] See Charles Tilly, *From Mobilization to Revolution* (New York: Random House, 1978), esp. 191; and Peter Amann, "Revolution: A Redefinition," in *Why Revolution? Theories and Analyses*, ed. Clifford Paynton and Robert Blackey (Cambridge, Mass.: Schenkman, 1971), 58–59.

[6] Thus, Theda Skocpol refers to prerevolutionary governments as "old regime states in crisis." *States and Social Revolutions: A Comparative Analysis of France, Russia and China* (Cambridge: Cambridge University Press, 1979). State power may decline for a variety of reasons. The demand for resources may exceed the ability of existing institutions to provide them (as in France), the coercive apparatus may dissolve after a military defeat (as in Russia), or the legitimacy of the existing order may be challenged on moral grounds (as in Iran).

[7] See Samuel P. Huntington, *Political Order in Changing Societies* (New Haven: Yale University Press, 1968), 266; and Ellen Kay Trimberger, *Revolution from Above: Military Bureaucrats and Development in Japan, Turkey, Egypt, and Peru* (New Brunswick, N.J.: Transaction Books, 1978).

[8] A. S. Cohan writes that "in a revolution, one system of legality is substituted for another." *Theories of Revolution: An Introduction* (New York: Wiley, 1975), 25; see also Lyford P. Edwards, *The Natural History of Revolution* (Chicago: University of Chicago Press, 1970), 107–12.

[9] Thus, revolutionary states ordinarily adopt new names, flags, anthems, and social practices, such as the French revolutionary calendar or the reimposition of the women's *chador* in Iran.

a fight, there are likely to be violent struggles among competing revolutionary factions.[10] The issues at stake are enormous, because the process of redefining a political community places everyone at risk. Until a new order is in place, no one is safe from exclusion, and the temptation to use force to enhance's one's position is difficult to resist. The possibility that winners will take all and losers will lose everything heightens the level of suspicion and insecurity. Fears of plots and conspiracies abound. Disagreements over specific policies can become life-or-death struggles, if they are seen as reflecting an inadequate commitment to the revolutionary cause.

In sum, revolutions are deadly serious contests for extremely high stakes. The collapse of the old regime places all members of society on shaky ground. Conflicts can be resolved only by tests of strength, and no one's interests or safety are assured. As a result, revolutions are usually violent and destructive, especially when they involve the replacement of the existing elite by previously excluded members of society.[11]

*Capabilities*

Owing to the features just described, revolution usually reduces a state's capabilities in the short term. The demise of the old regime hinders any efforts to mobilize resources for war (at least until the new regime acquires the institutional capacity to tax and allocate resources), and the armed forces will be severely disrupted if they have not collapsed completely. In the absence of a viable central authority, previously suppressed groups may assert new claims, and certain regions or groups may try to gain their independence, thereby adding to the new regime's burdens and reducing its overall capabilities.

In addition, many revolutionary elites will be poorly prepared for running a government or managing its diplomacy, and key members of the old regime are likely to flee the country or to be purged by the new

[10] The estimated death tolls confirm the ubiquity of violence in modern revolutions: France, at least 35,000 dead; Russia, 500,000; China, 1 million; Cuba, 5,000; Iran, 17,000; Mexico 250,000; Nicaragua, between 30,000 and 50,000. These estimates are based on Melvin Small and J. David Singer, *Resort to Arms: International and Civil Wars, 1816–1980* (Beverly Hills, Calif.: Sage, 1986); and Donald Greer, *The Incidence of the Terror in the French Revolution* (Cambridge: Harvard University Press, 1935).

[11] As noted in chapter 1, these characteristics are most apparent in mass revolutions. The level of violence is usually lower in an elite revolution, because the revolutionaries typically seek less radical goals, the old regime usually collapses more rapidly, and the new leaders already control elements of a new state apparatus and can establish their authority more easily. See Ellen Kay Trimberger, "A Theory of Elite Revolutions," *Studies in Comparative International Development* 7, no. 3 (1972); and Erik Allardt, "Revolutionary Ideologies as Agents of Structural and Cultural Change," in *Social Science and the New Societies,* ed. Nancy Hammond (East Lansing: Social Science Research Bureau, Michigan State University, 1973), 154.

regime.[12] Thus, the new regime may lack experienced diplomats, trained commanders, and disciplined armies, unless it has also fought a civil war and therefore controls a military establishment of its own. In the latter case, however, its strength will be sapped by the destruction caused by the civil war. Uncertainty about the future cripples economic activity and encourages the flight of capital and expertise, reducing the capabilities of the new state even more.

The damage produced by a revolution is often temporary, and its magnitude is difficult to estimate in any case. By definition, successful revolutionary organizations are good at mobilizing social power and directing it toward specific political ends. Although a revolution harms a state's power in the short term, therefore, it is likely to improve it in the long run.[13] Measuring the precise impact of a revolution on the balance of power will be especially difficult, however, if the new order is based on a radically different model of social and political organization. Thus, while a revolution may appear to create an inviting window of opportunity, at the time it is unclear how large the window is and how long it is going to remain open.

### Revolutionary Ideologies, State Preferences, and Elite Perceptions

In a revolution, the old ruling elite is replaced by individuals committed to different goals and infused with a radically different worldview. When a revolutionary movement takes power, therefore, its ideology shapes both the preferences of the new regime and its perceptions of the external environment. Unfortunately, most revolutionary ideologies contain ideas and themes that can create (or exacerbate) conflicts of interest and magnify perceptions of threat.

Successful revolutions are rare, because even weak and corrupt states usually control far greater resources than their internal opponents. States have better access to the means of violence and can use these tools to monitor, suppress, or coopt potential challengers.[14] It is not surprising, therefore,

---

[12] As Lenin once admitted, the Bolsheviks "really did not know how to rule." Quoted in John Dunn, *Modern Revolutions: An Introduction to the Analysis of a Political Phenomenon* (Cambridge: Cambridge University Press, 1972), 18–19, 47; see also William Henry Chamberlin, *The Russian Revolution 1917–1921* (1935; reprint, Princeton: Princeton University Press, 1987), 1:351.

[13] See Theda Skocpol, "Social Revolutions and Mass Military Mobilization," *World Politics* 40, no. 2 (1988), and Ted Robert Gurr, "War, Revolution, and the Growth of the Coercive State," *Comparative Political Studies* 21, no. 1 (1988).

[14] Indeed, some writers assert that revolution is impossible so long as the armed forces retain their loyalty and cohesion. See Katherine C. Chorley, *Armies and the Art of Revolution* (London: Faber and Faber, 1943); Jonathan R. Adelman, *Revolution, Armies, and War: A Politi-*

that most revolutionary movements are rapidly extinguished, and would-be revolutionaries often end up in prison, in exile, or dead. Indeed, it is perhaps more surprising that revolutions ever succeed.

The inherent difficulty of overthrowing an existing state is compounded by the familiar problems of collective action.[15] Because some of the benefits from a revolution are indivisible (once provided, they are available to all), individual citizens can profit from a revolution even if they do nothing to help bring it about. Moreover, each individual's contribution is too small to determine the outcome, so a rational actor would inevitably choose a "free ride" rather than incur the risks and costs of joining a revolutionary movement. Indeed, if people were motivated solely by self-interest and guided by an accurate assessment of costs and benefits, then the lack of willing participants would make revolutions impossible.[16]

A number of scholars have suggested that revolutionary movements can overcome the free-rider problem by offering positive inducements or threatening negative sanctions.[17] Yet this explanation is only partly satisfying. Although specific incentives such as food or protection may help convince uncommitted individuals to support a revolutionary movement, they do not explain either why individuals will risk their lives to expand the movement or how an organization gets started in the first place, before it was able to provide these benefits. Given the high probability of failure and the risks that revolutionaries face, the payoffs would have to be enormous for joining a revolutionary movement to be a ratio-

---

cal History (Boulder, Colo.: Lynne Rienner, 1985); Anthony James Joes, From the Barrel of a Gun: Armies and Revolutions (Washington, D.C.: Pergamon-Brassey's, 1986); and John Ellis, Armies in Revolution (New York: Oxford University Press, 1974).

[15] See Mancur Olson, The Logic of Collective Action: Public Goods and the Theory of Groups (Cambridge: Harvard University Press, 1971); and Russell Hardin, Collective Action (Washington, D.C.: Johns Hopkins University Press/Resources for the Future, 1982).

[16] Applications of collective-goods theory to the problem of revolution include Gordon Tullock, "The Paradox of Revolution," Public Choice 11 (fall 1971); Philip G. Roeder, "Rational Revolution: Extensions of the 'By-Product' Model of Revolutionary Involvement," Western Political Quarterly 35, no. 1 (1982); Morris Silver, "Political Revolution and Repression: An Economic Approach," Public Choice 17 (spring 1974); Samuel L. Popkin, The Rational Peasant: The Political Economy of Revolution in Vietnam (Berkeley: University of California Press, 1979); Michael Taylor, "Rationality and Revolutionary Collective Action," in Rationality and Revolution, ed. Michael Taylor (Cambridge: Cambridge University Press, 1988); James DeNardo, Power in Numbers: The Political Strategy of Protest and Rebellion (Princeton: Princeton University Press, 1985); Edward N. Muller and Karl-Dieter Opp, "Rational Choice and Rebellious Collective Action," American Political Science Review 80, no. 2 (1986); and Mark I. Lichbach, The Rebel's Dilemma (Ann Arbor: University of Michigan Press, 1995).

[17] See Jeffrey Race, "Toward an Exchange Theory of Revolution," in Peasant Rebellion and Communist Revolution in Asia, ed. John Wilson Lewis (Stanford: Stanford University Press, 1974); Joel S. Migdal, Peasants, Politics, and Revolution: Pressures toward Political and Social Change in the Third World (Princeton: Princeton University Press, 1974); and the references in n. 16 above.

nal choice.[18] And testimony from several revolutionary leaders suggests that they did not expect to be rewarded at all.[19] According to Che Guevara, who lost his life trying to foment revolution in Bolivia, "Each guerrilla must be prepared to die, not to defend an ideal, but to transform it into reality."[20] So the puzzle remains: how do revolutionary movements convince potential members to bear the costs and risks of this activity, and how do revolutionaries sustain their commitment through prolonged, difficult, and uncertain struggles?[21]

Part of the answer lies in the possibility that participation in a revolution is motivated as much by moral commitments as by narrow self-interest. For those who believe that abolishing the present order is a moral imperative, individual benefits are secondary or irrelevant.[22] More fundamentally, perceptions of costs and benefits ultimately rest on subjective beliefs about the consequences of different choices. If individuals believe that a revolution is possible and will bring them great benefits—irrespective of the actual possibilities—they will be more likely to support it, particularly if they are also convinced that success requires their participation.[23] Revolutionary move-

[18] As Charles Tilly notes, "why and how . . . the group committed from the start to fundamental transformation of the structure of power . . . forms remains one of the mysteries of our time." *From Mobilization to Revolution*, 203.

[19] That revolutionaries are often surprised to gain power suggests that they were not motivated by prospects of future gain. Lenin told a socialist youth group in January 1917, "We of the older generation may not live to see the decisive battles of this coming revolution," and the Sandinista leader Daniel Ortega admitted that as late as July 1979, he did not expect to see the revolution succeed in Nicaragua. Ayatollah Khomeini was reportedly surprised by the speed with which the shah's regime collapsed as well. Chamberlin, *Russian Revolution*, 1:131, 323; Robert Pastor, *Condemned to Repetition: The United States and Nicaragua* (Princeton: Princeton University Press, 1987), xiv; and Marvin Zonis, "A Theory of Revolution from Accounts of the Revolution," *World Politics* 35, no. 4 (1983), 602.

[20] Quoted in Robert Blackey, *Revolutions and Revolutionists: A Comprehensive Guide to the Literature* (Santa Barbara, Calif.: ABC-Clio, 1982), 405.

[21] "How do we account for . . . the willingness of people to engage in immense sacrifice with no evident possible gain (the endless parade of individuals and groups who have incurred prison or death for abstract causes)?" Douglass C. North, *Structure and Change in Economic History* (New York: W. W. Norton, 1981), 10–11.

[22] Chamberlin describes Lenin's "intense faith" in Marxism in *Russian Revolution*, 1:135, 140. For a general discussion, see James B. Rule, *Theories of Civil Violence* (Berkeley: University of California Press, 1988), 35–39.

[23] Recent sociological research suggests that political organizations encourage collective action by promoting beliefs about the seriousness of the problem, the locus of causality or blame, the image of the opposition, and the efficacy of collective response. See David A. Snow, E. Burke Rochford, Jr., Steven K. Worden, and Robert D. Benford, "Frame Alignment Processes, Micromobilization, and Movement Participation," *American Sociological Review* 51, no. 4 (1986); David A. Snow and Robert Benford, "Ideology, Frame Resonance, and Participant Mobilization," in *From Structure to Action: Comparing Social Movement Research across Cultures*, ed. Bert Klandermans, Hanspeter Kriesi, and Sidney Tarrow (Greenwich, Conn.: JAI Press, 1988); and Jeffrey Berejikian, "Revolutionary Collective Action and the Agent-Structure Problem," *American Political Science Review* 86, no. 3 (1992), 652–55.

ments therefore try to convince potential members, first, that seeking to overthrow the existing order is the morally correct position; second, that doing so will bring significant benefits; and third, that the probability of success is high *if* they act.

Persuading uncommitted individuals of these "facts" is one of the principal functions of a revolutionary ideology, either as a means of gaining the strength needed to challenge the old regime and overcome rival contenders for power or as an instrument for sustaining popular support and legitimizing their subsequent right to rule.[24] Let us examine some of the forms that this all-important ideology can take.

An ideology is a normative theory of action. Ideologies "explain" prevailing social conditions and provide individuals with guidelines for how to react to them. In nonrevolutionary societies, for example, the dominant ideology discourages disobedience and free-riding by persuading citizens "to conceive of justice as coextensive with the existing rules, and accordingly, to obey them out of sense of morality," in the words of Douglass North. By contrast, "the objective of a successful counterideology is to convince people not only that the observed injustices are an inherent part of the system but also that a just system can come about only by active participation of individuals in the system."[25] Revolutionary ideologies present a critique of the current system (as Marx's analysis of capitalism did), together with a strategy for replacing it.[26] In addition, North writes, a revolutionary ideology serves to "energize groups to behave contrary to a simple, hedonistic, individual calculus of costs and benefits. . . . Neither maintenance of the existing order nor its overthrow is possible without such behavior."[27] To nourish this altruistic behavior, revolutionary ideologies tend to emphasize three key themes.

First, revolutionary groups usually portray opponents as intrinsically evil and incapable of meaningful reform.[28] This theme enhances the moral basis

---

[24] Thus, Sandinista leader Humberto Ortega admitted having exaggerated the feasibility of revolution: "Trying to tell the masses that the cost was very high and that they should seek another way would have meant the defeat of the revolutionary movement." Quoted in Tomas Borge et al., *Sandinistas Speak* (New York: Pathfinder, 1982), 70–71.

[25] North, *Structure and Change*, 53–54.

[26] According to Mark Hagopian, "There are three structural aspects of revolutionary ideology: *critique*, which lays bare the shortcomings of the old regime; *affirmation*, which suggests or even spells out in detail that a better society is not only desirable but possible; and in recent times, *strategic guidance*, which tells the best way to make a revolution." *The Phenomenon of Revolution* (New York: Dodd, Mead, 1974), 258.

[27] North, *Structure and Change*, 53–54. According to Ted Robert Gurr, "one of the most potent and enduring effects of 'revolutionary appeals' is to persuade men that political violence can provide value gains commensurate to or greater than its cost in risk and guilt." *Why Men Rebel* (Princeton: Princeton University Press, 1970), 215–16.

[28] Jack A. Goldstone, "The Comparative and Historical Study of Revolutions," *Annual Review of Sociology* 8 (1982), 203.

for revolutionary participation: if the current system is unjust and cannot be improved, then efforts at compromise are doomed, and revolution is the only acceptable alternative. It was this issue that ultimately separated Lenin and the Bolsheviks from the "Economists" in Russia and from social democrats such as Karl Kautsky; where the latter believed that tsarism and capitalism could be reformed, the Bolsheviks denied that compromise was possible and remained committed to overthrowing both.[29] Portraying enemies as irredeemably hostile can also strengthen the solidarity of the revolutionary movement and enhance its discipline by making any ideological variations appear treasonous. Indeed, the tendency to view the world in Manichean terms can leave a revolutionary organization prone to fratricidal quarrels in which dissenters are castigated as traitors and blamed for any setbacks that occur.[30]

This element of revolutionary ideologies is similar to the popular propaganda that emerges within nation-states during wartime, and for many of the same reasons. Revolutions and wars are violent and dangerous; in order to justify the costs that are inherent in both activities, leaders try to portray opponents as evil or subhuman.[31] After all, if one's enemies are truly wicked, then compromising with them would be both risky and immoral, and eliminating them forever may be worth a great sacrifice. In each case, compromise will give way to more radical solutions.

The second theme is that victory is inevitable. A revolutionary movement will not get very far unless potential supporters believe their sacrifices will eventually bear fruit. Thus, revolutionary ideologies are inherently optimistic: they portray victory as inevitable despite what may appear to be overwhelming odds. To reinforce this belief, the ideology may invoke irresistible or divine forces to justify faith in victory. For Marxists, for example, the "laws" of history led inexorably toward proletarian revolutions and the establishment of socialism.[32] For Islamic fundamentalists, optimism rests on faith in God. Revolutionaries may also cite the successes of earlier movements to sustain confidence in their own efforts; thus, the Sandinistas saw

---

[29] Edward Hallett Carr, *The Bolshevik Revolution, 1917–1923* (New York: Macmillan, 1950–53), 1:11.

[30] Lewis A. Coser, *Greedy Institutions: Patterns of Undivided Commitment* (New York: Free Press, 1974), 110.

[31] For examples of this tendency, see John Dower, *War without Mercy: Race and Power in the Pacific War* (New York: Pantheon, 1986); and John MacArthur, *Second Front: Censorship and Propaganda in the Gulf War* (New York: Hill and Wang, 1992).

[32] Thus, the inaugural issue of *The American Socialist,* published by an obscure Trotskyite splinter group, proclaimed, "We are part of the stream of history. We are confident of our future because we believe we have the correct understanding and tactic[s] and . . . the grit and tenacity to carry on. Do not anybody despair because of our small numbers. . . . We are like the American abolitionists of a hundred years ago. We are like Garrison and Wendell Phillips and Frederick Douglass and John Brown." Quoted in Coser, *Greedy Institutions,* 111–12.

Castro's victory in Cuba as evidence that their own efforts in Nicaragua could succeed.[33]

Optimism can also be encouraged by dismissing an opponent's apparent superiority as illusory. Mao Tse-tung argued that "reactionaries" were "paper tigers," and Lenin described imperialism as containing both the power to dominate the globe *and* the seeds of its inevitable destruction at the hands of the proletariat.[34] Depicting opponents in this way is an obvious method for sustaining commitment within the movement: no matter how hopeless a situation appears to be, success is assured if the revolutionary forces simply persevere.

At the same time, the real difficulties of the struggle demand that revolutionary movements temper their optimism with elements of caution. Even if victory is inevitable, for instance, it may require heroic efforts and repeated sacrifices. Such beliefs address the free-rider problem directly: if potential members are convinced that victory is inevitable regardless of whether they joined or not, then the temptation to let others bear the burdens of the struggle would be too strong. Thus, Mao warned his followers to "despise the enemy strategically while taking full acount of him tactically": overcoming the enemy would require careful preparation and repeated sacrifices, but victory was assured because the enemy was vulnerable.[35] In the same way, Lenin warned his followers that faith in victory should neither lead to overconfidence nor preclude setbacks and tactical retreats along the path to power.[36]

The worldview of most revolutionary movements will thus exhibit a strong tension between optimism and prudence. Two important questions, therefore, are which of these tendencies will exert the greatest influence on the perceptions and behavior of the new state, and how its external situation and the responses of other powers will affect the relative weight given to these competing imperatives.

The third key theme is an insistence that the revolution has universal meaning. Specifically, revolutionary movements often believe that the prin-

---

[33] See the testimony in Dennis Gilbert, *Sandinistas: The Party and the Revolution* (London: Basil Blackwell, 1988), 5, 56.

[34] Lenin "Imperialism: The Highest Stage of Capitalism," in his *Selected Works,* 1:667–768.

[35] Peter Van Ness, *Revolution and Chinese Foreign Policy: Peking's Support for Wars of National Liberation* (Berkeley: University of California Press, 1970), 40–41. Mao also told his followers that imperialism was "rotten and had no future" and "we have reason to despise them." Yet he cautioned, "We should never take the enemy lightly . . . and concentrate all our strength for battle in order to win victory." Mao Tse-tung, *Selected Works* (Beijing: Foreign Languages Press, 1965), 4:181; and Tang Tsou and Morton Halperin, "Mao Tse-tung's Revolutionary Strategy and Peking's International Behavior," *American Political Science Review* 59, no. 3 (1965), 89.

[36] In 1919, Lenin warned, "We may suffer grave and sometimes even decisive defeats. . . . If, however, we use all the methods of struggle, victory will be certain." *Selected Works,* 3:410–11.

ciples of the revolution are relevant for other societies and should not be confined within the boundaries of a single state. In extreme cases, the ideology may go so far as to reject the nation-state as a legitimate political unit and call for the eventual elimination of the state system itself.

That revolutionary ideologies contain universalist elements should not surprise us. If the failures of an old regime are the result of external forces such as the "tyranny of kings," "capitalist exploitation," or "Western interference," then action beyond the state's own borders may be necessary to eliminate these evils once and for all. Such views promise adherents an additional reward for their sacrifices: the revolution will not only be good for one's own society but will ultimately benefit others as well. Moreover, in order to attract popular support, revolutionary ideologists tend to portray their new political ideas as self-evident truths—creating a strong bias toward universalism. After all, how can a self-evident political principle be valid for one group but not others? Could the Jacobins argue that the "Rights of Man" applied only to the French? Could Marx's disciples claim that his inexorable "laws of history" were valid in Russia alone? Could the Iranian revolutionaries think that an Islamic republic was essential for Persians but not for other Muslims?

A few caveats are in order here. These ideological themes are neither necessary nor sufficient conditions for revolutionary success. One or more may be missing in some cases. Nor do revolutions automatically occur whenever some group adopts these ideological formulas. The likelihood of a revolution is also affected by a number of other conditions and by the old regime's ability to respond to the challenge.[37] But it is striking that, as we shall see, the ide-

[37] For macro theories of revolution, see Skocpol, *States and Social Revolutions;* and Jack A. Goldstone, *Revolution and Rebellion in the Early Modern World* (Berkeley: University of California Press, 1991). On the importance of political opportunities, social networks, and mass communication in facilitating (revolutionary) collective action, see Tilly, *From Mobilization to Revolution,* chaps. 3–4; Doug McAdam, "Micromobilization Contexts and Recruitment to Activism," in Klandersman, Kriesi, and Tarrow, *From Structure to Action;* and Sidney Tarrow, *Power in Movement: Social Movements, Collective Action, and Politics* (Cambridge: Cambridge University Press, 1994). Susanne Lohmann has recently analyzed the problem of collective action as a signaling game in which decisions to rebel are based on an individual's personal "threshold for action" and the information he or she receives about the likelihood that others will act as well. Information indicating that the old regime has weakened will lower the expected costs of protest and allow potential dissidents to send "costly" (i.e., credible) signals of their own willingness to act. Under certain conditions, seemingly isolated acts of protest can produce a "cascade" of such information and trigger a sudden outburst of revolutionary activity. See her article "Dynamics of Informational Cascades: The Monday Demonstrations in Leipzig, East Germany, 1989–91," *World Politics* 47, no. 1 (1994); as well as the related works by DeNardo, *Power in Numbers;* Dennis Chong, *Collective Action and the Civil Rights Movement* (Chicago: University of Chicago Press, 1991); Mark Granovetter, "Threshold Models of Collective Behavior," *American Journal of Sociology* 83, no. 6 (1978); and Timur Kuran, "Sparks and Prairie Fires: A Theory of Unanticipated Revolution," *Public Choice* 61, no. 1 (1989). These perspectives complement the focus on ideology I have adopted here. In my account, revolution-

ological programs of revolutionary movements as varied as those of the American Founding Fathers, the Russian and Chinese Communists, and the Iranian fundamentalists all incorporated variations on these three principles. Moreover, even when the social and organizational prerequisites are present, it is hard to imagine a mass revolution succeeding without some kind of ideological program that justifies revolt and also gives participants a reason to believe they will win.[38] In short, although the inherent difficulty of revolution and the logic of the free-rider problem do not require that revolutionary movements adopt these ideological formulas, such tenets are likely to give them an advantage over rivals who lack a similar set of ideas.

Revolutionary ideologies should not be seen as wholly different from other forms of political belief. Indeed, often they are simply more extreme versions of the patriotic ideals that established regimes use to encourage individual sacrifice. Just as states in war portray their enemies as evil, victory as certain, and their own goals as pure and idealistic ("to make the world safe for democracy," "to promote a new world order," etc.), revolutionary movements encourage similar sacrifices through the three ideological themes described above. Because the risks are great and the odds of success low, however, revolutionary movements will try to indoctrinate members even more enthusiastically than other states. And whereas states ordinarily abandon wartime propaganda when the conflict is over, revolutionary movements that face continued internal opposition may continue using the ideology as a mobilizational device even after the struggle for power has been won.

The elements of revolutionary ideology identified here will be most common in mass revolutions. Because elite revolutions originate within elements of the existing state bureaucracy and are usually less violent, they face less severe collective-action problems than other revolutionary movements. And because such revolutions ordinarily arise in response to the threat of foreign domination, elite leaders can rely primarily on nationalism to mobilize their followers and legitimize the seizure of power. As a result, elite revolutions present less fertile ground for the Manichean worldview and universalistic ambitions that mass revolutions often foster.

By definition, revolutions are conducted by movements that oppose the policies of the old regime. If they succeed in taking power, they invariably attempt to implement policies designed to correct the objectionable features of the old order. Thus, all revolutions entail the emergence of a new state

---

ary ideologies seek to lower the individual threshold for rebellion by portraying the existing regime as evil and doomed to defeat. In other words, revolutionary ideologies try to create conditions in which an "informational cascade" is more likely to occur.

[38] According to Franz Borkenau, "if violence is the father of every great upheaval, its mother is illusion. The belief which is always reborn in every great and decisive historical struggle is that this is the last fight, that after this struggle all poverty, all suffering, all oppression will be a thing of the past." "State and Revolution," 74–75.

whose preferences differ in important ways from those of the old regime. The new government is virtually certain to adopt new domestic and foreign policies, even at the risk of provoking both internal and external opposition.

The revolutionary process will shape the perceptions of the new ruling elite as well. The ideologies of many revolutionary movements describe opponents as incorrigibly evil and destined for the dustbin of history. As we shall see, this trait encourages them to assume the worst about their enemies and intensifies each side's perceptions of threat. This is most true of mass revolutions, but elements of these ideas appear in elite revolutions are well.

## Uncertainty and Misinformation

In the wake of revolutions, uncertainty about the balance of power grows, and so does the danger of war via miscalculation. Estimating intentions is harder, and prior commitments and understandings are called into question as soon as the new leaders take power.

Other states are equally uncertain about the new regime's true aims and its willingness to bear costs and run risks; the old regime's reputation for credibility, restraint, prudence, and so on is of little or no use. Thus, other states have to start from scratch in gauging how the new regime is likely to behave. The same is also true in reverse: the new regime cannot know exactly how others will respond, although it can use their past behavior as a rough guide to their future conduct. These conditions magnify the importance of ideology. Lacking direct experience, the revolutionary regime will rely on its ideology to predict how others will behave, while the other powers will use the same ideology as a guide to the likely conduct of the new regime.

The problem of uncertainty is not confined to relations between the revolutionary state and other powers. In addition, states observing a revolution cannot know how other actors in the system will respond to it. Revolutions thus exert direct and indirect effects on the foreign policies of other states, which must respond both to the new regime and to the uncertain reactions of the entire international community.

Third, revolutions exert unpredictable effects on other societies. As discussed at greater length below, a central issue in the aftermath of a revolution is the likelihood of its spreading to other states. The question of whether (or how easily) it will spread is of tremendous importance to both sides, yet neither side can form a reliable answer. This problem stems partly from sheer ignorance about political conditions in other countries but even more importantly from the fundamental incalculability of a revolutionary upheaval. As Timur Kuran has shown, an individual's willingness to rebel is a form of private information that cannot be reliably estimated in advance, especially when there is a threat of repression, giving the potential revolutionaries a strong incentive to misrepresent their true preferences.[39] As a result, neither the new revolutionary regime nor its potential adversaries can obtain an accurate assessment of the odds that the revolution will move beyond its original borders, a situation creating additional room for miscalculation. And because an individual's true level of support (or opposition) to the new regime cannot be directly observed, neither the new regime nor its foreign counterparts can estimate either its own popularity or the likelihood of counterrevolution.

Unfortunately, the available evidence on these issues is virtually certain to be ambiguous. A mass revolution will always attract some adherents in other countries—thereby supporting the new regime's hopes and its neighbors' worries—but neither side will know if these sympathizers are merely isolated extremists or the tip of a subversive iceberg. Similarly, there will almost always be some evidence of internal resistance after a revolution, yet neither the new regime nor its adversaries will know how strong or widespread such sentiments are. Because these appraisals are central to each side's decisions and yet unreliable at best, the danger of miscalculation is especially severe.

To make matters even worse, the information that both sides receive is likely to be biased by the transnational migration of exiles and revolutionary sympathizers. Revolutions invariably produce a large population of exiles who flee abroad to escape its consequences.[40] Many of them are members of the old regime, and therefore hostile to the revolutionary government and eager to return to power. They tend to settle in countries that are sympathetic to their plight, where they may try to obtain foreign assistance for their counterrevolutionary efforts. To do so, they will portray the new regime as a grave threat to other states and will stress its potential vulnerability to counterrevolutionary action. Moreover, despite their obvious biases, exiles are often seen as experts on conditions in their home country at a time when other sources of information are scarce, so their testimony is overvalued.[41] In much the same way, revolutionary sympathizers flock to

[39] See Timur Kuran, "Sparks and Prairie Fires," and "Now Out of Never: The Element of Surprise in the Revolutions of 1989," *World Politics* 44, no. 3 (1991); but see also Nikki Keddie, "Can Revolutions Be Predicted; Can Their Causes Be Understood?" *Contention* 1, no. 2 (1992); and Jack A. Goldstone, "Predicting Revolutions: Why We Could (and Should) Have Foreseen the Revolutions of 1989–91 in the USSR and Eastern Europe," *Contention* 2, no. 2 (1993).

[40] Yossi Shain, *The Frontier of Loyalty: Political Exiles in the Age of the Nation-State* (Middletown, Conn.: Wesleyan University Press, 1989).

[41] This is not a new phenomenon. As Machiavelli observed: "How vain the faith and promises of men are who are exiles from their own country.... Whenever they can return to their country by other means than your assistance, they will abandon you and look to the other means, regardless of their promises to you.... Such is their extreme desire to return to their homes that they naturally believe many things that are not true, and add many others on purpose; so that, with what they really believe and what they say they believe, they will fill you with hopes to that degree that if you attempt to act upon them, you will incur a fruitless expense, or engage in an undertaking that will involve you in ruin." *The Prince and the Discourses* (New York: Modern Library, 1950), 388–89.

the new capital after the revolution, eager to learn from its experiences, lend support to its efforts, or seek assistance for their own struggles.[42] Such groups portray their home countries as both hostile and ripe for revolution, in order to obtain external support for their efforts. In the revolutionary state, these newcomers are regarded as having special knowledge about conditions back home, despite their obvious interest in providing a distorted picture. The two-way, parallel migration of exiles and sympathizers is a feature of most revolutions, and it increases the danger that each sides' perceptions and policies will be based on biased evidence.

Finally, revolutions damage the normal channels of communication between states at precisely the time when the need for accurate information is greatest, hindering even more the ability of both sides to understand the information they do have. Diplomatic representatives are often withdrawn or replaced and intelligence networks disrupted, making it more difficult for each side to determine what the other is doing and why. A shortage of adequate facilities and trained personnel can also impair the new regime's ability to evaluate others' conduct and to communicate its intentions. These various sources of uncertainty enhance the probability of miscalculation, as we shall see.

In sum, the process of revolution exerts a profound influence on the state that emerges from it, as well as its peers. Revolutions reduce a state's capabilities in the short term (although they often produce dramatic increases over time). Revolutionary movements are often based on optimistic and universalistic ideologies that portray opponents as irredeemably hostile, and they come to power in circumstances where accurate information about capabilities, intentions, and future prospects is difficult or impossible to obtain. These characteristics help explain how revolutions encourage international conflict.

## WHY REVOLUTIONS CAUSE CONFLICT AND WAR

### *The Balance of Power and Windows of Opportunity*

By altering the balance of power, revolutions intensify the security competition between states in at least two ways. First, other states may see the revolutionary state's weakness as an opportunity to improve their relative positions—either by seizing valuable territory or by seeking important diplomatic concessions—or as a chance to attack a state that was previously protected by the old regime. In either case, the revolution creates a window of opportunity for others to exploit.

---

[42] Examples are ubiquitous: the American Thomas Paine traveled to France in the 1790s, along with would-be revolutionaries from the rest of Europe, and socialists such as John Reed, Louise Bryant, and Emma Goldman journeyed to Russia after the Bolshevik seizure of power in 1917. Havana, Tehran, and Managua have been minor meccas for foreign revolutionaries as well.

Second, revolutions can exacerbate security competition *among* other states. If a foreign power becomes concerned that one of its rivals will take advantage of the revolution in order to improve its own position, the foreign power may be forced to take action either to obtain spoils for itself or to prevent its rival from doing the same thing. Thus, the window of opportunity created by the revolution may inspire conflict among third parties so that they intervene, even if they have no particular quarrel with the new regime.[43]

## Ideology, Intentions, and Spirals of Suspicion

The movements that revolutions bring to power are by definition opposed to most (if not all) of the policies of the old regime. States with close ties to the old regime will naturally view the revolution as potentially dangerous and its new initiatives as a threat to their own interests. For purely rational reasons, therefore, revolutionary states and foreign powers are likely to experience sharp conflicts of interest and to regard each other's intentions with suspicion.

In addition, actions that one state takes to increase its security—such as strengthening its military forces—will tend to reduce the security of other states.[44] The other states may consequently exaggerate the hostility or aggressiveness of their adversary, thereby inflating the level of threat even more. The resulting spiral of suspicion raises the odds of war, as compromise appears infeasible and both sides begin to search for some way to eliminate the threat entirely.[45]

Revolutionary states are prone to spirals of suspicion for several reasons. First, as noted above, a revolutionary regime will be unsure about other states' intentions, simply because it has little or no direct experience in dealing with them. Lacking direct evidence, it will fall back on ideology, which in most revolutionary situations tends to portray opponents as incorrigibly hostile.[46] Thus, even a mild diplomatic dispute is likely to escalate. Conces-

---

[43] Jennifer Bailey, "Revolution in the International System," in *Superpowers and Revolution*, ed. Jonathan Adelman (New York: Praeger, 1986), 19.

[44] This is the familiar security dilemma identified by John Herz in "Idealist Internationalism and the Security Dilemma," *World Politics* 2, no. 2 (1950). See also Jervis, "Cooperation under the Security Dilemma."

[45] Robert Jervis, *Perception and Misperception in International Politics* (Princeton: Princeton University Press, 1976), chap. 3. For important refinements to Jervis's presentation, see Charles L. Glaser, "The Political Consequences of Military Strategy: Expanding the Spiral and Deterrence Models," *World Politics* 44, no. 4 (1992).

[46] Thus, at the end of World War I, Lenin predicted that "world capital will now start an offensive against us." Quoted in Chamberlin, *Russian Revolution*, 2:155–56. He also told the Third Comintern Congress in June 1921 that "the international bourgeoisie . . . is waiting, always on the lookout for the moment when conditions will permit the renewal of this war" with Soviet Russia. Quoted in Leites, *Study of Bolshevism*, 405.

sions may be viewed with skepticism, because conflict is seen as inevitable and compromise as naive or even dangerous.

Second, revolutionary regimes may harbor suspicions based on historical experience. If the revolutionary leaders are eager to redress past wrongs (as is generally the case), they will be especially wary of the foreign powers they hold responsible for earlier transgressions. Thus, Mao Tse-tung's suspicions of the United States were based in part on past Western interference in China, and revolutionary forces in Mexico, Nicaragua, and Iran preoccupied themselves with the possibility of U.S. intervention for similar reasons.[47]

Under these conditions, revolutionary regimes, assuming the worst about other states, will interpret ambiguous or inconsistent policies in a negative light. Threats and signs of opposition simply confirm the impression of hostility, while concessions and signs of approval are regarded as insincere gestures masking the opponent's true intentions.[48] Unfortunately, the other states' policies are almost sure to be ambiguous, if only because it takes time for them to decide how to respond to the new situation. This problem is compounded by the difficulty of trying to understand the new political order, by the states' ignorance of the background and beliefs of the new regime, and by the obstacles to obtaining reliable information. Even when foreign powers are not especially hostile, therefore, some of their actions and statements will probably reinforce the suspicions of the revolutionary regime.

Third, a spiral of suspicion will be more likely if the elite (or a faction within it) exaggerates a foreign threat in order to improve its internal position, exploiting it either to rally nationalist support for the new leaders or to justify harsh measures against their internal opponents. Such exaggerations will be especially effective when there is some truth to the accusations: for example, if foreign powers that had been allied with the old regime now seem to be suspicious of the new government. This tactic can be dangerous if it magnifies a conflict that might otherwise have been avoided or minimized, but the risk can be reduced if the revolutionary elite continues to base its policy decisions on its true assessment of others' intentions rather than the myth it has manufactured. Maintaining such fine control is tricky, however. Even if the revolutionary leadership knows the myths to be myths, the campaign may be so convincing that it becomes the basis for policy. Moreover, efforts to enhance domestic support by exaggerating external threats can be self-fulfilling: if foreign powers do not recognize the real mo-

---

[47] See Mao Tse-tung, *Selected Works*, 4:447–50; Gilbert, *Sandinistas*, 153–75; and James A. Bill, *The Eagle and the Lion: The Tragedy of American-Iranian Relations* (New Haven: Yale University Press, 1988), 96–97.

[48] On the tendency to fit ambiguous information into existing beliefs, see Jervis, *Perception and Misperception*, 143–54.

tive behind such a campaign, they will take the revolutionary state's accusations at face value and conduct themselves accordingly. If they react defensively—as one would expect—it will merely confirm the bellicose image that they have been given.

Other states contribute to the spiral of hostility. To begin with, they may fail to understand that the revolutionary state's version of history probably differs from their own. Revolutionary states ordinarily emphasize past injustices, including what they regard as illegitimate foreign interference. But because all states view their own history in a favorable light, foreign powers will not understand why the new regime sees them as objects of hatred and suspicion and will consider the new state's defensive responses to be evidence of its aggressive character.[49] Thus, U.S. policy makers saw Chinese intervention in the Korean War as evidence of the expansionist tendencies of international Communism, in part because politicians such as Secretary of State Dean Acheson, who believed that U.S. policy in the Far East was in China's best interest, failed to appreciate that Western actions in the Far East had actually left a far more negative impression on the minds of China's new leaders.[50] Similar problems afflicted U.S. relations with Fidel Castro: because U.S. leaders such as President Dwight D. Eisenhower believed that U.S. policy had been largely beneficial for Cuba, they saw Castro's hostility as unjustified aggression rather than as an understandable (if excessive) reaction to past U.S. behavior.[51] Even where tangible grounds for conflict exist (as they did in both these cases), ignorance of the historical basis for suspicion will cause the foreign powers to misinterpret the revolutionary state's bellicosity.

Foreign powers may also start a negative spiral if the new regime's domestic programs affect their interests adversely. Such a situation is a legitimate basis for conflict, of course, but the threat will be magnified if actions taken for internal reasons are also viewed as evidence of aggressive intent. Groups whose interests are harmed (such as foreign corporations whose assets have been seized) may try to convince their home governments that the new regime is a threat to security, in the hope of obtaining diplomatic or military support. Thus, Castro's land reform program exacerbated the spiral of hostility between the United States and Cuba, and Arbenz's land reforms in Guatemala moved the United Fruit Company to organize a public

---

[49] Stephen Van Evera, *Causes of War*, vol. 2: *National Misperceptions and the Roots of War* (Ithaca: Cornell University Press, forthcoming), chap. 11; and E. H. Dance, *History the Betrayer: A Study in Bias* (London: Hutchinson, 1960).

[50] Richard Ned Lebow, *Between Peace and War: The Nature of International Crisis* (Baltimore: Johns Hopkins University Press, 1981), 205–16; and Jervis, *Perception and Misperception*, 70–72.

[51] Richard Welch, *Response to Revolution: The United States and the Cuban Revolution, 1959–1961* (Chapel Hill: University of North Carolina Press, 1985), 41.

relations campaign that formed the backdrop for the U.S.-led coup that overthrew him.[52]

To make matters worse, revolutions alter international relations in ways that exacerbate perceptions of hostility. First, each side is likely to underestimate the other's sense of vulnerability, leading it to discount the role of defensive motivations in explaining the other side's conduct. In addition to the burdens of organizing a government and rebuilding a damaged society, revolutionary states usually face continued domestic opposition. Fearful of having only a precarious hold on power, they are more likely to overreact to threats.[53] Yet revolutionary states also try to portray themselves as firmly in control, in order to discourage counterrevolution at home and to attract recognition abroad. If this public relations effort is successful, however, other states will underestimate the extent to which the revolutionary state's actions are driven by insecurity, interpreting its defensive actions as a sign of aggressive intent rather than as a reaction to legitimate fears. Furthermore, the other states may not recognize, first, that a new regime must build a reputation for defending its interests in order to deter future challenges and, second, that this will motivate it to respond vigorously when conflicts of interest arise.

The same tendency can occur in reverse as well. Fully aware of its own weaknesses, a revolutionary state may find it hard to understand why it is considered dangerous. If so, it may view the opposition of other states as evidence of their intrinsic hostility rather than as a response to its own actions. Foreign powers will be concerned with building a reputation as well, in order to teach the new regime that they cannot be exploited. Thus, both sides will be prone to see even purely defensive policies as signs of aggressive intent, especially when real conflicts of interest are also present.

A second exacerbating factor is the pernicious influence of exiles and revolutionary sympathizers. As suggested above, exiles from the revolutionary state have an incentive to portray the new regime as especially hostile, in order to convince other states to support their counterrevolutionary ambitions. Similarly, revolutionary sympathizers from other countries are likely to reinforce the new regime's own suspicions by portraying foreign governments as deeply hostile. The more vocal and visible these groups are, the

---

[52] On Cuba, see Richard Moss, "The Limits of Policy: An Investigation of the Spiral Model, The Deterrence Model, and Miscalculations in U.S.–Third World Relations" (Ph.D. diss., Princeton University, 1987), 160–64, 193–94. On Guatemala, see Richard H. Immerman, *The CIA in Guatemala: The Foreign Policy of Intervention* (Austin: University of Texas Press, 1982); and Stephen Schlesinger and Stephen Kinzer, *Bitter Fruit: The Untold Story of the American Coup in Guatemala* (Garden City, N.Y.: Anchor Books, 1983).

[53] According to George Pettee, "revolutionists enter the limelight, not like men on horseback, as victorious conspirators appearing in the forum, but like fearful children, exploring an empty house, not sure that it is empty." *The Process of Revolution* (New York: Harper Brothers, 1938), 100–101.

[36]

greater the tendency for both sides to conclude that the host country supports their aims. A large and vocal population of exiles will be seen as a sign that the host country is hostile to the revolution, just as a large and vocal group of foreign sympathizers will be taken as evidence that the new regime is actively seeking to spread its ideals elsewhere. Taken together, the parallel migration of exiles and sympathizers and the testimony they provide to their hosts will strongly reinforce each side's beliefs that the other is inherently dangerous.

A third factor inflating the perception of hostility is the loss of expertise that accompanies a revolution, particularly when revolutionary governments purge people with ties to perceived or potential enemies. The Iranian revolutionaries removed officials with close links to the United States, and Communist China persecuted its own "America Hands" in the 1950s. Ironically, as the treatment of the State Department's "China Hands" suggests, the same process may occur within the nonrevolutionary states as well.[54] By removing experienced individuals, each side further reduces its capacity to understand the other. Thus, the personnel changes set in motion by a revolution will exacerbate the prevailing uncertainty and reinforce mutual suspicion.

Because revolutions unleash a variety of forces that make it more difficult for the revolutionary state and its neighbors to assess each others' intentions accurately, each is likely to view the other as more hostile than it really is. Such a conclusion hampers their ability to reach a satisfactory modus vivendi and strengthens the position of those who favor direct action to eliminate the threat.

Each side's tendency to exaggerate the other's hostility helps explain why security competition increases after a revolution, but it does not explain why *war* occurs. After all, the United States and the Soviet Union were extremely hostile for much of the Cold War, but neither saw actual war as an attractive option for dealing with the situation. Thus, the next question is why war *is* often seen as a reasonable response.

### Revolution, the Offense-Defense Balance, and War

All else being equal, war is more likely when national leaders believe that offense is easier than defense. When offense is easy, states are less secure yet simultaneously have greater incentives to try to improve their relative positions. At the same time, using force promises greater benefits because it will be simpler to gain a decisive victory over the opponents. Thus, offense dominance both raises the perceived level of threat and suggests that it will be

---

[54] The "China Hands" were a group of China experts accused of disloyalty and purged from the State Department during the McCarthy era. See E. J. Kahn, *The China Hands: America's Foreign Service Officers and What Befell Them* (New York: Viking, 1975).

easy to reduce. The result is more international competition and a higher risk of war.[55]

Revolutions are a powerful source of this danger. In addition to creating distorted perceptions of hostility, revolutions also encourage both sides to exaggerate their own vulnerability and also the vulnerability of their opponents. This tendency is partly due to the inherent difficulty of estimating the balance of power after a revolution, which makes it more likely that each will exaggerate its military prospects. In addition, the belief that the revolution will either spread to other countries or readily succumb to counterrevolutionary pressure magnifies this sense of vulnerability. Unable to estimate with high confidence the likelihood of either possibility, all sides will tend to assume the worst. For both military and political reasons, therefore, a revolution heightens each side's sense of threats and opportunities.

Taken together, these factors encourage both parties to believe that the other presents a grave threat, yet they also encourage the belief that the threat can be eliminated fairly easily. Furthermore, these perceptions may encourage third parties to intervene either to eliminate a potential revolutionary threat or to prevent other powers from gaining an advantage by doing it themselves. Once again, we can best understand these dynamics by examining revolutionary states and foreign powers separately.

Why are revolutionary states simultaneously insecure and overconfident?

To begin with, the inherent optimism of most revolutionary ideologies encourages the new leaders to overstate the odds of victory, so they become more willing to contemplate the use of force. Arguments of this sort are difficult to counter without appearing disloyal; if victory is inevitable and opponents are destined for the dustbin of history, then expressing doubts about the certainty of victory betrays a lack of confidence in the revolution and could easily undermine one's political position at home.

Second, the optimism of revolutionary states rests on the belief that opponents will be undermined by the irresistible spread of revolutionary ideas. This hope reflects the universalism common to many revolutionary ideologies and the assumption that their opponents will be unable to fight effectively owing to lack of popular support. Mao's claim that "a single spark can ignite a prairie fire" nicely conveys this faith in the catalytic effects of revolutionary action, as does the so-called *foco* theory of guerrilla warfare developed by Che Guevara.[56] This view is also fueled by the ten-

---

[55] See the references in n. 2 above.

[56] On the basis of his experience in the Cuban revolution, Guevara argued that acts of violence by a small revolutionary band (the *foco*) could spark a successful revolution even if strong indigenous support were lacking. The strategy was a dismal failure, and Guevara was killed trying to implement it in Bolivia. See Che Guevara, *Guerrilla Warfare* (New York: Monthly Review Press, 1961); and also Regis Debray, "Revolution in the Revolution? Armed Struggle and Political Struggle in Latin America," *Monthly Review* 19, no. 3 (1967).

dency for rebellious collective action to occur in distinct waves or cycles. Although most dissident social movements do not lead to a revolution, the leaders of a revolutionary state are likely to interpret signs of turbulence in other societies as evidence that their own victory is merely the first of many.[57]

Revolutionary states can be further misled if they give too much credence to the testimony of foreign sympathizers, whose desire for external support inspires them to exaggerate the prospects for revolution back home. Such testimony will encourage active efforts to export the revolution (which will exacerbate tensions with other states) and fortify the new regime's confidence when it contemplates war. Moreover, their own success in gaining power against seemingly impossible odds may convince the revolutionary leaders that they can triumph over more powerful international opponents (this tendency will be compounded if other societies show signs of a similar level of discontent, even if rebellious action elsewhere does not lead to a full-fledged revolution). Furthermore, divisions within the revolutionary elite may encourage overly ambitious objectives, particularly if a willingness to export the revolution becomes a litmus test of revolutionary convictions.[58]

Finally, and somewhat paradoxically, a revolutionary state's own vulnerability may cause its interest in expansion to grow, at least in ideological terms. Fearing that their hold on power is fragile, revolutionary leaders are likely to view domestic opponents as potential fifth columns for their external foes. Exporting the revolution becomes the only way to preserve their positions at home: unless opposing states are swiftly overthrown, the argument runs, they will eventually join forces with domestic counterrevolutionaries in order to crush the revolutionary state. To avoid this fate, the revolutionaries may conclude their only hope is to strike first.

Meanwhile, foreign powers are also both insecure and overconfident after a revolution. Why them as well?

Other states fear the spread of revolutionary ideas, especially when the ideas challenge their own form of government directly. But they also think this threat an easy problem to solve. Because of the disorder that accompanies a revolution, other states view the new regime as weak and vulnerable, especially because of the inherent difficulty of estimating a new state's ability to fight. (By definition, revolutionary states rest on novel forms of social organization; revolutionary movements succeed because they exploit new

---

[57] Sidney Tarrow, *Struggle, Politics, and Reform: Collective Action, Social Movements, and Cycles of Protest*, Occasional Paper 21, Western Studies Program (Ithaca: Center for International Studies, Cornell University, 1989).

[58] This is one variant of the domestic politics approach discussed in chapter 1. When a revolutionary movement is deeply divided, extremists may advocate an aggressive foreign policy as a means of undermining the revolutionary credentials of their more moderate opponents.

ways to mobilize previously untapped sources of social power. Unfortunately, the novelty of these institutions renders any meaningful evaluation of their impact on national capabilities nearly impossible.) Ideological biases may amplify this tendency, because states based on different political principles have trouble acknowledging that a revolutionary government could be popular or effective. (This problem affected U.S. perceptions of revolutionary states such as China, Cuba, and Nicaragua, for instance; because U.S. leaders believed that Communism was illegitimate and immoral, they had difficulty recognizing these regimes as independent states commanding substantial popular support.[59]) And if they believe that a revolutionary state is inherently unpopular, the other states will exaggerate their own ability to confront it successfully.

The uncertainty surrounding a revolution contributes to the problem; as discussed above, foreign powers will exaggerate the threat of subversion. Having witnessed an unexpected revolutionary upheaval, mindful of the confident proclamations of the revolutionary forces, and aware that some members of their own society might harbor similar ideas (especially when there are clear signs of unrest), other states are likely to see contagion as more likely than it really is. The universalism of most revolutionary ideologies compounds these worries, because the other states fear that an alliance of like-minded revolutionary powers could leave them adrift in a hostile ideological sea.

Even in the absence of clear evidence of the revolution spreading, other states cannot be completely confident that subversive movements do not lurk beneath the surface. European fears of a Jacobin conspiracy and the U.S. "Red scares" of the 1920s and the 1950s illustrate the tendency for foreign powers to misread the ideological appeal (and therefore the offensive power) of revolutionary states. Because the threat these states pose is not simply a function of material capabilities, revolutions will seem even more dangerous than they are. And a similar logic applies to counterrevolutions: the inevitable signs of internal discord will encourage other states to try to reverse the revolution, even when it is impossible to determine the chances of success.

Once again, the perception of the threat from a revolutionary state and its susceptibility to outside pressure will be exacerbated by testimony from self-interested exiles and revolutionary sympathizers. The former portrays the revolutionary state as both a dangerous adversary and a disorganized, unpopular, and vulnerable target, while the latter depicts foreign powers as

[59] Thus, Assistant Secretary of State Dean Rusk claimed that the Communist regime in China was "a colonial Russian government . . . it is not Chinese." Quoted in Michael J. Schaller, *The United States and China in the Twentieth Century* (New York: Oxford University Press, 1979), 125.

both hostile and ripe for revolution. And if their respective hosts do not discount this testimony accordingly, they are more likely to fall into a precarious web of fear and overconfidence.

Thus, in addition to altering the balance of power, revolutions also shape perceptions of intent and estimates of the offense-defense balance in especially dangerous ways. Both the revolutionary regime and the leaders of outside states view the other's existence as a serious challenge, yet neither can estimate the danger accurately. Lacking reliable information about the magnitude of the threat or their ability to overcome it, both will rely on ideology to fill in the gaps in their understanding, and will be susceptible to self-interested testimony from émigrés or itinerant revolutionaries, particularly when this advice confirms preexisting beliefs. Therefore, although each side fears the other, it is also likely to conclude that the threat can be eliminated at relatively low cost. In short, the beliefs that opponents are hostile, dangerous, *and* vulnerable readily combine to support preventive and preemptive wars.

When a revolution topples an apparently viable regime, it is not surprising that other states fear that they might be next. Similarly, if the revolutionary state has suffered extensive damage and faces continued internal opposition, its leaders have reason to worry that their success will be short lived. As subsequent chapters will show, however, both sides are usually wrong.

Revolutions are a relatively poor export commodity, and although counterrevolutionary efforts face somewhat better prospects, reversing a revolution from outside usually proves more difficult than its advocates expect.[60] If each side's hopes and fears were accurate, the struggle between them would be a swift and decisive triumph for one side or the other. But instead of a wave of revolutionary upheavals or the swift collapse of the new regime, the normal result is either a brief, inconclusive clash (such as the Allied intervention in Russia or the Bay of Pigs invasion) or a protracted, bloody struggle (such as the Iran-Iraq war or the *contra* war in Nicaragua). The final irony, therefore, is that each side's perceptions of threats and vulnerabilities are usually mistaken.

Why are revolutions hard to export, and why do foreign interventions fail? First, the universalist ideological rhetoric notwithstanding, a revolution

---

[60] Examples of successful counterrevolutions include the Austro-Prussian intervention in Belgium in 1790, the Russian and Austrian interventions in Italy and Greece in the 1830s, the U.S.-backed coups in Iran, Guatemala, and Chile, the U.S. invasion of Grenada in 1983, and the Vietnamese overthrow of the Khmer Rouge in Cambodia in 1979. With the exception of Cambodia, however, none of these regimes came to power through a prolonged revolutionary struggle, and none attempted (let alone accomplished) a thorough social transformation. Moreover, these are all cases where the intervening powers were overwhelmingly larger and stronger than the governments they overthrew.

[41]

is, above all, a national phenomenon. A campaign to export a revolution to other countries will immediately bring it into conflict with the national loyalties of the intended recipients. And the principle that people who conceive of themselves as a nation are entitled to their own independent state has proven to be a far more powerful social force in modern history than any notion of universal revolutionary solidarity.[61] Foreign populations are likely to view efforts to export the revolution as unwarranted acts of aggression, in turn making it easier for the ruling elites to resist the revolutionary forces. Even if conditions in other countries resemble those that produced one revolution in a general way, the special circumstances that enabled that one revolution to succeed are unlikely to exist elsewhere. Even if social unrest does transcend national boundaries and the success of one movement does inspire like-minded individuals abroad, actually causing a revolution to occur in a foreign country is another matter altogether.

Second, until a revolution actually occurs, other states may not have taken the possibility seriously, but once the danger is demonstrated, potential victims will take steps to avoid a similar fate (for example, through defensive alliances, internal reforms, or more extensive repression). Thus, the Cuban Revolution inspired the U.S. "Alliance for Progress" in Latin America (intended to forestall additional "Cubas" by promoting economic and political development) and encouraged Latin American oligarchies to suppress their domestic opponents more vigorously. Again, the point is not that revolutions pose no danger, but rather that other states can usually take a number of steps to contain the threat.

Efforts to support a counterrevolution fail for somewhat different reasons. Revolutionary leaders are usually dedicated, highly motivated individuals who have been successful precisely because they are good at organizing support in the face of impressive obstacles. They are likely to be formidable adversaries, because the same skills will aid their efforts to mobilize the nation for war.[62] Foreign interventions also fail, because they provide the domestic legitimacy that a revolutionary regime needs: the same nationalist convictions that prevent a revolution from adapting smoothly to other states will also complicate foreign intervention against a revolutionary regime. And there is an inherent paradox in trying to use exiles as the core of the counterrevolutionary movement: if these groups require extensive foreign assistance in order to challenge the new regime, their ability to command indigenous support is probably limited and their prospects for success comparatively low.

[61] See Ernest Gellner, *Nations and Nationalism* (Ithaca: Cornell University Press, 1983), 1–7; and Eric J. Hobsbawm, *Nations and Nationalism since 1780: Programme, Myth, Reality* (Cambridge: Cambridge University Press, 1990), 9–12.
[62] Skocpol, "Revolutions and Mass Military Mobilization."

To summarize: the pressure for war produced by a revolution results from two parallel myths: the belief that the revolution will spread rapidly if it is not "strangled in its crib," and the belief that such a reversal will be easy to accomplish. Among other things, this argument implies that war would be most likely when the revolutionary state espouses a universalist ideology, because such ideologies can easily be regarded as a potent (though unmeasurable) source of threat by other states. Contrary to these expectations, however, the normal result is neither a swift tide of revolutionary contagion nor the quick and easy ouster of the new regime. Instead, the more frequent result is a prolonged struggle between the unexpectedly resilient revolutionary regime and its surprisingly impervious opponents.

The explanation outlined in this chapter may also provide a more complete explanation of why revolutionary states tend to alter their behavior over time. Many of the problems caused by a revolution arise from misjudging the balance of power, the intentions of others, and the probability of contagion or counterrevolution. From this perspective, "socialization" is simply the process by which both sides acquire greater information about each of these factors. As evidence accumulates, the uncertainty that permits exaggerated perceptions of threat to flourish declines proportionately. Even if the new regime does not abandon its ultimate objectives, it is likely to modify its short-term behavior in accordance with this new information. Relations between the revolutionary states and the rest of the system will become increasingly "normal," assuming, of course, that each side is capable of evaluating and revising its policies in light of experience.[63]

Two caveats should be noted at this point. First, because elite revolutions feature less extreme ideological visions and exert less dramatic internal effects than mass revolutions, they will have less effect on the balance of threats, and so the risk of war will be lower than it is after a mass revolution. Second, the level of conflict will be greatest when the revolution creates a new state whose characteristics and ideological foundations depart sharply from the domestic orders of the other great powers. By contrast, if a revolution brings a state into conformity with prevailing sociopolitical forms, then the new regime will be seen as less hostile and the danger of contagion may be slim to nonexistent. One cannot understand the international impact of a revolution by looking solely at the revolutionary state; one must also consider the external environment in which the revolution occurred.

---

[63] David Armstrong, *Revolution and World Order: The Revolutionary State in International Society* (Oxford: Clarendon Press, 1993), esp. 302–304. For a useful survey of the literature on how states learn, see Jack Levy, "Learning and Foreign Policy: Sweeping a Conceptual Minefield," *International Organization* 48, no. 2 (1994).

## TESTING THE THEORY

As shown in figure 1, the theory outlined above identifies several independent, mutually reinforcing mechanisms linking revolution and war. It predicts that revolutions will lead to sharper security competition between states and increase the probability of war. Indeed, the theory suggests that strong pressures for war will be present even when other factors intervene to prevent it.

In each of the case studies that follow, I explore whether the different mechanisms identified in this chapter were present and, if so, whether they had the predicted effects. In general, the theory can be considered supported if, first, the revolution was followed by increased security competition or war; second, conflict and war occurred for the reasons identified in the theory; third, one or more of the causal mechanisms identified in the theory was absent or muted and war did not occur; fourth, the predicted pressures for war were present but other factors intervened to prevent it; and fifth, these effects would have been unlikely to occur had the revolution not taken place.

More specifically, the theory is supported either if other states saw the revolution as altering the balance of power, and sought to take advantage of this window of opportunity, or if they were inclined to use force in order to prevent other states from doing the same thing. By contrast, if other states did not view the revolution as a potential opportunity (owing to a perceived shift in the balance of power), that would count against this part of the theory.

*Figure 1.*

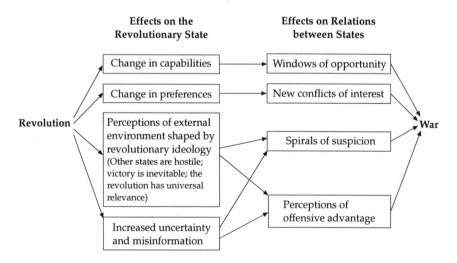

The theory is also supported if the new regime and other states consistently exaggerate each other's hostility, especially if these spirals reflected ideological predispositions. The occurrence of a serious dispute does not necessarily mean that a spiral of suspicion occurred; rather, one or both sides must have also misinterpreted the other's actions and exaggerated its hostility.[64] The theory gains further credence if these errors were fueled by uncertainty or problems of communication arising from the revolution, or by the transnational activities of counterrevolutionary exiles or revolutionary sympathizers. Again, this element of the theory is undermined if the revolution in question caused little change in either side's perceptions of intent or if a subsequent dispute was based solely on a legitimate clash of interest that both sides evaluated more or less accurately.

Evidence that the possible spread of revolution (or counterrevolution) magnified each side's perceptions of insecurity or overconfidence supports the theory, especially if these beliefs were central to the decision for war. By contrast, the theory loses credibility if war occurred when the possibility of exporting the revolution was either absent or dismissed, or if both sides believed that the revolution was likely to spread but were able to establish good relations nonetheless.

The theory I have set forth in this chapter explains why revolutions intensify security competition between states and increase the probability of war. I do not mean to imply that revolutions are a unique cause of war or that the dynamics that link revolutions and international conflict do not apply in other situations. However, I do regard revolutions as an especially powerful source of these dangers and consider war to be very likely in the aftermath of a successful revolution. In other words, a revolution is a sufficient but not necessary cause of security competition and war. The question is whether the effects of major revolutions support this general argument. To provide an answer, I begin by examining the international consequences of the French Revolution.

---

[64] It can also be difficult to determine if statements indicating suspicion or hostility are evidence of genuine fears or merely propaganda intended for other purposes. Even if it is propaganda, it is unlikely to be effective when there is not some basis for it, and such campaigns can take on a life of their own if elites begin to believe their own rhetoric or become trapped by public opinion.

[45]

# [3]

## *The French Revolution*

"Not until statesmen had at last grasped the nature of the forces that had emerged in France and had grasped that new political conditions now obtained in Europe, could they foresee the broad effects all this would have on war."

—Carl von Clausewitz

In this chapter I explore relations between revolutionary France and the other European powers from 1789 to 1799, with particular emphasis on the wars of the First and Second Coalitions. The period illustrates the link between revolution and war in an especially vivid way and provides strong support for the arguments advanced in the previous chapter.

First, as balance-of-threat theory would suggest, the French Revolution made war more likely by altering the balance of power. France's apparent weakness invited other states to seek gains either at French expense or in other areas, because they believed France could not oppose them effectively. Although neither Prussia nor Austria was strongly committed to overthrowing the new French leaders, the two states' desire to exploit the power vacuum created by the revolution helped place them both on a collision course with the new regime.

Second, the drive to war was fueled by the effects of the revolution on each state's intentions and by the ways that these intentions were perceived by others. The revolution altered French foreign policy objectives (both for ideological reasons and because competing factions within France used foreign policy to challenge their internal opponents), and it also distorted other states' perceptions of French intentions in especially dangerous ways.

Third, these fears were exacerbated by each side's belief that its opponents might be able to impose their will with relatively little effort, either through subversion, propaganda, or a rapid military campaign. French leaders were preoccupied with the danger of counterrevolution—based on suspicions of treason, rumors of aristocratic plots, and the possibility of foreign interference—while foreign leaders came to worry that the revolution in France would spread to their own societies. As we shall see, both sides'

[46]

fears were overstated: the French were able to spread their revolution only through direct military conquest, and foreign efforts to reverse the revolution in France were never very effective. Nonetheless, each side's belief in its own vulnerability intensifed its perceptions of threat and encouraged efforts to eliminate the danger before it became irresistible. Instead of the swift and bloodless victories that both sides anticipated, however, the result of these decisions was a quarter-century of recurring warfare.

And fourth, these problems were exacerbated by the poor information available to national leaders. Throughout this period, political leaders repeatedly miscalculated the balance of power, misread each other's intentions, and exaggerated the prospects for revolution and counterrevolution. Such problems are hardly unusual in international politics, but the revolution aggravated them by severing the normal channels of information between governments, by encouraging a variety of unofficial representatives (such as the French émigrés) to purvey a host of self-serving myths, and by forcing statesmen to base policy decisions on estimates of probabilities that were inherently unknowable (such as the revolutionary potential of a given society).

This chapter is divided into four parts. The first describes the origins and ideological foundations of the revolution and the causes of the war of 1792. In the second I examine the expansion of the war in 1793 and the subsequent struggle between France and the First Coalition. I turn in the third part to the War of the Second Coalition. Finally I consider the arguments advanced in chapter 2 in light of these events.

## THE REVOLUTION IN FRANCE AND THE ORIGINS OF THE WAR OF 1792

### Avant le Déluge: *France and Europe under the Old Regime*

French prestige and influence declined steadily after 1750, a trend underscored by its defeat in the Seven Years War (1756–63), its paralysis during the Polish succession of 1764 and the first partition of Poland in 1772, and the various reverses suffered by its Swedish and Ottoman allies. An apparent French triumph in the War of American Independence proved to be a hollow victory, as it did little to damage England and contributed to the growing fiscal crisis in France.

England was France's traditional rival, owing to a combination of geographic proximity, colonial competition, and conflicting security interests. An attempt to improve relations through a commercial treaty in 1785 failed to overcome English suspicions, and the growth of French influence in the Low Countries (culminating in the Franco-Dutch alliance of 1785) eventually led England and Prussia to invade Holland in 1787. The invaders ousted the pro-French Patriot Party and restored the pro-English Stadholder, William of Orange, in yet another demonstration of French impotence.[1]

Austria and France had been formally allied since 1756, but the tie was increasingly seen as a burden by both countries. Yet it endured, because France wanted to keep Austria from allying itself with England, and Austria wanted to keep France away from Prussia.[2] France was also allied to Spain via the Family Compact of 1761, an agreement based on dynastic solidarity between the two Bourbon houses and mutual hostility to England. These assets did not outweigh France's many liabilities, however, and France's international position on the eve of the revolution was not auspicious.[3]

Conflicts among the other great powers, endemic in this period, would play an important role in shaping foreign responses to events in France. Austria and Prussia had been rivals since the 1740s, with each one primarily concerned with enhancing its position at the expense of the other. Emperor Joseph II of Austria also hoped to exchange his Belgian possessions for Bavaria (thereby ridding himself of some unruly subjects and consolidating Austria's position in Central Europe), but his efforts to do so were repeatedly thwarted by foreign opposition. Austria did manage to isolate Prussia by allying with Russia in 1781, but Joseph was eventually forced to enter the Russo-Turkish war in 1788 in order to maintain the connection and to prevent Russia from monopolizing the fruits of victory. The Hapsburgs also faced considerable internal unrest during this period (partly a reaction to Joseph's reform program), including a conservative revolt in the Netherlands in 1789.[4]

Prussia's small size and relative weakness encouraged an expansionist foreign policy, and King Frederick William made several unsuccessful at-

[1] On Anglo-French relations prior to the revolution, see T. C. W. Blanning, *The Origins of the French Revolutionary Wars* (New York: Longman, 1986), 45–51; M. S. Anderson, "European Diplomatic History," in *New Cambridge Modern History*, vol. 8: *The American and French Revolutions, 1763–93*, ed. Albert Goodwin (Cambridge: Cambridge University Press, 1965), 267–68; and J. H. Clapham, "Pitt's First Decade," in *Cambridge History of British Foreign Policy*, ed. A. W. Ward and G. P. Gooch (New York: Macmillan, 1922), 1:159–70. The Patriot revolt in Holland is described by Simon Schama, *Patriots and Liberators: Revolution in the Netherlands, 1780–1813* (New York: Random House, 1977), chap. 3; and Alfred Cobban, *Ambassadors and Secret Agents: The Diplomacy of the First Earl of Malmesbury at the Hague* (London: Jonathan Cape, 1954).
[2] See Blanning, *French Revolutionary Wars*, 40–45; J. H. Clapham, *The Causes of the War of 1792* (1892; reprint, New York: Octagon Books, 1969), 5–8; and Paul W. Schroeder, *The Transformation of European Politics, 1763–1848* (Oxford: Clarendon Press, 1994), 42–43.
[3] See Derek McKay and H. M. Scott, *The Rise of the Great Powers, 1648–1815* (New York: Longman, 1983), 215–16.
[4] On the Belgium-Bavaria exchange, see Schroeder, *Transformation of European Politics,* 26–35. On Joseph's reforms and the Belgian revolt, see Robert R. Palmer, *The Age of the Democratic Revolution: A Political History of Europe and America, 1760–1800,* (Princeton: Princeton University Press, 1959, 1964), 1:341–57, 374–83.

tempts to acquire additional territory. Prussia was allied with England and Holland, but the alliance was strictly defensive and England refused to back most of Frederick William's diplomatic gambits, including his proposal for an attack on Austria in 1790. As events in France began to cast a shadow over the European system, Frederick William was already contemplating several new ploys for territorial aggrandizement, ranging from an alliance with France to an attack upon France or an additional partition of Poland.[5]

Relations among the great powers were complicated further by the growth of Russian power and the unstable situation in Poland. Catherine II had used the Austro-Prussian rivalry to win concessions from both, while seizing territory from the Ottoman Empire and establishing de facto control of Poland after the first partition in 1772. When Russia was distracted by the war with Turkey and an opportunistic invasion by Sweden in 1788, a group of Polish reformers convened a new Diet and proclaimed a new constitution. Although the effort temporarily succeeded, it was only a matter of time before Catherine would attempt to reassert Russian primacy.[6]

Thus the European system was in a state of considerable fluidity when the revolution in France began. France was formally allied with Austria and Spain (though the relationship with Austria was strained) and openly hostile to England. England was equally suspicious of France, formally allied to Prussia and Holland, and wary of Russia. Austria was allied with France and Russia and bogged down in a war against the Ottoman Empire while keeping a watchful eye on Prussia. Both Austria and Prussia were interested in territorial revisions, and the internal turmoil in Poland and the Low Countries added to the endemic instability of the system.

### Ideological Underpinnings

Identifying the ideological roots of the French Revolution is especially challenging because none of the leading participants began with a blueprint for the future political order that was well thought out.[7] Without being able to consult an explicit revolutionary program, therefore, students of the period must try to identify the central ideas that informed political debate and drove political action, while recognizing that this vocabulary shifted in re-

[5] See Robert Howard Lord, *The Second Partition of Poland: A Study in Diplomatic History* (Cambridge: Harvard University Press, 1915), 75–82; Blanning, *French Revolutionary Wars*, 51–55; and Clapham, "Pitt's First Decade," 190–97.

[6] See Palmer, *Democratic Revolution*, 1:422–29; Lord, *Second Partition*, chaps. 1, 5–6.

[7] As the Jacobin Camille Desmoulins later recalled: "In all France there were not ten of us who were republicans prior to 1789." Quoted in Henri Peyre, "The Influence of Eighteenth Century Ideas on the French Revolution," in his *Historical and Critical Essays* (Lincoln: University of Nebraska Press, 1968), 72.

[49]

sponse to the revolutionary process itself.[8] The concepts that shaped the revolution were not fixed, but they did provide the intellectual arsenal that rival groups employed both to understand the events in which they were immersed and to rally support and discredit opposition. And while these ideological underpinnings did not determine the course or outcome of the revolution, they did form the elements from which it was built.[9]

What are the main ideas that shaped the revolution in France? At the risk of oversimplifying, I have identified four interrelated themes in prerevolutionary political discourse that merit particular attention.

The first key theme was a commitment to reason and natural law, together with the concomitant belief that political action could correct existing social ills. In addition to undermining support for the Church, the notion that human affairs could be ordered according to the dictates of reason was a potent solvent to a conception of society based on privileged orders and monarchical authority.[10] This discourse implied that departures from tradition were permissible, provided they were based on reason, and faith in the power of reason helped created a new faith in politics and its unlimited capacity for action.[11]

A second theme was a broad ideological assault on the legitimacy of the absolutist state. This discourse contained several distinct but mutually reinforcing strands: one focusing on "justice" (defined as restraint on monarchical will), another extolling liberty and equality and attacking the institutions of aristocratic privilege, and a third challenging the image of the king as

---

[8] This war of ideas took place in a society that was experiencing an explosion in publishing, making it possible to disseminate contending opinions more rapidly and widely than ever before. See Robert Darnton and Daniel Roche, eds., *Revolution in Print: The Press in France, 1775–1800* (Berkeley: University of California Press, 1989); Jeremy Popkin, *Revolutionary News: The Press in France 1789–1799* (Durham: Duke University Press, 1990); and Colin Jones, ed., *The Longman Companion to the French Revolution* (New York: Longman, 1988), 260–62.

[9] "The ideology embraced by the National Assembly . . . was . . . less a blueprint than a set of architectural principles that could be applied to the construction of quite different sociopolitical orders." William Sewell, "Ideologies and Social Revolutions: Reflections on the French Case," *Journal of Modern History* 57, no. 1 (1985), 71. See also Daniel Mornet, *Les Origines intellectuelles de la révolution française (1715–1787)* (Paris: Armand Colin, 1933), esp. 477; Peyre, "Influence of Eighteenth Century Ideas"; and Roger Chartier, *The Cultural Origins of the French Revolution*, trans. L. G. Cochrane (Durham: Duke University Press, 1989).

[10] "The Enlightenment insisted on the universal applicability of reason to human affairs. It had scorn for all privilege no matter how ancient or venerable." Sewell, "Ideologies and Social Revolutions," 65.

[11] François Furet argues that "the very bedrock of revolutionary consciousness" is the belief that "there is no human misfortune not amenable to a political solution." *Interpreting the French Revolution*, trans. Elborg Forster (Cambridge: Cambridge University Press, 1981), 25. As products of the Enlightenment, the revolutionaries "believed in the absolute efficacy of politics—which they thought capable of recasting the body social and regenerating the individual." Bronislaw Baczko, "Enlightenment," in *A Critical Dictionary of the French Revolution*, ed. François Furet and Mona Ozouf, trans. Arthur Goldhammer (Cambridge: Harvard University Press, 1989), 662–64; and see Chartier, *Cultural Origins*, 198.

God's chosen representative. If not revolutionary by themselves, each of these strands nourished doubts about the existing order and cleared the way for a fundamental change.[12]

Third, the wide-ranging challenge to absolutism featured a continuing debate on the nature of the political community. Over time, the image of France as the personal possession of a sovereign king was supplanted by the idea that sovereignty was held by a single people united by language, territory, blood, and other "natural" characteristics. This transformation from subjects to citizens was already evident in 1788, when Abbé Sieyès declared that the Third Estate was "everything appertaining to the nation."[13] The revolution completed this process by replacing an abstract notion of the king as the sovereign authority with a concept of "popular sovereignty" in which the nation was the embodiment of the "general will."[14]

Finally, under the influence of Rousseau, Montesquieu, and others, the ideological foundations of the French Revolution also contained a powerful moral dimension, centered on the concept of *virtue*. The importance attached to virtue helped discredit the old regime (which was seen as corrupt) and legitimated efforts to inculcate proper conduct as part of creating a new political order. A belief in reason and in the limitless possibilities of politics also implied that "human action no longer encounters obstacles or limits, only adversaries, preferably traitors."[15] This tendency reached its peak during the Reign of Terror, when the Jacobins used the machinery of the state to promote virtue among the citizens, while seeking to eliminate any individuals whose opposition to the general will exposed their evil natures.[16]

---

[12] See Keith Michael Baker, *Inventing the French Revolution: Essays on French Political Culture in the Eighteenth Century* (Cambridge: Cambridge University Press, 1982), esp. 25–27; Jeffrey Merrick, *The Desacralization of the French Monarchy in the Eighteenth Century* (Baton Rouge: Louisiana State University Press, 1990); and Robert Darnton, *The Literary Underground of the Old Regime* (Cambridge: Harvard University Press, 1982).

[13] Sieyès added that "the Nation is prior to everything, it is the source of everything.... Its will is always the supreme law." His attack on privilege placed these orders outside the political community; in his words, "the nobility does not belong to the social organization at all.... whatever is not of the third estate may not be regarded as belonging to the nation. What is the third estate? Everything!" Joseph Emmanuel Sieyès, "What Is the Third Estate?" in *A Documentary Survey of the French Revolution*, ed. John Hall Stewart (New York: Macmillan, 1951), 44.

[14] According to Leah Greenfeld, "the Nation replaced the king as the source of identity and focus of social solidarity, as previously the king had replaced God." *Nationalism: Five Roads to Modernity* (Cambridge: Harvard University Press, 1993), esp. 160–68. See also Alfred Cobban, "The Enlightenment and the French Revolution," in his *Aspects of the French Revolution* (New York: George Braziller, 1968), 25.

[15] Furet, *Interpreting the French Revolution*, 26.

[16] See Carol Blum, *Rousseau and the Republic of Virtue: The Language of Politics in the French Revolution* (Ithaca: Cornell University Press, 1986), chaps. 8 and 10; and also Alfred Cobban, "The Fundamental Ideas of Robespierre," in his *Aspects of the French Revolution*; and Norman Hampson, *Will and Circumstance: Montesquieu, Rousseau, and the French Revolution* (Norman: University of Oklahoma Press, 1983).

[51]

These four broad and interrelated themes formed the worldview of the revolutionary vanguard in France. They set the terms and limits of debate throughout the revolutionary period and encouraged a number of specific attitudes and actions.[17] The appeal to reason and natural law contributed to the optimism that is essential for revolutionary action, and this attitude was strongly reinforced by the extraordinary events of 1789–91. The revolutionaries' own experience seemed to prove that society could be transformed according to the dictates of reason, and the possibilities for political and personal transformation were soon regarded as virtually limitless. This belief helped discredit the voices of moderation and encouraged the revolutionaries' faith that they could overcome any obstacle.

Like any ideology, the worldview of the French Revolution contained obvious ambiguities and contradictions. On the one hand, faith in the preeminence of reason and the operation of universal laws encouraged the revolutionaries in France to view their achievements as a world-historical event whose principles were of universal validity. On the other hand, the simultaneous redefinition of the political community in terms of the French "nation" encouraged more self-interested and particularistic conceptions, a tendency reinforced by existing animosities (such as the rivalry with England).

Furthermore, the revolutionary process created a profound tension between the explicit goal of liberty and the implicit principle of national unity. It replaced the authority of the king with the authority of "le peuple," and it linked popular sovereignty to equality and Rousseauist notions of the general will (rather than placing it within a framework of individual rights and representative institutions). The revolution was supposed to free citizens from monarchical tyranny and arbitrary government authority, and create a *nation* consisting of a single body shorn of privileged orders.[18] In the absence of a theory of representation, however, these principles left France without a legitimate avenue for disagreement. Given the presumption of unity, the only outlet for opposition was conspiracy, which was also the most obvious explanation for any failure to achieve the revolution's lofty goals. Thus, any sign of dissent was a potential hazard to the unity of the nation, leaving revolutionary France peculiarly vulnerable to fears of plots and conspiracies.[19]

Although the French Revolution was not the product of a self-conscious revolutionary movement originating under the ancien régime, its underly-

[17] As Sewell puts it, ideologies "are at once constraining and enabling. They block certain possibilities, but they also create others." "Ideologies and Social Revolutions," 60.

[18] As Furet points out, "the 'people' were defined by their aspirations, and as an indistinct aggregate of individual 'right' wills. By that expedient, which precluded representation, the revolutionary consciousness was able to reconstruct an imaginary social cohesion in the name and on the basis of individual wills." *Interpreting the French Revolution*, 27.

[19] See Norman Hampson, *Prelude to Terror: The Constituent Assembly and the Failure of Consensus, 1789–1791* (London: Basil Blackwell, 1988), esp. 106–107; and Furet, *Interpreting the French Revolution*, 51–55.

ing principles resemble the ideal type set forth in chapter 2. The revolutionaries were confident of their ability to reshape politics, society, and even
human nature itself, strongly inclined to consider their opponents inherently evil and deserving of extermination, and prone to uphold their own
experience as a model for others. As we shall see, these views, which continued to shape perceptions and political debate once the revolution was
underway, had a powerful influence on relations between revolutionary
France and the rest of Europe.

### The Dismantling of the Ancien Régime and
### the Initial Foreign Response

The immediate cause of the French Revolution was the fiscal crisis triggered by French aid to the American colonies during their War of Independence, which broke the back of the archaic French tax system.[20] The nobility
successfully resisted Louis XVI's efforts to impose new taxes in 1787, forcing
the king to summon the Estates General for the first time since 1614. Under
pressure from liberal nobles and provincial authorities, Louis and his ministers agreed to double the size of the Third Estate (representing the com-
moners) in January 1789. They resisted demands to grant each deputy a
single vote, however, in favor of the traditional practice of each order voting
in unison.[21]

The first decisive break came when the representatives of the three estates
met at Versailles in May. After a month of futile debate over the voting procedure, representatives of the Third Estate designated themselves a new National Assembly and invited members of the other orders to join. Louis
reluctantly accepted this measure on June 23, but he also began assembling
troops near the capital in preparation for a *coup de main* against the defiant
deputies. Before he could launch his coup, however, the fear of an aristocratic reaction sparked a popular uprising in Paris and began to undermine
the loyalty of the royal garrisons. Supporters of the Assembly had already
begun to mobilize the Parisian population, and an angry mob stormed the
fortress of the Bastille on July 14. Informed that he could no longer count on
his troops' allegiance, Louis agreed to disperse the regiments surrounding
Paris and declared his support for the National Assembly on July 17. A new

---

[20] See Doyle, *Origins of the French Revolution*, 43–53; Jean Egret, *The French Pre-Revolution,
1787–88*, trans. Wesley D. Camp, (Chicago: University of Chicago Press, 1977); and John Francis Bosher, *French Finances, 1770–1795: From Business to Bureaucracy* (Cambridge: Cambridge
University Press, 1970).

[21] The First Estate represented the clergy, the Second Estate the nobility, and the Third Estate everyone else. Representatives for each order were chosen through local elections, and
the local assemblies drew up petitions of grievances (known as *cahiers de doléances*) for consideration by the king and Estates General.

municipal government was formed in Paris, the Marquis de Lafayette became commander of the new National Guards, and the first wave of émigrés departed, including the king's brothers, the comte d'Artois and comte de Provence.[22]

The upheaval in Paris was accompanied by similar events in the provinces. The departure of the émigré aristocrats increased concerns about a reactionary conspiracy and helped spark the "Great Fear" that engulfed France from July 20 to August 4. Inspired by reports of armed brigands, food shortages, and aristocratic plots, rural mobs began burning chateaux, destroying manorial records, and seizing noble property. Provincial notables began forming "permanent committees" to restore order, and these bodies began to supplant the municipal institutions of the ancien régime as royal authority waned.[23]

Meanwhile, the deputies (now designated the National Constituent Assembly) were launching a direct assault on the institutions of the ancien régime. The deputies voted to abolish the feudal order "in its entirety" on the night of August 4 and approved the famous Declaration of the Rights of Man and the Citizen on August 27. Over the next twenty-six months, the Assembly abolished noble and clerical privileges and reorganized the institutions of local government and the judiciary. The deputies also voted to confiscate Church property in November 1789, banned religious orders in February 1790, and passed a new Civil Constitution of the Clergy that placed the church under the formal control of the state in July. Clerical opposition to these measures prompted a further decree in November 1790 that required priests to swear an oath of allegience to the constitution or be removed from office.[24]

Predictably, these steps provoked considerable opposition. The king refused to sanction the August decrees, and renewed fears of a royalist coup

---

[22] On these events, see William Doyle, *The Oxford History of French Revolution* (New York: Oxford University Press, 1988), 107–11; D. M. G. Sutherland, *France 1789–1815: Revolution and Counterrevolution* (New York: Oxford University Press, 1986), 47–48, 59–68; George Rudé, *The Crowd in the French Revolution* (London: Oxford University Press, 1959); and Georges Lefebvre, *The French Revolution*, trans. Elizabeth M. Evanson (vol. 1) and John Hall Stewart and James Friguglietti (vol. 2) (New York: Columbia University Press, 1962, 1964); 1:120–24. On the disintegration of the army, see Samuel F. Scott, *The Response of the Royal Army to the French Revolution: The Role and Development of the Line Army, 1787–1793* (Oxford: Clarendon Press, 1978), 51–59; and Jean-Paul Bertaud, *The Army of the French Revolution: from Citizen-Soldiers to Instrument of Power*, trans. Robert R. Palmer (Princeton: Princeton University Press, 1988), 22–29.

[23] The classic analysis of the Great Fear is Georges Lefebvre, *The Great Fear of 1789: Rural Panic in Revolutionary France*, trans. Joan White (Princeton: Princeton University Press, 1973). On the provincial revolts, see Lynn A. Hunt, "Committees and Communes: Local Politics and National Revolution in 1789," *Comparative Studies in Society and History*, 18, no. 3 (1976); and Sutherland, *France*, 70–76.

[24] For the texts of these decrees, see Stewart, *Documentary Survey*, chap. 2; for summaries, see Sutherland, *France*, 88–99; and Michel Vovelle, *The Fall of the French Monarchy, 1787–1792*, trans. Susan Burke (Cambridge: Cambridge University Press, 1984), 146–62.

led an unruly mob to invade Versailles on October 5 and bring the royal family back to Paris, where the king's activities could be monitored more easily. The anticlerical measures angered many priests and parishioners, economic conditions worsened, and the émigré exodus continued. When the king's brothers began to solicit aid for a restoration from the other European governments, the rumors of an "aristocratic conspiracy," once entirely a myth, began to acquire a real basis.[25]

Over the next ten months, the debate over the constitution saw the emergence of several contending factions within the Assembly. These groups were not formal political parties but loose alignments of delegates who shared similar views on salient political issues. The largest faction was that of the moderates, which was eventually centered around a group meeting at the Feuillant Club. Composed primarily of liberal nobles such as the Marquis de Lafayette and members of the upper bourgeoisie, the Feuillants favored a constitutional monarchy, the strict protection of property rights, limited suffrage, and a laissez-faire economic policy. The Feuillants' main rivals were their former associates in the Société des Amis de la Constitution, popularly known as the Jacobin Club, from whom they had split in July 1791. The Jacobins were more distrustful of the king and more supportive of popular democracy, although they shared the Feuillants' desire to safeguard private property and were not yet opposed to the institution of the monarchy. More radical groups included the Société des Amis des Droits de l'Homme et du Citoyen (known as the Cordeliers Club) and the various popular associations that were then emerging among the artisans and poorer classes of Paris.[26]

The next phase followed Louis's unsuccessful attempt to flee from Paris in June 1791.[27] The royal family was captured and returned to Paris on June 25, but this new evidence of the king's attitude sparked renewed fears of a counterrevolutionary conspiracy and brought calls by the more radical deputies for the abolition of the monarchy. The moderates still hoped to persuade the king to accept the new constitution, however, and tried to discourage foreign intervention by treating Louis leniently. A commission of inquiry accepted the Feuillants' claims that the king had been abducted and declared Louis innocent of treason but suspended his royal functions provisionally. The verdict intensified the divisions within the revolutionary

[25] See Sutherland, *France,* 82–85, 124; Lefebvre, *French Revolution,* 1:130–35; and Hampson, *Prelude to Terror,* 77–81.

[26] This account does not do justice to the diverse political groups that emerged after 1789; for a summary, see Jones, *Longman Companion to the French Revolution,* 170–91. For background, see Michael Kennedy, *The Jacobin Club in the French Revolution: The First Years* (Princeton: Princeton University Press, 1981), esp. chap. 15; and Patrice Gueniffey and Ran Halevi, "Clubs and Popular Societies," in Furet and Ozouf, *Critical Dictionary,* 458–72.

[27] The abortive escape is described in detail in J. M. Thompson, *The French Revolution* (Oxford: Basil Blackwell, 1943), 198–210.

movement, and Lafayette and the National Guards were forced to suppress a radical demonstration in the Champ de Mars in August. Louis finally agreed to accept the constitution on September 14, and the Constituent Assembly disbanded pending the election of a new Legislative Assembly.[28]

At first, the main effect of the revolution in the international arena was to isolate France. Both allies and adversaries now discounted French power and influence and tended to focus their attention on other matters. At the same time, there were signs that the revolution might affect other states' interests adversely, and this fear grew as the revolution progressed.

The potentially threatening character of the French Revolution to foreign states had become apparent once the National Assembly began drafting a constitution in August 1789. By proclaiming that all men had the right to govern themselves, the universalist language of the Declaration of the Rights of Man constituted an implicit challenge to the legitimacy of the other European states. The decrees abolishing the feudal regime in France also threatened the traditional privileges of several foreign rulers, most notably in Alsace and Avignon.[29] The Assembly now claimed these territories on the basis of "popular sovereignty," an innovation that called the legal framework of the European political order into question. If the Assembly could rescind an existing treaty merely by invoking the will of the people, then no prior treaty (including any guaranteeing the present borders) was safe. Moreover, the notion of exclusive sovereignty based on the national will clashed with the heterogeneous and overlapping lines of authority that still held sway in much of Europe, especially in Germany. From the very beginning, therefore, the principles of the revolution posed a possible danger to political stability in Europe.[30]

These inherent conflicts were magnified by some predictable side-effects of the revolutionary process itself. Not only had the events of 1789 generated an enthusiastic response from intellectuals throughout Europe, but Paris quickly became a magnet for revolutionary sympathizers from other

[28] See Sutherland, *France*, 127–31.

[29] Alsace had been ceded to France by the Treaty of Westphalia in 1648, but the treaty also preserved the feudal rights of several German princes "in perpetuity." The electors of Trier, Cologne, and Mainz, the bishop of Basel, the duke of Württemberg, and the margrave of Baden protested the Assembly's action. Leopold II backed their claims in his capacity as Holy Roman Emperor. A rebellion in Avignon in June 1790 ousted the papal authorities, and the population voted to petition the Assembly for absorption by France, which granted the request in February 1791. See Sydney Seymour Biro, *The German Policy of Revolutionary France: A Study in French Diplomacy during the War of the First Coalition, 1792–1797*, (Cambridge: Harvard University Press, 1957), 1:39–42; and Blanning, *French Revolutionary Wars*, 77, and *The French Revolution in Germany: Occupation and Resistance in the Rhineland, 1792–1802* (London: Oxford University Press, 1983), 61–62.

[30] See David Armstrong, *Revolution and World Order: The Revolutionary State in International Society* (Oxford: Clarendon Press, 1993), 85; and Schroeder, *Transformation of European Politics*, 71–73.

countries. Such men saw events in France as heralding a new age of universal liberty, and they offered their own support for the revolution while seeking French assistance for their own ambitions at home. In June 1790, for
example, a sympathetic German baron named Jean-Baptiste (Anacharsis)
Cloots, self-proclaimed *orateur du genre humain*, brought an international
delegation before the Assembly to praise the revolution as "a trumpet . . .
[that] has reached to the four corners of the globe, . . . a choir of 25 million
free men [that] has reawakened people entombed in a long slavery."[31] But as
Georges Lefebvre notes, "separation from their homeland induced errors of
fact and judgment: they easily confused desires with reality and passed on
their delusions to their French comrades." Moreover, their presence in Paris
and their activities there came to be seen as threatening by other states.[32]

In the same way, the émigrés who left France after 1789 sought assistance
in restoring the old regime by telling foreign leaders that the revolution was
a serious threat to other countries and by portraying the new regime as illegitimate, unpopular, and vulnerable.[33] Although they achieved only mixed
results, they contributed to the growth of antirevolutionary sentiments in
several European capitals.[34] More importantly, their activities fueled the revolutionaries' recurring fears of an aristocratic conspiracy, even though foreign monarchs did not oppose the revolution until the summer of 1791.[35]
Thus, just as the migration of foreign revolutionaries exaggerated the danger France seemed to pose to other states, spurring hopes and fears of additional upheavals elsewhere, the émigrés simultaneously reinforced foreign
fears about the revolution and French perceptions of foreign hostility.[36]

Despite these omens, foreign reactions to the revolution were initially
rather mild. Some European leaders took steps to contain the spread of revolutionary ideas, but they ignored the émigrés' calls for action and made lit-

---

[31] Quoted in Blanning, *French Revolutionary Wars*, 74. See also Albert Mathiez, *La Révolution
et les étrangers: cosmopolitisme et défence nationale,* (Paris: Renaissance du Livre, 1918), chaps.
3–4; Lefebvre, *French Revolution*, 1:180; Jacques Godechot, *La Grande nation: L'Expansion révolutionnaire de la France dans le monde de 1789 à 1799,* 2d ed. (Paris: Aubier Montaigne, 1983),
151, 213; and Palmer, *Democratic Revolution*, 2:53–55.

[32] See Lefebvre, *French Revolution*, 1:181 and passim; and Robert R. Palmer, *The World of the
French Revolution* (New York: Harper and Row, 1967), 84–86.

[33] Thus, the comte d'Artois told Frederick William in January 1790 that the French people
were "sighing for foreign help." Quoted in Clapham, *Causes of the War of 1792*, 23–24. Émigré
agents also claimed the revolution was the work of an international network (the "Society of
Propaganda") whose aim was to foment revolution throughout Europe. As one royalist put
it, "If this should not be true, it would at least be worth it to spread the story." Quoted in
Palmer, *Democratic Revolution*, 2:51–52.

[34] See Lefebvre, *French Revolution*, 1:188.

[35] See Blanning, *French Revolution and Germany*, 47–58, and *French Revolutionary Wars*, 85;
and Biro, *German Policy*, 1:36–37.

[36] Lefebvre observes that the role the émigrés played abroad "bore close resemblance to
that of political refugees in France." *French Revolution*, 1:188.

tle or no effort to organize a counterrevolutionary campaign until the revolution was nearly two years old. Emperor Leopold expelled the émigrés' emissary in January 1791 and forced d'Artois to depart for Mantua in May. The royal family's own search for foreign support was unsuccessful, despite the close family connections between Louis and his queen and several ruling houses of Europe. Although Marie Antoinette maintained an active correspondence and Louis dispatched a personal emissary to negotiate for foreign assistance, their efforts brought only words of encouragement and counsels of patience.[37]

One reason for restraint was the favorable reaction that the revolution had produced among many European elites. If men such as Edmund Burke were suspicious, artists and intellectuals such as Kant, Fichte, Blake, and Beethoven all welcomed the apparent triumph of liberty in France.[38] This favorable view was shared by prominent political leaders: Thomas Jefferson described events in France as "the first chapter of the history of European liberty," and the leader of the English Whigs, Charles James Fox, called the fall of the Bastille "the greatest and best event that has happened in the world." Other Englishmen—including Prime Minister William Pitt—were reminded of England's own revolution and were flattered that France seemed to be following a similar path.[39] Although elites in Russia, Sweden, and Spain tended to see the revolution as illegitimate and dangerous, liberal monarchs such as Joseph II and Leopold I were more sympathetic.[40]

European statesmen also welcomed the revolution because it reduced French power, thereby decreasing the danger that prerevolutionary France had

[37] The queen's efforts to enlist foreign support are chronicled in Alfred Ritter von Arneth, ed., *Marie Antoinette, Joseph II, und Leopold II: Ihr Briefwechsel* (Leipzig: K. F. Kohler, 1866); and O. G. de Heidenstam, *The Letters of Marie Antoinette, Fersen, and Barnave* (New York: Frank Maurice, n.d.).

[38] On European reactions to the revolution, see Lefebvre, *French Revolution*, 1:179–87; Albert Soboul, *The French Revolution, 1787–1799*, trans. Alan Forrest and Colin Jones (New York: Vintage, 1975), 216–18; Palmer, *Democratic Revolution*, 2:16–27, 53; George Rudé, *Revolutionary Europe, 1783–1815* (New York: Harper Torchbooks, 1964), 180–82; G. P. Gooch, "Germany and the French Revolution," *Transactions of the Royal Historical Society*, ser. 3, no. 10 (1916), esp. 55–56; Vovelle, *Fall of the French Monarchy*, 137–41; Alfred Cobban, ed., *The Debate on the French Revolution* (London: Adam and Charles Black, 1960); and Philip Anthony Brown, *The French Revolution in English History* (London: Crosby Lockwood and Son, 1918), 29–50.

[39] Pitt told the House of Commons in February 1790 that "whenever the situation of France shall become restored, . . . France will enjoy just that kind of liberty which I venerate; . . . [I cannot] regard with envious eyes, an approximation in neighbouring states to those sentiments which are the characteristic features of every British subject." Quotations from Michael H. Hunt, *Ideology and U.S. Foreign Policy* (New Haven: Yale University Press, 1987), 98; Brown, *French Revolution in English History*, 38–39; John Holland Rose, *Life of William Pitt* (New York: Harcourt Brace, 1924), 1:551; Cobban, *Debate on the French Revolution*, 68–69.

[40] In August 1790, for example, the Spanish foreign minister, Count Floridablanca, described the French democrats as "a wretched set. . . . If I had my way, I would put a cordon along the frontier, as if for a plague." Quoted in Clapham, *Causes of the War of 1792*, 33.

posed and creating opportunities to profit at French expense. This attitude was nowhere more apparent than in England: to Pitt, France was "an object for compassion," while the duke of Leeds, then foreign secretary, remarked in 1789, "I defy the ablest heads in England to have planned, or its whole Wealth to have purchased, a Situation so fatal to its Rival, as that to which France is now reduced by her own Intestine commotions." His successor, Lord Grenville, rejoiced that France would not "for many years be in a situation to molest the invaluable peace we now enjoy," and the English ambassador at the Hague, William Eden (later Lord Auckland), judged that France had "ceased to be an object of alarm" and would be "of little importance with respect to its external politics." Even Burke, whose worries focused on the spread of subversive ideas, referred to the French as "the ablest architects of ruin . . . in the world."[41] Thus, when the émigrés offered them colonial concessions in exchange for British support, England's leaders chose the more immediate benefits of neutrality. As James Burges, undersecretary of state for foreign affairs, wrote Auckland in December 1790: "We have felt too strongly the immense advantages to be derived by this country from such a state of anarchy and weakness as France is at present plunged in to be so mad as to interfere in any measure that may . . . tend to [give] France . . . the power to injure us."[42]

France's reduced power was equally apparent to the eastern monarchies. Frederick William saw the revolution as a blow to the Franco-Austrian alliance and began contemplating the acquisition of French territory once the Convention of Reichenbach ended his plans for war against Austria.[43] Similarly, Catherine II's hostility toward the revolution did not blind her to its strategic benefits: the revolutionary crisis had left France unable to come to the aid of Poland, Sweden, or Turkey, and Catherine's subsequent denunciations of the new regime were partly intended to draw Prussian and Austrian attention westwards so as to free Russia's hand in the east.[44] Some

[41] See Rose, *Life of Pitt*, 1:542–43; Blanning, *French Revolutionary Wars*, 79–80, 132; Rudé, *Revolutionary Europe*, 181; and Harvey Mitchell, *The Underground War against Revolutionary France: The Missions of William Wickham, 1794–1800* (Oxford: Clarendon Press, 1965), 14. Such views were not confined to the English; one French agent reported in May 1790 that "England has nothing more to fear from France and can without qualms and without fear assume the supremacy of the [New and Old] worlds." Quoted in Albert Sorel, *L'Europe et la révolution française* (Paris: E. Pion, Nourrit, 1883–1912), 2:91.

[42] Quoted in Clapham, *Causes of the War of 1792*, 16. Auckland shared Burges's view, writing Grenville, "I heartily detest . . . the whole system of the *Democrates* [sic] . . . but I am not sure that the continued course of their struggles . . . would not be beneficial to our political interests, and the best security to the permanence of our prosperity." Quoted in Mitchell, *Underground War*, 19.

[43] The court in Berlin reportedly believed that "the great popular revolution in France will prevent that country effectually from interfering in any shape in favour of the Imperial courts." Clapham, "Pitt's First Decade," 190.

[44] In November 1791, Catherine reportedly told her secretary that she was "racking her brains to push the Courts of Vienna and Berlin into the French enterprise, so that she might have her own elbows free." Quoted in Lord, *Second Partition of Poland*, 274; and see also Clapham, "Pitt's First Decade," 190.

Austrian officials were pleased to watch French power decline, and Leopold began exploring a renewed alliance with England. Thus, the initially mild reaction of the other great powers was partly due to the strategic benefits that each hoped to gain from the disarray in France.

The belief that the revolution posed little danger at first was reinforced by the caution and circumspection that characterized French diplomacy from 1789 to 1791. When the Spanish seizure of English fishing vessels in the Nootka Sound brought the two nations to the brink of war in 1790, for example, the Assembly's de facto refusal to honor the Family Compact left Spain isolated and forced Madrid to beat a hasty retreat.[45] Louis did order the arming of fourteen ships of the line as a precautionary measure in May, but this move led the Assembly to decree that any declaration of war was subject to their approval. In a further burst of idealism, the deputies also voted to renounce "the undertaking of any war with a view of making conquests" and declared that France would not use force "against the liberty of any people."[46] By limiting royal authority over the conduct of foreign policy, these measures appeared to reduce French influence even more. The Assembly was equally unresponsive when Austria suppressed a revolt in the Netherlands later in the year, reinforcing the prevailing image of French impotence.

In addition, despite having renounced feudalism in August 1789, the Assembly treated the feudal rights of foreign powers cautiously. It offered to indemnify the Rhenish princes whose lands had been appropriated in Alsace and refrained from annexing Avignon until the pope had openly declared his own opposition to the revolution. Nor was the threat to the existing order that the Declaration of the Rights of Man and the renunciation of feudalism embodied as novel or as far-reaching as it first appeared: the French monarchy had violated the rights of foreign princes on numerous occasions before the revolution, and other rulers had acted similarly in their own realms. The situation in Avignon was equally muddled, as the French claim to the territory rested on both the notion of popular sovereignty and a number of traditional legal precedents. Given that annexation was common under the old regime, the Assembly's assertion of French sovereignty over a small enclave lying entirely within French borders hardly

---

[45] The tepid French response may have been partly due to English bribes to the comte de Mirabeau, the dominant figure in the Assembly during this period. See John Ehrman, *The Younger Pitt*, vol. 1: *The Years of Acclaim* (New York: E. P. Dutton, 1969), 553–68; Rose, *Life of Pitt*, 1:577–81; and Clapham, "Pitt's First Decade," 198–200.

[46] The decree was incorporated in the Constitution of 1791, and the comte de Mirabeau declared that "the moment is not far off when liberty will acquit mankind of the crime of war." Quoted in Gunther E. Rothenburg, "The Origins, Causes, and Extension of the Wars of the French Revolution and Napoleon," in *The Origins and Prevention of Major Wars*, ed. Robert I. Rotberg and Theodore K. Rabb (Cambridge: Cambridge University Press, 1988), 206; and see Stewart, *Documentary Survey*, 260.

posed a radical threat to the existing order. Until 1791, in short, the revolution in France simply did not appear that dangerous.[47]

Foreign reactions were further muted by the unpopularity of the émigrés and the obviously self-serving nature of their testimony. Although the émigrés were greeted warmly by some rulers (and were subsidized by Catherine the Great), their extravagance and vanity won them few friends in foreign courts and made them something of a nuisance in their adopted places of residence.[48] Moreover, the French royal family usually opposed their efforts, fearing that a restoration conducted under the auspices of the émigrés would weaken royal authority even more than the Assembly had.[49] Louis repeatedly rejected the émigrés' suggestions that he flee, preferring to make his own arrangements, and Louis explicitly warned Leopold not to support the émigrés (which the Austrian ruler was loath to do in any case). Contacts with émigré agents did reinforce Prussian revisionism (though Frederick William hardly needed encouragement), but England and Austria remained largely immune from their blandishments.[50] During the Nootka Sound dispute, for example, the British ambassador in Paris, Lord Gower, wrote that "the aristocratical party has little to hope from peace and shews evident signs of wishing to profit by the confusion which a war would certainly occasion." During the summer, the discovery that counterrevolutionary groups were trying to provoke a war between England and France by blaming the revolution on English interference led Pitt to send two agents to France to reassure the Assembly of England's pacific intentions and convince it not to support Spain.[51] Thus, the royalists' efforts to sound the alarm generally fell flat at this stage.

Last but by no means least, the revolution in France received modest attention because the great powers were preoccupied by more pressing problems elsewhere. Russia was at war with Turkey and Sweden and faced a direct challenge from the Poles, while Prussia was backing the Polish rebels

---

[47] See Lefebvre, *French Revolution*, 1:196–97; Blanning, *French Revolutionary Wars*, 76–78; Clapham, *Causes of the War of 1792*, 19–21; and Schroeder, *Transformation of European Politics*, 73.

[48] On the activities of the émigrés and foreign responses to them, see Blanning, *French Revolution in Germany*, 52–53, 60–61; Biro, *German Policy*, 1:42–45; Lefebvre, *French Revolution*, 1:187–88; and Massimo Boffa, "Emigrés," in Furet and Ozouf, *Critical Dictionary*, 326–28.

[49] Rivalry between the crown and the nobility predated the revolution. The comtes d'Artois and Provence sought to limit royal authority and preserve noble and provincial privileges. See Albert Goodwin, "Calonne, the Assembly of French Notables of 1787 and the Origins of the *Révolte Nobiliaire*," *English Historical Review* 61, nos. 240–41 (1946).

[50] See Lord, *Second Partition of Poland*, 159; and also J. Holland Rose, "The Comte d'Artois and Pitt in December 1789," *English Historical Review* 30, no. 118 (1915).

[51] Pitt's instructions convey his desire to remain aloof: "In the present circumstances the utmost care is necessary to use no language which can lead to an expectation of our taking measures to forward the internal views of any political party." Quoted in Mitchell, *Underground War*, 17–18.

and concocting its own schemes for aggrandizement. Austria's army was bogged down against the Turks, unrest at home was spreading, the Netherlands were in open revolt, and Prussia's restless revisionism remained a serious concern. England and Spain were at loggerheads for most of 1790, and Pitt was more concerned about the balance of power in the East than the collapse of England's rival across the Channel. Spain, Sweden, and the Rhenish princes were genuinely alarmed by the revolution but were too weak to act alone. Although events in France were of great interest, other problems still took precedence.

This analysis suggests that the wars between France and the rest of Europe did not arise from irreconcilable ideological antipathies. Foreign powers took note of the revolution, some with misgivings, but they did not regard it as an immediate threat on either military or ideological grounds.[52]

By contrast, the revolutionary forces in France were already worried about a counterrevolutionary conspiracy between the émigrés, the papacy, and various foreign monarchs. Their suspicions were partly justified, as both Louis and the émigrés had been seeking foreign assistance since the end of 1790. These efforts were largely unsuccessful, however, and relations between the émigrés and the king remained strained and suspicious. In short, genuine fears of an "aristocratic plot" helped drive the revolution in increasingly radical directions, but the alleged conspiracy was a chimera at this point. The stage was set for a spiral into war, partly intended and partly inadvertent.

### The Causes of the War of 1792

Relations between France and the rest of Europe deteriorated dramatically in 1791. An underlying cause was the end of the war with Turkey, which allowed Austria and Russia to shift their attention back to European affairs. Another contributing factor was the reform movement in Poland, which helped bring Austria and Prussia together and increased Catherine's desire to regain control in Warsaw. The three main causes of war in 1792, however, were the dynastic ambitions of the other great powers (especially Prussia), the struggle for power within France, and a series of regrettable miscalculations on both sides. The ideology of the revolution intensified mutual perceptions of threat and reinforced the belief that the enemy could be defeated quickly and painlessly. As we shall see, these beliefs turned out to be either erroneous or self-defeating and led to nearly a quarter century of war.

First we turn to Prussia's territorial ambitions. Despite the favorable opportunities created by the revolution in France, the revolt in Poland, and the

---

[52] Blanning, *French Revolutionary Wars*, 120–23 and passim.

outbreak of war in the East, Prussia had failed to gain a single inch of territory. When his plans to attack Austria were thwarted, Frederick William reversed course and sought an alliance *with* Leopold in order to pursue territorial gains at Russian, Polish, or French expense. In September 1790, a Prussian envoy proposed that Austria and Prussia act together to restore Louis to the throne, in exchange for territorial compensations in Flanders, Alsace, and Germany. Leopold rejected Prussia's entreaties at this time, and Frederick William turned to other equally unsuccessful schemes.[53] Undaunted by past failures, he repeated his offer for an alliance with Austria in June 1791, and Leopold was now more receptive. The Austrian monarch had become concerned about the fate of the royal family in France and wanted to convince the Assembly to halt its campaign against them. Leopold was also aware of the royal family's plans to escape, and he intended to organize an armed demonstration on the French border in order to convince the Assembly to adopt a more moderate policy. This plan crumbled when the royal escape miscarried, but Leopold still believed that foreign threats would have a moderating effect on the Assembly.[54]

Leopold's change of heart led to the signing of a formal convention between Austria and Prussia in July 1791. The convention committed the two states to aid each other in the event of internal rebellion, to support a free constitution in Poland, and to promote a European concert to regulate internal developments in France. But despite its outward appearance, the convention was not intended to be the first step toward a counterrevolutionary invasion. Instead, Leopold regarded it as a means of limiting Russian influence in Poland and moderating great power rivalries, and his objectives in France were still quite limited. The emperor aimed neither to start a war nor to undermine the National Assembly; he merely sought to strengthen the moderates and protect the royal family.[55] Frederick William wanted land, not counterrevolution, and he was willing to intervene in France in order to obtain territorial compensations rather than to defend monarchical institu-

---

[53] Frederick William backed an Anglo-Dutch-Prussian effort to force Russia to both restore the status quo ante with the Ottoman Empire and give up its predominant position in Poland, but the ploy failed when Catherine stood firm and the English Parliament refused to support the policy. On this incident (known as the Ochakov affair), see John Ehrman, *The Younger Pitt*, vol. 2: *The Reluctant Transition* (Stanford: Stanford University Press, 1983), chap. 1.

[54] Leopold and his sister corresponded regularly during this period. The queen's pleas heightened his concern over events in France but did not convince him to support a counterrevolutionary invasion. Von Arnath, *Marie Antoinette, Joseph II, and Leopold II,* 143–47, 156–69, 181–82, 188–93, 200–203, 240–41.

[55] Leopold supported the Constitution of 1791, and the Austrian chancellor, Prince Kaunitz, told the Prussian ambassador, "If Louis XVI can come to an agreement with the National Assembly about the constitution, there must be no war." When Louis accepted the constitution in September, Leopold declared that the need for a European concert had evaporated. See Heinrich von Sybel, *History of the French Revolution,* trans. Walter C. Perry (London: J. Murray, 1867), 1:362, 368; and Schroeder, *Transformation of European Politics,* 90.

tions. Although both monarchs used counterrevolutionary rhetoric to justify their actions, neither saw their rapprochement as the beginning of a counterrevolutionary crusade.[56]

Given these reservations, Leopold's efforts to pressure the Assembly were quite circumspect. He had already invited the other European powers to form a union to defend the French monarchy in July, but despite some stern language, the so-called Padua Circular was a symbolic gesture that did not commit him in any way. Meeting in Pillnitz at the end of the month (with the émigré comte d'Artois in attendance as well), Leopold and Frederick William issued a declaration calling for a European concert against the revolution. Like the Padua Circular, the Declaration of Pillnitz was purely symbolic, and joint action remained conditional on unanimous participation by the other powers. England was firmly committed to neutrality, however, which rendered the threat to intervene meaningless. This subtlety was lost on the deputies in the Assembly, in part because the Declaration implied that the émigrés and the foreign monarchs were in close collaboration.[57]

Leopold's attempt to encourage moderation seemed to work perfectly at first. The threat of foreign intervention strengthened the Feuillants' position in the Assembly and facilitated their efforts to preserve the king's position, while Louis' decision to accept the new constitution seemed to eliminate the need for intervention from abroad. With the Feuillants in control of the Assembly and the key ministries, the risk of war appeared to be fading by the fall of 1791.[58] Unfortunately, domestic politics in France now erupted and soon drove Europe over the brink.

The second major cause of war was the struggle for power in France and the Girondin campaign for war. The Feuillants' decision to preserve the

[56] Leopold did tell the Prussian ambassador, "the Jacobins are stirring up revolts throughout the whole of Italy. It is necessary to root out the evil at once." He offered no specific proposal for doing so, however, and warned, "We must proceed with extreme caution, and allow matters to come to such a pass that the nation itself will feel the necessity of a change in its condition." Most importantly, he emphasized that intervention would have to be conducted by a general concert of all the European powers, which he knew to be a remote possibility. Von Sybel, *French Revolution*, 1:351–52.

[57] The declaration stated that the two monarchs "trust that the [European] powers . . . will [employ] the most effective means for enabling the King of France to consolidate . . . the foundations of a monarchical government. . . . In which case [*alors et dans ce cas*] their said Majesties . . . are resolved to act promptly . . . with the forces necessary." And as Leopold assured his chancellor, Prince Kaunitz, "*Alors et dans ce cas* is for me the Law and the Prophets— if England fails us, the case I have put is nonexistent." In referring to the monarchs having received "requests and representations of M. le Comte d'Artois," the declaration also contributed to French fears of an aristocratic conspiracy. See Stewart, *Documentary Survey*, 221–26; Clapham, *Causes of the War of 1792*, 77–79; Blanning, *French Revolutionary Wars*, 88; Ross, *European Diplomatic History*, 36–39; Goodwin, "Reform and Revolution in France," 693–96; Schroeder, *Transformation of European Politics*, 89–90.

[58] The Feuillants obtained 264 seats in the first elections, the Jacobins received 136, and over 350 were uncommitted. See Lefebvre, *French Revolution*, 1:213; and Sutherland, *France*, 132.

monarchy after the flight to Varennes and their suppression of popular forces at the Champs de Mars had further polarized internal politics in France, and the Austro-Prussian rapprochement, the exodus of émigrés, the Padua Circular, and the Declaration of Pillnitz all combined to reinforce the fear that an aristocratic conspiracy was bent on crushing the revolution.

To counter these dangers and strengthen their own influence in the Assembly, a faction of the Jacobin movement known as the Girondins began to advocate war in the fall of 1791. Led by a former journalist, Jean-Pierre Brissot de Warville, the Girondins believed that war would either expose the king's disloyalty or force him to break ranks with the émigrés once and for all. In either case, the danger of counterrevolution would be reduced and the Girondins' own positions enhanced. The Girondins also feared the consequences of another popular uprising and thought a successful war would consolidate the nation and bring the revolutionary process to an end.[59]

The Girondin recipe for war contained several volatile ingredients. Its centerpiece was the familiar assertion that France faced a vast counterrevolutionary conspiracy linking the royal family, the émigrés, the dissident clergy, and several foreign powers.[60] France's opponents were portrayed as irrevocably hostile, implying that war was inevitable and France must seize the initiative. As Brissot told the Assembly in October, "It is not merely necessary to think of defense, the [counterrevolutionary] attack must be anticipated; you yourselves must attack."[61] The loyalty of the king was repeatedly questioned, and defenders of the monarchy now risked being labeled enemies of the revolution. The Girondins persuaded the Assembly to decree the death penalty for counterrevolutionaries and to issue an ultimatum demanding that several neighboring rulers expel the émigrés from their territories. These measures were intended to reduce the direct threat of counterrevolution and force the king to reveal his true loyalties.[62] Louis ve-

[59] The Girondins (so named because many came from the department of Gironde) were known to contemporaries as "Brissotins," in reference to Brissot de Warville. See M. J. Sydenham, *The Girondins* (London: Athlone Press, 1961); Alison Patrick, *The Men of the First French Republic: Political Alignments in the French Convention of 1792* (Baltimore: Johns Hopkins University Press, 1972); and "Girondins" in Jones, *Longman Companion*, 176–180.

[60] Brissot's first speech on foreign affairs raised the specter of a vast conspiracy against the revolution, and he accused the king of "secret schemes" in December. See Blanning, *French Revolutionary Wars*, 99–100; Clapham, *Origins of the War of 1792*, 135; Simon Schama, *Citizens: A Chronicle of the French Revolution* (New York: Knopf, 1989), 592–93; and F. L. Kidner, "The Girondists and the 'Propaganda War' of 1792: A Reevaluation of French Revolutionary Foreign Policy from 1791 to 1793," (Ph.D diss., Princeton University, 1971), 70–74.

[61] Clapham, *Causes of the War of 1792*, 27, 115, 135. On the central place of "plots" in the mindset of the revolution, see Furet, *Interpreting the French Revolution*, 55–70.

[62] As Brissot told the Jacobin Club in December 1791, "The accepted leader of the nation will be forced to rule in accordance with the Constitution. If he does his duty, we will support him wholeheartedly. If he betrays us—the people will be ready." Quoted in Sydenham, *Girondins*, 104.

toed the antiémigré decrees on November 12, but he also endorsed an ulti-matum demanding that the elector of Trier disperse the émigré armies the following month, and the Girondins' attempt to provoke a confrontation backfired when the elector promptly agreed to the French demands. The king's popularity soared, and the danger of war temporarily receded.

In addition, the Girondins argued that a successful war would rally pub-lic opinion behind the Assembly and undermine the counterrevolutionary forces within France. As Brissot told the Jacobin Club in December 1791: "A people which has just won its liberty after ten centuries of slavery needs a war in order tò bring about its consolidation." They also claimed that war would permit more active efforts to suppress internal opponents, because "in time of war, measures can be taken that would appear too stern in time of peace."[63]

The Girondin orators also successfully stirred the emotions of the deputies by repeatedly invoking French glory and national honor. In his ini-tial speech, Brissot began by reciting a list of alleged offenses committed by foreign powers and told the delegates, "You must avenge your glory, or con-demn yourselves to eternal dishonor." His associate Maximin Isnard pro-claimed, "The French people have become the foremost people of the universe. As slaves, they were bold and great; are they to be feeble and timid now that they are free?" Brissot addressed the same theme in a speech at the Jacobin Club in December: "Louis XIV could declare war on Spain be-cause his ambassador had been insulted . . . are we who are free, should we for a moment hesitate?" Another Girondin, Jean Baptiste Mailhe, pro-claimed that the French nation would "disappear from the face of the earth rather than violate her oath." That oath, Brissot reminded the delegates, was a simple one: "The Constitution or death!"[64]

These invocations of patriotism and national pride led to a final theme: that the war would be easy and a glorious victory inevitable. Echoing the optimistic predictions of the foreign representatives in Paris, the Girondins claimed that foreign peoples would rise up to overthrow the despots who sought to suppress liberty. "In the face of our brave patriots," predicted one speaker, "the allied armies will fade away like the shades of night in the face of the rays of the sun." The German exile Anacharsis Cloots told the As-sembly, "The German and Bohemian peasants will resume their war against their . . . seigneurs; the Dutch and the Germans, the Italians and the Scandi-

---

[63] Brissot also argued, "War at such a time as this would be a blessing to the nation, and the only calamity that we should fear is that there will not be a war," and he maintained that "we need spectacular treason cases; the people are ready!" Another Girondin suggested that France "designate the place for traitors beforehand, and let it be the scaffold!" Quoted in Soboul, *French Revolution,* 236–37; Clapham, *Causes of the War of 1792,* 135–36; and Lefebvre, *French Revolution,* 1:219.

[64] Blanning, *French Revolutionary Wars,* 100–101, 112.

navians, will shake off and shatter their chains with fury." Brissot described the war as "a crusade for universal liberty," and Isnard proclaimed, "If the cabinets try to raise up against France a war of kings, we shall raise up a war of peoples against kings. . . . At the moment that the enemy armies begin to fight with ours, the daylight of philosophy will open their eyes and the peoples will embrace each other in the face of their dethroned tyrants and an approving heaven and earth."[65]

If world revolution was imminent and lacked only the French spark to ignite it, then the war would be swift and would bring enormous benefits. As Mailhe reminded the Assembly: "Humanity will doubtless suffer, when one considers that in decreeing war you are also decreeing the death of several thousand men; but consider also that you are perhaps decreeing the liberty of the entire world. . . . Outside France despotism is in its death throes and a prompt attack will precipitate its final agony."[66]

This extraordinary optimism also rested on an inflated sense of France's military capabilities and an unwarranted disregard for its opponents. Claiming that free peoples would fight more fiercely than the mercenary armies of the old regime, one of the deputies suggested that "Louis XIV with 400,000 slaves, knew how to defy all the powers of Europe; can we, with our millions of free men, fear them?" Another asked, "What is the [French] army?" and provided his own answer: "It is the entire population." Yet another declared that "if the French people once draws the sword, it will fling the scabbard far away. Inflamed by the fire of freedom, it can . . . singlehanded change the whole face of the earth and make the tyrants tremble on their thrones of clay." Brissot argued that "every advantage is now on our side, for every Frenchmen is a soldier, and a willing soldier at that! Where is the power on earth . . . who could hope to master six million free soldiers?" This confidence was reinforced by misleading reports from the minister of war, who believed that a short war would rally the nation around the constitution and presented the Assembly with an overly rosy picture of the nation's readiness for war.[67]

The Girondins also argued that the diplomatic environment was unusually favorable. They predicted that Sweden, Russia, and England would re-

---

[65] The president of the Assembly, Henri Grégoire, declared that "if the princes of Germany continue to favor preparations against the French, the French will not carry fire and the sword to them, they will carry liberty. It is up to them to calculate the possible consequences of an awakening of nations." Another Girondin predicted, "If the Revolution has already marked 1789 as the first year of French liberty, the date of the 1st of January 1792 will mark this as the first year of universal liberty." Quotations from Blanning, *French Revolutionary Wars*, 109–10; Kidner, "Girondists and the 'Propaganda War,' " 77; and Schama, *Citizens*, 594, 597.

[66] Quoted in Blanning, *French Revolution in Germany*, 63.

[67] See Blanning, *French Revolutionary Wars*, 108–109; Von Sybel, *French Revolution*, 1:385. For evidence of France's lack of readiness, see Lefebvre, *French Revolution*, 1:229; but see also Scott, *Response of the Royal Army*, esp. 161–62; and Bertaud, *Army of the French Revolution*, 49–74.

main neutral, while Prussia would abandon Austria and ally with France. Here was logic at its most contradictory: on the one hand, war was necessary because France was threatened by a vast aristocratic conspiracy; on the other hand, victory was certain because a key member of the opposing coalition was actually a French ally!

In short, the Girondins' campaign for war was inspired primarily by their desire to undermine the Feuillants and the king and to stave off the counterrevolution they believed was imminent. Brissot and company may not have believed all of their own arguments, of course, and their position was neither internally consistent nor supported by a careful survey of the available evidence.[68] The key point, however, is that these arguments touched a sympathetic chord within the Assembly and helped convince the deputies to take an increasingly bellicose position toward the émigrés, the Austrians, and the king. By portraying France's foes as implacably hostile, by linking them with the king, émigrés, and internal opposition, and by persuading the Assembly that the campaign would be short, cheap, and glorious, the Girondins cast war as an ideal solution to the present turmoil.

Momentum for war increased after the Girondins' opponents also concluded that it would advance their own political fortunes. By the fall of 1791, for example, Lafayette was convinced that a short, victorious war would rally popular support behind the new constitution and establish the king's authority. Hence, his followers supported the Girondin campaign for war, but for their own reasons.[69] Ironically, Louis XVI also decided to support a war at this point, because he believed that France was unprepared and a rapid defeat would undermine the Assembly's authority and permit him to negotiate his own restoration.[70] By January, therefore, a number of the contenders for power were in favor of war, each convinced that it would strengthen his own position and weaken his internal rivals.

The Girondins' efforts were aided by the fact that some of their arguments were partly true. The king's acceptance of the constitution was insincere, and although there existed no antirevolutionary "aristocratic plot," the royal fam-

---

[68] The contradictions in the Girondins' position are noted by Kidner, who concludes that they did not seriously expect to spread revolution. See "Girondists and the 'Propaganda War,'" 84, 91–92 and passim.

[69] See Albert Mathiez, *The French Revolution,* trans. Catherine Alison Phillips (New York: Alfred A. Knopf, 1928), 139–40; Blanning, *French Revolutionary Wars,* 99–100; and Lefebvre, *French Revolution,* 1:217–18.

[70] Louis told an advisor, "The physical and moral state of France is such that it is impossible for her to carry on [this war] for half a campaign, but it is necessary that I should appear to enter upon it whole-heartedly .... My course of action should be such that the nation may find its only resource in its troubles in throwing itself in to my arms." The queen shared this view, arguing that "the fools" in the Assembly "do not see that [threatening the Electors] is a service to us, for if we begin [to fight them], it will be necessary ... for all the powers to intervene." Quoted in Mathiez, *French Revolution,* 140–42.

ily had been in contact with various counterrevolutionary groups and did hope to reverse the revolution at an opportune moment.[71] The hostility of the émigrés was not a fabrication either, even if the actual threat they posed was minimal. And, while there was no European concert against the revolution, Prussia and Austria had made hostile gestures at Pillnitz, and Sweden, Russia, and Spain had expressed even greater antipathy to the new order in France. Finally, the ease with which the revolts in Holland and Belgium had been suppressed in 1787 and 1790 gave the deputies in the Assembly a reasonable basis for fearing that they might suffer a similar fate. Although the Girondins tailored their arguments to suit their political goals, their assertions gained credibility because there was considerable evidence to support them.

In addition to the roles of Prussian ambition and internal French developments, the decision for war was encouraged by a series of misperceptions and miscalculations between France and its main adversaries that intensified perceptions of hostility and strengthened the prowar factions on both sides. The first error arose from Leopold's belief that the Padua Circular and the Declaration of Pillnitz had strengthened the Feuillants and convinced the Assembly to moderate its policies. Unaware that the Feuillants' earlier ascendancy had had little to do with his threats or that conditions within France were changing rapidly, Leopold failed to recognize that further attempts to intimidate the the Assembly would have very different effects.

As we have seen, the Girondins' first attempt to provoke a confrontation in November 1791 had backfired when Louis demanded the dispersal of the émigré armies and the German electors complied. Unfortunately, Leopold now chose this moment to try to repeat his actions of the previous August. As head of the Holy Roman Empire, he sent a formal protest regarding the usurping of the imperial princes' feudal rights in Alsace on December 3 and approved the Imperial Diet's resolution on this issue. On December 21, the Austrian chancellor, Prince Wenzel Anton von Kaunitz, informed the Assembly that Austria would defend the elector of Trier if he were threatened, bluntly warning that armed action by France would lead to "inevitable consequences not only from the head and members of the Holy Roman Empire but also from the other sovereigns who have united in a concert for the maintenance of public order and for the security and honour of monarchs."[72]

Despite the insulting tone of the Austrian démarche, Leopold and Kaunitz did not want war, and the emperor advised the electors to accept the French demands.[73] Instead, their threats were intended to strengthen the

---

[71] See Kidner, "Girondists and the 'Propaganda War,' " 119–22.

[72] Quoted in Blanning, *French Revolutionary Wars*, 102; and see also Clapham, *Causes of the War of 1792*, 132–33.

[73] See Alfred von Vivenot and H. Zeissberg, eds., *Quellen zur Geschichte der Deutschen Kaiserpolitik Österreichs während der Französichen Revolutionskriege, 1790–1801* (Vienna: Wilhelm Braumüller, 1873–90), 1:304, 316.

moderates and to force the Assembly to turn to the king. The Austrians did not know that the Feuillants were no longer in control, however, and Kaunitz's note merely aroused French suspicions and further undermined the moderates. On January 25, 1792, the Assembly voted to issue a counterultimatum demanding that Leopold renounce any agreements or treaties directed against France. Louis promptly vetoed the motion, reminding the deputies that the Constitution of 1791 gave him primary responsibility for the conduct of foreign policy and pointing out that he had already requested assurances of Leopold's peaceful intentions.[74]

Louis's opposition stymied the Girondins temporarily, but momentum for war was restored when Austria tried yet again to intimidate the Assembly. The Austrian Council of State had already decided on January 17 to reactivate the "European concert" and demand that France disband its forces on the border, restore the German princes' feudal rights, renew Louis's traditional privileges and freedoms, return Avignon to the papacy, and confirm its adherence to all existing treaties. Still convinced that their campaign of intimidation was working (an illusion sustained by a conciliatory message from French foreign minister Antoine Delessart), Austria now sought to transform the convention with Prussia into a formal military alliance, and Kaunitz dispatched another caustic note to Paris on February 17.[75] Yet even these steps were not intended to lead to war, as Leopold and Kaunitz still believed an armed demonstration with Prussia would be sufficient to strengthen the forces of moderation and restore the position of the king.[76]

Frederick William and his ministers welcomed the proposal for an alliance, and a formal treaty was signed on February 7. The Austrians still hoped to avoid war (although acquisitive ambitions were beginning to emerge in Vienna as well), but Prussia's leaders saw the situation primarily as an opportunity to expand. Their zeal was further increased by their awareness of Russia's designs on Poland, which created the alluring possibility that Prussia might receive several Polish territories it had long coveted as compensation for its efforts in France.[77]

---

[74] See Blanning, *French Revolutionary Wars*, 105; Clapham, *Causes of the War of 1792*, 145–48; Kidner, "Girondins and the 'Propaganda War,' " 95–102.

[75] Delessart had tried to satisfy the Assembly's demands without provoking Austria to war, but his measured reply unwittingly reinforced the Austrians' faith in their minatory diplomacy. See Clapham, *Causes of the War of 1792*, 154–55, 164–66; Von Sybel, *French Revolution*, 1:426–27; Blanning, *French Revolutionary Wars*, 116; and Lefebvre, *French Revolution*, 1:224.

[76] See Schroeder, *Transformation of European Politics*, 89, 95–97; and also Vivenot and Zeissberg, *Geschichte der Deutschen Kaiserpolitik*, 1:323–41, esp. 327–30.

[77] According to Robert Lord, "From the first moment when the enterprise against France appeared possible, Frederick William's dominant aim—the first and last word of his policy—was territorial aggrandizement." *Second Partition of Poland*, 230–33. See also Blanning, *French Revolutionary Wars*, 114–15; Von Sybel, *French Revolution*, 2:6–11, 22; and Clapham, *Causes of the War of 1792*, 156, 171–72.

Prussia's desire for action was based on the same sort of optimistic beliefs that the Girondins had promulgated so effectively within France. Influenced by the testimony of émigré and royal agents (who portrayed the new regime as unpopular and vulnerable) and by the successful suppression of earlier revolts in Holland and Belgium, the Prussians assumed that the campaign would be short and easy. The belief that the revolution had sapped French strength was widespread, in part because the exodus of the émigrés had robbed the army of many of its officers. Catherine the Great believed that "a corps of 10,000 men would be sufficient to traverse [France] from one end to the other," while a Prussian diplomat reported that "France is without disciplined armies, without experienced generals, without money, and the highest degree of anarchy reigns in all departments." Similarly, one of Frederick William's chief advisors predicted, "The comedy will not last long. The army of lawyers will be annihilated in Belgium and we shall be home by the autumn."[78] Austria's leaders assumed that the threat of invasion would quiet the Assembly as it had the previous summer, although a few officials were beginning to favor ambitious schemes of their own. Thus, if the Girondins envisioned war as a triumphant crusade for liberty, their opponents believed it either would be avoided entirely or would lead to a swift and lucrative victory.

As T. C. W. Blanning writes, "with all three combatants believing their side to be invincible and their opponents on the verge of collapse, the scene was set for the final lurch into war."[79] The Austrian note of February 17 provoked an uproar in the Assembly and led to Delessart's impeachment. The remaining Feuillant ministers resigned, and Louis reluctantly appointed a new cabinet containing several Girondins. For foreign minister he chose Charles-François Dumouriez, an ambitious general who believed that the Austrian Netherlands were ripe for revolt and hoped to establish his own rule there following a successful invasion.[80]

Dumouriez began by attempting to isolate the Austrians, who were coping with Leopold's unexpected death on March 1. He obtained assurances of neutrality from England, Holland, Spain, and Switzerland, but his efforts to sever Prussia and the German states from Vienna failed completely. His first message to Austria (on March 19) was mild, but a second note nine

[78] Quoted in Crane Brinton, *A Decade of Revolution: 1789–1799* (New York: Harper and Row, 1934), 84; and Blanning, *French Revolutionary Wars*, 115–16.

[79] Blanning, *French Revolutionary Wars*, 115–16.

[80] Dumouriez told the Council of Ministers on March 22, "All these [Belgian] provinces are permeated by the spirit of liberty and shaken by recent revolution.... They will join forces with our troops and will easily drive the dispersed hordes of Austrian mercenaries from their towns." Quoted in Patricia Chastain Howe, "Charles-François Dumouriez and the Revolutionizing of French Foreign Affairs in 1792," *French Historical Studies* 4, no. 3 (1985–86), 386–87; and see also Lefebvre, *French Revolution*, 1:224; and Clapham, *Causes of the War of 1792*, 177–78.

days later demanded that Austria renounce the concert against France or face "the sternest measures." Dumouriez had already warned the Assembly's Diplomatic Committee that Austrian reinforcements were transforming Belgium and Liège into a "formidable military state." He now argued that a preemptive strike was preferable to letting France's enemies complete their preparations. A harsh Austrian reply to Dumouriez's first message brought fresh denunciations within the Assembly, and Austrian agents in France now reported that war was imminent.[81]

On April 20, Dumouriez presented to the Assembly a formal report listing France's motives for war. Louis bowed to the inevitable and asked the Assembly for a formal declaration of war against "the king of Austria and Hungary." Although several prominent Jacobins (notably Maximilien Robespierre) opposed the decision, the motion passed with only seven dissenting votes.[82] Austria and Prussia had already begun mobilizing their forces, and the first shots were to be fired by the end of the month.[83]

The origins of the war of 1792 support several of my hypotheses about the relationship between revolution and war. First, the war was not simply the result of ideological antipathies between the old-regime monarchies of Austria and Prussia and the new regime in France. France was still officially a monarchy when the war broke out, and Frederick William of Prussia had been willing to negotiate an alliance with France in 1790. Dumouriez sought a similar arrangement in 1792 and explored the possibility of an alliance with England as well. Even more significantly, the French decided to invite the duke of Brunswick to command the French armies; his reputation as a commander was clearly more important to the Assembly than his status within the ancien régime.[84] These events suggest that internal differences

[81] On Dumouriez's efforts to shake the Austro-Prussian alliance, see Sorel, *L'Europe et la révolution française*, 2:352–56; and Howe, "Dumouriez and French Foreign Affairs," 385–87.

[82] Robespierre had opposed war since November, arguing with remarkable foresight that it would either restore the monarchy or usher in a military dictatorship. He ridiculed the universalist pretensions of the Girondins, arguing that "no one likes an armed missionary, and no more extravagant idea ever sprang from the idea of a politician than to suppose that one people has only to enter another's territory with arms in its hands to make the latter adopt its Constitution." See J. M. Thompson, *Robespierre* (Oxford: Basil Blackwell, 1988), 202–209; Georges Michon, *Robespierre et la guerre révolutionnaire* (Paris: Marcel Rivière, 1937), 51–55; and Von Sybel, *French Revolution*, 1:395–96. An equally prophetic warning was given by Henri Becquet, a deputy from Haute-Marne; see Thompson, *French Revolution*, 261.

[83] The Austrians deployed fifty thousand men to the frontiers on April 12, eight days before the formal declaration of war by the French Assembly. Frederick William ordered his own army to mobilize for war on April 24, but Prussia did not declare war for several months.

[84] The duke of Brunswick had won renown as a general in the Seven Years War and was considered a reformer within his own domains. Ironically, he was eventually appointed commander of the Austro-Prussian armies, and he led the initial invasion of France. See Von Sybel, *French Revolution*, 1:397–98; and Biro, *German Policy*, 1:56–57.

were less significant than Girondin rhetoric implied; similarly, while foreign monarchs were concerned about the long-term impact of events in France, neither Prussia nor Austria went to war to defend the monarchical principle.

Second, although the impact of the revolution on the balance of power played a role in causing the war, the importance of this factor should not be overstated. Perceptions of French weakness fueled Prussian acquisitiveness and encouraged the belief that victory would be swift, but Prussia would not have gone to war on its own, and the decline of French power also encouraged other states to concentrate on more pressing issues. England remained neutral, Russia and Austria concerned themselves with events in the East, and even Frederick William preferred to gain territory from Poland than from France. French weakness made these gambits seem feasible, but the war did not arise solely (or even primarily) from the desire to exploit France's difficulties.

Third, several significant misperceptions, which both exacerbated and were reinforced by the ideology of the revolutionary movement and the internal struggle for power in France, clearly contributed to the outbreak of the war. The revolution had fostered a profound sense of insecurity within France, culminating in the belief that the king, the émigrés, the clergy, and several foreign monarchs were conspiring to restore the ancien régime. This fear helped the Girondins persuade the Assembly that a foreign war was unavoidable and that it would help preserve the revolution. Their arguments rested on erroneous beliefs about the influence of the émigrés and the hostility of Austria and Prussia, resulting from their misreading of the Austro-Prussian rapprochement, the Padua Circular, and the Declaration of Pillnitz. Austria's clumsy attempts to browbeat the Assembly merely reinforced these tendencies and facilitated the Girondins' efforts.

Interestingly, the revolution did not provoke a similar degree of insecurity in Austria or Prussia, whose responses were not driven by a strong sense of French bellicosity.[85] Leopold and Frederick William were worried about the spread of revolutionary ideas and by aspects of French behavior, but neither went to war for that reason. Rather, Frederick William's decisions reflected his perennial desire to expand (bolstered by the testimony of certain émigrés), while Austria was forced into war by the French response to their earlier threats and its own latent expansionism.[86] The fear of contagion was

[85] That the sense of threat was limited may have been partly due to the modest scope of the changes within France. Although royal authority had been sharply curtailed and the position of the king was still precarious, the Constitution of 1791 not only retained the monarchy but gave the king a substantial role.

[86] Kaunitz seems to have discounted the danger of revolutionary subversion prior to the war, writing in November 1791, "The alleged danger of the possible effects that the bad example of the French could have on other peoples is nothing but a wild-eyed panic, a chimera contradicted by the facts." Quoted in Vivenot and Zeissberg, *Geschichte der Deutschen Kaiserpolitik*, 1:286.

[73]

more prevalent in Spain, Sweden, Russia, and the smaller German states, but leaders there were not actively involved in the initial decisions for war. In partial contrast to the predictions set forth in chapter 2, therefore, the spiral of suspicion that led to the war of 1792 was essentially one-sided.

Fourth, the revolution had obvious and important effects on perceptions of the offense-defense balance, such that the use of force appeared more attractive. This factor was most evident in the Girondin campaign for war, which rested on the claims that Europe was ripe for revolt, foreign mercenaries would be no match for "free" soldiers, and France would win a quick and costless victory. France's opponents evinced equal optimism, based on the widespread assumption that the revolution had left France in no condition to fight. These perceptions were at least partly influenced by self-serving testimony from the émigrés or the revolutionary exiles in Paris, which helps explain why their forecasts were so inaccurate.

Finally, lack of information was an important contributing factor. Because they were unfamiliar with the subtleties of old-regime diplomacy, the deputies failed to realize that Leopold's warnings were largely empty gestures. Similarly, because they had no reliable information about the rapid shifts in French domestic politics, Leopold and Kaunitz could not know that their efforts to browbeat the Assembly into a more moderate stance were having the opposite effect. The dearth of information played a key role in driving the spiral to war, therefore, as Austria's actions unintentionally confirmed French fears and fortified the extremists.

With some qualifications, therefore, the war of 1792 illustrates many of the mechanisms that link revolution and war. The upheaval in France caused a destabilizing shift in the balance of power, an exaggerated perception of hostility, an internal struggle for power in which foreign policy was a potent political issue, and visions of a mutual offensive advantage that inflated both sides' confidence that they could improve their positions through war.

## The War of the First Coalition

When war broke out in April 1792, the combatants anticipated a short war and did not expect it to spread. Although the French proclaimed that they would wage a "war against kings," they delayed the declaration of war against Prussia, in an attempt to isolate Austria, and proceeded to launch a traditional limited war against the Austrian Netherlands. Austrian and Prussian war aims were unfocused, and both powers were soon distracted by the Russian invasion of Poland in May.[87] Divisions within the allied coali-

---

[87] See Schroeder, *Transformation of European Politics*, 102–107.

tion helped the revolutionary government survive the initial clashes, and the conflict soon expanded throughout Europe and beyond.

### The Second Revolution and the Expansion of the War

Contrary to the optimistic predictions of the Girondins, the war began with a series of embarrassing French defeats. The Army of the North invaded the Austrian Netherlands on April 28, but the inexperienced French troops broke and ran at their first encounter with the Austrian forces. A French general was murdered by his own troops, and the remaining commanders declared an offensive impossible and refused to move.[88]

The debacle further polarized the political climate in France. The generals blamed the defeat on lack of discipline and ministerial incompetence, while the Girondins accused the army and king of disloyalty, and Brissot warned that a secret "Austrian Committee" was at work to betray the country.[89] Given the initial belief that victory would be swift, treason seemed the only possible explanation for the initial setbacks. To stave off counterrevolution, the Assembly voted to deport the dissident clergy and dissolve the king's Swiss Guards, and ordered the deployment of provincial National Guards (known as *fédérés*) around Paris. Louis promptly vetoed these measures, dismissed the Girondin ministers, and reappointed the Feuillants. Now convinced that the radicals were intent on destroying the constitution, Lafayette left his troops and returned to Paris, where he tried unsuccessfully to rally the Assembly and the National Guard against the Jacobins. These events reunited opposition to the king, and the deputies overrode the royal veto on July 3 and authorized the *fédérés* to come to Paris to celebrate the anniversary of the fall of the Bastille. The Assembly declared the country "in danger" on July 11 and decreed a new troop levy the following day.[90]

*The Founding of the First Republic.* Demands to abolish the monarchy were growing by this point, exacerbating the divisions within the Jacobin move-

---

[88] These events led Kaunitz to abandon his normal pessimism, and he predicted that France would fall in a single campaign. Another Austrian official declared that "two regiments of Hungarian hussars, with whips as their arms, would suffice to terminate the farce." Quoted in Biro, *German Policy*, 1:74. On the failure of the initial campaign, see Ross, *European Diplomatic History*, 49–50; and Scott, *Response of the Royal Army*, 116–17.

[89] Girondin accusations about the "Austrian committee" turned out to be partially true, as agents of the queen had sent information about French military plans to the Austrian commanders. See Soboul, *French Revolution*, 242–44; Sutherland, *France*, 145; and Mathiez, *French Revolution*, 149–50.

[90] See Mathiez, *French Revolution*, 148–56; and Norman Hampson, *A Social History of the French Revolution* (London: Routledge and Kegan Paul, 1963), 137–46.

ment.[91] The Girondins were alarmed by the popular agitation in Paris and the growing strength of the more radical Montagnards, and they began negotiating with Louis for reappointment after the Feuillant cabinet resigned on July 10.

The struggle for power reached a climax after France's opponents made yet another ill-advised attempt to intimidate the Assembly. When the Austro-Prussian invasion finally got underway in July, concern for the royal family led the duke of Brunswick to issue an ultimatum threatening the destruction of Paris if its members were harmed. The so-called Brunswick Manifesto was actually the brainchild of a royalist émigré, and like Leopold's earlier démarches, the declaration merely intensified French fears and undermined the king's position even more.[92]

Spurred on by Jacobin propaganda, deteriorating economic conditions, and the fear of foreign occupation, the population of Paris rose in protest on August 9. Angry *sans-culottes* replaced the municipal government with a new body—known as the Paris Commune—and a mob of Parisians and *fédérés* stormed the Tuileries and forced the royal family to take refuge with the Assembly. Alarmed by the popular insurgency and fearing for their own safety, the deputies voted to recognize the Commune as a legitimate body and to suspend the king pending election of a national convention based on universal male suffrage.[93] Executive leadership (including the management of foreign policy) would be conducted by a provisional executive council, and the Ministry of Foreign Affairs was assigned to Pierre Hélène-Marie Lebrun, a parvenu journalist and protégé of Dumouriez.[94] In a burst of revolutionary fervor, the Assembly voted to bestow French citizenship on a number of foreign sympathizers and approved a motion renouncing conquests and expressing its desire for "fraternity with all peoples."[95]

After another outburst of mob violence and a hasty series of elections, the new National Convention convened in Paris on September 21. The deputies

---

[91] A delegation from the *fédérés* in Paris demanded the suspension of the king on July 17, claiming that "without the treason of the enemies of the interior, the others [i.e., Austria, Prussia, and the émigrés] were not to be feared or rather they would not exist." Quoted in Sutherland, *France*, 147.

[92] For the text of the manifesto, see Stewart, *Documentary Survey*, 306–11; on its origins and effects, see H. A. Barton, "The Origins of the Brunswick Manifesto," *French Historical Studies* 5, no. 2 (1967); and Biro, *German Policy*, 1:68–71.

[93] See Doyle, *History of the French Revolution*, 184–89; and Lefebvre, *French Revolution*, 1:229–35.

[94] The Executive Council was first led by Danton and later by Georges Roland, while the Diplomatic Committee of the Assembly included Brissot and several of his associates. See J. T. Murley, "The Origin and Outbreak of the Anglo-French War of 1793" (Ph.D. diss., Oxford University, 1959), 5–21.

[95] See Palmer, *Democratic Revolution*, 2:54–55; and Sorel, *L'Europe et la révolution française*, 3:15.

immediately voted to abolish the monarchy and place the king on trial and began to mobilize the nation for war. In less than six months, the war had destroyed both the monarchy and the Constitution of 1791 and given birth to the First Republic.[96]

*Revolutionary Expansion.* By the end of the year, what had begun as a defensive struggle against a counterrevolutionary expedition had become an offensive war of conquest. This dramatic improvement in France's military fortunes was partly the result of an outpouring of patriotic feeling, which filled the ranks of the French forces with enthusiastic if unskilled volunteers.[97] Equally important, however, were the rivalries and distractions that weakened France's opponents. The Austro-Prussian invasion was first delayed by negotiations over contributions and compensations and then undermined by overconfidence, mutual suspicions, and a preoccupation with events in Eastern Europe. As a result, Austria contributed only 70,000 of its 200,000 troops and Prussia sent only 40,000 out of 170,000. The invading force did not cross the French border until August 19, and its slow rate of advance gave the French invaluable time to prepare.[98]

The tide turned on September 20, when a body of French artillery halted a Prussian assault at the Battle of Valmy. With his army weakened from disease and bad weather, Brunswick called off the advance and began negotiations with Dumouriez (who had resigned from the cabinet in June and taken command of the French Army of the North). These parleys continued for over a month, and though Frederick William kept up appearances by declining an offer of alliance and ordering Brunswick to issue another threatening manifesto, his enthusiasm for the war was fading rapidly. Dumouriez eventually permitted the Prussian forces to withdraw unchallenged, and Frederick William informed the Austrians in late October that he would require additional compensation in Poland if he were to continue the war.[99] The Prussian forces had left French territory by the end of Octo-

---

[96] In September, Jacobin efforts to rally the population and reports that the foreign armies were advancing on Paris led to the murder of over a thousand imprisoned criminals who were mistakenly believed to be counterrevolutionaries. See Sutherland, *France,* 154–55; Thompson, *French Revolution,* 302–309; Patrice Gueniffy, "Paris Commune," and François Furet, "Terror," in Furet and Ozouf, *Critical Dictionary,* 138–39, 520–22.

[97] Samuel F. Scott reports that "during 1792 more than 70,000 men enlisted in the line army, an impressive achievement under any circumstances." *Response of the Royal Army,* 165; also see Bertaud, *Army of the French Revolution,* 66–74.

[98] Ross, *European Diplomatic History,* 51–52.

[99] The negotiations between France and Prussia are recounted in Biro, *German Policy,* 1:79–87; Sorel, *L'Europe et la révolution française,* 3:53–55, 77–96; Von Sybel, *French Revolution,* 2:139–48, 172–77, 185–88; Karl A. Roider, Jr., *Baron Thugut and Austria's Response to the French Revolution* (Princeton: Princeton University Press, 1987), 100–101; and Schroeder, *Transformation of European Politics,* 118–20.

ber, while a French army occupied Savoy and Nice and another moved into the Rhineland.[100]

J. T. Murley notes, "Had the Republic been prepared to compromise with the Austro-Prussian Coalition, a general peace might have resulted."[101] The main issue was whether the French would insist on imposing republican institutions in the areas it had conquered or permit these peoples to choose their own rulers without interference. The latter outcome was not inconceivable, as the negotiations between France and Prussia had shown that the Executive Council was willing to cooperate with foreign monarchs and the Assembly had passed a resolution renouncing foreign conquests in August. Moreover, the Executive Council had reaffirmed that France would not "interfere in the internal government of other peoples," and the Girondin leaders knew that ending the war would reduce the fear of counterrevolution and aid their ability to control the popular forces. They were increasingly concerned about the costs of the war as well, and some worried that a campaign of expansion would both jeopardize efforts to reach a separate peace with Prussia and contradict the revolutionary ideals of liberty and self-determination.[102]

Yet other forces drew the Republic toward a policy of revolutionary expansion. This outcome was partly due to the ambitions of men such as Dumouriez—who saw the war primarily as an opportunity for personal advancement—as well as latent French hostility to Austria and the anticlerical sentiments that dominated the Assembly. These concerns—together with a desire for territorial aggrandizement—account for the Executive Council's decision to authorize an invasion "to enfranchise the oppressed peoples" in the Netherlands on October 6.[103]

Even more importantly, the policy of revolutionary expansion resulted from the same influences that had driven France to war seven months ear-

[100] The expedition into the Rhineland was based on the unfulfilled hope of a general uprising among the local population. Von Sybel, *French Revolution*, 2:165–72.

[101] See Murley, "Origin of the Anglo-French War," 98. Of course, peace in the west would not have ended the rivalries among the eastern powers, and might well have increased them.

[102] On October 8, Brissot wrote that while "it would suit us to be surrounded by allied republics, our Republic would lose itself in expanding." On October 24, the Diplomatic Committee of the Convention advised against further expansion and declared that the French were not "conquerors of territory but the benefactors of the human race." Similarly, Dumouriez's *Manifesto to the Belgians*, published at the beginning of his invasion, pledged, "We enter to help you plant the tree of liberty, but without involving ourselves at all in the constitution that you wish to adopt." All quoted in Murley, "Origin of the Anglo-French War," 118–19.

[103] Brissot wrote Dumouriez that "the French Republic should not have any boundary other than the Rhine," and Lazare Carnot justified annexation on the grounds that "the ancient and natural boundaries of France are the Rhine, the Alps, and the Pyrenees." Similarly, Danton argued for the annexation of Belgium by saying it was "pointless to fear overextending the Republic. Its boundaries have been set by nature." See Denis Richet, "Natural Borders," in Furet and Ozouf, *Critical Dictionary*, 758.

lier. French foreign policy was in the hands of leaders who still saw themselves as part of a universal movement for liberty and whose hostility to monarchical institutions had led them to depose their own king. Although these ideological principles could be used to justify nonintervention (as imposing liberty by force would violate the rights of the alleged beneficiaries), the belief that neighboring peoples were eager to receive the fruits of liberty obscured the possibility that they might actually not welcome the French assistance. Moreover, hostility to monarchical institutions increased French perceptions of threat so that expansion seemed necessary for security. Foreign Minister Lebrun told the deputies, "The moment of greatest danger will arrive next spring, when allied tyranny will make its last effort, and then we must repel the combined force of all the kings." In September, Danton told the Convention, "We have the right to say to the peoples: you shall have no more kings!" and warned that, were France to remain surrounded by monarchs, these peoples "would furnish us with an endless series of tyrants to combat."[104] The president of the Assembly, Henri Grégoire, endorsed a petition to annex Savoy by saying, "It in no way adds to the hatred of oppressors for the Revolution. . . . It adds to the resources by which we shall break their league. . . . All Governments are our enemies, all Peoples are our allies; either we shall fall or all peoples shall become free."[105] Having defined the war as a campaign against kings, it was hard to limit it so long as a single monarch remained on a throne. As in the winter of 1791–92, the beliefs that foreign powers were intrinsically hostile and that the revolution was part of a universal trend combined to justify a policy of expansion.

The impact of these beliefs was accentuated by rivalries between the Girondin and Montagnard factions and the chaotic nature of decision-making within the Convention. Although the Girondins controlled the Executive Council, they lacked an absolute majority in the Convention, and the Montagnards were more popular among the radical Parisian sections. To compensate for their moderation on domestic issues, therefore, the Girondins returned to the bellicose rhetoric they had used so successfully

[104] Danton's words were somewhat disingenuous, as he was simultaneously negotiating for a separate peace with Prussia. Yet his willingness to use such rhetoric in the Convention reveals his awareness of its political potency, and he told the Convention that it "should be a committee of general insurrection against all the kings in the universe, and I ask that in calling all peoples to the conquest of liberty [the National Convention] offer them all the means of repulsing tyranny. . . . The French cannot endure that peoples who aspire to liberty nevertheless give themselves a government contrary to their interests." Quoted in Albert Mathiez, *Danton et la paix* (Paris: Renaissance du Livre, 1919), 58; also see his *French Revolution*, 278; Norman Hampson, *Danton* (New York: Holmes and Meier, 1978), 89–93; and Murley, "Origin of the Anglo-French War," 102.

[105] Like Danton, Grégoire also maintained that spreading the revolution would protect France from its opponents. In his words: "When my neighbor keeps a nest of vipers, I have the right to smother them lest I become their victim." Quoted in Mathiez, *French Revolution*, 285.

the previous year. And as Murley points out, because the Convention still lacked fixed rules of procedure, "major decisions turned on the chance passions of unregulated debates, . . . exposed to the harangue of the demagogue, to the irresponsible maneouvre of faction and, above all, to the popular enthusiasms of the great mass of deputies." In this setting, ideologically inspired passions dominated and a careful assessment of interests and capabilities was virtually impossible.[106]

The key shift occurred on November 6, 1792, when Dumouriez's Army of the North defeated the Austrians at Jemappes and occupied the Austrian Netherlands, accompanied by two divisions of Belgian exiles.[107] The unexpected victory seemed to confirm the Girondins' optimistic predictions, and doubts about the policy of expansion were swept away in an outpouring of revolutionary fervor. Vergniaud described Jemappes as a "victory for all humanity" and the Montagnards now joined the chorus, with one deputy predicting that "the territory that separates Paris from Petersburg and Moscow will soon be Francicized, municipalized, and Jacobinized." Grégoire proclaimed, "A new era has opened . . . [and] this part of the globe will no longer contain either fortresses or foreign peoples." The Vicaire Episcopal of the Cathedral of St. Font held a celebratory Te Deum in which he predicted that "the French will proceed from conquest to conquest, their glory will be envied by all nations, [and] the spectacle of their happiness will excite the emulation of all peoples." Lebrun christened his infant daughter "Civilis-Victoires-Jemappes-Dumouriez" and expressed his hope that the French would soon "deliver their Batavian brothers from the Stadholder's yoke." In the same spirit, Brissot told a friend, "We cannot be at ease until Europe, all Europe, is ablaze," and he called for further "upheavals of the globe, these great revolutions that we are called upon to make."[108]

This heady atmosphere was quickly transformed into action. On November 16, the Convention voted to open the River Scheldt to international shipping, even though it would violate several existing treaties and threaten

---

[106] Murley also describes the Convention as "a running faction fight rather than a debate between organized parties" and concludes that "the internal conflict was an important, perhaps a decisive factor in the official conduct of the war and foreign policy." "Origin of the Anglo-French War," 97–98, 114. On the Girondins' motivations, see Lefebvre, *French Revolution*, 1:273.

[107] Pressure from foreign revolutionaries in Paris had already led the Assembly to establish a Belgian-Liègeois Legion in April 1792, and Batavian, Allobrogian (for the Savoyards and Swiss), and Germanic legions were formed later in the year. See Palmer, *Democratic Revolution*, 2:56; and Kidner, "Girondists and the 'Propaganda War,'" chap. 3.

[108] Brissot also advised Dumouriez not to "busy oneself any longer with these projects of alliance with Prussia or England; [these are] sorry structures that are bound to disappear." These quotations are from Murley, "Origin of the Anglo-French War," 125–28; Palmer, *Democratic Revolution*, 2:60; and Richet, "Natural Borders," 758. Even Kidner, who argues that the Girondists were not committed to a "propaganda war," concedes that Brissot's ambitions in this case were genuine. "Girondists and the 'Propaganda War,'" 232–35, 267–68.

long-standing English interests.[109] An equally rash and even more ominous step was the so-called Decree on Liberty of November 19, which declared that France would "grant fraternity and aid to all peoples who wish to recover their liberty." The decree was not the result of a well-formed plan for exporting the revolution; on the contrary, it was an impromptu response to foreign requests for protection against counterrevolution. Yet with an "excess of oratory and a deficit of deliberation," the deputies once again succumbed to a vision of a universal crusade for liberty and approved the motion after a cursory debate.[110]

The November 19 decree was followed by a second decree, on December 15, intended to provide specific guidance to the French military leaders in the conquered regions. The new measure ordered French commanders to abolish feudal institutions in the occupied regions and to finance these actions by confiscating property from the privileged orders. The decree was partly a response to the mounting costs of the war, but it was also intended to give the Convention greater control over ambitious generals like Dumouriez.[111] In practice, the decree was a license to use the wealth of the occupied regions to pay for French occupation and to support pro-French factions within them. By this step, "the revolutionaries progressed from a war of prudence to a war of propaganda to a war of imperial expansion."[112]

Like their predecessors in the Legislative Assembly, the deputies in the Convention had fallen victim to a fictitious image of irreducibly hostile monarchies, restive foreign subjects, and irresistible revolutionary momentum. The rhetoric behind their actions was often instrumental, and some of the deputies were aware of the hazards of a revolutionary war *à outrance*.[113] But depicting the war in such stark and universal terms committed them to a policy of expansion that they never examined carefully, and both their rhetoric and their behavior reinforced foreign fears about French intentions and the possibility that the revolution might spread.[114]

---

[109] Lebrun was apparently responsible for this initiative, which was designed to win the support of Belgian merchants. See Kidner, "Girondists and the 'Propaganda War,' " 227–30.

[110] See Blanning, *French Revolutionary Wars*, 136–37; Stewart, *Documentary Survey*, 381; Biro, *German Policy*, 1:112–14; and Kidner, "Girondists and the 'Propaganda War,' " 230–38.

[111] To preserve his popularity, Dumouriez had refused to levy forced requisitions, arranged elections for a Belgian assembly, and agreed to preserve the property and tithes of the ruling classes, in exchange for a loan to support his own forces and an independent Belgian army. The Convention began to fear that Dumouriez would become strong enough to take independent action, correctly as it turned out. See Schama, *Patriots and Liberators*, 153; Ross, *European Diplomatic History*, 62–63; and Palmer, *Democratic Revolution*, 2:76–78. The text of the December 15 decree is in Stewart, *Documentary Survey*, 381–84.

[112] Blanning, *French Revolutionary Wars*, 136.

[113] Lebrun tried unsuccessfully to qualify the Decree on Liberty shortly after its passage, and various foreign revolutionaries (most notably the Dutch) were disappointed by the paltry support they received from France.

[114] By December, some Girondin leaders were convinced that war was necessary to keep the

*England's Entrance into the War.* Nowhere were these fears more evident
or important than in England. As described earlier, England's leaders had
seen the revolution as a favorable development at first and had maintained
a policy of steadfast neutrality despite entreaties from the émigrés and the
fulminations of Edmund Burke and others. This position did not waver as
the war with Austria and Prussia approached, and Pitt justified further re-
ductions in the military budget in February 1792 with the confident claim
that "there never was a time in the history of this country, when     we
might reasonably expect fifteen years of peace than at the present time."
England's leaders expected France to collapse quickly and anticipated further gains: according to Foreign Minister Grenville, "as soon as the German
troops arrive in Paris, whatever is the ruling party in Paris must apply to us
to mediate for them."[115]

Anglo-French relations began to deteriorate after the "Second Revolution" in August. The suspension of the king and the September Massacres
alarmed and repelled England's leaders, and the decision to recall the English ambassador (who was formally appointed to the now nonexistent
royal court) awoke French suspicions. Yet even the French victory at Valmy
did not provoke much concern, and Grenville congratulated the Cabinet in
November for having "the wit to keep ourselves out of this glorious enterprise. . . . We are not tempted by the hope of sharing the spoils in the division of France, nor by the prospect of crushing all democratic principles all
over the world. . . . We shall do nothing."[116]

Yet despite their desire to avoid a direct clash, France and England soon
saw each other both as a source of danger and as an obstacle that would be
easy to overcome. England's insecurity arose primarily from its fear of
French control over the Low Countries; as Grenville admitted on November

---

army from directly threatening public order. The minister of finance, Etienne Clavière, wrote
General Custine, "We must maintain a state of war; the return of our soldiers would increase the
disorder everywhere and ruin us" and Roland reportedly remarked, "It is necessary to march
the thousands of men whom we have under arms as far away as their legs will carry them, or
else they will come back and cut our throats." Quoted in Mathiez, *French Revolution,* 286.

[115] Quoted in Rose, *Life of Pitt,* 2:32. A British military representative in France reported that
the revolution had so weakened the discipline of the French Army that it could not "frustrate,
or even derange, the plans of the combined army of Austria and Prussia." Quoted in
Clapham, "Pitt's First Decade," 214.

[116] Grenville was willing to recognize the republic "once order was restored," and George
III remarked in September, "There is no step I should not take for the personal safety of the
French King and his family that does not draw this country into meddling with the internal
affairs of that ill-fated kingdom." Pitt greeted the storming of the Tuileries in August by saying "I can see no step that would not do more harm than good," and in November he hoped
that "some opportunity may arise which may enable us to contribute to the termination of
the war between the different powers in Europe, leaving France . . . to arrange its own affairs
as best it can." See Ehrman, *Reluctant Transition,* 202–205; Murley, "Origin of the Anglo-
French War," 41–43, 48, 195; and Rose, *Life of Pitt,* 2:60–61.

14, "The conquest of Flanders ... has brought the business to a much nearer issue here than any reasonable man could believe a month ago." A British warning against reopening the River Scheldt arrived too late to stop the decree of November 16, but Pitt and Grenville immediately reaffirmed their commitment to defend Holland "against any attempt to invade it or disturb its government."[117] This warning, which was explicitly intended to deter France from further expansion, shows how worried England's leaders were about French intentions.[118] These concerns were heightened by the Decree on Liberty, French support for the Dutch Patriot Party, and reports of Dumouriez's plans to invade Holland.[119] The independence of the Low Countries remained England's overriding concern from November forward and provided its primary motive for war.

A growing fear that the revolution might spread to England itself intensified these perceptions of threat. Pressure for parliamentary reform had been building within the country for more than a decade, and the revolution in France had already provoked a lively debate over the relative merits of the English and French constitutions.[120] A poor harvest and high prices fueled popular discontent and the growth of various radical associations, leading George III to issue a proclamation banning seditious writings in May.

The rising visibility of these radical movements seemed especially worrisome as Anglo-French relations deteriorated, because many English radicals were strongly pro-French. The popular societies welcomed the French victories at Valmy and Jemappes, and a dozen radical groups sent messages expressing their support for the revolution to the Convention and predicted

[117] Quoted in Murley, "Origin of the Anglo-French War," 198; and J. Holland Rose, "The Struggle with Revolutionary France," in Ward and Gooch, *British Foreign Policy*, 1:226–27.

[118] After the French conquest of Belgium, Grenville stated, "The only probable means of averting the danger is to meet it with firmness. . . . The King's intentions should be early and publicly notified, both to give encouragement to the Dutch Government . . . and to apprize those who may have hostile intentions of all the extent of those consequences which must arise from the execution of their plans." Quoted in J. Holland Rose, "Documents Relating to the Rupture with France in 1793, Part 1," *English Historical Review* 27, no. 105 (1912), 119.

[119] British intelligence had intercepted a letter from Dumouriez stating that he was "counting on carrying liberty to the Batavians as I have to the Belgians." Lebrun expressed similar ambitions in a letter to Dumouriez on November 22, and Dumouriez responded by predicting that "the Batavian Legion will promptly push the Revolution to the point where it will break out at the moment I appear on the Dutch border." See Rose, *Life of Pitt*, 2:73–74, 76, 84; Blanning, *French Revolutionary Wars*, 141; and Murley, "Origin of the Anglo-French War," 235, 272.

[120] The reform movement in England and the effects of the revolution are examined in Albert Goodwin, *The Friends of Liberty: The English Democratic Movement in the Age of the French Revolution* (Cambridge: Harvard University Press, 1979); esp. chaps. 4 and 6; H. T. Dickinson, *British Radicalism and the French Revolution* (London: Basil Blackwell, 1985); Clive Emsley, *British Society and the French Revolution, 1793–1815* (Totowa, N.J.: Rowman and Littlefield, 1979); Mark Philp, ed., *The French Revolution and British Popular Politics* (Cambridge: Cambridge University Press, 1991); and Colin Jones, ed., *Britain and Revolutionary France: Conflict, Subversion, and Propaganda* (Exeter, England: University of Exeter, 1985).

that similar upheavals would soon occur in England.[121] The fear of revolutionary subversion was compounded by the bellicose rhetoric emanating from the Convention itself, on the one hand, and the enthusiastic welcome the deputies had extended to foreign sympathizers, on the other.[122] British leaders were also concerned by the growing number of French agents in London, and especially by émigré warnings of a French-backed plot to overthrow the government.[123]

These developments brought a swift end to English complacency. By November 18, Pitt said that "the unexpected turn of events in France is but too much likely to give encouragement to the forces of disorder in every part of the world," and Home Secretary Henry Dundas warned that "if the spirit of liberty and equality continues to spread with the same rapidity, . . . it must soon break out in open sedition." These dangers were blamed on "secret machinations" and "dangerous and unprincipled emissaries." Lord Auckland told one confidant at the end of November, "We may expect in about six months to be walking about on all fours in the woods, at least as many of us as can save our throats from the knife of liberty."[124] In response, the government called out the militia in December and began a campaign to discredit the radical forces and promote popular support for the government.[125]

---

[121] A radical society in Rochester wrote Lebrun that "a great part of this generous nation is ready to make common cause with France," and emissaries from the Society for Constitutional Information appeared at the Convention in November and stated that "after the example given by France, revolutions will become easy. . . . [It] would not be extraordinary if in a much less space of time than can be imagined, the French should send addresses of congratulations to a National Convention of England." A delegation of Irish and English radicals told the deputies, "It is for the French nation to free all Europe," adding that these beliefs were shared by "the vast majority of our compatriots." For these and similar statements, see Goodwin, *Friends of Liberty*, 244–67, 501–12; Rose, *Life of Pitt*, 70–71; and Marianne Elliott, *Partners in Revolution: The United Irishmen and France* (New Haven: Yale University Press, 1982), 55.

[122] Pitt told one French agent that the Decree on Liberty "must be considered as an act of hostility to neutral nations." When the agent explained that the Decree had been passed in a "moment of fermentation" and was not a general invitation to revolt, Grenville invoked the "public reception given [by the Convention] to promoters of sedition in this country" as evidence of France's revolutionary aims. Quoted in Rose, "Struggle with Revolutionary France," 232–33, and *Life of Pitt*, 2:80–81; and Goodwin, *Friends of Liberty*, 256–57.

[123] Lebrun began sending agents to England at the end of August in an attempt to ascertain the government's intentions and boost public support for neutrality. This policy reflected lingering French suspicions of England, the revolutionaries' distaste for traditional diplomacy, and their predilection for direct appeals to the people. Murley, "Origin of the Anglo-French War," 32–40, 63–83.

[124] Quoted in Murley, "Origin of the Anglo-French War," 185, 202.

[125] The royal proclamation calling out the militia declared: "The utmost industry is still being employed by evil-disposed persons within this Kingdom, *acting in concert with persons in foreign parts*, with a view to subverting the laws and established constitution of this realm and to destroy all order and government therein." Quoted in Murley, "Origin of the Anglo-French War," 217–18 (emphasis added); and Dickinson, *British Radicalism and French Revolution*, chap. 2.

Ironically, the French government discounted English warnings because its members shared many of the same beliefs about England's revolutionary potential. This erroneous assessment was based on ill-informed and self-serving reports from the French agents in London, reinforced by the enthusiastic but unreliable testimony of English radicals. In September, a French agent advised Lebrun, "We can always count on [English] neutrality"; the same agent reported one month later, "Our victories have had a marked impact on popular opinion . . . which is more favorable day by day." French agents were soon predicting an imminent upheaval, assuring Lebrun that "all that is needed is a little spark to cause a terrible explosion."[126] The former French ambassador, Bernard Chauvelin, abandoned his initial caution and reported a financial panic in the City of London, a naval mutiny, and an uprising in Ireland, while another agent suggested that "to the eyes of an outside observer, England offers precisely the same prospect that France did in 1789. . . . All the symptoms indicate that revolutionary movements cannot be far off." With his own prejudices thus reinforced, Lebrun reassured the Convention, "If the court of St. James adopts a policy of severity and resistance, it will inevitably provoke an insurrection. . . . The results would be fatal for the monarchy and the government."[127]

These optimistic visions were sustained by French ignorance about the true state of popular opinion and party politics in England. Misinterpreting Pitt's retreat in the Ochakov affair with Russia in 1791 and overestimating the influence of Whig leader Charles Fox, Lebrun and others convinced themselves that Parliament would not support a war. The idea that England would do anything to remain neutral was confirmed by French diplomats at the Hague, whose accounts of the negotiations with England and Holland conveyed a misleading impression of English spinelessness. And even if England were to resist, French leaders believed that war would provoke a financial crisis in London and an uprising against the government.[128]

Thus, French intransigence remained intact, scuttling efforts to achieve a diplomatic solution. Lebrun and his agents tried several times to continue the negotiations, but the belief that England could not afford to fight led them to drive an excessively hard bargain. Even when it became clear that

---

[126] Other reports reinforced these views. One agent wrote Lebrun, "Each cry in favor of the French Republic has been followed by a cry against the abuses of the English government," and another reported that Ireland "awaits only the moment of explosion, and the first cannon-shot fired by Great Britain will be the signal for a general insurrection." Quoted in Murley, "Origin of the Anglo-French War," 143–45.

[127] Quoted in Blanning, *French Revolutionary Wars*, 152–53; and Goodwin, *Friends of Liberty*, 257–61, esp. n. 234.

[128] See Murley, "Origin of the Anglo-French War," 222–40. In January, a Girondin deputy told the Convention, "The credit of England rests on fictitious wealth, the real riches of the people are scattered everywhere" (i.e., in vulnerable overseas colonies). Quoted in Rose, *Life of Pitt*, 2:102.

England would not back down, Lebrun refused to rescind the opening of the Scheldt and continued making threatening remarks in the Convention. His freedom of action was constrained in any case, as the deputies were all too willing to take on another adversary. As one deputy told the Convention: "We have no reason to fear war [with England] since our fishing boats are ready to carry 100,000 men across the Channel, who will put an end to the contest on the ruins of the Tower [of London]."[129] French optimism increased further when Geneva voted to place itself under French protection—a step that reinforced an image of irresistible revolutionary momentum—and when the Dutch Patriots reported that Zeeland was defenseless and urged an immediate attack. By this time, the atmosphere in the Convention would have made it nearly impossible for Lebrun to avoid a war even if he had wanted to.[130]

English expectations were equally optimistic. By December, fears of an immediate uprising had faded and a rift in the Whig Party had given Pitt a comfortable majority in Parliament. The French Army of the North had been weakened by desertions, and several Prussian triumphs in December restored an image of French inferiority, convincing Pitt that "it will be a short war, and certainly ended in one or two campaigns." English confidence was heightened by a sense of fortunate timing; as Pitt told the lord chancellor in January, war was "inevitable, and the sooner begun the better."[131] Adding to the support for the war was the prospect of colonial expansion, with the *Times* of London predicting that the loss of France's Caribbean possessions would be such a blow that "it would require ages for France to recover to the political balance of Europe that preponderancy, which she enjoyed previous to the Revolution."[132]

By the end of December, therefore, both England and France were convinced that the other was unalterably aggressive and yet easy to defeat. These conditions made war virtually inevitable, and when Chauvelin told Grenville on December 27 that France would not rescind the Decree on Lib-

---

[129] Similarly, the Navy Minister, Gaspard Monge, issued a proclamation declaring that he would "effect a landing in England, throw 50,000 red caps of liberty upon the shore, and raise the English republic on the ruins of the throne." See Von Sybel, *French Revolution*, 2:304; and Rose, *Life of Pitt*, 2:95, 102–103.

[130] See Blanning, *French Revolutionary Wars*, 156–57.

[131] Pitt reportedly believed that "the nation was now prepared for war, which might not be the case six weeks hence . . . [France] had only six ships of the line in the Mediterranean, we upwards of twenty. . . . The Dutch were quite right, and in earnest. . . . Russia will to go all lengths, Spain was ready to join, and all the little Powers only waited our giving the signal." Grenville shared this view, writing to Auckland, "To you privately I may say that our confidence . . . is very great indeed." Quoted in Blanning, *French Revolutionary Wars*, 154.

[132] Quoted in Michael Duffy, "War, Revolution, and the Crisis of the British Empire," in Philp, *French Revolution and British Politics*, 118–19. English optimism was also based on the expectation that other states (such as Austria) would do most of the fighting on the Continent.

erty or reverse the opening of the River Scheldt, the foreign minister coldly dismissed his explanations of the decree, declared that the French position on the Scheldt was unacceptable, and warned that England would never allow France to "make herself, either directly or indirectly, sovereign of the Low Countries, or general arbitress of the rights and liberties of Europe." The line was now drawn, and although Lebrun made several last-minute efforts to continue the negotiations, the Convention was uncompromising.[133] Chauvelin was ordered to leave England on January 21, 1793, and the news of his expulsion sparked another outburst in Paris. The Executive Council authorized the invasion of Holland on January 31; the Convention voted an official declaration of war on February 1.[134]

The fundamental cause of the conflict was a clash of aims and interests—centered on the Low Countries—but each side exaggerated the other's hostility in precisely the manner described above in chapter 2. English officials overstated the importance of the Decree on Liberty and failed to recognize the ambivalence France's new leaders felt about their role as Europe's revolutionary vanguard. A clear sign of this ambivalence was the Executive Council's earlier refusal to authorize an invasion of Holland, despite Dumouriez's desire to do so and the repeated entreaties of the Dutch Patriots. English leaders did not realize that the bellicose rhetoric emanating from France was partly a product of the political struggle within the country; if they had, they might have discounted some of the deputies' inflammatory statements and gone to greater lengths to find a modus vivendi. British officials also overstated the degree of coordination between France and the various radical movements in England; although French agents did meet with radical leaders on several occasions, there is no evidence of an active French attempt to promote a revolution in England. English officials also took the large number of French agents in England as evidence of French hostility, but most of these men were there for other purposes and none of them had a significant impact on English attitudes.[135] Lebrun tried to convince En-

---

[133] See David Williams, "The Missions of David Williams and James Tilly Matthews to England (1793)," *English Historical Review* 53, no. 212 (1938); and Murley, "Origin of the Anglo-French War," 455–92.

[134] On January 31, Jean Marie Collot d'Herbois told his fellow Jacobins, "Our soldiers will plant the tree of liberty . . . under the windows of King George, [who] will leave his palace as Louis Capet left the Tuileries." Danton told the Convention the following day, "No power can stop us. It is fruitless to fear the wrath of kings. You have thrown down the glove. That glove is the head of a king. . . . The tyrants of England are dead. The people will be free." Brissot seems to have had doubts as war approached, but he also believed that "if we had hesitated, the Mountain would have taken power from us." Murley, "Origin of the Anglo-French War," 499–502.

[135] In addition to conducting unofficial negotiations, French agents in England were trying to locate the sources of forged French currency, to find the thieves who had stolen the French crown jewels, and to monitor the activities of French émigrés. Unfortunately, "the mere presence of so many French agents in London . . . helped to give greater credibility to stories passed on to the Home Office by French émigré sources" (Goodwin, *Friends of Liberty*, 261).

[87]

gland's leaders that the November 19 decree was an isolated act rather than a blueprint for expansion; however, his own conduct was inconsistent and did little to undo the damage.[136]

French observations of England were equally distorted. Perceptions of a threat from England first arose after the withdrawal of the British ambassador in August, a step France mistakenly interpreted as evidence of monarchical hostility. Lebrun was soon convinced that Pitt was engaged in a variety of anti-French conspiracies, and French leaders interpreted the Anti-Sedition and Alien acts as anti-French gestures. They were also upset by the cordial (albeit reserved) welcome given to French émigrés in England.[137] Pitt's decision to call up 20,000 sailors in December and halt grain shipments to France in January was correctly seen as evidence of English opposition, but the French seem not to have realized their own role in triggering these responses.

Indeed, what is perhaps most striking is the degree to which English opposition was based on France's *external* conduct rather than its internal arrangements. Auckland proposed recognizing the republic at the beginning of November. Even after the invasion of the Netherlands, Home Secretary Dundas argued that "the strength of our cause consists in maintaining that we have nothing to do with the internal politics of foreign nations." When Catherine II invited England to join a concert against France in December, Grenville's reply stressed that England would confine its actions to opposing "the intrigues and ambitious plans pursued by France" while abstaining from "any interference in the interior government of that country." Thus, English opposition was based on the danger of French expansion and not on hostility to the revolution itself, a distinction the French missed completely.[138]

This spiral of hostility was exacerbated by several factors: Lebrun's inexperience, rivalries between the main French agents in England, and these agents' need to adopt extreme positions in London in order to protect their credibility at home. These factors did not cause the conflict, of course, but

[136] See Marianne Elliott, "French Subversion in Britain in the French Revolution," in Jones, *Britain and Revolutionary France*, 41–42, and *Partners in Revolution*, 53–54.

[137] In October, for example, Lebrun believed England was about to sign an offensive alliance with Spain, and he later accused England of directing Prussian and Genevan resistance to French demands. Murley, "Origin of the Anglo-French War," 84.

[138] Grenville's instructions to the British ambassador in Russia outlined the following war aims: "the withdrawing of [French] arms within the limits of French territory; the abandoning of their conquests; the rescinding of any acts injurious to the sovereignty or rights of any other nations; and the giving, in some public and unequivocal manner, a pledge of their intention no longer to foment troubles and to excite disturbances against their own Governments." See Rose, "Struggle with Revolutionary France," 220–30, "Documents Relating to the Rupture with France," 122, and *Life of Pitt*, 2:100.

they contributed to French misperceptions and hindered efforts to reach a negotiated settlement.[139]

Finally, it should be noted that English and French expectations were both mistaken, particularly on the crucial question of whether the revolution was likely to spread. These errors confirm both the inherent difficulty of gauging a society's revolutionary potential, as well as the danger that revolutionary elites and foreign leaders will draw unwarranted conclusions based on their ideological predispositions, unexpected events in one country, and the biased information at their disposal.

The expansion of the war in 1793 arose from a combination of insecurity and overconfidence that strikingly resembled the forces that had led to war with Austria and Prussia the previous year. Once again, the Girondins had sought to strengthen their internal position by invoking foreign threats and universalistic ambitions. Although their arguments seemed vindicated by the conquest of Belgium, Savoy, and the Rhineland, the Girondins eventually became trapped by radical sentiment within the Convention and lost control of foreign policy. The deputies' enthusiasm overrode earlier counsels of prudence and moderate voices were silenced by the fear of damaging their own revolutionary credentials.

Both English and French leaders were convinced of each other's hostility by the end of 1792; even worse, they also believed that the other was not a very formidable adversary. These beliefs arose from each side's ideological predispositions; the domestic conflicts within France; biased information from émigrés, revolutionary agents, and sympathizers; and the inherent difficulty of gauging the broader appeal of French revolutionary ideals. Taken together, they left both sides more willing to use force. Thus, the expansion of the war in 1793 is largely consistent with the theory set forth in chapter 2.

## The Conduct of the War

England's entry soon brought most of Europe into the anti-French coalition. England and Holland were already allied. Spain and Sardinia declared war on France in March, along with Naples, Tuscany, Venice, and Modena. Portugal joined England shortly thereafter, as did Hanover, Baden, Hesse-Castel, and Hesse-Darmstadt. The Imperial Diet of the Holy Roman Empire declared war on France in April, and England worked to strengthen the

---

[139] Chauvelin had tried to reassure Paris about English intentions in September and warned that the activities of other French agents were confirming English suspicions. By November, however, as a result of his desire to retain his influence in Paris, he took a more radical position and wrote Lebrun that "the spectacle given to other countries by France will accelerate the era of revolution." Murley, "Origin of the Anglo-French War," 78, 82, and passim.

[89]

coalition by negotiating bilateral alliance treaties (or loans or subsidies) with Austria and Prussia.[140]

The War of the First Coalition supports the idea that social revolutions are both difficult to reverse and hard to export. The Republic proved to be a far more formidable adversary than its opponents expected: it was adept at mobilizing the nation's resources for war, and the patriotic sentiments aroused by the revolution enhanced France's military power and reduced its vulnerability to counterrevolution. At the same time, the war was hardly the swift parade of revolutionary upheavals that the Girondins had predicted. Although France eventually established "sister republics" in the areas it conquered, those regimes were dependent on French military support, and they cost thousands of lives to create and maintain. Repeated efforts to ignite a rebellion in Great Britain failed (because France was unable to land an army there), and the "sister republics" are more accurately seen as the products of imperial expansion rather than of revolutionary contagion.

The evolution of French policy during the War of the First Coalition also substantiates the claim that revolutionary states will moderate their conduct in response to external pressure. In fact, the survival of the revolution was due in large part to its leaders' willingness to subordinate their universalistic idealism to a narrower conception of national interest. These ideals were not repudiated completely, but their impact on foreign policy declined as the French Republic responded to the demands of the war.

Domestic rivalries within France continued to affect relations with other states as well. The republic, still divided into hostile factions, was obsessed with fears of foreign plots. These conditions made it more difficult for France to take advantage of its military achievements and negotiate a favorable peace, even when its opponents were willing to offer one.

*The Jacobin Dictatorship.* The republic faced its greatest challenge in the spring and summer of 1793. The volunteers who had flocked to defend *la patrie* in 1792 returned home after their triumphs in the fall, and the French armies shrank from roughly 450,000 in November to less than 300,000 in February.[141] Meanwhile, the anti-French coalition had been strengthened by its new members, and these shifts enabled Prussia to recapture most of the left bank of the Rhine by the end of April. The Army of the North suffered similar setbacks: Dumouriez invaded Holland on February 1, but his outnumbered forces were forced to withdraw after an Austrian army beat them badly at Neerwinden and Louvain in March. Alarmed by the execution of

[140] Lefebvre, *French Revolution*, 2:4; Ross, *European Diplomatic History*, 66–67; and John M. Sherwig, *Guineas and Gunpowder: British Foreign Aid in the Wars with France, 1793–1815* (Cambridge: Harvard University Press, 1969), 17–33.

[141] Lynn, *Bayonets of the Republic*, 53. Biro reports that the French army in Belgium declined from roughly 100,000 troops to about 45,000. *German Policy*, 1:112.

the king and upset by the Convention's policy of requisitions (which alienated the Belgian population and threatened his own ambitions there), Dumouriez negotiated an armistice with the Austrian commanders and tried to launch a coup to restore the monarchy. His troops refused to follow him, however, and Dumouriez was forced to defect to the Austrians. This unexpected act of treason sparked a new wave of suspicion within France—if its leading general could not be trusted, who could? Meanwhile, the Austrian and Prussian armies continued a slow advance in the north while Sardinia and Spain advanced in the south, placing the republic in imminent danger once again.[142]

The new regime also faced growing unrest in the provinces and the imminent loss of several valuable colonies. Motives for provincial resistance ranged from die-hard royalism to the defense of local autonomy, and the struggle was exacerbated by conscription, economic hardship, and the various anticlerical measures adopted since 1789. By the summer, "federalist" uprisings had broken out in several areas and a full-scale civil war was raging in the Vendée. An English squadron landed at Toulon in August to support the counterrevolutionary uprising there, and England also invaded the French colonies at Tobago and Santo Domingo in April and September. With France now facing both foreign invasion and internal rebellion, Pitt told the House of Commons in June that "every circumstance concurs to favor the hope of being able completely to accomplish every object of the war."[143]

Yet not only did the revolutionary regime survive, it was to regain the initiative in the fall of 1793 and begin a campaign of expansion that would destroy the First Coalition and create a substantial European empire. This unexpected reversal of fortune was the result of the mobilization of the republic by the Committee on Public Safety and the self-defeating rivalries within the enemy coalition.

In the spring of 1793, the French Republic's efforts to mobilize for war led to the creation of a Committee on General Security, to deal with suspected counterrevolutionaries, and a Committee on Public Safety (CPS), to coordinate the activities of each ministry. The Convention imposed the death penalty on émigrés and dissident priests and established a revolutionary tribunal to try suspected counterrevolutionaries. It also began dispatching so-

---

[142] The actual threat was more apparent than real, as members of the Coalition were deeply divided in their war aims and none of them intended to march on Paris and restore the old regime. See Schroeder, *Transformation of European Politics*, esp. 128–30.

[143] Quoted in Ehrman, *Reluctant Transition*, 284. On the provincial revolts, see Doyle, *History of the French Revolution*, chap. 10; Norman Hampson, *A Social History of the French Revolution* (London: Routledge and Kegan Paul, 1963), 158–61, 170–75; and Sutherland, *France*, 66–82. British aid to the French counterrevolutionaries is described in detail in Mitchell, *Underground War*; and Maurice Hutt, *Chouannerie and Counterrevolution: Puisaye, the Princes, and the British Government in the 1790s*, 2 vols. (Cambridge: Cambridge University Press, 1983).

called *représentants en mission* to oversee the mobilization effort in the provinces and to suppress counterrevolutionary resistance.[144]

Meanwhile, repeated military setbacks during this period brought the struggle between the Girondins and the Montagnards to a climax. The stalemate between them was finally broken by another popular uprising in Paris: a new Commune was formed on May 31 and thousands of angry *sans-culottes* surrounded the Convention and forced it to remove and arrest twenty-nine Girondin leaders. The upheaval left the Montagnards in control of the Convention and the government, although their own freedom of action was constrained by the threat of another popular uprising.[145]

The ouster of the Girondins cleared the way for more extreme measures. The CPS was reorganized and given near-dictatorial powers, and a new and more radical constitution was approved in August.[146] The CPS began a brutal campaign against provincial rebels and suspected counterrevolutionaries, aided by local revolutionary committees and paramilitary bands known as *armées révolutionnaires*.[147] In August, the CPS proclaimed the famous *levée en masse*, which made all French citizens eligible for national service. French armed strength increased to nearly 600,000 men by the fall of 1793 and more than a million one year later, and new military industries were created and manned.[148] The Law of the General Maximum imposed price controls in September, a Law on Suspects enhanced the CPS's powers to arrest potential traitors, and the Law of 14 Frimaire, Year II (December 5, 1793), gave it authority over all public officials and legislated the denunciation of traitors before revolutionary tribunals.[149]

These measures were accompanied by a deliberate effort to transform the symbolic and moral bases of French society. The CPS adopted the metric system in August and replaced the Christian calendar with a revolutionary one as part of an overt campaign of dechristianization.[150] In addition to en-

---

[144] See Hampson, *Social History*, 168–69.

[145] On the fall of the Girondins, see Mathiez, *French Revolution*, chap. 10.

[146] The Constitution of the Year I was suspended until the end of the war and was never implemented. For its text, see Stewart, *Documentary Survey*, 454–68; for its background, see Marc Bouloiseau, *The Jacobin Republic, 1792–1794*, trans. Jonathan Mandelbaum (Cambridge: Cambridge University Press, 1983), 67–68; and Thompson, *French Revolution*, 360–63.

[147] The definitive treatment of the *armées révolutionnaires* is Richard Cobb, *The People's Armies*, trans. M. Elliott (New Haven: Yale University Press, 1987). On the revolutionary committees, see John Black Sirich, *The Revolutionary Committees in the Departments of France, 1793–94* (Cambridge: Harvard University Press, 1943).

[148] The text of the decree is in Stewart, *Documentary History*, 472–74. For discussions of its effects, see Lynn, *Bayonets of the Republic*, 56–61; Ross, *European Diplomatic History*, 80; and Bertaud, *Army of the French Revolution*.

[149] These decrees are in Stewart, *Documentary Survey*, 477–90.

[150] The new calendar dated Year I from the founding of the republic on September 22, 1793. There were twelve months of thirty days each and a five-day festival period. See Mona Ozouf, "Revolutionary Calendar," in Furet and Ozouf, *Critical Dictionary*, 538–47.

couraging popular patriotism, these efforts reflected the beliefs that the republic required new symbolic and moral foundations and that direct government action should be taken to promote civic virtue.

The establishment of the Jacobin dictatorship did not bring the struggle for power to an end; if anything, factional quarrels became even more intense. At one extreme were the so-called Hébertists (after the radical leader Jacques-René Hébert), who favored economic policies to benefit the poor, radical dechristianization, rigorous measures against hoarders and political criminals, and the aggressive export of revolution.[151] At the other extreme stood Danton and the Indulgents, who favored a negotiated peace, the relaxation of the Terror, and a return to constitutional rule. Between them stood Robespierre, Louis-Antoine de Saint-Just, and their followers, who were increasingly suspicious of both groups and preoccupied with establishing a "Republic of Virtue."[152] Fostering conflict among these groups was a paranoid political climate in which accusations of treason and fears of foreign plots abounded. Under these conditions, virtually any disagreement could be interpreted as a sign of disloyalty. Or as Saint-Just put it in March 1794: "Every faction is then criminal, because it tends to divide the citizens . . . [and] neutralizes the power of public virtue." In the Jacobin Republic, dissent had become an act of treason.[153]

Although the leaders of the Republic did not abandon all of their ideological aims and continued to rely on unconventional diplomatic means, the CPS abandoned their predecessors' utopian approach to foreign policy in favor of a more hardheaded realpolitik. Evidence of this deradicalization was most apparent in the declining commitment to the universalist goal of "promoting liberty," on the one hand, and the priority given to exploiting other peoples rather than liberating them, on the other. In contrast to its earlier support for foreign revolutionaries, for example, the Convention rejected a request for the formation of an Italian legion in February 1793.[154] The Convention revoked the Decree on Liberty in April and declared that henceforth it would "not in-

---

[151] The Hébertists were also known as "ultras" or "enragés." See Denis Richet, "Hébertists," in Furet and Ozouf, *Critical Dictionary*, 363–69; and Schama, *Citizens*, 805–17.

[152] The belief that domestic opponents constituted the main threat to the revolution was a consistent theme in Robespierre's political thought. David P. Jordan, *The Revolutionary Career of Maximilien Robespierre* (New York: Free Press, 1985), 170–172.

[153] Robespierre also warned of the danger of factions in the fall of 1793, telling the Convention that "whoever seeks to debase, divide, or paralyze the Convention is an enemy of our country, whether he sits in this hall or is a foreigner." Quotations from R. R. Palmer, *Twelve Who Ruled: The Year of the Terror in the French Revolution* (Princeton: Princeton University Press, 1941), 71, 291, and also see 263–66.

[154] In a report to the Diplomatic Committee, Lazare Carnot suggested that the simplest means of establishing a universal republic would be "to establish within the bounds Nature has traced for us [such] prosperity [that] . . . neighboring peoples . . . will be led to imitate [us]. . . . The first interest to consult is that of the [French] Republic itself." Quoted in Biro, *German Policy*, 1:220 n. 268.

terfere in any manner in the government of other powers."[155] By the fall, Robespierre was insisting the revolution should be spread not by force but by example, telling the Convention that "the French are not afflicted with a mania for rendering any nation happy and free despite itself."[156] Similarly, when it became clear that efforts to "promote liberty" via propaganda and subversion were undermining French relations with several neutral powers (such as the United States and the Swiss Confederation), France's leaders recalled their agents and suspended their subversive efforts.[157]

The waning of revolutionary internationalism was accompanied by a growing xenophobia, once again triggered by the pervasive fear of foreign plots.[158] In December, Robespierre accused foreign revolutionaries such as Anacharsis Cloots of dragging France into a dangerous and unprofitable war, informing the Jacobin Club, "I distrust without distinction all those foreigners . . . who endeavour to appear more republican and energetic than we are."[159] While serving as *représentant en mission* in Alsace in December, Saint-Just disbanded a group of local republicans who advocated universal liberty; one of his assistants advised Robespierre "not to listen to these cosmopolitan charlatans and to trust only in ourselves." The CPS denied a petition for assistance from a group of Dutch revolutionaries in March, and it eventually dissolved the foreign legions that the Assembly had created in 1792. Thus, by 1794 the earlier visions of a universal crusade for liberty had faded almost completely.[160]

Moderation was also apparent in French policy toward neutral states. Despite an improving military posture, pressure from local officials, and the

---

[155] As Danton told the deputies: "In a moment of enthusiasm you passed a decree whose motive was doubtless fine . . . [but] this decree appeared to commit you to support a few patriots who might wish to start a revolution in China. Above all we need to look to the preservation of our own body politic and lay the foundation of French greatness." Quoted in Blanning, *French Revolution and Germany*, 70; and see also Stewart, *Documentary Survey*, 426–27.

[156] Robespierre also emphasized the need to stop "our generals and our armies [from interfering] in [others'] political affairs; it is the only means of preventing intrigues which can terminate our glorious revolution." Quoted in Biro, *German Policy*, 1:188–89.

[157] See Eugene R. Sheridan, "The Recall of Edmund Charles Genet," *Diplomatic History* 18, no. 4 (1994); and David Silverman, "Informal Diplomacy: The Foreign Policy of the Robespierrist Committee on Public Safety" (Ph.D. diss., University of Washington, 1974), 56–65, 94, 96–103.

[158] The fear of foreign plots, magnified by Dumouriez's treason, helped lead to the ouster of the Girondin leaders in June. These fears grew in the fall, when a Montagnard deputy informed the CPS that the republic faced a vast foreign conspiracy whose members included Convention deputies, foreign ministry officials, and Marie-Joseph Herault de Sechelles, a member of the CPS itself. See Mathiez, *Révolution et les étrangers*, 164–66; and Silverman, "Informal Diplomacy," 106–107.

[159] Quoted in Mathiez, *French Revolution*, 419; and see also Silverman, "Informal Diplomacy," 130.

[160] Quoted in Silverman, "Informal Diplomacy," 108 n. 5.

massacre of several French sailors by a group of English seamen, the CPS chose to respect Genoese neutrality during the fall of 1793. When an attempt to undermine English commerce with a discriminatory Navigation Act damaged relations with neutral states and brought French foreign trade to a standstill, the CPS promptly suspended the act and embarked on efforts to rebuild ties with neutral powers.[161]

As noted earlier, the exigencies of war had also forced the republic to abandon its idealistic principles and systematically exploit conquered regions in order to sustain its war effort. The tension between universal ideals and selfish national interests was already apparent in the fall of 1792, and the decree of December 15, 1792, was the first step toward a more self-serving policy. The issue was moot so long as France was on the defensive, but when its military fortunes improved, the Convention ordered army commanders to renounce "every philanthropic idea previously adopted by the French people with the intention of making foreign nations appreciate the values and benefits of liberty." Now, the French armies were to "behave towards the enemies of France in just the same way that the powers of the Coalition have behaved towards them . . . and exercise . . . the customary rights of war." In a sharp departure from its original ideals, therefore, the republic was now justifying the exploitation of occupied territories on the grounds that other great powers acted the same way![162] As the French armies continued to advance, the exploitation of conquered territory became a way of life. The CPS established agencies of evacuation to coordinate the exploitation of foreign resources in May 1794, and Carnot, who was responsible for military mobilization, declared, "We must live at the expense of the enemy . . . , we are not entering his territory to bring him money."[163] Even measures of apparent restraint masked self-interested motives: prior to the occupation of Holland in January 1795, the CPS informed its generals that "the interest of the Republic is to reassure the Dutch so that they do not emigrate with their riches. . . . It is necessary to safeguard the rights of property so that Holland will furnish us with provisions."[164]

---

[161] See Silverman, "Informal Diplomacy," 86–87, 92, 135–38.

[162] Quoted in Blanning, *French Revolution in Germany*, 72; and see also Biro, *German Policy*, 1:191–92, 207–208.

[163] When the French reoccupied Belgium in July, Carnot declared that "all that is found in Belgium must be sent back to France. . . . It is necessary to despoil the country and make it impossible to furnish means for the enemy to return." Although Carnot emphasized that French requisitions should be confined to the rich and that the occupiers should respect Belgian customs, these restrictions were usually ignored in practice. See Silverman, "Informal Diplomacy," 228–30; and Biro, *German Policy*, 1:230.

[164] Quoted in Schama, *Patriots and Liberators*, 181. French policy in the Rhineland was even more severe, and the winter of 1793–94 became known as the "Plunder Winter." See Blanning, *French Revolution in Germany*, chap. 3; and Biro, *German Policy*, 1:205–207.

A final sign of deradicalization was France's intermittent effort to improve its diplomatic position and negotiate an end to the war. During his tenure on the first CPS, Danton tried unsuccessfully to attract Sweden, Denmark, the Ottoman Empire, and several other states into an alliance with France, while simultaneously seeking to isolate Austria by courting Prussia. Similarly, Lebrun made an indirect offer to support the Prussian acquisition of several smaller German states in April and extended Prussia a free hand in Poland in May. These concessions led to direct negotiations between French and Prussian agents. The minister of the interior told the Convention that peace might be imminent, but the negotiations were cut off when Danton was removed from the CPS in July.[165]

French leaders' efforts to initiate talks with England and Austria were less successful. Lebrun made a tentative overture to England through a Welsh tea dealer and intriguer named James Tilly Matthews, and although the Montagnards permitted Lebrun to continue his efforts after his arrest in June, these informal contacts failed to bear fruit.[166] France also sent envoys to several Italian courts to see if they would renew an alliance with France in exchange for the release of Marie Antoinette, but this overly subtle attempt to probe Austrian intentions led nowhere.[167] Danton held private discussions with an English agent in December 1793 (with the apparent approval of the CPS). An agent was instructed to open indirect negotiations with England at about the same time, while England made overtures to France via Phillipe Noël, the French envoy at Venice. Foreign Minister François Deforgues established indirect and direct contacts with Prussia in a further attempt to separate it from Vienna, and there is even some evidence that Robespierre sent an agent to explore the possibility of peace with Austria in May 1794.[168]

These efforts failed for a number of reasons. France's bargaining position was initially quite weak, and the Coalition had little reason to make peace when its opponent seemed ready to collapse. The domestic climate within France was unfavorable as well, as any effort to pursue peace left one exposed to accusations of treason. Indeed, pressure from the Hébertists eventually led the Convention to outlaw negotiations with states that did not recognize the republic, resulting in the severing of direct diplomatic contacts with all countries except the United States and the Swiss Confederation.[169]

---

[165] On these various offers, see Biro, *German Policy*, 1:163–65; Von Sybel, *French Revolution*, 3:47–53; and Alphonse Aulard, "La diplomatie du premier Comité de salut public," in his *Etudes et leçons sur la révolution française*, 3d ser. (Paris: Felix Alcan, 1902), 121–22, 205.

[166] Williams, "Missions of Williams and Matthews," 660–65 and passim.

[167] Aulard, "Diplomatie du premier Comité de salut public," 135–36.

[168] Silverman, "Informal Diplomacy," 110–12, 140–47. Historians remain divided over whether the latter negotiations actually took place; see Biro, *German Policy*, 1:222–36.

[169] The April 1793 decree renouncing support for "foreign patriots" had also imposed the death penalty for proposing negotiations with states "which have not previously solemnly recognized ... the French nation... [and] its sovereignty." Stewart, *Documentary Survey*, 426–27.

This constraint forced Foreign Minister Deforgues to rely on indirect contacts, via neutral agents, and confined subsequent peace overtures to obscure and unreliable back channels. In addition, key members of the Coalition had different aims and interests, making it difficult to devise a settlement that would be acceptable to all. Finally, as a result of a series of French victories in the fall of 1793, an immediate peace seemed less necessary and the republic hardened its diplomatic position. Although states such as Prussia were increasingly willing to settle, prominent Jacobins now argued that only all-out war would gain them acceptable terms. As one member of the CPS, Bertrand Barère, told the Convention in January: "In wars of liberty there is only one means: it is to ruin and exterminate the despots. . . . There is neither peace nor truce, nor armistice, nor any treaty to make with the despots until the Republic is consolidated, triumphant, and dictating peace to the nations."[170] Such statements reveal that the process of deradicalization was still incomplete. They also illustrate how domestic divisions prevented France from splitting the alliance even when a separate peace was within reach.

In short, although the French Republic had not abandoned all of its ideological principles, its policies in 1793–94 were a striking departure from the lofty visions that had driven France to war in 1792–93. And by mobilizing its latent potential and moderating its more unrealistic schemes, revolutionary France escaped defeat once again.

Divisions within the opposing coalition played a key role in the survival of the revolution as well. Austria and Prussia were increasingly at odds; each blamed the other for their poor performance in 1792, and Frederick William's commitment to the war declined even more after Prussia and Russia signed a secret agreement for a second partition of Poland in January 1793. Once the Allies reconquered Belgium in the summer of 1793, he announced that Prussia would continue the war only if he were granted another subsidy. He ordered his generals to leave the French Army intact and to give only limited assistance to his Austrian ally. The allied advance resumed after England agreed to provide additional funds, but Prussia's commitment to the Coalition remained shaky at best. It vanished entirely after Austria and Russia mended fences and arranged a final partition of Poland in 1794, and Frederick William soon decided to abandon the war with France in order to preserve his gains in the east.[171]

---

[170] Barère also invoked the fear of traitors by asking, "Who then dare to speak of peace? [Only] aristocrats, the rich, . . . the friends of conspirators, . . . bad citizens, false patriots. . . . What we need today is redoubled boldness against conspirators, . . . redoubled scrutiny against men who call themselves patriots." Quoted in Silverman, "Informal Diplomacy," 156–59; see Leo Gershoy, *Bertrand Barère: A Reluctant Terrorist* (Princeton: Princeton University Press, 1962), 157–59; 207–208.

[171] In the words of Paul Schroeder, "the allied coalition was wrecked more by internal divisions than French victories." *Transformation of European Politics*, 138; also see Sherwig, *Guineas and Gunpowder*, 27–48.

England's leaders tried to transform the coalition into a unified alliance, but their own priorities were far from clear and not always compatible with the aims of its putative allies. Having entered the war solely to halt French expansion, the government gradually came to view the restoration of the monarchy as an essential strategic objective.[172] English leaders were themselves divided on what strategy to follow. Like their allies, they proved unable to resist the lure of territorial acquisitions. Even though the main road to victory lay in the battlefields of the Low Countries and the Rhineland, England sent nearly seven thousand troops to seize the French colonies in the Caribbean and another five thousand to support a counterrevolutionary uprising at Toulon.[173] These diversions weakened the coalition's military effort and rekindled Spanish opposition to English colonial expansion, leaving Spain more susceptible to subsequent French blandishments.

Instead of banding together against revolutionary France, in short, the members of the First Coalition were more interested in acquiring territory for themselves than in forging a strategy that might have made such acquisitions possible. The combined effects of French mobilization and allied disunity were soon apparent: French victories at Hondschoote and Wattignies halted the Allied advance in the fall of 1793, and an Allied attempt to resume the initiative in April 1794 was soundly defeated. The French armies won a decisive victory at Tourcoing in May and had reoccupied Brussels, Antwerp, and Liège by midsummer, along with most of the left bank of the Rhine. The Spaniards and Sardinians were driven back in the south, and the counterrevolutionary rebellions inside France were beginning to subside as well. By the fall of 1794, the threat to the republic had been lifted and France had resumed its expansionist course.

*From Thermidor to the Directory.* As noted earlier, the easing of the foreign danger in the spring allowed rifts to reemerge within the CPS and the Convention. Convinced that the Indulgents and the Hébertists posed threats to the revolution, Robespierre and his followers now took the offensive against both. After mending fences with Danton and cultivating the *sans-culottes* with a series of generous economic decrees, the CPS brought the Hébertists

---

[172] Thus, the commissioners in Toulon were informed that "the acknowledgement of an hereditary monarchy . . . affords the only probable ground for restoring regular government in France," and a royal manifesto in October 1793 invited the French to "join the Standard of an Hereditary Monarchy, . . . in order to unite themselves once more under the Empire of Law, of Morality, and of Religion." In 1794, Pitt remarked that he "had no idea of any peace being secure, unless France returned to a monarchical system." Quoted in Mitchell, *Underground War*, 34; Cobban, *Debate on the French Revolution*, 460–62; and McKay and Scott, *Rise of the Great Powers*, 273.

[173] See Michael Duffy, *Sugar, Soldiers, and Seapower: The British Expeditions to the West Indies and the War against Revolutionary France* (Oxford: Clarendon Press, 1987); and Ehrman, *Reluctant Transition*, esp. 303.

before the Paris tribunal and executed them on March 23. Danton and several associates followed them to the guillotine two weeks later, leaving Robespierre and his supporters free to wage war against suspected counterrevolutionaries in the name of the Republic of Virtue. The law of 22 Prairial (June 10, 1794) streamlined the work of the revolutionary tribunals and broadened the list of capital offenses, and the guillotines claimed over two thousand victims in the next two months alone.[174]

The Great Terror marked the final stage of the Jacobin republic. Now convinced that Robespierre sought to establish a personal dictatorship, a faction within the CPS organized a coup. Robespierre defended his actions by again invoking the danger of a counterrevolutionary conspiracy, but the deputies had finally turned against him and he was arrested and subsequently executed on 9 Thermidor (July 27, 1794), along with Saint-Just and several others.

The Jacobin dictatorship had saved the republic, but Robespierre's successors began dismantling it as soon as he was gone.[175] The Jacobin Club was banned in November, and a White Terror soon arose against suspected Jacobins. The end of the revolutionary dictatorship did not bring political stability, however, and food shortages, rising prices, and an extremely cold winter sparked violent demonstrations by the Parisian *sans-culottes* in Germinal and Prairial, Year III (April–May 1795). Unlike in past upheavals, however, the demonstrators were quickly suppressed by government troops.[176] Even more important, the end of the Terror allowed royalists, Girondins, émigrés, and loyal Catholics to reenter political life. Given the enduring divisions within French society (which had been exacerbated by the revolution and the Terror), it was now nearly impossible for any government to gain broad popular support.

The political weakness of the Thermidorean regime was institutionalized by the Constitution of the Year III. Enacted in September 1795, the new constitution established a bicameral Assembly chosen by indirect elections, with suffrage restricted to males over twenty-one and participation in the

---

[174] The ouster of the Hébertists and Dantonists is described in Thompson, *French Revolution*, 452–60. For Robespierre's vision of the ideal republic, see Palmer, *Twelve Who Ruled*, 275–77; and Thompson, *Robespierre*, 450–55, 485–96. On the magnitude of the Terror, see Donald Greer, *The Incidence of the Terror in the French Revolution: A Statistical Interpretation* (Cambridge: Harvard University Press, 1935); and Schama, *Citizens*, 836–37.

[175] The Convention quickly repealed the law of 22 Prairial, curtailed the use of terror, abolished price controls, suspended the *levée en masse*, and abandoned reliance on the *représentants en mission*. Several Girondin deputies were readmitted to the Convention, and the CPS also offered an amnesty to the rebels in the Vendée and partially restored freedom of religion. See Lefebvre, *French Revolution*, 2:137–42; Stewart, *Documentary Survey*, 538–552; and Denis Woronoff, *The Thermidorean Regime and the Directory, 1794–1799*, trans. Julian Jackson (Cambridge: Cambridge University Press, 1984), 1–10, 20–22.

[176] According to Lefebvre, the government's victory over the popular forces in Paris on 3 Prairial marks "the date which should be taken as the end of the Revolution. Its mainspring was now broken." *French Revolution*, 2:144–45.

second electoral stage limited by strict property qualifications. Executive powers were assigned to a five-man Directory chosen by the two legislative Councils, and one-third of each Council and one of the five directors were to be replaced each year.[177] Intended as a safeguard against dictatorship, these measures deprived the executive of stability and authority. Not only was the executive vulnerable to disputes among the directors, but its membership was constantly changing owing to the rotation of deputies in the Councils.[178] Moreover, by seeking to restore the moderate order envisioned in the Constitution of 1791 (minus the monarchy, of course), the Directory guaranteed its own unpopularity. Royalists rejected it because there was no king, die-hard republicans opposed the property restrictions and preferred the more egalitarian Constitution of 1793, and both groups remained fearful that the other might regain power. Thus, the Directory rested on an extremely narrow political base and faced repeated challenges from resurgent royalists and unrepentant republicans alike.[179] Even before the constitution was completed, evidence of increasing royalist strength led the leaders of the Convention to decree that two-thirds of the seats in the new Councils would be chosen from among their own ranks. This measure, which guaranteed that moderate republicans would control the new Councils, provoked a two-day uprising by Parisian royalists on 12–13 Vendémiaire , Year IV (October 4–5, 1795). Hardly an auspicious beginning, this turmoil was a clear indication of the Directory's shaky foundation.[180]

These problems were compounded by irregular food supplies, growing disparities of income, alternating periods of inflation and deflation, and enduring budgetary problems. Recurrent counterrevolutionary disturbances did nothing to help the French economy, and although the Directory exploited its foreign conquests relentlessly, these gains were negated by the

[177] For the text of the new Constitution, see Stewart, *Documentary Survey*, 571–612; for analyses of its provisions, see Woronoff, *Thermidorean Regime and Directory*, 29–31; Martyn Lyons, *France under the Directory* (Cambridge: Cambridge University Press, 1975), 18–20; Sutherland, *France*, 272–75; and Lefebvre, *French Revolution*, 2:160–64.

[178] The director to be replaced each year was chosen by drawing lots. For the changing composition of the Directory, see Jones, *Longman Companion to the French Revolution*, 82–83; Albert Goodwin, "The French Executive Directory—A Revaluation," in *The French Revolution: Conflicting Interpretations*, ed. Frank Kafker and James M. Laux, 2d ed. (Malabar, Fla.: Krieger, 1989); and M. J. Sydenham, *The First French Republic* (Berkeley: University of California Press, 1974), 323–41.

[179] According to Sutherland, "the Directory has a totally justified reputation as one of the most chaotic periods in modern French history." *France*, 279. For a dissenting view, see Goodwin, "French Executive Directory."

[180] The Vendémiaire uprising marked the political debut of Napoleon Bonaparte, whose troops fired the "whiff of grapeshot" that helped defeat the royalist groups. See Rudé, *Crowd in the French Revolution*, chap. 11; Jacques Godechot, *The Counterrevolution: Doctrine and Action, 1789–1804*, trans. Salvator Attanasio (Princeton: Princeton University Press, 1971), 260–62; Sydenham, *First French Republic*, 76–82; and Harvey Mitchell, "Vendémiaire: A Revaluation," *Journal of Modern History* 30, no. 3 (1958), 191–202.

damage done to French foreign trade. The Directory did much to stabilize French fiscal policy over the longer term, but the short-term costs were severe and contributed greatly to the country's political weakness.[181]

*The Foreign Policy of the Directory.* The political divisions within France and the weakness of the new regime had important effects on French foreign policy and its conduct of the war. To begin with, there was no consensus on what France's war aims should be.[182] Royalists favored the renunciation of prior French conquests, seeing that as the swiftest route to peace and a restoration of the monarchy. Moderates within the Directory sought only limited territorial acquisitions, on the grounds that further expansion would undermine French power and lead to incessant warfare.[183]

The dominant position, however, was held by the advocates of "natural borders," whose ranks included most of the leading figures of the Thermidorean period and the first Directory. According to this view, France's borders had been "ordained by nature" and consisted of the Atlantic, the Pyrenees, the Alps, and most importantly, the Rhine. To obtain these limits, France would have to annex Belgium and the entire left bank of the Rhine, including German states belonging to Prussia and Austria or falling under Francis II's protection in his capacity as head of the Holy Roman Empire.

To justify prolonging the war, supporters of *"les grandes limites"* argued that expansion to the Rhine would greatly enhance French security. As Merlin de Douai told the Convention in December 1794: "We want [a peace] guaranteed by our own power and the powerlessness of our enemies ever to harm us." Another member of the CPS, François-Antoine Boissy d'Anglas, told the Convention that the borders designated by nature would protect France from "all invasion . . . for a long series of centuries," and Jean-Jacques Cambacérès, a prominent Thermidorean, declared, "When a nation has risen in arms against invasion, . . . it should use its power to ensure that [its rights] will be respected forever." Others suggested that France required additional territory in order to counter the Prussian and Austrian gains in Poland and

[181] Economic conditions and policies under the Directory are summarized in Sydenham, *First French Republic*, 96–100, 182–86; Goodwin, "French Executive Directory," 326–32; Woronoff, *Thermidorean Regime and the Directory*, chap. 4; Lyons, *France under the Directory*, chaps. 4–5, 12; and Michel Bruguière, "Assignats," in Furet and Ozouf, *Critical Dictionary*, 426–36.

[182] On the different positions, see Ross, *European Diplomatic History*, 110–112; Lyons, *France under the Directory*, 190–91; Woronoff, *Thermidorean Regime and the Directory*, 27, 61–63; and Biro, *German Policy*, 2:488–98, 500–506.

[183] Thus, Carnot told the CPS in July 1794, "We could, if we so wished, plant the liberty tree on the banks of the Rhine and unite to France all the former territory of the Gauls, but however seductive this system might be, . . . France can only weaken herself and sow the seeds of an endless war by expanding her territory in this way." It should be noted that Carnot's views on this issue fluctuated greatly. See Richet, "Natural Borders," 760–61; Biro, *German Policy*, 1:235, 263, 2:504–505; and Blanning, *French Revolution in Germany*, 75.

preserve the balance of power; as Jean-François Reubell put it, "The object of the pacification of France should be not so much to acquire indemnities, as to restore that equilibrium on which its safety depends." Supporters of expansion also emphasized the wealth of the neighboring regions and argued that annexation would redeem France's inflated currency, bolster the French economy, and sustain its military effort. And to combat the assertion that occupation or annexation would be unpopular, advocates claimed that the local populations believed "they have all to gain by being French."[184]

The advocates of expansion lacked the political power to impose their preferences arbitrarily, and obtaining the "natural borders" would in any case require additional military successes. So long as Reubell was the dominant figure in the Directory, however, this group had the greatest influence over French war aims. Reubell was especially interested in protecting the French position in his native Alsace, and his control over foreign policy ensured that the goal of *les grandes limites* was never entirely abandoned.[185]

Several other factors strengthened the expansionist thrust of French foreign policy and reduced the prospects for peace. The first was economic: because the ravaged French economy could not keep the army supplied, it had become reliant on requisitions and levies from the occupied territories. Thus, the Directory told General Moreau that he should "nourish the Army with the fruit of its courage" and reminded General Jourdan that "the great art of war is to live at the expense of the enemy."[186]

France's dependence on the lands it occupied was compounded by the independence of local representatives and military commanders and also by the opportunities for personal enrichment that occupation afforded. The Directory had abandoned the Jacobin system of central supply and given private contractors the task of supplying the army. This policy allowed the generals even greater freedom of action and created a powerful domestic constituency whose financial well-being was sustained by war.[187] To make

[184] These quotations are from Biro, *German Policy*, 1:263, 335, 427–38, 2:513; and Blanning, *French Revolution in Germany*, 74.

[185] See Gerlof D. Homan, *Jean-François Reubell: French Revolutionary, Patriot, and Director (1747–1807)* (The Hague: Martinus Nijhoff, 1971), esp. 89.

[186] As Blanning notes, "neither in nature, scope, nor intensity was the exploitation of the Rhineland exceptional. The conditions which dictated exploitation—the penury of the government, the size of the armies, the scale of the war—applied with roughly equal force to all other parts of French-occupied Europe." See his *French Revolution in Germany*, chap. 3, esp. 127–28; and Biro, *German Policy*, 2:650–60.

[187] Thus, one French official admitted, "Our expedition [across] the Rhine . . . was due entirely to pecuniary considerations. . . . Our incursion into a rich and defenseless country was to procure us the money of which we were in such dire need." Quoted in Geoffrey Best, *War and Society in Revolutionary Europe, 1770–1870* (London: Oxford University Press, 1982), 92–93. On the growing independence of the army, see Lyons, *France under the Directory*, 155–58. According to Woronoff, by 1796 "the war was no longer concerned with national defense, but with conquest—or even merely plunder." *Thermidorean Regime and the Directory*, 64–67, 74.

matters worse, the deep divisions within French society and the lack of broad popular support forced the Directory to rely on the army to keep itself in power. Bonaparte's "whiff of grapeshot" had halted the Vendémiaire uprising, and military support would be needed to defuse the royalist challenge in Fructidor, Year V (September 1797) and the neo-Jacobin resurgence of Floréal, Year VI (April 1798). Thus, the Directory had become dependent on the goodwill of its generals, and the army and its suppliers had become addicted to expansion, a combination wholly fatal to any serious effort to make peace.

There is also evidence that the directors feared that peace would bring adverse domestic consequences—and greater royalist influence—unless they obtained tangible gains from the war. Abbé Sieyès told a Prussian diplomat in May 1795, "We need to obtain a glorious peace," and he later warned that the Directory "would be lost if peace were made." Other directors feared that peace would expose them to charges of corruption, force the discharge of proroyalist troops, and reveal that economic hardship in France was due to their own mistakes rather than the war. The danger of direct military interference was equally worrisome; as one of the directors put it, "Make peace! And what will you do with the generals? Would they cultivate greens?"[188]

In short, although several directors recognized that a negotiated settlement was desirable, six years of revolution and war had created a formidable engine of expansion. Some of the directors now opposed further expansion, and in the words of Martyn Lyons, the foreign policy of the Directory "oscillated between the defence of [the] natural frontiers, . . . and the creation of semi-independent sister republics," depending on shifts of military fortune and which faction enjoyed the dominant position in the executive.[189] Despite the growing desire for peace and several promising diplomatic opportunities, therefore, the Directory was unable to take France out of the war.

*The Collapse of the First Coalition.* France's inability to make peace was especially tragic in light of its favorable military position. Amsterdam had fallen to the French in January 1795, and Dutch sympathizers quickly proclaimed a "Batavian Republic" and signed a one-sided treaty of alliance in May.[190] Tuscany made peace in February, and peace talks between Prussia

---

[188] Quoted in Biro, *German Policy*, 1:375, 2:509–10; and see also Rothenburg, "Wars of the French Revolution," 214–15.

[189] See Lyons, *France under the Directory*, 190–91; and also Blanning, *French Revolution in Germany*, 75.

[190] The text of the treaty is in Stewart, *Documentary Survey*, 567–71. For details on the occupation and negotiations, see Schama, *Patriots and Liberators*, 178–210; and Palmer, *Democratic Revolution*, 2:180–92.

and France took on new life. Frederick William, whose finances were dwindling rapidly, had no reason to continue fighting now that his ambitions in Poland had been satisfied.[191] His decision was simplified by England's reluctance to grant additional subsidies and Vienna's collusion with Russia in a third partition of Poland, and Prussia and France signed a peace treaty in Basel in April. The German princes of the Holy Roman Empire accepted Prussian mediation in their own negotiations with France, and Spain signed a peace treaty with France at the end of July.[192]

England's efforts to hold the Coalition together were undermined by military setbacks of its own. Although England had seized several French and Dutch colonies, the occupation of Toulon had to be abandoned at the end of 1793 and the expedition to Santo Domingo had turned into a costly quagmire.[193] The French conquest of Holland had confined English forces on the continent to Hanover, and an amphibious landing in Brittany in June 1795 was a total failure. Convinced by French émigrés that the expedition would spark a large counterrevolutionary uprising, the English landed an army of some thirty-three hundred émigrés at Carnac on June 27, where they were joined by several thousand members of the local resistance. But the quarrelsome émigrés failed to coordinate their actions with their local allies, and the expedition was quickly "trapped like rats" (as the French commander put it) on the narrow Quiberon Peninsula. Efforts to evacuate them were only partially successful, and more than six hundred émigrés were captured and executed. The fiasco marked the émigrés' last major effort to spark an armed counterrevolution in France.[194]

By the fall of 1795, therefore, the main counterrevolutionary efforts in France had been quelled and the coalition against France had been reduced to England, Austria, and a handful of German and Italian states. The fate of the Rhineland awaited a final peace settlement with Austria and the lesser German states, but the Convention had already voted to annex Belgium and Liège on 9 Vendémiaire, Year III. The decision not to annex the left bank outright also reflected France's reluctance to antagonize Prussia (which it hoped to draw into an alliance at a later date), and

[191] Frederick William told an English envoy in February that despite his "invariable abhorrence of the French principles, . . . it was necessity alone that governed his conduct, and . . . another campaign would completely exhaust his treasure." Quoted in Biro, *German Policy*, 1:340.
[192] The Treaty of Basel established a neutral zone along the northeastern border and permitted French troops to remain in Prussian territory on the left bank of the Rhine pending "the general pacification between France and the Germanic Empire." See Stewart, *Documentary Survey*, 563–67; and Biro, *German Policy*, vol. 1, chaps. 8–9. On the negotiations between France and Spain, see Von Sybel, *French Revolution*, 4:357–66.
[193] See Duffy, *Sugar, Soldiers, and Seapower*, pt. 1.
[194] A detailed account of the Quiberon raid is in Hutt, *Chouannerie and Counterrevolution*, 2:269–325.

the Directory made delicate inquiries regarding peace with Austria at about this time as well.

Unfortunately for France, the dismantling of the Jacobin dictatorship had undermined its capacity to mobilize the nation for war, and its military forces fell to fewer than 450,000 men by the fall of 1795.[195] Russia joined the Coalition in September (though it did not participate in the fighting), and the final partition of Poland allowed Austria to devote greater attention to France. England granted Austria another loan in May, and Austria won a series of important victories in September and October and were threatening the French positions by November.[196] Convinced that more favorable terms would be forthcoming, the Austrians now rejected the French peace offers. England's response was similar: although Pitt had begun secret peace negotiations following the passage of the new French constitution in September, the talks foundered over the Directory's refusal to relinquish Belgium.[197]

The campaigns of 1796–97 struck the final blow against the First Coalition. The Directory intended the brunt to fall on Germany while the Army of Italy tied up Austrian forces and acquired "bargaining chips" for subsequent negotiation. The French armies resumed the offensive in May, took Frankfurt and Nuremburg by the end of July, and occupied Munich and Ulm in August. Combined with Bonaparte's victories in Italy (see below), these successes led to renewed peace talks with Austria and a series of armistices with the lesser German states. The prospect of a Franco-Austrian settlement convinced Prussia to cede its territories on the left bank in exchange for territorial concessions elsewhere, and the new understanding was enshrined in the Treaty of Berlin in July. Although it remained contingent on the Imperial Diet's consent, the agreement brought France closer to formal annexation of the Rhineland.[198] Military reversals soon undermined these diplomatic achievements, however; Austrian forces under Charles V defeated the French forces at Altenkirchen in September and drove another French army back across the Rhine shortly thereafter.

[195] Alan Forrest reports that France had 750,000 men in arms in September 1794, fewer than 500,000 a year later, only 400,000 in July 1796, and roughly 325,000 by September 1798. *Conscripts and Deserters: The Army and French Society during the Revolution and Empire* (New York: Oxford University Press, 1989), 34.
[196] Austria's victories were facilitated by the dilatory conduct of the commander of the French Army of the Rhine, Jean-Charles Pichegru, who was collaborating with a group of royalist émigrés and receiving bribes from English intelligence agents in Switzerland. See Mitchell, *Underground War*, 60–63, 118–24; Woronoff, *Thermidorean Regime and the Directory*, 53–54; Palmer, *Democratic Revolution*, 2:227.
[197] In addition to retaining Belgium, the French insisted that England relinquish its colonial conquests, and Pitt concluded that England would have to wait "for the return of reason in our deluded enemy." Quoted in Ehrman, *Reluctant Transition*, 607; see also Rose, "Struggle with Revolutionary France," 261–65; and Ross, *European Diplomatic History*, 115–16.
[198] On the Treaty of Berlin, see Biro, *German Policy*, 615–19.

In Italy, by contrast, the French armies won a series of stunning victories that eventually forced Austria to negotiate in earnest. Under the command of Napoleon Bonaparte, the Army of Italy took Piedmont in April, forced Sardinia to make peace in May, and followed up these victories with a successful invasion of Lombardy. Milan fell on May 15. Venice, Verona, and the papacy had agreed to armistices by the end of June. The French then defeated a detachment of Austrian reinforcements in August and trapped them at Mantua, which fell after a long siege in February 1797.

Although Reubell and several other directors opposed "revolutionizing" Italy for fear that it would prolong the war, Bonaparte had ignored their objections and set up a number of "republican" governments in the wake of his victorious army.[199] After establishing a new regime in Lombardy and proclaiming a "Cispadane Republic" in December 1796, he created "Venetian" and "Ligurian" republics in May and June and, in July, combined Lombardy and the Cispadane Republic into the "Cisalpine Republic." Together with the Batavian Republic in Holland, these new states comprised the "sister republics" of revolutionary France. Nominally independent and equipped with constitutions similar to the French, they endured the same "benefits" of French occupation that Belgium and the Rhineland had. The systematic looting of the conquered regions sustained the French troops in the field and swelled the personal fortunes of French commanders, but the policy cost the French whatever local support they initially enjoyed and left the sister republics entirely dependent on French backing.[200]

Bonaparte renewed his attacks in March, and the Austrians were now willing to negotiate. Eager to seal his triumph, Bonaparte ignored the Directory's preference for territory on the Rhine and negotiated a preliminary peace that gave Belgium and Lombardy to France and compensated Austria with Venice and its Adriatic provinces, but deferred the status of the Rhineland to a later congress. The Directory, in no position to oppose France's most successful general, quickly ratified his fait accompli. Bonaparte then raised the stakes by demanding the left bank of the Rhine and several other concessions, and Austria was forced to accede. After six months of negotiations, the state of war between Austria and France was formally ended in October 1797 by the Treaty of Campo Formio.[201]

England's deteriorating military position had brought it back to the negotiating table as well, but a peace agreement remained elusive. England faced a serious fiscal crisis and rising public discontent. In addition, Spain

---

[199] On the directors' reservations, see Homan, *Jean-Francois Reubell*, 135.

[200] Godechot estimates that the French conquests in Italy paid 45 million livres to France during 1796 alone and even more in subsequent years. *Grande nation*, 439–41.

[201] For the text of the treaty, see Stewart, *Documentary Survey*, 702–709; for insightful analyses of the negotiations, see Schroeder, *Transformation of European Politics*, 166–72; and Roider, *Thugut and Austria's Response*, 240–61.

had realigned with France in 1796, and its cabinet was increasingly alarmed by French support for the Irish independence movement (including an attempted invasion by a French expeditionary force in December 1796). Talks between Lord Malmesbury and French foreign minister Delacroix began in October 1796, but the English terms were too one-sided and the negotiations soon broke down.[202] Although a victory over the Spanish fleet at Cape St. Vincent in February stiffened English resolve temporarily, the pressure for peace resumed after Austria signed the preliminary agreement at Leoben and the Royal Navy was rocked by a series of mutinies in April.

When negotiations between England and France resumed in July, England now indicated it would accept the annexation of Belgium in exchange for the French and Dutch colonies at Ceylon, the Cape of Good Hope, and Martinique. Unfortunately, this promising initiative was soon derailed by political divisions within France and England's renewed hopes for a royalist restoration. Although some émigré leaders continued to insist that the old regime be restored in its entirety, other prominent royalists had begun to downplay these ambitions to attract popular support.[203] The result was a stunning defeat for the Directory in the elections of Germinal, Year V (April 1797), which left the two Councils divided between republicans who favored a harsh peace and the moderates and royalists who were willing to offer more generous terms in order to end the war quickly.[204] The Directory was itself divided by this time, and the royalist leaders assured their English patrons that better peace terms would be available once they gained control. Thus, internal divisions within France both prevented the Directory from offering acceptable terms and encouraged England to stand firm in the hope of obtaining a better deal.

With their positions in jeopardy, a triumvirate of Barras, Reubell, and La Révellière-Lépeaux turned to the army once again. Backed by the minister of war, General Hoche, and by Bonaparte (whose prestige was now unmatched), the triumvirs launched a coup on 17 Fructidor, Year V (September

---

[202] On French support for the Irish rebels, see Elliott, *Partners in Revolution;* the 1796 invasion is analyzed in chapter 4. See also E. H. Stuart Jones, *An Invasion That Failed* (Oxford: Oxford University Press, 1950). On the Anglo-French peace talks, see Ehrman, *Reluctant Transition,* 641–50.

[203] According to Martyn Lyons, "the story of [royalist] attempts to seize power is one of consistent self-delusion and failure." *France under the Directory,* chap. 3, esp. 37. Counterrevolutionary activities are described in Godechot, *Counter-revolution;* Sutherland, *France 1789–1815,* 286–92; Doyle, *History of the French Revolution,* chap. 13 and 127–31; Jones, *Longman Companion,* 194–200; Palmer, *Democratic Revolution,* 2:225–28, 244–55; and Massimo Boffa, "Emigrés" and "Counterrevolution," in Furet and Ozouf, *Critical Dictionary,* 324–36, 640–48. English support for the royalists is described in detail in Hutt, *Chouannerie and Counterrevolution;* and Mitchell, *Underground War,* 124–35, 150–61.

[204] Only 11 out of 216 deputies were reelected at this time, reducing support for the current directors from roughly two-thirds of the Councils to about one-third. Sydenham, *First French Republic,* 121–27.

3, 1797). The main royalist leaders were arrested, and Carnot and Barthélemy were ousted from the Directory, while 198 royalist deputies were removed from the Councils. Royalist newspapers were closed, former émigrés were given ten days to leave French soil, and a number of anticlerical measures were restored. The Fructidor coup ended the danger of a royalist restoration, but it also showed that the Directory could not survive without violating its own constitution. The coup also brought the peace talks with England to an end; when the French representative declared that France would neither grant colonial concessions nor relinquish its prior annexations, his English counterpart broke off the negotiations.[205]

The First Coalition lay in ruins by the end of 1797. Prussia was firmly neutral, Austria had made peace, and Spain, Sardinia, and the sister republics in Holland and Italy were formally allied with France. England was France's sole remaining opponent, but it could do little without a strong continental ally.

The story of the War of the First Coalition illustrates the difficulties that revolutionary states and other powers face when attempting to gauge the balance of threats. The war expanded in part because England and France saw each other as both threatening and vulnerable, and it continued because France could not sustain its military effort and because the Coalition was divided by conflicting interests and ambitions. Since the leading members of the Coalition had trouble assessing the true level of threat, they failed either to muster sufficient power to overthrow the revolutionary regime, on one hand, or to offer sufficient concessions to persuade it to make peace, on the other. The problem was compounded by a lack of information on each side and a concomitant tendency to rely on biased sources. As a result, Lebrun and the Convention exaggerated the prospects for a revolution in England in 1792–93, and the Directory felt emboldened to support an uprising in Ireland. Similarly, the Coalition's war effort was partly sustained by the belief that the revolutionary government was unpopular and by exaggerated hopes of a counterrevolutionary restoration. In each case, incomplete or biased information reinforced expectations of victory and discouraged efforts to make peace.

Domestic politics within France contributed to the expansion and continuation of the war as well. Under the CPS, negotiations were inhibited by the danger of appearing disloyal, while the Directory's efforts to pursue peace were hampered by several factors: disagreements among the directors, their fragile hold on power, and the army's growing interest in expansion. These internal divisions also helped sustain the Coalition's hopes, at least until the republic's victories in 1796–97 forced all save England to make peace.

[205] On the coup of Fructidor V, see Sutherland, *France 1789–1815*, 305–07; Sydenham, *French Republic*, 140–48; and Lefebvre, *French Revolution*, 2:197–206.

Finally, the course of the war also illustrates how a revolutionary state will modify its initial goals in the face of external pressure. The goal of spreading liberty had been abandoned by 1795, and though the directors continued to offer lip service to republican ideals by giving the sister republics French-style constitutions, they treated these areas as assets to be exploited rather than as fraternal associates in an idealistic campaign for liberty.[206] The war also bore an increasing resemblance to a traditional struggle for power, with the contenders wrangling over colonial possessions and territorial compensations rather than rival ideological visions.

## THE WAR OF THE SECOND COALITION

### *The Armed Truce*

The peace that followed the collapse of the First Coalition was little more than an intermission. The Directory was unhappy with the Treaty of Campo Formio (because it deferred acquisition of the left bank of the Rhine), and it faced a new challenge to its authority at home, this time from the left. Jacobinism had made a brief resurgence after the royalist uprising in Vendémiaire III, when the Councils had relaxed the existing anti-Jacobin measures in order to suppress the royalists. Support for the Jacobins was further enhanced by such factors as chronic economic problems, growing disparities of wealth, and the military setbacks of 1795–96, which recalled the dangers of 1793 and cast doubt on the Directory's ability to lead the nation in war.

The Directory had responded by closing the remaining Jacobin political clubs and banning former Montagnards from Paris, but Jacobin influence began to reemerge after the antiroyalist coup of Fructidor, Year V.[207] Left-wing newspapers and political associations became increasingly active, and with nearly 60 percent of the deputies due for replacement in the next election, the danger of a Jacobin victory began to eclipse the fear of a royalist restoration.[208] The directors imposed new restrictions on the Jacobin clubs,

---

[206] Thus, a French general argued that "Holland has done nothing to avoid being classed among the general order of our conquests. It was the ice, the indefatigable courage of our troops and the talents of our generals that delivered her and not any revolution. It follows from this that there can be no reason to treat her differently from any conquered country." Quoted in Schama, *Patriots and Liberators*, 201.

[207] The first challenge had come not from the Jacobins but from the even more radical Conspiracy of the Equals, led by François-Noel ("Gracchus") Babeuf. Babeuf tried to launch an insurrection against the Directory by organizing a clandestine party and infiltrating the army, but the plot was betrayed by an informer and Babeuf was executed in May 1797. See R. B. Rose, *Gracchus Babeuf: The First Revolutionary Communist* (Stanford: Stanford University Press, 1978); Palmer, *Democratic Revolution*, 2:231–44; and James H. Billington, *Fire in the Minds of Men: Origins of the Revolutionary Faith* (New York: Basic Books, 1980), 72–78.

[208] Sutherland, *France*, 309.

eventually passing a decree that required incumbent deputies to verify the elections of new members. These maneuvers enabled the directors to remove 127 deputies (most of them suspected Jacobins) in the so-called Coup of Floréal, Year VI. The Directory had managed to cling to power once again, but the episode further underscored its political weakness.[209]

Despite its earlier successes, France's strategic position remained problematic. England remained defiant and its fortunes were reviving after the setbacks of the previous year: the naval mutinies had been quelled by midsummer, a series of fiscal reforms and tax increases had restored the government's credit, the threat of invasion had made the English public more receptive to patriotic appeals, and the destruction of the Dutch fleet at Camperdown in October had bolstered English morale and preserved its maritime superiority. England had also extricated itself from Santo Domingo by the fall of 1798, freeing resources for new campaigns elsewhere. Although Pitt had been willing to acknowledge French possession of the Low Countries during the peace talks in 1797, England's leaders were increasingly committed to overthrowing the revolutionary regime and restoring the balance of power in Europe. Naval power could not accomplish these objectives unaided, however, so England still needed continental allies.[210]

*French Expansionism.* There was no shortage of candidates for constructing a new coalition. The Austrian government was equally unhappy with the Treaty of Campo Formio, and Baron Thugut of Austria began exploring new alliance possibilities before the ink on the treaty was dry.[211] There were hints that Prussia might join a new coalition and Russia was beginning to take a more active role as well.[212] Yet given the conflicting interests and mistrust

[209] The results were ratified by the law of 22 Floreal, which gave a legal veneer to a clear violation of constitutional procedure. See Sydenham, *First French Republic*, 170–75; and Isser Woloch, *Jacobin Legacy: The Democratic Movement under the Directory* (Princeton: Princeton University Press, 1970), chap. 10.

[210] See Rose, *Life of Pitt*, 2:328–33; Ian R. Christie, *Wars and Revolutions: Britain, 1760–1815* (Cambridge: Harvard University Press, 1982), 241–42; Piers Mackesy, *Statesmen at War: The Strategy of Overthrow, 1798–99* (London: Longman, 1974), 2–9; A. B. Rodger, *The War of the Second Coalition, 1798–1801* (London: Oxford University Press, 1964), 7–8; Duffy, *Sugar, Soldiers, and Seapower*, 298–311; and John M. Sherwig, "Lord Grenville's Plan for a Concert of Europe, 1797–99," *Journal of Modern History* 34, no. 3 (1962).

[211] In a note to a confidant, Thugut remarked, "Peace! But where is it? I do not see it in the treaty [of Campo Formio] . . . and the execution of it will perhaps be only a second volume of the preliminaries." The future foreign minister, Louis Cobenzl, told Thugut, "We are only concluding a truce which will allow us to reestablish ourselves in Italy more easily than by means of the most successful military campaign; in any case, settling matters in Germany will give us twenty reasons for beginning the war again if we wish to." Quoted in Roider, *Thugut and Austria's Response*, 260–61; and Mackesy, *Statesmen at War*, 9.

[212] Catherine II had died in 1796, but the new tsar, Paul I, shared her anti-Jacobin sentiments and was alarmed by the growth of French influence in Italy and the eastern Mediterranean. See Norman E. Saul, *Russia and the Mediterranean, 1797–1807* (Chicago: University of

among the potential members, the formation of a second anti-French coalition could have been prevented had the Directory refrained from further efforts to expand. But the coup of 18 Fructidor had left the conduct of foreign policy in the hands of Reubell—a consistent advocate of the "natural borders"—and the Jacobin resurgence in 1797 magnified the pressures for an expansionist policy. Taking a hard line at the Congress of Rastatt, the Directory forced the Imperial Diet to acknowledge French sovereignty over the entire left bank of the Rhine (including several territories that had been excluded at Campo Formio). Negotiations between Austrian and French representatives accomplished nothing, and Thugut was increasingly convinced that Austria would have to resume the war once conditions favored it.[213]

At the same time, the creation of additional sister republics in Italy and Switzerland and the consolidation of French influence in Belgium and Holland had reinforced an image of limitless French ambition. Although the Directory had not intended to "revolutionize" Rome, struggles between local radicals and conservatives led to the death of a French general, an invasion of the the papal territories, and the establishment of a "Roman Republic" in February 1798. French intervention enabled a group of Swiss sympathizers to launch their own revolt in January, which led to the establishment of a "Helvetic Republic" in April. The Kingdom of Piedmont was occupied and annexed the following year, confirming France's aggressive reputation.[214]

Why was the Directory unable to stop the expansion? In part because the French armies were still dependent on foreign plunder and the Directory on military backing. War had become an economic and political necessity despite the widespread desire for peace, and abandoning the sister republics would have entailed dismantling the army in the middle of a war—with untold domestic and international consequences. As Reubell told a Prussian diplomat in January 1799, "War has become our element . . . the nation has become martial." Or as Bonaparte later recalled, "To exist [the Directory] needed a state of war as other governments need a state of peace."[215]

---

Chicago Press, 1970), 32–39, and "The Objectives of Paul's Italian Policy," in *Paul I: A Reassessment of His Life and Reign*, ed. Hugh Ragsdale (Pittsburgh: Center for International Studies, University of Pittsburgh, 1979), 31–43; and Rodger, *War of the Second Coalition*, 11–12.

[213] See Lefebvre, *French Revolution*, 2:227–28; and Roider, *Thugut and Austria's Response*, 264, 283, and passim.

[214] Thugut concluded, "We must either accept the status quo in Italy and in Switzerland or come to a new rupture with France." He chose the latter option because he believed that "if the French continue to hold Switzerland, revolution in the Swabian Circle first and then in all of Germany is inevitable." Quoted in Roider, *Thugut and Austria's Response*, 283–84. On these events, see Palmer, *Democratic Revolution*, 2:372–80, 402–13; Woronoff, *Thermidorean Regime and the Directory*, 153–54; and Godechot, *La Grande nation*, 198–202.

[215] Albert Sorel offers a similar verdict: "War alone assured the existence of the Directory, and war could only be sustained by war itself." *Europe et la révolution française*, 5:283; and see also Woronoff, *Thermidorean Regime and the Directory*, 167; and Lyons, *France under the Directory*, 204.

In addition to the army's interest in conquest and plunder, further efforts to extend French control were encouraged by the desire to safeguard past conquests and put additional pressure on England. In the words of one director, France now aimed "to unite Holland, France, Switzerland, [and] the Cisalpine and Ligurian republics by an uninterrupted continuity of territory . . . a nursery of excellent soldiers and a formidable strategic position." Thus, the Rhineland was sought as a strategic barrier, and the establishment of the Helvetic Republic was inspired in part by a desire to control the strategic passes between France and Italy and halt the espionage activities of English and émigré agents in Switzerland. Similarly, although France's policies toward the Batavian Republic were affected by its own domestic politics, its underlying objective was to strengthen a key ally and guarantee its continued loyalty.[216]

*The Expedition to Egypt.* French expansionism after Campo Formio helped ensure that a Second Coalition would rise to replace the First, despite the many conflicts between France's putative opponents.[217] The decisive event, however, was the French expedition to Egypt in May 1798. Because England's naval supremacy made a cross-Channel invasion problematic, Bonaparte proposed an expedition to conquer Egypt instead.[218] In addition to enhancing French control of the eastern Mediterranean, the conquest of Egypt would pose a direct challenge to the British position in India, which was regarded as the key to England's wealth. It would also bring France's military power to bear against England and facilitate French commerce in the eastern Mediterranean. Napoleon and Talleyrand assured the Directory that the Egypt's defenders were weak and the population "would greet us with rapture." They also promised that England's fear of invasion would prevent the Royal Navy from interfering, and that France's expedition would not provoke any adverse foreign response. Over the objections of Reubell and La Révellière-Lépeaux (who favored consolidating the French hold on the Continent), the expedition was approved in March 1798 and set sail from Toulon in May.[219]

---

[216] See Blanning, *French Revolutionary Wars*, 178. Reubell supported the "revolutionizing" of Switzerland as a military necessity, remarking, "I have never deserved better of my country than by pushing this revolution with all my strength." Swiss wealth was an additional incentive, and France used the Bern treasury to finance Bonaparte's expedition to Egypt later in the year. See Gerlof D. Homan, "Jean-Francois Reubell, Director," *French Historical Studies* 1, no. 4 (1960), 431–32; and Palmer, *Democratic Revolution*, 2:200.

[217] Blanning, *French Revolutionary Wars*, 192; Sherwig, *Guineas and Gunpowder*, 101–103; and Mackesy, *Statesmen at War*, 12–13.

[218] After Campo Formio, Bonaparte had advised the Directory "to concentrate all our activity on the Navy and destroy England. That accomplished, Europe will lie at our feet" (quoted in Rodger, *War of the Second Coalition*, 11). He was ordered to prepare for an invasion but soon realized that the risks were too great.

[219] As Blanning points out, these arguments echo the Girondins' earlier optimism; the French were again choosing to expand the war in the belief that victory would be swift and easy. See his *French Revolutionary Wars*, 181–83; Rodger, *War of the Second Coalition*, 15–30; and Woronoff, *Thermidorean Regime and Directory*, 146–48.

The Egyptian expedition was a product of Bonaparte's personal ambition and the desire to end the stalemate with England. The directors' political weakness played a role as well, as they were in no position to defy France's most popular and successful general. Sending him away at his own request may have appeared an ideal solution.

If the solution seemed ideal, its actual consequences were not.[220] Bonaparte's troops seized Malta in June and reached Egypt in July, where they made short work of the Mameluke defenders. However, the situation was reversed when an English squadron destroyed the French fleet at the Battle of the Nile, leaving Napoleon and his army stranded. Not only did this defeat end any possibility of a French challenge in India (where a French-backed uprising was rapidly collapsing), it also brought Russia and Turkey into the war against France. Contrary to Talleyrand's assurances, the invasion of Egypt had encouraged a rapprochement between the two eastern rivals, and the destruction of the French fleet cast doubt on French invincibility. Russia and the Ottoman Empire began joint operations to retake the Ionian Islands in the fall. The sultan also prepared an army to reconquer Egypt. In response, Bonaparte led an expedition to Syria in an attempt to disrupt the Ottoman preparations, but his forces were repulsed, with heavy losses, by a combination of Ottoman troops and English seapower.

In addition to squandering some of France's best troops and isolating its most successful general, the results of its expedition to Egypt was to restore England's control of the Mediterranean and bring two new powers into the war against France.[221] It also prevented France from exploiting the Irish revolt in May 1798; although a belated expedition managed to land a French battalion in Ireland in August, the invaders were quickly defeated and the opportunity to strike a direct blow against England was lost.[222]

### The Renewal of the Coalition

French expansionism had forced Austria back toward war, but the fear of a Prussian alliance with France, together with England's refusal to grant a

---

[220] R. R. Palmer calls the expedition to Egypt possibly "one of the worst strategic blunders ever made." *Democratic Revolution*, 2:499. Also see Blanning, *French Revolutionary Wars*, 179–82. For a contrasting view, see Edward Ingram, *Commitment to Empire: Prophecies of the Great Game in Asia, 1797–1800* (Oxford: Clarendon Press, 1981).

[221] See J. Holland Rose, "The Political Reactions of Bonaparte's Eastern Expedition," *English Historical Review* 44, no. 173 (1929).

[222] Marianne Elliott argues, "The failure of the French to arrive had baffled the Irish leaders and was the most important single reason for the indecision of the leaders, the consequent erosion of United [Irish] strength, and the confused campaign that followed." The rebel force consisted of 800 French soldiers and 500 Irish recruits, facing roughly 20,000 English soldiers. *Partners in Revolution*, 214.

new loan, kept Vienna on the fence for some time.[223] The Austrian government, understandably reluctant to resume a war in which its own territories would be most at risk and its own troops would do most of the fighting, held on to hopes that the Directory would offer additional concessions. These reservations faded when it became clear that France would not give ground and Tsar Paul I offered to send a corps to Austria to fight against the French. As a first step, Austria sent troops into the Swiss canton of the Grisons in October, where they stood ready to invade the Cisalpine and Helvetic republics.

The final push came after King Ferdinand of Naples launched an ill-fated invasion of the Roman Republic in the fall. A French counterattack routed the Neapolitan forces and led to the proclamation of the "Parthanopean Republic" in January 1799. Although its alliance with Naples was purely defensive (and Ferdinand had been warned to avoid any provoking the French), Austria's refusal to come to Ferdinand's aid reinforced Paul's fear of Austrian duplicity. He threatened to withdraw his troops unless Vienna declared war immediately. France made the Austrian decision easier by demanding that Austria expel the Russians or face war. Austria promptly rejected the ultimatum, and French units were crossing the Rhine even before the formal declaration of war in March.

Ironically, although both Grenville and Thugut sought to forge a unified concert against France, their conflicting aims and mutual mistrust made this impossible. Austria was formally allied with Russia but not with England, and efforts to draw Prussia into the coalition failed completely. Agreement on war aims was equally elusive, because the three main allies had very different objectives. England and Russia sought to overthrow the revolutionary government and reduce France to its original size, in order to establish a balance of power on the continent that would maximize their influence there and free them to pursue territorial advantages elsewhere. By contrast, Austria was largely indifferent to the nature of the French government. It sought a territorial settlement that would contain future French expansionism, compensate Austria for its previous sacrifices, and enable it to protect itself against its other rivals. As Piers Mackesy observes, "in the absence of agreed Coalition aims, the major allies would allow their divergent political aims to distort the planning of their strategy and disrupt its execution."[224]

---

[223] Relations between England and Austria were severely strained by Austria's refusal to ratify a loan agreement in 1797 (which had embarassed the Pitt government and shaken English finances temporarily), as well as by Austrian resentment at having to bear the brunt of the costs of the war and English anger over Vienna's decision to make peace at Campo Formio. See Sherwig, *Guineas and Gunpowder*, 100–103; Mackesy, *Statesmen at War*, 12–14, 30–32; and Roider, *Thugut and Austria's Response*, 270–73.
[224] *Statesmen at War*, 70; and see also Ross, *European Diplomatic History*, 187–88. For accounts sympathetic to Austria, see Schroeder, *Transformation of European Politics*, 192–97, and "The Collapse of the Second Coalition," *Journal of Modern History* 59, no. 2 (1987); and Roider, *Thugut and Austria's Response*, chap. 11.

Thus, the conduct of the war followed the same familiar pattern: the Coalition's early successes were undermined by internal disagreements that allowed France to emerge victorious once again—but not, however, before a series of serious setbacks. An initial French offensive in Germany was repulsed, and Austrian troops under Archduke Charles had driven the French forces out of southern Germany and the Helvetic Republic by mid-June. A combined Austro-Russian army under Marshal Alexander Suvorov swept the French from northern Italy, the sister republics promptly collapsed, and a combined Anglo-Russian force staged an amphibious landing in Holland in August.[225] The Coalition seemed poised to carry the war directly into France, where the combination of a new conscription law and the Allies' initial successes had sparked new counterrevolutionary uprisings in Toulouse, the Vendée, and Brittany.[226] The French Republic now faced its most serious challenge since 1793. The result was another swing to the left in the elections of Germinal, Year VI and a brief attempt to resurrect the revolutionary spirit of 1793–94. Jacobin clubs reopened throughout France, and the Councils decreed the mobilization of five classes of conscripts in June, along with new restrictions on émigré families and other suspected dissidents. These policies were obviously reminiscent of the revolutionary Terror of 1793–94, yet memories of the earlier period helped ensure that these new measures were but a pale imitation of the earlier mobilization. A proposal to declare *la patrie en danger* was rejected in September and the other decrees were never fully implemented.[227]

Fortunately for France, the Second Coalition now succumbed to the same internal divisions that had undermined its predecessor. Ever mistrustful of Austria (which he suspected of harboring territorial ambitions in Switzerland), Grenville proposed that the Austrian army in Switzerland be replaced by 65,000 Russians under Marshal Suvorov and General A. M. Rimsky-Korsakov. Supplemented by Swiss volunteers (which were expected to number 20,000), this force would then clear the French from the rest of Switzerland and launch the main invasion into France itself. Despite his own misgivings, Thugut accepted this strategy in the interest of allied cohesion. He was also eager to see Suvorov's forces depart from Italy (where the conduct of the Russian soldiers was sowing discord between Vienna and St. Petersburg), and he worried that the allied armies would be left without adequate supplies. Accordingly, Thugut proposed that Charles's forces move north out of Switzerland, leaving a residual force to remain in contact with

---

[225] According to A. B. Rodger, the French army had only 250,000 men with whom to defend the border from Holland to Italy. *War of the Second Coalition*, 151, 158–59; and also Ross, *European Diplomatic History*, 194–95.

[226] Godechot, *Counter-Revolution*, esp. chap. 13.

[227] Palmer, *Democratic Revolution*, 2:564–65; Lefebvre, *French Revolution*, 2:246–49; Sydenham, *First French Republic*, 198–203; and Woloch, *Jacobin Legacy*, 369–70.

the Russians. This step would relieve the logistical burden, protect the Upper Rhine from a French counterattack, preserve Austrian interests in southern Germany, and facilitate efforts to link up with the Anglo-Russian expeditionary force in Holland. The English and Russian ambassadors accepted Thugut's suggestions, and the bulk of Charles's army headed north toward Mainz in late August.

This decision proved fatal to the Coalition's plans for a coordinated assault on revolutionary France. Rimsky-Korsakov turned out to have only 28,000 troops (instead of an anticipated 45,000), and the efforts to raise Swiss volunteers yielded a mere 2,000 men. The orders to Suvorov were delayed and Thugut neglected to remind Charles to remain in Switzerland until Suvorov had arrived. As a result, writes Karl Roider, "Switzerland gradually become not the staging area for the overwhelming allied invasion force . . . but a weak point in the allied cordon." The French seized the opportunity and attacked, driving the Austro-Russian forces from Zurich on September 25–26 and forcing them back into Hapsburg territory for the winter.[228]

The French victories ended the danger of a foreign invasion and enabled France to send reinforcements to Holland in October, where the Anglo-Russian expeditionary force remained on the narrow Helder Peninsula. Testimony from Orangist exiles in England had convinced Grenville and Pitt that the landing would spark an uprising against the French, but the anticipated revolt never materialized.[229] Pressed by the onset of winter, the Anglo-Russian force signed an armistice permitting them to evacuate their troops in return for the release of 8,000 French and Dutch prisoners. The latest wave of internal revolts was subsiding as well, and disgust over his allies' conduct led the tsar to withdraw from the Coalition in October. Once again, an attempt to combine against revolutionary France had fallen victim to overconfidence, conflicting aims and interests, and the intrinsic difficulty of a coordinating allied strategy over a vast geographic area.

*Brumaire and Beyond.* Although France had survived this latest danger, its government did not. The machinations of the previous two years had cost the Directory whatever legitimacy it had once possessed, and the directors'

[228] Earlier accounts view the decision to send Charles's army northward as a product of Austria's selfish desire to retake the Netherlands: Ross, *European Diplomatic History*, 208–12; Sherwig, *Guineas and Gunpowder*, 123; Rodger, *War of the Second Coalition;* and Mackesy, *Statesmen at War.* More recent research offers a different interpretation, which is the one I adopt here: Roider, *Thugut and Austria's Response*, 308–27; and Schroeder, "Collapse of the Second Coalition," and *Transformation of European Politics*, 200–206.

[229] In the words of the British commander Sir Ralph Abercrombie, "The grounds on which this great undertaking were founded have failed. We have found no cooperation in the country." Quoted in Palmer, *Democratic Revolution*, 2:568. See also Schama, *Patriots and Liberators*, 389–96; and Rodger, *War of Second Coalition*, 176–94.

attempts to rein in the army had cost them the military's support as well. The purge of Prairial, Year VII left Abbé Sieyès in charge of the Directory, an inveterate schemer who now conspired to establish a new government that could eschew the use of terror, protect bourgeois interests, and arrange a final end to the war. Because he regarded the legal procedure for revising the constitution as too cumbersome and time-consuming, Sieyès decided another coup was necessary.[230]

The stage was now set for Bonaparte, who had abandoned his army in Egypt and staged a dramatic return to Paris just as France's military fortunes began to rise. Despite his failure in Egypt and his callous disregard for his troops' welfare, Bonaparte's prestige was undimmed and he quickly endorsed Sieyès's plans. The plot was launched on 17 Brumaire, Year VIII (November 8, 1799). After warning of a fictitious Jacobin conspiracy, the real conspirators persuaded the Councils to reassemble a few miles outside Paris, where they would be at the mercy of the troops assigned to protect them. The directors then resigned in favor of Bonaparte, who appeared before the Councils to receive their approval. The deputies greeted Bonaparte with open hostility, however, and drove him from the chamber. Rallied by Napoleon's brother Lucien, troops loyal to the conspirators removed the defiant deputies. The remainder then appointed Bonaparte, Sieyès, and Roger Ducos as "provisional consuls" pending the drafting of a new constitution.

Sieyès's plot backfired when Bonaparte ignored his erstwhile partners and quickly established himself as the unchallenged leader of France. As Burke and Robespierre had warned many years before, the revolution in France had ended in a military dictatorship. The war continued until French victories at Marengo and Hohenlinden forced Austria to negotiate a separate peace in February 1801. Pitt resigned and peace talks began the following month. The final treaty was completed at Amiens in March 1802. England formally recognized the new French state and the Batavian, Cisalpine, Ligurian, and Helvetian republics and agreed to return all of its colonial conquests save for Ceylon and Trinidad. The treaty was a clear triumph for France, if not for the revolution: the revolutionary period was now over and the Napoleonic era had begun.[231]

---

[230] Amendments to the Constitution had to be proposed by the Council of Elders on three separate occasions in nine years and ratified by the Council of Five Hundred. An "assembly of revision" would then have three months to make final changes. See Stewart, *Documentary History*, 608–09.

[231] This period of the war is analyzed in Piers Mackesy, *War without Victory: The Downfall of Pitt, 1799–1802* (Oxford: Clarendon Press, 1984); Gunther E. Rothenberg, *Napoleon's Great Adversaries: The Archduke Charles and the Austrian Army, 1792–1814* (Bloomington: Indiana University Press, 1982), chap. 3; Ross, *European Diplomatic History*, chap. 7; Sherwig, *Guineas and Gunpowder*, 126–143; and Christie, *Wars and Revolutions*, 249–61.

## Conclusions: The French Revolution and Balance-of-Threat Theory

The evidence presented in this chapter supports the main propositions advanced in chapter 2. As predicted, the revolution increased the level of security competition among the European states. Conflict was a constant feature of European politics before 1789 and some sort of war might well have occurred had the revolution never occurred, but the revolution in France was largely responsible for the wars that did occur and the shape that they ultimately took. By weakening France in the short term and casting doubt on the legitimacy of existing political forms, the revolution created both new problems to resolve and new opportunities for other rulers to exploit. The struggle for power within France sabotaged Austrian emperor Leopold's efforts to preserve the French monarchy and promote a concert of mutual restraint, leading directly to the declaration of war in 1792. The war delivered the final blow to the monarchy, and French attempts to spread the revolution soon brought the rest of Europe into the war. The republic survived the initial assault but eventually became dependent on a diet of conquest and exploitation that made a negotiated settlement extremely elusive.

The dynamics that led to war also support the basic theory laid out in the previous chapter. The revolution created inviting shifts in the balance of power, encouraged states to view one another's intentions as excessively malign, and fostered an exaggerated belief in the efficacy of military force and the prospects for both revolutionary and counterrevolutionary subversion. These problems were compounded by uncertainty and biased information, which were themselves a by-product of the revolutionary experience.[232]

### The Balance of Power

The revolution in France altered the balance of power in Europe, and these shifts contributed to the outbreak of war in two closely related ways. First, Prussia saw France's apparent weakness as an opportunity either to acquire territory directly from France or to obtain it elsewhere in compensation for helping restore Louis to his throne. A similar motive played a minor role for Austria as well—particularly after the death of Leopold—as Francis II and his ministers came to see war against France as a way to obtain international approval for the coveted Bavarian-Belgian exchange.[233]

---

[232] As Paul Schroeder points out, "Europe in the 1780s was not heading inexorably toward revolution, but toward war, whether or not there was revolution." *Transformation of European Politics*, 51–52. Nevertheless, the French Revolution was the immediate cause of the wars of the 1790s, and largely for the reasons I set forth in chapter 2.

[233] See Blanning, *French Revolutionary Wars*, 115.

Second, the belief that the revolution had left France defenseless boosted its adversaries' confidence that victory would be swift and the cost low. Their calculations were not entirely mistaken, as the French armies did perform poorly at first and would have had difficulty meeting a full-fledged invasion. In the end, however, the allies' belief that the French "army of lawyers" would not fight effectively was self-defeating, as it encouraged Austria and Prussia to wage only a half-hearted campaign.

Shifts in the balance of power also contributed to the expansion of the war in 1793. French capabilities were on the rise by the fall of 1792, and England decided to enter the war as a direct response to the French conquest of the Austrian Netherlands and Liège and the danger this posed to Holland.[234] The French victories at Valmy and Jemappes had partly dispelled the image of French impotence, but Pitt and Grenville still believed that the war would offer an easy opportunity to expand England's colonial holdings at French expense. Once again, this view was not entirely unwarranted, and only the extraordinary efforts of the Committee on Public Safety and divisions within the allied coalition allowed the republic to avoid defeat in 1793.

Thus, the French case supports the claim that revolutions cause war by altering the balance of power and creating seemingly large windows of opportunity. Yet it also demonstrates that this effect is only part of the story. Prior to 1792, Prussia was the only state that saw the revolution as an opportunity for aggrandizement.[235] Frederick William was unwilling to act alone, however, and Leopold and Kaunitz consistently opposed war, believing that Louis' acceptance of the constitution in September 1791 had eliminated the need for military action. Although Francis II was more acquisitive and adventuresome, Austria would not have gone to war had the French Assembly taken a less belligerent position from November 1791 onward. By itself, therefore, the effect of the revolution on the balance of power would not have led to war. Similarly, England's leaders were less concerned with French capabilities per se than with the purposes for which French power was being used. As noted earlier, England's leaders still saw France as relatively weak, and both Grenville and Pitt emphasized that they were primarily concerned with French actions (such as the closing of the River Scheldt) and not with the nature of the French government or its relative position in the European system.

The growth of French power after 1793 had other effects as well. The desire to balance the threat from revolutionary France played a central role in the formation of the First and Second coalitions, although the divisions that

---

[234] Not only was England eager to keep the Belgian and Dutch coastlines out of French hands, but they were worried that the Dutch fleet might fall under the control of the French as well.

[235] Catherine the Great is a partial exception to this claim. She saw the revolution as a means of distracting the other powers and gaining a free hand in the east.

undermined both of these alliances suggests that the sense of threat was not overwhelming. Moreover, it was the policies pursued by successive French governments that led to these countervailing coalitions, not simply the growth in French power. Thus, Russia and the Ottoman Empire entered the war in 1798 not because France was becoming too powerful (although this was a concern) but because France's activities in the eastern Mediterranean, and above all Bonaparte's expedition to Egypt, betrayed limitless ambitions and posed an immediate threat to Russian and Ottoman interests.

### Perceptions of Intent

The revolution also profoundly affected France's intentions and its willingness to use force. From 1789 to 1791, French assertiveness declined as a consequence of military weakness and a preoccupation with internal events. The Assembly gradually adopted more aggressive policies, however, including the annexation of Savoy and Alsace, the de facto renunciation of the Austro-French alliance, and the ultimatums demanding that the German princes expel the émigrés. The Decree on Liberty in November 1792 marked an even more dramatic departure from diplomacy of the old regime, and if the quest for "natural borders" did not begin with the revolution, the new regime placed more weight on this goal than its immediate predecessor had. Thus, the revolution did influence French aims and objectives in ways that contributed to foreign perceptions of threat.

This case also supports the claim that revolutionary states are especially prone to spiral toward enmity with other powers. The pervasive fear of an aristocratic conspiracy between the king, the émigrés, the papacy, the dissident clergy, and various foreign rulers helped radicalize the revolution between 1789 and 1791 and formed the centerpiece of the Girondin campaign for war in 1791–92. The flight to Varennes reinforced these suspicions, and events such as the Padua Circular, the Declaration of Pillnitz, the formation of the Austro-Prussian alliance, and Austria's imprudent démarches in 1791–92 merely confirmed the Girondin image of a monolithic counterrevolutionary bloc. Impressions of irreconcilable foreign hostility increased even more during the war; for example, the dire warnings contained in the Brunswick Manifesto helped spark the abolition of the monarchy and the September Massacres and reinforced the prevailing image. This tendency to view opponents as irrevocably hostile reached its peak during the Terror, when any sign of dissent could be seen as treason.

The revolutionaries' suspicions were not without some basis, of course. Indeed, the deputies were correct to doubt the king's commitment to the constitution, as they were to suspect that the royal family was seeking foreign assistance. Domestic opposition to the revolution was widespread, and the antipathy of the émigrés was self-evident. Moreover, some foreign rulers

[120]

(such as Catherine of Russia, Gustav Adolphus of Sweden, and Charles IV of Spain) were openly hostile. But there was no European concert to reverse the revolution, and the French greatly exaggerated Austrian (and to a lesser extent) Prussian hostility: Prussia hungered for territory but did not care where it came from, and Frederick William even sought an alliance with France on more than one occasion. Leopold wanted to protect the royal family and defend the rights of the German princes, but he hoped to accomplish these goals through diplomatic pressure rather than open warfare.[236] The émigrés' activities reinforced French fears of a counterrevolutionary coalition, but their entreaties had little influence on foreign powers.

Interestingly, neither Austria nor Prussia exaggerated French hostility very much. Frederick William was motivated more by greed than by fear, and Leopold's concerns about the royal family, the German princes, and the bellicose Legislative Assembly were clearly justified. Austria and Prussia contributed to the spiral by acting in ways that confirmed French suspicions, but their perceptions of French intentions turned out to be fairly accurate. Thus, spirals of negative sentiment prior to the war of 1792 were largely confined to France alone.

By contrast, the expansion of the war in 1793 was based on exaggerated perceptions of hostility on both sides. English impressions of French intentions were critical to its decision for war; had France rescinded the November 19 decree and agreed to keep the River Scheldt closed, England would almost certainly have remained neutral. By December, however, England's leaders were convinced that France sought to control the Low Countries and to export its principles to other societies, an assessment based on such actions as the Decree on Liberty and the friendly reception given to English radicals at the Convention in Paris.

These fears were not without some basis, but England's leaders clearly overstated the strength of the French commitment to revolutionary expansion. Although Pitt and Grenville saw the Decree on Liberty as strong evidence of French ambitions, the Convention and the CPS were actually ambivalent about supporting foreign revolutionary movements; the Decree was an impulsive act and was rescinded less than five months later. France did not try to foment revolution in England until after war was declared, and Lebrun and others eventually recognized that reports from French agents predicting an imminent revolution in England were erroneous. In short, although England's fears of French aggression were not unwarranted, their inferences were at least partly inflated.

---

[236] Paul Schroeder argues that Leopold was trying to use the threat from revolutionary France to promote a general concert of the European powers that would dampen their competition in other areas (*Transformation of European Politics*, 89–90). Whatever Leopold's ultimate aims were, it is clear that the French misread them.

For their part, France's leaders viewed England as potentially hostile even before the invasion of the Low Countries, and failed to appreciate England's strong desire to remain neutral. As a result, they saw English opposition to their policy of expansion as evidence of innate hostility and did not recognize their own role in forcing England to make common cause with their enemies. The shared belief that the other side was irrevocably hostile may have led both states to overlook possibilities for a peaceful resolution of the dispute, and to the extent that these beliefs were exaggerated, spiraling contributed to the expansion of the war.

The French case reveals that spirals of suspicion can arise from several distinct sources. One obvious source is ideology: by portraying opponents as irrevocably evil or aggressive, revolutionary ideologies encourage their adherents to see the behavior of potential adversaries in the worst possible light. Spiraling may also arise from domestic political competition, particularly if one faction decides to overemphasize a foreign danger in order to bolster its internal position. The Girondins did exactly that in the fall and winter of 1791–92, and their efforts were critical to solidifying French perceptions of an external danger and driving the Assembly to declare war in April. Their efforts might well have failed, however, if the deputies had been less disposed to see foreign monarchs as potentially hostile or if certain rulers' actions had not appeared to confirm the Girondins' accusations.

Ignorance about domestic conditions within a revolutionary state may provide a third source of spiraling. For example, Austria's démarches in 1791–92 were intended to strengthen the moderates and undermine the radicals, but they had precisely the opposite effect. Similarly, England's leaders misread the French commitment to revolutionary expansion because they were unaware that the Decree of November 19 was an act of revolutionary bravado and did not know of the disagreements within France on the entire question of supporting foreign revolutionaries.

### *Offense, Defense, and the Export of Revolution*

The wars of the French Revolution support the hypothesis that revolutions make war more likely by affecting perceptions of the offense-defense balance. They also illustrate why these beliefs are usually incorrect or self-defeating, and why revolutions are harder to export or to reverse than either side expects.

As we have seen, this tendency is partly due to the effects of a revolution on perceptions of the balance of power. By causing a short-term decline in the new state's military capabilities, revolutions encourage other states to believe that the new regime will be easy to overcome. Such a belief convinced Austria, Prussia, and England to go to war against France in 1792 and 1793. That is also why their military efforts were relatively modest and

[122]

their attention so easily distracted. On the other hand, an outpouring of revolutionary fervor may convince the revolutionary government that its military strength has grown, inspiring it to run greater risks. This is precisely what happened in France in 1791–92, most obviously in the Girondins' lavish claims about the ability of "free soldiers" to overcome the armies of the old regime.

To be sure, the nationalist energies unleashed by the revolution in France did liberate armies from the cumbersome logistical and doctrinal constraints of eighteenth-century warfare and improve the prospects for decisive battles and rapid wars of conquest. Yet the offensive implications of this military innovation should not be overstated. It took many years before the strategic and tactical implications of these changes were fully realized: the Girondin visions of a rapid and relentless revolutionary advance turned out to be grossly exaggerated. Although France won a number of impressive victories between 1792 and 1799, it suffered equally impressive losses and was often close to defeat.[237] In short, while the Girondins correctly foresaw that the revolution would increase France's offensive capabilities, they overestimated the magnitude of this effect.

The diplomacy of the French Revolution also confirms that the possibility of revolutionary contagion or counterrevolutionary subversion intensifies the security dilemma between the revolutionary state and its adversaries, making both sides more willing to use force. The ability to subvert other states is an especially potent form of offensive power because it enables one state to "conquer" another at virtually no cost. The revolutionary forces in France were preoccupied by the fear of counterrevolution, and so they confined the royal family in the Tuileries from 1789 onward, imposed harsh measures against émigrés and dissident priests, issued ultimatums to the émigrés' foreign hosts, and eventually declared war on Austria in April 1792. They were also worried about the possibility of foreign invasion, but this fear was linked to the belief that foreign enemies and internal traitors were collaborating to restore the old order.

In addition, the Girondin campaign for war rested on the claim that revolutionary contagion would enable France to win a swift, easy victory. Even if the Girondins used this argument solely to enhance their internal positions, the fact that many deputies embraced it suggests that it struck a sympathetic chord among the revolutionary elite. The unexpected successes of the revolution at home, the optimistic testimony from the foreign revolutionaries, and the universalist beliefs that had inspired the revolution all contributed to the Assembly's confidence in the offensive power of its

[237] See Peter Paret, "Napoleon and the Revolution in War," in his edited *Makers of Modern Strategy: From Machiavelli to the Nuclear Age* (Princeton: Princeton University Press, 1986), 124–27.

ideals. French military successes in the fall of 1792 seemed to confirm these rosy visions, and an unwarranted belief in England's revolutionary potential encouraged France to risk expanding the war in February 1793. Although faith in a universal crusade for liberty faded quickly, a lingering belief in the power of subversion continued to shape French foreign policy for the rest of the decade and contributed to the length of the war.[238]

France's opponents exhibited similar tendencies, albeit not as powerfully. By 1791, virtually all of the European powers feared the spread of revolution, and all had taken steps to suppress suspected Jacobins. The scope and impact of these fears varied widely, however, and neither Austria, Prussia, nor England went to war for this reason alone. Ironically, fear of Jacobinism was probably most pronounced in Sweden, Russia, and Spain, yet the first two states remained neutral for most of the decade and the last was one of the first to abandon the Coalition.

Finally, the belief that the new regime was illegitimate and would therefore be easy to overthrow made war more attractive than peace in the eyes of its opponents. Monarchists in France welcomed the outbreak of war because they thought France would lose and the Assembly would be discredited by the defeat. Austria, Prussia, and England were convinced that the revolutionaries lacked popular support, and England provided subsidies to a variety of counterrevolutionary groups from 1794 onward.[239] Encouraged by optimistic testimony from royalists within France and émigrés outside, British faith in the fragility of the revolutionary regime led to the disastrous expedition to Quiberon in 1795 and the ill-fated Anglo-Russian landing in Holland in 1799. Similarly, assuming that the royalists would soon gain control of the Councils, England rejected a possible peace settlement in the summer of 1797 only to have its hopes dashed by the coup of Fructidor V. In each of these cases, an exaggerated sense of the fragility of the revolutionary government and the potency of the counterrevolutionary forces made opponents of the revolutionary regime more willing to start or to continue the war.

In short, conflict between France and its opponents was fueled by each side's beliefs about the likelihood of revolutionary contagion and the chances for a successful counterrevolution. Both dangers turned out to be greatly exaggerated; the revolution did not spread to any other states in Europe except where forcibly implanted by French troops. None of France's opponents faced a serious internal challenge during the war, and foreign support for counterrevolutionary efforts within France were even less suc-

---

[238] France's efforts to aid the Irish rebels reflected its continued hopes for a successful revolt against English rule there. The formation of additional sister republics after the Treaty of Campo Formio was partly based on beliefs about the universal applicability of French principles.

[239] See Mitchell, *Underground War*; and W. R. Fryer, *Republic or Restoration in France, 1794–1797* (Manchester, England: Manchester University Press, 1965).

cessful. Thus, the French case, contrary to both sides' expectations, supports one of my central claims: except when the disparity of power between the two sides is very large, revolutions are both hard to export and difficult to reverse.

Against this interpretation, it might be argued that the French expansion after 1794—and especially the creation of the "sister republics"—shows that the foreign fears of revolutionary contagion were justified. Similarly, the recurring revolts within France and the near-victories by France's opponents in 1793 and 1799 could be taken as evidence that French fears and Allied hopes for a counterrevolution were not unwarranted. One could even argue that, had Austria and Prussia focused their strength against France in 1792 and fought more energetically, the revolution would have been crushed long before the mobilization of 1793–94 began. Each of these arguments implies that the security dilemma was real and intense and that the use of force was justified even if it did not have the anticipated effects.

Although not without merit, these points are ultimately unpersuasive. France's conquests in Italy and Holland did enable them to place local "patriots" in power and to equip them with constitutions similar to its own, but the sister republics were the product of French military expansion and not of revolutionary contagion. Nor was their creation an easy or spontaneous event; although the Girondins had claimed that the "liberty of the whole world" would cost only a few thousand deaths, establishing the sister republics had cost France and its foes close to a million lives by 1802. The sister republics remained utterly dependent on French support, and efforts to promote revolutionary upheavals in the absence of French occupation consistently failed, most notably in the case of the botched expedition to Ireland in response to the abortive rebellion of 1798.[240] These failures confirm the difficulty of spreading a revolution when other states retain their political cohesion and military effectiveness. Revolutionary France was able to "export" its principles only where its armies were able to destroy the existing political order.

Similarly, while the revolutionaries may have worried about the danger of a restoration and France's enemies had high hopes for such an event, the actual danger of a counterrevolution was slight. The revolutionary regime did face recurring internal revolts (at times backed by France's foreign adversaries), but they were poorly coordinated and dominated by local concerns. They were therefore incapable of challenging the revolutionary government in Paris, which was able to deal with them in piecemeal fash-

---

[240] Although R. R. Palmer views the French Revolution as part of a wave of "democratic revolutions," he acknowledges that "nowhere, except in far-off Poland, was there any revolt against a government with which France was at war. There was no revolution in aid of France. It was perfectly evident that the foreign revolutionaries were entirely dependent on the French." *Democratic Revolution*, 2:117, 330–31, 340.

ion. The counterrevolutionary movement was weakened further by internal divisions and the uncompromising positions adopted by the pretender Louis XVIII (the former comte de Provence), and other émigré leaders undermined their efforts to attract support within France itself.[241] Although, unsurprisingly, the revolutionary government took the royalist threat seriously, it was able to suppress these various challenges fairly easily.

The difficulty of exporting *or* reversing a revolution reminds us why revolutions are rare. Even weak or divided states retain enormous advantages over their internal opponents. Just as it was easy for other states to repress local "democrats" (as long as their territory was free of French troops), so it was also easy for the revolutionaries in France to overcome their domestic rivals once they had established control of the state and the army. In short, the export of revolution *or* counterrevolution was largely a function of military success; it was not determined by the popular appeal of ideological principles.

Finally, although it is possible that an all-out invasion in the spring of 1792 could have toppled the Assembly and restored the king's authority, this scenario ignores the possibility that such a vigorous invasion would have instead accelerated the radicalization of the revolution and brought the monarchy down even more quickly. There is also no guarantee that the foreign invaders would not have been stopped by the same sort of popular mobilization that halted them in 1792 and 1793. Most important of all, Austria and Prussia were willing to go to war precisely because they believed it would be easy; had they foreseen that war would require a more substantial effort, they would have been more reluctant to confront France during the latter half of 1791 and more inclined to seek a peaceful accommodation with the new regime. And if they had done so, it would have defused the paranoia pervading the Assembly and rendered war far less likely. Thus, this political "cult of the offensive" was both destabilizing and self-defeating. In particular, the very beliefs that led Austria and Prussia into the war with France also made them less likely to adopt the one strategy that might have brought success.

### Uncertainty, Information, and Miscalculation

Each of these causes of war was exacerbated by uncertainty and lack of information. France's opponents miscalculated the balance of power in part because the military potential of revolutionary France rested on ideas and institutions (such as the *levée en masse*) that were previously unknown. This fact helps explain why the various anti-French coalitions found it difficult to implement a unified strategy. Although each member agreed that France

[241] See Fryer, *Republic or Restoration*, 11–19, 108, 184–85.

was a threat, the precise magnitude of the danger was impossible to state with confidence. The danger seemed much clearer to England and Austria than to Prussia or Russia (especially after 1795), and even Austria was distracted by events in Eastern Europe and its concern for the future of the Holy Roman Empire.

Lack of information also fueled the spiral of suspicion between France and its adversaries. Austria's attempts to threaten the Assembly were based on outdated information about political conditions within France, while the French failed to appreciate the subtleties in both the Padua Circular and the Declaration of Pillnitz. Similarly, English perceptions of French hostility were reinforced by the Decree on Liberty, but English officials did not understand its impromptu origins and did not appreciate how weak the French commitment to revolutionary internationalism really was. These problems, partly due to the slow pace of communications, were amplified by the breakdown in diplomatic relations and the resulting need to rely on unreliable, unofficial channels. Thus, the Anglo-French negotiations during the winter of 1792 were undermined by the activities of inexperienced agents in London, and Foreign Minister Lebrun was forced to pin his later hopes for peace on an unofficial emissary (the English radical David Williams) and on a personal initiative by a Welsh tea dealer, James Tilly Matthews, who was subsequently confined to an asylum!

As suggested in chapter 2, lack of information may also explain why both sides exaggerated the potential for both revolutionary contagion and counterrevolutionary subversion. The French knew that the revolution had attracted favorable responses from some foreign groups, and also that some of their adversaries faced significant internal opposition. They had little basis for judging the strength of these sentiments, however, or the ability of foreign rulers to quell or coopt them. Lacking adequate information about others' preferences and forgetting that their own revolution had encouraged other rulers to take preventive measures, the French overstated the likelihood that other societies would imitate their own experience. France's foreign opponents could not gauge the level of radical support either, nor could they determine whether pro-French forces within their own societies were an irrelevant minority or a sign of imminent revolt. Efforts to estimate the prospects for a counterrevolution in France faced the same difficulties: France's leaders had no idea how many of their compatriots favored a restoration, and the Coalition could not dismiss royalist reports that the French people, groaning under Jacobin repression, were ready to rise up against the republic as soon as the opportunity beckoned.

In the absence of reliable information, both sides fell back on ideology or other sources that were obviously biased. Raising the level of misinformation was the testimony of the émigrés who had fled from France and the foreign revolutionaries who had flocked to it. The émigrés portrayed the revolution as a grave threat to the rest of Europe while stressing its unpopularity at home and the ease with which it could be overturned. Their efforts were not always successful, but their testimony did contribute both to foreign suspicions of France and to French fears of a looming aristocratic menace.

· The foreign revolutionaries in France had similar effects in reverse. Their presence in Paris made Europe appear ripe for revolution, and the testimony of such people as Anacharsis Cloots and the English and Irish delegations to the Convention in November 1792 strengthened the universalist hopes of the French radicals. French policy soon became more discriminating and support for foreign revolutionaries declined, but groups such as the United Irishmen continued to receive French backing throughout the war. And just as the French took the activities of the émigrés as evidence of a foreign conspiracy against the revolution, their opponents saw the presence of the foreign revolutionaries in Paris as proof of the revolution's universalistic ambitions.

Finally, the diplomacy of revolutionary France also supports the claim that radical regimes will moderate their ideological ambitions in the face of external pressure. After renouncing foreign conquest in 1791 and launching a "crusade of liberty" in 1792, revolutionary France quickly reverted to the familiar pursuit of self-interest. French armies began to plunder their neighbors instead of liberating them, and support for foreign revolutionaries was largely abandoned. French diplomats eventually engaged in the same sort of territorial barters that the European states had practiced for centuries. By 1797, the Directory was willing to cede the Republic of Venice to the Hapsburgs at Campo Formio in exchange for territory elsewhere, a sure sign that the original principles of the revolution no longer held sway.

To summarize: I believe that the origins and course of the French revolutionary wars provide considerable support for my main arguments about the relationship between revolution and war. The revolution tempted other states to take advantage of a favorable shift in the balance of power, led both sides to exaggerate the hostility of their opponents, and created erroneous perceptions of vulnerability and overconfidence that cast the use of force in a more attractive light.

# [4]

## *The Russian Revolution*

"What, are we going to have foreign affairs?"
—V. I. Lenin, October 1917

"I shall issue some revolutionary proclamations to the peoples and then close up shop."
—Leon Trotsky, as commissar for foreign affairs, 1917

"Lenin . . . was one of the greatest realists, as well as one of the greatest fanatics."
—William Henry Chamberlin, 1935

The Russian Revolution caused a dramatic shift in the Eurasian balance of power that threatened the interests of the other great powers and pressed them to intervene in the subsequent civil war. The Bolsheviks and the Western powers regarded each other with suspicion if not outright hostility, and the belief that the 1917 revolution in Russia might spark similar upheavals elsewhere led the Soviet government to venture several ill-fated attempts to accelerate the process. The uncertainties unleashed by the revolution made accommodation more difficult, because both sides based their actions on unfounded hopes and fears and were unable to maintain consistent policies in the face of conflicting information.

Coexistence became feasible once these illusions were challenged. By the early 1920s, Western fears of a rising Bolshevik tide were declining, along with the hope that Bolshevik rule in Russia would be short-lived. Soviet leaders were more confident about their own ability to hold power but also were beginning to recognize that the revolution was unlikely to spread quickly. As mutual perceptions of threat declined, a more "normal"—albeit guarded—relationship began to emerge. Efforts to establish normal relations fell short of each side's expectations, however, and the international position of the Soviet Union deteriorated sharply after 1924.

This chapter consists of five parts. In the first I describe Russia's foreign relations from the collapse of the tsarist empire to the end of World War I, focusing on the Bolsheviks' initial responses and the Allied decision to intervene. Next I examine the diplomacy of the Russian Civil War, the Entente's confused attempts at dealing with the Soviet regime, and the brief but bloody war between Russia and Poland in 1920. In the third part, I turn to the new regime's efforts to normalize relations under the guise of "peaceful coexistence," and in the fourth I describe how this process was gradually reversed under the doctrine of "socialism in one country." Finally, I summarize the evidence and consider its theoretical implications.

FROM THE FEBRUARY REVOLUTION
TO THE END OF WORLD WAR I

In February 1917, the Romanov dynasty collapsed after thirty months of war. The monarchy was replaced by a Provisional Government, led by Alexander Kerensky, which shared power with the "soviets," or councils, of workers and soldiers that had brought down the tsar. The leader of the Bolshevik Party, V. I. Lenin, returned from exile in April, and though they remained a distinct minority, the Bolsheviks' organization and internal discipline proved to be a potent political asset. Kerensky's attempt to continue the war discredited his leadership, and the Provisional Government was finally toppled by a Bolshevik coup d'état in October.

### The Bolshevik Worldview

Once in power, the Bolsheviks' prospects were not auspicious, however, as Germany still occupied large areas of Russian territory, and authority within the former tsarist empire was disintegrating rapidly.[1] The Soviet response to these challenges was shaped by a set of core beliefs that are remarkably consistent with the ideal type presented above in chapter 2. First, the Bolsheviks believed that capitalism was by its very nature hostile to socialism and that the imperialist powers would inevitably try to overthrow them. In Lenin's words: "International imperialism . . . could not, under any circumstances, under any conditions, live side by side with the Soviet Republic. . . . In this sphere a conflict is inevitable."[2] At the same time, Lenin believed that the capitalist world was itself deeply divided by the inevitable

---

[1] By the summer of 1918, at least twenty-four separate governments had been proclaimed on the territory of prerevolutionary Russia. See Edward Hallett Carr, *The Bolshevik Revolution, 1917–1923* (New York: Macmillan, 1950–53), 1:287–89, 340; William Henry Chamberlin, *The Russian Revolution, 1917–1921* (1935; reprint, Princeton: Princeton University Press, 1987); 1:348, 378–81; and George F. Kennan, *Soviet-American Relations*, vol. 2: *The Decision to Intervene* (Princeton: Princeton University Press, 1958), 416.

[2] Vladimir I. Lenin, *Selected Works* (Moscow: Progress Publishers, 1970–71), 2:581; and Carr, *Bolshevik Revolution*, 3:115.

competition for markets and resources. As he later recalled, "If capital were to unite, we should be crushed. . . . Fortunately for us, it is in the nature of capital that it cannot unite."[3]

As orthodox Marxists, Lenin and his followers also thought that a worldwide socialist revolution was inevitable and that their own survival depended on it. If the transition to socialism had begun in "backward" Russia, then more advanced capitalist societies such as Germany or Great Britain could not be far behind. Having previously advised that "any day may come the crash of European imperialism," Lenin told his associates in September 1917, "We are *on the eve of a worldwide revolution*."[4]

The idea that the survival of Soviet Russia hinged on the spread of revolution flowed logically from the Bolsheviks' awareness of their own weakness and their perception of imperialism as irredeemably hostile. Lenin told the Congress of Soviets in March 1918, "We are in no condition to accept battle at the moment," and though he warned against staking everything "on the assumption that the German revolution will begin immediately," he also argued that "the workers of the most backward country [Russia] will not be able to hold the banner [of revolution] unless the workers of all advanced countries come to their aid." Or as Trotsky put it: "If the peoples of Europe do not arise and crush imperialism, we shall be crushed—that is beyond doubt."[5]

The Bolsheviks' commitment to world revolution and their disregard for traditional diplomatic practice were apparent in the so-called Decree on Peace, issued November 8, 1917. The decree invited the "class-conscious workers of England, France, and Germany" to "bring to a successful end the cause of peace, . . . and the liberation of all who labor." Another declaration called for the Muslims of "Russia and the East" to overthrow the imperialist "robbers and enslavers."[6] Nor was the commitment to world revolution merely rhetorical: the Soviet government allocated 2 million rubles to aid "the left internationalist wing of the labor movement of all countries" in December, and the new Soviet ambassador to Germany, Adolf Joffe, devoted

[3] Thus, Lenin argued, "We were able so easily to pass from victory to victory . . . due only to a special combination of international circumstances that temporarily shielded us from imperialism." Quoted in Richard H. Ullman, *Anglo-Soviet Relations, 1917–1921*, vol. 1: *Intervention and the War* (Princeton: Princeton University Press, 1961), 120–21; and Lenin, *Selected Works*, 2:581, 629.

[4] Lenin, *Selected Works*, 2:385.

[5] Quoted in Carr, *Bolshevik Revolution*, 3:17–18; and Lenin, *Selected Works*, 2:583, 586–87, 634, 639. Nikolai Bukharin offered a similar view in 1918, arguing, "The Russian revolution will either be saved by an international revolution, or it will perish under the blows of international capital." Quoted in Dmitri Volkogonov, *Lenin: A New Biography* (New York: Free Press, 1994), 184.

[6] See Jane Degras, ed., *Soviet Documents on Foreign Policy* (London: Oxford University Press, 1951–53), 1:1–3, 15–17.

most of his energies to financing opposition groups.[7] The Soviet government renounced Russia's foreign debts in February and began publishing
various tsarist treaties in an attempt to undermine the governments of the
Entente. These steps had little immediate impact, but they do convey the
Bolsheviks' initial rejection of "bourgeois" diplomacy and their desire to foment unrest in other countries.[8]

The Bolsheviks' faith in world revolution, however, was most apparent in
their handling of the peace talks with Germany. When negotiations began in
January 1918, the Bolshevik Party soon split between the advocates of an
immediate peace (most notably Lenin) and supporters of a policy of revolutionary war. Led by Bukharin and Grigory Zinoviev, the latter group argued
that the German terms were too harsh, that revolution in Europe was imminent, and that a peace agreement with Germany would betray foreign revolutionary forces on the eve of their triumph. Even Lenin could not persuade
this faction to accept the German peace offer, despite the fact that by this
time Russia had lost all capacity to resist.[9]

Instead, the Party adopted Trotsky's compromise policy of "no war, no
peace." In an attempt to prolong the negotiations so that the anticipated
revolution in Germany could begin, Trotsky declared that Russia would
neither sign nor fight. The Germans merely resumed their advance and
forced the Bolsheviks to sue for peace two weeks later, after a protracted
debate between advocates of "revolutionary war" and those who believed
that ending the war was necessary to keep the Soviet experiment alive.
Unlike some of his more idealistic colleagues, Lenin's commitment to
world revolution was tempered by his awareness of Russia's profound
weakness. Instead of counting on an upheaval in the West, Lenin sought a
"breathing space" in which to recover. As he told his colleagues in March,
"Yes, we shall see the world revolution, but for the time being it is a very
good fairy-tale. . . . If the revolution breaks out, everything is saved. Of
course! But . . . if it does not achieve victory tomorrow—what then?"
Lenin's views finally prevailed, and the treaty was ratified by the Congress of Soviets on March 15.[10]

---

[7] Joffe later admitted providing more than 10 million rubles to revolutionary groups in
Germany. See Carr, *Bolshevik Revolution*, 3:18–19, 76–78, 94–95; Kurt Rosenbaum, *Community
of Fate: German-Soviet Diplomatic Relations, 1922–28* (Syracuse: Syracuse University Press,
1965), 2–3; Degras, *Soviet Documents*, 1:126–28; and John W. Wheeler-Bennett, *Brest-Litovsk:
The Forgotten Peace—March 1918* (London: Macmillan, 1956), 348–61.

[8] Soviet disdain for conventional diplomatic practice is also revealed in their use of the title
"commissar" rather than "minister" and the term "plenipotentiary representative" in place
of "ambassador." See Leon Trotsky, *My Life* (New York: Grosset and Dunlap, 1960), 337–38;
and Carr, *Bolshevik Revolution*, 3:68–69.

[9] For accounts of the negotiations, see Wheeler-Bennett, *Brest-Litovsk*, 183–97; and Louis
Fischer, *The Life of Lenin* (New York: Harper and Row, 1964), 191–95.

[10] Lenin, *Selected Works*, 2:589.

Within a few months of their gaining power, therefore, the Bolsheviks' belief that revolution would soon spread to the rest of Europe had given way to caution. The regime now sought to forestall a full-scale imperialist assault by maneuvering among the capitalist powers, until the anticipated wave of revolutionary upheavals eliminated the danger once and for all.

### The Origins of Allied Intervention

During 1917, the Entente's primary concern was to keep Russia in the war. They continued to provide the Provisional Government with military supplies and tried unsuccessfully to persuade Japan to send an expeditionary force to bolster the eastern front.[11] Foreign involvement in Russia increased steadily after the Bolsheviks seized power. By the end of the year, British, French, American, Chinese, and Japanese troops had arrived in northern Russia, Siberia, Transcaucasia, and the trans-Caspian region, usually in league with various anti-Bolshevik groups. The various decisions to intervene illustrate the ways that revolutions increase the level of security competition.

*Britain and France.* Until World War I came to an end in November 1918, the goal of defeating the Central Powers dominated British and French responses to the revolution. Bolshevik opposition to the war was well known, and a separate peace between Russia and Germany would have enabled Germany to shift the bulk of its forces to the western front and give the Central Powers access to Russian grain and other vital supplies. Accordingly, British and French policy after the Bolshevik coup focused on preventing the Central Powers from exploiting Russia's collapse.

Determining the best way to do this was not easy, however, and officials in both countries often differed over how to proceed.[12] Nonetheless, the Entente warned the Soviet regime that a separate peace with Germany would "be followed by the most serious consequences" and tried to encourage loyal Russian forces to continue the war on their own. The British War Cabinet authorized the distribution of £10 million to support Cossack forces in the Don River basin in December 1917, with an equivalent sum to be distributed to Russian groups who were willing to fight on the Rumanian or Ukrainian fronts. France offered the new Ukrainian regime de facto recog-

[11] See L. P. Morris, "The Russians, the Allies, and the War," *Slavonic and Eastern European Review* 50, no. 118 (1972); and James W. Morley, *The Japanese Thrust into Siberia, 1918* (New York: Columbia University Press, 1957), 29–31.

[12] See Michael Jabara Carley, *Revolution and Intervention: The French Government and the Russian Civil War, 1917–1919* (Montreal: McGill/Queen's University Press, 1983), 33–35, and "The Origins of the French Intervention in the Russian Civil War, January–May 1918: A Reappraisal," *Journal of Modern History* 48, no. 4 (1976); and Ullman, *Intervention and the War*, 83–84.

nition and financial support if it would continue the war with Germany, and Britain and France signed a formal convention dividing responsibility for supporting pro-Entente forces in the Ukraine and the Cossack territories. The British also dispatched a squadron of armored cars and a military aid mission to support the independence movement in Transcaucasia, and eventually sent aid to Cossack forces in the trans-Baikal region as well.[13]

Britain and France wanted Japan and the United States to send troops to protect the Trans-Siberian Railway and maintain a lifeline to Rumania, which was still at war with the Central Powers. Intervention was also seen as a way to prevent Germany from seizing the military supplies that the Allies had previously shipped to the tsarist government, now languishing in vast stockpiles in Archangel and Vladivostok. Supporters of these schemes argued that the Russians would welcome some form of foreign intervention, that anti-Bolshevik forces were growing in strength, and that intervention would be the first step toward extensive Japanese participation on the eastern front.[14]

These initiatives were not based on hostility to Bolshevik rule per se, however. Instead, the decision to aid the Cossacks and the other anti-Bolshevik groups was motivated by the overriding Entente objective of defeating the Central Powers.[15] British and French officials recognized that foreign intervention might drive the Bolsheviks and Germans closer together, so representatives of both powers made several attempts to reach a modus

[13] See George F. Kennan, *Soviet American Relations*, vol. 1: *Russia Leaves the War* (Princeton: Princeton University Press, 1956), 89–94, 170; Carley, *Revolution and Intervention*, 28–31; Ullman, *Intervention and the War*, 22, 40–54, 305–306; Louis Fischer, *The Soviets in World Affairs: A History of the Relations between the Soviet Union and the Rest of the World, 1917–1929*, 2d ed. (Princeton: Princeton University Press, 1951), 2:836; and George A. Brinkley, *The Volunteer Army and Allied Intervention in South Russia, 1917–1921* (Notre Dame: University of Notre Dame Press, 1966), 28–30.

[14] There were 648,000 tons of war materiel in Vladivostok and 212,000 tons of food and ammunition in Archangel by the end of 1917. In March, the leaders of France, Britain, and Italy sent a joint note to the United States warning of German domination of Russia and declaring that "since Russia cannot help herself she must be helped by her friends." The note recommended an appeal to Japan to intervene, noting that "no steps could usefully be taken . . . which had not the active support of the United States," and asked for "favourable consideration from the U.S. government." See David Lloyd George, *War Memoirs of David Lloyd George* (Boston: Little, Brown, 1934–37), 6:165–66; Ullman, *Intervention and the War*, 87, 93–94, 109; and Kennan, *Russia Leaves the War*, 300–303, 460–67.

[15] On December 22, an inter-Allied conference authorized relations with the Bolsheviks "through unofficial agents," stressed the need to prevent a separate peace, stated that the Allies' main goals were "to save Rumania" and "prevent Russian supplies from reaching Germany," and agreed that "it would be very desirable" if the Allies could persuade "the southern Russian Armies to resume the fight." *Foreign Relations of the United States, 1918, Russia* (Washington, D.C.: U.S. Government Printing Office, 1931), 1:330–31. Two months later, the British foreign secretary, Arthur Balfour, reminded a British agent in Petrograd that "internal affairs in Russia are no concern of ours. . . . We only consider them in so far as they affect the war." Quoted in Ullman, *Intervention and the War*, 74.

vivendi with the new regime.[16] The British sent a sympathetic young diplomat, R. Bruce Lockhart, to Petrograd in January 1918, where he soon became a vocal advocate of cooperation with Russia's new leaders.[17] Until March, the continuing threat of German invasion led Lenin and Trotsky to invite support from the Entente—as a hedge against renewed fighting with Germany and as a way to discourage Western intervention. Trotsky, hinting that Russia might reenter the war in exchange for Western aid, requested French, Italian, and U.S. assistance in reorganizing the Russian Army.[18] Entente officials clearly regarded these overtures with suspicion, but their response suggests that they would have considered supporting the Soviet regime had the Bolsheviks been willing to resume fighting.[19] This possibility was remote, however, as aid from the Entente would have taken months to arrive and the German Army would have made short work of the Soviet government in the interim. Thus, British and French efforts to persuade the Bolsheviks to reenter the war were stillborn from the start, and pressure for direct intervention grew steadily after the Treaty of Brest-Litovsk.

The growing interest in intervention was partly due to the deteriorating situation on the western front.[20] The Entente powers increasingly believed that the Bolsheviks were German agents or were under German control, a view reinforced by the Treaty of Brest-Litovsk, the arrival of a new German ambassador in Moscow, and the German and Turkish advance into south-

[16] Balfour and the British ambassador to Russia, Sir George Buchanan, warned that a complete break might "hasten the organization of [Russia] by German officials along German lines" and cautioned against giving "the Russians a motive for welcoming into their midst German officials and German soldiers as friends and deliverers." See Lloyd George, *War Memoirs*, 5:111–14; and Ullman, *Intervention and the War*, 23–24, 31–33.

[17] See Ullman, *Intervention and the War*, 58–62.

[18] On March 5, Trotsky told Lockhart and Raymond Robins (head of the U.S. Red Cross mission in Moscow) that Russia might resume the war in exchange for economic and military aid from the Entente. When a German-Finnish invasion of northern Russia seemed likely in April, Trotsky ordered the Murmansk soviet to accept British and American military aid and invited the Allies to submit "a full and proper statement of [the] help they could furnish." See C. K. Cumming and Walter W. Pettit, eds., *Russian-American Relations: March 1917–March 1920* (New York: Harcourt, Brace and Howe, 1920), 81–85; Ullman, *Intervention and the War*, 72–76, 159–63; Carley, *Revolution and Intervention*, 37–38; and Carr, *Bolshevik Revolution*, 3:43–50.

[19] In a message requesting U.S. intervention in April, Balfour stated, "If the Bolshevist government will cooperate in resisting Germany, it seems necessary to act with them as the *de facto* Russian government." In addition, Allied military engineers reportedly aided Russian efforts to destroy rail lines in the path of the German Army. See Ullman, *Intervention and the War*, 161–64; Carley, *Revolution and Intervention*, 37–38, and "Origins of French Intervention," 420–21, 428; Carr, *Bolshevik Revolution*, 3:43–50; and Kennan, *Decision to Intervene*, 112–23.

[20] Germany shifted forty divisions from the eastern front after the Russian surrender and launched a major offensive in April 1918. A British War Office memorandum declared in June, "Unless Allied intervention is undertaken in Siberia forthwith, *we have no chance of being ultimately victorious*, and shall incur serious risk of defeat in the meantime." Quoted in Ullman, *Intervention and the War*, 129.

ern Russia and Ukraine.[21] These events convinced Lockhart that further attempts to accommodate the Bolsheviks would be futile, and he joined Ambassador Joseph Noulens of France in arguing that intervention was necessary to prevent a German takeover.[22]

In addition to the legitimate fear that Germany would exploit Russian raw materials and strengthen its forces in the west, British and French leaders were also fretting over a host of far-fetched scenarios about the strategic consequences of Soviet rule. The Entente powers worried that Germany might capture the military stockpiles in Archangel and Vladivostok and rearm the 800,000 German and Austrian prisoners of war in Siberia, thereby permitting them to rejoin the fighting in the west. British officials were also concerned about their imperial possessions in the Near East and India, and a British Imperial General Staff memorandum warned that Germany would "make use of the pan-Turanian movement and of Mahommedan fanaticism to fan into a flame the ever glowing embers of a religious war, in order to loose on India the pent-up tide of Moslem invasion." By July, the chief of the General Staff advised the War Cabinet that "unless . . . democratic Russia can be reconstituted as an independent military power, it is only a question of time before most of Asia becomes a German colony, and nothing can impede the enemy's progress towards India." In an even more bizarre fantasy, British military planners also worried that a German advance across Russia would enable the Germans to ship disassembled U-boats to Vladivostok, where they could be reassembled and used against Allied shipping in the Pacific![23]

Underlying these dire visions was the assumption that Russia was rapidly falling under German domination and only prompt intervention by the Entente could stave off disaster. In fact, however, most of the worries were groundless. Given the decrepit state of the Russian railway network, a German attempt to seize the Allied military stores would have come up against the same logistical problems that had prevented tsarist Russia from using these same supplies during the war. The "threat" from German U-

[21] The belief that the Bolsheviks were German agents was reinforced by a set of reportedly official documents obtained by Edgar Sisson, head of the U.S. propaganda office in Moscow. These documents, which suggested that the Bolsheviks were taking orders from Berlin, were actually forgeries produced by anti-Bolshevik forces. See Kennan, *Russia Leaves the War,* 441–57, and "The Sisson Documents," *Journal of Modern History* 28, no. 2 (1956).

[22] Noulens stated this belief in a public interview on April 23, strengthening Bolshevik suspicions about Allied intentions. See James Bunyan, *Intervention, Civil War, and Communism in Russia: April–December, 1918* (Baltimore: Johns Hopkins Press, 1936), 71–72; Kennan, *Decision to Intervene,* 210–11; and Carley, *Revolution and Intervention,* 58–60. Lockhart and Noulens began providing financial support to several anti-Bolshevik factions; Lockhart was subsequently arrested and expelled by the Soviet government. See Ullman, *Intervention and the War,* 186–90, 231–35.

[23] See Kennan, *Decision to Intervene,* 71–74, 77–82; and Ullman, *Intervention and the War,* 87–88, 156–58, 304–6.

boats in Vladivostok was absurd for the same reason, and instead of repatriating German and Austrian prisoners to support the German war effort, the Bolsheviks were more interested in recruiting them for revolutionary activities in their home countries. In any event, under the chaotic conditions in Russia, the prisoners could scarcely have reached the western front quickly and even then would have been in no condition to fight.

By May 1918, therefore, Britain and France had abandoned their efforts to cooperate with the Bolshevik regime, yet neither state could spare the men that would have been needed to intervene.[24] While continuing to press the United States and Japan to take action, therefore, Britain and France decided to use the Czechoslovak Legion, a force of fifty thousand Czech and Slovak prisoners of war originally recruited in Russia to fight against the Central Powers. The Entente had previously decided to transport the legion to the western front via Vladivostok and the troops had begun to move across Russia in March. In April, however, the British suggested that the legion remain in Russia to provide order and protect Allied interests. As a result, Britain and France ordered part of the legion to head north toward Archangel while the remainder continued east toward Vladivostok.[25]

Relations between the Czechoslovak Legion and various local soviets quickly deteriorated, and a series of misunderstandings soon led to armed clashes.[26] This development was a golden opportunity for the Bolsheviks' opponents; Ambassador Noulens urged the Czechs and Slovaks to resist Soviet efforts to disarm them, and ordered French military representatives in Russia not to try to resolve the dispute. The Czechs and Slovaks decided to fight their way across Russia by rail and had seized most of the key towns along the Trans-Siberian Railway by the end of June. Encouraged by reports of growing opposition to Bolshevik rule, Prime Minister Clemenceau of France agreed that the Czechoslovak Legion could remain in Russia "to constitute a center of resistance around which Siberian and Cossack elements could gather. . . [and] to prepare the way for . . . Allied intervention from the east." By July, these developments convinced the Supreme War Council to recommend the dispatch of U.S. and Japanese troops to Russia "to prevent the unlimited military and economic domi-

---

[24] According to Carley, "By the end of April 1918 Paris was thoroughly committed to overthrowing the Bolshevik regime." British planning for intervention in Siberia and northern Russia began in May. See Carley, *Revolution and Intervention*, 53; and Ullman, *Intervention and the War*, 193–94.

[25] The saga of the Czechoslovak Legion is recounted in Kennan, *Decision to Intervene*, chaps. 6 and 12; Ullman, *Intervention and the War*, 151–56, 168–72; Bunyan, *Intervention, Civil War, and Communism*, chap. 2; and John Swettenham, *Allied Intervention in Russia, 1918–1919* (London: George Allen and Unwin, 1967), 88–99.

[26] In the words of James Morley, "To send the Czechs through Siberia was to roll a powder keg through a forest fire. An explosion was inevitable." *Japanese Thrust*, 235.

nation of Russia by Germany . . . [and] to bring assistance to the Czecho-Slovak forces."[27]

*The United States.* Across the Atlantic in Washington, President Woodrow Wilson had seen the collapse of tsarism as a liberal triumph that removed his reservations about an alliance with Russia.[28] The Bolshevik coup was more problematic, but Wilson initially regarded the Bolsheviks as well intentioned, if naive.[29] His intimate advisor, Colonel Edward House, predicted moderate forces would soon regain power, and both he and Wilson were confident that Russia would choose to remain part of the liberal alliance against the autocratic Central Powers. A number of U.S officials were less optimistic, however, and virtually all favored a hands-off policy until the situation in Russia was clearer.[30]

Pressed by Secretary of State Robert Lansing and others to counter Bolshevik propaganda (and hoping to coopt the Bolsheviks into his vision of the postwar order), Wilson paid particular attention to the situation in Russia in his "Fourteen Points" speech in January 1918. The sixth of his points called for the "evacuation of all Russian territory" by foreign armies and advised other states to give Russia "a sincere welcome into the society of free nations under institutions of her own choosing." Wilson condemned Germany's territorial demands, praised the "true spirit of modern democracy" that he believed to be emerging in Russia, and lauded the "voice of the Russian people" that "will not yield either in principle or in action."[31] Despite the growing evidence to the contrary, Wilson was still convinced that liberalism would emerge triumphant and Russia would continue to resist the Central Powers.

His optimism soon faded. The dissolution of the Constituent Assembly in January cast doubt on the Bolsheviks' commitment to democracy. Wilson

[27] See Ullman, *Intervention and the War*, 172; Carley, *Revolution and Intervention*, 64–66; and *Foreign Relations, 1918, Russia*, 2:241–46.

[28] Wilson told Congress in April 1917 that Russia "was always in fact democratic at heart . . . and the great, generous Russian people have been added . . . to the forces fighting for freedom." Quoted in N. Gordon Levin, *Woodrow Wilson and World Politics: America's Response to War and Revolution* (New York: Oxford University Press, 1968), 42–43; and see also Kennan, *Russia Leaves the War*, 14–26; and Betsy Miller Unterberger, *America's Siberian Expedition, 1918–1920: A Study of National Policy* (Durham: Duke University Press, 1956), 8–10.

[29] In November, Wilson said to a group of labor leaders, "Any body of free men that compounds with the present German government is compounding for its own destruction," and he told his cabinet that the actions of Lenin and Trotsky "sounded like *opéra bouffe*, talking of armistice when a child would know Germany would . . . destroy any chance for the democracy they desired." Quoted in Levin, *Wilson and World Politics*, 58–59.

[30] See Levin, *Wilson and World Politics*, 68; Kennan, *Russia Leaves the War*, 156–57, 174–78; and David W. McFadden, *Alternative Paths: Soviets and Americans, 1917–1920* (New York: Oxford University Press, 1993), chap. 2.

[31] See Cumming and Pettit, *Russian-American Relations*, 68–74; and Kennan, *Russia Leaves the War*, 253–55.

grew more concerned after the Congress of Soviets answered his message of congratulations with a bellicose call for world revolution.[32] An image of the Bolshevik regime as hostile and illegitimate began to take shape, and U.S. officials began considering more extensive ways to influence or replace it.

Unlike its British and French allies, however, the United States rejected direct intervention until the summer of 1918. Wilson and his advisors, aware of Japanese ambitions in the Far East, did not want to give Japan an opportunity to increase its own influence on the mainland. U.S. leaders also feared that intervention would push Russia closer to Germany, and they opposed diverting military assets from the main struggle in Europe. Wilson himself was reluctant to help former tsarist elements regain power: his experiences with the Mexican Revolution (discussed in chapter 6 below) having taught him there were limits to what outside forces could accomplish in a revolutionary situation.[33]

The breakthrough came in June, when the United States agreed to send troops to support a British and French expeditionary force in northern Russia.[34] The Soviet government tried to head off intervention by offering a series of economic concessions in May, but these gestures did not reverse the growing perception of the Soviet regime as unfriendly and illegitimate. The revolt of the Czechoslovak Legion overcame the rest of Wilson's reservations, and he approved a plan for joint intervention by seven thousand U.S. and seven thousand Japanese troops in July.[35]

At the most general level, the U.S. decision to intervene was shaped by Wilson's idealistic faith in the strength of Russian liberalism. Pressure from Britain and France played a key role as well, and Wilson told one confidant

[32] Wilson's message had expressed "the sincere sympathy which the people of the United States feel for the Russian people" and pledged that the United States "would avail itself of every opportunity to secure for Russia once more complete sovereignty and independence." In response, the Soviet government proclaimed, "The happy day is not far distant when the laboring masses . . . will throw off the yoke of capitalism and will establish a socialistic state of society." See *Foreign Relations 1918, Russia,* 1:399–400; Chamberlin, *Russian Revolution,* 1:406; and Kennan, *Russia Leaves the War,* 509–14.

[33] See Kennan, *Russia Leaves the War,* 323–24, 466–67; and Unterberger, *America's Siberian Expedition,* 25, 31–33. Wilson compared the Russian and Mexican situations in a speech in June, saying that "we cannot make anything out of Russia." Quoted in Eugene P. Trani, "Woodrow Wilson and the Decision to Intervene in Russia: A Reconsideration," *Journal of Modern History* 48, no. 3 (1976), 444.

[34] Under pressure from the other members of the Entente, Wilson had briefly approved a proposal for Japanese intervention on March 2, but he withdrew his approval three days later. See Kennan, *Decision to Intervene,* 460–83; and Unterberger, *America's Siberian Intervention,* 30–34.

[35] For Wilson, the intervention in northern Russia was intended to safeguard the allied military stores, while intervention in the Far East was designed to aid the evacuation of the Czechoslovak forces, but his written orders also referred to helping "steady any efforts at self-government or self-defense in which the Russians themselves may be willing to accept assistance." See Carr, *Bolshevik Revolution,* 3:87–88; and Kennan, *Decision to Intervene,* chaps. 16–17 and 483.

that he agreed to the intervention because it was an endeavor "upon which [the United States' allies] have so much set their hearts." Wilson was also encouraged to act by the former tsarist ambassador in Washington and other prominent Russian exiles, and he shared the British and French fear that Russia was falling under German control. U.S. ambassador David Francis had reported that the German ambassador "was practically dictator in Moscow"; British and French officials sounded similar alarms throughout this period. The growing belief that the Bolsheviks were either pro-German or German agents removed the fear that intervention might force Russia and Germany together, and some U.S. officials favored sending troops out of a fear that the Bolsheviks' internal opponents might turn toward Germany if they were unable to obtain Allied support. Wilson, who suspected that Japan was going to intervene anyway, decided that a U.S. presence would be the best way to keep Japan's ambitions in check. This objective linked U.S. intervention to Wilson's overall vision of a liberal Russian future: by preventing foreign powers from controlling Russia's destiny, the U.S. presence would help bring the liberal forces in Russia to the fore. Finally, the plight of the Czechoslovak Legion provided a moral basis for intervention, as sending U.S. forces to "rescue" them was consistent with Wilsonian idealism and his commitment to national self-determination. Thus, on July 6, 1918, Wilson finally agreed to send approximately seven thousand U.S. troops to Vladivostok "to guard the line of communication of the Czecho-Slovaks . . . and cooperate with [them]," while stressing "that there is no purpose to interfere with [the] internal affairs of Russia."[36]

*Japan.* For Japan, the Russian Revolution presented both a threat and an opportunity. On the one hand, the revolution threatened Japan's control over the former German territories it had seized at the beginning of the war and jeopardized the favorable concessions it had obtained from Russia in 1916. The Japanese government also worried that foreign intervention in Russia might lead to a long-term increase in Western influence in the region.[37] On the other hand, the collapse of Russian power gave Japan the chance to expand its territorial control and political influence in Siberia and northern China. Given Western interests in the area, however, it had to pursue this objective without alarming the other great powers.[38] Japanese mili-

[36] See *Foreign Relations, 1918, Russia*, 2:262–63, 287–90. On these various motives, see Trani, "Wilson and the Decision to Intervene," 442–445; Levin, *Wilson and World Politics*, 70–71, 91–95, 109; Kennan, *Russia Leaves the War*, 94, 147–48, and *Decision to Intervene*, 365–69, 378–79; and Unterberger, *America's Siberian Expedition*, 30.

[37] In addition to a secret defense pact, Russia had agreed to turn over part of the Chinese Eastern Railway to Japan in exchange for military aid. See Morley, *Japanese Thrust*, 55, 94; Kennan, *Russia Leaves the War*, 312–13; and Ian Nish, *Japanese Foreign Policy, 1869–1942* (London: Routledge and Kegan Paul, 1977), 106–11.

[38] On Japanese ambitions, see Morley, *Japanese Thrust*, 50–59.

tary leaders had begun preparing plans for intervention in Russia within a week of the Bolshevik coup, but they preferred to maximize their own freedom of action and took no interest in British or French schemes for using Japanese troops against the Central Powers. Instead, Japanese advocates of intervention hoped to obtain an invitation from the United States that would enable them to expand their country's influence without damaging relations with the West.[39]

These concerns did not mean Japan was idle. Two warships were sent to Vladivostok in January, and British and Japanese troops went ashore in April after local disturbances left several Japanese citizens dead. Japanese agents were also providing financial and military assistance to Cossack forces in Siberia, as well as to an independent regime in Harbin set up by General Dmitri Horvath, the former governor-general of the Chinese Eastern Railway. In addition, the Japanese government negotiated an agreement with the Chinese government in an attempt to coordinate their actions in the Chinese Eastern Railway Zone.[40]

Pressure to act increased throughout the spring of 1918. In March, General Horvath's decision to allow a group of U.S. railroad experts to assist in the management of the Chinese Eastern Railway spurred Japanese concerns about U.S. influence, while Britain and France again invited Japan to intervene "as far west as possible for the purpose of encountering the Germans." Japanese officials were still divided, however, and the Cabinet refused to move without "the moral and material support of the United States." And in the event that intervention did take place, the Japanese insisted that they be allowed to command the expedition.[41]

By convincing Wilson to act, the Czech uprising removed the main obstacle to Japan's ambitions. The United States proposed that each state limit its forces to seven thousand men and guarantee "not to impair the political or territorial sovereignty of Russia." Because these conditions threatened Japan's larger objectives, a series of delicate negotiations ensued between the rival factions in Japan and between Japan and the United States. The Japanese government eventually fashioned a reply that appeared to satisfy the U.S. conditions without significantly restricting Japan's freedom of action, and by October Japan had landed more than seventy thousand troops in Siberia.[42]

*Soviet Responses.* British and French troops began to arrive in northern Russia in July. The Soviet authorities in Archangel were ousted by a pro-

[39] Morley, *Japanese Thrust*, 122–23.

[40] Morley, *Japanese Thrust*, 118–21, 161–65.

[41] See *Foreign Relations, 1918*, Russia, 2:202–3; Ullman, *Intervention and the War*, 202; Kennan, *Decision to Intervene*, 384; and Morley, *Japanese Thrust*, 213–16, 226, 229–31.

[42] See *Foreign Relations, 1918*, Russia, 2:262–63; and Morley, *Japanese Thrust*, chap. 12 and 307–10.

Entente coup in early August, and some fifty-five hundred U.S. troops joined the European forces in September. The expeditionary force's stated purpose was to guard the military stockpiles and rendezvous with the Czechoslovak Legion, but it soon found itself engaged in combat operations against Bolshevik units. U.S. and Japanese troops reached the Far East in September, along with token British and French contingents, and British units entered Transcaucasia and the trans-Caspian region with the aim of countering German and Turkish influence and protecting the approaches to India.

Although these activities were not directed against Soviet rule per se, they reinforced the Bolsheviks' impression of imperialist hostility.[43] In addition to undertaking a concerted effort to rebuild Russia's military power, the Soviet government began to move closer to Germany as the threat from the West increased. Germany's desire to evade the Allied blockade and Russia's own economic difficulties led to a trade agreement between the two states in May, and Soviet foreign minister G. V. Chicherin endorsed an earlier German proposal for intervention in Karelia in August, saying that "an open military alliance was impossible in the state of public opinion, but parallel action in fact was possible." Russia's leverage improved as Germany's military position decayed, and Germany agreed to modify the Treaty of Brest-Litovsk in August.[44]

These shifts did not mean that the Bolsheviks had abandoned their revolutionary aims. A Soviet diplomat at Brest-Litovsk told his German counterpart that he hoped "to start a revolution in your country also," and at the signing of the treaty the Soviet representative said to the head of the German delegation, "This triumph of imperialism and militarism over the international proletarian revolution will prove only temporary and transitory." Lenin informed his colleagues the Soviet government had violated the antipropaganda provisions of the peace treaty "thirty or forty times," and the Soviets continued their efforts to recruit supporters among captured German and Austrian prisoners of war.[45] Thus, the tilt toward Ger-

[43] Lenin told the Central Committee in July that the Czechoslovak Legion's uprising was "one link in the chain long since forged by the systematic policy of British and French imperialists to throttle Soviet Russia. . . . What we are faced with here is a systematic, methodical, and evidently long-planned counter-revolutionary military and financial campaign against the Soviet Republic." Lenin, *Selected Works*, 3:29–30.

[44] Lenin wrote in August 1918, "*I shall not hesitate one second* to enter into [an] 'agreement' with the German imperialist vultures if an attack upon Russia by Anglo-French troops calls for it." See Lenin, *Selected Works*, 3:47; Carr, *Bolshevik Revolution*, 3:79–85; Gerald Freund, *Unholy Alliance: Russian-German Relations from the Treaty of Brest-Litovsk to the Treaty of Berlin* (New York: Harcourt, Brace, 1957), 23; Wheeler-Bennett, *Brest-Litovsk*, 427–46; and Degras, *Soviet Documents*, 1:96–98.

[45] The Soviets convened an "All-Russian Congress of Internationalist Prisoners of War" in April 1918, which Lenin later called "the real foundation" of the Third International. See Carr, *Bolshevik Revolution*, 3:71–76.

many was merely a temporary expedient, not a fundamental shift in Soviet intentions.

Finally, the foreign powers' decision to intervene dissolved the few remaining contacts between the Soviet regime and the Entente. An abortive uprising in August and the wounding of Lenin by a member of an opposition party triggered a "Red Terror" by the secret police, as well as a sharp rise in hostility toward the Allied powers. After the British naval attaché was murdered by a mob attacking the British embassy in September, the British government promptly detained several Bolshevik representatives in England and harshly denounced the Soviet regime. British, French, and U.S. diplomats were withdrawn in August, and the Soviet government arrested and detained hundreds of Allied citizens in Moscow and Petrograd. At the time World War I ended, therefore, relations between the Bolsheviks and the West were going from bad to worse.[46]

The diplomatic history of Soviet Russia and the other great powers during the first year of Soviet rule supports my theory in several ways. First, foreign states' responses to the revolution were motivated primarily by their concern for the balance of power. The Allies did not intervene in Russia because hostility to Bolshevism per se; rather, they sought to prevent Germany from exploiting Russia's collapse. This preoccupation with the balance of power and the war in Europe helps elucidate why the Entente tried to persuade the Bolsheviks to reenter the war while simultaneously providing aid to the Bolsheviks' internal opponents. The Central Powers welcomed the revolution for the same reasons that the Entente opposed it, and the emerging alignment between Moscow and Berlin during the final months of the war was an obvious attempt to balance against a common enemy.

By opening up an enormous power vacuum in Eurasia, the Russian Revolution also created tempting opportunities for a number of other states, most notably Japan. Japanese expansion was driven both by the government's own acquisitiveness and by the fear that other powers might exploit the situation if it did not. As one Japanese official put it, failure to act might confine Japan to policing activity "while England and America are getting the gravy."[47] The awareness of Japan's ambitions had a major impact on U.S. policy, and Wilson's desire to rein in Japanese expansion played a key role in overcoming his initial reluctance to intervene. Similar motives were also at work in France; although fear of Germany was the primary factor motivat-

[46] On the Red Terror, see Chamberlin, *Russian Revolution*, vol. 2, chap. 23. Balfour termed the attaché's murder an "abominable outrage" and warned that unless Britain received a satisfactory reply it would "make every endeavour to secure that [the Soviet government] shall be treated as outlaws by the governments of all civilized nations." Quoted in Ullman, *Intervention and the War*, 288–91.

[47] Quoted in Morley, *Japanese Thrust*, 216.

ing France's support for intervention in Russia, the French were also worried that inaction on their part would enable the other great powers to supplant their own prewar preeminence—and this worry both encouraged intervention and made it more difficult for outside powers to coordinate their actions.

The first year of Bolshevik rule also illustrates how states exaggerate each other's hostility in the wake of revolution. The Bolsheviks were already inclined to view foreign responses in the most negative way; for example, although Allied aid to various non-Bolshevik groups was motivated mainly by the desire to prevent the Central Powers from exploiting Russia's collapse, to the Bolsheviks it was evidence of innate imperialist ill will. Similarly, the revolt of the Czechoslovak Legion was seen as a deliberate imperialist plot (which it was not), and the Bolsheviks failed to recognize that the Allied military intervention was either in response to local events (such as the attacks on Japanese citizens in April) or directed primarily against Germany. Given that the Entente Powers were backing the Bolsheviks' domestic opponents, however, their disavowal of any desire to interfere in Russia's internal affairs was clearly disingenuous, and it is hardly surprising that Lenin dismissed their offers of support as a transparent ploy intended to undermine the Soviet regime.[48]

In the same way, the Entente saw the Soviet decision to leave the war as unambiguous evidence of Bolshevik perfidy and concluded that the Bolsheviks were either German agents or under German control. This inference was entirely erroneous: the Treaty of Brest-Litovsk had been a bitter pill that the Bolsheviks swallowed with great reluctance. The Entente was also alarmed by the growing ties between Germany and Russia during the spring of 1918, failing to realize that the alignment was formed against the threat of Allied intervention rather than being based on sympathy with Germany. Indeed, Lenin believed that Soviet policy should be "equally hostile to the English and the Germans" and eagerly anticipated a revolutionary upheaval in Germany.

Of course, the tensions between Soviet Russia and the outside world were not due solely to these misunderstandings. The Bolsheviks' animosity toward the outside world was abundantly clear, and both the Central Powers and the Entente were opposed to Bolshevik rule. Nonetheless, the evidence suggests that neither side understood the real motives behind each other's conduct and both drew exaggerated conclusions about their opponents' hostility.

Third, responses to the revolution were shaped by beliefs about the possibility that the revolution might spread. The Bolsheviks rejected the initial

---

[48] Lenin rejected Allied aid offers, saying, "The members of the Anglo-French bourgeoisie are laying a trap for us: 'Just come along, my little dears, and go to war *right now*. . . . Germany will strip you bare . . . and will give us better terms in the west, and incidentally Soviet power will go to the devil.' " Quoted in Kennan, *Russia Leaves the War*, 502.

German peace offer on the grounds that a revolution was about to engulf Germany; in other words, they believed that Marxist propaganda, together with the example they had already set, would form a potent offensive weapon that could destroy a powerful opponent virtually overnight. These hopes were soon dashed, however, and Lenin eventually persuaded his colleagues to ground Soviet diplomacy in the realities of power rather than an unpredictable revolutionary timetable. Similarly, the Entente's decision to intervene was based on exaggerated fears about the strategic implications of the revolution. Advocates of intervention believed the Central Powers could easily exploit vast areas of Russian territory, while simultaneously arguing that a modest Allied effort would prevent such a calamity. Thus, an unrealistic sense of what military force could accomplish helped persuade the Allied leaders that intervention was both necessary and feasible.[49]

Finally, each side's responses were affected by a pervasive lack of reliable information. This problem was due partly to a general breakdown in communications within Russia, as well as to the Soviet decision to move most foreign representatives to the isolated town of Vologda. As a result, contacts between the Soviet government and the Entente began to dissolve at precisely the moment when accurate data was most needed. The dearth of trustworthy information hampered efforts to formulate clear and consistent policies, if only because advocates of different positions could not marshal compelling evidence to support their recommendations.[50]

To make matters worse, the information that was available was often misleading. Foreign governments were bombarded by intense lobbying from allies, domestic groups, the Czech leaders, and assorted Russian exiles, each conveying "information" intended to sway national leaders in the desired direction.[51] Allied intervention was inspired in large part by the fear that

[49] Such views were not universal. Balfour noted that "Russia, however capable of fighting, is not easily overrun. Except with the active good will of the Russians themselves, German troops . . . are not going to penetrate many hundreds of miles into that vast country." Similarly, Wilson reportedly told the British ambassador in May that "no military man with whom he [Wilson] had talked had been able to convince him that there was any practical scheme which would recreate a Russian front." Quoted in David Lloyd George, *War Memoirs*, 5:114; and Unterberger, *America's Siberian Expedition*, 52–53.

[50] Thus, Balfour answered complaints about the Allies' indecision by noting that they had "determined their policy as quickly as could reasonably be expected in the face of the varying opinions expressed by their agents, the contradictory reports which poured into them from Russia, and the novelty of the problems presented to them for solution." Quoted in Ullman, *Intervention and the War*, 191–92.

[51] Kennan argues that the former tsarist embassy in Washington "played an important part in shaping the initial American response to the Bolshevik seizure of power," but former ambassador Boris Bakhmetev's influence declined sharply after 1918. See Kennan, *Decision to Intervene*, 322–23; 360–61; McFadden, *Alternative Paths*, 48–50; Linda Killen, "The Search for a Democratic Russia: Bakhmetev and the United States," *Diplomatic History* 2, no. 3 (1978); and Robert J. Maddox, "Woodrow Wilson, the Russian Embassy, and Siberian Intervention," *Pacific Historical Review* 36, no. 4 (1967).

Russia was falling under German influence—a belief supported by U.S. ambassador Francis's report that the German ambassador "was practically dictator in Moscow" and the testimony of various anti-Bolshevik groups. The decision to intervene was also driven by the mistaken fear that Germany would try to seize the Allied military stockpiles in Archangel and Vladivostok, even though the German troops were hundreds of miles away. Even worse, Wilson agreed to send U.S. troops to Murmansk in order to protect the allied military stockpiles, but the stores were actually in Archangel, and most of the supplies had already been removed by the Bolsheviks. Thus, the purpose for which U.S. troops were originally sent to northern Russia had been rendered obsolete before the expeditionary force even arrived, in a vivid illustration of the inadequate information available on the other side of the ocean.[52]

The decision to intervene in Siberia was based on equally inaccurate notions about conditions in Russia. Intervention was intended to aid the Czechoslovak Legion and prevent Germany from gaining a strategic advantage, based on the fear that German and Austrian prisoners of war would extend German influence across Siberia or return west to reinforce the Central Powers. A group of Western military attachés led by William Webster and W. L. Hicks reported that the prisoners of war were not a serious threat, but their assessment was not received until the momentum for intervention was far advanced. As Kennan notes, "here again the lack of an effective orderly arrangement for representation and information-gathering abroad prevented the United States government from assembling and utilizing correctly the best information available." The belief that the Czechs were in imminent danger was equally erroneous, and by the time U.S. troops arrived, the Czech forces had occupied Vladivostok and were aiding military operations by anti-Bolshevik forces. Finally, Wilson's desire to aid "liberal" forces in Russia showed scant appreciation for the chaotic political situation there, where none of the competing factions could reasonably be labeled "liberal." Like that of the other members of the Entente, in short, the U.S. involvement in Russia was founded on inaccurate and misleading information from the beginning.[53]

---

[52] Wilson himself referred to the situation in Russia as "kaleidoscopic," and complained, "As soon as we have thought out a working plan there is a new dissolution of the few crystals that had formed there." Quoted in Trani, "Wilson and the Decision to Intervene," 454; and see also Ullman, *Intervention and the War*, 194–95; and Kennan, *Decision to Intervene*, 418–19.

[53] In addition, a prophetic warning against intervention from the U.S. vice consul in Archangel was delayed in transmission and failed to reach Washington until after the decision had been made. See *Foreign Relations, 1918, Russia*, 2:230–31; Kennan, *Decision to Intervene*, 74–82, 363–65, 400–401; Levin, *Wilson and World Politics*, 104–105; and Unterberger, *America's Siberian Expedition*, 45–47. On this general point, see Kennan, *Russia Leaves the War*, 190.

## The Great Powers and the Russian Civil War

### Why Did Intervention Continue?

As Allied intervention in Russia was motivated primarily by fear of Germany, the surrender of the Central Powers in November 1918 should have spurred the Entente to withdraw their troops without delay.[54] Instead, foreign involvement in Russia increased after the armistice, and its objective shifted from defeating Germany to overthrowing Bolshevik rule. Yet Western policy remained inconsistent: the Allies backed several desultory efforts to eliminate Bolshevik rule in Russia while simultaneously engaging in sincere but erratic attempts to reach a modus vivendi with the Soviet regime.[55] Soviet policy was equally contradictory; while trying to persuade the Entente to recognize their government and to cease its support for the anti-Bolshevik Whites, the Soviet leaders also reaffirmed their commitment to world revolution and conducted a propaganda campaign that reinforced Western suspicions.

Overall, the history of foreign involvement in the Russian Civil War further supports my central arguments. Soviet Russia and the Entente Powers saw each other as a serious threat, but each expected the threat to collapse quickly if it were challenged. Relations between Russia and the outside world were also affected by rivalries among the great powers, exaggerated perceptions of hostility, and the inevitable uncertainties that accompany a revolutionary upheaval.

*The Rise and Fall of the Whites.* By the time World War I ended, Russia was already engulfed in a bitter civil war. The Czechoslovak Legion's uprising and the Allied intervention had combined to halt the spread of Bolshevik control in Siberia in 1918, and a coalition of anti-Bolshevik forces set up an All-Russian Provisional Government in Omsk in September. Two months later, a group of tsarist officers ousted the socialist members of the regime and appointed Admiral Alexander Kolchak "supreme ruler" of the White forces in Siberia.[56] Bolstered by British and French assistance and support

---

[54] Lloyd George later wrote that with the end of World War I "every practical reason for continuing our costly military efforts in Russia disappeared," and Winston Churchill recalled that the armistice "had altered all Russian values and relations. . . . Every argument which had led to intervention had disappeared." See David Lloyd George, *The Truth about the Peace Treaties* (London: Victor Gollancz, 1938), 1:317; and Winston S. Churchill, *The World Crisis—1918–1928: The Aftermath* (New York: Charles Scribners, 1929), 165–66.

[55] In August, the chairman of the British Eastern Committee, Lord Curzon, complained, "The situation is so complex, and the difficulties of arriving at a decision . . . are so great that, in some instances, it would be no exaggeration to admit that there is no policy at all." Quoted in Churchill, *Aftermath*, 244. Chamberlin agrees: "One searches in vain . . . not only for a consistent Allied policy, but even for a steadfast policy on the part of the individual Allied powers." *Russian Revolution*, 2:151.

[56] The origins of the Kolchak regime are described in Richard Luckett, *The White Generals: An Account of the White Movement and the Russian Civil War* (New York: Viking, 1971), 214–23;

from anti-Bolshevik exiles, Kolchak's forces launched a major offensive in the spring of 1919. Their advance brought them within six hundred miles of Moscow by May, but a Soviet counterattack in June soon sent Kolchak's army reeling back across Siberia. Omsk was abandoned in November, and Kolchak himself was captured and executed by the Red Army in February 1920.[57]

A more serious challenge to the Bolsheviks came from the "Volunteer Army" led by General Anton Denikin. Denikin joined forces with several Cossack groups in 1918, and his forces also received considerable military aid from Britain and France. The Volunteer Army began an offensive in March 1919 and was only two hundred fifty miles from Moscow by early October. This proved to be the high-water mark of the Whites' fortunes, however. Denikin's troops were repulsed by a Red Army counterattack at the end of the month. The Volunteer Army was soon in full retreat, and Denikin resigned his command and fled into exile in April 1920. His successor, General Pyotr Wrangel, managed to restore the Whites' morale and launch another abortive offensive in June, but the Volunteer Army no longer posed a real danger to Bolshevik rule.[58]

The last White offensive was an unsuccessful assault on Petrograd by General Nikolai Yudenich's "Northwestern White Army," a force of roughly seventeen thousand partisans, prisoners of war, and former tsarist officers, based in Estonia. Beginning a mere hundred miles from its objective, the Northwestern Army had reached the outskirts of the city by October 20. Strengthened by reinforcements from Moscow and Trotsky's inspiring leadership, the defenders soon drove Yudenich's forces back across the border, where they were disarmed and disbanded by the Estonian government.[59] Although the Soviet government still faced the remnants of the Volunteer Army and numerous rural revolts, victory over the Whites was virtually certain by the spring of 1920.

---

W. Bruce Lincoln, *Red Victory: A History of the Russian Civil War* (New York: Simon and Schuster, 1989), 234–49; and Richard M. Connaughton, *The Republic of the Ushakovka: Admiral Kolchak and the Allied Intervention in Siberia, 1918–1920* (London: Routledge, 1990), 89–101. For evidence that British officers planned the coup that brought Kolchak to power; see Ullman, *Intervention and the War,* 279–84.

[57] This summary is based on Lincoln, *Red Victory,* chap. 7; Footman, *Civil War in Russia,* chap. 5; Chamberlin, *Russian Revolution,* 2:184–205; Connaughton, *Republic of Ushakovka,* chaps. 9–12; and Luckett, *White Generals,* 223–28, 260–67, 293–99, 307–14, 343–47.

[58] See Lincoln, *Red Victory,* chaps. 6 and 13; Luckett, *White Generals,* 174–95, 247–60, 271–93, 322–40, 348–84; Brinkley, *Volunteer Army and Allied Intervention,* chaps. 6–8; Chamberlin, *Russian Revolution,* vol. 2, chaps. 27, 32–33, 35; and Peter Kenez, *Civil War in South Russia, 1919–1920: The Defeat of the Whites* (Berkeley: University of California Press, 1977).

[59] See Ullman, *Britain and the Russian Civil War,* 285, 254–56. See also Lincoln, *Red Victory,* chap. 8; and Luckett, *White Generals,* 269–70, 299–306, 314–22.

*Foreign Involvement in the Russian Civil War.* Ironically, although Prime Minister David Lloyd George was extremely skeptical about the merits of intervention, Great Britain was more extensively involved in Russia than any of the other members of the Entente.[60] The British reinforced the expeditionary force in northern Russia after the armistice, and the Allied troops fought several engagements against Red Army units before finally being withdrawn in October 1919.[61] There was also a small British contingent in Siberia, reinforced by a battalion from India and four thousand Canadians, although British activities there were limited to arming and training Kolchak's armies. Britain recognized Kolchak's regime as the legitimate government of Russia following his successful offensive in the spring of 1919, but its support dwindled rapidly after the Bolsheviks gained the upper hand. The British mission in Siberia withdrew in March 1920, ending what Lord Curzon, now foreign secretary, termed a "highly discreditable enterprise."[62]

In southern Russia, Britain provided extensive military aid to Denikin's Volunteer Army, and British troops occupied Baku, Batum, and Tbilisi after the Central Powers withdrew. British advisors helped train and direct the Volunteer Army, British naval units provided artillery support on several occasions, and British pilots and tank units performed minor combat roles during Denikin's drive towards Moscow. When the Soviet counteroffensive threatened to destroy the Volunteer Army in the fall of 1919, the British helped evacuate the survivors and then withdrew most of their own troops. The remainder departed in June and July 1920, thereby ending direct British involvement in the civil war.[63]

---

[60] On November 14, three days after the armistice, the War Cabinet decided "to remain in occupation at Murmansk and Archangel for the time being; to continue the Siberian Expedition; to try to persuade the Czechs to remain in Western Siberia, to give General Denikin . . . all possible help in the way of military material; [and] to supply the Baltic States with military materials." Quoted in Brinkley, *Volunteer Army and Allied Intervention*, 75. British operations in Russia between November 1918 and October 1919 cost over £28 million, and Britain also provided between £20 and £50 million in military assistance to the White armies during the same period. See Ullman, *Anglo-Soviet Relations*, vol. 2: *Britain and the Russian Civil War* (Princeton: Princeton University Press, 1968), 365–68; Chamberlin, *Russian Revolution*, 170; and Churchill, *Aftermath*, 246, 250, 256.

[61] The British Commonwealth contributed 6,300 soldiers to the expeditionary force, while the United States and France sent 5,200 and 1,700 respectively. See Ullman, *Britain and the Russian Civil War*, 20–28, 178–81, 190–203; Swettenham, *Allied Intervention*, 53–54, 70–82, 187–231; and John Silverlight, *The Victors' Dilemma: Allied Intervention in the Russian Civil War* (New York: Weybright and Talley, 1970), 172–98.

[62] Britain and France provided Kolchak with 200,000 uniforms, 500 million cartridges, 2,000 machine guns, 400 heavy guns, 135 airplanes, and a small number of tanks. See *Foreign Relations, 1919, Russia* (Washington, D.C., U.S. Government Printing Office, 1937), 389. British units also provided artillery support for the Whites on two occasions. See Ullman, *Britain and the Russian Civil War*, 28–36, 253.

[63] Ullman reports that the Volunteer Army received "more than 1,200 guns and nearly 2 million shells, 6,100 machine guns, 200,000 rifles, 500 million rounds of small-arms ammuni-

In the Baltic, the British gave direct military aid to the Northwestern Army and to the independent governments of Estonia, Lithuania, and Latvia. The Royal Navy maintained the blockade of Russia that had been imposed during the latter stages of World War I. It also conducted several dramatic raids against Soviet naval bases during the summer of 1919. Lithuania and Latvia fell to the Bolsheviks in January 1919, but artillery support and supplies from British naval forces helped Estonia retain its independence through the winter.[64]

It was the French government that had been first to advocate intervention in Russia in 1918, but the struggle on the western front prevented them from playing a major role. After the war, however, France quickly reaffirmed the Anglo-French convention dividing southern Russia into French and British zones, and dispatched eighteen hundred troops to Odessa in December. Their objective, according to Prime Minister Georges Clemenceau, was to achieve "the isolation of Russian Bolshevism with a view to bringing about its destruction."[65] The expedition proved to be a complete fiasco. Poorly informed about the chaotic political conditions in Ukraine, the French soon found themselves facing Red Army units, Ukrainian separatists, and several hostile partisan groups. Efforts to convince the Ukrainians and the Whites to join forces against the Bolsheviks proved fruitless, and the expeditionary force was forced to withdraw in April.[66]

Subsequent French involvement was limited to a small contingent in northern Russia, a military mission in Siberia (intended to lead the Czechoslovak Legion), and a training mission that was sent to aid Kolchak. These measures were meant to restore France's prewar position once the Bolsheviks were overthrown. However, French influence with Kolchak never equaled that of Great Britain, and the Czechoslovak Legion was a de-

---

tion, more than half a million complete uniforms, 629 trucks and ambulances, 279 motorcycles, 74 tanks, 6 armored cars, 100 aircraft, twelve 500-bed general hospitals, 25 field hospitals, and large amounts of communications and engineering equipment." *Britain and the Russian Civil War*, 212–16. Also see Richard H. Ullman, *Anglo-Soviet Relations, 1917–1921*, vol. 3: *The Anglo-Soviet Accord* (Princeton: Princeton University Press, 1972), 86–87, 337; Lincoln, *Red Victory*, 198; Brinkley, *Volunteer Army and Allied Intervention*, 93–94, 100; and Luckett, *White Generals*, 259–60.

[64] The Allied blockade of Russia was originally intended to prevent the shipment of war materiel from Russia to Germany; it was kept in place as a means of weakening the Soviet regime. See Geoffrey Bennett, *Cowan's War: The Story of British Naval Operations in the Baltic, 1918–1920* (London: Collins, 1964); and Ullman, *Britain and the Russian Civil War*, 52–58, 273.

[65] See Brinkley, *Volunteer Army and Allied Intervention*, 75.

[66] The French commander later described the expedition as "the complete failure of a ridiculous adventure." Quoted in Carley, *Revolution and Intervention*, 176; and see also John Reshetar, *The Ukrainian Revolution, 1917–1920* (Princeton: Princeton University Press, 1952), esp. 233–49; Arthur Adams, *Bolsheviks in the Ukraine: The Second Campaign, 1918–1919* (New Haven: Yale University Press, 1963), 95–99, 192–200; and Kenez, *Civil War in South Russia*, 178–202.

moralized and ineffective force by the time the French military mission arrived.[67]

Unlike that of the other great powers, U.S. involvement in Russia did not increase after the armistice with Germany. The United States had already sent fifty-five hundred troops to the Murmansk-Archangel region and roughly nine thousand troops to Siberia, and their activities there reflected the deep ambivalence that characterized U.S. policy throughout this period.[68]

While Britain and France hoped to link the expeditionary force in the north with elements of the Czechoslovak Legion and other anti-Bolshevik groups, Wilson had restricted U.S. involvement to the protection of the Allied military stores. The armistice with Germany superseded this objective, of course, and Wilson announced in February that American forces would be withdrawn "at the earliest possible moment that weather conditions . . . permit." The U.S. contingent eventually returned home in June 1919, after engaging in several skirmishes with Red Army units in the winter and spring.[69]

The U.S. involvement in Siberia was even more limited. U.S. troops did not engage in combat operations, and direct U.S. support for Kolchak was confined to modest amounts of humanitarian aid.[70] Instead, U.S. efforts centered on maintaining the Chinese Eastern and Trans-Siberian railways, resulting in a series of confrontations with Japanese troops who were seeking to gain control of the railway zone. The United States and Japan tried to alleviate these problems by negotiating an Inter-Allied Railway Agreement in January 1919, but tensions persisted throughout the year.[71] Wilson was repeatedly pressed to recognize the Kolchak government and support it economically or militarily, but Kolchak's deteriorating military position and

---

[67] See Carley, *Revolution and Intervention*, 78–80, 190–92; Ullman, *Britain and the Russian Civil War*, 32–35.

[68] See Kennan, *Decision to Intervene*, 426; Swettenham, *Allied Intervention*, 54.

[69] See *Foreign Relations of the United States, 1919, Russia*, 617–18; and Ernest M. Halliday, *The Ignorant Armies* (New York: Harper, 1958), 195–96.

[70] The U.s. government assisted the relief efforts of the Red Cross, YMCA, and U.S. War Trade Board and helped ship rifles and other supplies purchased by the Russian mission in Washington, using credits extended to the Provisional Government in 1917. See *Foreign Relations, 1919, Russia*, 325–26, 389, 401–402, 424–25, 435; Unterberger, *America's Siberian Expedition*, 150, 162; and John W. Thompson, *Russia, Bolshevism, and the Versailles Peace* (Princeton: Princeton University Press, 1967), 284.

[71] The Chinese Eastern Railway Zone was formally part of China, but Russia had held de facto control for several decades and the railway was managed by a Russian company. A technical mission led by John Stevens had been supervising operations on the Far Eastern Railway since 1917 and continued its activities until the Japanese withdrawal in 1922. See Unterberger, *America's Siberian Expedition*, 9–10 and chap. 6; Kennan, *Decision to Intervene*, 64–65, and *Russia Leaves the War*, 287–90; *Foreign Relations, 1919, Russia*, 573–78, 588–94; Peter S. H. Tang, *Russian and Soviet Policy in Outer Mongolia and Manchuria, 1911–1931* (Durham: Duke University Press, 1959), 123–28; and Pauline Tompkins, *American-Russian Relations in the Far East* (New York: Macmillan, 1949), 119–33.

Wilson's continued reservations kept the United States from offering the Omsk regime direct assistance. U.S. officials moved steadily toward withdrawal as Kolchak's prospects faded, although concern over Japanese ambitions and the desire to safeguard the remaining Czechoslovak troops delayed the departure until April 1920.[72]

Because the Japanese decision to intervene was not inspired by the goal of defeating Germany, it is not surprising that their presence in Russia did not decline after the war in Europe ended. In addition to the expedition to Vladivostok, Japan sent troops to the Chinese Railway Zone and Russia's Maritime Province and provided arms and advisors to Cossack forces in the trans-Baikal region and to General Horvath's regime in Harbin.[73] These activities aroused increasing controversy, however, and Japan eventually withdrew its forces from the Amur and trans-Baikal regions early in 1920. Support for a policy of expansion was still strong, however, and hardliners within the army eventually used the massacre of several hundred Japanese civilians by a group of Bolshevik partisans in Nicolaevsk in May 1919 to justify the seizure of Vladivostok, the Maritime Province, and the northern half of Sakhalin Island.[74]

*Explaining Intervention.* Intervention in Russia can be explained with a look at three broad themes: the balance of power, the growing fear of Bolshevism, and the impact of uncertainty.

For Great Britain, the desire to profit from Russia's distress gradually overcame the initial doubts about the merits of continued involvement in Russia.[75] Great Britain and Russia had been rivals in Asia for decades, and many British officials gladly saw a weak and divided Russia as a less serious threat to their imperial interests. The British government moved quickly to support the independent states in the Baltic region and Transcaucasia, and British strategic planners also hoped to gain control of the rich Baku oil fields, if only to deny them to France. In addition, British officials worried

---

[72] Levin argues that Wilson's policy was a compromise between his reluctance to intervene and his desire to see liberal forces triumph. See *Wilson and World Politics*, 227–29; and also Unterberger, *America's Siberian Expedition*, chap. 10.

[73] See Morley, *Japanese Thrust*, 93–100, 172–76, and chap. 9; and Tatsuji Takeuchi, *War and Diplomacy in the Japanese Empire* (Chicago: University of Chicago Press, 1935), 204–209.

[74] The decision to seize these regions had been made prior to the incidents at Nicolaevsk. See Carr, *Bolshevik Revolution*, 1:356–57; Canfield F. Smith, *Vladivostok under Red and White Rule: Revolution and Counterrevolution in the Russian Far East, 1920–1922* (Seattle: University of Washington Press, 1975), 33–43; and John Albert White, *The Siberian Intervention* (Princeton: Princeton University Press, 1950), 286–92.

[75] Some British leaders also believed that they had a moral obligation to the Russians who had remained loyal to the Entente during the war. See Ullman, *Britain and the Russian Civil War*, 11–14; Thompson, *Russia, Bolshevism, and Versailles*, 54; Brinkley, *Volunteer Army and Allied Intervention*, 91–94; and W. P. Coates and Zelda K. Coates, *Armed Intervention in Russia, 1918–1922* (London: Victor Gollancz, 1935), 135–37.

that Germany might "restore order" in Russia and eventually forge a powerful revisionist alliance. If the original goal of British intervention was now irrelevant, in short, new goals had emerged to replace it.[76]

French policy during this period revealed similar concerns. Although French hostility to Bolshevism exceeded that of the other great powers, its overriding goal was the future containment of Germany. The French government therefore supported the creation of independent buffer states in Eastern Europe and the reconstitution of a stable Russian government in which they enjoyed predominant influence. The expedition to Odessa and French support for Kolchak were also based on the desire to protect French investments in Russia and prevent other great powers from gaining a foothold there once the Bolsheviks were gone.[77]

U.S. and Japanese policy evinced a similar attention to relative position. Japan sought to expand its influence in the Far East while preventing other states from doing the same thing, whereas Wilson's commitment to a liberal world order led him to oppose any attempts to exploit Russian weakness. Thus, in addition to countering Japanese expansion in Siberia, the United States aimed to preserve Russian unity by declining to recognize the new governments in the Baltic and Transcaucasia.[78]

Although foreign intervention in revolutionary Russia was originally inspired by other motives, in short, the intervening powers also saw it as a way to protect or enhance their relative positions. This motivation was most apparent in the case of Japan, but competition among the Entente reemerged once the Central Powers had been defeated. As Lenin had fore-

[76] In November, both Lloyd George and Balfour questioned the wisdom of British involvement in Russia, and the chief of the Imperial General Staff recommended that Britain "liquidate" its commitments as soon as possible. Less than a month later, however, the General Staff warned of French influence in the Caucausus and stated, "It would be most undesirable for the approaches to India from South Russia, the Black Sea, and Turkey . . . to be placed at the disposal of an ambitious military power, which, although friendly to us at the moment, is our historical world rival." See Thompson, *Russia, Bolshevism, and Versailles*, 51–56; Ullman, *Britain and the Russian Civil War*, 11–15, 54–55, 66–86; and Silverlight, *Victors' Dilemma*, 86–91.

[77] At times, the French also favored creating pro-French states in the Crimea and Ukraine, as a further buffer against Germany and as an avenue for French trade and investment. French officials also tried to establish several *banques d'émission* to issue new currency in the White areas of Russia, in order to weaken the Bolshevik regime and enhance France's own influence. See Carley, *Revolution and Intervention*, chaps. 7–8; Arno J. Mayer, *Politics and Diplomacy of Peacemaking: Containment and Counterrevolution at Versailles, 1918–1919* (New York: Alfred A. Knopf, 1967), 181–83; Unterberger, *America's Siberian Expedition*, 214; Thompson, *Russia, Bolshevism, and Versailles*, 57–59; Brinkley, *Volunteer Army and Allied Intervention*, 75–77, 88–90; and Silverlight, *Victors' Dilemma*, 118–19.

[78] Wilson also encouraged Kolchak to recognize the autonomy of these regions until their final status could be determined. In the end, however, Wilson favored allowing the Russians "to fight it out among themselves" and made aid to the Whites conditional on pledges to implement democratic reforms. See Levin, *Wilson and World Politics*, 109–110, 197–207, 224–26, 231; and *Foreign Relations, 1919, Russia*, 367–70.

seen, these concerns both encouraged continued foreign involvement in Russia and made it harder for the intervening powers to coordinate their activities.

Foreign powers were also encouraged to intervene in Russia by their growing fear of ideological contagion. This concern had lain dormant as long as Germany posed the greater danger, but the threat of revolutionary subversion began receiving more attention after the Central Powers' defeat. In December 1918, Curzon justified British intervention in southern Russia by claiming that "anarchy, disorder or Bolshevism there" would "inevitably" affect the British position in the Near East and India. In the same spirit, Winston Churchill accused the Bolsheviks of seeking "to make the soldiers mutiny against their officers, to raise the poor against the bourgeois, . . . the workmen against the employers, . . . [and] to paralyze the country by general strikes." According to General Sir Henry Wilson, chief of the Imperial General Staff, by October 1918 the British Cabinet was united in the belief that "our real danger now is not the Boches but Bolshevism."[79]

Other Allied officials held similar views. Woodrow Wilson told his Cabinet that "the spirit of the Bolsheviki is lurking everywhere." U.S. Secretary of State Robert Lansing described Bolshevism as "the most hideous and monstrous thing that the human mind has ever conceived" and lamented that it was now "spreading westward." The commander of the Allied armies, Marshal Ferdinand Foch, agreed to allow German units to remain in Eastern Europe to protect the local population "against the horrors of Bolshevism," and the French General Staff described Russia as "an immense hotbed of anarchist propaganda." Not to be outdone, the Quai d'Orsay now declared that the danger from Bolshevism was "more fearful for humanity" than a German victory would have been.[80]

This fear of Bolshevism was magnified by a belief that World War I had left Europe especially vulnerable to revolutionary subversion. The war had discredited the old European order, the German and Austro-Hungarian monarchies had already collapsed, and famine and poverty were widespread. As a French General Staff memorandum put it, "this new and monstrous form of imperialism represented a danger all the more fearful as it arose at the precise moment when the impending end of the war would provoke in every country a grave social and economic crisis." Lloyd George re-

[79] Even before the war was over, a British Foreign Office memorandum warned of the danger presented by the Bolshevik "doctrine of irreconcilable class war." Quoted in Ullman, *Britain and the Russian Civil War*, 11, 67; Churchill, *Aftermath*, 274–75; and Thompson, *Russia, Bolshevism, and Versailles*, 21.

[80] Lansing also believed that Bolshevism "finds its adherents among the criminal, the depraved, and the mentally unfit" and "seeks to devour civilized society and reduce mankind to the state of beasts." Quotations from Thompson, *Russia, Bolshevism, and Versailles*, 14–15, 29–30; and Carley, *Revolution and Intervention*, 106–10.

portedly believed that revolution in England was not out of the question; both he and French premier Clemenceau thought "anything was possible in Italy"; and Wilson regarded Central Europe as especially vulnerable. Fear of Bolshevism also raised Japan's interest in Siberia, which it saw as a potential buffer against Communist subversion. Thus, intervention was sustained by two key elements of threat: the belief that Soviet Russia was hostile and the fear that Bolshevism might be contagious.[81]

Despite the widespread consensus that Bolshevism was a threat, however, there was little agreement on how to respond to it.[82] One barrier to cooperation has already been noted: once Germany was defeated, each member of the Entente began pursuing its own interests even when this interfered with the shared goal of containing Bolshevism.[83] A second barrier was the lack of reliable information on the conditions in Russia or the likelihood that the revolution would spread. The effects of this lack were mixed, however, as it both encouraged attempts to isolate the Soviet leadership and discouraged an all-out effort to remove it. In the end, the Allies did enough to sustain the Whites and solidify Soviet animosity, but not enough to replace the Soviet regime with one more to their liking.[84]

Not surprisingly, supporters of all-out intervention (such as Churchill, Foch, and Clemenceau) saw Bolshevism in Russia as a particularly grave threat and stressed that ousting the Bolsheviks would be relatively easy.[85] By

[81] House also believed that "Bolshevism is gaining ground everywhere," and a confidential memorandum by Lloyd George stated that "the whole of Europe is filled with the spirit of revolution." See Charles Seymour, ed., *The Intimate Papers of Colonel House,* (Boston: Houghton Mifflin, 1926–28), 4:118–19; Thompson, *Russia, Bolshevism, and Versailles,* 14, 389–91; Levin, *Wilson and World Politics,* 186–93; Carley, *Revolution and Intervention,* 110; Carr, *Bolshevik Revolution,* 3:126–30; Smith, *Vladivostok under Red and White Rule,* 34, 43; and Chamberlin, *Russian Revolution,* 2:152.

[82] On February 14, Churchill proposed sending "volunteers, technical experts, arms, munitions, tanks [and] aeroplanes" to the Whites; two weeks later, Foch suggested that the Allies equip and train a large body of Poles, Finns, Czechs, Rumanians, and Greeks for intervention in Russia, thereby eliminating the need for Allied troops. He offered a less ambitious plan for aid to Poland and Rumania on March 17 and reiterated the proposal ten days later, but each of these suggestions was vetoed by Great Britain and the United States. In May, Lloyd George suggested that Allied troops in northern Russia should "march to meet Kolchak," but Wilson rejected the suggestion. Churchill and others again pressed for Allied action during the fall of 1919, without success. See Ullman, *Britain and the Russian Civil War,* 119–28, 136–40, 164–65, 222–23, 261–62; and Thompson, *Russia, Bolshevism, and Versailles,* 134–40.

[83] According to Thompson, "There was more improvization than far-sighted planning, more disparity than unity of purpose, and more inconsistency than steadfastness in the various policies and plans of the Western statesmen." *Russia, Bolshevism, and Versailles,* 60; and also Bradley, *Allied Intervention,* 132–33.

[84] Churchill later recalled that "enough foreign troops entered Russia to incur all the objections which were patent against intervention, but not enough to break the then gimcrack structure of the Soviet power." See Churchill, *Aftermath,* 285.

[85] The French chief of staff endorsed Churchill's February 14 proposal for intervention by noting that the Red Army had "irremediable sources of weakness," that its successes were

contrast, opponents of intervention argued that removing the Bolsheviks would be costly and difficult, that the war-weary Allied populations would not support the effort, and that foreign intervention would merely increase popular support for the Bolshevik regime. Thus, Lloyd George opposed Churchill's proposal for an anti-Bolshevik crusade by arguing that "aggression against Russia is a way to strengthen Bolshevism in Russia and create it at home," and Wilson countered proposals for military action by saying, "To attempt to arrest a revolutionary movement by means of deployed armies is like trying to use a broom to sweep back the tide." Opponents also maintained that relief aid to Europe would be a better antidote; as Wilson put it, "The only way to take action against Bolshevism was to eliminate its causes."[86]

Without reliable information about conditions in Russia or the likelihood that the revolution would spread or collapse, neither side could marshal definitive evidence to support its policy recommendations. Advocates of intervention pointed to the Whites' successes during the spring and summer of 1918 while opponents invoked the growing strength of the Red Army, the sheer size of Russia's territory, and the dissension and corruption that afflicted the Whites. In the absence of solid information about Bolshevik and White Russian prospects, however, weighing the pros and cons of alternative policies proved to be extremely difficult.[87]

Evidence of Bolshevik intentions was equally ambiguous. The Soviets had made no secret of their revolutionary aims, of course, and the image of Bol-

---

due to the fact that "it has never encountered adversaries superior to it as regards either numbers, supplies, or moral[e]," and, in conclusion, that "even though numerically inferior, regular Allied troops would easily defeat it. . . . Such a success could be won at very slight cost." On February 25, Marshal Foch made a sweeping proposal for intervention and argued that "the Eastern problem would not be more difficult to solve than the Western problem. . . . To fight against such an enemy, troops . . . need not be strongly organised or of superior quality. . . . But great numbers were required which could be obtained by mobilizing the Finns, Poles, Czechs, Rumanians, and Greeks, as well as the Russian pro-Ally elements still available. . . . If this were done, 1919 would see the end of Bolshevism, just as 1918 had seen the end of Prussianism." See *Foreign Relations, 1919, Paris Peace Conference* (Washington, D.C.: U.S. Government Printing Office, 1942–47), 4:10–13, 122–23; and Thompson, *Russia, Bolshevism, and Versailles*, 182–84.

[86] In November 1918, Balfour noted that Britain "would certainly refuse to see its forces . . . dissipated over the huge expanse of Russia in order to carry out political reforms in a State which is no longer a belligerent Ally." Quoted in Lincoln, *Red Victory*, 272; and Ullman, *Britain and the Russian Civil War*, 11, 126, 139. See also Levin, *Wilson and World Politics*, 204–205; *Foreign Relations, 1919, Peace Conference*, 3:648–50; Thompson, *Russia, Bolshevism, and Versailles*, 94, 100; Mayer, *Politics and Diplomacy*, 457–58; and Carley, *Revolution and Intervention*, 112.

[87] As Ullman points out, "From the departure of Bruce Lockhart from Russia at the end of September 1918 until the arrival in Moscow of the first British mission in March 1921—London had no overt official source of information about conditions within the territory controlled by the Soviet regime." See *Britain and the Russian Civil War*, 173–77; and Thompson, *Russia, Bolshevism, and Versailles*, 378–84.

shevik aggressiveness was reinforced by the Red Terror that swept Moscow in September 1918, together with Joffe's subversive activities in Germany and a bellicose message from the Soviet commissar for foreign affairs, György Chicherin, to Wilson in October 1918.[88] On the other hand, the Soviet government also made several conciliatory gestures at the end of the war and seemed genuinely interested in a formal peace settlement. Thus, Lansing, Churchill, and Foch concluded that the Soviet government was irrevocably hostile while Lloyd George and Wilson thought some form of accommodation might be possible, and both sides found evidence to support their positions.[89]

These uncertainties help explain why the Allied leaders could not agree on a consistent policy toward the Bolshevik regime. In some cases, lack of information encouraged greater involvement; for example, the disastrous expedition to Odessa was largely the result of France's ignorance about political conditions there. Similarly, Wilson's early faith in the strength of "liberal" forces in Russia accounts in part for his own decision to intervene, and he moved to end U.S. intervention once he realized this view was incorrect.[90]

On balance, uncertainty about the situation in Russia probably did more to restrain intervention than to promote it. In December 1918, for example, Lloyd George noted "the absolute contradiction between information supplied from Russia by men of equally good authority" and complained that "Russia was a jungle in which no one could say what was within a few yards of him." Four months later, he told the House of Commons that "there is no longer even an entity that could accurately be called 'Russia' " and declared it impossible to know which authorities actually controlled what territories. Because Russia was a volcano "still in fierce eruption," he concluded that the prudent course was to keep one's distance while trying to prevent the lava from spreading. Aid to the Whites was justified by the need to honor wartime commitments and support for the border states was a way to contain the Bolshevik "eruption," but the unclear situation within Russia advised against a direct Allied attempt to remove the Bolsheviks by force.[91] Similarly, Wilson admittedly privately that his impressions of Russia

[88] See Degras, *Soviet Documents*, 1:112–20; and *Foreign Relations, 1918, Russia*, 1:680–91.

[89] In January 1918, Lansing wrote that Lenin and Trotsky "were so bitterly hostile to the present social order . . . that nothing could be said which would gain their favor or render them amenable to reason." See Arno J. Mayer, *Political Origins of the New Diplomacy, 1917–1918* (New Haven: Yale University Press, 1959), 343. His view had not changed by November 1919, when he warned the British and French governments that Lenin and the other Bolsheviks would never "give up permanently the dream of a world-wide revolution and loyally enter into friendly relations with governments which are not communistic." See *Foreign Relations, 1919, Russia*, 129–30.

[90] Lloyd George shared Wilson's skepticism, but his freedom of action was constrained by Conservative opposition. See Thompson, *Russia, Bolshevism, and Versailles*, 240; Levin, *Wilson and World Politics*, 231–32; and Ullman, *Anglo-Soviet Accord*, 9–11.

[91] See Lloyd George, *Truth about the Peace Treaties*, 1:325–30; and Ullman, *Britain and the Russian Civil War*, 96–97, 153–55, 173–77.

were based on "indefinite information," and he told the other Allied leaders in May that he no longer felt "the same chagrin that he had formerly felt at having no policy in regard to Russia. It had been impossible to have a policy hitherto." Now, he argued, "the proper policy of the Allied and Associated Powers was to clear out of Russia and leave it to the Russians to fight it out among themselves."[92]

Given this pervasive uncertainty, it is hardly surprising that Allied ambitions rose whenever the Whites did well and fell whenever they faltered. In the spring of 1919, for example, the establishment of a short-lived Communist regime in Hungary and Kolchak's successful offensive in Siberia brought renewed calls to recognize the Whites and provide them with additional military support. Even Lloyd George now endorsed plans for a joint offensive by Kolchak's White Army and the Allied expeditionary force in northern Russia, with the aim of eliminating the Soviet regime once and for all. The information upon which these hopes were based was already outdated, however, and the pledge of additional military support did not reach Kolchak until after the Red Army had launched the counteroffensive that would destroy his army and cost him his life.[93] The offensives by Denikin and Yudenich rekindled Allied hopes in the summer and fall and sparked new debates over Allied involvement, but the eventual failure of these campaigns fed the growing awareness that the Soviet regime would be around for some time.

### The Failure of Accommodation

The Entente's halfhearted efforts to overthrow the Soviet regime were accompanied by equally feeble attempts to include Russia in the postwar peace settlement. Despite having sent additional troops to Russia and provided the White armies with generous military assistance, the Western powers repeatedly disavowed any desire to interfere in Russia's internal affairs and tried to end the civil war on several occasions. These contradictory and unsuccessful initiatives exemplify the obstacles that can hamper efforts to improve relations with a revolutionary regime.

*The Soviet Peace Offensive.* The Soviets started trying to reach a modus vivendi with the Entente as soon as World War I ended. Like the Treaty of Brest-Litovsk, the Soviets' peace offensive was based on a candid appraisal of their present weakness—and on their optimistic faith that the revolution would eventually spread to other countries. Lenin was well aware that in-

[92] Quoted in Frederick S. Calhoun, *Power and Principle: Armed Intervention in Wilsonian Foreign Policy* (Kent: Kent State University Press, 1986), 232, 238.

[93] See Ullman, *Britain and the Russian Civil War*, 164–65; and *Foreign Relations, 1919, Russia*, 632–33.

ternational socialism was still "weaker than international imperialism . . . and must do everything to avoid battle with it." He was also convinced that the survival of Soviet Russia depended on divisions between the capitalist countries and warned at the end of World War I, "Now world capital will start an offensive against us."[94] In addition to the negative sentiments of the Whites and their Western supporters, hostility to Bolshevism was also apparent in the suppression of the Spartacist movement in Germany in January 1919, the murder of Rosa Luxemburg and Karl Liebknecht by government security forces in Berlin, and the deaths of four Russian Red Cross delegates at the hands of a group of Polish gendarmes. Allied support for the independence movements in the Baltic and Transcaucasia and their decision to allow German troops to remain in Eastern Europe as a "barrier to Bolshevism" further confirmed the Bolsheviks' belief in a powerful capitalist alliance bent on their destruction.

At the same time, Lenin and his associates maintained that prospects for a world revolution had never been brighter. In a letter to the Central Committee on October 3, Lenin called for "an army of three million" to aid the "international worker's revolution," and subsequent messages urged Soviet diplomats in Berlin and Stockholm to devote greater efforts to propaganda work. A Central Committee resolution on October 22 summed up this blend of optimism and pessimism perfectly: "On the one hand, we have never been so close to an international proletarian revolution as we are now; on the other hand, we have never been in such a perilous position as we are now."[95] Their response was a strategy of appeasement intended to divide the imperialist forces and buy time for the revolution to spread. Thus, apart from a few minor lapses (such as the harsh letter from Chicherin to Wilson in October 1918), the Soviet government began to emphasize its desire for an accommodation with the West.[96]

The first clear sign of this policy was a resolution issued by the Sixth All-Russian Congress of Soviets on November 8, 1918. The resolution offered generous economic concessions in exchange for a peace agreement, an offer that Soviet emissary Maxim Litvinov repeated during talks with Western representatives in December. On December 23, Litvinov sent a letter to the Allied governments proposing negotiations for "a peaceful settlement of all

[94] Quoted in Thompson, *Russia, Bolshevism, and Versailles,* 86; and Chamberlin, *Russian Revolution,* 2:155. Lenin also told Karl Radek, "The gravest moment has arrived. Germany is beaten. The Entente's road to Russia is cleared. Even if Germany does not take part in the campaign against us, the hands of the Allies are free." Quoted in Piero Melograni, *Lenin and and the Myth of World Revolution: Ideology and Reasons of State, 1917–1920* (Atlantic Highlands, N.J.: Humanities Press, 1989), 28.

[95] See Lenin, *Selected Works,* 3:55–56; Bunyan, *Intervention, Civil War, and Communism,* 149–50; and Carr, *Bolshevik Revolution,* 3:91–97.

[96] According to Thompson, "from October 1918 to January 1919 the Soviet government officially proposed peace to the Western powers on at least seven different occasions." *Russia, Bolshevism, and Versailles,* 88; and see also Ullman, *Britain and the Russian Civil War,* 87 n. 50.

the outstanding questions," which he followed with a conciliatory message to Wilson the next day. Addressing the "one-sided accusations against Soviet Russia," Litvinov appealed to Wilson's "sense of justice and impartiality," reiterated the Bolshevik desire for peace, and called for the Entente to withdraw its troops, lift the blockade, and "come to an understanding with the Soviet Government."[97]

*Allied Responses.* The Soviet peace offensive received a favorable response from Britain and the United States. The Imperial War Cabinet authorized preliminary talks with Litvinov, and Wilson sent a young diplomat, William H. Buckler, to meet with Litvinov in Stockholm in January. Litvinov told Buckler his government was "prepared to compromise on all points, including the Russian foreign debt, protection to existing foreign enterprise, and the granting of new concessions in Russia." He also declared that Bolshevik propaganda would end as soon as a peace settlement was reached, and stated that the "Russians realize that in certain western countries conditions are not favorable for a revolution."[98]

In response, Britain and the United States made several attempts to end the civil war and terminate their involvement in Russia. Buckler's talks with Litvinov convinced the Allies to approve a British proposal for negotiations on "conditions for a general settlement," and the Allied representatives at the Paris Peace Conference overcame French objections and voted on January 21 to invite representatives of the "organized groups now contending for the leadership and guidance of Russia" to a conference to be held at the Prinkipo Islands in mid-February.[99] The Soviet government accepted the proposal on February 4, 1919. The decision reflected its overwhelming desire to end the civil war and its confidence that any concessions it might be forced to make would be reversed once the revolution had spread to the West.[100] The leaders

[97] Litvinov also requested outside aid and technical support to help the Soviet government "exploit [Russia's] natural richness . . . for the benefit of all countries." See Degras, *Soviet Documents*, 1:123, 129–32; and *Foreign Relations 1919, Russia*, 1–2. For a description of other Soviet activities along these lines, see McFadden, *Alternative Paths*, 176–80.

[98] See *Foreign Relations 1919, Russia*, 15–17.

[99] See *Foreign Relations 1919, Russia*, 2–3, 30–31; Thompson, *Russia, Bolshevism, and Versailles*, 93–95 and passim; Ullman, *Britain and the Russian Civil War*, 95–100. French foreign minister Stephen Pichon protested that France would "make no contract with crime," and Ambassador Noulens made a dramatic presentation in which he portrayed the Soviet government as both an awesome menace and a weak and vulnerable foe. See *Foreign Relations, 1919, Peace Conference*, 3:623–42; and Mayer, *Politics and Diplomacy*, 427.

[100] See Degras, *Soviet Documents*, 1:137–39; Thompson, *Russia, Bolshevism, and Versailles*, 115–18; and McFadden, *Alternative Paths*, 202–205. Trotsky had already declared, "All that we cede now will come back to us, because Soviet Russia gives in to the imperialists only temporarily," and Chicherin remarked that "Brest-Litovsk had shown that such [imperialist] annexations could be only of short duration." Quoted in Piotr S. Wandycz, *Soviet-Polish Relations, 1917–1921* (Cambridge: Harvard University Press, 1969), 102.

of the various ex-Russian territories accepted the Allied invitation as well, but the representatives of the anti-Bolshevik Whites refused to participate, on the grounds that negotiations would legitimize Bolshevik rule.[101] The French government encouraged the Whites to reject the invitation, and conservatives in Britain and the United States waged a fierce press campaign against any contact with the Bolshevik "criminals." The date for the conference soon passed and the "Prinkipo proposal" merely confirmed each side's belief in the immutable malice of the other.[102]

The next attempt to reach an accommodation with the Soviet regime began in February, when Wilson authorized an unofficial mission to Moscow by William Bullitt, a journalist attached to the U.S. delegation in Paris. The mission was originally intended to gather information about social and political conditions in Russia, but as Bullitt later recounted, some Entente officials decided to use the opportunity "to obtain from the Soviet Government an exact statement of the terms on which they were ready to stop fighting." Members of the British and U.S. delegations gave Bullitt several specific proposals for ending the civil war and restoring normal relations between Russia and the West and asked him to determine whether these terms would be acceptable to the Bolsheviks.[103]

Bullitt's observations in Russia convinced him that the Soviet regime enjoyed substantial popular support and was governing effectively in the territories it controlled. The Soviet leaders accepted his proposals with only minor modifications. Their willingness to concede vast amounts of territory to the Whites in exchange for the cessation of Allied assistance testifies to the importance they attached to ending foreign intervention and to Lenin's belief that the White armies could not survive on their own.[104]

---

[101] See Mayer, *Politics and Diplomacy*, 432–39; Thompson, *Russia, Bolshevism, and Versailles*, 123–24; and Nadia Tongour, "Diplomacy in Exile: Russian Emigrés in Paris, 1918–1925," (Ph.D. diss., Stanford University, 1979), 132–33.

[102] The failure of the Prinkipo proposal is analyzed in Richard K. Debo, *Survival and Consolidation: The Foreign Policy of Soviet Russia, 1918–1921* (Montreal: McGill/Queen's University Press, 1992), 31–33; Chamberlin, *Russian Revolution*, 2:157–59; McFadden, *Alternative Paths*, chap 8; Ullman, *Britain and the Russian Civil War*, 107–17; Thompson, *Russia, Bolshevism, and Versailles*, 119–30; Mayer, *Politics and Diplomacy*, 436–49; and Carley, *Revolution and Intervention*, 152–53.

[103] These proposals were worked out by Bullitt, Edward House, and Philip Kerr, Lloyd George's private secretary, and Wilson was not informed of this step (although Lloyd George probably was). The lack of clear agreement on the purpose of the mission contributed to its failure and underscored Soviet impressions of Western perfidy. See Debo, *Survival and Consolidation*, 44–49; McFadden, *Alternative Paths*, chap. 9; Thompson, *Russia, Bolshevism, and Versailles*, 149–56; and Ullman, *Britain and the Russian Civil War*, 145–46.

[104] As Lenin told a British journalist in 1920, "We proposed this treaty [to Bullitt] with the knowledge that if peace were signed, those [White] governments could never hold out." Quoted in McFadden, *Alternative Paths*, 231; and also see Thompson, *Russia, Bolshevism, and Versailles*, 154, 164–75. For Bullitt's report, see *Foreign Relations, 1919, Russia*, 85–95.

Bullitt hurriedly cabled these terms to Paris on March 16 but returned there to find that nothing had been done. As it turned out, the proposals he had submitted in Moscow did not even reflect a consensus among U.S. officials (let alone the Entente as a whole), and both Lloyd George and Wilson faced strong domestic opposition to any compromise with the Bolshevik regime.[105] Bullitt's own progressive sympathies made it easier for conservatives to discount his testimony, and though his conduct in Moscow showed him to be a tough and effective negotiator, the terms he achieved still contained significant flaws. Bullitt's efforts also fell victim to bad timing, as the agenda of the peace conference had shifted by the time he returned to Paris and his sponsors now chose to focus their energies on other issues.[106]

With hindsight, the Bullitt mission is best seen as a lost opportunity for the Allies to end their involvement in Russia on far better terms than they ultimately obtained. The concessions offered to Bullitt did not mean that the Bolsheviks had abandoned their revolutionary ambitions, and a sincere effort to follow up on Bullitt's initiative would hardly have guaranteed a significant improvement in Soviet relations with the West; however, the Soviets' response suggested that they were willing to pursue more or less normal relations with the Allied powers, even if out of necessity rather than conviction.[107] And since their acceptance of virtually all Bullitt's conditions had gained them nothing, it is hardly surprising that they saw this episode as additional evidence of imperialist hostility.

The final attempt to reach an accommodation with the Soviet regime during the first half of 1919 was the so-called Hoover-Nansen plan, which linked Western relief aid to a ceasefire between the Red Army and the Whites. The proposal suffered the same dim fate as its predecessors. The

---

[105] Wilson refused to meet with Bullitt upon the latter's return to Paris, and Lloyd George answered Bullitt's pleas by waving a copy of the conservative *Daily Mail* and saying, "As long as the British press is doing this kind of thing, how can you expect me to sensible about Russia?" Lloyd George later recalled, "Personally I would have dealt with the Soviets as the *de facto* government of Russia. So would President Wilson. But we both agreed that we could not carry to that extent our colleagues at the [peace conference] nor the public opinion of our own countries which was frightened by Bolshevik violence and feared its spread." See his *Truth about the Peace Treaties*, 1:331; Debo, *Survival and Consolidation*, 50; Levin, *Wilson and World Politics*, 214–15; and Ullman, *Britain and the Russian Civil War*, 153–56.

[106] The agreement called for a cease-fire and a joint pledge of noninterference in domestic politics but did not explain how either provision would be enforced. It also required an end to Allied support for the Whites, which in effect meant abandoning the policy the Entente had followed for over a year.

[107] The Bolshevik decision to accept Bullitt's proposals was clearly controversial; Zinoviev refused to speak with Bullitt, and Trotsky referred to the delegation as "eavesdroppers" sent "to assess whether we should hold firm or not." Chicherin defended the compromise, warning that a refusal would lead to renewed support for the Whites, and Lenin reminded several party gatherings that "our country alone cannot overthrow world imperialism. . . . We have to make concessions [to it]." See Debo, *Survival and Consolidation*, 47–48; and McFadden, *Alternative Paths*, 228–30.

French government reluctantly endorsed it on April 16 but Kolchak and the émigré Political Committee protested that relief aid would merely prolong Bolshevik rule.[108] The Soviet government did not even learn of the proposal until May 4, and then responded by blaming food shortages in Russia on the civil war and the Allied blockade and pointing out that the political issues raised in the proposal could only be addressed by formal peace talks. By the time this message was received, however, reports of Kolchak's early successes had reached Paris, and the Hoover-Nansen plan was quickly dropped. Like the Prinkipo proposal and the Bullitt mission, the speed with which this initiative was abandoned underscores the Entente's continued ambivalence about the proper approach to the new regime in Moscow.[109]

The failure of accommodation highlights some of the obstacles to improving relations with a revolutionary government. The first problem was the sheer difficulty of negotiating with an unrecognized regime: the Soviets were not present at the peace conference, and unlike the Whites, they had no community of sympathizers in Paris to lobby on their behalf. Communication was hampered further by the Entente's fear that contacts with the Soviet regime might imply recognition (although this objection did not prevent them from sending military attachés and other representatives to work directly with the Whites). As a result, negotiations were conducted either via erratic radio broadcasts or through semiofficial emissaries such as Bullitt. These constraints increased uncertainty and made detrimental misunderstandings more likely.[110]

Second, the opposition to accommodation was reinforced by anti-Bolshevik propaganda, much of it traceable to Russian exiles and the White forces themselves. Not only did the exiles' Political Committee in Paris enjoy close ties with the French government (which shared its anti-Bolshevik worldview), but the conservative opposition that constrained Lloyd George was fueled in part by misleading or fictitious reports from unreliable anti-Bolshevik sources.[111] Thus, the general lack of information was exacerbated by "facts" that were politically inspired and predictably biased.

Third, accommodation was hampered by disagreements among the Allies as a whole and within the individual Allied governments. These divisions

---

[108] On the origins and outcome of the Hoover-Nansen plan, see Levin, *Wilson and World Politics*, 217–18; Thompson, *Russia, Bolshevism, and Versailles*, 256–62; *Foreign Relations, 1919, Russia*, 100–102, 108–109; and McFadden, *Alternative Paths*, chap. 10.

[109] According to Ullman, the Allied commissioners did not receive the Soviet reply until May 14, because the French receiving station in the Eiffel Tower refused to relay the message. See *Britain and the Russian Civil War*, 160; and *Foreign Relations, 1919, Russia*, 111–15, 351–54.

[110] See Thompson, *Russia, Bolshevism, and Versailles*, 160–61.

[111] These reports, published in a British government white paper, contained accusations that the Bolsheviks had nationalized women and established "commissariats of free love," that they were using Chinese torturers, and that churches were being converted into brothels. See Ullman, *Britain and the Russian Civil War*, 141–44, 173–77.

were partly due to normal political rivalries but were enlarged by the persistent dearth of information. The consequence was a stalemate: the Whites received enough support to continue but not enough to win, and the Allies never followed up on the Soviets' favorable responses to their halfhearted proposals for détente.[112]

Finally, the failure of accommodation reflected the basic truth that the Bolsheviks were more interested in a settlement than the Allies were. No Western leader wanted Russia to remain under Bolshevik control, and even those who opposed intervention were unwilling to pursue accommodation in the face of domestic opposition or reports of White successes. The result was a self-defeating mixture of confrontation and conciliation that simultaneously reinforced Soviet perceptions of threat and helped them strengthen their hold on power.

### The Diplomacy of Isolation

After the demise of the Hoover-Nansen plan, the Soviet government suspended its efforts at accommodation in favor of greater reliance on revolutionary propaganda. An international congress of socialist parties convened in Moscow in March, and the delegates responded to a fiery speech by an Austrian representative by voting to establish the Third Communist International, or Comintern.[113] The congress also called for colonial revolts against the imperialist powers (a theme that the Bolsheviks repeated throughout the year), and Foreign Minister Chicherin began propaganda broadcasts encouraging foreign workers to oppose intervention in Russia.[114]

Soviet reliance on propaganda during this period was partly ideological in origin and partly a matter of necessity. The failure of the peace offensive confirmed Soviet beliefs about capitalist hostility and the inevitability of

---

[112] As an Italian delegate later recalled: "We had to choose in Russia between two policies equally logical and defendable. The first is that of intervention; to go to Moscow if necessary and crush Bolshevism by force. The second consists in regarding Bolshevism as a government *de facto*, and to establish relations with it, if not cordial at least more or less normal. We did not know how to adopt either one or the other and we have suffered the worst consequences for pursuing both at the same time. Without going to war, we are in a state of war with Russia." Quoted in Wandycz, *Soviet-Polish Relations*, 104.

[113] The Austrian delegate, Karl Steinhardt, told the congress that "all eyes [in Europe] are turned toward revolutionary Russia. They are only waiting for her to give them the password to go into action." Quoted in Melograni, *Lenin and World Revolution*, 56; and see also James W. Hulse, *The Forming of the Communist International* (Stanford: Stanford University Press, 1964), 19–20; and Carr, *Bolshevik Revolution*, 3:118–26.

[114] As Chicherin described Soviet diplomacy during this period: "We write fewer notes to governments but more appeals to the working classes." *Two Years of Soviet Foreign Policy: the Relations of the Russian Socialist Federal Soviet Republic with Foreign Nations, from November 7, 1917, to November 7, 1919* (New York: Russian Soviet Government Bureau, 1920), 35. Also see Carr, *Bolshevik Revolution*, 3:122–23, 235–36; and Degras, *Soviet Documents*, 1:150–178.

war, while evidence of unrest in the West sustained the hope that the spread of revolution would undermine the imperialist powers and provide Soviet Russia with new allies. As Lenin told the Eighth Party Congress in March 1919: "We are living not merely in a state, but in *a system of states;* and it is inconceivable that the Soviet republic should continue to exist for a long period side by side with imperialist states. Ultimately one or the other must conquer."[115] Although a Communist uprising in Berlin was crushed in January, the Bolsheviks were heartened by mutinies that forced the French expeditionary force to withdraw from the Ukraine and by the establishment of a Soviet republic in Hungary in March. Indeed, when a Soviet government was proclaimed in Bavaria in April, Lenin declared, "Our victory on an international scale is now completely secure." The head of the Comintern, Gregor Zinoviev, echoed this assessment by predicting that within a year, one would begin to forget that there was ever a struggle over Communism in Europe. Lenin made a similar forecast two months later, saying that "this July will be our last difficult July, and next July we shall greet the victory of the international Soviet republic."[116] Although statements such as these were probably intended to bolster morale, they also reveal a continued faith in the inevitability of world revolution. As it happened, neither the Hungarian nor Bavarian regime would last more than a few months, and an attempted Communist uprising in Vienna was to be crushed in June.[117] For the moment, however, these events reinforced the Soviets' faith in Europe's revolutionary potential and encouraged their continued efforts to promote it.

The Soviet government also believed that the threat of revolution might convince the Allies to abandon their support for the Whites. Chicherin's radio broadcasts were intended to hasten this process, and the British Socialist Party's "Hands Off Russia" campaign in February 1919 and an abortive general strike later in the spring convinced Soviet leaders that revolutionary propaganda was an effective way to undermine public support for intervention. As Lenin told a British journalist early in the year, "England may seem to you untouched, but the microbe is already there."[118] The

---

[115] Quoted in Carr, *Bolshevik Revolution,* 3:115 (emphasis in the original).

[116] As Lenin told the Comintern Congress in March, "When we hear how quickly the idea of Soviets is spreading in Germany and even in Britain, it is very important evidence that the proletarian revolution will be victorious." See Lenin, *Selected Works,* 3:162, 176–77; and Carr, *Bolshevik Revolution,* 3:129.

[117] On these events, see Werner T. Angress, "The Takeover that Remained in Limbo: The German Experience, 1918–1923," and Paul Ignotus, "The First Two Communist Takeovers of Hungary: 1919 and 1948," in *The Anatomy of Communist Takeovers,* ed. Thomas T. Hammond (New Haven: Yale University Press, 1975); Mayer, *Politics and Diplomacy,* chaps. 17, 21, 24; and Peter Pastor, *Hungary between Wilson and Lenin* (Boulder, Colo.: East European Quarterly, 1976).

[118] Quoted in Carr, *Bolshevik Revolution,* 3:128. For descriptions of domestic conditions in Europe, see Mayer, *Politics and Diplomacy,* 559–62 and chaps. 18–20, 25; and Walter Kendall, *The Revolutionary Movement in Britain, 1900–1921* (London: Weidenfeld and Nicolson, 1969), 187–95.

[165]

Bolsheviks' faith in these tactics was based partly on their own isolation; lacking reliable information about social conditions in Europe, they exaggerated the strength of socialist forces in the West and failed to recognize how different conditions in Europe were from those in Russia in 1917.

Finally, the Soviets relied on propaganda simply because they had no other options. Attempting to spark other proletarian revolutions was not only consistent with Bolshevik ideology, it was the only policy available once the peace offensive failed. Even if full-fledged revolutions did not occur elsewhere, the threat of domestic disturbances might persuade the Entente to abandon its support for the Whites. Nor was this hope entirely fanciful, as the fear of domestic unrest was one reason why Lloyd George and others had opposed an all-out effort to topple the Soviet regime in the first place.

*Hints of Detente.* The failure of the Whites forced the Entente to reconsider its policy toward Soviet Russia, and Lloyd George began to sketch an alternative approach in November 1919. After acknowledging that Denikin's offensive had been "temporarily checked," he suggested that "other methods must finally be resorted to for restoring peace and good government" in Russia. The prime minister defended the Allies' past actions by claiming they had given the anti-Bolshevik forces a fair chance, but he emphasized that "we cannot, of course, afford to continue so costly an intervention in an interminable civil war." Although he qualified his remarks to mollify British Conservatives, Lloyd George was signaling a major shift in British policy.[119]

Evidence of the change was soon apparent. Negotiations for a prisoner exchange began in November—marking the first significant contact between the Entente and the Bolsheviks since the demise of the Hoover-Nansen plan—and a final agreement was signed in February 1920.[120] The Entente began to abandon counterrevolution in favor of a policy of containment, and this new objective was tacitly approved at an inter-Allied conference in December. Convinced that a permanent division of the former tsarist empire would reduce the threat to British imperial interests, the British offered de facto recognition to Estonia, Georgia, Armenia, and Azerbaijan in early 1920, seeking to use them as a barrier against further Soviet encroachments.[121]

Lloyd George invoked the classic liberal arguments about the benefits of trade to justify his new policy. He stressed the contribution that Russian

---

[119] The Bolsheviks did not miss the change, and Chicherin subsequently announced, "Relations between Britain and Russia are quite possible in spite of the profound differences between Britain's and Russia's regime. . . . We are ready even to make sacrifices for the sake of a close economic connection with Britain." Quoted in Carr, *Bolshevik Revolution*, 3:151–52; and see also Thompson, *Russia, Bolshevism, and Versailles*, 349–52; and Ullman, *Britain and the Russian Civil War*, 304–307.

[120] See Ullman, *Britain and the Russian Civil War*, 339–43.

[121] Ibid., 322–25; and Thompson, *Russia, Bolshevism, and Versailles*, 330–35, 344–45.

grain could make to alleviating famine and high food prices in Europe and argued that trade would exert a "civilizing" influence on Soviet behavior as well. On January 16, 1920, the Allies agreed to lift the blockade and commence trade with Russia for the first time since 1918. As the prospects for a successful counterrevolution were fading, in short, the Entente was turning to a combination of containment and détente.

The Soviet government was clearly interested in expanding its ties with foreign powers. In addition to the negotiations for a prisoner exchange with Great Britain, the Soviet government began peace talks with Poland and Estonia and signed a formal treaty with the latter in February 1920.[122] Relations with Germany were beginning to show signs of life as well; the suppression of the Spartacist uprising in Berlin and the collapse of the Bavarian Soviet had reduced the German fear of Bolshevism, and the harsh peace terms imposed by the Entente made collaboration with Russia more attractive. Soviet-German cooperation was supported by their mutual antipathy to Poland, and Germany's rejection of an Allied request to renew the blockade of Russia in October was clear evidence of a growing détente. A prisoner exchange soon followed, and Germany withdrew its remaining forces from the Baltic region, thereby sowing the seeds for a future rapprochement.[123] The appeals for economic links expressed during Moscow's earlier peace offensive were renewed, and efforts to initiate talks with Western governments and private business interests began in earnest later in the year.[124]

Finally, the Soviet government was also starting to show a renewed commitment to traditional Russian interests. The Ministry of Foreign Affairs issued a formal protest when the Paris Peace Conference awarded the Aland Islands to Finland, and it repeated its protests when Norway received Spitzbergen. Thus, as Carr points out, despite its initial disdain for "bourgeois" diplomacy, "the Soviet government found itself almost involuntarily in the posture of defending, not the interests of world revolution, but na-

---

[122] Lenin termed the peace treaty with Estonia of "gigantic historical significance" and took up the phrase "peaceful coexistence" shortly thereafter. See Jon Jacobson, *When the Soviet Union Entered World Politics* (Berkeley: University of California Press, 1994), 18; and Xenia Eudin and Harold Fisher, *Soviet Russia and the West: A Documentary Survey* (Stanford: Stanford University Press, 1957), 7–9.

[123] See Freund, *Unholy Alliance*, 42–52. The Soviet-German rapprochement was facilitated by discussions between Karl Radek, a Polish member of the Bolshevik Party who had been arrested in Germany in 1918, and a series of German officials who visited him in prison. See Edward Hallett Carr, "Radek's 'Political Salon' in Berlin, 1919," *Soviet Studies* 3, no. 4 (1952); Lionel Kochan, *Russia and the Weimar Republic* (Cambridge: Bowes and Bowes, 1954), 16–18; and Warren Lerner, *Karl Radek: The Last Internationalist* (Stanford: Stanford University Press, 1970), 85–90.

[124] As early as October 1919, Lenin had remarked, "We are decidedly for an economic understanding with America—with all countries but especially with America." See McFadden, *Alternative Paths*, 267.

tional interests which any government of Russia would be obliged to defend."[125]

By the spring of 1920, foreign involvement in the Russian Civil War was nearly over. The new regime had proved stronger than it looked, and the Entente was now abandoning its modest attempts to overthrow it and searching for other ways to defuse the danger. The Soviet commitment to world revolution remained intact, but the Bolsheviks, still acutely aware of their own weakness, were actively interested in a settlement with the West.[126] Unfortunately, the first moves toward a more normal relationship were temporarily interrupted by the Russo-Polish war.

### The Russo-Polish War and the Balance of Threats

The first clash between Soviet and Polish troops took place in February 1919, after Soviet troops entered border areas claimed by the new government in Warsaw. Intermittent fighting continued throughout the year, with the Poles capturing Wilno in April and extending their holdings as far as Minsk by autumn.[127]

Poland's new leaders disagreed about the final form that the new state should take, but the main factions all favored expanded borders that would provide greater security against both Russia and Germany.[128] The Poles declined Soviet proposals for peace negotiations, and in December the Polish head of state, Joseph Piłsudski (who was also commander-in-chief of the army), ordered the Ministry of Military Affairs to prepare for "a definitive settlement of the Russian question" in April 1920.[129]

The Polish invasion began on April 25. Mistakenly believing that the bulk of the Red Army was in the south, Piłsudski concentrated his forces there in

---

[125] See Carr, *Russian Revolution*, 3:157–58; and Degras, *Soviet Documents*, 1:169–170, 181–82.

[126] In an interview with the *Manchester Guardian* in October, Lenin reiterated Soviet willingness to abide by the terms agreed upon during Bullitt's visit to Moscow in March. See Thompson, *Russia, Bolshevism, and Versailles*, 354.

[127] In Churchill's apt phrase, "The War of the Giants has ended; the quarrels of the pygmies have begun." See Norman Davies, *White Eagle, Red Star: The Polish-Soviet War, 1919–1920* (New York: St. Martin's, 1972), 21, 27. Other accounts of the war include Wandycz, *Soviet-Polish Relations*; Thomas C. Fiddick, *Russia's Retreat from Poland, 1920: From Permanent Revolution to Peaceful Coexistence* (New York: St. Martin's, 1990); Ullman, *Anglo-Soviet Accord*, chaps. 4–6; Warren Lerner, "Attempting a Revolution from Without: Poland in 1920," in Hammond, *Anatomy of Communist Takeovers*; Lincoln, *Red Victory*, chap. 12; and James M. McCann, "Beyond the Bug: Soviet Historiography of the Soviet-Polish War of 1920," *Soviet Studies* 36, no. 4 (1984).

[128] See Davies, *White Eagle, Red Star*, 29–30; Wandycz, *Soviet-Polish Relations*, 94–100, 104–10, 118–22; and Joseph Rothschild, *East Central Europe between the Two World Wars*, 3d ed. (Seattle: University of Washington Press, 1979), 31–34.

[129] Piłsudski held secret talks with Bolshevik representatives in the fall of 1919 and agreed to stay out of the civil war, in part because the Whites refused to acknowledge Polish independence. See Degras, *Soviet Documents*, 1:177–78; Davies, *White Eagle, Red Star*, 86–87.

the hopes of landing a knock-out blow. The invaders encountered only light opposition and swept rapidly across the Ukraine, occupying Kiev on May 6 and pushing across the Dnieper River a few days later. The Poles' initial success was short-lived, however, and a Soviet counteroffensive soon had them racing back west nearly as fast as they had come. Poland's belligerence had already cost it most of its international support, but the possibility that the Red Army might invade Poland reawakened Western concerns. Lloyd George was especially worried that the war would interfere with the negotiations for a trade agreement that had just commenced in London, and Great Britain issued a formal démarche on July 11 warning that if Soviets crossed the boundary set by the peace conference, "the Allies would feel bound to assist the Polish nation to defend its existence with all the means at their disposal."[130]

The note also invited the Soviets to attend a conference in London to settle the remaining border issues in the east. On July 16, however, the Soviet Politburo rejected British mediation and ordered the Red Army "to continue and step up the offensive." Chicherin offered to begin bilateral talks with the Poles—noting that the Soviet government had already signed peace treaties with several Baltic states "without the participation of other parties"—and he also announced that the Soviets would send an "enlarged" delegation to the next round of trade talks in London, in order to reach a "final" peace.[131] More ominously, his response implied that a peace settlement would require adjustments in Poland's internal arrangements, and indeed the Soviets subsequently insisted that the Polish Army be replaced by a militia "organized among the workers."[132]

The Soviet decision to invade Poland is best seen as a calculated risk.[133] Lenin's support for this step is somewhat surprising, as he had opposed

---

[130] In April, Lloyd George said the Poles "have gone rather mad" and described them as "a menace to the peace of Europe." See Debo, *Survival and Consolidation*, 215; Ullman, *Anglo-Soviet Accord*, 48, 137–39; and W. P. Coates and Zelda Coates, *A History of Anglo-Soviet Relations* (London: Lawrence and Wishart, 1944), 35.

[131] See Degras, *Soviet Documents*, 194–97; Ullman, *Anglo-Soviet Accord*, 148–49, 168–69; and Branko Lazitch and Milorad M. Drachkovitch, *Lenin and the Comintern* (Stanford: Hoover Institute Press, 1972), 1:273.

[132] As Pyotr Wandycz points out, this condition was "equivalent to a demand for complete surrender." See Wandycz, *Soviet-Polish Relations*, 245–47; Degras, *Soviet Documents*, 1:196, 201–202; and Carr, *Bolshevik Revolution*, 3:213.

[133] The decision to invade Poland remains the object of controversy. The traditional view is that Lenin insisted on an attempt to impose Bolshevism by force, overruling Trotsky, Stalin, and the Polish Communists; see Carr, *Bolshevik Revolution*, 3:209–10; Ullman, *Anglo-Soviet Accord*, 165–70, 184–85; Lerner, "Revolution from Without," 98–102, and "Poland in 1920: A Case Study in Foreign-Policy Decision Making under Lenin," *South Atlantic Quarterly* 72, no. 3 (1973); Wandycz, *Soviet-Polish Relations*, 213–15; and Davies, *White Eagle, Red Star*. For alternative interpretations, see Fiddick, *Russia's Retreat from Poland*; and Melograni, *Lenin and the Myth of World Revolution*, 97–102, 112–13.

precipitous attempts to export the revolution since the seizure of power in 1917. He still believed the imperialist powers were intent on overthrowing the Soviet regime, however, and he seems to have viewed a Soviet Poland both as a barrier to imperialist pressure and as a bridge to Germany, which was still the main object of the Bolsheviks' revolutionary hopes. Finally, the invasion coincided with the Second Comintern Congress in Petrograd, and a socialist takeover in Poland at that moment would have strengthened Moscow's claims to primacy within the international socialist movement.[134]

The Soviets did not expect to conquer Poland solely by force of arms; rather, the invasion would allow the Polish workers and peasants to overthrow the bourgeois government and establish an independent Soviet regime.[135] And Lenin was adamant about what he would do if this assumption were incorrect: "If the expected uprising does not occur, . . . would it be fitting to push military operations more thoroughly, risking a dangerous turn of events? Without doubt, no!" Thus, the invasion of Poland was a gamble but a limited one, and Lenin was unwilling to raise the stakes if his hopes turned out to be incorrect.[136]

His error was soon apparent: the Polish proletariat did not rise up to welcome the invading Red Army, and a Polish counterattack at the outskirts of Warsaw split the Soviet forces and sent them scurrying back across the border. Peace negotiations commenced in Riga in November, and a final peace treaty was concluded in March 1918.[137]

*The Balance of Threats.* The war between Russia and Poland supports the general proposition that revolutions alter the balance of threats in ways that make war more likely. By affecting the balance of power, perceptions of intent, and assessments of the offense-defense balance, the revolution in Rus-

---

[134] Lenin saw the Poles' actions as intended "to strengthen the barrier and to deepen the gulf which separates us from the proletariat of Germany," and he told a group of European socialists that "if Poland gives itself to Communism, the universal revolution would take a decisive step. . . . [It] would mean Germany shortly falling due, Hungary reconquered, the Balkans in revolt against capitalism, Italy shaken up, it would mean bourgeois Europe cracking apart in a formidable hurricane." Quoted in Davies, *White Eagle, Red Star,* 114; and Fiddick, *Russia's Retreat from Poland,* 122–23. See also Vladimir I. Lenin, *Collected Works* (London: Lawrence and Wishart, 1966), 31:305; Lazitch and Drachkovitch, *Lenin and the Comintern,* 1:274–77; and Carr, *Bolshevik Revolution,* 3:187–201.

[135] In May 1920, the president of the Soviet Executive Central Committee, Mikhail Kalinin, had predicted, "If we deliver the first blow, the Polish proletariat will deliver the second and final one. . . . The western capitalists . . . will only succeed in founding yet another Soviet state with which we will enjoy close relations with the proletariat of the West." Quoted in Davies, *White Eagle, Red Star,* 114.

[136] Quoted in Fiddick, *Russia's Retreat from Poland,* 123–24; and see also Lerner, "Revolution from Without," 105.

[137] The Treaty of Riga was quite favorable to Poland, which received considerable territory in the east and financial compensations as well. See Eudin and Fisher, *Soviet Russia and the West,* 18.

sia heightened Soviet-Polish animosity and made the use of force appear especially attractive.

First we examine the issue of the balance of power. The underlying cause of the Russo-Polish war was each side's sense of insecurity. For the Poles, expansion was seen as essential to ensure their long-term security against Germany and Russia. Piłsudski "described himself as a "realist, without prejudices or theories," and Poland's unhappy past had taught him that Poland would either be "a state equal to the great powers of the world, or a small state that needed protection of the mighty." He saw the revolution in Russia and the German defeat in World War I as a once-in-a-lifetime opportunity and believed that the conquest of the borderlands would give Poland the size and strength it needed to survive. Failing to seize this chance, by contrast, would doom Poland to permanent inferiority.[138]

Soviet behavior reflected similar concerns. In addition to the ideological commitment to world revolution, Soviet leaders saw the creation of additional Soviet republics as the best way to protect Soviet Russia from outside interference. If Poland remained independent and tied to the West, Russia would be cut off from Europe and the prospects for subsequent revolutions would decrease. Even before the Red Army had crossed the Polish border, in fact, Trotsky had declared that the existence of an independent bourgeois Poland was a threat to Soviet Russia.[139] If the Polish government were overthrown, however, Russia would be more secure in the short term and better able to support revolutionary efforts elsewhere. Moreover, the restoration of Russian authority in the borderlands would eliminate the threat of further Polish encroachments or a renewed counterrevolutionary invasion.

By contrast, ideological antipathies played only a secondary role. Although Piłsudski declared Bolshevism to be a "purely Russian disease" and sought to push this "foreign way of life" as far from Poland as possible, his main focus was on the balance of power. Poland's leaders were equally hostile to the Whites; as Piłsudski put it, "Irrespective of what her government will be Russia is terribly imperialistic." The head of the Polish Socialist Party opposed Allied proposals for Polish intervention in Russia by saying, "We want to be neither the advance guard nor the gendarmerie of the East," and the leader of the Populist Party stated, "A struggle against Bolshevism in particular is neither our aim nor our task." Instead, the Polish Supreme Command emphasized that the main goal was territory, because the "reduction of Russia to her historical frontiers is a condition of [Poland's] existence." On the Soviet side, ideology exacerbated Soviet fears and inflated their hopes of spreading the revolution, but as Pyotr Wandycz notes, even

---

[138] Quoted in Wandycz, *Soviet-Polish Relations*, 94, 159–60; and also see Lerner, "Poland in 1920," 409.

[139] See Lerner, "Revolution from Without," 98.

in their case "ideological motives blended with the requirements of Russian *raison d'état.*"[140]

In sum, relations between bourgeois Poland and revolutionary Russia displayed the classic symptoms of an intense security dilemma. Both states saw their own expansion as necessary for their security and expansion by the other as a serious threat.

The security dilemma between Russia and Poland was compounded by a second factor, perception of intent. Each side believed that the other was hostile, sentiments that were reinforced by ignorance and ideology, combined with the adversary's subsequent behavior. Thus, relations between Soviet Russia and Poland confirm the tendency for revolutionary states to enter a spiral of suspicion with other powers. The shared belief that war was inevitable provided both sides with a powerful incentive to initiate it as soon as circumstances seemed favorable.

Polish behavior gave the Soviet government ample grounds for suspicion. The murder of four Russian Red Cross officials by Polish security forces in January 1919 was a clear warning, and Poland's refusal to negotiate and its steady movement east convinced Lenin and Trotsky that their efforts at accommodation had simply invited further aggression. The Polish invasion in April merely confirmed Soviet perceptions of threat and increased their incentive to replace the Polish state with a Soviet regime.[141]

These perceptions of Polish hostility were magnified by the belief that Poland was a tool of the Entente. Lenin believed that with the Polish capture of Wilno the Entente "became even more impudent," and he saw the invasion as imperialism's latest attempt to overthrow the Soviet regime.[142] The Bolsheviks still feared a renewal of Allied support for the Whites, and Wrangel's spring offensive seemed too well timed to be purely coincidental. This image of implacable imperialist aggression was reinforced when King George of England sent a message congratulating the Poles on the two hundredth anniversary of the Polish Constitution of 1791, which the Soviets incorrectly saw as an endorsement of the Polish invasion.[143]

---

[140] See Wandycz, *Soviet-Polish Relations*, 94, 107–108, 126–27, 198, 287.

[141] As one Bolshevik leader declared in July, "With these people [the Poles] there can be no peace. . . . [The] historical strife between Russia and Poland must end by friendship and unification of the Russian and Polish Soviet republics." See Wandycz, *Soviet-Polish Relations*, 174, 221; and Fiddick, *Russia's Retreat from Poland*, 29.

[142] In May, Lenin told a group of soldiers that Poland's invasion had been "instigated by the Entente," and he later declared that "international capital . . . was the chief force driving the Poles into a war with us." See Lenin, *Selected Works*, 3:431, and *Collected Works*, 31:301. For Lenin's reaction to the seizure of Wilno, see Wandycz, *Soviet-Polish Relations*, 128.

[143] Some Bolshevik leaders saw the British government as divided between hardline anti-Bolsheviks and moderate advocates of accommodation, but Lenin told Trotsky that the talks in England "have shown *with full clarity* that England is helping and will help both the Poles and Wrangel. *There is absolutely only one line.*" Lenin's appraisal was incorrect, as the British had rejected Polish requests for military aid in the fall of 1919 and did little to aid the Poles.

Polish suspicions of Russia were equally intense. In addition to reacting to a long history of Russian domination, the Poles understandably read the Bolsheviks' early attempts to establish "Soviet" republics in the Baltic states and Byelorussia as evidence of expansionist intentions. Piłsudski was convinced that a war with Soviet Russia was inevitable, and he viewed the various Soviet peace offers simply as attempts to buy time.[144]

The defensive expansionism that drove subsequent Soviet and Polish policies underscored each state's worst fears. Poland began planning an all-out offensive in December 1919, and Lenin told Trotsky in February to "get ready for war with Poland." Soviet preparations just strengthened the Poles' desire to strike first.[145]

Momentum for war was increased by mutual perceptions of an offensive advantage. In addition to believing that war was inevitable, both sides believed that they would win a swift and decisive victory. The repatriation of Polish units at the end of World War I had brought the Polish Army up to a strength of 590,000 troops, and an assault on Pinsk in March 1920 had been surprisingly easy. In addition, the Poles were aware that Russia had been weakened by the revolution and distracted by the civil war, an assessment shared by foreign military experts and several Soviet leaders as well.[146]

The Poles also recognized that this opportunity was unlikely to last. Victories over Kolchak and Yudenich allowed the Soviets to focus more attention on Poland, and Soviet troop strength in the west increased steadily after January 1920. Concerned that the Soviets would draw out the peace talks in order to build up their forces, Piłsudski decided to seize the opportunity before the window closed. Thus, the Polish invasion of the Ukraine in April 1920 contains elements of preventive and preemptive war: Piłsudski attacked while the balance of power still favored Poland and "to forestall by his offensive an attack by Soviet troops."[147]

---

See Ullman, *Anglo-Soviet Accord*, 137–47, 163, 173–83; Fiddick, *Russia's Retreat from Poland*, 45, 100–101, 168; Wandycz, *Soviet-Polish Relations*, 161–62, 211–12; Davies, *White Eagle, Red Star*, 92–93, 172–73, 220, "Lloyd George and Poland, 1919–20," 132–54; and Marjan Kukiel, "The Polish-Soviet Campaign of 1920," *Slavonic Review* 8, no. 1 (1929), 59.

[144] See Davies, *White Eagle, Red Star*, 26–27, 65; Wandycz, *Soviet-Polish Relations*, 144–45.

[145] Piłsudski told a French journalist in March, "My impression of Bolshevik behavior is that peace is out of the question. I know the Bolsheviks are concentrating large forces on our front. They are making a mistake. . . . Our Army is ready." See Davies, *White Eagle, Red Star*, 88, 98–99; Wandycz, *Soviet-Polish Relations*, 167, 178.

[146] Piłsudski referred to White and Red Russia as "cadavers" and tried to get Wrangel to renew the war in southern Russia so as to stretch the Soviet forces even further. See Davies, *White Eagle, Red Star*, 83–85; Brinkley, *Volunteer Army*, 209–10; Wandycz, *Soviet-Polish Relations*, 141, 147–49, 167, 173; and Ullman, *Anglo-Soviet Accord*, 32–34.

[147] This assessment was made by a group of Soviet historians. Similarly, French general Maxime Weygand later termed the Polish assault a "preventive offensive." See Wandycz, *Soviet-Polish Relations*, 194; and Davies, *White Eagle, Red Star*, 87–88.

When the tide turned in June, however, the Soviets succumbed to their own optimistic delusions. The march on Warsaw was predicated on the belief that the campaign would be over before the Entente could come to Poland's rescue; and by the hope that the Polish proletariat would greet the Red Army as liberators. Despite their awareness of Poland's anti-Russian propensities, their ideological commitment to world revolution left the Soviets vulnerable to this kind of optimism even in the face of considerable contrary evidence. Polish Communists warned Lenin that a revolution in Poland was unlikely, but his normal caution evaporated in the face of the Red Army's successful advance and other apparently encouraging signs. His hopes for a revolution in the West had been renewed by the failure of the right-wing Kapp putsch in Germany in March 1920 (which he saw as analogous to the Kornilov revolt that had preceded the Bolshevik seizure of power in 1917). The first signs from Poland seemed favorable as well, and reports from England and France suggested strong public opposition to any attempt to aid the Poles.[148]

Uncertainty and misinformation contributed to all these miscalculations. Soviet Russia and Poland correctly saw each other as hostile, but the level of animosity was blown out of proportion and the benefits of using force exaggerated. The Soviets erroneously blamed Polish expansionism on imperialist hostility and played up the revolutionary prospects in Poland, while mistakenly viewing working-class opposition to Allied intervention as evidence of Europe's own revolutionary potential.[149] For their part, the Poles overstated their own ability to attract popular support in the borderlands and underestimated the Bolsheviks' military capability and political resolve. Thus, not only was each side relatively ignorant about the other's true capabilities, but each misread its own ability to impose a political solution by force.

In sum, the Russo-Polish war presents a vivid illustration of how revolutions foster security competition and war. Both Russia and Poland faced serious security problems that neither could solve without endangering the

---

[148] Lenin's optimism about revolutionary prospects in Europe was nicely expressed in a message to Stalin in July: "The situation in Comintern is splendid . . . it is time to encourage revolution in Italy. . . . For this to happen, Hungary must be sovietized, and maybe also the Czech Lands and Romania." He later maintained that attacking Poland would help sovietize Lithuania and Poland and aid the revolution in Germany, and that even failure "will teach us about offensive war . . . . We will help Hungary, Italy, and at each step we will remember where to stop." Quoted in Volkogonov, *Lenin,* 388; and also see Lerner, "Revolution from Without," 102–103.

[149] France supported the Polish initiative, but the Polish government made its decisions independently. See Michael Jabara Carley, "Anti-Bolshevism in French Foreign Policy: The Crisis in Poland in 1920," *International History Review* 2, no. 3 (1980), and "The Politics of Anti-Bolshevism: The French Government and the Russo-Polish War, December 1919 to May 1920," *Historical Journal* 19, no. 1 (1976).

other. Both sides saw the other as aggressive, and these perceptions of hostility grew as each state took steps to protect itself. The revolution in Russia had created a seemingly large window of opportunity, and with Poland and Russia both preparing for a war they regarded as inevitable, it is not surprising that the Poles moved first. Ideology reinforced the Soviet belief that Poland was a cat's paw of the Entente and fueled their hopes for an uprising there (although Moscow reversed course when the anticipated uprising failed to occur). Thus, by altering each side's evaluation of the balance of threats, the revolution in Russia made war with Poland virtually inevitable.

## THE STRATEGY OF "PEACEFUL COEXISTENCE"

By late 1920, the failure of Communist revolts in Germany, Hungary, and Austria had cast doubt on Soviet hopes that the revolution would soon spread to the rest of Europe. The abortive invasion of Poland merely reinforced this trend, and Soviet officials began to abandon the belief that war with the West was inevitable and imminent. Instead, Lenin now foresaw an indefinite period of "peaceful coexistence."[150] Soviet Russia was badly in need of peace and economic reconstruction after seven years of war and revolution, and the Bolsheviks also believed that their capitalist opponents needed Russian markets and raw materials. Western hopes that the White armies would soon eliminate the Soviet regime had proved equally mistaken, and leaders on both sides saw the restoration of economic ties as the best way to accelerate recovery and enhance security. This more cooperative approach yielded a number of tangible benefits—although Soviet efforts to build more normal relations were repeatedly compromised by lingering suspicions and their continued commitment to world revolution.

### The Anglo-Soviet Trade Agreement

As noted earlier, Lloyd George had begun to advocate the restoration of trade with Russia at the end of 1919, and he told the House of Commons in February 1920, "We have failed to restore Russia to sanity by force. I believe we can save her by trade." A broad spectrum of British business, labor, and political leaders endorsed this policy, arguing that it would help revive Britain's sagging economy. They also pointed out that other countries

---

[150] As Lenin put it in November 1920: "Today we have to speak, not merely of a breathing space, but of there being a serious chance of a new and lengthy period of development." Quoted in Teddy J. Uldricks, "Russia and Europe: Diplomacy, Revolution, and Economic Development in the 1920s," *International History Review* 1, no. 1 (1979), 61; and see also Jacobson, *When the Soviet Union Entered*, 18–19.

would capture the Russian market if Britain failed to act, and that access to Russian grain would improve Europe's food supply.[151]

The chief motive behind the trade negotiations, however, was political.[152] The government was worried about the impact of Bolshevik propaganda on the British Empire, and Lloyd George saw the restoration of trade as a way to persuade the Soviet government to abandon its subversive activities.[153] Accordingly, the British insisted that any trade agreement include "a mutual undertaking to refrain from hostile actions or measures against the other party and from direct or indirect official propaganda." The fear of Bolshevik subversion, which had once justified support for the Whites, now became a rationale for accommodation.[154]

The Soviet government accepted the British invitation to begin trade talks in June 1920 and sent Leonid Krasin, a Soviet official with extensive business experience, to conduct the negotiations. Despite each side's obvious interest in restoring commercial ties, the negotiations faced several impressive obstacles. British conservatives still mistrusted the Bolsheviks, and their suspicions were not allayed by the Soviets' public commitment to exporting their revolution. The British government was facing renewed unrest in Ireland, several rebellious colonies, a threatened strike by the Miners' Federation, and the formation of a trade union Council of Action to oppose British involvement in the Russo-Polish war. Opponents of the trade talks blamed working-class agitation on the presence of the Soviet delegation, and Field Marshal Sir Henry Wilson began preparations for a military campaign against the Council of Action in August. Sir Basil Thomson, chief of intelli-

---

[151] Lloyd George told Parliament, "The withdrawal of Russia from the supplying markets is contributing to high prices, high cost of living, and to scarcity and hunger. Russia supplied before the war one-fourth of the whole export wheat of the world. . . . The world needs it." Quoted in Coates and Coates, *Anglo-Soviet Relations*, 15–16; and see also Ullman, *Anglo-Soviet Accord*, 15–20, 37; Alfred L. P. Dennis, *The Foreign Policies of Soviet Russia* (New York: E. P. Dutton, 1924), 381–83; Lloyd C. Gardner, *Safe for Democracy: The Anglo-American Response to Revolution, 1913–1923* (London: Oxford University Press, 1984), 328; and Stephen White, *Britain and the Bolshevik Revolution: A Study in the Politics of Diplomacy, 1920–24* (New York: Holmes and Meier, 1979), 15–16.

[152] According to Thompson and White, Lloyd George "had never abandoned his hopes for some sort of peaceful settlement in Russia," and the trade talks provided a cover for discussions whose "real substance had remained pre-eminently political throughout." See Thompson, *Russia, Bolshevism, and Versailles*, 347; and White, *Britain and the Bolshevik Revolution*, 7.

[153] The First Congress of the Communist International in March 1919 had anticipated "open risings and unrest in all colonies" and the liberation of "colonial slaves" by the victorious proletariat. Zinoviev called for a "holy war against British imperialism" at a "Congress of Peoples of the East" in September, the Soviet government established a school for training Asian revolutionaries in Tashkent, and fifteen hundred Bolshevik agents were reported to be in India. See Carr, *Bolshevik Revolution*, 3:245–60; Ullman, *Anglo-Soviet Accord*, 349–51, 357–67; and White, *Britain and the Bolshevik Revolution*, 82–96, 98–104, 116–24.

[154] They also demanded that the Soviet government undertake "not to join in military activities or propaganda conducted by the Asiatic peoples against British interests or the British Empire." Degras, *Soviet Documents*, 1:192–93.

gence for the Home Office, told the Cabinet in September, "The Russian Trading Delegation has become a greater menace to the stability of this country than anything that has happened since the Armistice." And where Lloyd George believed that these dangers could be defused by a combination of an armistice in Poland, a trade agreement with Russia, and the ban on Bolshevik propaganda, to his Conservative opponents the threat of revolution was a sufficient reason to abandon the talks forthwith.[155]

Soviet officials were equally suspicious, and Lenin warned Krasin that "that swine Lloyd George has no scruples or shame in the way he deceives: don't believe a word he says and gull him three times as much."[156] They also exaggerated the revolutionary potential of the British working class, and their misplaced optimism nearly derailed the negotiations completely.[157] In August, the new Soviet negotiator in London, Lev Kamenev, misled the British government regarding the peace terms the Soviets had offered to Poland in order to buy time for the Red Army to reach Warsaw.[158] Kamenev also held several meetings with members of the Council of Action and other left-wing groups and gave £75,000 to the left-wing *Daily Herald*, thereby violating the pledge not to interfere in British domestic politics. The exposure of these deceptions led conservatives to demand the immediate expulsion of the Soviet trade delegation, and Lloyd George promptly informed Kamenev that he was no longer welcome.[159]

---

[155] See Ullman, *Anglo-Soviet Accord*, 51–52, 222–24, 265–85. On the Council of Action, see White, *Britain and the Bolshevik Revolution*, 43–51.

[156] Chicherin wired Krasin that the Foreign Office was "playing a most perfidious and base double-faced game," and Lenin argued that British proposals for a ceasefire in Poland were intended "to snatch victory out of our hands with the aid of false promises." Kamenev's own views were more moderate, and he told Lloyd George in August that he was aware that "neither Poland nor Wrangel had the direct support of the British Government." See Ullman, *Anglo-Soviet Accord*, 116–17, 121–22, 166; and Rohan Butler and J. P. T. Bury, eds., *Documents on British Foreign Policy, 1919–1939*, 1st ser. (London: H.M. Stationery Office, 1958), 8:686.

[157] Soviet officials knew that Lloyd George's interest in a trade agreement was based in part on his desire to end Bolshevik propaganda, and Chicherin told Krasin to "make it clear that we are able to cause [England] serious damage in the East if we so wish." He added: "Picture to them what will happen if we send a Red Army to Persia, Mesopotamia, and Afghanistan. We are awaited and yearned for there, and it is only the moderation of our policy which causes a slow development [of the revolutionary situation] in that country." Quoted in Ullman, *Anglo-Soviet Accord*, 122.

[158] Kamenev omitted the Soviet demand that the Polish Army be disarmed and replaced by a "worker's militia" organized under Russian auspices. Ironically, Chicherin had tried to convince Kamenev to make this demand public in order to stimulate revolutionary attitudes among British workers. See Ullman, *Anglo-Soviet Accord*, 253–64.

[159] After meeting with representatives from the Council of Action on August 7, Kamenev wired Chicherin that "the workers are coming forward on our side, not because we are right or wrong, but because they must be with Russia at all costs, and on any terms." Similarly, after Soviet hopes for the conquest of Poland had faded, Lenin was still instructing Kamenev to "use all your forces to explain [Lloyd George's treacherous aggression] to the British workers. Write articles for them yourself . . . teach them how to agitate among the masses. In this

Lloyd George was still committed to restoring normal relations, however, and he managed to exempt Krasin from the charges leveled at Kamenev. The basic terms for an agreement had been in place since June, but disputes over a final prisoner exchange and several other issues delayed the final signature until March 1921. In addition to the economic arrangements, each party agreed to "refrain from hostile action . . . and from conducting outside its own borders any hostile propaganda." The Soviets specifically pledged not to interfere in India or Afghanistan; Britain made a similar commitment regarding the territories of the former Russian Empire.[160]

The Anglo-Soviet trade agreement illustrates some of the other obstacles that can impede efforts to normalize relations with a revolutionary regime. First, in addition to each side's suspicions and the complications raised by the Russo-Polish war, the negotiations were prolonged by the inherent difficulty of measuring the level of threat that a revolutionary power represents. In 1920, the Bolshevik threat to British interests was based not on Russian economic or military power but on the appeal of Bolshevik *ideas*, yet no one knew how broadly appealing these ideas really were. Men such as Basil Thomson recognized that the Council of Action was primarily an antiwar movement and not a revolutionary organization, but they could not be certain that pro-Bolshevik sentiment was not growing beneath the surface. Indeed, Sir Henry Wilson eventually became convinced that Lloyd George himself was a Bolshevik and tried to organize a campaign to force him from office.[161] In the same way, Kamenev's misconduct while in England followed from the belief that England was ripe for a revolution, even though his efforts to encourage one merely hardened Conservative attitudes and jeopardized the process of accommodation. Thus, uncertainty about Britain's revolutionary potential made both sides less willing to compromise.

Interestingly, other forms of uncertainty may have facilitated the negotiations. Because of their ignorance about economic conditions in Russia, the British may have exaggerated the economic benefits of trade and thereby overstated their own interest in accommodation. Similarly, the claim that a trade agreement would strengthen Russian "moderates" reveals both wishful thinking and the British leaders' continued failure to understand the basic nature of the Soviet system. Interest in the trade agreement was also fueled by unwarranted concerns about Communist subversion in the rest of the British empire, which increased the desire to silence Soviet propaganda.[162]

---

lies your chief task." Ullman, *Anglo-Soviet Accord*, 224–25, 254, 269. On Kamenev's expulsion, see Butler and Bury, *British Documents*, 783–91.

[160] The text of the agreement is reprinted in Ullman, *Anglo-Soviet Accord*, 474–78.

[161] For the details of this fascinating episode, see Ullman, *Anglo-Soviet Accord*, 274–81, 307–308.

[162] Ullman, *Anglo-Soviet Accord*, 415–19, 438–43.

Thus, despite enduring suspicions, continued insecurity, deep domestic opposition, and a host of misconceptions, Britain and Russia managed to take the first step toward a more normal relationship. Above all else, their willingness to do so reveals a growing recognition of the postwar balance of threats. Although Churchill and Curzon continued to oppose the trade agreement on the grounds that Soviet Russia "makes no secret of its intentions to overthrow our institutions everywhere," the claim that the Soviet government could be toppled easily was now untenable. Lloyd George drew the obvious conclusion: if Bolshevism could not be eliminated, then Britain should come to terms with it. Similarly, although Soviet leaders had not abandoned their hope for a world revolution, they were beginning to realize that it might not be imminent and were becoming increasingly aware of their own economic liabilities.[163] Agreeing to mute their propaganda offensive was a small price to pay for recognition and the restoration of trade, which they believed would foster recovery and discourage a renewed imperialist offensive. Not surprisingly, similar calculations were beginning to shape Soviet relations with a number of other countries as well.

### Soviet Diplomacy in Asia

The Soviet government saw the developing world as a natural ally in the struggle against imperialism, and the liberation of the colonial areas received particular attention at the Second Comintern Congress in July and August of 1920.[164] The Soviets began cultivating close ties with Persia, Afghanistan, Turkey, and China during this period. In each case, the desire to enhance the security of the Soviet state proved stronger than the commitment to world revolution.

Before World War I, Persia's position in international politics was defined by the Anglo-Russian Convention of 1907, which gave Russia a sphere of influence in the north of Persia and Britain a sphere of influence in the south. The Soviet government renounced these treaty rights in January 1918, and British forces moved into the vacuum as Russia withdrew. The pro-British Cabinet of Vusūq al-Dawlah signed a new Anglo-Persian treaty on August

---

[163] In November, Lenin admitted, "Though we have not yet won a world victory . . . we have fought our way into a position where we can coexist with the capitalist powers, who now are forced to have trade relations with us." In December, he acknowledged that "the speed, the tempo, at which revolution is developing in the capitalist countries is far slower than it was in our country." Quotations from Ullman, *Anglo-Soviet Accord*, 412; and Lazitch and Drachkovitch, *Lenin and the Comintern*, 1:540.

[164] At the congress, Lenin called for "the closest alliance, with Soviet Russia, of all the national and colonial liberation movements." Lenin, *Selected Works*, 3:434; and Carr, *Bolshevik Revolution*, 3:251–59.

9, 1919; had it been ratified, the agreement would have given Britain de facto control over much of Persia's foreign and domestic policy.[165]

Britain's attempt to solidify its influence in Persia sparked a storm of protests, however, and the situation was complicated further when Mirza Kūchik Khān, a dissident nationalist, proclaimed an independent "Republic of Gilan" in northern Persia and began receiving aid and military backing from the Soviet regime in Azerbaijan. The British withdrawal from northern Persia following a Soviet raid on Enzeli shook Persian confidence in British protection, and the Persian government quickly dispatched an envoy to Russia to negotiate the resumption of relations.

British officials responded by arranging for a Persian colonel, Reza Shah, to conduct a coup d'état in January 1921.[166] This move appeared to backfire when Reza denounced the Anglo-Persian agreement and signed a formal treaty of friendship with the Soviet government in February 1921. The Soviets again renounced any special privileges in Persia, but the treaty authorized their entry "should a third power intervene with armed force" on Persian territory.[167] Reza Shah carefully maintained his freedom of action, however, suppressing local Communists and refusing to allow the Soviet ambassador to enter Tehran until all Soviet forces had withdrawn from Persian soil. The Soviets abandoned Kūchik Khān as relations with Tehran improved, and the "Republic of Gilan" quickly collapsed. All told, the initial course of Soviet-Persian relations offered an early indication of Moscow's willingness to disregard immediate revolutionary objectives for the sake of tangible diplomatic benefits.[168]

Soviet relations with Afghanistan followed a similar pattern. Prior to World War I, Afghanistan lay largely within the British sphere of influence, but the revolution in Russia inspired Emir Amanullah to declare war on

[165] The Soviets renounced any "spheres of influence and exclusive interests" in Persia at Brest-Litovsk, and Lenin sent a formal message to the government of Persia "repudiating all Tsarist privileges and agreements that are contrary to the sovereignty of Persia." See R. K. Ramazani, *The Foreign Policy of Iran, 1500–1941: A Developing Nation in World Affairs* (Charlottesville: University of Virginia Press, 1966), 148–51; Carr, *Bolshevik Revolution*, 3:232 n. 2; George Lenczowski, *Russia and the West in Iran, 1918–1948* (Ithaca: Cornell University Press, 1949), 49–50; and Harish Kapur, *Soviet Russia and Asia, 1917–1927* (Geneva: Michael Joseph, 1966), 154.

[166] For an account of the coup that stresses the British role, see Ullman, *Anglo-Soviet Accord*, 355–57, 376–88; for a version downplaying it, see Ramazani, *Foreign Policy of Iran*, 176–77.

[167] The Soviet-Persian treaty was an obvious attempt to balance against Great Britain, but Reza Shah recognized that Russia was a potential threat as well. He therefore tried to maintain cordial relations with Britain and the United States, a policy consistent with Persia's traditional practice of seeking third powers to balance British and Soviet pressure. See Ramazani, *Foreign Policy of Iran*, 203–11, 308–309.

[168] The Soviet ambassador told Khan, "Soviet Russia at this time regards all revolutionary movements as not only fruitless but also harmful. Therefore, Soviet Russia has adopted a new form of policy as evidenced by its new treaty with the government of Iran." Quoted in Ramazani, *Foreign Policy of Iran*, 191.

Britain in April 1919 and request aid from Moscow. The Soviet government was in no position to help, however, and Amanullah's forces were soon defeated. Britain acknowledged Afghan independence in August, and Lenin subsequently sent a telegram to the emir proposing a trade agreement and a treaty of friendship directed against "the most rapacious imperialist government on Earth—Great Britain."[169]

This offer led directly to the Soviet-Afghan treaty of February 1921. Ideological solidarity played no role in this agreement (if anything, Amanullah's pan-Islamic beliefs were a potential threat to Soviet control in Central Asia), and the treaty failed to prevent a number of serious disagreements between Moscow and Kabul.[170] Like the Persians, the Afghanis were primarily interested in balancing between Britain and Russia, and the Soviet-Afghan treaty was followed by a similar agreement with Great Britain in November.

Russia's policy toward Afghanistan offers further evidence of its pragmatic approach to diplomatic relations with the border states, particularly in areas where the threat of imperialist interference was especially acute. E. H. Carr notes, "What was significant in all this was not the extension of propaganda for world revolution but the succession of Soviet Russia to the traditional Russian role as Britain's chief rival in central Asia."[171]

Soviet policy toward Turkey also sought to counter Western (especially British) influence. Tsarist Russia and the Ottoman Empire had been rivals for centuries, but Soviet Russia and the new Turkish state found themselves united by a number of common interests. Clandestine discussions between Karl Radek and several prominent members of the Young Turk movement had already raised the possibility of a Soviet-Turkish alliance against British imperialism. Chicherin broadcast a radio message warning of the dangers of imperialism and proposing Soviet-Turkish cooperation to "expel the European robbers" in September 1919. Until the summer of 1920, however, Soviet hopes rested primarily on the Turkish Communist movement.[172]

As discussed at length below in chapter 6, foreign interference in Turkey eventually caused a nationalist revolution led by Mustafa Kemal Pasha, a prominent Ottoman general. In April 1920, when the revolt was well underway, Kemal sent a formal note to Moscow proposing diplomatic rela-

---

[169] Lenin's message congratulated the Afghan people on their struggle against "foreign oppressors" and referred to the "wide possibilities for mutual aid against any attack by foreign bandits on the freedom of others." Quoted in Fischer, *Soviets in World Affairs*, 1:285–86.

[170] The main dispute concerned the emir of Bokhara, who was ousted by a Bolshevik "Young Bokharan" movement in September 1920. The emir fled to Afghanistan while his supporters tried to oust the new government, and this incident delayed the Soviet-Afghan treaty for several months. See Kapur, *Soviet Russia and Asia*, 222–28; Carr, *Bolshevik Revolution*, 3:290–92.

[171] *Bolshevik Revolution*, 3:292.

[172] Ibid., 3:244–47.

tions and a joint "struggle against foreign imperialism which threatens both countries."[173]

The harsh peace terms imposed at Versailles accelerated the Soviet-Turkish rapprochement. Turkey and Russia began direct negotiations in Moscow in July, and a Soviet representative arrived in Ankara in November. A friendship treaty emphasizing "their solidarity in the struggle against imperialism" was signed in March 1921; six months later, the Treaty of Kars settled the remaining border disputes between the new Turkish state and the Soviet republics of Georgia, Armenia, and Azerbaijan.[174]

Despite these favorable developments, Russia and Turkey faced several enduring disputes during this period. Both states still coveted parts of Transcaucasia, and Kemal's overt anti-Communism was an obvious irritant as well. Soviet self-interest soon overcame any ideological inclinations, and Russia sent a military delegation to Ankara in November 1921 and agreed to provide a subsidy of 3.5 million gold rubles and enough arms and ammunition for three divisions. This gesture did little to bind Turkey to Moscow, however, and when the Greeks withdrew following their final defeat in 1922, Kemal moved away from Moscow and suppressed the Turkish Communist Party even more vigorously. Turkey also reversed its earlier position on the Turkish Straits and agreed to negotiate a new arrangement with the Western powers. The Soviets' response to these setbacks was restrained, a policy that paid off when Turkey insisted that Russia be invited to participate in the negotiations for a new straits regime.[175]

On the whole, Soviet relations with Persia, Afghanistan, and Turkey are best seen as attempts to balance against a common threat. They are thus entirely consistent with the dictates of realpolitik. At the same time, Bolshevik ideology clearly affected Moscow's evaluation of alternative partners. The 1921 friendship treaties both stabilized Soviet relations with three of its neighboring countries and presented a worrisome threat to Western influence in the developing world. Although maintaining these connections required Moscow to overlook the persecution of local Communist groups, it was a small price to pay for such obvious diplomatic benefits.

The Far East did not at first appear to be an area of great revolutionary potential. The "Congress of Peoples of the East" held in Baku in 1920 focused primarily on the Near East and South Asia, and the first "Congress of Toilers of the Far East" did not meet until January 1922. The Soviet government played a only minor role in the founding of the Chinese and Japanese

[173] Quoted in ibid., 248; and also see Salahi Ramsdan Sonyel, *Turkish Diplomacy, 1918–1923: Mustafa Kemal and the Turkish National Movement* (Beverly Hills, Calif.: Sage, 1973), 39–42.

[174] In an obvious attempt to exclude the Entente, the Treaty of Kars also declared that Russia and Turkey would negotiate a new treaty governing the Straits of Constantinople. See Degras, *Soviet Documents*, 1:237–42, 263–69; and Kapur, *Soviet Russia and Asia*, 107.

[175] See Kapur, *Soviet Russia and Asia*, 109–14, 124–30.

Communist parties, neither of which was a significant political force at this stage.[176] Lack of interest in the Far East was also a function of timing, as Soviet hopes for an imminent "world revolution" had begun to fade by the time the civil war was over and contact with the Far East restored. As a result, Soviet policy in the Far East initially eschewed direct efforts to foment revolution and focused on reasserting traditional Russian interests.

The task of restoring Soviet power in the Far East was complicated by the turbulent situation in China and the ambiguous status of Outer Mongolia and Manchuria. The overthrow of the Manchu dynasty in 1911 had failed to produce an effective government, and China was now ruled by a set of competing warlords. The official government in Beijing saw the collapse of Russian power in 1917 as a chance to reassert its authority over Outer Mongolia and the Chinese Eastern Railway, and China also sent a token force to Vladivostok during the Allied intervention and set up a satellite regime in the Mongolian capital of Urga in the fall of 1919.[177]

The Soviets' policy toward China was quite conciliatory at first, a position that reflected their own weakness. They offered to establish diplomatic relations immediately and renounced Russia's former privileges in Mongolia and Manchuria. Communications between Moscow and the Far East had been cut off by the civil war, however, and this offer did not reach Beijing until March 1920. Circumstances had changed dramatically by then: a group of rival warlords had ousted the Beijing government, the Whites were nearing defeat, and foreign involvement in the civil war was drawing to a close. When a Chinese delegation finally arrived in Moscow in October 1920, therefore, the Soviet government abandoned its earlier offers and insisted on its former rights to the Chinese Eastern Railway. After several false starts and a protracted series of negotiations, the two sides signed a treaty resolving the railway issue and establishing de jure recognition in May 1924. Although Chicherin hailed the agreement as a "historic step in the emancipation of the Eastern peoples," the Sino-Soviet treaty in fact marked the restoration of Russia's former predominance over the official government in Beijing.[178]

[176] The Chinese Communist Party had fewer than one hundred members at its founding in 1921, and Zinoviev told the Congress of the Toilers of the Far East in January 1922 that the Communist parties in the East "represent at present only small groups." See Xenia Eudin and Robert C. North, *Soviet Russia and the East, 1920–1927: A Documentary Survey* (Stanford: Stanford University Press, 1957), 222.

[177] See Allen S. Whiting, *Soviet Policies in China, 1917–1924* (New York: Columbia University Press, 1954), 26–28; Tang, *Russian and Soviet Policy*, 115–21, 360–65; Carr, *Bolshevik Revolution*, 3:491; and Bruce A. Ellemann, "Secret Sino-Soviet Negotiations on Outer Mongolia, 1918–1925," *Pacific Affairs* 66, no. 4 (1993–94).

[178] The treaty renounced several earlier concessions and acknowledged Chinese sovereignty in Outer Mongolia, but it also gave Moscow the dominant role in managing the Chinese Eastern Railway. Allen Whiting observes, "whatever good intentions may have

The reestablishment of Russian power was even more apparent in the conquest of Outer Mongolia. The turmoil in China had enabled a Cossack adventurer named Baron von Ungern-Sternberg to seize power in Urga in February 1921, but his regime was quickly ousted by Soviet troops in July. A Provisional People's Government "invited" the Soviet troops to remain, and the new "Mongolian People's Republic" signed a treaty restoring Russia's traditional predominance in November.[179]

The Japanese withdrawal from Siberia gave an additional boost to Russia's reemergence in the Far East. Pressure from the United States and Great Britain, together with the costs of occupation and the ascendancy of a moderate faction in Tokyo, had led Japan to begin a withdrawal from Siberia in 1922. Talks between Japanese and Soviet representatives were unsucccessful at first, but discussions resumed in January 1923 and culminated in an agreement on "basic rules of relations" two years later.[180] The agreement established normal diplomatic and consular relations and committed both powers to additional negotiations on a range of other issues. It also committed the signatories "to live in peace and amity with each other" and to refrain from "any act overt or covert liable in any way whatever to endanger the order and security" in either state's territory. Negotiations to replace the 1907 Russo-Japanese Fishery Convention began shortly thereafter, and a new agreement was eventually signed two years later.[181]

These advances were possible because both sides were willing to overlook ideological differences for the sake of tangible diplomatic benefits.[182] For the Japanese, détente with the Soviet Union provided a counterweight to British and U.S. pressure. Japanese officials also hoped that access to the Russian market would spur their sputtering economy. The Soviets shared the hope that trade would accelerate their own recovery, but they also sought to prevent the capitalist powers from forming an anti-Soviet bloc in the Far East. Soviet-Japanese cooperation was based entirely on self-

prompted the revolutionary foreign policy of self-denial in 1917–1918, by 1923 Soviet Russia was looking at the Far East exactly as had Tsarist Russia." See his *Soviet Policies in China,* 28–30, 200; and also Eudin and North, *Soviet Russia and the East,* 128–30, 245–48, 316–18; Tang, *Russian and Soviet Policy,* 138–41, 148–78; and Degras, *Soviet Documents,* 1:212–15.

[179] See Thomas T. Hammond, "The Soviet Takeover of Outer Mongolia: Model for Eastern Europe?" in his *Anatomy of Communist Takeovers;* and Carr, *Bolshevik Revolution,* 3:500–502, 511–23.

[180] See Carr, *Bolshevik Revolution,* 1:355–63, 3:536; George Alexander Lensen, *Japanese Recognition of the USSR: Soviet-Japanese Relations, 1921–1930* (Tokyo: Sophia University with the Diplomatic Press, 1970), 11; and Debo, *Survival and Consolidation,* 381–89.

[181] Lensen, *Japanese Recognition,* 177–95 and chap. 9; Eudin and North, *Soviet Russia and the East,* 253; and Edward Hallett Carr, *Socialism in One Country, 1924–1926* (New York: Macmillan, 1958–64), 3:870–76.

[182] This policy required certain compromises; for example, the Soviets agreed to refrain from revolutionary activities in Japan and to observe the elaborate religious etiquette of the imperial court. See Lensen, *Japanese Recognition,* 318, 345.

interest, therefore, and as Lensen notes, "neither party lowered its guard."[183] The Japanese government continued to repress local Communists and kept the Soviet representatives in Japan under surveillance, but these policies did not prevent the two states from making deals. As in Turkey, Persia, and elsewhere, in short, spreading revolution remained a secondary objective.[184]

Viewed as a whole, Soviet relations in Asia were recovering rapidly by the end of 1924. The Soviet government had signed treaties of friendship with Persia, Afghanistan, and Turkey; Japan was withdrawing from Russian soil and moving toward recognition, and Moscow had regained control of most of Siberia and Outer Mongolia and reestablished its primacy in the Chinese Railway Zone. These achievements were facilitated by Moscow's willingness to subordinate its revolutionary goals to more immediate political imperatives, but the lingering commitment to world revolution would have more pernicious effects in the years to come.

### Alliance of Outcasts: The Soviet-German Rapprochement

Allied intervention had pushed Soviet Russia toward Germany even before World War I was over; after the war, the two states were drawn together by their shared status as pariahs and their mutual hostility toward Poland and the Entente. Germany was also the main object of the Bolsheviks' revolutionary ambitions, however, and Soviet policy toward the Weimar Republic combined efforts to cultivate close political and military ties with shakier attempts to spark a proletarian revolution. Repeated failures taught the Soviets to focus on direct diplomatic and military cooperation, but because their faith in Germany's revolutionary potential proved extremely resilient, this learning process was surprisingly slow and erratic.[185]

*Origins.* At the end of World War I, Soviet-German relations were not promising. The Bolsheviks viewed the Social Democratic Party in Germany with contempt and expected it to collapse in the face of continued revolutionary agitation. Relations were also troubled by the presence of German military units in the Baltic region, where they fought against both Allied

---

[183] Japan refused an offer of Soviet aid after a major earthquake in 1924, fearing that the aid mission might be an instrument of Communist subversion. The Japanese Communist Party disbanded in 1924 and was reconstituted in 1925–26, but government repression kept it on the fringes of Japanese political life. See Lensen, *Japanese Recognition,* 137–43; Eudin and North, *Soviet Russia and the East,* 272–79; and Carr, *Socialism in One Country,* 3:883–94.

[184] Lensen concludes in his detailed study of Soviet-Japanese relations, "In the late 1920s, the Russian leaders took pains not to jeopardize Soviet-Japanese relations by overt subversion." *Japanese Recognition,* 361.

[185] See Edward Hallett Carr, *German-Soviet Relations between the Two World Wars* (Baltimore: Johns Hopkins University Press, 1951), 25–26.

and Bolshevik forces during the civil war.[186] Although German officials were already contemplating a closer relationship with Russia, the belief that Bolshevism was both potentially threatening and unlikely to survive dictated a cautious response. Thus, when some German officers proposed an alliance with Soviet Russia against the Versailles Treaty, the commander of the German Army, Wilhelm Groener, stated that "an alliance with Russia, that is with Bolshevism, is something for which I cannot take the responsibility."[187]

Resentment of the harsh terms imposed at Versailles soon overruled these reservations. As one German diplomat later recalled, most of his colleagues "were more sympathetic to the West than to the East" but the Versailles Treaty revealed that "the West was much the more dangerous foe." This view was especially pronounced within the German military, where an alliance with Russia was expected to provide an outlet for German industry in the short term and to improve Germany's bargaining position over time.[188] Groener's successor, General Helmut von Seeckt, believed that the danger of Communist subversion did not preclude closer ties between the two governments, and he soon decided that "a political and economic agreement with Russia [would be] an irrevocable purpose of our policy."[189]

Progress toward rapprochement was swift. Germany had already refused to honor the Allied blockade of Russia in November 1919, and the two states signed an agreement for the release of prisoners in April 1920 and exchanged diplomatic representatives in June. Berlin took a decidedly pro-Soviet position during the Russo-Polish war, refusing to permit the Allies to send military supplies to the Poles across German territory and briefly raising the possibility of territorial adjustments in the event of a Soviet victory.[190] By the end of 1920, Von Seeckt had established a special bureau to study the "possibilities of cooperation with the Red Army" and powerful external forces were now pushing the two countries together despite their ideological differences. Lenin observed in November: "The German bourgeois government madly hates the Bolsheviks, but the interests of the inter-

[186] See Robert G. Waite, *Vanguard of Nazism: The Free Corps Movement in Postwar Germany, 1918–1923* (Cambridge: Harvard University Press, 1952), chap. 5.

[187] At the same time, Groener told the cabinet that Germany "must do what is required to secure Russia's friendship in the future." See Freund, *Unholy Alliance*, 39–40, 43. There is some ambiguous evidence of informal military cooperation between Russia and Germany in October 1919; for details, see Carr, *Bolshevik Revolution*, 3:247, 361.

[188] Quoted in Freund, *Unholy Alliance*, 49–50; and Carr, *Bolshevik Revolution*, 312–19.

[189] Quoted in Freund, *Unholy Alliance*, 46.

[190] On Germany and the blockade, see Robert H. Haigh, David S. Morris, and Anthony R. Peters, *German-Soviet Relations in the Weimar Era: Friendship from Necessity* (Totowa, N.J.: Barnes and Noble, 1985), 61–62. During the Russo-Polish war, some German officials feared that the Red Army might continue on to Germany, while Von Seeckt and others believed that a Soviet victory would be a powerful blow against the entire Versailles system. See Freund, *Unholy Alliance*, 69–73; and Werner T. Angress, *Stillborn Revolution: The Communist Bid for Power in Germany, 1921–23* (Princeton: Princeton University Press, 1963), 80–81.

national situation are pushing it towards peace with Soviet Russia against its own will." And Lenin left no doubt that Russia would welcome these overtures, because "so long as we are alone and the capitalist world is strong, . . . [we are] obliged to utilize [these] disagreements" in the capitalist world. A preliminary economic accord was completed by mid-February, leaving the two states on the brink of a de facto alliance.[191]

Yet despite the failure of the Spartacist uprisings in Berlin in January 1919 and the collapse of the short-lived Communist republic in Bavaria in May, the Soviet government had not lost all hope in the revolutionary potential of the German working class. In March 1920, an abortive coup by right-wing forces (the so-called Kapp putsch) sparked a general strike in Berlin and a brief Communist uprising in the Ruhr. Lenin now predicted that "the time is not far off when we shall march hand in hand with a German Soviet government." Soviet diplomats helped smuggle arms and explosives to Communist groups in Germany, and Soviet officials began to intervene directly in the internal politics of the German working-class movement. These efforts paid off in October 1920, when Zinoviev persuaded a majority of the Independent Socialist Party to unite with the German Communist Party (KPD) and join the Comintern. Three months later, Comintern officials arranged the replacement of the KPD leader, Paul Levi, by officials more amenable to Soviet influence.[192]

These developments culminated in the KPD's attempt to launch a proletarian uprising in March 1921. The party's new leaders were convinced that international and domestic conditions were ripe for revolution, and a delegation from the Executive Committee of the Comintern arrived in Germany at the beginning of March and began to press for an armed insurrection. The KPD proceeded to launch a violent but poorly planned revolt on March 23. Their belief that millions of non-Communist workers would rise up and join them proved false, and the "March action" was quickly crushed.[193]

---

[191] Quoted in Carr, *Bolshevik Revolution*, 3:330–31. As usual, Lenin saw cooperation with capitalist states as a temporary expedient and not a permanent option. In a prescient passage, he noted that "Germany wants revenge, and we want revolution. For the moment our aims are the same, but when our ways part, they will be our most ferocious and greatest enemies." Quoted in Dennis, *Foreign Policies of Soviet Russia*, 154–55; and see also Lionel Kochan, *Russia and the Weimar Republic* (Cambridge: Bowes and Bowes, 1954), 38–39; and Gordon A. Craig, *The Politics of the Prussian Army* (London: Oxford University Press, 1964), 409.

[192] Lenin's statement is quoted in Freund, *Unholy Alliance*, 62. On the Spartacist uprisings and Russian manipulation of the KPD, see Angress, *Stillborn Revolution*, 13–31, 91–100. On the brief career of the Bavarian Soviet Republic, see Allan Mitchell, *Revolution in Bavaria, 1918–1920: The Eisner Regime and the Soviet Republic* (Princeton: Princeton University Press, 1965).

[193] The March action is described in detail by Angress in *Stillborn Revolution*, chap. 4, and "The Takeover That Remained in Limbo: The German Experience, 1918–1923," in Hammond, *Anatomy of Communist Takeovers*, 176–80. Carr reports that KPD membership declined from 450,000 to 180,000 following the March action, and the debacle "set in motion a wave of recriminations which continued for many years to split the party." *Bolshevik Revolution*, 3:337.

A new sense of realism had set in by the time the Third Comintern Congress met in Moscow in June. Lenin now admitted that "the development of the world revolution . . . did not proceed along the direct line we anticipated," and Trotsky told the delegates, "We are not so immediately near . . . to the world revolution. In 1919 we said to ourselves: 'it is a question of months.' Now we say: 'it is perhaps a question of years.' " When viewed alongside the Anglo-Soviet trade agreement and the friendship treaties with Turkey, Afghanistan, and Iran, such statements were a clear sign that hopes for an immediate world revolution was declining. According to E. H. Carr, "a new and well-grounded pessimism about the prospects of the European revolution confirmed and reinforced the drive towards a temporary accommodation with the capitalist world."[194]

By weakening the German left, the debacle in March 1921 made it easier for the German government to move closer to Moscow without fear of leaving itself vulnerable to revolutionary subversion. At the same time, the Allied announcement of the final reparations bill and the French decision to enforce the reparations clause by occupying parts of the Ruhr had increased Germany's interest in an alignment with Russia. Germany and Russia signed a secret agreement in April for the production of German aircraft and munitions in Russia, the economic agreement negotiated in January was completed in May, and the two states agreed to exchange new diplomatic representatives shortly therafter. A German military delegation arrived to provide advice for the restoration of Russia's military industries, and covert meetings between Soviet and German officers continued through the fall.[195]

*Rapallo and After.* The conference in Genoa in April 1922 brought the Soviet-German rapprochement out into the open. The conference was originally intended to create an international consortium for European reconstruction, including the restoration of regular commerce with Russia. As part of the new policy of peaceful coexistence, Chicherin had issued a formal note in October 1921 stating Russia's willingness to make concessions on the debt issue and proposing a conference "to consider the claims of the Powers against Russia and of Russia against the Powers, and to draw up a definite treaty of peace between them." Following a suggestion from Lloyd George, the Supreme Allied Council agreed to combine the two goals and issued a resolution calling for an economic and financial conference "to remedy the paralysis of the European system."[196]

---

[194] Quotations from Eudin and Fisher, *Soviet Russia and the West*, 82–84; and Carr, *Bolshevik Revolution*, 3:338, 385.

[195] See Freund, *Unholy Alliance*, 93–94; Craig, *Politics of the Prussian Army*, 409–11; and Hans W. Gatzke, "Russo-German Military Collaboration during the Weimar Republic," *American Historical Review* 63, no. 3 (1958).

[196] The Soviet note is in Degras, *Soviet Documents*, 1:270–72; the resolution by the Supreme Allied Council is quoted in Eudin and Fisher, *Soviet Russia and the West*, 98. Lenin personally

Unfortunately, the collapse of the Briand government in France returned René Poincaré to power in January 1922, and his steadfast refusal to alter the reparations arrangements ended any possibility of creating an international body for European recovery. Relations with Russia became the main item of discussion by default, and the German delegates began to fear that the Western powers were about to make a separate deal with Russia. To avoid complete isolation, they accepted a Soviet invitation for a clandestine meeting in the nearby town of Rapallo and signed an agreement restoring diplomatic relations between Germany and Russia and committing both powers to consult each other before signing international economic agreements. The Rapallo agreement prevented the Allies from excluding either power from a more general settlement and offered the first sign of an overt Soviet-German alignment.[197]

Soviet-German cooperation expanded considerably the following year. The two states exchanged ambassadors after Rapallo and signed a convention for military cooperation in August. The Soviets supported Germany when the French occupied the Ruhr in January 1923; *Izvestiya* declared, "Soviet Russia *in her own vital interests* cannot permit the final subjugation and destruction of Germany by . . . France and her vassals," and Bukharin announced that the Red Army would probably intervene if Poland tried to take advantage of Germany's present weakness.[198]

The blossoming Soviet-German relationship was soon threatened by another misguided outburst of revolutionary enthusiasm. The Soviets' faith in an imminent world revolution had declined steadily after the March action in 1921, but this objective revived whenever conditions seemed more encouraging. Germany was now reeling from a combination of hyperinflation and domestic political paralysis, and the crisis helped the KPD recover from its earlier setbacks. Several Soviet officials saw the fall of the Cuno cabinet in August as a sign that the German revolution was finally at hand and convinced themselves that the German proletariat would rise up once the initial blow had fallen. Lenin's second stroke had removed him as a restraining influence and the KPD gradually succumbed to Soviet pressure. The day of the insurrection was fixed for November 7, and the campaign began with the appointment of KPD chief Heinrich Brandler and several other KPD members to ministerial posts in the state government of Saxony. The German chancellor, Gustav Stresemann, quickly obtained emergency powers and ordered the army into Saxony to dissolve the local government. At-

---

edited Chicherin's speech to the conference in order to eliminate any revolutionary rhetoric that might alarm the other great powers. See Uldricks, "Russia and Europe," 62 n. 27.

[197] As Freund points out, "more important than the formal contents of the treaty was the fact that Germany and Russia had dared to sign it." *Unholy Alliance*, 118.

[198] See Freund, *Unholy Alliance*, 125–26, 142–46, 152–53.

tempts to organize a general strike were ineffective and the KPD decided to cancel the insurrection. Owing to a failure in communications, however, the KPD organization in Hamburg went ahead and began the revolt, but it was easily suppressed by government forces. The German revolution had fizzled once again, further discrediting the advocates of world revolution. [199]

Beginning in 1920, the Soviet Union and the capitalist powers had made a genuine attempt to establish more normal relations. Soviet leaders began to acknowledge that world revolution might not occur for quite some time—so capitalism and socalism could be forced to coexist indefinitely—and they were increasingly confident that the Soviet regime would survive. Western leaders had reached similar conclusions; although the Soviet regime could not be removed at an acceptable cost, the danger that Bolshevism would spark a wave of revolutionary upheavals seemed less worrisome as well. As their perceptions of threat declined, in short, both sides became more willing to explore a more normal relationship.

The effects of this development were readily apparent. The British Labour Party took office for the first time in January 1924 and Britain and Italy extended de jure recognition to the Soviet Union the following month. A host of other countries (Austria, Denmark, Greece, Hungary, Mexico, and Sweden) soon followed suit, and France finally took the plunge in October. As one Soviet commentator proudly declared in March, the Soviet Union was becoming "a full-fledged member on the chessboard of international diplomacy."[200]

---

[199] According to Werner Angress, "in their eagerness to revive the revolutionary wave in Europe, the Bolshevik leaders succumbed to wishful thinking, to a misjudgment of the true situation in Germany, and to the temptation to sponsor a 'German October' uprising." See *Stillborn Revolution*, 378, 394–97; Isaac Deutscher, *The Prophet Unarmed, Trotsky: 1921–1929* (London: Oxford University Press, 1959), 142–44; Lerner, *Radek*, 123–25; and Edward Hallett Carr, *The Interregnum: 1923–24* (New York: Macmillan, 1954), 201–204, 212–15.

[200] See Eudin and Fisher, *Soviet Russia and the West*, 191–92, 235; Carr, *Interregnum*, 251–52. The United States was the main exception to this trend; it refused to recognize a power "whose conceptions of international relations are so alien to its own, so utterly repugnant to its moral sense." *Foreign Relations of the United States, 1920* (Washington, D.C.: U.S. Government Printing Office, 1936), 3:463–68. Nonrecognition did not prevent the United States from providing extensive relief aid during a devastating famine in 1921–22, but Soviet officials regarded the relief mission with suspicion and did not revise their hostile image of the United States. U.S. business firms did begin establishing economic ties with Russia, however, and U.S. exports to Russia quadrupled between 1923 and 1924 while imports increased sevenfold. The United States was responsible for one-third of Soviet foreign trade in 1925 and by 1927 U.S. investments in Russia were second only to Germany's. See Benjamin M. Weissman, *Herbert Hoover and Famine Relief to Soviet Russia, 1921–23* (Stanford: Stanford University Press, 1974); Joan Hoff Wilson, *Ideology and Economics: U.S. Relations with the Soviet Union, 1918–1933* (Columbia: University of Missouri Press, 1974); Peter G. Filene, *Americans and the Soviet Experiment, 1917–1933* (Cambridge: Harvard University Press, 1967).

The year 1924 was the high-water mark of peaceful coexistence, and Soviet relations with the outside world deteriorated sharply thereafter. Efforts to integrate the Soviet Union into the world economy had failed to generate the expected levels of foreign trade and investment, and the Western powers continued to regard the USSR with considerable suspicion.[201] A series of diplomatic setbacks convinced key Soviet officials that the danger of an imperialist war was growing and contributed to the growing consensus on the need for heightened military preparations.[202]

Tragically, these perceptions of threat were based on a fundamental misreading of Western intentions. The Western powers were not engaged in a new campaign to overthrow Bolshevism; instead, their seemingly hostile reactions were for the most part defensive responses to the activities and rhetoric of the Comintern and the Soviet government's reluctance to explicitly disavow the export of revolution. This reluctance also gave conservatives in the West abundant ammunition with which to oppose a further accommodation with Moscow, and the Manichean nature of the Bolsheviks' ideology made them especially prone to take such setbacks as evidence of imperialist plots, even when their own actions were in fact responsible for them. Thus, the deterioration of Soviet foreign relations after 1924 provides another example of the tendency for revolutionary states to engage in self-defeating spirals of suspicion with foreign powers.

These perceptions of threat played a key role in shaping the emerging doctrine of "socialism in one country."[203] First enunciated by Bukharin in 1923 and formally adopted at the Fourteenth Party Congress in December 1925, the new policy proclaimed that the Soviet Union could build socialism without waiting for the revolution to spread to other countries. Strengthening the Soviet Union was now portrayed as the best way to hasten revolutions elsewhere, and foreign Communists were expected to support the Soviet Union even when doing so jeopardized their own revolutionary prospects.[204] Fi-

---

[201] According to Ullman, the trade agreement with England "resulted in precious little trade—only [£]108 million in the first five years, 282 million in the first decade." See Ullman, *Anglo-Soviet Accord,* 454; and also Uldricks, "Russia and Europe," 69.

[202] See Uldricks, "Russia and Europe," 66–68; and Jacobson, *When the Soviet Union Entered,* 147–50. On Soviet military capabilities, see John Erickson, *The Soviet High Command: A Military-Political History, 1918–1941* (London: Macmillan, 1962), chap. 7; and Mark von Hagen, *Soldiers in the Proletarian Dictatorship: The Red Army and the Soviet Socialist State, 1917–1930* (Ithaca: Cornell University Press, 1990), 202–67.

[203] On "socialism in one country," see Nollau, *International Communism,* 92–96; Eudin and Fisher, *Soviet Russia and the West,* 255–59, 283–85, 289–91; Carr, *Socialism in One Country,* 2:chap. 12; and Jacobson, *When the Soviet Union Entered,* 140–43.

[204] As Stalin put it in 1927, "he is a *revolutionary* who, without reservation, unconditionally, openly and honestly . . . is ready to protect and defend the USSR." Quoted in Degras, *Soviet Documents,* 2:243.

nally, because the West was unlikely to help the Soviet Union acquire the economic and military capacity it needed, the Soviet people would have to do this on their own. Although world revolution remained the touchstone of Soviet foreign policy, the emphasis increasingly shifted toward advancing Soviet state interests.

## The Transformation of the Comintern

The waning faith in world revolution and the priority attached to Soviet state interests was clearly evident in the evolution of the Comintern. Convinced that the Bolshevik triumph in Russia had demonstrated the value of a disciplined, vanguard party of dedicated revolutionaries, Lenin's goal in founding the Comintern was to put this principle to work on a worldwide scale.[205] Accordingly, the platform of the First Comintern Congress in 1919 declared that its aim was to subordinate "so-called national interests to the interests of the international revolution," based on the firm belief that "the epoch of the communist revolution" was at hand.[206]

Yet as we have seen, the initial wave of revolutionary optimism passed quickly. The invasion of Poland brought a burst of renewed hope to the Second Comintern Congress in August 1920, but Lenin cautioned the delegates that "in the great majority of capitalist countries the preparations of the proletariat . . . have not been completed, indeed in many cases have not even been systematically begun." Accordingly, he warned, "The immediate task is to accelerate the revolution, taking care not to provoke it artificially before adequate preparations have been made."[207] Consistent with Lenin's belief that success required a disciplined and centralized revolutionary movement, the Second Congress approved a set of twenty-one conditions for membership, intended to eliminate "reformist" or social-democratic tendencies. Foreign parties were required to accept the decisions of the congress and the Executive Committee of the Comintern (ECCI), and members refusing to accept the Twenty-one Points were expelled. By imposing Bolshevik organizational principles, the congress laid the foundation for Russian dominance within the allegedly "international" movement.[208]

[205] Julius Braunthal, *History of the International*, vol. 2: *1914–43*, trans. John Clark (New York: Praeger, 1967), 177.

[206] Text presented in Jane Degras, ed., *The Communist International, 1919–1943: Documents* (London: Oxford University Press, 1956–65), 1:17–24.

[207] Comintern president Gregor Zinoviev told the congress that "the decisive hour is approaching," and he later recalled that the delegates had followed the progress of the Red Army in Poland "with breathless interest." Quoted in Carr, *Bolshevik Revolution*, 3:188; and Degras, *Communist International*, 1:117–18.

[208] See Degras, *Communist International*, 1:168–72; and also Braunthal, *History of the International*, 170–73; Borkenau, *World Communism: A History of the Communist International* (Ann Arbor: University of Michigan Press, 1962), 197–99; and Carr, *Bolshevik Revolution*, 3:193–96.

Revolutionary hopes had faded further by the Third Congress in July 1921, and Russian primacy was increasingly evident. Zinoviev acknowledged prior to the Congress that "the tempo of the international proletarian revolution is . . . somewhat slowed down," and Lenin told the assembled delegates that "the international revolution we predicted is developing, but not along the straight line we expected." The congress approved a set of theses declaring that "the first period of the post-war revolutionary movement . . . seems in essentials to be over" and concluded that "world revolution will require a fairly long period of revolutionary struggle."[209]

The prospects for rapid revolutionary advances had declined even more by the Fourth Congress in November 1922. Lenin's report struck a pessimistic tone, and he warned that "all the parties which are preparing to take the direct offensive against capitalism in the near future must now give thought to the problem of preparing for a possible retreat." Even the normally exuberant Zinoviev cautioned against "precipitate action and unprepared risings," and Karl Radek, the Polish Bolshevik now serving as ECCI secretary, told the delegates that "the conquest of power as an immediate task of the day is not on the agenda."[210] In response, the congress abandoned the narrow sectarianism of the Twenty-one Points and directed foreign Communists to form "united fronts" with non-Communist labor parties.[211]

The failure of the October 1923 uprising in Germany accelerated these trends. The Fifth Comintern Congress in the summer of 1924 conceded that "the bourgeoisie had succeeded almost everywhere in carrying out successfully its attack on the proletariat." This theme continued at the fifth ECCI plenum in March 1925, with Stalin announcing that "in the center of Europe, . . . the period of revolutionary upsurge has already ended." This view was reinforced by the parallel claim that the Soviet order had stabilized itself as well, which implied that the two systems might coexist for some time. This conclusion strengthened the case for a policy of "socialism in one

---

[209] In his own speech, Trotsky conceded that in 1918–19 "it seemed . . . that the working class would in a year or two achieve State power . . . [but] History has granted the bourgeoisie a fairly long breathing spell." Quotations from Carr, *Bolshevik Revolution,* 3:384; Eudin and Fisher, *Soviet Russia and the West,* 82–87; and Degras, *Communist International,* 1:230, 243.

[210] See Lenin, *Selected Works,* 3:719; Carr, *Bolshevik Revolution,* 3:443–48; Eudin and Fisher, *Soviet Russia and the West,* 122; and Braunthal, *History of the International,* 257.

[211] The aim was to unite the working class under Communist leadership, though the official line alternated between endorsing tactical alliances with the leaders of non-Communist labor parties (the united front "from above") and attempting to persuade members of rival parties to join the Communists (the united front "from below"). See Degras, *Communist International,* 1:307–22; Eudin and Fisher, *Soviet Russia and the West,* 201–202; Carr, *Bolshevik Revolution,* 389–92, 406–12, 422–25, and *Socialism in One Country,* 3:79–81, 525–30, 937–38; and Borkenau, *World Communism,* chap. 12.

country," and the theme of stabilization remained a central tenet of Comintern doctrine for the next four years.[212]

Soviet authority within the Comintern increased as faith in world revolution faded. The Third Congress had declared that "unconditional support of Soviet Russia remains . . . the cardinal duty of the communists of all countries," and despite Lenin's warning that the Comintern was becoming "too Russian," the Fourth Congress approved a reorganization of the ECCI that eliminated the autonomy of the foreign parties and in Braunthal's words, made them "sections of the Russian Communist Party, ruled by the Politburo." This trend was completed at the Fifth Congress in 1924, which confirmed the authority of the ECCI and imposed even greater uniformity and discipline within the Comintern itself, with the Russian Communist Party serving as the model for the rest.[213]

The transformation of the Comintern from an international revolutionary organization to an subordinate agency of the Soviet state reveals a great deal about the evolution of Soviet foreign policy after 1917. The primacy of the Communist Party of the Soviet Union was due to its status as the only party to have successfully gained power, reinforced by the growing dependence of foreign Communist parties on financial subsidies from Moscow. The emergence of the new doctrine was also influenced by the power struggle that followed Lenin's death in January 1924. The slogan of "socialism in one country" was an effective weapon in Stalin's campaign against Trotsky (who maintained that the creation of socialism required a world revolution but later become a leading advocate of increased economic ties with the capitalist states) because it appealed to Russian national pride and allowed Stalin to ,portray his rival as both overly pessimistic and prone to adventurism. Most important of all, "socialism in one country" was the obvious response to dim revolutionary prospects abroad; if world revolution was not on the agenda, then protecting Soviet Russia was the next best thing.[214]

[212] Zinoviev told the congress, "We misjudged the tempo (of world revolution): we counted in months when we had to count in years." In June, Stalin told an audience at Sverdlov University that there would be no proletarian revolution in the West "for ten or fifteen years." These quotations are from McKenzie, *Comintern and World Revolution*, 51; Carr, *Socialism in One Country*, 3:73, 287; and Richard Lowenthal, *World Communism: The Disintegration of a Secular Faith* (London: Oxford University Press, 1964), 292 n. 6.

[213] This was known as the policy of "Bolshevization." See Braunthal, *History of the International*, 261–63; Carr, *Bolshevik Revolution*, 3:445–50, *Socialism in One Country*, 3:92–94, 283, and *Foundations of a Planned Economy, 1926–1929* (London: Macmillan, 1969–1978) 3:122.

[214] Stalin's campaign against Trotsky provided another motive for "Bolshevization," as strict discipline over foreign Communists kept Trotsky from rallying support within the Comintern, where his popularity and prestige remained high. See Carr, *Socialism in One Country*, 3:90–94, 293–300; Deutscher, *Prophet Unarmed*, 146–51, 284–90; and Robert C. Tucker, *Stalin as Revolutionary, 1878–1919: A Study in History and Personality* (New York: Norton, 1973), 384–90.

## The Deterioration of Soviet Foreign Relations

*Relations with the West.* The Soviet strategy of peaceful coexistence was intended to gain recognition and more normal relations with potentially hostile powers. Its successes included the Baltic peace treaties, the Anglo-Soviet trade agreement, the rapprochement with Germany, the friendship treaties with Turkey, Afghanistan, and Persia, and the wave of diplomatic recognitions in 1924. But these advances were undermined by repeated attempts to export the revolution beyond Russia's borders (as in Poland in 1920 and Germany in 1921 and 1923), and the tension between these conflicting objectives impaired Soviet efforts to improve relations with the other major powers.[215] The conflicts eventually triggered sharp Western responses that reignited Soviet fears of an imperialist war and led to a sharp deterioration in the Soviet Union's international position.

This first evidence of trouble was a sudden decline in Anglo-Soviet relations. The Labour government in Britain fell in October 1924, and the Conservative Party's return to power was aided by the publication of the so-called Zinoviev letter, a clever forgery by a group of anti-Bolshevik exiles that seemed to show the Soviet government to be actively working to topple the British government. The Conservative government rejected a new trade agreement that the Labour Party had negotiated the previous year, and Anglo-Soviet relations soon reached their lowest point since 1923.[216]

Soviet relations with France were marred by continued wrangling over the tsarist debts and by French accusations that the Soviets were aiding rebel forces in Morocco. An even more worrisome development was the emerging détente between Germany and the Western powers, beginning with the Dawes plan in August 1924 and culminating in the Locarno treaty of 1925 and Germany's entry into the League of Nations the following year. Zinoviev described the Locarno negotiations as "a direct attempt at a break, an immediate preparation for war against the Soviet Union," and Stalin announced that "the danger of intervention is again becoming real."[217]

---

[215] Thus, the British government threatened to abrogate the trade agreement in May 1923 unless the Soviet Union ceased its propaganda activities in Asia and gave way on a number of other issues. See White, *Britain and the Bolshevik Revolution,* 159–61; Degras, *Soviet Documents,* 1:396–97; Eudin and Fisher, *Soviet Russia and the East,* 184–88; Coates and Coates, *Anglo-Soviet Relations,* 102–19; Carr, *Interregnum,* 168–73; and Jacobson, *When the Soviet Union Entered,* chap. 5.

[216] See Carr, *Socialism in One Country,* 3:34; and Lewis Chester, Stephen Fay, and Hugo Young, *The Zinoviev Letter* (London: Heinemann, 1967). For a recent assessment of this incident, see Jacobson, *When the Soviet Union Entered,* 137–39.

[217] The Dawes plan created less onerous arrangments for the payment of German war reparations, and the Locarno treaty guaranteed Germany's western border and normalized relations with its wartime adversaries. As Stalin told the Fourteenth Party Congress, "If the Dawes Plan is fraught with a revolution in Germany, the Locarno Treaty is fraught with a

The Soviet government responded by reinforcing its diplomatic position and intensifying efforts to rebuild its internal strength, while seeking to avoid a war for which it was obviously unprepared. New nonaggression treaties were negotiated with Turkey, Afghanistan, and Persia, and a similar pact with Lithuania was completed in September 1926.[218] The Soviets also took steps to strengthen ties with Germany, beginning with a new commercial agreement in October 1925. Chicherin paid official visits to Poland and France to remind Germany of the benefits of its Russian connection, and his efforts paid off when the Soviet Union and Germany signed a new nonaggression treaty in April 1926. Soviet officials were increasingly convinced that Germany was not a reliable partner, however, especially after the Social Democrats began a public campaign against the covert military relationship with the Soviet Union.[219]

Similar setbacks occured during 1926 and 1927. The Soviet government's unwise endorsement of a general strike in England prompted new denunciations by British Conservatives, and British officials also blamed a series of anti-Western strikes in Shanghai on Soviet interference. The Foreign Office eventually issued a formal protest against Soviet activities in February 1927. The British government broke diplomatic relations and suspended trade in May after a raid on the office of the Soviet trade mission in London uncovered evidence of Soviet espionage.[220] Relations with France remained distant as well, and though negotiations on the thorny issue of Russian debts had resumed in 1924, the talks made little progress. Relations deteriorated further after the Soviet ambassador signed a bellicose Communist proclamation and the French government insisted on his recall.[221] Soviet relations with Poland

---

new war in Europe." Similarly, Chicherin's report to the CPSU Central Committee in October 1924 warned of a "recently opened offensive of world imperialism," and Radek greeted 1925 by declaring in *Pravda* that the Soviet Union was entering "a period of international dangers." Quotations from Uldricks, "Russia and Europe," 73; Jacobson, *When the Soviet Union Entered*, 144, 146; and Carr, *Socialism in One Country*, 3:248–49.

[218] See Eudin and Fisher, *Soviet Russia and the West*, 277–83, 323–37; Carr, *Socialism in One Country*, 3:38–40, and *Foundations of a Planned Economy*, 3:37–46.

[219] The German ambassador to Russia called the Soviet-German alignment "a marriage of necessity," and a former German diplomat suggests that "no love was lost between the policy makers of the two states; it was a purely pragmatic arrangement between two governments sharing a few problems and having a few enemies in common." By 1927, an *Izvestiya* correspondent warned that "ultimately the German bourgeoisie, capitalist Germany, will take its stand where its fundamental class interests dictate." See Gustav Hilger and Alfred G. Meyer, *The Incompatible Allies: A Memoir-History of German-Soviet Relations, 1918–1941* (New York: Macmillan, 1953), 150; Jacobson, *When the Soviet Union Entered*, 128, 160–62, 185–86; Uldricks, "Russia and Europe," 75; and R. Craig Nation, *Black Earth, Red Star: A History of Soviet Security Policy, 1917–1991* (Ithaca: Cornell University Press, 1992), 60.

[220] See Eudin and Fisher, *Soviet Russia and the West*, 341–45; Carr, *Foundations of a Planned Economy*, 3:18–30; and Coates and Coates, *Anglo-Soviet Relations*, 251–90.

[221] The declaration called for the "defeat of all bourgeois states which wage war against the Soviet Union," and retired general Ferdinand Foch added to the tensions by stressing the continued threat of Bolshevism in a public interview. See Carr, *Foundations of a Planned Economy*, 3:64–65.

and the Baltic states were equally guarded, and Piłsudski's return to power in 1926 and the assassination of the Soviet ambassador in Warsaw in June 1927 gave the Soviet government additional grounds for concern. Taken together, these developments reinforced the growing Soviet belief that the capitalist powers were preparing to wage a counterrevolutionary war against them.

*The Chinese Debacle.* The deterioration of the Soviet position in Europe was matched by an even more dramatic decline in its position in China. In addition to reestablishing relations with the official government in Beijing, Moscow had been carefully cultivating Sun Yat-sen's Guomindang (GMD) movement since the early 1920s. Although Sun was not a Marxist, he shared the Soviets' opposition to imperialism and saw their success in Russia as a model for his own efforts in China. He had agreed to permit members of the newly formed Chinese Communist Party (CCP) to join the GMD as individuals in June 1922 (though he rejected proposals for a formal alliance between the two parties), and Sun and a Soviet emissary issued a joint statement in January 1923 reaffirming Soviet support for the "completion of [China's] national unification and . . . full national independence." This announcement was immediately endorsed by the ECCI, which described the GMD as "the only serious national revolutionary group in China," and the CCP was ordered to unite with it despite Sun's belief that the Soviet system was not appropriate for China. Thus, even as the Soviet treaty with the Beijing government neared completion, Moscow was moving to align itself with one of Beijing's main opponents.[222]

Until 1927, the tacit alliance between the GMD and the CCP provided the clearest example of the "united front" doctrine in action, and China became the object of the Soviet government's most extensive and sustained effort to export revolution. The Soviet government provided extensive material support to the GMD; Sun sent his chief of staff, Chiang Kai-shek (Jiang Jieshi), to Moscow for military training; and the Soviets assigned Michael Borodin, an experienced Bolshevik agent, to serve as the Comintern representative at GMD headquarters in Canton (Guangzhou). Soviet military aid strengthened the GMD armies, and Borodin contributed to transforming the GMD into a more disciplined and effective organization.[223]

---

[222] The joint statement is reprinted in Degras, *Soviet Documents*, 1:370–71; and see also Gottfried-Karl Kindermann, "The Attempted Revolution in China: 1924–27," in Hammond, *Anatomy of Communist Takeovers*, 194–95. The Comintern also directed the CCP to "oppose every GMD attempt to court the capitalist powers" and warned that the CCP "must not . . . merge with the GMD and . . . must not furl up its own banner." Quoted in Eudin and North, *Soviet Russia and the East*, 141, 217–19, 343–46; and Carr, *Socialism in One Country*, 3:690–91.

[223] On Borodin and his role, see Dan Jacobs, *Borodin: Stalin's Man in China* (Cambridge: Harvard University Press, 1981); and Lydia Holubnychy, *Michael Borodin and the Chinese Revolution, 1923–25* (Ann Arbor, Mich.: University Microfilms for the East Asian Institute of Columbia University, 1979); Robert C. North, *Moscow and Chinese Communists* (Stanford: Stan-

This policy seemed to pay off handsomely at first. CCP membership was growing rapidly, and Soviet optimism continued to rise after Sun Yat-sen's death in March 1925 and a series of violent labor disputes in Chinese industrial centers.[224] Because the GMD was hostile to imperialism and far stronger than the Chinese Communists, however, Soviet interests still seemed better served by courting the former rather than by trying to sponsor an independent social revolution by the CCP.[225]

In the end, Soviet hopes proved illusory and the united front ended in disaster. The GMD split into left- and right-wing factions after Sun Yat-sen's death in 1925, and the latter group became increasingly worried about Communist influence. Chiang Kai-shek was now the dominant figure within the GMD, but his plans for a military campaign against the northern warlords placed him at odds with his Soviet advisors, who wanted to consolidate Communist influence within the GMD before trying to subdue their other opponents. Thus, when Borodin left Canton in March 1926 to consult with other Chinese leaders, Chiang arrested a number of prominent CCP leaders and purged the rest.[226]

The Soviets responded with a series of fatal blunders. Convinced that a social revolution was impossible and that Chiang was still a reliable partner, Stalin ignored his recent coup and continued to endorse the united front. The Great Northern Campaign was launched in July 1926, and the GMD armies had seized most of central and eastern China by the end of the year. The campaign brought an upsurge in peasant support, inspiring the left wing of the GMD and the CCP to advocate more aggressive efforts to prepare an agrarian uprising. Stalin rejected this suggestion to avoid alienating Chiang further, although Borodin did try to curtail Chiang's authority by

---

ford University Press, 1963), 72–76; Carr, *Socialism in One Country*, 3:694–700; and C. Martin Wilbur and Julie Lien-ying How, *Missionaries of Revolution: Soviet Advisors and Nationalist China, 1920–27* (Cambridge: Harvard University Press, 1989), chap. 2.

[224] CCP influence was especially strong in the so-called May 30 movement in Shanghai. CCP membership increased from roughly 1,000 in May 1925 to 30,000 in July 1926 and nearly 60,000 by April 1927, and membership in the associated Socialist Youth Corps rose from 2,000 in 1925 to 35,000 in 1927, with nearly one million workers and farmers under their political control. See Kindermann, "Attempted Revolution in China," 205; and Carr, *Foundations of a Planned Economy*, 3:789–90.

[225] Zinoviev told the Fourteenth Party Congress in December 1925: "There were moments when the young Chinese Communist Party and the leaders of the Shanghai trade unions [were] in favor of sharpening the conflict to the point of armed insurrection. . . . Comintern gave a directive against these moods, recommending the party to execute a gradual putting on of brakes." Quoted in Carr, *Socialism in One Country*, 3:738–39.

[226] See Wilber and How, *Missionaries of Revolution*, 103–106, 188–95, 250–51; Kindermann, "Attempted Revolution in China," 195–97, 206; North, *Moscow and Chinese Communists*, 85–87; and James Pinckney Harrison, *The Long March to Power: A History of the Chinese Communist Party, 1921–27* (New York: Praeger, 1972), 77–80.

shifting the GMD headquarters to Wuhan and arranging to remove Chiang from his party posts.[227]

Chiang quickly reestablished his primacy. When pro-CCP laborers in Shanghai launched a violent uprising in February 1927, Chiang kept his own forces outside the city while the workers battled the local authorities. Still convinced that Chiang could be trusted, Stalin ordered the Communist forces to hide their weapons and avoid a direct conflict with Chiang's forces, telling the ECCI that Chiang and the Right-GMD had to be "utilized to the end, squeezed like a lemon and then thrown away." But it was Chiang who did the squeezing: after reaching an agreement with the local warlords, his troops began a bloody campaign against the disarmed and helpless Communists in Shanghai. "Within a few days," writes Robert North, "the Shanghai Communists and their labor supporters were all but annihilated." Stalin still refused to permit the CCP to withdraw from the united front, however, and ordered it to maintain its alliance with the Left-GMD and to purge the united front of "unreliable elements."[228] The Left-GMD saw this order as a threat to their own positions and promptly expelled the Communists from Wuhan in July. With the united front in ruins and the CCP now isolated, Stalin at last authorized an armed insurrection. These poorly planned uprisings were crushed, and by the end of 1927 the Soviet Union's entire Chinese policy lay in ruins.[229]

The debacle in China illustrates why exporting a revolution is difficult, particularly when a revolutionary state tries to guide the revolution from afar. Soviet officials misjudged events in China because they were poorly informed about conditions there and because they tried to apply principles that had worked in Russia to a fundamentally different set of circumstances. Soviet efforts to promote revolution in China may have aided the eventual triumph of the CCP by helping it acquire greater discipline and organizational coherence, but a successful revolution would take place only after the Chinese Communists abandoned unquestioned obedience to Moscow and developed their own revolutionary strategy.[230]

*Prelude to Stalinism: The War Scare of 1927.* The deterioration of the Soviet Union's international position culminated in the so-called war scare of 1927, which ended with the expulsion of Trotsky and Zinoviev and cleared the way for Stalin's "revolution from above." Although some authors have

---

[227] See North, *Moscow and Chinese Communists*, 90–93.

[228] Ibid., 97, 105–107.

[229] To make matters worse, the warlord regime in Beijing had broken relations with Moscow and executed twenty Communists in April, after a raid on the Soviet embassy uncovered evidence of subversive activities.

[230] See Wilber and How, *Missionaries of Revolution*, 416–17. For a general account of the debacle in China, see Conrad Brandt, *Stalin's Failure in China, 1924–1927* (Cambridge: Harvard University Press, 1958).

interpreted this episode as a Stalinist hoax devised to undermine his domestic rivals, the available evidence suggests that the Soviet fear of war was genuine.[231] Stalin had warned in October 1926 that "the period of peaceful coexistence was fading into the past," and Bukharin issued an even more ominous warning in January. Their statements triggered a flurry of hoarding and other signs of public alarm, which Stalin sought to dispel in March. These events suggest that the war scare was a genuine response to international trends and did not originate with Stalin alone.[232]

The war scare became overt at the Central Committee Plenum in April 1927, when Stalin's opponents attempted to blame him for the Soviet Union's deterioriating international position. By arguing that war was imminent, however, they unwittingly undermined their own positions. Stalin accused his opponents of sowing dissension in the face of a growing external threat and declared that "the chief contemporary question is the threat of a new imperialist war . . . against the Soviet Union in particular."[233]

Stalin's counterattack discredited his opponents and the war scare passed quickly, but it was more than just a manifestation of the internal struggle for power. Soviet diplomats, worried about the risk of war, went to great lengths to persuade France and Germany not to imitate Britain's decision to break relations. The Soviet delegation to the World Economic Conference stressed the danger of war and the need for economic ties between the two social systems, and Litvinov made a dramatic appeal for total disarmament at a League of Nations conference in November. Finally, Stalin's report to the Fifteenth Party Congress in December 1927 warned that the period of "peaceful coexistence" was giving way to "a period of imperialist attacks" and he reminded the party, "Our task consists in postponing the war, in buying ourselves off by paying a tribute to the capitalists, and in taking all measures to maintain peaceful relations."[234] Thus, the fear of war seems to

---

[231] Examples of the "hoax" interpretation include Adam B. Ulam, *Expansion and Coexistence: Soviet Foreign Policy, 1917–1973* (New York: Praeger, 1974), 165–66; Fischer, *Soviets in World Affairs,* 2:739–42; and Robert V. Daniels, *The Conscience of the Revolution* (Cambridge: Harvard University Press, 1960), 285–86.

[232] In March, Bukharin declared, "We have no guarantee against an invasion of our country. It is of course not a question of today or tomorrow, or even of next month, but we have no guarantee whatever that it may not come in the spring or the autumn." Stalin's view at this point was much less alarmist, and he argued the Soviet Union's "active policy of peace . . . makes war with our country difficult." Quoted in Alfred G. Meyer, "The War Scare of 1927," *Soviet Union/Union Sovietique* 5, no. 1 (1978), 4–6; and see also John Sontag, "The Soviet War Scare of 1927," *The Russian Review* 34, no. 1 (1975).

[233] Foreign observers reported that the fear of war was evident "even among cautious members of the [Soviet] government" and there was another wave of hoarding during the summer. Quoted in Meyer, "War Scare," 9–16; and see also Degras, *Soviet Documents,* 2:233–35; Carr, *Foundations of a Planned Economy,* 3:8–11; and Fischer, *Soviets in World Affairs,* 2:740.

[234] For these quotations and further discussion, see Meyer, "War Scare," 3, 24–25; Carr, *Foundations of a Planned Economy,* 3:27; Sontag, "Soviet War Scare," 72–73; and Eudin and Fisher, *Soviet Russia and the West,* 407–409.

have been genuine, even if it also gave Stalin a golden opportunity to eliminate his principal rivals. It also provided a rationale for the brutal strategy of autarky and forced industrialization that Stalin initiated several years later, for if the West was unremittingly bent on war, then the Soviet Union needed the capacity to defend itself and could not expect the capitalist states to help them acquire the necessary forces.

Yet as noted earlier, Soviet perceptions of a growing capitalist danger were largely a mirage. None of the Western powers was planning to attack the Soviet Union, and their anti-Soviet policies were for the most part defensive responses to Soviet actions. Unfortunately, the Soviets' enduring belief in capitalist hostility and their long-range commitment to world revolution combined to undo the progress achieved after 1921 and prevent the Soviet Union from taking its place as a fully accepted member of the international community.

In one sense, the doctrine of "socialism in one country" was the culmination of a process that had begun as soon as the Soviets gained control. Having successfully seized state power, the Bolsheviks automatically acquired an interest in preserving their position within a particular geographic area. In practice, this meant defending the security of the Soviet state, so when the revolution failed to spread as expected, Russia's new leaders concentrated on enhancing their hold on power within their own borders. Soviet diplomacy began forging working relations with a number of foreign powers, and the Comintern was converted from an international revolutionary party into an obedient tool of Soviet policy.

In another sense, however, "socialism in one country" marked a return to the harsh and conflictive image of international relations that had dominated Soviet perceptions during the civil war. Soviet officials gave up their hopes of integrating Russia into the world economy and became increasingly fearful of a renewed imperialist war. If world revolution was no longer seen as imminent, neither was normalization. Thus, the Soviet Union would have to go it alone, and Stalin's formula of autarky, forced industrialization, and the primacy of Soviet state interests was the logical (and tragic) result.

## CONCLUSION: THE RUSSIAN REVOLUTION AND BALANCE OF THREAT THEORY

The international impact of the Russian Revolution was to intensify the level of security competition between states. To be sure, the revolution did reduce the level of conflict briefly by taking Russia out of World War I, and a weakened Russia would have been a ripe source of conflict even if Nicholas II had retained his throne. By dissolving the tsarist empire and bringing to power a messianic and xenophobic revolutionary movement, however, the Bolshevik revolution raised the level of international tension substantially. In the short term, it opened a window of opportunity and gave other states additional incentives to intervene. Over the longer term, it created a new state that was fundamentally hostile to the prevailing international order and openly committed to spreading its principles to other countries. Because one simply cannot imagine tsarist Russia adopting such a policy or having the same impact on the other great powers, we may safely infer that the revolution was responsible for the intense suspicions that characterized Soviet foreign relations after 1918.

### The Balance of Power

The revolution in Russia caused a major shift in the balance of power in Eurasia. As the theory in chapter 2 predicts, this shift exacerbated existing incentives for conflict and created a number of new ones.

The initial motive behind Allied intervention in Russia was the fear that the revolution would shift the balance of power in favor of Germany. After the war, European intervention was fueled by the Allies' concern over Russia's place in the postwar balance of power and by each great power's desire to enhance its position vis-à-vis the others. A similar pattern occurred in the Far East: Japan and China endeavored to take advantage of Russia's weakness while the United States tried to check Japanese ambitions and support the largely nonexistent forces of Russian liberalism. The Russo-Polish war sprang from similar roots, insofar as Poland's leaders believed that expansion was necessary for their long-term security and that Russia's weakness was an opportunity Poland could not ignore.

The détente that began after the civil war can also be traced to states' growing awareness of the true balance of power. The end of the Russo-Polish war offers the most obvious example; according to Pyotr Wandycz, "peace became possible only after both sides tried to accomplish their aims and failed. At that point there was no alternative."[235] Similarly, the Allies withdrew from Russia after recognizing that removing the Bolsheviks would require a much larger commitment of men and money than they were willing to undertake. Balance-of-power logic is also revealed in the rapprochement between Soviet Russia and Weimar Germany and the friendship treaties with Afghanistan, Turkey, and Iran. In each case, isolated powers joined forces to counter a specific external threat, despite their obvious ideological differences.

[235] *Soviet-Polish Relations,* 290; and see also Carr, *Bolshevik Revolution,* 3:216.

The diplomacy of the Russian Revolution highlights the tendency for revolutionary states to assume the worst about other states' intentions, an assumption that is usually reciprocated. Although both the Soviets and the onlookers had legitimate grounds for suspicion, each side interpreted the other's actions in ways that reinforced its initial suspicions and inflated the perceived level of threat even more. In the end, the Soviet susceptibility to a highly paranoid view of world politics helped derail the initial process of normalization and ensured that Soviet foreign relations would remain deeply conflictive for several more decades.

The belief that the capitalist world was intrinsically hostile was a central tenet of Bolshevik ideology, so Soviet Russia tended to view the behavior of other powers in the least generous terms possible. The Soviets saw Western support for the Whites as directed primarily against them (though the policy was originally inspired by fear of Germany), and they interpreted the Entente's offers of support prior to Brest-Litovsk as an insincere attempt to lure them to their doom. Allied policy at the Paris Peace Conference was seen as hostile and duplicitous, and the Soviets subsequently accused Britain and France of instigating the Polish invasion in 1920 as well. These inferences were all of dubious validity: the Allies were sincerely interested in supporting the Russian war effort, on condition the Bolsheviks be willing to resume fighting; Allied policy at the peace conference owed more to uncertainty and internal disagreements than to any careful plan to overthrow Soviet Russia; and the Polish invasion, which was Piłsudski's own doing, was condemned by most Western officials. Yet the Soviets clung to their idea of imperialism as intrinsically hostile, even after the capitalist powers had begun to trade with Russia and several had provided extensive relief aid during the famine in the Ukraine in 1921–22. The belief that Soviet Russia could at best achieve a temporary accommodation with capitalism justified the Bolsheviks' continued efforts to subvert the Western powers and impeded the establishment of more normal relations despite the other great powers' genuine interest in relaxing tensions.

The Entente powers also failed to appreciate how their own actions reinforced Soviet suspicions. Allied intervention in Russia during World War I was driven by the incorrect belief that the Bolsheviks were German agents, and the Treaty of Brest-Litovsk was seen as evidence of pro-German sympathies rather than as a desperate concession to German power. Subsequent Soviet peace offers never received adequate attention (because Allied statesmen did not trust them and were loathe to confer recognition on the new regime), and accommodation was further discouraged by the belief that it would do no good. Although Wilson and Lloyd George wanted to respond favorably to the Soviet peace offensive, their efforts foundered in the face of opposition from France, the White leaders, and conservatives at home. Finally, the Allies do not seem to have realized that the Soviet government would inevitably regard their stated disinterest in interfering in Russia as wholly insincere, since Allied troops were already present on Russian soil and the Entente was already supporting the Whites militarily. The result was the worst of all possible worlds: these inconsistencies appeared to the Soviets as evidence of imperialist duplicity, while the Entente believed their own actions to have been part of a genuine if not very extensive effort to bring peace to a divided and war-ravaged Russia.

Conflict between Russia and the West was not due solely to this sort of misperception, of course, and both sides also had legitimate grounds for suspicion. The Bolsheviks did aspire to lead a worldwide movement that would usher in the socialist epoch; for this reason, conservatives such as Lansing, Foch, and Churchill regarded Bolshevism as the embodiment of evil, and even such moderates as Lloyd George and Wilson preferred that Russia be governed by a non-Bolshevik regime. At the same time, however, both sides seem to have underestimated the existing willingness to compromise. They therefore may have neglected to pursue promising opportunities for accommodation; for example, a deal along the lines of either the Prinkipo proposal or the terms worked out by Bullitt in March 1919 would have been no worse, and probably considerably better, than continued Western involvement in the civil war. Given the mutual suspicions and the absence of established channels of communication, however, these possibilities never had much chance.[236] Similarly, a less confrontational policy would have made it easier for the Soviets to end Western intervention and obtain the economic assistance they so desperately needed.

While it never vanished completely, the extreme hostility that shaped international relations during the Russian Civil War began to ease after 1920. Both the Soviets and their peers abroad remained wary, but they were increasingly willing to attempt limited forms of cooperation. Lenin's New Economic Policy was seen by many as a sign of moderation, and the Soviets agreed to suspend hostile propaganda as part of the Anglo-Soviet trade agreement (though these activities continued under the auspices of the Comintern). Soviet representatives attended international conferences in Genoa and Lausanne in 1922 and 1923, and the government signed friendship treaties with Turkey, Iran, and Afghanistan despite the anti-Communist policies that each regime pursued at home. By 1925 Moscow had established diplomatic relations with most of the other great powers and was playing an increasingly active role in other international forums. As each side's image as incorrigibly aggressive eroded, the level of threat declined and more normal relations became possible. The tragedy of Soviet diplo-

---

[236] On this point, see Thompson, *Russia, Bolshevism, and Versailles*, 379–80, 396–97.

macy lies in the fact that Bolshevik ideology predisposed them to assume the worst about their adversaries, and to interpret any setback as evidence of renewed imperialist aggression. And from the Soviet perspective, the greater tragedy is that their own self-defeating actions undoubtedly left them unnecessarily isolated and insecure.[237]

### Offense, Defense, and the Export of Revolution

The early history of revolutionary Russia supports the hypothesis that revolutions nourish a state's perceptions of a particular sort of offensive advantage. The Bolsheviks were convinced that a worldwide socialist revolution was inevitable and their long-term survival depended on it. Although Lenin warned against placing too much hope in an imminent world revolution, the belief that their triumph in Russia would soon be repeated elsewhere affected Soviet policy at several critical moments. The assumption of a forthcoming wave of revolutions across Europe cost them considerable territory at Brest-Litovsk. It also meant the Soviets viewed the formation of the Hungarian and Bavarian Soviets, the Kapp putsch in Germany, the army mutinies and labor disturbances in France, and the "Hands Off Russia" movement in England as signs that the revolutionary tide was still rising. The decision to invade Poland in 1920 rested on similar expectations, as did the Soviets' continued reliance on propaganda and subversion despite the negative responses these activities provoked.

Over time, however, a steady diet of failure eroded Soviet hopes for an imminent upheaval in the West. Indeed, where the Second Congress of the Comintern had breathlessly tracked the Red Army's progress in Poland, the Third Congress admitted that "the world revolution . . . will require a prolonged period of revolutionary struggle."[238] Although Soviet hopes rebounded on occasion, the ideal of world revolution was gradually subordinated to the more immediate need to enhance the power, security, and status of the Soviet state. But because the goal of world revolution was never formally abandoned, other states remained wary long after the danger had faded.

Perceptions of the offense-defense balance affected foreign responses to the revolution as well, in mixed ways. During World War I, advocates of Allied intervention argued that the Central Powers could easily exploit vast areas of Russia while a modest Allied force could avert this possibility at relatively low cost. After the war, Soviet hopes that the revolution would spread to Europe were mirrored by Western fears that the Bolsheviks might be right. Many Western statesmen believed Europe was vulnerable to revolutionary subversion in the aftermath of World War I, justifying their sup-

---

[237] See Uldricks, "Russia and Europe," 80–81.
[238] Quoted in Eudin and Fisher, *Soviet Russia and the West*, 87.

port for the Whites during the civil war and playing a key role in the Entente's decision not to recognize the new regime.[239] The belief that the Soviet regime was fragile and unpopular encouraged these policies as well: support for the Whites made more sense if the Bolsheviks were vulnerable, and accommodation would be unnecessary if the Soviet regime were about to collapse.[240] Thus, the impression of Soviet Russia as both dangerous and vulnerable led to repeated attempts to isolate or overthrow it, even if these efforts were not especially extensive.

Indeed, despite the widespread consensus that Bolshevism was a threat, there was little agreement on how to respond to it. The differences were based largely on competing assessments of the offense-defense balance, and in particular, on the expected cost of trying to overcome the new regime. Churchill and Clemenceau thought Bolshevik Russia would be relatively easy to remove, while Wilson and Lloyd George believed intervention would merely increase the appeal of Bolshevism both at home and abroad. And once it became clear that ousting the Soviet regime would require a major Western effort—owing to both Russia's vast size and the Bolsheviks' unexpected staying power—the Allies abandoned their halfhearted efforts to topple it and turned to a combination of containment and accommodation instead.

Thus, perceptions of a profound offensive advantage over Soviet Russia were not universal, especially with respect to the prospects for foreign intervention. Although they regarded the Soviet regime as illegitimate and unpopular, the leaders of the Entente quickly realized that their own populations would not support a large-scale effort to overturn it. As a result, they were forced to pin their hopes on the corrupt, contentious Whites or on stillborn schemes for action by various Eastern European forces. The Allies' awareness that intervention in Russia would not be easy stands in marked contrast to the cavalier approach to intervention that France's enemies adopted in 1792–93, and is the main reason why the revolution in Russia did not lead to a larger war.[241]

---

[239] According to William Chamberlin, "probably the decisive factor in bringing about a continuation of the policy of limited intervention was the fear, by no means unreasonable or ungrounded in 1919, that Bolshevism in one form or another might spread to other European countries." *Russian Revolution*, 2:152.

[240] In November 1917, the British Foreign Office reported that "Bolshevism was probably on its last legs," and U.S. ambassador David Francis declared, "This Bolshevik government can not survive." According to Phillip Knightley, "in the two years from November 1917 to November 1919, the *New York Times* reported no fewer than ninety-one times that the Bolsheviks were about to fall or, indeed, had already fallen." See Robert K. Murray, *Red Scare: A Study of National Hysteria, 1919–1920* (New York: McGraw-Hill, 1964), 40; and Phillip Knightley, *The First Casualty: The War Correspondent as Hero, Propagandist, and Mythmaker* (New York: Harcourt Brace Jovanovich, 1975), 138.

[241] Even Churchill opposed the use of conscripts in Russia, and recalled that "it would not have been right after the Great War was over, even had it been possible, to use British, French, or American troops in Russia." *Aftermath*, 286.

The Russian Revolution confirms that expectations about the likelihood of a revolution spreading (or collapsing) will have a powerful effect on relations between a revolutionary state and its main foreign adversaries. It also suggests that states' initial assessments are not cast in stone, and the security competition sparked by a revolution can ease once each side's initial expectations are dispelled.

## Uncertainty and Misinformation

Uncertainty and misinformation helped magnify each side's perceptions of threat, thereby contributing to the security competition that followed the Russian Revolution. During World War I, for example, British and French responses to the revolution were based on a series of unlikely scenarios—involving the seizure of Allied supplies, the arming of German and Austrian prisoners of war, and the possible use of Vladivostok as a German U-boat base. The worries were baseless, but the Western powers could not simply reject them out of hand. The United States was vulnerable to this problem as well, as revealed by Wilson's decision to send U.S. troops to northern Russia to guard Allied stores that were no longer there. France's expedition to Odessa in 1918 was based on its ignorance about conditions in the Ukraine, just as British aid to the Whites was sustained in part by inaccurate estimates of their true military prospects. From the very beginning, therefore, a lack of information contributed to the growing conflict between Moscow and the West.

Lack of information also undermined several early attempts at accommodation. The severing of diplomatic relations and the withdrawal of Western diplomats left the Allies without a reliable way to ascertain if support for Bolshevism was growing or declining and made it difficult for either side to determine what the other was doing and why. Accommodation was also impeded by the near impossibility of communicating directly with the Soviet regime. The Bolsheviks had been excluded from the peace conference, and communication with Moscow was further impaired by the Allies' reluctance to take steps that might signal their acceptance of the Soviet regime. As a result, the two sides were forced to rely on unreliable radio communications or on unofficial emissaries who were all too easy to disregard. These obstacles introduced additional delays and ensured that positive efforts would be overtaken by events. The isolation of Soviet Russia also meant that the anti-Bolshevik exiles (whose ranks included many former tsarist officials) became Russia's main voice in the West. As one would expect, the exiles opposed any understanding with the new regime, and their testimony reinforced Allied intransigence at several crucial moments.[242]

---

[242] See Tongour, "Diplomacy in Exile"; Kennan, *Decision to Intervene*, chap. 14; and Ullman, *Britain and the Russian Civil War*, 141–44, 173–77.

Most important of all, neither the Soviets nor the Entente powers could gauge the potential for either revolution or counterrevolution in the wake of the Bolshevik victory in Russia. Fear of Bolshevism justified Western efforts to overthrow the new regime (or at least to keep it at arm's length), while Soviet hopes for world revolution accounted for the invasion of Poland in 1920 and their continued willingness to engage in counterproductive acts of revolutionary subversion.

## Socialization and Learning

Finally, the early history of Soviet foreign relations lends partial—but only partial—support to neorealist claims about the socializing effects of anarchy. On the one hand, Soviet leaders did moderate their revolutionary aims in order to advance specific diplomatic objectives, and they proved to be adept practioners of traditional balance-of-power politics. Moreover, as each side gained a more accurate estimate of the balance of threats, the level of security competition declined, prospects for cooperation increased, and Soviet foreign relations took on a more normal cast. On the other hand, Bolshevik ideology continued to shape both its avowed objectives and its perceptions of foreign powers, even when the policies that emerged exacerbated its isolation and insecurity. Such behavior is difficult to reconcile with a purely structural theory such as neorealism, which reminds us that foreign policy is never determined solely by structural factors. With hindsight, it is all too obvious that Leninist ideology was a serious handicap for Soviet diplomacy. Both the commitment to world revolution and the deep suspicion of other states endured because, first, the evidence against them was not clear-cut; second, they were a central part of the CPSU's claim to rule; third, they had been institutionalized in the Comintern and in the CPSU itself; and fourth, the Communist system inhibited critical debate about fundamental principles. As a result, although the Soviet Union made tactical adjustments in response to changing conditions, it did not formally abandon its revolutionary agenda until 1986, when it was already on its last legs.[243]

The diplomacy of the fledgling Soviet state backs my theory that revolutions intensify security competition between states and raise the probability of war. Moscow's relations with most other states deteriorated badly after 1917, several foreign powers tried to overthrow the new regime, foreign troops occupied portions of Russian territory until 1924, and Russia and Poland fought a brief but intense war in 1920. Relations between Russia and

---

[243] 1986 marked the first time when a congress of the Communist Party of the Soviet Union omitted an assessment of the "world revolutionary process." See Jacobson, *When the Soviet Union Entered*, 30.

the outside world improved slightly from 1921 to 1924, but efforts to establish more cordial relations ultimately failed to overcome the mutual perceptions of threat, keeping the Soviet Union in a self-imposed state of partial isolation.

This unfortunate result was due primarily to the enduring legacy of Bolshevik ideology. Although the revolution in Russia had not spread as they had anticipated, the Soviet leaders were unable or unwilling to give up the long-range goal of world revolution. They quickly learned to make tactical adjustments for the sake of immediate advantages (something Leninist ideology had long endorsed), but external pressures did not induce them to abandon the overthrow of capitalism as a long-term objective. And holding fast to this policy had very real costs, as it greatly increased the number of potential enemies the Soviets faced and would make it far more difficult to attract allies in the future.

Unlike the French case, however, the revolution in Russia did not lead to a war among the great powers. In addition to the sheer size of Soviet Russia (and the innate defensive advantage that this produced), the absence of great-power war is also explained by the massive bloodletting that had taken place between 1914 and 1918. Despite the intense fears of Bolshevism and their deep suspicion of Soviet intentions, none of the European powers was in a position to make a serious effort to oust the Soviet regime. This observation reminds us that understanding the foreign relations of revolutionary states requires a broad perspective. Beyond the preferences and capabilities of the new regime, one must also consider the aims and capacities of the other states in the system.

# [5]

## *The Iranian Revolution*

We have in reality, then, no choice but to . . . overthrow all treacherous, corrupt, oppressive, and criminal regimes.
—Ayatollah Ruhollah Khomeini

Nobody is ever ready for a revolution.
—Gary Sick, White House aide for Iran, 1977–81

Like the French and Russian revolutions, the Islamic upheaval in Iran confirms that revolutions raise the level of security competition between states. By altering the regional balance of power, the revolution in Iran both threatened other states and created opportunities for them. It also triggered spirals of hostility between the new regime and several other countries, which raised the level of threat even further. The fear that the revolution would spread made the danger seem greater, and lingering opposition within Iran fed the new regime's fears of foreign plots and gave its rivals the impression that it would be easy to overturn. Foreign responses to the revolution were also affected by uncertainty and misinformation, which exacerbated each side's perceptions of threat.

The hopes and fears that accompanied the revolution turned out to be greatly exaggerated. Although the Iranian example did encourage fundamentalists in other countries, it was not the sole (or even the most important) cause of the Islamic resurgence, and Iranian efforts to export the revolution to other countries have been largely unsuccessful. Foreign beliefs that the new regime would collapse turned out to be equally misguided; the Islamic Republic has survived diplomatic isolation, economic difficulties, a costly war, and internal conflicts that have endured for over fifteen years. Again we find that revolutions are both hard to spread and hard to reverse.

Finally, the Iranian Revolution offers only modest support for neorealist claims about the socializing effects of the international system. As in the Soviet case, key members of the revolutionary elite sought to moderate Iranian diplomacy in order to improve its international position. Their efforts were erratic and incomplete, however, for several reasons: the evidence in favor of moderation was ambiguous, the commitment to a radical foreign policy was central to the legitimacy of the clerical regime, and the revolutionary government was torn between competing factions and thus unable to sustain a consistent line.

This chapter consists of three main sections. First I describe the origins of the Islamic Republic and summarize its ideological foundations. After that, I examine the foreign policy of the new regime and describe how other states responded, focusing primarily on its first decade in power. Finally, I compare the evolution of Iran's foreign relations against the propositions developed in chapter 2.

## THE ORIGINS OF THE ISLAMIC REPUBLIC

### The Fall of the Shah

In simple terms, the regime of Shah Muhammad Reza Pahlavi fell because the shah's reformist policies alienated a broad spectrum of Iranian society that he was unable to coopt yet unwilling to suppress by brute force.[1] Opposition to the shah arose from, first, the economic and social dislocations generated by his rapid modernization program; second, clerical resistance to the intrusion of alien values and the shah's attempt to reduce their influence; and third, the widespread perception that the shah was a U.S. puppet and the head of a corrupt and decadent elite.[2]

The revolutionary crisis began late in 1977, after the shah's decision to relax police controls and judicial procedures had revived the liberal opposition and sparked several clashes between antigovernment demonstrators and the shah's internal police. The challenge grew in January 1978, after an insulting attack on the radical clergy in a government newspaper triggered a series of riots by theology students, in which seventy students were killed. The riots began an escalating cycle of popular demonstrations through the

---

[1] Accounts of the Iranian revolution include Said Amir Arjomand, *The Turban for the Crown: The Islamic Revolution in Iran* (London: Oxford University Press, 1988); Dilip Hiro, *Iran under the Ayatollahs* (London: Routledge and Kegan Paul, 1985); Shaul Bakhash, *The Reign of the Ayatollahs: Iran and the Islamic Revolution* (New York: Basic Books, 1984); John D. Stempel, *Inside the Iranian Revolution* (Bloomington: Indiana University Press, 1981); Farideh Farhi, *States and Urban-Based Revolutions: Iran and Nicaragua* (Urbana: University of Illinois Press, 1990); and Misagh Parsa, *Social Origins of the Iranian Revolution* (New Brunswick: Rutgers University Press, 1989).

[2] Opposition to the shah included the liberal National Front, the pro-Communist Tudeh Party, the Liberation Movement (which advocated a synthesis of Islam with modern Western thought), left-wing guerrilla organizations such as the Sazman-i Mujahedin-i Khalq-i Iran (or Islamic Mujahedin) and the Sazaman-i Cherikha-yi Feda'i Khalq-i Iran (or Marxist Feda'i), and Muslim clerics such as Khomeini. See Ervand Abrahamian, *Iran between Two Revolutions* (Princeton: Princeton University Press, 1982), chap. 10, and *The Iranian Mojahedin* (New Haven: Yale University Press, 1989); and Stempel, *Inside the Iranian Revolution*, 42–56.

spring and summer, and a mass demonstration in Tehran drew nearly five hundred thousand participants in September. The shah declared martial law and ordered the military to suppress the demonstrations, but these actions merely united the liberal opposition and the radical clerics. By November, a series of strikes had shut down the bazaars, universities, government offices, banks, and much of the oil industry.

The radicalization of the revolution was due in part to the shah's refusal either to make bold concessions or to order a massive crackdown. His indecision was exacerbated by his deteriorating health and an inability to obtain clear and consistent advice from the United States, which did not appreciate the seriousness of the crisis until very late.[3] Strikes and demonstrations continued through December, with the army rank and file becoming increasingly reluctant to use force against the opposition. Support from Washington was evaporating as well, as U.S. officials belatedly realized that the shah might be beyond saving. In desperation, the shah at last offered to negotiate with the opposition. After persuading Shahpour Bakhtiar, a prominent member of the liberal National Front, to lead a caretaker government, the shah agreed to leave the country for a "vacation" and to accept a greatly diminished role. It was a meaningless agreement, as the Pahlavi state was dissolving rapidly by this point and authority had already begun to pass into the hands of local governing bodies (or *komitehs*), many of which were controlled by clerics loyal to Ayatollah Ruhollah Khomeini, the intellectual spiritual leader of the opposition. Khomeini returned to a tumultuous welcome on February 1, and the Supreme Council of the Armed Forces declared itself neutral ten days later. Bakhtiar immediately resigned and went into hiding, marking the final end of the Pahlavi state.

### Khomeini's Revolutionary Program

Many diverse groups participated in the anti-shah coalition, but Ayatollah Ruhollah Khomeini was clearly its dominant figure. Khomeini had opposed the shah's regime since the early 1960s, when his criticisms of Iran's dependence on the United States had led to his arrest and subsequent exile in Iraq. He began extolling a radical doctrine of Islamic government while in exile and built an extensive network of supporters among the clergy. This

[3] Accounts of U.S. handling of the revolution vary in assigning blame, but all agree that American decision-makers were deeply divided and U.S. advice was inconsistent. See Gary Sick, *All Fall Down: America's Tragic Encounter with Iran* (New York: Random House, 1985); James A. Bill, *The Eagle and the Lion: The Tragedy of American-Iranian Relations* (New Haven: Yale University Press, 1988), chap. 7; Zbigniew Brzezinski, *Power and Principle: Memoirs of the National Security Advisor, 1977–1981* (New York: Farrar Straus Giroux, 1983), 354–98; William Sullivan, *Mission to Iran* (New York: W. W. Norton, 1981); and Stempel, *Inside the Iranian Revolution*, chap. 14. The shah's memoirs place the blame for his ouster on the United States; see Mohammad Reza Shah, *Answer to History* (New York: Stein and Day, 1980).

combination of ideology and organization would prove to be a potent revolutionary weapon.[4]

The central element of Khomeini's revolutionary program was his insistence that the shah's regime be replaced by a government based on Islamic law. Khomeini also argued that the clergy should play an active and direct role in the political system, to ensure that it conformed to Islamic principles.[5] In the absence of direct guidance from the Prophet Muhammed or his chosen successors, he argued, Islamic government should be based on the "guardianship of the jurisprudent" (*velayet-e faqih*). "Since the rule of Islam is the rule of law," he wrote, "only the jurists, and no one else, should be in charge of the government. They are the ones who can govern as God ordered."[6] Thus, not only did Khomeini reject the separation of religion and politics, but his vision of Islamic government placed the clergy in a position of primacy.[7]

Khomeini's blueprint for Islamic government rested on several other core beliefs. First, he regarded all other forms of government as illegitimate, because they were not based on Islam, and believed that the major world powers were innately hostile and aggressive. Dividing the world into "oppressors" (the superpowers, their allies, and their various puppets) and the "oppressed" (the victims of imperialist exploitation, such as Iran), Khomeini accused the Western powers of deliberately seeking "to keep us backward, to keep us in our present miserable state so that they can exploit our riches, our underground wealth, our lands, and our human resources." For this reason, he argued, the imperialist powers had "separated the various segments of the Islamic *ummah* (community) from each other and artificially

---

[4] See Bakhash, *Reign of the Ayatollahs*, 35–44; Abrahamian, *Iran between Two Revolutions*, 475–79, and *Khomeinism: Essays on the Islamic Republic* (Berkeley: University of California Press, 1993), 10–12; and Arjomand, *Turban for the Crown*, 94–102.

[5] Khomeini declared that "Islam is political or it is nothing" and insisted that "this slogan of the separation of religion and politics and the demand that Islamic scholars not intervene in social and political affairs have been formulated and propagated by the imperialists; it is only the irreligious who repeat them." *Islam and Revolution: Writings and Declarations of Imam Khomeini*, trans. Hamid Algar (Berkeley, Calif.: Mizan Press, 1981), 37–38.

[6] Quoted in Abrahamian, *Iran between Two Revolutions*, 477.

[7] "If a worthy individual possessing [knowledge of the law and justice] arises and establishes a government, he will possess the same authority as the Most Noble Messenger [the Prophet Mohammed] . . . and it will be the duty of all people to obey him." Khomeini, *Islam and Revolution*, 62. For summaries of Khomeini's theory of Islamic government, see Farhang Rajaee, *Islamic Values and World View: Khomeini on Man, the State, and International Politics* (Lanham, Md.: University Press of America, 1983); David Menashri, "Khomeini's Vision: Nationalism or World Order?" in his edited *Iranian Revolution and the Muslim World* (Boulder, Colo.: Westview, 1990); Marvin Zonis and Daniel Brumberg, *Khomeini, the Islamic Republic of Iran, and the Arab World* (Cambridge: Harvard Center for Middle Eastern Studies, 1987); and Gregory Rose, "*Velayet-e Faqih* and the Recovery of Islamic Identity in the Thought of Ayatollah Khomeini," in *Religion and Politics in Iran: Shi'ism from Quietism to Revolution*, ed. Nikki Keddie (New Haven: Yale University Press, 1983).

created separate nations." In addition to "corrupting the minds and morals of the people," the oppressors had replaced the judicial process and political laws of Islam with "European importations" and "installed their agents in power." According to Khomeini, therefore, the only way to end foreign exploitation was to overthrow agents such as the shah and establish a government based on Islamic principles.[8]

This Manichean worldview precluded any compromise with the shah or his foreign patrons. Khomeini told his followers in November 1978, "If you give [the shah] a breathing spell, tomorrow neither Islam nor your country nor your family will be left for you. Do not give him a chance; squeeze his neck until he is strangled." He was particularly suspicious of the United States, whose support for the shah qualified it as the "Great Satan," but the Soviet Union and the other major powers were seen as equally hostile.[9] For Khomeini, the superpowers were driven by an incorrigible lust for power and were especially dangerous for Iran. Even after the shah was gone, Khomeini warned that the great powers sought "to break Iran into pieces, to stage a coup d'état and pave the way for the . . . supervision of foreigners." Neither patience nor conciliation could remove the danger, because the "Satans are making plans [against Islam] for a century from now."[10]

Second, Khomeini rejected existing state boundaries as "the product of the deficient human mind" and emphasized that "Muslims are one family, even if they are subject to different governments and even if they live in regions remote from one another." Accordingly, he called for active efforts to spread the revolution beyond Iran's borders, declaring that "we have in reality, then, no choice but to . . . overthrow all treacherous, corrupt, oppressive, and criminal regimes." He also argued that his doctrine of Islamic government would end the artificial divisions imposed by the West and

---

[8] "It is the duty of all of us to overthrow the *taghut,* i.e., the illegitimate political powers that now rule the entire Islamic world. The government apparatus of tyrannical and anti-popular regimes must be replaced by institutions serving the public good and administered according to Islamic law. In this way an Islamic government will gradually come into existence." Khomeini, *Islam and Revolution,* 34–35, 48–50, 136, 147. See also Shireen T. Hunter, *Iran and the World: Continuity in Revolutionary Decade* (Bloomington: Indiana University Press, 1990), 37–41; and Richard Cottam, "Iran—Motives behind Its Foreign Policy," *Survival* 28, no. 6 (1986).

[9] In 1964, Khomeini had declared, "America is worse than Britain; Britain is worse than America. The Soviet Union is worse than both of them." For these quotations, see Arjomand, *Turban for the Crown,* 102; and Khomeini, *Islam and Revolution,* 185.

[10] Khomeini also warned, "Neither the West nor the East will leave us alone. They will try everything in their power to prevent Iran from settling down." Quoted in W. R. Campbell and Djamchid Darvich, "Global Implications of the Islamic Revolution for the Status Quo in the Persian Gulf," *Journal of South Asian and Middle Eastern Studies* 5, no. 1 (1981), 42; and see also Rajaee, *Islamic Values,* 75–78; and Roy Parviz Mottahedeh, "Iran's Foreign Devils," *Foreign Policy* 38 (1980).

recreate a unified Muslim *ummah*. And though the Muslim world was the primary object of his revolutionary ambitions, Khomeini and his followers occasionally suggested that the ultimate goal was the creation of a global community that would transcend the existing state system altogether.[11] In addition, Khomeini argued that failure to spread the revolution would leave Iran vulnerable to the "oppressors" or their various puppets. Once in power, he declared, "We should try to export our revolution to the world. . . . If we remain in an enclosed environment we shall definitely face defeat." Thus, there were both offensive and defensive justifications for an expansionist policy; although he repeatedly denied that it would involve the use of force, spreading the revolution beyond Iran was both a means to ensure Iran's security and an end in itself.[12]

Third, like other revolutionary ideologies, Khomeini's worldview combined long-term optimism with an emphasis on sacrifice and discipline. He preached, "The Quran says 'And hold fast . . . to the cable of Allah, and do not separate. . . . [All your] political social and economic problems will be solved." Similarly, he exhorted his followers, "*Know that it is your duty to establish an Islamic government*. Have confidence in yourselves and know that you are capable of fulfilling this task."[13] Noting that "all the prophets began as lonely individuals, . . . but they persisted," he emphasized that "it is only through the active, intentional pursuit of martyrdom that unjust rulers can be toppled."[14] Indeed, he suggested, a single individual could spark a revolution: "Even if only one true human being appears, [the imperialists] fear

[11] Quotations from Rouhallah K. Ramazani, *Revolutionary Iran: Challenge and Response in the Middle East* (Baltimore: Johns Hopkins University Press, 1986), 20–21; Rajaee, *Islamic Values,* 77; Menashri, "Khomeini's Vision," 43; and Khomeini, *Islam and Revolution,* 47–48, 50–51. Khomeini also stated, "We say we want to export our revolution to all Islamic countries as well as to the oppressed countries. . . . Export of our revolution means that all nations grow aware and save themselves." Quoted in Maziar Behrooz, "Trends in the Foreign Policy of the Islamic Republic," in *Neither East Nor West: Iran, the Soviet Union, and the United States,* ed. Nikki R. Keddie and Mark J. Gasiorowski (New Haven: Yale University Press, 1990), 14–15.

[12] Quoted in Ramazani, *Revolutionary Iran,* 24–26, and "Khumayni's Islam in Iran's Foreign Policy," in *Islam in Foreign Policy,* ed. Adeed Dawisha (Cambridge: Cambridge University Press, 1983), 19–20; Rajaee, *Islamic Values,* 82–85; and Campbell and Darvich, "Global Implications," 44–46.

[13] He also stressed the need for action, advising Iranians, "Rid yourselves of your depression and apathy. . . . An Islamic government will definitely be established," and he stated that the "unity of truth and . . . the expression of God's oneness . . . will guarantee victory." The quotations are from Rajaee, *Islamic Values,* 85; Khomeini, *Islam and Revolution,* 37, 137; and Rose, "*Velayet-e faqih* and the Recovery of Islamic Identity," 186–87.

[14] Quoted in Rajaee, *Islamic Values,* 85; and Zonis and Brumberg, *Khomeini, Iran, Arab World,* 27–28; and Khomeini's speech in Foreign Broadcast Information Service, *Daily Report, South Asia,* July 15, 1983, I/1–3. Ten years after the revolution, Khomeini recalled, "Anyone who did not believe in struggle 100 percent would easily flee the arena under the pressure and threats of the pseudo-pious. . . . The only way available was struggle through blood; and God paved the way for such a course." See Foreign Broadcast Information Service, *Daily Report, Near East/South Asia,* February 23, 1989, 45.

[215]

him, because others will follow him and he will have an impact that can destroy the whole foundation of tyranny, imperialism, and government by puppets."[15]

Not surprisingly, the ideology of the Iranian revolutionaries left them deeply suspicious of most foreign powers (especially the United States). Khomeini and his followers also saw their revolution as a model for other states—especially other Muslim countries—and favored active efforts to spread the revolution beyond Iran's borders. Finally, their own success reinforced the growing belief that revolutionary Islam was an irresistible force that could overcome seemingly insurmountable obstacles.

### The Consolidation of Clerical Power

Clerical power was consolidated in three main phases. During the first, from February to November 1979, the main institutions of the new state were established and the more moderate forces were checked by pressure from the clergy and the radical left. Khomeini selected a moderate politician, Mehdi Bazargan, to head the Provisional Government, but Bazargan was forced to share power with the so-called Revolutionary Council, a secret group of mostly clerical advisors. Bazargan submitted a draft constitution in June, but protests from the clergy and the left led to the convening of an "Assembly of Experts" that proceeded to transform the original document into a blueprint for a theocratic state.[16] The final blow against Bazargan came when the shah's entry into the United States for medical treatment ignited a wave of protests in Iran and demands that the shah be returned to Iran to stand trial. Bazargan met with U.S. national security advisor Zbigniew Brzezinski in an attempt to resolve the dispute, and Khomeini issued a statement urging Iranian students "to expand with all their might their attacks against the United States and Israel" in order to compel the return of the shah.[17] When a group of students seized the U.S. embassy on November 4 and Khomeini endorsed their action, Bazargan had no choice but to resign.

The second phase, from November 1979 to June 1981, was dominated by a prolonged struggle for power between the new president, Abolhassan Bani-Sadr, and the clerical forces of the Islamic Republic Party led by the Ayatollah Muhammed Beheshti. Unlike Bazargan, Bani-Sadr favored a radical

---

[15] Khomeini, *Islam and Revolution,* 39; and see also Mary Heglund, "Two Images of Husain: Accommodation and Revolution in an Iranian Village," in Keddie, *Religion and Politics,* esp. 228–30; and Arjomand, *Turban for the Crown,* 99–100.

[16] The text of the Constitution of the Islamic Republic of Iran is reprinted in *Middle East Journal* (hereafter *MEJ*) 34, no. 2 (1980), 181–204; and see also Bakhash, *Reign of the Ayatollahs,* 74–75.

[17] See "Chronology," *MEJ* 34, no. 1 (1980), 50.

transformation of Iran along Islamic lines.[18] He opposed direct clerical rule, however, and believed that government positions should be given to individuals with technical expertise rather than religious qualifications. He also sought to improve Iran's international position by resolving the hostage crisis with the United States.[19]

These positions placed Bani-Sadr at odds with the radical clergy, which waged a relentless campaign to limit his power. The IRP dominated the parliamentary elections in March 1980, and Bani-Sadr found himself in a protracted struggle against the party's efforts to expand its control.[20] Although Khomeini implored the two sides to resolve their differences and even formed a three-man commission to mediate between them in March 1981, disputes between the clergy and the president remained intense.[21] Bani-Sadr eventually sought support from liberals, moderate clerics, and the left-wing Islamic Mujahedin, and this step convinced Khomeini that Bani-Sadr had become a threat to the clerical regime. The ayatollah relieved him from his position as commander-in-chief in June and the Majlis (Parliament) soon ordered his arrest, forcing Bani-Sadr to flee into exile in July.

The third phase, from July 1981 to February 1983, featured a violent struggle between the IRP and the radical left.[22] The Mujahedin launched a bloody wave of terrorism following Bani-Sadr's removal. A bomb blast at the headquarters of the IRP in June killed seventy-four IRP officials, including the Ayatollah Beheshti. Bani-Sadr's successor, Mohammed Rajai, was killed by another bomb on August 30 (along with Prime Minister Muhammed Bahonar). The clergy responded with a brutal campaign of repression. Official executions totaled over twenty-six hundred by November 1981, and over twelve thousand dissidents were killed in clashes with the Revolutionary Guards or in official executions between 1981 and 1985.[23]

---

[18] The son of an ayatollah, Bani-Sadr had studied sociology and law in Tehran and was jailed for opposition activities in the 1960s. He became part of Khomeini's entourage during the latter's exile in France and returned with him to Tehran in February 1979.

[19] See Bakhash, *Reign of the Ayatollahs*, 114–17; Behrooz, "Foreign Policy of the Islamic Republic," 18–19; and Abolhassan Bani-Sadr, *My Turn to Speak: Iran, the Revolution, and Secret Deals with the United States*, trans. William Ford (Washington, D.C.: Brassey's, 1991), 22–25.

[20] See Abrahamian, *Iranian Mojahedin*, 60–65; Bakhash, *Reign of the Ayatollahs*, esp. 100–110; and David Menashri, *Iran: A Decade of War and Revolution* (New York: Holmes and Meier, 1990), 133–35, 168–74, 181–83.

[21] Khomeini asked the contestants to settle their differences and serve "the interest of the nation" in September and implored them to stop "biting one another like scorpions" in February. See "Chronology," *MEJ* 35, no. 1 (1980), 46; no. 2 (1981), 215; no. 3 (1981), 367.

[22] The principal left-wing groups in Iran were the Islamic Mujahedin, the Marxist Feda'i, and the Communist Tudeh Party. All three groups favored radical domestic change and an end to imperialist exploitation but opposed the establishment of a theocratic state.

[23] The chief prosecutor, Ayatollah Sadeq Khalkhali, declared that "these deaths are not merely permissible, they are necessary." See Abrahamian, *Iranian Mojahedin*, 68–69, 219–22.

The threat from the Mujahedin was largely eliminated by the end of 1982, and in February 1983, the government moved to suppress the (Communist) Tudeh Party, removing the last independent political organization of any consequence. The presidency, prime ministry, and speakership of the Majlis were all in clerical hands, the IRP dominated the Majlis, and the clergy had established effective control over the armed forces and Revolutionary Guards. Although low-level opposition continued throughout the rest of the decade and splits *among* the religious leaders became more and more apparent, the leaders of the Islamic Republic no longer faced a serious threat to their rule.

### Conflict and Compromise in the Islamic Republic

The basic institutions of the Islamic Republic were in place by the end of 1983. The IRP dominated the Majlis and the ministries, and the army and Revolutionary Guards were all controlled by clerics loyal to Khomeini. The new regime had begun to reorder Iranian society along Islamic lines, bringing dramatic changes in law, education, and popular mores.[24] Opposition from within the senior clergy had been stilled as well, leaving Khomeini as the ultimate arbiter of Iran's Islamic future.[25]

Despite these achievements, deep political differences soon began to divide Iran's new rulers.[26] In broad terms, the contest pitted a comparatively moderate group led by Majlis speaker Ali Akbar Hashemi-Rafsanjani, President Said Ali Khamenei, and Foreign Minister Ali Akbar Velayati against a more radical faction led by Prime Minister Mir-Husayn Musavi, Ayatollah Husayn Ali Montazeri, and Ayatollah Ali Akbar Mohtashemi. The pragmatists downplayed the importance of exporting the revolution, supported the private sector, and advocated enhancing Iran's international position by increasing its ties with other countries. By contrast, the radicals sought to maintain the ideological purity of the revolution, and they emphasized the

[24] See Menashri, *Iran*, 137–38, 192–97, 225–28, 271–76.

[25] Khomeini was the only grand ayatollah to endorse direct clerical rule, and several equally eminent clerics (most notably Kazem Shariatmadari) criticized Khomeini's position as contrary to Islam. Shariatmadari's personal prestige was no match for Khomeini's control over the main state institutions, however, and he was placed under house arrest and subsequently discredited by his later involvement in an unsuccessful coup. See Menashri, *Iran*, 70–73, 129–30, 239–40; Bakhash, *Reign of the Ayatollahs*, 67–68, 89–90, 223; Hiro, *Iran under the Ayatollahs*, 139–43, 218–19; and Shahrough Akhavi, "Clerical Politics in Iran since 1979," in *The Iranian Revolution and Islamic Republic*, ed. Nikki Keddie and Eric Hooglund (Syracuse: Syracuse University Press, 1986), 59–62, 88–89.

[26] In September 1984, Majlis speaker Rafsanjani admitted that the Islamic Republican Party's Central Council "does not enjoy a unity which is a *sine qua non* for its ability to be active and advance the [party's] goals," and he described "this very fundamental problem" as "a significant challenge." See Menashri, *Iran*, 307–308; and Shahrough Akhavi, "Elite Factionalism in the Islamic Republic of Iran," *MEJ* 41, no. 2 (1987), 184.

export of Islamic fundamentalism, the use of state power to aid the "oppressed," the removal of Western influence, and steadfast opposition to the United States and its regional allies.[27]

The pragmatists slowly gained the upper hand throughout the 1980s, although the process was erratic and the basic divisions would remain intact after Khomeini's death in 1989. Khomeini called repeatedly for the "elimination of differences," but he also shifted his own position in order to prevent either faction from gaining undisputed control. As a result, periods of deradicalization alternated with occasional outbursts of extremism. By 1985, Rafsanjani and his supporters had begun to curb the excesses of "Islamization" and Iranian officials were signaling their desire to restore Iran's contacts with the outside world. In addition to a détente with Saudi Arabia and several Western states, Iran began seeking advanced U.S. weaponry from a number of Israeli intermediaries. This policy was a direct response to the demands imposed by Iran's war with Iraq and marked a noteworthy departure from its public antipathy toward Israel and the "Great Satan."[28] The initiative came to an abrupt end when Rafsanjani's internal opponents leaked word of his negotiations with the United States. The news brought intense criticism from the radicals, but Khomeini condemned this new threat to unity, and Rafsanjani and the moderates emerged in an even stronger position. Khomeini continued to back them, and the trial and subsequent execution of Mehdi Hashemi, former head of the bureau dealing with foreign revolutionaries, was a major setback for the radicals.[29]

As Rafsanjani and the pragmatists continued to consolidate their position during 1988, evidence of a renewed drive toward moderation was apparent. The most obvious sign was the ceasefire with Iraq—which entailed abandoning the oft-repeated goal of toppling Saddam Hussein—but Khomeini also agreed to a series of administrative initiatives that curtailed the role of religious authorities. Both Khomeini and Rafsanjani made statements stressing that religious principles must "adapt to the requirements of time and place," and the speaker later declared that although "the law

[27] The membership of each faction changed over time, and some individuals supported one side on certain issues but not on others. See Akhavi, "Elite Factionalism"; Ramazani, "Iran's Foreign Policy"; *Middle East Contemporary Survey* (hereafter *MECS*), vol. 8: 1983–84 (Tel Aviv: Dayan Center for Middle East and African Studies/Shiloah Center, 1986), 430–33; *MECS 1988* (Boulder, Colo.: Westview, 1990), 493–94; and Shireen T. Hunter, *Iran after Khomeini* (New York: Praeger, 1992), 36–39.

[28] See Menashri, *Iran*, 322–25, 374–75.

[29] Hashemi was believed to be responsible for leaking word of the arms deals. Another sign of internal differences was the decision to disband the Islamic Revolution Party in 1987. Rafsanjani admitted in 1986 that there were "two relatively powerful factions in our country. . . . They may in fact be regarded as two parties without names." He termed the decision to disband the party "temporary" and said that it might be revived "if the consensus which led to its formation in 1979 is available again." See Robin Wright, *In the Name of God: The Khomeini Decade* (New York: Simon and Schuster, 1989), 162.

should follow Islamic doctrine . . . priority will be given to government decisions over doctrine." Khomeini also issued a formal edict (or *fatwa*) declaring that the authority of the Islamic state was the same as it had been in the time of Muhammed, implying that government decisions could supersede Islamic law. "Our government," he declared, "has priority over all other Islamic tenets, even over prayer, fasting, and the pilgrimage to Mecca." Thus, after having overthrown one regime in the name of Islamic law, Khomeini in effect declared that the Islamic Republic could disregard Islam if the interests of the state required it. Other signs of liberalization included the open endorsement of birth control by several prominent theologians, the implementation of a law permitting the registration of new political parties, and public calls for greater freedom of expression in universities and more flexibility in the veiling of women. These steps did not imply a new tolerance toward all domestic opponents, however, and several radical clerics and a large number of suspected leftists were reportedly executed later in the year.[30]

As before, however, these acts of moderation were followed by a subsequent tilt toward the revolutionary purists. The occasion for this shift was the publication of Salman Rushdie's novel *The Satanic Verses*, whose satirical portrayal of Muhammed had already sparked protests in other Muslim countries. In February 1989, Khomeini stunned the world by sentencing Rushdie (who lived in England) to death and publicly exhorting "zealous Muslims" to carry out his order. Iran offered a $2.6 million reward to Rushdie's executioner, and Khomeini declared that the entire episode was divinely intended to warn Iran against an overly "pragmatic" foreign policy.[31]

Khomeini's sudden reversal was meant to ensure that Iran's revolutionary ideals were not entirely abandoned. If compromise and moderation had been necessary to save the revolution in 1988, Khomeini now saw a need to rekindle ideological purity and revolutionary commitment. According to David Menashri, "Rushdie's book served the revolution just as the American hostages had in 1979; it unified the revolutionary forces against the external demonical enemy and stirred up passions around an issue which all believers could . . . identify with."[32]

---

[30] In January 1989, Khomeini also approved a series of legislative reforms that further diluted the authority of religious experts and gave greater priority to state (as opposed to theological) interests. For these quotations and events, see *MECS 1988*, 472–73, 486–88; and Wright, *In the Name of God*, 172–73.

[31] This sudden return to a bellicose ideological posture forced the moderates to adopt more extreme rhetoric themselves, and Rafsanjani at one point suggested that the Palestinians should kill five U.S., French, or British citizens for every Arab killed in the Israeli-occupied West Bank or Gaza Strip. See Foreign Broadcast Information Service, *Daily Report, Near East/South Asia*, February 23, 1989, 44–48; *MECS 1988*, 494; and Wright, *In the Name of God*, 201.

[32] See *MECS 1988*, 495.

The condemnation of Rushdie was Khomeini's last important political act. His health deteriorated in the spring and he died on June 3, 1989, at the age of eighty-six. His passing allowed Rafsanjani and the moderates to resume their efforts to adapt the principles of "Islamic government" to contemporary political conditions. Not surprisingly, the transition to the post-Khomeini era began with new signs of moderation.

The first step was the selection of President Ali Khamenei to succeed Khomeini as supreme jurisprudent. This decision was a further retreat from Khomeini's original blueprint for Islamic government, because Khamenei was not an accomplished theologian. A sweeping series of constitutional amendments was approved by a national referendum in July. The new constitution dropped the requirement that the supreme jurisprudent be a senior religious leader (thereby legitimizing Khamenei's selection as Khomeini's successor), abolished the position of prime minister, and strengthened the powers of the presidency.[33] Rafsanjani was elected president by an overwhelming margin in July, further cementing the moderates' hold on power. Rafsanjani emphasized that his main priority would be reconstruction and economic recovery, and his new cabinet was dominated by technocrats chosen for their administrative competence rather than their ideological purity. Although the radicals were not silenced and the pragmatists had not wholly abandoned the principles of the Islamic revolution, the leaders of the regime seemed to be increasingly willing to sacrifice doctrinal purity for the sake of political stability, economic recovery, and international acceptance.[34]

The radicals suffered yet another defeat in the 1991 elections, leading some observers to conclude that Rafsanjani's position was more powerful than ever.[35] Yet the scales quickly swung back when Khamenei announced a crackdown on "Western culture" in the summer of 1992 and reaffirmed the death sentence on Salman Rushdie, Iran's hostility to the United States, and its commitment to spreading the revolution.[36] Khamenei and the radicals began to strip Rafsanjani of many of the powers he had previously accumulated and forced him to abandon his efforts to establish better relations with the West. The radical resurgence was partly a response to Rafsanjani's failed attempts to liberalize the economy, but it also reflected the incomplete insti-

[33] See Hunter, *Iran after Khomeini*, 25–26; *MECS 1989* (Boulder, Colo.: Westview, 1991), 344, 348–53; and Abrahamian, *Khomeinism*, 34–35.

[34] See *MECS 1989*, 341–62.

[35] See R. K. Ramazani, "Iran's Foreign Policy: North and South," *MEJ* 46, no. 3 (1992), 394–95; and Said Amir Arjomand, "A Victory for the Pragmatists: The Islamic Fundamentalist Reaction in Iran," in *Islamic Fundamentalism and the Gulf Crisis*, ed. James Piscatori (Chicago: American Academy of Arts and Sciences, 1991).

[36] On July 29, 1992, Ayatollah Khamenei warned, "One must never believe that the United States, the everlasting enemy of Islam, has put an end to its antagonism. . . . The United States is the main enemy of Islam and will remain so." *Middle East International*, no. 431 (August 7, 1992), 13.

[221]

tutionalization of the revolutionary regime and the radicals' fear that further moves toward moderation would jeopardize their own claim to rule.[37]

The Islamic revolution in Iran is still a work in progress. Although the revolution created a strong state apparatus, authority remains divided, and neither the moderates nor the radicals have been able to eliminate the other faction or reduce its base of support. It has thus been difficult for the Islamic Republic to sustain a coherent set of policies, and as we shall see, this endemic inconsistency has had especially pernicious effects on Iran's foreign relations.

## THE FOREIGN RELATIONS OF REVOLUTIONARY IRAN

### *Foreign Policy under the Shah*

Under the shah, Iranian foreign policy was directed toward the long-term goal of becoming a major world power. The foundation of this policy was the shah's alliance with the United States, which had grown in importance after the Nixon administration decided to use Iran as one of its "twin pillars" in the Persian Gulf region. This policy fed the shah's own ambitions; Iran's oil wealth fueled a massive arms buildup; and the United States became inextricably identified with the shah's regime.[38]

Predictably, prerevolutionary Iran's relations with the Soviet Union were less favorable. The shah was understandably wary of his large northern neighbor and perennially worried about leftist subversion within Iran itself. Iran's role as the West's "regional policeman" irritated the Soviets, as did the shah's opposition to revolutionary movements and radical states elsewhere in the Middle East.[39] Yet despite these disagreements and Iran's close ties with the United States, the Soviet Union and Iran maintained cordial diplomatic and economic relations, and their 1921 treaty of friendship and cooperation remained in force.[40]

---

[37] On these events, see "Iran, the Sequel: New Actors, but the Same Lines," *New York Times*, January 23, 1994, 4:4; and also *Middle East International*, no. 430 (July 24, 1992), 13; no. 432 (August 21, 1992), 11; no. 438 (November 6, 1992), 12; no. 439 (November 20, 1992), 3–5.

[38] Useful surveys of the U.S.-Iranian relationship include Mark J. Gasiorowski, *U.S. Foreign Policy and the Shah: Building a Client State in Iran* (Ithaca: Cornell University Press, 1991); Bill, *Eagle and Lion*, chaps. 1–6; and R. K. Ramazani, *The United States and Iran: The Patterns of Influence* (New York: Praeger, 1982).

[39] Iran helped the sultan of Oman suppress the Soviet-backed Dhofar rebellion in the early 1970s, and the shah was especially hostile to Soviet clients such as Gamal Abdel Nasser of Egypt and the Baath parties in Syria and Iraq.

[40] See Sepehr Zabih, "Iran's International Posture: De Facto Non-Alignment within a Pro-Western Alliance," *MEJ* 24, no. 3 (1970), 313; Alvin Z. Rubinstein, *Soviet Policy towards Turkey, Iran, and Afghanistan: The Dynamics of Influence* (New York: Praeger, 1982); and Aryeh Yodfat, *The Soviet Union and Revolutionary Iran* (London: Croom Helm, 1984), 25–43.

Within the Middle East, Iran's foreign policy grew more assertive as its military and economic power increased. Iran seized several islands in the Persian Gulf in 1971, and its support for the Kurdish insurgency in Iraq forced Baghdad to accept its terms in a long-standing dispute over the Shatt al-Arab waterway. Relations with Saudi Arabia and the other gulf states were friendly but guarded; although the gulf monarchies shared the shah's opposition to radicalism of any sort, they were also worried by Iran's military power and the shah's regional ambitions. Relations with Egypt improved dramatically after its realignment with the United States, but relations with Syria, Libya, and South Yemen remained hostile. These tensions help explain Iran's tacit alignment with Israel, based on a combination of factors including shared opposition to the main Arab powers, Israel's interest in the Iranian Jewish community, covert cooperation between the Israeli and Iranian intelligence services, and their shared ties to the United States.[41]

Overall, Iran's foreign policy under the shah combined a pro-Western orientation with an ambitious effort to build Iran's military power and expand its regional role. The shah's immediate ambitions were limited, however; although Iran annexed small portions of foreign territory on several occasions, the shah did not seek to transform the existing state system or eliminate any of his immediate neighbors. And though he occasionally invoked Islamic symbols to attack his Arab opponents, Islam played little or no role in Iran's foreign policy prior to the revolution.

### Aims and Ambitions of the Islamic Republic

Although the revolutionary coalition was divided on many issues, there was widespread agreement on the broad outlines of Iran's postrevolutionary foreign policy. The new regime was strongly opposed to foreign (especially U.S.) interference and committed to an explicit policy of nonalignment. Prime Minister Bazargan announced this new policy in February 1979, and the principle of nonalignment was formally enshrined in the Constitution of the Islamic Republic later in the year.[42] The constitution committed Iran to work for the unity of all Islamic peoples and openly endorsed efforts to export the revolution to other countries.[43] Although Khomeini at

[41] On the origins of the Iranian-Israeli relationship, see Uri Bialer, "The Iranian Connection in Israel's Foreign Policy, 1948–1951," *MEJ* 39, no. 2 (1985).

[42] The constitution calls for "the complete expulsion of colonialism and the prevention of foreign influence" and explicitly forbids foreign military bases or any agreements "allowing a foreign power to dominate . . . the affairs of the country." "Constitution of the Islamic Republic," 189, 201–202.

[43] The constitution states that it "provides the basis for trying to perpetuate this revolution both at home and abroad," and it emphasizes the importance of "expanding international relations with other Islamic movements . . . to pave the way to form the world unity of followers." Ibid., 185.

times stated that Iran would not use force to spread its revolution, some of his remarks (and those of several of his followers) were less restrained.[44] The new regime also undertook to aid other victims of imperialism, and the new constitution proclaimed that Iran would "protect the struggles of the weak against the arrogant, in any part of the world."[45]

These principles constituted a near-total reversal of the shah's foreign policy. In addition to moving to a nonaligned position, the commitment to spreading Khomeini's ideas of Islamic government challenged the legitimacy of the existing state system and threatened the stability of Iran's immediate neighbors. Not surprisingly, the establishment of the Islamic Republic had dramatic effects on Iran's international position.

## The United States and Revolutionary Iran

The effects of the revolution were most apparent in Iran's relations with the United States. The revolutionaries blamed the United States for the injustices of the shah's rule, and they were especially worried that the United States would try to repeat the 1953 coup that had restored the shah to his throne. For their part, the Americans were concerned by the loss of an important ally, the impact of the revolution on world oil supplies, and the possibility that the shah's ouster would permit the Soviet Union to expand its own influence in an important strategic area.[46]

Yet U.S.-Iranian relations seemed fairly encouraging at first. Prime Minister Bazargan announced that Iran would continue exporting oil to the United States, and when a group of radical students invaded the U.S. embassy compound in Tehran in February 1979, the Bazargan government quickly removed them and tightened security around the embassy. President Carter declared that the United States "would attempt to work closely with the existing government of Iran," and U.S. diplomats and intelligence officials maintained extensive contacts with the Bazargan government and tried to cultivate more radical figures such as Bani-Sadr as well. Carter also

[44] According to Khomeini, Iran would "export our revolution to the whole world. Until the cry 'There is no God but God' resounds over the whole world, there will be struggle." Quoted in Wright, *In the Name of God*, 108. In 1981, Foreign Minister Musavi declared that one of the objectives of Iran's foreign policy was to "carry the message of Iran's Islamic revolution to the [entire] world," and Ayatollah Ali Meshkini stated that the goal of the revolution was "to impose the Qur'an over the entire world." In 1982, then-president Ali Khamenei called on prayer leaders from forty countries to use their mosques as "prayer, political, cultural and military bases," in order to "prepare the ground for the creation of Islamic governments in all countries." Quoted in Menashri, "Khomeini's Vision," 48–49; and Bakhash, *Reign of the Ayatollahs*, 234–35.

[45] "Constitution of the Islamic Republic," 202; and see also Ramazani, *Revolutionary Iran*, 23–24, and "Khumayni's Islam," 21–22; and Rajaee, *Islamic Values*, 79–81.

[46] See Bill, *Eagle and Lion*, 277–78; and Warren Christopher et al., *American Hostages in Iran: The Conduct of a Crisis* (New Haven: Yale University Press, 1985), 2.

authorized shipments of gasoline and heating oil to alleviate temporary shortages in Iran and agreed to ship spare parts to the Iranian armed forces in October.[47]

There were several obvious points of tension, however. Secretary of Defense Harold Brown's statement that the United States would use military force "if appropriate" to protect its access to Persian Gulf oil alarmed Iran's new leaders, and the violent reprisals that followed the shah's departure disturbed many American observers. The U.S. Senate condemned the summary executions conducted by the Revolutionary Courts in May—an action Iran denounced as "clear interference." The new regime refused to accept the credentials of the U.S. ambassador-designate in June, expelled several U.S. journalists in July, and canceled a $9 billion arms deal in August.[48] Unable to establish direct contact with Khomeini or his supporters during this period, the Carter administration was forced to pin its hopes on such moderates as Bazargan. Bazargan and Foreign Minister Ibrahim Yazdi were interested in developing a cordial relationship with the United States, but their authority was evaporating rapidly at this point. The radical clergy opposed any attempt at a rapprochement, and relations between the two states worsened as the mullahs tightened their hold on power. The final break came when Carter agreed to permit the shah to fly to New York for medical treatment in October. This decision triggered a new wave of anti-U.S. demonstrations and raised new fears that the United States was preparing a counterrevolutionary coup. Bazargan met with U.S. national security advisor Brzezinski in an attempt to resolve the dispute, but his efforts ended with the seizure of the U.S. embassy and the onset of a major hostage crisis.

The United States responded to the seizure of its embassy by freezing Iranian assets, organizing an international embargo, and deploying additional military forces in the region. It began transmitting propaganda broadcasts into Iran in order to undermine the Ayatollah and eventually attempted an unsuccessful rescue mission in April 1980. The continuing power struggle in Iran impeded efforts to resolve the crisis through negotiation, largely because Bani-Sadr lacked the authority to make a deal and because supporters of a settlement were vulnerable to accusations of insufficient revolutionary zeal.[49] The breakthrough finally came in the fall of 1980, when Iran agreed to release the hostages in exchange for roughly $11 billion in frozen Iranian assets and other financial commitments.[50]

[47] See Bill, *Eagle and Lion,* 286–93.
[48] Ibid., 280–82.
[49] "Chronology," *MEJ* 34, no. 4 (1980), 475. The sheer difficulty of communicating with the Iranian regime was a serious obstacle as well, and virtually all accounts of the hostage crisis emphasize the confusion that U.S. negotiators faced in trying to deal with the Islamic Republic.
[50] The most complete account of the hostage negotiators (though written entirely from the U.S. perspective), is Christopher et al., *American Hostages in Iran.* See also Sick, *All Fall Down,*

By confirming each side's impression that the other was unremittingly hostile, the hostage crisis cast an enduring shadow over U.S.-Iranian relations. U.S. pressure on Iran strengthened the revolutionaries' image of American hostility, and the radical clergy used the threat of the "Great Satan" to undermine Bazargan and Bani-Sadr and to consolidate their own positions.[51] The abortive rescue mission also revealed that the United States still controlled significant intelligence assets within the country and reinforced Iranian fears of U.S. military action, while Iran's bellicose rhetoric and disregard for traditional diplomatic norms solidified its reputation as an aggressive revolutionary state. Iran's subsequent actions (such as its support for the Lebanese Shiites who kidnapped several U.S. citizens and conducted the suicide bombing of the U.S. Marine barracks in Beirut in 1983) merely sealed Iran's aggressive reputation in Washington.

These developments convinced the United States to increase its support for conservative Arab regimes such as Saudi Arabia and to tilt towards Iraq during the Iran-Iraq war. Initially concerned that an Iraqi victory would upset the regional balance of power, the U.S. government had quietly allowed Israel to ship several billion dollars' worth of U.S. arms and spare parts to Iran in 1981 and 1982. When the tide of battle turned in Iran's favor, however, the U.S. State Department began a diplomatic campaign to persuade other states to deny military equipment to Iran. The United States began providing intelligence information to Iraq in 1982 and replenished the stockpiles of Jordan, Saudi Arabia, and Kuwait when they transferred U.S.-made weaponry to Baghdad. The United States reestablished diplomatic relations with Iraq in 1984 and began covertly supporting Iranian exile groups during this period as well.[52]

---

chaps. 9–15; Bill, *Eagle and Lion*, 293–304; Pierre Salinger, *America Held Hostage: The Secret Negotiations* (Garden City, N.Y.: Doubleday, 1981); Brzezinski, *Power and Principle*, chap. 13; and Hamilton Jordan, *Crisis: The Last Year of the Carter Presidency* (New York: G. P. Putnam, 1982).

[51] As Rafsanjani remarked after the hostage settlement, "America continues to remain our enemy, and, accordingly, we are America's enemy. . . . This will continue for a long time." Quoted in Menashri, *Iran*, 205; and see also Campbell and Darvich, "Global Implications of the Iranian Revolution," 49.

[52] See Anthony Cordesman, *The Iran-Iraq War and Western Security, 1984–1987: Strategic Implications and Policy Options* (London: Jane's, 1987), esp. 79; "U.S. Said to Aid Iranian Exiles in Combat and Political Units," and "U.S. Secretly Gave Aid to Iraq Early in Its War against Iran," *New York Times*, March 7, 1982, A1, A12; January 26, 1992, A1, A4; Dilip Hiro, *The Longest War: The Iran-Iraq Military Conflict* (London: Routledge, 1991), 96; Ralph King, *The Iran-Iraq War: The Political Implications*, Adelphi Paper no. 219 (London: International Institute for Strategic Studies, 1982), 53.

The main departure from this policy was the notorious Iran-*contra* arms deal.[53] This initiative rested on the hope that supplying arms would strengthen "moderate forces" within the Islamic Republic, who would help obtain the release of the U.S. hostages in Lebanon and work to improve U.S.-Iranian relations. This goal also reflected U.S. concerns that Iran was increasingly vulnerable to Soviet pressure or subversion, as well as the expectation that the threat from Moscow would make Iran more receptive to U.S. overtures.[54]

In the summer of 1985, U.S. and Israeli officials began negotiating to sell advanced weapons to Iran in exchange for the release of U.S. citizens held by pro-Iranian groups in Lebanon. Lacking both direct access to the revolutionary government and accurate information about internal developments within Iran, the U.S. government—or more precisely, the cabal within the National Security Council that conducted the negotiations—decided to use a shady Iranian arms merchant, Manucher Ghorbanifar, as their principal intermediary. The initiative was soon taken over by Oliver North, a marine officer assigned to the U.S. National Security Council, and he and former U.S. national security advisor Robert C. McFarlane eventually made a secret visit to Tehran in May 1986 in an unsuccessful venture to get the hostages released. The continuing power struggle between moderates and extremists in Iran brought the negotiations to an end in November 1986, but not before the U.S. had sent Iran nearly sixteen hundred antitank missiles, assorted spare parts, and valuable intelligence information on Iraqi military deployments.

The attempt to trade arms for hostages improved neither the situation in Lebanon, the position of the Iranian "moderates," nor the state of U.S.-Iranian relations. Although the Shiites released one U.S. hostage in September 1985

---

[53] The best account of the Iran-*contra* affair is Theodore Draper, *A Very Thin Line: The Iran-Contra Affairs* (New York: Simon and Schuster, 1991). See also James A. Bill, "The U.S. Overture to Iran, 1985–86: An Analysis," in Keddie and Gasiorowski, *Neither East Nor West*, 166–79; Peter Kornbluh and Malcolm Byrne, eds., *The Iran-Contra Scandal: The Declassified History* (New York: New Press, 1993); and Samuel Segev, *The Iranian Triangle: The Untold Story of Israel's Role in the Iran-Contra Affair* (New York: Free Press, 1988).

[54] At the request of the National Security Council, the Central Intelligence Agency prepared a new intelligence estimate on Iran in May 1985. It predicted that "the Khomeini regime will face serious instability," warned that Tehran's leadership "seems to have concluded that improvement of relations with the Soviet Union is essential to Iranian interest," and recommended that the United States begin active efforts compete for influence in Iran. In response, a National Security Council memorandum suggested that U.S. allies be encouraged to provide Iran with "selected military equipment . . . on a case-by-case basis." The texts of these memoranda are printed in the *Report of the President's Special Review Board* ("Tower Commission"), February 26, 1987, B-6:7; B-7:8; and the *Joint Hearings before the House Select Committee to Investigate Covert Arms Transactions with Iran and the Senate Select Committee on Secret Military Assistance to Iran and the Nicaraguan Opposition*, 100th Congress, 1st sess. (Washington, D.C.: U.S. Government Printing Office, 1988), vol. 100-10:512–18.

and another in July 1986, they replaced them by kidnapping two more U.S. citizens in September 1986. The exposure of the secret arms shipments embarrassed the Reagan administration and alarmed its Arab allies, who saw the initiative as a hypocritical departure that undercut efforts to contain Iran. Moreover, the revelation that Iranian government officials had held secret negotiations with the "Great Satan" revived Iranian fears about U.S. influence and forced pragmatists such as Rafsanjani to revert to more hard-line positions. In sum, the "arms for hostages" scheme was a fiasco from start to finish.

Rafsanjani made several cautious overtures to the United States early in 1987, but relations between the two countries deteriorated after the "arms for hostages" scheme unraveled.[55] In an attempt to cut Iraq's oil revenues and reduce Arab support for Baghdad, Iran had begun laying mines in the Persian Gulf and threatening to attack oil shipments from Saudi Arabia and Kuwait. To restore its credibility with the gulf Arabs and bring additional pressure to bear on Iran, the U.S. eventually agreed to place Kuwaiti tankers under U.S. registry and provide a naval escort for tankers using Kuwaiti and Saudi ports. This decision led to repeated confrontations between the U.S. and Iranian forces: a U.S. fighter fired on an Iranian F-14 in August, and U.S. naval units sank an Iranian ship laying mines in the gulf the following month. In October, U.S. naval forces sank three Iranian gunboats after they fired on a U.S. helicopter and destroyed several Iranian oil platforms in retaliation for missile attacks on two U.S. tankers. The Senate banned oil imports from Iran in September, and President Reagan announced a complete ban on Iranian imports and an embargo on "militarily useful" exports in October, while minor clashes between U.S. and Iranian forces continued into the following year. Finally, the U.S. destroyer *Vincennes* mistakenly shot down an Iranian civilian airliner on July 2, killing all 290 people aboard.

The tragedy brought defiant protests from Tehran, but it also seems to have convinced Khomeini to end the war. Rafsanjani announced that concluding the war would allow Iran to follow a more "open" foreign policy, but in fact it did not lead to a significant improvement in U.S.-Iranian relations. The hostages in Lebanon remained a sore point and U.S. officials were no longer willing to make concessions to hasten their release. The United States rejected an Iranian offer to mediate in exchange for the release of additional Iranian assets in August, and the Iranian government denounced a conciliatory letter from former president Carter to Khomeini and Rafsanjani as a "new trick." Although Iran's deputy foreign minister hinted that relations with the United States might be restored, Rafsanjani declared that

[55] In April, Rafsanjani declared that normal relations with the United States would be possible once it stopped threatening Iran. He later stated that Iran would help obtain the release of U.S. hostages in Lebanon if the Americans showed goodwill by releasing frozen Iranian assets, adding that relations need not remain poor "until doomsday." "Chronology," *MEJ* 41, no. 4 (1987), 601.

public opinion was still not ready for such a step. Finally, the radical turn signaled by Khomeini's condemnation of author Salman Rushdie in February ended any possibility of a rapprochement between the two states.[56]

Khomeini's death began a brief period of moderation in Iran's foreign policy, but relations with the United States stayed chilly at best. In August, however, Rafsanjani made a public speech declaring that the hostage problem could be solved peacefully, and Iran reportedly helped obtain the release of two U.S. hostages later in the year.[57] Iran remained neutral in the 1991 Gulf War (though it did express concern about the enormous Western presence in the Persian Gulf region) and Rafsanjani made several cautious overtures to the United States as part of his effort to resuscitate Iran's stagnant economy and end its international isolation.[58]

These veiled feelers failed to elicit a favorable response from Washington, however, and a radical resurgence in 1992 soon removed any possibility of a détente. Although Rafsanjani expressed his continued desire for improved relations with the West and specifically requested "goodwill gestures" from the United States, his efforts were hamstrung by radical opposition within Iran and by U.S. concerns about Iran's support for international terrorism and the potential spread of Islamic fundamentalism. Indeed, the Clinton administration labeled Iran "an international outlaw" and a "pariah" in May 1993, as part of a policy of "dual containment" aimed equally at Baghdad and Tehran.[59] Despite the costs to both powers, in short, relations between

[56] See Wright, *In the Name of God*, 256–57; "Iranian Dismisses Prospects of Thaw with Washington," *New York Times*, February 6, 1989, A1. Minister of the Interior Ali Akbar Mohtashemi blamed U.S. and British intelligence agencies for the publication of Rushdie's book and called it part of a "new war against Islam," and Khomeini declared that it was useless for Iran to act in a pragmatic manner thinking that the West would "humanely reciprocate." "Chronology," *MEJ* 63, no. 3 (1989), 483.

[57] The United States also paid Iran $287 million for military equipment ordered by the shah but never delivered, thereby resolving the last financial dispute stemming from the 1980 hostage crisis. See *MECS 1991* (Boulder, Colo.: Westview, 1992), 32–33; Hunter, *Iran after Khomeini*, 123.

[58] In April 1990, one of Rafsanjani's associates wrote an article calling for improved relations with the U.S., and another advisor told a *New York Times* reporter that Washington and Tehran could enjoy a "marriage of convenience." In March 1991, Rafsanjani declared that the U.S. presence in the Persian Gulf was "not useful" but also "not a threat to Iran," and he later suggested that Iran needed a "prudent policy" so it could "help people without being accused of engaging in terrorism, without anyone being able to call us fanatics." The radical clerics were uncompromising, however, and even Rafsanjani suggested that the United States would have to make the first move in order to overcome Iranian suspicions. See *MECS 1991*, 384–86, 394–96; and Hooshang Amirahradi, "Iran and the Persian Gulf Crisis," in his and Nader Entessar's edited *Iran and the Arab World* (New York: St. Martin's, 1993), 109–10, 118–19.

[59] U.S. concerns increased after the terrorist bombing of the World Trade Center in New York in February 1993 and were reinforced by Tehran's vocal support for the fundamentalist movements in Sudan, Egypt, and Algeria. See *Middle East International*, no. 444 (February 19, 1993), 10; no. 452 (June 11, 1993), 3–4; and no. 453 (June 25, 1993), 12–13; "Fearing More Hostility from Iran, U.S. Considers Moves to Isolate It," *New York Times*, May 27, 1993, A1, A4.

the United States and Iran remained estranged more than fifteen years after the fall of the shah.[60]

## The Soviet Union and Revolutionary Iran

The Soviet Union welcomed the Iranian Revolution at first, because it overthrew an important U.S. ally and gave the Soviets an opportunity to expand their own influence. As the campaign to oust the shah gathered momentum in the fall of 1978, Soviet premier Leonid Brezhnev stated that the Soviet Union opposed "foreign interference by anyone." The warning was reiterated in January 1980 and Brezhnev informed the Bazargan government that he hoped "good neighborly relations will develop fruitfully."[61] Iranian foreign minister Karim Sanjavi replied that Iran "genuinely wants friendly relations with the USSR," and the Soviet government subsequently vetoed a UN Security Council resolution calling for economic sanctions in response to the detention of the U.S. hostages. The Soviets condemned the U.S. rescue mission in April, agreed that Iran could ship goods across Soviet territory in the event of a U.S. blockade, and issued frequent warnings about America's hostile intentions. The pro-Soviet Tudeh Party supported Khomeini and the radical clergy against both Bazargan and Bani-Sadr, and the Soviets endorsed Iran's request for an investigation of the shah's rule by the UN Security Council. The Islamic Republic also established close ties with Soviet allies such as Libya, Syria, South Yemen, and the Palestine Liberation Organization, indicating that the fall of the shah had brought Moscow and Tehran closer together.[62]

But it soon became apparent that the establishment of the Islamic Republic had created as many problems for the Soviet Union as it had solved. To begin with, the revolution introduced an element of instability into a region on the Soviets' southern border, which increased the risk of U.S. military involvement and raised concerns about the impact of Islamic fundamentalism on the Muslim population of the Soviet Union. Khomeini and his followers saw Soviet Communism as an atheistic ideology that was every bit as objectionable as Western capitalism, and Khomeini soon declared, "We are in con-

---

[60] A useful guide to the present state of U.S.-Iranian relations is Geoffrey Kemp, *Forever Enemies? American Policy and the Islamic Republic of Iran* (Washington, D.C.: Carnegie Endowment for International Peace, 1994).

[61] Quoted in Hiro, *Iran under the Ayatollahs*, 283. In 1981, Brezhnev termed the Iranian Revolution a "major international event" and said that, "for all its complications and contradictions, it is still fundamentally an anti-imperialist revolution." Quoted in Karen Dawisha and Hélène Carrère d'Encausse, "Islam in the Foreign Policy of the Soviet Union: A Double-Edged Sword?" in Dawisha, *Islam in Foreign Policy*, 170.

[62] See Menashri, *Iran*, 99; Hunter, *Iran and the World*, 85, and "Soviet-Iranian Relations in the Post-Revolution Period," in *Iran's Revolution: The Search for Consensus*, ed. R. K. Ramazani (Bloomington: Indiana University Press, 1990), 86.

flict with international communism to the same extent as we are against the Western exploiters. . . . The danger of communist power is not less than that of America."[63] Iran's new leaders were well aware of earlier Soviet attempts to dominate Iran, and the new regime abrogated the 1921 Soviet-Persian friendship treaty in November 1980. Iran accused the Soviet Union of supplying arms to the Kurds and other rebellious ethnic minorities, and President Bani-Sadr warned that the Soviet Union "sought to divide Iran" in order to extend its control to the Indian Ocean.[64] The Soviet invasion of Afghanistan was another source of tension, both because Afghanistan was a Muslim country and because the invasion reinforced Iranian fears about Soviet intentions.[65] Iran's fear of Communist subversion was another sore point, and as noted earlier, Iran eventually banned the Tudeh Party and expelled eighteen Soviet diplomats in April 1983.[66] Finally, the Iraqi invasion in September 1980 posed a serious dilemma for the Soviet Union, as Iraq, a long-standing ally, was heavily dependent on Soviet weaponry. The Soviets declared they would remain neutral and offered to sell arms to Iran, but their support for Iraq would remain a contentious issue for the rest of the decade.[67]

By the mid-1980s, Soviet relations with Iran were much worse than they had been under the shah. Early hopes that the revolution might take on a "progressive" character had been dashed, and Iran's military successes against Iraq threatened to shift the regional balance of power and boost the ideological appeal of Islamic fundamentalism.[68] Cooperation between

[63] Quoted in Menashri, *Iran*, 156. In 1980, then-foreign minister Sadeq Qotbzadeh told Soviet foreign minister Andrei Gromyko, "Our Imam has described the United States as a great satan. Unfortunately, you too have proved in practice that you are no less satanic than the United States." Quoted in Yodfat, *Soviet Union and Revolutionary Iran*, 71.

[64] See Menashri, *Iran*, 99; "Chronology," *MEJ* 34, no. 2 (1980), 171; and Richard K. Herrmann, "The Role of Iran in Soviet Perceptions and Policy, 1946–1988," in Keddie and Gasiorowski, *Neither East Nor West*, 78–80.

[65] Foreign Minister Qotbzadeh called the invasion of Afghanistan "a hostile measure . . . against all Muslims of the world." Quoted in Hiro, *Iran under the Ayatollahs*, 284. Similarly, Khomeini condemned "the savage occupation of Afghanistan by the aggressive plunderers of the East" and hoped that "the noble Muslim people of Afghanistan will achieve victory . . . and be delivered from the clutches of the so-called champions of the working class." Quoted in Zalmay Khalilzad, "Soviet Dilemmas in Khomeini's Iran," in Rosen, *Iran since the Revolution*, 121.

[66] Rafsanjani called the Tudeh Party a "disreputable party with a filthy record" in November 1982, and Radio Tehran announced in May 1983 that "the mercenary leaders of that party . . . were laying the foundations of a . . . creeping *coup d'état* so that they could . . . drag the country in the direction they wished." "Chronology," *MEJ* 37, no. 2 (1983), 246; and Yodfat, *Soviet Union and Revolutionary Iran*, 132, 142–44.

[67] An Iranian mob attacked the Soviet embassy in Tehran in December 1980, and the Soviets suspended arms shipments to Iraq for a year. Shipments resumed after a series of Iranian victories in 1982. See Hiro, *Iran under the Ayatollahs*, 287; Yodfat, *Soviet Union and Revolutionary Iran*, 81, 134–36; Menashri, *Iran*, 207; "Chronology," *MEJ* 37, no. 2 (1983), 246; and 42, no. 2 (1988), 466.

[68] See Hunter, "Soviet-Iranian Relations," 90.

[231]

Moscow and Tehran was confined to economic affairs, as the Soviet Union had become an increasingly important avenue for Iranian foreign trade once Iran's major ports were damaged in the war with Iraq. The two states eventually signed a major economic agreement, in February 1982, and subsequent trade deals helped compensate for the loss of trade between Iran and the West.[69] Rafsanjani described relations as "somewhat improved" in 1985; Prime Minister Musavi called the Soviet approach to the Iran-Iraq war "more realistic." Tensions reemerged after Iraqi president Saddam Hussein visited Moscow in December and got a renewed pledge of Soviet arms. Musavi now accused the Soviets of having "long desired access to southern waters through Iran," while Foreign Minister Velayati declared that "Iran will never accept Soviet domination."[70]

Both Iran's refusal to end the war with Iraq and the continued Soviet presence in Afghanistan remained major sources of strain, and talks between Velayati and Soviet president Andrei Gromyko in February 1987 were described as "businesslike." Khomeini repeated his condemnation of Soviet support for Iraq; President Khamenei called Soviet policy in the gulf a "grave error" in April, and Iranian gunboats attacked a Soviet tanker in May. The U.S. reflagging operation and the resulting confrontation between the U.S. and Iran brought Moscow and Tehran closer together in the summer, however, and Rafsanjani accepted an invitation to visit the Soviet Union at some point in the future. The Soviets also persuaded the UN Security Council to delay imposition of an arms embargo against Iran in the fall, but Iran's continued suspicions and the Soviets' reluctance to jeopardize their opening to the West kept the emerging detente from developing further.[71]

Relations improved sharply following the Iranian ceasefire with Iraq and the Soviet withdrawal from Afghanistan. The Soviets offered to aid Iran's postwar reconstruction, and Deputy Foreign Minister Vorontsov admitted that "mistakes had been made" in Moscow's earlier dealings with Iran.[72] Another series of economic agreements was completed in the fall of 1988, and Khomeini called for improved relations between the two countries in a personal message to Gorbachev in January 1989. Soviet foreign minister Eduard Shevardnadze met with Khomeini during a visit to Iran in February, when

[69] There were also reports that Soviet intelligence officials were advising the Revolutionary Guards and that the Soviet Union and Iran had signed a secret military agreement in May 1982, but these stories were probably fabrications by exile groups hoping to obtain more support from the West. See Yodfat, *Soviet Union and Revolutionary Iran*, 98–99, 101, 132; and Menashri, *Iran*, 249.

[70] Quoted in Menashri, *Iran*, 363–64; and Hunter, "Soviet-Iranian Relations," 94.

[71] On these events, see *MECS 1987* (Boulder, Colo.: Westview, 1989), 414–15; Hunter, *Iran and the World*, 90–92; and Robert O. Freedman, "Gorbachev, Iran, and the Iran-Iraq War," in Keddie and Gasiorowski, *Neither East Nor West*, 122–28.

[72] Quoted in Hunter, "Soviet-Iranian Relations," 97–99.

the Soviets reportedly passed on intelligence information about a U.S. spy ring within the Iranian armed forces. The rift with the West occasioned by the Rushdie affair in February 1989 pushed Iran even closer to the Soviet Union, and Khomeini endorsed Shevardnadze's call for improved ties by saying that Iran wanted better relations in order to resist the "devilish acts of the West." Rafsanjani visited the Soviet Union three weeks after Khomeini's death, and Gorbachev told him, "Our country supports your anti-imperialist revolution. . . . We are ready to go as far as Iran is ready to meet us." The two states signed a series of agreements for technical, cultural, scientific, and economic cooperation, and their subsequent joint declaration referred to "strengthening Iran's defense capability," suggesting that Iran was preparing to obtain weapons directly from the Soviet Union. Foreign Minister Velayati praised the policy of glasnost then underway in the Soviet Union, and Rafsanjani declared that the Soviets now "comprehended the reality of the [Islamic] revolution."[73] Thus, despite the ideological differences that still survived, relations between Iran and the Soviet Union were assuming a more normal footing as the Soviet Union itself began to come apart.

## Relations with Medium Powers

Iran had enjoyed good political relations with Western Europe and Japan under the shah, based largely on Iran's importance as an oil supplier. The revolution damaged Iran's relations with each of these states, but the effects were generally not as severe as in the case of the United States.

*Great Britain.* Great Britain's earlier involvement in Iran had left a legacy of suspicion. Attacks on the British embassy and several representatives of the Anglican Church led London to withdraw most of its diplomatic personnel in 1980.[74] Britain supported the imposition of economic sanctions after the seizure of the U.S. embassy and reluctantly joined the U.S.-led embargo in June 1980.[75] The arrest of a group of Iranian students following a vi-

---

[73] Khomeini's message also described Communism as an obsolete ideology and suggested that Gorbachev should embrace Islam instead. For these quotations, see Manshour Varasteh, "The Soviet Union and Iran, 1979–89," in Ehteshami and Varasteh, *Iran and the International Community*, 57–59; "Chronology," *MEJ* 43, no. 3 (1989), 483; Hunter, *Iran and the World*, 94; Carol R. Saivetz, "The Soviet Union and Iran: Changing Relations in the Gorbachev Era," in *Iran at the Crossroads: Global Relations in a Turbulent Decade*, ed. Miron Rezun (Boulder, Colo.: Westview, 1990), 195–96; *MECS 1989*, 365; and Herrmann, "Role of Iran in Soviet Perceptions," 89.

[74] Khomeini once termed Britain "the aged wolf of imperialism." Quoted in Geoffrey Parsons, "Iran and Western Europe," in Ramazani, *Iran's Revolution*, 71.

[75] British participation in the embargo was limited to contracts signed after June 1980. See Robert Carswell and Richard Davis, "The Economic and Financial Pressures: Freeze and Sanctions," in Christopher et al., *American Hostages in Iran*, 198–99.

olent demonstration at the Iranian embassy in London was a further source of tension, leading Rafsanjani to warn of an "appropriate reaction" unless the students were released.[76]

Subsequent efforts to improve relations foundered over Iran's extreme sensitivity to any sign of British opposition. The trade embargo was lifted after the release of the U.S. hostages, and Britain adopted a carefully neutral position in the Iran-Iraq war. Britain allowed an "Iranian Purchasing Office" to remain in London, where it conducted some of Iran's dealings in the private arms markets, and a visit by a British trade mission in May 1983 fueled expectations of a rapid increase in Anglo-Iranian trade.[77] Yet relations between the two countries remained fragile; Britain refused to accept the credentials of an Iranian envoy in 1986, and Iran responded by rejecting a British diplomat's credentials shortly thereafter. The arrest of an Iranian diplomat for shoplifting in May 1987 led to the arrest and beating of a British diplomat in Tehran, triggering a series of tit-for-tat expulsions that ended with the two states breaking diplomatic relations. British naval forces participated in the multinational effort to escort merchant shipping in the Persian Gulf in 1987, and the British government shut down the Iranian Purchasing Office in London after a British vessel was fired upon by Iranian forces. The British supported the UN effort to impose an arms embargo on Iran in order to force acceptance of Resolution 598, and Foreign Minister Geoffrey Howe declared that although "the door was ajar" to improved relations, "the ball was in the Iranian hand."[78]

Movement toward détente between Britain and Iran resumed in June 1988, beginning with an agreement on compensation for the damage to their respective embassies. A decision to restore diplomatic relations was announced in September, and relations were formally reestablished two months later. The Rushdie affair reversed this positive trend, however; Rushdie went into hiding in Great Britain, Iran severed relations once again, and the Majlis voted to suspend commercial ties as well. Although Rafsanjani and the moderates resumed efforts to normalize relations in the early 1990s, the reaffirmation of the *fatwa* against Rushdie and the radical resurgence at the end of 1992 blocked any significant improvement in Anglo-Iranian relations.

*France.* Unlike the United States, Great Britain, or the Soviet Union, France had no prior imperial role in Iran. In addition, the French government had granted Khomeini political asylum following his deportation from Iraq in 1978, and one might have expected Franco-Iranian ties to have

---

[76] "Chronology," *MEJ* 35, no. 1 (1981), 46.
[77] Parsons, "Iran and Western Europe," 80.
[78] See *MECS 1987*, 413–14; and "Chronology," *MEJ* 41, no. 4 (1987), 602.

profited from this favorable historical legacy. Yet relations between France and revolutionary Iran were still strained, despite several well-intentioned efforts to establish a cordial relationship.

Tensions between France and Iran arose from several separate issues. France had become the preferred haven for the anti-Khomeini opposition, including former prime minister Bakhtiar, former president Bani-Sadr, Islamic Mujahedin leader Masoud Rajavi, and several members of the Pahlavi family. The revolutionary government accused France of providing asylum to "criminal leaders" and held it responsible for "attacks against the clergy." A congratulatory message from President François Mitterand following Rajai's election in 1981 was denounced as a lie, and the assassination of a number of exile leaders on French soil both angered and alarmed the French.[79] Relations were strained further when a group of Iranian exiles seized a French-built missile boat previously ordered by the shah. French officials recovered the ship and transferred it to Iran but refused to turn over the hijackers despite strong Iranian protests. In Lebanon, Iran's support for radical Shiite groups clashed with France's traditional support for the Lebanese Christians; pro-Iranian factions kidnapped several French citizens; and a terrorist truck bomb killed fifty-eight French soldiers in the UN peacekeeping force.[80] A final issue was French military support for Iraq: in addition to selling billions of dollars of weapons to the Iraqis, France also leased them five warplanes equipped with Exocet antiship missiles, which greatly enhanced their ability to attack Iran's oil and shipping facilities.[81]

France sought to normalize relations with the Islamic Republic in 1986 in an attempt to obtain the release of its Lebanese hostages. A French parliamentary delegation visited Tehran in January, middle-level officials exchanged visits in May and September, and France subsequently agreed to repay $330 million of a $1 billion loan provided by the Pahlavi regime, in exchange for the release of two French hostages. It also agreed to expel a number of members of the Mujahedin as a goodwill gesture. This détente evaporated the following year, however, after the French tried to interrogate Vahid Gordji, an Iranian translator whom they suspected of participating in a series of terrorist bombings. Gordji took refuge in the Iranian embassy, which the French promptly blockaded, leading Iran to surround the French

---

[79] "Chronology," *MEJ* 36, no. 4 (1982), 72. The shah's nephew was assassinated in Paris in 1979, former prime minister Bakhtiar narrowly escaped an attack in 1980 (a subsequent attempt in August 1991 succeeded) and General Ghulam Ovaisi, commander-in-chief of the army under the shah, was murdered in Paris in February 1984. See Parsons, "Iran and Western Europe," 75; Hiro, *Iran under the Ayatollahs*, 267; and "Killing Off Iranian Dissenters: Bloody Trail Back to Tehran," *Washington Post*, November 21, 1993, A1.

[80] See Hunter, *Iran and the World*, 150; and George Joffee, "Iran, the Southern Mediterranean, and Europe," in Ehteshemi and Varasteh, *Iran and the International Community*, 87–88.

[81] See Hiro, *Longest War*, 82, 123–27; Mark Heller, *The Iran-Iraq War: Implications for Third Parties* (Tel Aviv: Jaffee Center for Strategic Studies, 1984), 39–40; and *MECS 1987*, 412.

embassy in Tehran and arrest a French diplomat on various fabricated charges. France broke diplomatic relations, imposed an embargo on Iranian oil, and sent French warships to join the U.S.-led flotilla in the Persian Gulf.[82]

Gordji was finally deported in December 1987, and the end of the Iran-Iraq war paved the way for a slightly more durable détente.[83] Diplomatic relations were restored in June 1988 after France expelled fourteen members of the Islamic Mujahedin and agreed to repay another $300 million of the Iranian loan. The oil embargo was soon lifted, and French foreign minister Roland Dumas visited Tehran in February 1989. Khomeini's campaign against Salman Rushdie slowed the process of normalization at this point, but diplomatic ties were not cut off. Both sides seemed interested in establishing a less acrimonious relationship (though the French decision to try two Iranian citizens for the murder of former prime minister Bakhtiar had cast yet another shadow over Franco-Iranian relations at the end of 1994).[84]

*Other Medium Powers.* In contrast to its relations with Britain and France, Iran's dealings with other medium powers were fairly benign. West Germany joined the Western appeal for release of the U.S. hostages and supported the economic embargo but did not take a strong position. The West German government served as an intermediary during the hostage crisis; Foreign Minister Hans-Dietrich Genscher became the first Western leader to visit the Islamic Republic in July 1984.[85] Germany had become one of Iran's largest trading partners by 1986, and a brief rift following a West German television broadcast mocking Khomeini healed quickly.[86] Germany helped dilute UN Resolution 598 to make it more palatable to Iran, and Tehran returned the favor by facilitating the release of two German hostages in Lebanon in September 1988. The German government responded with uncharacteristic sharpness to the death threat against Salman Rushdie, recalling their ambassador for "consultations" and hinting of economic sanctions, but a complete rift was avoided and German-Iranian relations resumed their generally cordial nature after Khomeini's death. Iran remained Germany's largest Middle Eastern trading partner, and an Iranian diplomat ad-

---

[82] See "Chronology," *MEJ* 42, no. 1 (1988), 94–95; *MECS 1987*, 412–13.

[83] President Khamenei remarked that France had given up its bullying and was trying to normalize relations, while Prime Minister Musavi stated that recent progress in relations had been "very good" and he hoped "this tendency will continue and expand." *MECS 1987*, 413.

[84] Evidence of this trend includes the French decision to repatriate two Iranians accused of murdering the brother of the head of the anti-Khomeini Islamic Mujahedin. See "France Sends Two Murder Suspects Back to Iran, Stirring Wide Protest," *New York Times*, January 4, 1994, A5.

[85] Genscher reported that Iran "sought better relations with the West," a view that overlooked the divisions on this issue within Iran. See "Chronology," *MEJ* 39, no. 1 (1985), 112.

[86] Iran responded by expelling two German diplomats in February 1987. *MECS 1987*, 409.

mitted in October 1993 that the German and Iranian security agencies had engaged in "close collaboration" for several years. Germany had continued to take a softer line toward Iran than the other Western powers, but its decision to place an Iranian diplomat on trial for the murder of several Kurdish exiles introduced a discordant note in the harmony between Berlin and Tehran in 1992.[87]

Relations between Iran and Japan have followed a similar pattern. Strong U.S. pressure persuaded Japan to reduce its oil purchases and impose other economic sanctions during the hostage crisis, but Japan has gone to some lengths to preserve its economic links with Iran.[88] Rafsanjani visited Japan in June 1984, and Iranian officials praised Japan's lack of an imperialist past and its achievements as a non-Western power. Minor tensions arose from Japan's refusal to complete a petrochemical project begun prior to the revolution, and from its oil purchases from other Arab states, but Japan has succeeded in maintaining an essentially neutral position.[89]

The Islamic Republic also established cordial relations with China and several less powerful states. China and Iran were brought together in part by their fear of the Soviet Union (especially after the invasion of Afghanistan), and Iran's difficulties in obtaining arms from the West led naturally to arms deals with China and North Korea. The Islamic Republic also cultivated economic and political ties with several Eastern European states and a number of smaller European Community powers, suggesting that its Islamic ideology did not interfere with efforts to improve relations with smaller states, regardless of their internal arrangments or external commitments.[90]

## Iran and the Arab World

Under the shah, Iran's relations with most of the Arab world were guarded at best. In addition to inheriting the historical rivalries between Persians and Arabs and the Sunni-Shiite division within Islam, the shah was openly hostile to pan-Arabism and especially to "Arab socialists" such as Gamal Abdel Nasser of Egypt or the Baath regimes in Syria and Iraq. Al-

---

[87] See *Middle East International*, no. 461 (October 22, 1993), 13, and no. 463 (November 19, 1993), 11.

[88] Japan had replaced the United States as Iran's largest trading partner by 1982. See Kamran Mofid, "The Political Economy of Iran's Foreign Trade since the Revolution," in Ehteshami and Varasteh, *Iran and the International Community*, 150–51; and Hunter, *Iran and the World*, 193–96.

[89] Menashri, *Iran*, 365; and Hunter, *Iran and the World*, 162.

[90] Iran purchased $600 million worth of Chinese arms in 1986 and $1 billion worth in 1987, and there were reports of negotiations for the purchase of Scud missiles from North Korea in the early 1990s. R. K. Ramazani, "Iran's Resistance to the U.S. Intervention in the Persian Gulf," in Keddie and Gasiorowski, *Neither East nor West*, 44–45.

though the shah and the conservative Arab monarchies shared a pro-Western orientation and an aversion to radical political movements of any kind, the gulf states were also concerned by Iran's growing power, the shah's regional ambitions, and Iran's close ties with Israel. By introducing a powerful ideological dimension into Iran's foreign policy, however, the revolution intensified mutual perceptions of threat and helped trigger a bitter and protracted war with Iraq.

*The Iran-Iraq War.* Given that Iran and Iraq had been rivals since their emergence as independent states, and that Iran had held the upper hand since the early 1970s, it is hardly surprising that Iraq welcomed the fall of the shah at first. The Iraqi government sent a congratulatory message to Khomeini upon the founding of the Islamic Republic and invited Bazargan to visit Baghdad, but relations soon deteriorated and President Saddam Hussein decided to launch a full-scale invasion of Iran in September 1980.[91]

The Iranian threat to Iraq sprang from several sources. Iranian control of the Shatt al-Arab threatened Iraq's only port, thereby jeopardizing Iraq's foreign trade, especially its oil exports. Moreover, the Islamic Republic had refused to withdraw from several territories it promised to vacate as part of the Algiers accord in 1975 and had resumed its support for the Kurdish insurgents within Iraq. Iraq responded in kind, sending material aid to Arab and Kurdish rebels within Iran.

Most important of all, Khomeini's universalist ideology directly challenged its Arab neighbors, and especially secular regimes such as the Iraqi Baath. Shiites make up roughly 55 percent of the Iraqi population, and among them the revolution in Iran had clearly sparked greater restiveness.[92] Under the leadership of Muhammed Baqir al-Sadr, a cleric with ties to Khomeini, a fundamentalist movement known as Al-Dawa al-Islamiya (Islamic Call) had become increasingly active in the 1960s. Iran began providing rhetorical and material support to the Shiite underground in Iraq in

[91] Iraq praised Iran's "independent foreign policy" after the latter withdrew from the Central Treaty Organization (CENTO) in the spring of 1979, and then-president Ahmad al-Bakr offered "best wishes for the friendly Iranian people" and called for "the closest ties of friendship" between Iran and the Arab states in April. See Ramazani, *Revolutionary Iran*, 58–59; Jasim M. Abdulghani, *Iraq and Iran: The Years of Crisis* (Baltimore: Johns Hopkins University Press, 1984), 181–82; Philip Robins, "Iraq: Revolutionary Threats and Regime Responses," in *The Iranian Revolution: Its Global Impact*, ed. John L. Esposito (Miami: Florida International University Press, 1990), 83; and Efraim Karsh, "Military Power and Foreign Policy Goals: The Iran-Iraq War Revisited," *International Affairs* 64, no. 1 (1987–88), 87.

[92] Baath concerns were nicely revealed by President Hussein's warnings in February and June 1980 that Iraq might break up into separate Sunni, Shiite, and Kurdish portions if preventive steps were not taken. See Amazia Baram, "Mesopotamian Identity in Ba'thi Iraq," *Middle Eastern Studies* 19, no. 4 (1983), 445 and n. 85, and "The Impact of Khomeini's Revolution on the Radical Shi'i Movement of Iraq," in Menashri, *Iranian Revolution and the Muslim World*, 140–43.

the fall of 1979, and Iranian officials made no secret of their desire to replace the Baath regime in Iraq with another Islamic republic. Khomeini named Sadr head of the "Supreme Council of the Islamic Revolution of Iraq," and al-Sadr began to issue increasingly explicit calls for a Shiite uprising. A group of Shiites of Iranian origin tried to assassinate Iraqi deputy premier Tariq Aziz in April 1980, and Khomeini now declared that "the people and Army of Iraq must turn their back on the Baath regime and overthrow it."[93] Iraq responded by increasing its support for Iranian dissidents and launching a crackdown against Al-Dawa adherents. Sadr was arrested and executed and over 35,000 Shiites were deported, while the government began a major campaign to improve living conditions in the remaining Shiite communities in order to reduce their receptivity to Iranian propaganda. The war of words escalated throughout 1980, with neither side attempting to conceal its hostility.[94]

Iraq's decision to invade was primarily a response to its fear of Iranian fundamentalism, but it also reflected Iraq's larger ambitions within the Arab world. In addition, Iraqi officials were convinced that the revolution in Iran had created a set of unusually promising conditions: the military balance seemed to favor them, the Iranian armed forces had been weakened by purges and desertions, and the new regime faced a challenge from Kurdish insurgents and several other dissident ethnic groups.[95] The Iraqis also believed that the predominantly Arab population of Khuzistan (an oil-rich province adjacent to the border) would support the invasion and turn

[93] Quoted in Abdulghani, *Iraq and Iran*, 189. On these points see Baram, "Impact of Khomeini's Revolution," 141–42; Hanna Batatu, "Iraq's Underground Shi'a Movements: Characteristics, Causes, and Prospects," *MEJ* 35, no. 4 (1981); Robins, "Revolutionary Threats and Regime Responses," 85–92; Zonis and Brumberg, *Khomeini, Iran, Arab World*, 62–67; King, *Iran-Iraq War*, 8–9; and Halliday, "Iranian Foreign Policy," 95–96.

[94] Iranian officials described the Baath as "fascist and racist" and as being a "bunch of atheists." Iraqi leaders portrayed Khomeini's religious views as "a medieval sectarian philosophy" and called the Islamic Republic a backwards regime of "dwarf Persians." Iranian foreign minister Qotzbadeh announced, "We have decided to overthrow the Ba'thist regime of Iraq," and Khomeini warned that if Iraq attacked Iran, "the Iranian Army would advance toward Baghdad to . . . overthrow the regime there." Abdulghani, *Iraq and Iran*, 181–92.

[95] Roughly 23,000 Iranian military officers had been executed or purged or had fled into exile by 1986. The army lost 50 percent of the officers between the ranks of major and colonel, the air force lost 50 percent of its pilots, and the regular army dropped from 285,000 men to approximately 150,000. See Karsh, "Military Power and Foreign Policy," 89–90, William F. Hickman, *Ravaged and Reborn: The Iranian Military 1982*, Staff Paper (Washington, D.C.: Brookings Institution, 1982), 8–18; Sepehr Zabih, *The Iranian Military in Revolution and War* (London: Routledge, 1988), chap. 5; Nikola B. Schahgaldian with the assistance of Gina Barkhordarian, *The Iranian Military under the Islamic Republic* (Santa Monica, Calif.: Rand Corp., 1987), 17–27; Gregory F. Rose, "The Post-Revolutionary Purge of Iran's Armed Forces: A Revisionist Assessment," *Iranian Studies* 17, nos. 2–3, (1984); and Nader Entessar, "The Military and Politics in the Islamic Republic of Iran," in *Post-Revolutionary Iran*, ed. Hooshang Amirahmadi and Manoucher Parvin (Boulder, Colo.: Westview, 1988), esp. 61–65.

against the government in Tehran. This sense of optimism was encouraged by the testimony of Iranian exiles in Baghdad, including former prime minister Bakhtiar and several former Iranian generals.[96] The window of opportunity would not last forever, and the threat would increase dramatically once the Islamic Republic began to mobilize Iran's superior resources.

Given these beliefs, the temptation to eliminate the threat through the use of force proved irresistible. At a minimum, Iraq's leaders sought to restore its former position in the Shatt al-Arab, create a buffer zone along the border, and persuade Iran to halt its support for dissident Shiites in Iraq. At most, they hoped to annex Khuzistan—thereby acquiring some of Iran's most valuable oil fields—and perhaps to topple or divide the new regime as well. Any of these outcomes would reduce the threat from Iran and enhance Iraq's overall position.[97]

Unfortunately for Hussein, the decision to invade was based on several profound miscalculations. The danger that the revolution in Iran would spread to Iraq turned out to be minimal, as the vast majority of Iraqi Shiites remained loyal to Baghdad; even the execution of Muhammed al-Sadr in June 1980 did not cause significant unrest. Similarly, the Arab population of Khuzistan did not rise up and welcome the Iraqi invaders, and the Iraqi Army proved to be a less potent offensive weapon than Hussein had hoped. Far from undermining the Islamic Republic, the invasion enabled the Iranian clergy to invoke Iranian nationalism and traditional Arab-Persian animosities as a means of rallying popular support. Like the Austro-Prussian invasion of 1792 and the Allied intervention in Russia in 1918, the Iraqi attack also justified extensive efforts by the revolutionary state to repress internal dissent, thereby facilitating the consolidation of the clerical regime.[98]

Most important of all, Hussein and his advisors misjudged the resolve and the fighting capacities of the Islamic Republic. Although Iran's military effort suffered from poor leadership, inadequate supplies, and rivalries within the revolutionary elite, the enthusiasm and commitment of the Rev-

---

[96] See Renfrew, "Who Started the War?" 98; Hiro, *Longest War*, 2; King, *Iran-Iraq War*, 8–10; Efraim Karsh, *The Iran-Iraq War: A Military Analysis*, Adelphi Paper no. 220 (London: International Institute for Strategic Studies, 1987), 11–13; and Jiman Tagavi, "The Iran-Iraq War: The First Three Years," in Rosen, *Iran since the Revolution*, 67.

[97] Iraqi officials denied any annexationist ambitions, but Hussein added that "if the [Khuzistanis,] Baluchis, or Azerbaijanis want their stand and decision to be different, then this will be another matter." Another Iraqi official warned that "Arabistan [Khuzistan] oil will remain Iraqi" unless Iran agreed to negotiate, and Iraqi deputy prime minister Tariq Aziz commented that "Five small Irans would be better than one big Iran." Similarly, Hussein declared, "We are for [Iran's] fragmentation, weakening, destruction, and instability as long as it is an enemy of the Arab nation and Iraq." Hiro, *Longest War*, 46; Hunter, *Iran and the World*, 106; and Abdulghani, *Iraq and Iran*, 205, 209.

[98] Bani-Sadr remarked in October 1980: "The war is very useful for us. It consolidates our Islamic Republic." Quoted in *MECS 1979–80* (New York: Holmes and Meier, 1981), 27; and see also *MECS 1981–82* (New York: Holmes and Meier, 1984), 543.

olutionary Guards and regular army more than compensated for these deficiencies. Like the revolutionary regimes in France and Russia, the Islamic Republic was able to direct the fervor that had toppled the old regime against a foreign invader.[99] Indeed, the revolutionary government refused to consider anything less than total victory, and its refusal to compromise would keep the war going for nearly eight years.[100]

The war itself can be divided into four main phases.[101] During the first phase, Iraq seized approximately ten thousand square miles of Iranian territory, capturing the city of Khorramshahr and laying siege to the refinery center at Abadan. The Iraqi advance halted at the end of November, and for the next twelve months there was little change in the adversaries' positions. Iran's military performance improved steadily throughout the year, however, and by September 1981 its army had lifted the siege of Abadan and made a number of minor gains. Both sides began attacking each other's oil facilities during this phase, but neither was able to land a decisive blow.[102]

The second phase began with a successful Iranian offensive in March 1982. A second advance in May retook Khorramshahr, and Hussein now ordered a complete Iraqi withdrawal. Iran rejected an offer to return to the status quo ante and launched a counterinvasion of Iraq in July, intended "to deliver the Iraqi nation from this accursed [Baath] party." In Khomeini's words, it was time for the Iraqi people to "rise up and install the Islamic government that you want. . . . Greet your Iranian brothers, so you can cut off the hands of the Ba'thists."[103]

Iran's decision to carry the war onto Iraqi soil was based on an exaggerated sense of its own military capabilities and ideological appeal.[104] Iran's

[99] See Hickman, *Ravaged and Reborn;* Schahgaldian, *Iranian Military;* and Theda Skocpol, "Social Revolutions and Mass Military Mobilization," *World Politics* 40, no. 2 (1988), 164–68.

[100] When the war broke out in 1980, Khomeini declared, "There was absolutely no question of peace or compromise and we shall never have any discussions with them." Bani-Sadr predicted that Iraq would lose the war "whatever they do and however much it costs us." He also estimated the war "would last fifteen days if Iraq received no outside assistance, otherwise until the last of 36 million Iranians are dead." Quoted in Ramazani, *Revolutionary Iran,* 64; and *MECS 1979–80,* 21.

[101] In addition to the sources cited below, this account is based on Hiro, *Longest War;* Shahram Chubin and Charles Tripp, *Iran and Iraq at War* (Boulder, Colo.: Westview, 1988); and Ephraim Karsh, *The Iran-Iraq War: A Military Analysis,* Adelphi Paper No. 220 (London: International Institute for Strategic Studies, 1987).

[102] See Anthony H. Cordesman, *The Gulf and the Search for Strategic Stability: Saudi Arabia, the Military Balance in the Gulf, and Trends in the Arab-Israeli Military Balance* (Boulder, Colo.: Westview, 1984), 545–49.

[103] See "Khomeini Urges Iraqis to Revolt," *Washington Post,* July 15, 1982, A1, A16.

[104] At the outset of the war, Khomeini told his followers that they "should never have any fear of anything. . . . With the weapons of faith and Islam, we shall succeed and we shall win." In 1984, Speaker Rafsanjani declared, "The faith of the Islamic troops is stronger than Iraq's superior firepower." Prime Minister Musavi stated the following year, "The power of faith can outmanoeuvre a complicated war machine used by people bereft of sublime reli-

leaders were convinced that the invasion would trigger an uprising by the Iraq's Shiite majority and that the creation of an Islamic republic in Iraq would accelerate the spread of revolutionary Islam throughout the region.[105] This belief was consistent with Khomeini's universalist ideology and was reinforced by reports of disturbances among the Iraqi Shiites and testimony from members of Al-Dawa who fled to Tehran during the war.[106]

Contrary to these expectations, however, the Shiite population in Iraq did not rise up to welcome the Iranian invaders. Furthermore, Iran's gains led the gulf states and a number of Western powers to tilt toward Iraq, and the third phase of the conflict was to be a bloody war of attrition. This phase also witnessed the escalation of air attacks on oil shipments and population centers, as well as Iran's covert efforts to obtain arms from the "Great Satan" in exchange for the U.S. hostages in Lebanon.

The stalemate was broken by Iran's seizure of the Fao Peninsula in February 1986, but this success was Iran's last important victory. Another offensive in January 1987 gained additional territory, but Iran's forces suffered heavy losses and failed to destroy Iraq's ability to resist. Iran's manpower reserves were dwindling after six years of fighting, and the military balance had shifted toward Iraq as the war entered its final phase. The Iranian decision to escalate the tanker war led the United States and several other powers to take an even more active role, and Iran could not match the scope or effectiveness of the Iraqi missile attacks, which resumed the following year.[107]

Strengthened by foreign assistance and the use of poison gas, Iraq recaptured the Fao Peninsula in April 1988 and regained the Majnoon Islands in June. Facing growing popular discontent, a deteriorating economy, and declining hopes of victory, Rafsanjani and the other moderates convinced

---

gion." Quoted in Ramazani, *Revolutionary Iran*, 64; Chubin, "Iran and the War," in Rezun, *Iran at the Crossroads*, 134; and Chubin and Tripp, *Iran and Iraq at War*, 42.

[105] As early as October 1979, Ayatollah Montazeri had predicted that if the Imam Khomeini ordered the Iraqi Shiites to rebel against the Baath, "the entire Iraq nation would rise." Foreign Broadcast Information Service *Daily Report: Middle East/North Africa*, October 22, 1979, R-7. In March 1982, President Khamenei declared: "The future government of Iraq should be an Islamic and popular one. . . . There is no difference between the two nations of Iran and Iraq in accepting the Imam as their leader. . . . The Imam is not limited by geographical frontiers." And in June 1982, Khomeini announced that "if Iran and Iraq unite and link up with one another, the smaller nations of the region will join them as well." Quoted in Bakhash, *Reign of the Ayatollahs*, 232, 235.

[106] See Robins, "Revolutionary Threats and Regime Responses," 88–93; and Hiro, *Longest War*, 61–62, 88.

[107] In February 1987, Rafsanjani admitted, "We cannot see a bright horizon now, so far as ending the war in its present form is concerned." Quoted in Ramazani, "Iran's Resistance," 48; and see also Wright, *In the Name of God*, 154–57; and Cordesman, *Gulf and the West*, 317–18, 422–32.

Khomeini that continuing the war might jeopardize the survival of the Islamic Republic itself. Calling the decision "more deadly for me than taking poison," Khomeini finally agreed to a ceasefire on July 18.[108]

Like the wars of the French Revolution and the Russo-Polish war, the Iran-Iraq war was a direct consequence of the revolution itself. Both Iran and Iraq saw the other as a potential threat, and each exaggerated its ability to reduce the danger through the use of force. The Iraqi invasion was driven by its fear that the revolution might spread, together with its beliefs that Khomeini's regime was unpopular, its military forces were weak and disorganized, and an invasion would spark a sympathetic uprising among the Arabs of Khuzistan. All three beliefs turned out to be erroneous, and the Iraqi offensive soon ground to a halt. Khomeini and company then succumbed to similar delusions, overstating their own ability to export the revolution and failing to realize that military success would merely cause other states to oppose them more vigorously. Instead of the swift and easy victory that both sides seem to have expected, the result was a long and bloody war of attrition. The war had helped Khomeini and his supporters consolidate their hold on power, but Khomeini's quest for total victory ultimately left both states far worse off than they had been before.

*Containing the Revolution: The Persian Gulf and Lebanon.* Although Iran's other Arab neighbors had hoped that the Islamic Republic would be less assertive than its predecessor, the revolution was still a serious threat. The Persian Gulf states shared Iraq's concern that the revolution would spread, exacerbated by Khomeini's claims that monarchical institutions were "un-Islamic," his accusations that the conservative Arab states were corrupt puppets of the "Great Satan," and repeated Iranian statements confirming their desire to export the revolution.[109] Several gulf states were especially worried about unrest among their own Shiite populations, whom they feared would be susceptible to Khomeini's message. The Saudi royal family was also concerned that the revolution would open a door for Soviet encroachments in the region; the Soviet invasion of Afghanistan and reports of growing Soviet influence within Iran did little to assuage their fears. A third danger was the possibility of direct attack, which became increasingly real as the Iran-Iraq war escalated.

---

[108] Khomeini emphasized that the decision "was made only on the basis of expediency," and he warned that "our nation should not consider the matter closed." Hiro, *Longest War*, 243. Useful discussions of the cease-fire process include Chubin, "Iran and the War"; Wright, *In the Name of God*, 173–78, 184–91, 254–55; *MECS 1988*, 207–18, 476–77; Sigler, "Legacy of the Iran-Iraq War," 149–51; and Gary Sick, "Slouching Toward Settlement: The Internationalization of the Iran-Iraq War, 1987–1988," in Keddie and Gasiorowski, *Neither East Nor West*, 220–22, 238.

[109] See Jacob Goldberg, "Saudi Arabia and the Iranian Revolution," in Menashri, *Iranian Revolution and the Muslim World*, 156–57.

Several subsequent incidents reinforced these underlying tensions. There were serious disturbances among the Shiites in Saudi Arabia's eastern province in November 1979 and February 1980, clearly inspired by events in Iran and encouraged by Iranian propaganda.[110] Iran also began to use the annual pilgrimage to Mecca (the *hajj*) as a means of spreading the revolution, which led to repeated confrontations with Saudi officials.[111] There were pro-Khomeini demonstrations in Kuwait and Bahrain in 1979; Iran attacked three Kuwaiti oil facilities in October 1981; an Iranian agent led an unsuccessful coup attempt in Bahrain in December; and a group of Iranian-backed Iraqi exiles conducted a series of terrorist bombings in Kuwait in 1983.[112]

The gulf states responded to the threat by arresting or deporting potential dissidents, providing greater economic benefits to their own Shiite populations, trumpeting their own Islamic credentials, and stressing Arab nationalism rather than Islamic solidarity. In addition to improving their own defense capabilities through increased arms purchases, the gulf states formed the so-called Gulf Cooperation Council in January 1981 to coordinate joint responses to the threat of Iranian subversion.[113] Saudi Arabia and Kuwait overcame their earlier fears of Iraqi ascendancy and began providing Baghdad with extensive financial support; aid increased as Iraq's plight worsened, and the two monarchies eventually loaned Iraq approximately $40 billion to finance its war effort.[114]

Iran initiated a brief détente with Saudi Arabia in the mid-1980s, in an attempt to persuade the Saudis to reduce their support for Iraq. Rafsanjani informed Riyadh that Iran "had no intention of controlling Ka'ba and Mecca,"

[110] See Goldberg, "Saudi Arabia," 160, and "The Shi'i Minority in Saudi Arabia," in *Shi'ism and Social Protest*, ed. Juan R. I. Cole and Nikki R. Keddie (New Haven: Yale University Press, 1986), 230, 239–44; Zonis and Brumberg, *Khomeini, Iran, Arab World*, 52; and David Long, "The Impact of the Iranian Revolution on the Arabian Peninsula and the Gulf States," in Esposito, *Iranian Revolution*, 105–106.

[111] Clashes between Iranian pilgrims and Saudi security forces took place in 1979, 1980, and 1981, and Iranian officials repeatedly denounced Saudi control over the holy places in Mecca and Medina. The two states reached a partial compromise that permitted Iran to send a greater number of pilgrims after 1983, but the 1987 *hajj* ended in violent disturbances between the Iranian pilgrims and Saudi security forces that left over four hundred dead. When the Saudis limited Iran to forty-five thousand pilgrims in 1988, Iran chose to boycott the *hajj* entirely. See Goldberg, "Saudi Arabia and the Iranian Revolution," 164–65; Zonis and Brumberg, *Khomeini, Iran, Arab World*, 53–54; Menashri, *Iran*, 209–10, 252, 293, 333, 366–67; and *MECS 1986* (Boulder, Colo.: Westview, 1988), 149–51; *1987*, 172–76, 416–17; *1988*, 177–85; *1989*, 182–87; *1990* (Boulder, Colo.: Westview, 1992), 189–91.

[112] See Zonis and Brumberg, *Khomeini, Iran, Arab World*, 42–50; and Hunter, *Iran and the World*, 115.

[113] See Mahnaz Z. Ispahani, "Alone Together: Regional Security Arrangements in Southern Africa and the Arabian Gulf," *International Security* 8, no. 4 (1984); and Ramazani, *The Gulf Cooperation Council: Record and Analysis* (Charlottesville: University of Virginia Press, 1988).

[114] See Karsh and Rautsi, "Why Saddam Hussein Invaded Kuwait," 19 and n. 3.

and the Saudis responded by inviting Rafsanjani to visit Mecca during the
*hajj,* Saudi foreign minister Prince Saud visited Iran in May 1985, and Iranian foreign minister Velayati made a return visit to Riyadh in December. But
the period of détente did not last long.[115]

The gulf states increased their aid to Iraq after Iran captured the Fao
Peninsula in 1986, and clashes between Iranian pilgrims and Saudi security
forces during the 1987 *hajj* led Rafsanjani to proclaim that Iran must "uproot
the Saudi rulers . . . and divest the control of the holy shrines from
[them]."[116] The Saudis responded by denouncing the "insane fascist regime"
that had made Iran a "slaughterhouse." Iran remained bitterly hostile to
Kuwait as well, owing to the sheikdom's support for Iraq and its reliance on
U.S. and other Western backing. Kuwait expelled six Iranian diplomats after
a Iranian missile attack in 1987, and the Saudis later executed sixteen
Kuwaitis accused of terrorist activities "inspired by Tehran." Neither the
end of the war with Iraq nor Khomeini's death ended their mutual suspicions; although the smaller gulf states moved back to a more neutral position when the Iran-Iraq war ended, Iran and Saudi Arabia stayed estranged
until the Iraqi invasion of Kuwait in 1990.[117]

For the most part, Iran's initial efforts to export its revolution failed to ignite a wave of sympathetic uprisings in other Muslim countries. The principal exception to this conclusion was the rise of Islamic fundamentalism
among the Shiite population of Lebanon, where groups such as Hezbollah
and Islamic Jihad embraced Iran's anti-Western, pan-Islamic ideology and
acknowledged Khomeini as their inspiration and leader.[118] Iran sent approximately one thousand Revolutionary Guards to Lebanon in 1982, to
support the Shiite fundamentalists there, and gave nearly $500 million in fi-
nancial subsidies to its Shiite clients. Hezbollah and Islamic Jihad began to

[115] See Ramazani, *Revolutionary Iran,* 96–98. There are also reports of secret Saudi-Iranian
negotiations on possible scenarios for ending the Iran-Iraq war in 1984, but the talks apparently accomplished little. Gerd Nonneman, "The GCC and the Islamic Republic," in Ehteshami and Varasteh, *Iran and the International Community,* 107.

[116] Rafsanjani later declared, "If the world of Islam and its scholars decide so, we are ready
to fight under any circumstances for [the] liberation of Mecca." Quoted in *MECS 1987,* 417.

[117] For these incidents and quotations, see Goldberg, "Saudi Arabia and Iran," 163; *MECS
1989,* 366; *1990,* 366–69; Nonneman, "GCC," 116–23.

[118] According to Sayyid Ibrahim al-Amin, the official spokesman of Hezbollah: "We in
Lebanon do not consider ourselves as separate from the revolution in Iran. . . . We consider
ourselves . . . part of the army which the Imam wishes to create in order to liberate Jerusalem.
We obey his orders because we do not believe in geography but in the change." Another leading Hezbollah figure, Sheikh al-Tufayli, declared that "the leadership of the Islamic Republic
of Iran is the direction of all Muslims of the World," and an open letter from the leaders of
Hezbollah in 1985 proclaimed, "We are sons of the nation of Hezbollah, whose vanguard God
made victorious in Iran, and who reestablished the nucleus of a central Islamic state in the
world." See Martin Kramer, "Redeeming Jerusalem: The Pan-Islamic Premise of Hizballah,"
in Menashri, *Iranian Revolution and the Muslim World,* 113–14; and Zonis and Brumberg,
*Khomeini, Iran, Arab World,* 59.

challenge the other Shiite groups in Lebanon in the mid-1980s, in what was probably the most impressive demonstration of Iran's ideological reach.[119]

The impact of the revolution in Lebanon reflected several unusual circumstances. First, the Lebanese Shiites were already disaffected and radicalized by the late 1970s, and thus were more receptive to Iran's message than other Shiite communities; the Israeli invasion of Lebanon in 1982 and the intervention by the United States and several European countries in 1983 helped make Iran's anti-Western, anti-Israeli policies even more appealing. Second, many of the Lebanese Shiites who founded Hezbollah were part of the same clerical network as the pro-Khomeini forces in Iran.[120] Third, Hezbollah also received active support from Syria during the early 1980s, which sought to use the Shiite population of Lebanon to advance its own interests in the country. Finally, the protracted civil war in Lebanon had left the country without a central authority to suppress or coopt the fundamentalists.[121] Given these conditions—which were largely absent elsewhere in the Arab world—it is not surprising that the Iranian Revolution had a greater impact in Lebanon than anywhere else.

Yet despite these uniquely favorable circumstances, Iran was no more successful in establishing a second Islamic republic in Lebanon than it was in fomenting rebellion in the Persian Gulf. The Lebanese Shiites remained divided, and Syrian support for Hezbollah began to drop off after 1984. Moreover, Iran's ability to control its Lebanese affiliates declined steadily after the first outburst of revolutionary enthusiasm. Thus, Lebanon offers a strong demonstration of the inherent difficulty of spreading revolution: even when conditions are favorable, efforts to export an ideological movement in the absence of military occupation rarely succeed.[122]

*Other Islamic Movements.* The revolution in Iran also encouraged diverse Islamic groups in Sudan, Egypt, Algeria, and Tunisia, with whom the Islamic Republic eventually forged a variety of links. Iran and Sudan formed a close political alignment after a military coup brought the fundamentalist National Islamic Front to power in 1989, and Rafsanjani reportedly offered the new regime economic and military aid during a visit to Khartoum in 1991.[123]

[119] See Augustus Richard Norton, "Lebanon: The Internal Conflict and the Iranian Connection," in Esposito, *Iranian Revolution*, esp. 126.

[120] Interestingly, the most senior Shiite cleric in Lebanon, Ayatollah Said Muhammed Fadlallah, was not a disciple of Khomeini, and he rejected the latter's concept of *velayet-e faqih*. See Kramer, "Pan-Islamic Premise," 121–25.

[121] The former Iranian ambassador to Lebanon said in 1984 that "since the Republic of Lebanon does not have much power, there is no serious obstacle in the way" of an Islamic revolution. Quoted in Zonis and Brumberg, *Khomeini, Iran, Arab World*, 61.

[122] See Norton, "Lebanon," 130–33; and Hunter, *Iran and the World*, 126.

[123] According to news reports, Rafsanjani promised to supply Sudan with free oil, sell it arms, and send Revolutionary Guards to aid the government's efforts against the rebel movements in

Iran and Sudan are believed to have aided the election campaign of the Islamic Salvation Front in Algeria in 1992, and National Islamic Front leader Hassan al-Turabi repeatedly referred to a global Islamic resurgence based on "the experiences of Iran in heart of Asia, Sudan in the heart of Africa, and Algeria which is very near to the European continent."[124] Together with the rise of fundamentalism in Egypt and Algeria, these events sparked renewed fears of a rising Islamic tide posing an ominous threat to the West.[125]

Although the growth of Islamic fundamentalism clearly merits careful attention from Middle Eastern governments and their foreign allies, this phenomenon should not be seen as the emergence of an "Islamic monolith" or as a case where a revolution was successfully exported. In the first place, most contemporary Islamic movements predate the revolution in Iran, and their growing popularity is due more to indigenous trends than to the transmission of revolutionary ideas from Tehran. This qualification is especially true of Sudan—the only other regime that openly espouses fundamentalist principles—where the process of Islamization was not the result of a mass revolution. On the contrary, the Islamization campaign was begun by Jifar Nimeiri (a former general who seized power in the early 1970s) and completed following his ouster by a military coup in 1989.[126] Similar observations apply to North Africa as well. According to François Burgat, "Khomeinism was . . . not responsible for the creation of the Islamist movement" and none of his successors "could be considered to be the conductor of an Islamic orchestra responding to his solicitations."[127] Although the

the south. See *Middle East International,* no. 418 (February 7, 1992), 18–19; and "Fundamentalism Alters the Middle East's Power Relationships," *New York Times,* August 22, 1993, 4:1.

[124] See *Middle East International,* no. 416 (January 10, 1992), 7–8; no. 418 (February 7, 1992), 16–18; no. 421 (March 20, 1992), 17–18; no. 465, (December 17, 1993), 13; and *MECS 1991,* 183–84.

[125] In 1993, an unnamed U.S. official warned, "From the Iranian point of view, Sudan is strategically located: south to Africa, north and west to Egypt and North Africa. It gives the Iranians a strategic toehold, which can help promote its revolutionary cause in Algeria, Egypt, Tunisia, Sudan itself, and south." Quoted in "Fundamentalism Alters the Middle East's Power Relationships." For other examples of Western alarmism about the rise of Islamic fundamentalism, see John L. Esposito, *The Islamic Threat: Myth or Reality?* (London: Oxford University Press, 1992), chap. 6. For a predictably extreme assessment by a member of the Iranian opposition, see Mohammed Mohaddessin, *Islamic Fundamentalism: The New Global Threat* (Washington, D.C.: Seven Locks Press, 1993); for a critique, see Leon Hadar, "What Green Peril?" *Foreign Affairs* 72, no. 2 (1993).

[126] According to John O. Voll, "the Iranian revolution seems to have had little direct impact on Sudan. The basic developments of Islamization and Islamic revivalism . . . during the 1970s and 1980s were primarily shaped by the long traditions of Sudanese history. . . . The relationship between Sudan's Islamization program and the Iranian revolution tends to disprove the hypotheses that view the Islamic resurgence as a tightly bound network of events or even some form of international conspiracy." "Islamization in the Sudan and the Iranian Revolution," in Esposito, *Iranian Revolution,* 283, 288.

[127] See François Burgat and William Dowell, *The Islamic Movement in North Africa* (Austin, Tex.: Center for Middle Eastern Studies, 1993), 36–37. According to G. H. Jansen, "the Irani-

Egyptian and Tunisian governments have repeatedly accused Iran of supporting the Islamic radicals, their statements have clearly been intended to encourage foreign support and to provide a scapegoat for their own failures. Such reports should not be dismissed entirely, perhaps, but they should be discounted.[128]

The belief that Islamic fundamentalism is a unified movement directed or inspired by Iran also ignores the considerable diversity among the various fundamentalist groups. The Iranian revolution was conducted by Shiite Muslim *Persians,* while the other Islamic movements are led by Sunni Arabs. None of the Sunni movements have embraced Khomeini's doctrine of *velayet-e faqih,* and their specific political programs differ significantly as well.[129] Among other things, this diversity suggests that, should additional "Islamic" movements gain power in other countries, they are as likely to quarrel over the "correct" form of Islamic government as to cooperate in a jihad against the West.

Furthermore, despite the many problems that presently afflict a number of Middle Eastern governments, they have been able to contain the Islamic challenge through a combination of cooptation, repression, and external support.[130] If the revolution in Iran helped inspire fundamentalists elsewhere, it also gave fair warning to potential victims and encouraged them to join forces against the perceived danger. Although the more extreme movements have responded with violent campaigns against government officials and Western tourists and business interests, none of these regimes had fallen as of mid-1995. Iran has had more than fifteen years in which to replicate its own revolution; the ability of regimes as fragile, corrupt, and economically troubled as Egypt and Algeria to resist its efforts is compelling

---

ans may even flatter themselves that the Algerians are only following the Iranian example, but that would not be true. . . . If there has been any outside influence in Algeria it has come from Saudi Arabia." See *Middle East International,* no. 416 (January 10, 1992), 8.

[128] One recent congressional study noted that although Tunisian leaders blamed the rise of fundamentalist attacks on the "Tehran-Khartoum-Tunis axis," "no evidence has been released that these attacks were part of a 'Fundamentalism International' conspiracy to take power in Tunisia." George Pickard, *The Battle Looms: Islam and Politics in the Middle East,* a Report to the Committee on Foreign Relations, U.S. Senate, 103d Congress, 1st sess. (Washington, D.C.: U.S. Government Printing Office, 1993), 12. See also *Middle East International,* no. 417 (January 24, 1992), 5–6.

[129] See Bassam Tibi, "The Iranian Revolution and the Arabs: The Quest for Islamic Identity and the Search for an Islamic System of Government," *Arab Studies Quarterly* 8, no. 1 (1986).

[130] When the Islamic Salvation Front gained a majority in first stage of the December 1991 elections, the Algerian Army promptly canceled the second stage and began a brutal campaign against the Algerian fundamentalists. A similar campaign in Tunisia resulted in the arrest and sentencing of three hundred members of the main fundamentalist party in August 1992.

evidence of the advantages even weak states possess when facing a revolutionary challenge.[131]

To be sure, the revolution in Iran did inspire fundamentalist groups in a number of other Muslim societies, primarily by demonstrating that a movement based on Islamic principles could overthrow a seemingly impregnable regime. As in the French and Bolshevik cases, however, success in one context did not lead to rapid triumphs elsewhere. Most important of all, the claim that the revolution in Iran "caused" sympathetic upheavals elsewhere is almost certainly spurious; instead, it is merely one part of a much broader political process whose ultimate outcomes will take many forms.

*Iran's Arab Allies.* Although the revolution left Iran isolated from most of its neighbors, it did establish close alignments with a number of other "radical" states. The Syrian-Iranian relationship was probably the most important for the first decade after the revolution—an alignment based almost entirely on realpolitik. Despite serious ideological differences, the two states were united by their mutual antipathy to Iraq, Israel, and the United States. Syria backed Iran during the hostage crisis, provided modest amounts of Soviet weaponry from its own stockpiles, and aided the Kurdish insurgents within Iraq itself. Syria also shut down Iraq's oil pipelines in 1982, and it and Iran joined forces to support the Islamic fundamentalists in Lebanon in the early 1980s. Although President Hafez al-Assad still referred to Syria's alignment with Iran as "strategic" in 1986 and President Khameni described the relationship as "profound" and "brotherly" the following year, Syrian-Iranian ties were strained when Syria began to favor the more moderate Lebanese Shiite faction, Amal, over Hezbollah. The end of the Iran-Iraq war reduced the value of the Syrian-Iranian alignment, and Syria subsequently refused to allow Iran to send additional Revolutionary Guards and a shipment of arms to Lebanon in January 1990. Syria also joined the UN coalition against Iraq in the wake of the latter's invasion of Kuwait in August 1990 (a move that Iran regarded with misgivings), but relations between Tehran and Damascus remain cordial at present.[132]

Iran also enjoyed good relations with Libya, Algeria, and South Yemen for most of the 1980s, based primarily on their mutual opposition to the United States and Israel. Algeria also served as the principal intermediary with the United States during the hostage crisis, but relations deteriorated sharply

[131] See F. Gregory Gause III, "Revolutionary Fevers and Regional Contagion: Domestic Structures and the Export of Revolution in Middle East," *Journal of South Asian and Middle Eastern Studies* 14, no. 3 (1991).

[132] See Yosef Olmert, "Iranian-Syrian Relations: Between Islam and Realpolitik," in Menashri, *Iranian Revolution and Muslim World*, 172–75; Ramazani, *Revolutionary Iran*, 81–82; "Chronology," *MEJ* 40, no. 4 (1986), 699; *MECS 1987*, 419; *1989*, 367.

after the Algerian government voided the results of the 1991 elections and launched a major crackdown on the fundamentalist movement. The Islamic Republic also established cordial diplomatic relations with a number of revolutionary movements and Third World states during its first decade, being particularly friendly toward radical states such as Nicaragua, Cuba, and North Korea.[133] These policies, which were consistent with Khomeini's commitment to protecting the "oppressed" peoples against great-power dominance, confirm that Iran's postrevolutionary foreign policy had made a decisive break with the policies of the old regime.

## CONCLUSIONS: THE IRANIAN REVOLUTION AND BALANCE-OF-THREAT THEORY

The independent impact of revolutions on the level of security competition is probably most apparent in the Iranian case. The revolution altered virtually the entire spectrum of Iranian foreign relations and led directly to a protracted war with Iraq. Although Iran faced a number of opponents under the shah, it had not been involved in a major war since 1945, and it enjoyed good relations with most of the great powers. The revolution transformed U.S.-Iranian relations from a close alignment to one of bitter enmity; undermined Iran's wary but cordial relationship with the Soviet Union; caused the severing of diplomatic relations with several European states; and alarmed and provoked the gulf states and several other regional powers. It is virtually impossible to imagine these destabilizing events occurring had the shah retained his throne. Moreover, the evidence suggests that these effects occurred for most (if not all) of the reasons identified in chapter 2.

### The Balance of Power

*Superpower Responses.* Because of Iran's oil reserves and strategic location, both the United States and the Soviet Union viewed the revolution there in terms of its potential impact on the global balance of power. U.S. leaders feared that the fall of the shah had created a power vacuum that might be filled by the Soviet Union; indeed, some U.S. officials suspected that the So-

---

[133] Khomeini told the Nicaraguan minister of education during the latter's visit to Iran in 1983: "Your country is very similar to our country; but ours has more difficulty. . . . We should all try to create unity among the oppressed, regardless of their ideology and creed. Otherwise, the two oppressors of East and West will infect everyone like a cancerous tumor." Quoted in Hunter, *Iran and the World,* 236, n. 9.

viets had played an active role in bringing the shah down.[134] The ouster of the shah had direct strategic consequences as well, as the U.S. lost access to monitoring stations that provided intelligence data on Soviet missile tests, and U.S. officials worried that the Soviet Union might obtain secret military technology that had been sold to Iran.

The Soviet invasion of Afghanistan in December 1979 magnified these concerns. U.S. leaders saw the invasion as evidence of greater Soviet assertiveness: Carter warned that the invasion was "a stepping stone to possible control over much of the world's oil supplies." A U.S. Defense Department study argued that the Soviet Union might exploit the turmoil in Iran "in order to seize a historical opportunity to change the worldwide balance," and the United States established the so-called Rapid Deployment Force (RDF) to defend its interests in Southwest Asia.[135] Carter declared that "an attempt by any outside force to gain control of the Persian Gulf region . . . will be repelled by any means necessary." Taken together, the "Carter doctrine" and the creation of the RDF were primarily intended to deter any Soviet attempt to exploit the power vacuum in Iran.[136]

Concern for the balance of power was still evident even after it became clear the new regime was not pro-Soviet. For example, the American decision to provide arms to Tehran in 1985–86 was inspired by a 1985 Central Intelligence Agency report warning of a Soviet attempt to take advantage of Iran's "imminent" collapse.[137] Or as White House Chief of Staff Donald Regan put it, President Reagan "has this feeling, that we cannot allow Iran to fall into the

[134] According to former deputy secretary of state Warren Christopher, U.S. policy makers "had to be concerned with the reality that Iran's internal divisions made it weaker and therefore more vulnerable to Soviet opportunism." Zbigniew Brzezinski distributed copies of a *New Republic* article blaming the revolution on Soviet interference among other U.S. policy makers, and former National Security Council aide Gary Sick reports that this view "found a ready audience among many policy makers in the United States and elsewhere." CIA director Stansfield Turner stated, "I am sure that there is some Soviet influence behind it in one degree or another," and presidential candidate John Connolly suggested publicly that Iranian foreign minister Sadeq Qotbzadeh was a KGB agent. See Christopher et al., *American Hostages*, 2; Bill, *Eagle and Lion*, 277–78; Brzezinski, *Power and Principle*, 356, 372, 379, 386, 397, 444, 451, 485–500; Sick, *All Fall Down*, 106; Howard Hensel, "Moscow's Perspective on the Fall of the Iranian Monarchy," *Asian Affairs* 14, no. 2 (1983), 154; and "Connolly Tells of Belief Ghotbzadeh is in KGB," *New York Times*, January 14, 1980, A13.

[135] The Pentagon study also warned that Soviet conventional superiority in the region might force the United States to use nuclear weapons against a Soviet drive to the gulf. "Carter Embargoes Technology for Soviet," *New York Times*, January 5, 1980, A3; and "Study Says a Soviet Move in Iran Might Require U.S. Atom Arms," *New York Times*, February 2, 1980, 1:1, 4.

[136] "Transcript of President's State of the Union Address to Joint Session of Congress," *New York Times*, January 24, 1980, A12. For background, see Gary Sick, "The Evolution of U.S. Strategy towards the Indian Ocean and Persian Gulf Regions," in *The Great Game: Rivalry in the Persian Gulf and South Asia*, ed. Alvin Z. Rubinstein (New York: Praeger, 1983), 68–76.

[137] See Bill, *Eagle and Lion*, 310–11, and "U.S. Overture to Iran," 169, 173; and Draper, *Very Thin Line*, 148–51, 292–93.

Soviet camp." Similar motives underlay the decision to reflag Kuwaiti tankers and to provide a naval escort in 1987; Secretary of Defense Caspar Weinberger explained that failure to act "would have created a vacuum in the Gulf into which Soviet power would shortly have been projected."[138]

Not surprisingly, Soviet leaders welcomed the collapse of an important U.S. ally, although they were also concerned that instability and chaos within Iran might force the United States and its allies to take military action, thereby bringing Western military forces up against the Soviet border. Soviet general secretary Leonid Brezhnev issued an explicit warning against foreign intervention in Iran in November 1978, and the message was repeated on several subsequent occasions.[139] Soviet pronouncements and propaganda broadcasts repeatedly spoke of "American interference" and reminded Iranians of the dangers that Western intervention would pose for them, but these obviously self-serving efforts had little impact on Soviet relations with Iran.[140]

Paradoxically, although both superpowers were concerned that the revolution in Iran might tempt the other to intervene, they were aware that such a step might provoke a major confrontation, and this knowledge probably discouraged either party from taking direct action. The fear of a Soviet response clearly inhibited the United States during the hostage crisis, for example, and the Soviets did nothing to aid the leftist Islamic Mujahedin and Tudeh Party as they were being decimated by the Islamic Republican Party.[141] The Iranians seemed to be well aware of the benefits they derived from this bipolar stalemate, correctly inferring that each superpower would help protect them from the other.[142]

*Regional Responses.* The effects of the revolution on the balance of power within the region were even more profound. Before the shah's departure, for

---

[138] Quotations from Bill, "U.S. Overture to Iran," 169; and Ramazani, "Iran's Resistance to U.S. Influence," 37.

[139] Brezhnev's first warning stated that "any interference, especially military, in the affairs of Iran, a state directly bordering on the Soviet Union, would be regarded by the Soviet Union as a matter affecting its security interests." Quoted in Martin Sicker, *The Bear and the Lion: Soviet Imperialism and Iran* (New York: Praeger, 1988), 110. After the U.S. attempt to rescue the embassy hostages, Soviet foreign minister Andrei Gromyko declared, "We are against all measures of a military, or generally forcible, nature on the part of the United States or anyone else against Iran." Similarly, Brezhnev declared, "We are not going to intervene . . . [in the Iran-Iraq war]. And we resolutely say to others: Hands off these events." Quoted in Yodfat, *Soviet Union and Revolutionary Iran*, 77–79, 92.

[140] See Hensel, "Moscow's Perspectives," 156–57; Dennis Ross, "Soviet Views towards the Gulf War," *Orbis* 28, no. 3 (1984), 438–39; and Zalmay Khalilzad, "Islamic Iran: Soviet Dilemmas," *Problems of Communism* 33, no. 1 (1981).

[141] See Brzezinski, *Power and Principle*, 488–89, 493–94; Salinger, *America Held Hostage*, 106; and Gary Sick, "Military Options and Constraints," in Christopher et al., *American Hostages in Iran*, 150–55.

[142] See Hunter, *Iran and the World*, 58–59.

example, Crown Prince Fahd of Saudi Arabia declared that "the Arab states will have to support Iran and the Shah, because the stability of that country is important to the [entire] region . . . and any radical change will upset its security balance."[143] The conservative oil monarchies also worried that shah's departure would tilt the regional balance in favor of radical or pro-Soviet forces. Similar concerns were evident in Israel, which provided direct aid to the Islamic Republic despite its overtly anti-Zionist rhetoric. For Israel, Iran was still an effective counter to the more immediate threat it faced from states such as Iraq, and aiding the Iranian war effort was consistent with the same balance-of-power strategy that had inspired Israel's tacit alliance with the shah.[144]

The revolution's impact on the regional balance of power was also apparent in Iraq's decision to invade Iran in September 1980. The apparent weakness and vulnerability created by the revolution was not the only reason Iraq attacked, but it was clearly a central factor in its calculations. Thus, the Iraqi invasion was a direct response to the window of opportunity created by the revolution, even if that window turned out to be smaller than Saddam Hussein expected.[145]

Finally, although Khomeini criticized the state system as an illegitimate human invention and welcomed Iran's isolation from other states, the Islamic Republic was not immune from the competitive pressures of balance-of-power politics. Although Baathist Iraq was condemned as an atheistic state, Baathist Syria had become Iran's principal ally by 1982. Indeed, the pressure of war convinced Iran to purchase arms from a diverse array of suppliers—including Israel and the United States—solely for the purpose of improving its military capabilities. This does not deny ideology's effect on Iran's foreign policy, but it does suggest that external constraints set limits on the regime's ideological purity.

Thus, the effects of the revolution on the balance of power exacerbated the security competition between Iran and a number of other states and were an important cause of the war between Iran and Iraq.

*Perceptions of Intent*

The fall of the Pahlavi dynasty and its replacement by the Islamic Republic affected virtually every aspect of Iran's foreign policy. Whereas the shah

[143] Quoted in Menashri, *Iran*, 47.

[144] On Israel's military aid to Iran, see Segev, *Iranian Triangle*; Cordesman, *Gulf and Search for Stability*, 717; Brzezinski, *Power and Principle*, 504; and Hiro, *Longest War*, 118.

[145] See John W. Amos II, "The Iran-Iraq War: Conflict, Linkage, and Spillover in the Middle East," in *Gulf Security in the 1980s: Perceptual and Strategic Dimensions*, ed. Robert G. Darius, John W. Amos II, and Ralph H. Magnus (Stanford, Calif.: Hoover Institute Press, 1984), 58–60; Jack Levy and Mike Froelich, "Causes of the Iran-Iraq War," in *The Regionalization of Warfare*, ed. James Brown and William P. Snyder (New Brunswick, N.J.: Transaction Books, 1985), 137–39.

.ad been oriented toward the West and closely allied with the United States,
he Islamic Republic was suspicious of both. Whereas the shah had main-
:ained cordial if guarded relations with the Soviet Union, Khomeini viewed
it as the "lesser Satan," condemned its atheistic ideology, and denounced its
invasion of Afghanistan. The shah had supported Israel and the conservative gulf states and opposed the radical Arab regimes; by contrast, the Islamic Republic broke diplomatic relations with Israel, aided efforts to
overthrow the gulf states, and aligned itself with Syria, South Yemen, Libya,
and later Sudan. And where the shah's objectives vis-à-vis Iraq were limited
(he sought to dominate the region but did not try to overthrow the Iraqi
regime), revolutionary Iran was calling for the ouster of the Baath even before the war began.

These changes cannot be explained solely by shifts in the balance of
power. They were also products of the radically different worldview that inspired the revolution itself. Apart from its specifically Islamic content, the
ideology of revolutionary Iran arose from hostility to the shah and his policies, especially to his pro-Western orientation. It is not surprising that the
new regime therefore took steps that alarmed Iran's former allies.

Iran's foreign relations also support the hypothesis that revolutionary
states are especially prone to spirals of hostility. In particular, both sides
tended to take the very dimmest view of each other's actions and discounted the possibility that their own behavior might be responsible for the
opposition they were facing.

As one would expect, the tendency to spiral was most apparent in Iran's
diplomacy vis-á-vis the United States. Although both the Bazargan government and the Carter administration seemed genuinely interested in establishing a new relationship after the shah's departure, relations between the
United States and Iran soon deteriorated into a web of mutual suspicions.
Throughout this period, each side's defensive responses and hostile inferences were reinforced by insensitive or unwitting actions by the other.[146] In
the spring of 1979, for example, Iranian fears of a military coup inspired a
series of purges and executions by the Revolutionary Courts, prompting the
U.S. Senate to pass a condemnatory resolution. This action in turn derailed
an attempt to establish direct contact with Khomeini (who greeted the Senate resolution by calling the United States a "defeated and wounded

---

[146] In February 1979, Carter stated that the United States would "honor the will of the Iranian people" and expressed his willingness to "work closely with the existing government of
Iran." Foreign Minister Karim Sanjavi replied that Iran still sought "friendly relations" with
the United States, in the context of Iran's new policy of nonalignment. The United States
agreed to resume military shipments to Iran in October, and Prime Minister Bazargan and
Foreign Minister Ibrahim Yazdi (who had replaced Sanjavi in April) expressed their own
hope that relations "would soon take a turn for the better." See Menashri, *Iran,* 97; and
Behrooz, "Trends in the Foreign Policy of Iran," 16–17.

The Iranian Revolution

snake") and sparked mass demonstrations in Iran denouncing U.S. interference. The U.S. decision to permit the shah to enter the country for medical treatment in October angered the Iranian revolutionaries and raised new fears of a U.S. plot to place him back upon the throne; together, these events confirmed Iranian images of American aggressiveness and discredited the more moderate forces, thereby helping the more extreme forces consolidate their control.[147] On the other side, the seizure of the U.S. embassy and the prolonged detention of the hostages cemented U.S. hostility and solidified perceptions of Iran as a fanatical and dangerous regime.[148]

However, each side's interpretation was at least partly mistaken. Contrary to Iranian fears of a U.S.-backed counterrevolution, the United States had no intention of trying to restore the terminally ill shah; he had been permitted to enter the United States only after repeated requests from influential individuals such as David Rockefeller and Henry Kissinger.[149] And contrary to the U.S. image of unlimited Iranian bellicosity, the seizure of the embassy was inspired as much by conflicts within Iran as by an overt desire to harm the United States.[150] Although serious differences did exist, therefore, probably neither side was as aggressive as the other believed it to be.

Subsequent episodes heightened each side's paranoia. The abortive hostage rescue mission in April 1980 confirmed Iranian fears of U.S. military intervention and revealed that the United States still possessed an extensive intelligence network within their country, thereby reinforcing Iranian fears of U.S.-backed plots.[151] The trade embargo and the U.S. tilt toward Iraq during the Iran-Iraq war only strengthened the impression of U.S. aggression. To the extent that Iranians failed to recognize the role of their own actions in provoking these responses, they were more likely to view U.S. policy as evidence of innate U.S. hostility. Similarly, Americans who were unfamiliar with the history of U.S. involvement in Iran or who saw the prior U.S. role as beneficial would be inclined to consider Iranian actions as unjustifiedly hostile.

---

[147] Prior to his return to Iran, Khomeini warned that "America is an accessory" to the shah, and he later declared, "We will not let the United States bring back the Shah. This is what the Shah wants. Wake up. Watch out." Quoted in Hiro, *Iran under the Ayatollahs*, 315, 134–37. Meetings between U.S. general Robert Huyser and a group of Iranian military officers in January 1979 probably intensified Iranian fears of a U.S.-backed coup. See Sick, *All Fall Down*, 131–32; Menashri, *Iran*, 97–98, 114, 146–47; and Wright, *In the Name of God*, 75–76.

[148] In February 1979, a Gallup poll reported that 64 percent of all Americans held an "unfavorable" image of Iran, 21 percent expressed the most extreme negative rating, and 12 percent offered a mildly favorable view. In an identical poll taken after the seizure of the embassy, 90 percent reported an "unfavorable" image, with 60 percent giving Iran the most extreme negative rating. *Gallup Opinion Index*, no. 169 (August 1979), 41, and no. 176 (March 1980), 29.

[149] See Bill, *Eagle and Lion*, 321–40; and Sick, *All Fall Down*, 179–81.

[150] On the role of Iranian domestic politics in the seizure of the embassy, see Hiro, *Iran under the Ayatollahs*, 136–39; Wright, *In the Name of God*, 74–81; Sick, *All Fall Down*, 198–205; Abrahamian, *Iranian Mojahedin*, 57; and Arjomand, *Turban for the Crown*, 139–40.

[151] See Hiro, *Iran under the Ayatollahs*, 154–56, 319–20; Bill, *Eagle and Lion*, 302.

[255]

Even worse, gestures of accommodation tended to backfire, because they were seen as nefarious attempts to reestablish U.S. influence. For example, the premature U.S. effort to cultivate moderate forces after the shah's departure merely discredited these leaders and reinforced the radicals' belief that the United States was still trying to pull strings behind the scenes. Thus, Brzezinski's meeting with Bazargan in November 1979 helped force the latter's resignation, and Bani-Sadr's efforts to resolve the hostage crisis played a key role in discrediting him in the eyes of Khomeini and the clerics. This problem was exacerbated by the Iranians' fondness for conspiracy theories, which created fertile ground for the notion that the United States was still able manipulate events in Iran at will.[152] As a result, Iran blamed the United States for the assassinations of several leading clerics, the Iraqi invasion, and the activities of counterrevolutionary groups such as the Islamic Mujahedin.[153] These accusations were either without foundation or greatly exaggerated, but insofar as they reflected sincere Iranian beliefs rather than mere propaganda, they provide additional evidence of spiral dynamics at work.[154]

Lastly, the climate of suspicion and hostility between the United States and Iran made improving relations especially difficult. The United States did make conciliatory gestures on occasion, but the bulk of U.S. policy was hostile (for example, its support for the gulf states and the Iranian exiles, its efforts to deny Iran arms, and its gradual tilt towards Iraq). Not surprisingly, actions contrary to Iranian interests were seen as evidence of true U.S. preferences, while less harmful ones appeared as signs of U.S. duplicity. Thus, when the Senate passed a resolution condemning the executions by the Revolutionary Courts (an action that ran counter to the Carter administration's efforts to reach a modus vivendi with Iran), the clerics saw it as a direct challenge to the new regime. In the same way, when Rafsanjani and other moderates recognized that Iran was partly responsible for its own isolation, their efforts to cooperate with the United States in the Iran-*contra* arms deal were thwarted by extremists within Iran and by the incompetent bungling of the U.S. officials responsible for the initiative.[155] Because inter-

[152] On this pervasive Iranian tendency, see Abrahamian, *Khomeinism*, chap. 5; Sick, *All Fall Down*, 33–34, 48, 346 n. 4; Cottam, "Inside Revolutionary Iran," 16–17; Arjomand, *Turban for the Crown*, 129–30; and Salinger, *America Held Hostage*, 70–71.

[153] In fact, U.S. officials were upset by the Iraqi invasion because it interrupted negotiations for the release of the U.S. hostages. See Sick, *All Fall Down*, 320; Jordan, *Crisis*, 347; Christopher et al, *American Hostages in Iran*, 306; Ramazani, "Iran's Foreign Policy," 57; and Bani-Sadr, *My Turn to Speak*, 70, 76.

[154] Iran's suspicions were sometimes justified, as the United States did provide modest levels of aid to the *mujahedin* after they had been driven into exile and tilted toward Iraq in 1982. These decisions are consistent with the logic of spiraling: the U.S. was responding to Iranian behavior, but Iran interpreted its acts as evidence of intrinsic hostility rather than as a defensive reaction.

[155] Among other things, the mishandling of the first arms shipment in November 1985 (in which the U.S. sent Iran an obsolete version of the Hawk missile) and Oliver North's decision

nal disagreements on both sides made bridging the divide politically risky, attempts to "unwind" the spiral were confined to unofficial channels and unreliable intermediaries, whose deceptive conduct did nothing to dispel the mutual lack of trust.

Iran's relations with a number of other states indicate spiraling as well, although it is often difficult to distinguish between the results legitimate conflicts of interest and the effects of misperception. The Soviet Union was no more successful in shedding its satanic image than the United States, and Iran accused it of supporting Kurdish rebels and the Tudeh Party and repeatedly criticized Soviet support for Iraq. There was obviously some basis for each of these charges, but the tendency of Iranian leaders to equate the two superpowers suggests that they did not fully grasp the Soviet Union's genuine desire to improve relations.

Diplomacy with Britain and France also combined elements of spiraling with legitimate perceptions of hostility. On the one hand, there were very real conflicts of interest between these states and revolutionary Iran, based on six factors: Iran's support for terrorist activities on British and French soil; the kidnapping of British and French citizens by pro-Iranian forces in Lebanon; the attacks on British citizens in Iran by members of the Revolutionary Guards; British and French arms sales to Iraq during the Iran-Iraq war; French willingness to provide asylum for Bani-Sadr, Bazargan, and the leaders of the *mujahedin*; and European support for the U.S.-backed trade embargo during the hostage crisis. On the other hand, British and French moderation toward Iran (most clearly revealed by their halfhearted participation in the U.S. trade embargo and Britain's willingness to permit Iran to conduct its private arms dealings through an office in London) failed to lead to cordial relations. Instead, Iran's leaders saw British and French policy as fundamentally antagonistic and never made a serious attempt to reach a lasting modus vivendi. Iran's propensity for assuming the worst about the intentions of other states is also apparent in its extraordinary sensitivity to issues of status or autonomy. Thus, the British arrest of an Iranian official on shoplifting charges brought a disproportionate response from Tehran, while Iran's intransigence during the Gordji affair with France reflects the Islamic Republic's insensitivity to the degree to which its own behavior provoked others.[156]

---

to charge Iran vastly inflated prices for U.S. weaponry reinforced Iranian beliefs that the Americans could not be trusted and undercut the alleged U.S. objective of cultivating better ties. See Draper, *Very Thin Line*, 195–97, 274–75, 311, 377–79; and Bill, "U.S. Overture to Iran," 177.

[156] Revolutionary states are especially sensitive to diplomatic slights, and to any other actions that cast doubt on their legitimacy or status, perhaps because of their need to build a reputation. Specifically, as new members of the international system, revolutionary states may seek to deter future challenges by defending their prerogatives with particular vigilance. In addition, revolutionary elites may fear that a failure to respond could suggest a lack of revolutionary commitment and undermine their internal positions.

Another example of spiraling was Iran's tendency to attribute opposition from states such as Iraq, Saudi Arabia, and Kuwait to their internal corruption, lack of true Islamic character, or dependence on the United States, rather than seeing it as a direct response to Iran's aggressive actions. With the partial exception of Iraq (whose 1980 invasion combined offensive and defensive motives), the anti-Iranian measures that these states took (such as the formation of the Gulf Cooperation Council or support for the Iraqi war effort) were reactions to Iran's efforts to export its revolution and its escalating war with Iraq. Indeed, Iran's neighbors all genuinely tried to establish cordial relations with the new regime, but each shifted to policies of opposition once Iran's revisionist aims became clear. Thus, Iran's neighbors correctly read the impact of the revolution on Iranian intentions, and responded by joining forces to contain the threat.

By contrast, the mistaken belief that its neighbors were intrinsically hostile to the new regime seems to have played a key role in shaping Iran's foreign policy. The close ties between the United States and the conservative gulf states alarmed the revolutionary government, and Khomeini's belief that these states were puppets of the "Great Satan" suggests a genuine fear of a well-orchestrated U.S. effort to reverse the revolution.[157] Convinced that Iran's neighbors were inherently hostile, Khomeini could justify the export of revolution by saying, "If we remain in an enclosed environment we shall definitely face defeat." These perceptions of threat were not entirely illusory, of course, but they were clearly exaggerated. Thus, the suspicion that shaped Iran's policies toward most of its neighbors was the result of a spiral, insofar as the leaders of the Islamic Republic failed to recognize their own role in provoking others' responses.[158]

The revolution in Iran confirms that spirals may arise from at least two distinct causes. One potential source is cognitive: images of hostility may be so deeply ingrained in the minds of key elites that they view virtually any action by an opponent as evidence of malign intent. Another source is domestic politics, especially when authority is contested. Although Rafsanjani and others seem to have recognized Iran's own behavior as responsible for its isolation, the divisions within the revolutionary movement and the lack

---

[157] As noted earlier, Iranian officials blamed the United States for the Iraqi invasion in 1980 and accused Saddam Hussein of acting as the U.S. "deputy" in the region. Iranian fears of a U.S.-led coalition were increased by the Carter doctrine, the establishment of the Rapid Deployment Force and the related effort to forge closer security ties with a number of states in the region. The provision of AWACS aircraft to Saudi Arabia after the outbreak of the Iran-Iraq war was also seen as evidence of Arab collusion with the "Great Satan," as was the U.S. decision to reflag and escort Kuwaiti tankers in 1987. See Ramazani, "Iran's Resistance to U.S. Intervention," 38–39; Campbell and Darvich, "Global Implications of the Iranian Revolution," 41–42 n. 39, and 47–48.

[158] Ramazani, *Revolutionary Iran*, 24. Significantly, this statement was made in March 1980, well before the Iraqi invasion.

of an effective mechanism for resolving them prevented the more moderate or pragmatic elements from following through on their desire to improve relations.[159]

These episodes underscore the difficulty of reversing a spiral when authority on either side is divided. In such circumstances, gestures toward accommodation are likely to be attacked as a betrayal of revolutionary principles or as a direct threat to the revolution itself. Poorly executed efforts to improve relations may actually harm the situation, and the failure of each attempt will merely confirm the mutual antipathy.

The Iranian case also suggests that the normal prescription for avoiding or unwinding a spiral—by making concessions and other gestures of friendship in order to reduce the opponent's insecurity—may not work with a revolutionary regime. When power is contested and foreign regimes are viewed with suspicion, premature efforts at accommodation may be interpreted as an attempt to reestablish foreign control before the new regime consolidates itself. Under the circumstances, the allies of the old regime will be better off allowing the revolutionary process to run its course rather than trying to forge a close relationship right after the seizure of power.

### Offense, Defense, Contagion, and Counterrevolution

The Iranian experience also illustrates how revolutions intensify security competition by altering perceptions of the offense-defense balance, primarily through the belief that the revolution will be contagious. Khomeini and his followers clearly saw the Islamic Republic as a model for other societies and expected their revolution to spread throughout the Muslim world and beyond.[160] Khomeini had long regarded existing state boundaries as artificial creations, and he repeatedly emphasized the importance of unifying the entire Muslim community. After the revolution, he envisioned the Iranian model "spreading on a world wide scale and, God willing, . . . the way will be opened for the world government of the [twelfth imam]."[161] The Constitution

---

[159] In addition, hostility to the "Great Satan" was a central part of Khomeini's worldview and thus became deeply engrained in the ideology of the revolution. As a result, any serious effort to improve relations ran counter to the same set of beliefs that justified clerical rule.

[160] One of Khomeini's aides said in 1979: "Be patient. . . . We will both see the fate of the Saudi rulers six months after our return to Iran." Quoted in Menashri, "Khomeini's Vision," 51.

[161] According to the Shiite theory of occultation, the Twelfth Imam is the chosen successor to the Prophet Muhammed. He is believed to have been in hiding since the ninth century, but is destined to reappear and establish justice in conformity with Islam. The founder of the Islamic Republican Party, Ayatollah Mohammed Beheshti, echoed Khomeini's view by declaring that "Islam recognizes no borders," and another prominent ayatollah (Hussein Montazeri) declared, "Under Islam there is no differentiation between an Arab, a Persian, and others, and the government of the Islamic Republic of Iran is duty bound . . . to make consistent efforts to realize the political, economic, and cultural union of the Islamic world." Quoted in Ramazani, "Khumayni's Islam," 17; Behrooz, "Trends in Iran's Foreign Policy," 15;

of the Islamic Republic endorsed this objective, and Iran backed Shiite fundamentalists in Lebanon and the gulf states, broadcast revolutionary propaganda over Radio Tehran, and used the annual pilgrimage to Mecca to spread
its message among other Muslims.[162] Although Khomeini often insisted that
the export of revolution would be done by example and not "by the sword,"
pro-Iranian groups in Lebanon and the gulf states relied upon terrorism and
other violent acts with the apparent approval of the Iranian government.

Iran's leaders also believed that religious faith and revolutionary mobilization would enable them to gain victory even in the face of strong opposition. Khomeini told the Revolutionary Guards that victory "is achieved by
strength of faith." Other Iranian officials offered similar assessments; for example, the commander of the Revolutionary Guards declared, "Only an ideologically motivated army like ours . . . [is] capable of mobilizing the people
. . . until the Iraqi regime falls."[163] Despite the internal chaos produced by the
revolution and the fears of foreign intervention, the new regime adopted a
highly bellicose foreign policy, apparently unconcerned by the costs such a
policy might entail. Combined with the possibility of ideological contagion,
Iran's bellicose propaganda increased other states' perceptions of threat significantly.

These dynamics were most apparent in the Iran-Iraq war. A central cause
of the war was the Iraqi fear that Khomeini's version of Islamic fundamentalism would spread among Iraq's Shiite majority. Iran's leaders made no
secret of their desire to overthrow the Baath regime, and their support for
Al-Dawa intensified Iraqi concerns and made a preventive war more attractive.[164] Iraq's decision to attack was also fueled by expectations that the predominantly Arab population of Khuzistan would welcome its "liberation"
by the Iraqi army. Unfortunately for Iraq, they proved woefully mistaken.
The Arab population of Iran did not rise up to support them, and the Iraqi
invasion bogged down after less than two months. At the same time, the alleged danger of a popular uprising by the Iraqi Shiites proved to be minimal, and the Baath regime was able to suppress the Al-Dawa movement
with little difficulty. Thus, both of the assumptions underlying the Iraqi invasion, which were directly traceable to the revolution, turned out to be incorrect.

Similar misconceptions were at work on the Iranian side. Before the war,
Iran's verbal and material support for the Iraqi Shi'ites reflected their belief

---

and Foreign Broadcast Information Service, *Daily Report: Middle East/North Africa*, October 22,
1979, R-7.

[162] The constitution states that the armed forces and Revolutionary Guards are responsible
"not only for defending the borders but also for . . . fighting to expand the rule of God's law
in the world." "Constitution of Islamic Republic," 185–86.

[163] Quoted in Chubin and Tripp, *Iran and Iraq at War*, 40–42.

[164] Karsh, "Iran-Iraq War Revisited," 87–88.

that the revolution would soon spread to other states, as well as their fear that Iran would be vulnerable to foreign pressure if it did not.[165] When Iraq withdrew from Iran in June 1982, the Iranian decision to cross the border into Iraq was based primarily on the belief that the invasion would cause the Shiite population in Iraq to rise up against the Baath regime.[166] This hope proved to be just as illusory as Iraq's earlier expectations. Thus, both Iran and Iraq learned that revolutionary regimes can be formidable military opponents, and foreign populations rarely welcome armed invaders.

Iran's relations with its other neighbors reveal similar results. The gulf states were worried by the ideological challenge created by the Islamic Republic. Their concerns were exacerbated by hostile Iranian propaganda; its support for Shiite dissidents in Bahrain, Kuwait, Saudi Arabia, and elsewhere; and its use of the annual pilgrimage to Mecca to spread its revolutionary message.

Yet the immediate danger seems to have been greatly overestimated. Although the revolution did trigger mild responses within Iran's Arab neighbors and led to a number of acts of terrorism and subversion, the governments that were threatened by these developments were able to repress, expel, or coopt potential troublemakers fairly easily. And though the same forces of modernization and cultural alienation that helped cause the revolution in Iran have fed the Islamic resurgence in a number of other Arab states, Iran is still the only country to have experienced a mass-based Islamic revolution. Its support for foreign radicals is clearly irritating, but its ideological message has proven less compelling than many observers originally feared.[167]

This result confirms that even relatively weak states are usually stronger than most revolutionary movements. Events such as the Iranian Revolution are the product of particular domestic and international circumstances and specific historical contingencies, and thus they are relatively rare. Although conditions in other states may appear to be roughly similar, the circumstances will never be identical and the protagonists unlikely to respond in precisely the same way. Governments facing a revolutionary challenge can usually keep their opponents at bay through a combination of coercion and cooptation (as the shah did for nearly twenty-five years), and endangered states can join forces against the spread of ideological infection (as the gulf

[165] Thus Khomeini argued, "We must strive to export our Revolution throughout the world. . . . If we remain surrounded in a closed circle, we shall certainly be defeated." Bani-Sadr offered a similar assessment: "If we do not go out of Iran to help the revolution, others will come to our country to plot against us." Quoted in Hunter, *Iran and the World*, 41. The parallel between this view and Trotsky's justification for the export of revolution is striking.
[166] See Abdulghani, *Iraq and Iran*, esp. 210; Hiro, *Longest War*, 86, and *Iran under the Ayatollahs*, 212–13.
[167] Zonis and Brumberg, *Khomeini, Iran, Arab World*, 72.

[261]

states did by forming the Gulf Cooperation Council and backing Iraq). Given the asymmetry of power favoring existing regimes, it is not surprising that revolutions seldom spread.

This interpretation helps explain why the revolution had its greatest impact among the Shiite population of Lebanon. The Lebanese state was a hollow shell by 1979, so pro-Iranian groups such as Hezbollah were able to acquire considerable influence. Yet the fundamentalists in Lebanon proved to be no match for the Israeli and Syrian *states*, and their position deteriorated as soon as Damascus abandoned them. Thus, the Lebanese experience actually confirms the rule: revolutions are likely to spread only when the target state has been gravely weakened or has ceased to exist already.[168] The growth of Islamic fundamentalism in several other states does not undermine this conclusion significantly, as these groups continue to face stiff opposition from regimes whose performance in other areas is unimpressive. All things considered, the modest direct impact of the Iranian Revolution shows that these events do not travel very well.

### Uncertainty and Misinformation

Iran's relations with other states were also affected by uncertainty. In addition to bringing inexperienced and unfamiliar elites to power, the revolution's effects on existing channels of communication and information made it more difficult for either side to pursue its interests in a rational and well-informed manner.

As discussed earlier, Iraq's decision to invade in 1980 was based on imperfect knowledge about such crucial issues as the balance of military power, the danger of a pro-Iranian uprising among the Iraqi Shiites, and the likelihood that the Arabs of Khuzistan would welcome them. Although its armed forces appeared to have been gravely weakened by purges and defections, the explosion of martial enthusiasm unleashed by its opponent's revolution more than compensated for these deficiencies. And because its military power rested in part on such new military institutions as the Revolutionary Guards, it is not surprising that outsiders failed to anticipate how well the new regime would fight.[169]

In the same way, Iran's efforts to export its revolution (including its decision to carry the war into Iraq in 1982) betrayed its ignorance about political

---

[168] The formation of an Islamic government in Sudan supports this conclusion as well, insofar as the process of Islamization was actively promoted by the ruling elite itself.

[169] Most experts underestimated Iran's military power. A CIA estimate predicted that Iran would last only three weeks after the Iraqi assault, *Time* magazine concluded that the war was unlikely to last long, and two U.S. experts concluded in 1981 that "Iran's prospects for victory can be termed simply as 'bleak.' " See Wright, *In the Name of God*, 83–84; and *MECS 1979–80*, 43.

conditions elsewhere in the Arab world. Although Khomeini had lived in Iraq for nearly fourteen years, his experience was limited primarily to religious communities. As a result, his belief that the Iraqi Shiites would rise up against Hussein was based on a biased sample of Iraqi Shiites. The Iranian expectation that the revolution would soon spread to other Arab countries rested on equally inaccurate information about the revolutionary potential of these societies; instead of creating new Islamic republics, their efforts only encouraged potential victims to balance against them even more vigorously.

Iran's relationship with the United States also illustrates the obstacles that result from mutual ignorance. As a U.S. State Department desk officer complained after the shah's departure from Tehran, "We simply do not have the bios, inventory of political groups, or current picture of daily life as it evolves at various levels in Iran. Ignorance here of Iran is massive."[170] Preoccupied by its fears of a leftist takeover, the U.S. government did not establish direct contact with Khomeini during his first year in power, and efforts to contact other clerics were rare. Instead, the United States tried to cultivate the short-lived Bazargan government and conducted secret talks with Bani-Sadr without realizing that his authority was actually quite limited. Gary Sick reports that for several months after the embassy was taken, U.S. officials did not even know the precise number of U.S. hostages, and Undersecretary of State Warren Christopher told a congressional hearing in May 1980 that information about the numbers, identity, and motives of the Iranians occupying the U.S. embassy was "still quite misty and vague." Attempts to resolve the crisis were further handicapped by the sheer difficulty of communicating with a regime in which any contact with the "Great Satan" could be attacked as an act of disloyalty.[171]

Uncertainty and inaccurate information also played a crucial role in the Iran-*contra* imbroglio. The decision to provide arms to Iran was based on the following four beliefs: that Khomeini's regime was nearing collapse; that this collapse would make a Soviet takeover more likely; that the arms deal would strengthen the position of a group of Iranian "moderates" who were

[170] Quoted in Bill, *Eagle and Lion*, 276. U.S. ignorance is also revealed by Ambassador William Sullivan's prediction that Khomeini would play a "Gandhi-like" role in a post-shah Iran, by UN ambassador Andrew Young's comment that Khomeini "would one day be hailed as somewhat of a saint," and by Princeton professor Richard Falk's claim that Khomeini's entourage was "uniformly composed of moderate progressive individuals" with "a notable record of concern for human rights." Brzezinski, *Power and Principle*, 368; Wright, *In the Name of God*, 216; and Sick, *All Fall Down*, 166.

[171] In the absence of diplomatic relations, negotiations for the release of the hostages had to be conducted via third parties or else covertly. Gary Sick relied heavily on information from an unidentified Iranian American with contacts among the revolutionary leaders and the exile community in the United States, and White House Chief of Staff Hamilton Jordan met secretly with Iranian representatives several times in February 1980. See Sick, *All Fall Down*, 246 and chap. 12; Salinger, *America Held Hostage*, 245–46; and Jordan, *Crisis*, esp. 146–53, 159–68.

eager to restore relations with the United States; and that Iran could persuade the Lebanese Shiites to release the U.S. hostages.[172] These hopes were not based on hard information, however, but on testimony from self-serving "sources" such as Manucher Ghorbanifar, who managed to persuade gullible U.S. officials such as Oliver North that the sale of arms to Iran would pave the way for the release of the hostages in Lebanon and help bring about a U.S.-Iranian rapprochement.[173]

States never understand each other perfectly, of course, but the Iranian Revolution confirms how much worse this problem can be after a revolution. Lacking reliable information, Iran and its foreign adversaries relied on stereotypes, worst-case scenarios, and the testimony of self-interested exiles and sleazy middlemen. The result was a heightened sense of threat, a greater willingness to use force, and incompetent, doomed attempts to improve relations.[174]

## Socialization and Learning

The Iranian case offers partial—but hardly overwhelming—support for the neorealist claim that the constraints of international anarchy will force states with radical international goals to moderate their objectives. Iran's foreign policy objectives were extremely unrealistic at first, and its leaders did modify some of their goals in order to ensure the survival of the new regime. The Islamic Republic did not abandon all of its revolutionary aims, however, and it continues today to engage in bellicose policies toward a number of states despite the high cost these positions entail. This persistence was the result of internal divisions within Iran and the sacrosanct character of certain elements in Iran's revolutionary worldview.

As we have seen, the foreign policy of the Islamic Republic rested on a distinctly unrealistic set of ideologically inspired goals. Khomeini's ideology questioned the legitimacy of the existing state system. He initially welcomed Iran's international isolation as a means of preserving its independence and revolutionary purity. Although moderate leaders such as Bani-Sadr, Yazdi, and Qotbzadeh deplored the effects of these policies on

---

[172] Ironically, the original CIA estimate that helped launched the entire initiative was abandoned a year later. See *Secret Military Assistance to Iran and the Contras*, 427; and "Soviet Threat toward Iran Overstated, Casey Concluded," *Washington Post*, January 13, 1987, A1, A8.

[173] "Much of the trouble that beset the Americans in any effort to work out a new policy for Iran, in order to achieve a 'strategic opening' or to liberate the hostages or both, resulted from an almost total American ignorance of what was going on in Iran." Theodore Draper, *Very Thin Line*, 155.

[174] As Rafsanjani put in 1986: "The Americans . . . despite their satellites, spies, the CIA, and the rest are so immensely uninformed about our region; uninformed about our internal affairs; how many half-baked analyses they tend to make." Quoted in Chubin and Tripp, *Iran and Iraq at War*, 214.

Iran's international position, Iran's behavior in the immediate aftermath of the revolution showed little sensitivity to the limits imposed by the international system.[175]

As neorealism predicts, however, external constraints forced the Islamic Republic to moderate its conduct in several ways. One sign of learning was the growing professionalism of the Revolutionary Guards; over time, the war with Iraq forced Iran to worry more about military effectiveness and less about ideological purity. Similarly, Iran's willingness to obtain weapons from virtually any source—including the "Great Satan" and Israel—revealed its willingness to forgo its ideological scruples in order to deal with a serious external challenge.[176]

Iran also abandoned its isolationist policy and began seeking diplomatic and commercial relations with a number of other states. It condemned Iraq's "atheistic" Baathist ideology but did not hesitate to align itself with Syria, which was governed by a rival branch of the same Baath movement. And having previously stated that "We must become isolated in order to become independent," by 1984 Khomeini had announced that Iran "wanted relations with all countries" except the United States, Israel, and South Africa. Failure to establish such ties, he argued, "would mean defeat, annihilation, and being buried right to the end." Khomeini now told his followers, "We should learn the good things from foreigners and reject the bad things," and Foreign Minister Velayati warned that "if Iran is not present on the world scene, then important issues will be decided without it." President Khamenei called for "rational, sound, and healthy relations with all countries," and some Iranian officials conceded that the revolution was unlikely to spread anytime soon. As Prime Minister Musavi admitted in 1985, initially "our view . . . was that the Islamic Revolution would spread within a year as a chain reaction. . . . But it seems we were wrong in our initial assessments."[177] Other officials acknowledged that Iran's own actions had contributed to its isolation; in Rafsanjani's words, "If Iran had demonstrated a little more tactfulness . . . [Saudi Arabia and Kuwait] would not have supported Iraq." The decision to end the war with Iraq was another triumph of necessity over ideological conviction, and the constitutional revisions that followed Khomeini's death and Khamenei's selection as supreme jurispru-

[175] In November 1980, for example, former foreign minister Yazdi warned that the hostage issue "has not been handled well and politically we have lost in the world." Quoted in Sick, *All Fall Down*, 333.

[176] One source states that Iran obtained weapons from as many as forty-one different countries, spending roughly $2–3 billion per year. See Farhad Kazemi and Jo-Anne Hart, "The Shi'i Praxis: Domestic Politics and Foreign Policy in Iran," in Menashri, *Iranian Revolution and the Muslim World*, 66.

[177] These quotations are from Rouhallah K. Ramazani, "Iran's Foreign Policy: Contending Orientations," in his edited *Iran's Revolution*, 60; Menashri, "Khomeini's Vision," 52; and Shirin T. Hunter, "After the Ayatollah," *Foreign Policy* 66 (1987).

dent were equally striking departures from Khomeini's original blueprint for Islamic government.[178]

These signs of moderation should not obscure the durability of Iran's commitment to radical ends and revolutionary means, however. Iran has continued to violate a number of diplomatic norms, as revealed by its support for terrorist groups, its efforts to assassinate anti-Khomeini activists in several foreign countries, and the abuse and detention of foreign diplomats in Tehran.[179] Iran repeatedly used the annual *hajj* to spread its revolutionary message and to undermine the Saudi regime, and it has shown scant interest in normalizing relations with the United States or Israel. The Rushdie affair has jeopardized ties with Great Britain and France, and despite the continued deterioration of the Iranian economy and the obvious costs of its confrontational stance, Iran continues to back fundamentalist groups in a number of states and maintains a doctrine that is fundamentally hostile to the West. In short, although there has been some evidence of socialization since the fall of the shah, the process must be regarded as partial at best.

Iran's deradicalization has been limited in part because the evidence in favor of such a development was ambiguous. After the regime had accomplished a host of seemingly impossible feats during its first years in power (including the ouster of the shah, the successful defiance of the United States, and the repulse of the Iraqi invasion), the necessity for moderation was partially obscured by faith in Islam and trust in Khomeini's charismatic leadership. Events such as the U.S. withdrawal from Lebanon in 1983 may have reinforced this view as well, and the growth of Islamic activism throughout the Middle East undoubtedly helped sustain Iran's commitment to an ideologically oriented foreign policy.[180]

Even more importantly, Iran's ability to learn and adapt has been constrained by divisions within the revolutionary elite itself. Different factions have drawn different lessons from Iran's postrevolutionary experience, and where Rafsanjani and others have sought to downplay the export of revolution in order to cultivate diplomatic and commercial ties abroad, the hard-

[178] Quoted in Menashri, "Khomeini's Vision," 52. Rafsanjani's pragmatism was also revealed by his statement that "by the use of an inappropriate method [the export of revolution] . . . we have created enemies for our country," and he criticized Iranian extremists as "frozen in their beliefs." In a remarkable display of candor, Rafsanjani also endorsed Khamenei's selection as supreme jurisprudent in 1989 by saying that "familiarity with national issues" is "far more important than all other conditions such as [religious] knowledge [and even] justness." Quoted in *MECS 1988*, 475, 480; and *1989*, 352.

[179] See "Iran's Use of International Terrorism: An Unclassified Paper and Chronology," (Washington, D.C.: U.S. Department of State, 1987); Alex von Dornoch [pseud.], "Iran's Violent Diplomacy," *Survival* 30, no. 3 (1988); and "Killing off Iranian Dissenters."

[180] Khomeini remarked in 1983: "Were it not for divine assistance and for [Allah's] special blessing, we would never have possessed the strength to withstand a satanic regime [Iraq] armed to the teeth, which was dependent upon world powers." Quoted in Richard Cottam, "Iran's Perception of the Superpowers," in Rosen, *Iran since the Revolution*, 142.

liners have remained firmly committed to a radical Islamic vision. Khomeini contributed to this split by refusing to allow Rafsanjani and the pragmatists to either eliminate the hard-liners or move too far from the revolution's original ideals. Iranian foreign policy has remained erratic and inconsistent, therefore, and the Islamic Republic has failed to "learn" as rapidly as a unitary actor might.[181]

Compounding the problem are the presence of numerous competing power centers and the relative weakness of the executive branch. Presidential powers are limited by the constitution and subject to scrutiny by the supreme jurisprudent, while influential clerics control independent institutions whose actions are not subject to strict governmental control.[182] Iran's costly commitment to a "revolutionary" foreign policy also underscores that a revolutionary regime is not a blank state; on the contrary, its leaders often take power with a clear set of expectations and objectives. The ideological visions that inspire a revolution set the standards by which the new regime will be judged and provide the moral justification for its rule. Having waged a violent struggle in order to implement a particular vision of society, elites will find it difficult to reject these ideals openly (even if they depart from them in practice), especially when the ruling ideology is regarded as sacrosanct and unchallengeable. Although important members of the Iranian elite have been willing to modify their principles in light of changing conditions and new experiences, abandoning them completely would threaten the legitimacy of clerical rule and leave them open to the charge of betraying the revolution. As a result, core values such as anti-Americanism and the promotion of Islam in other countries remain central features of Iran's political agenda.

On the whole, the foreign policy of the Islamic Republic provides strong support for the main arguments of this book. The revolution in Iran raised concerns about the global balance of power and had even more profound effects on the balance of power within the region. The revolution disrupted relations between Iran and most of its neighbors and exacerbated the competition between the United States and Soviet Union as well. Iran and its adversaries saw each other as aggressive and dangerous, and although these perceptions were justified, Iran's rulers exaggerated the true degree of Western animosity. The fear that the revolution would spread increased for-

---

[181] Shahram Chubin, *Iran's National Security Policy: Capabilities, Intentions, and Impact* (Washington, D.C.: Carnegie Endowment for International Peace, 1994), esp. 71.

[182] In 1992, for example, Iranian relations with Western Europe and the U.S. deteriorated after Ayatollah Hassan Sanei, the head of the Fifteenth Khordad Foundation, announced that he had increased the reward for killing Rushdie and would send his own men to assassinate the author.

eign perceptions of threat further, and these various forces combined to leave Iran isolated for most of the 1980s.

As the theory suggests, uncertainty and lack of information damaged Iran's relations with most other states. As Iran and its neighbors began to form more accurate estimates of each other's capabilities and intentions, however, the belief that the revolution might soon spread began to fade. Although Khomeini's ideological legacy and the enduring rivalry among his successors have prevented an explicit repudiation of Iran's revolutionary program, efforts to establish more normal foreign relations have already begun and are likely to increase.

# [6]

## *The American, Mexican, Turkish, and Chinese Revolutions*

"As revolutions have begun, it is natural to expect that other revolutions will follow."

—Thomas Paine, 1791

What were the international effects of the American, Mexican, Turkish, and Chinese revolutions? Although the evidence presented here is not definitive, these four cases support the basic claim that revolutions intensify security competition and increase the risk of war. Each of them exhibited some or all of the destabilizing dynamics found in the three previous cases, and each state approached the brink of war at least once.

Yet three of these revolutions did not lead to all-out war. The absence of war following the American, Mexican, and Turkish revolutions is best explained by the participants' awareness that the use of force was likely to be costly and difficult. These revolutions did not foster powerful fears of contagion, and each took place in geopolitical circumstances that further discouraged the use of force. In other words, the relationship between these revolutionary states and foreign powers was characterized by a powerful condition of *defense* dominance. Thus, even when serious conflicts arose, the use of force was seen as neither necessary nor appealing. By contrast, fear of contagion and counterrevolution was widespread after the Chinese Revolution, whose international consequences were similar to those of the French, Russian, and Iranian cases.

### THE AMERICAN REVOLUTION

At first glance, the American Revolution seems an obvious exception to the main argument of this book. Contemporaries saw the War of American Independence and the creation of the United States as an event with poten-

[269]

tially far-reaching implications.[1] Unlike the other revolutions examined here, however, the new nation remained formally at peace with the other great powers for nearly three decades. By demonstrating that revolutions do not *necessarily* lead to war, therefore, this case presents an anomaly requiring explanation.

Closer examination suggests that the anomaly is not as significant as it first appears. Like other revolutionary leaders, U.S. statesmen were obsessed with questions of national security and combined awareness of their own vulnerability with a profound sense of optimism.[2] U.S. relations with other states suffered from misperceptions similar to those that have accompanied other revolutions, and the resulting tensions were exacerbated by internal divisions, the fear of subversion, and poor communication. Finally, although the revolution did not lead to war, the United States was involved in several "militarized disputes" and came very close to war on at least three occasions. The absence of open warfare was largely the result of geographic isolation, favorable timing, and the unique worldview of the revolutionaries themselves; war would have been far more likely under any other circumstances.

### The Diplomacy of the "New Republic"

*The War of Independence (1775–1783).* The diplomacy of the War of Independence supports several familiar propositions about the international effects of revolutionary change. Foreign powers saw the revolution largely in terms of the balance of power; France supported the rebellious colonies in order to weaken England and avenge the losses it had suffered in the Seven Years War, and Spain took advantage of England's defeat to improve its own position in the Western Hemisphere.[3]

The war also offers an example of a revolutionary movement modifying its initial preferences in response to external pressure. As the Model Treaty adopted by the Continental Congress in 1776 suggests, the Founding Fathers hoped to avoid foreign commitments and confine relations with foreign powers to the realm of commerce. The pressure of war forced them to abandon this idealistic stance, however, and the American Confederation

---

[1] For a persuasive argument that the American Revolution was a "real" revolution, see Gordon S. Wood, *The Radicalism of the American Revolution* (New York: Alfred A. Knopf, 1992).

[2] As E. Wayne Carp notes, "In fact, it is no exaggeration to say that war, threats of war, and domestic insurrections were the major preoccupations of Americans in the 1790s." "The Problem of National Defense in the Early American Republic," in *The American Revolution: Its Character and Limits,* ed. Jack P. Greene (New York: New York University Press, 1987), 35.

[3] See Richard W. Van Alstyne, *Empire and Independence: The International History of the American Revolution* (New York: John Wiley, 1965), esp. chaps. 4 and 8.

negotiated a formal treaty with France in 1778.[4] Yet an aversion to traditional diplomacy was still widespread, and several prominent American leaders recommended that the new nation forgo regular diplomatic relations with the other great powers.[5]

*Diplomacy under the Confederation (1783–1789).* The Treaty of Paris in 1783 acknowledged the formal independence of the American Confederation, and three main issues dominated its diplomacy for the rest of the decade. First, the colonists had expected the lure of American commerce to give them considerable leverage over the European powers, but trade with France remained modest, and England monopolized trade with its former colonies by denying U.S. vessels access to its home ports, Canada, or the West Indies. Under the Articles of Confederation, Congress lacked the authority to impose retaliatory restrictions, and the separate colonies soon found themselves in a damaging economic competition.[6] A second issue was payment for losses suffered during the War of Independence; the Treaty of Paris obliged the former colonies to compensate loyalists and British citizens for lost property, but the new Congress lacked the power to collect the necessary funds. As a result, Britain refused to withdraw from its network of forts along the northwestern frontier and continued to support a number of Indian tribes who were actively resisting the westward expansion of the new nation. Third, the United States and Spain were engaged in a protracted border dispute over Florida and the Mississippi Valley, and the federal government was too weak to force Spain into a more conciliatory position.[7] U.S. weakness was further underscored by the predations of the

---

[4] The principal architect of the Model Treaty, John Adams, had previously stated, "I am not for soliciting any political connection, or military assistance . . . from France. I wish for nothing but commerce." Quoted in Lawrence S. Kaplan, *Colonies into Nation: American Diplomacy 1763–1801* (New York: Macmillan, 1972), 91; and see also William Stinchcombe, "John Adams and the Model Treaty," in *The American Revolution and "A Candid World,"* ed. Lawrence S. Kaplan (Kent: Kent State University Press, 1977), 70.

[5] Felix Gilbert argues that the Founding Fathers rejected balance-of-power diplomacy in favor of an idealistic internationalism based on the writings of the French philosophes, but more recent research suggests that U.S. leaders placed great importance on the balance of power and paid scant attention to the philosophes' opinions. See Felix Gilbert, *To the Farewell Address: Ideas of Early American Foreign Policy* (Princeton: Princeton University Press, 1961); James Hutson, *John Adams and the Diplomacy of the American Revolution* (Lexington: University Press of Kentucky, 1980), "Intellectual Foundations of Early American Diplomacy," *Diplomatic History* 1, no. 1 (1977), and "Early American Diplomacy: A Reappraisal," in Kaplan, *American Revolution and "A Candid World,"* 49.

[6] See Charles R. Ritcheson, *Aftermath of Revolution: British Policy toward the United States, 1783–1795* (Dallas: Southern Methodist University Press, 1969), 18–45; Reginald Horsman, *The Diplomacy of the New Republic, 1776–1815* (Arlington Heights, Ill.: Harlan Davidson, 1985), 29–31; and Kaplan, *Colonies into Nation,* 158–63.

[7] The dispute had important implications for U.S. economic development, as Spain's control of New Orleans allowed it to prevent U.S. settlers from shipping goods via the river. See

Barbary pirates, who began attacking U.S. shipping once English protection was withdrawn.[8]

These issues cast doubt on the long-term viability of the republican experiment. The belief that republics were inherently unstable and suitable only for small nations such as Switzerland convinced many contemporaries that the Confederation would soon collapse, and U.S. leaders were increasingly worried about the threat of foreign subversion.[9] These pressures helped convince the thirteen former colonies to replace the Articles of Confederation with a constitution that would grant the federal government significantly more authority.[10]

*The Federalist Era: 1789–1801.* U.S. foreign policy acquired greater force and coherence under the new Constitution, but it also became the main issue dividing the emerging Federalist and Republican factions.[11] Led by Alexander Hamilton, the Federalists wanted to create a strong central state that could curb local factionalism and preserve U.S. independence in a world of hostile powers. Convinced that British capital and commerce were essential to establishing U.S. credit and restoring the U.S. economy, Hamilton opposed schemes for commercial retaliation against England and sought to downplay the alliance with France.[12]

By contrast, the Republican faction, led by Thomas Jefferson and James Madison, sought to preserve a predominantly agrarian republic and favored a close alliance with France. Viewing commerce as a potent diplomatic weapon, they called for discriminatory duties against states that refused to sign commercial treaties, and they believed the United States

Samuel F. Bemis, *Pinckney's Treaty: America's Advantage from Europe's Distress, 1783–1800* (New Haven: Yale University Press, 1960); and Arthur P. Whitaker, *The Spanish-American Frontier, 1783–1795: The Westward Movement and the Spanish Retreat in the Mississippi Valley* (Boston: Houghton Mifflin, 1927), esp. 8–10.

[8] See H. G. Barnby, *The Prisoners of Algiers: An Account of the Forgotten American-Algerian War, 1785–1797* (London: Oxford University Press, 1966); and Horsman, *Diplomacy of the New Republic*, 30–31.

[9] See Ritcheson, *Aftermath of Revolution*, 33–35.

[10] As Hamilton wrote in *Federalist No. 11*, "Under a vigorous national government, the natural strength and resources of the country, directed to a common interest, would baffle all the combinations of European jealousy to restrain our growth." Alexander Hamilton, John Jay, and James Madison, *The Federalist* (New York: Modern Library, 1937), 65. See also Frederick W. Marks, *Independence on Trial: Foreign Affairs and the Making of the Constitution* (Baton Rouge: Louisiana State University Press, 1973).

[11] The competing visions of the Federalists and Republicans are summarized in Alexander DeConde, *Entangling Alliance: Politics and Diplomacy under George Washington* (Durham: Duke University Press, 1956), 31–65; Paul Varg, *Foreign Policies of the Founding Fathers* (Lansing: Michigan State University Press, 1963), 73–80; and Richard Buel, Jr., *Securing the Revolution: Ideology in American Politics, 1789–1815* (Ithaca: Cornell University Press, 1972), 29–49.

[12] For a detailed description of Hamilton's "grand design," see Stanley Elkins and Eric McKitrick, *The Age of Federalism* (New York: Oxford University Press, 1993), 92–132.

could develop its economy without close ties to the former imperial power. Thus, where Hamilton saw Anglo-American commerce as an indispensable source of revenue and manufactured goods, to Jefferson and Madison it was a source of potential corruption and a threat to Republican ideals. Republicans also saw Hamilton's blueprint for a strong central state as a threat to liberty, and they generally opposed efforts to increase U.S. military preparedness.[13]

The differences between the Republican and Federalist prescriptions for U.S. foreign policy were compounded by the revolution in France and the outbreak of war in Europe. Jefferson and the Republicans saw the upheaval in France as another triumph for the cause of liberty, but Hamilton and the Federalists soon came to regard it as a threat to U.S. interests.[14] The Franco-American treaty of 1778 called for the United States to guarantee French possessions in the New World and authorized either power to dispose of prize vessels in the other's ports. But support for France would invite English retaliation and disrupt the commercial ties that lay at the heart of Hamilton's financial system. Despite Republican misgivings, therefore, the United States formally proclaimed its neutrality in April 1793.[15]

France saw U.S. neutrality as a betrayal of the 1778 alliance. Relations were strained further by the activities of Edward Charles Genet, the new French minister to the United States. Genet had received a tumultuous welcome upon his arrival in Philadelphia in April 1793, and he promptly commissioned a dozen U.S. ships to operate as privateers against English shipping. These acts were in clear violation of U.S. neutrality laws, but Genet answered requests to cease his activities by threatening to appeal directly to the American people. Even Francophiles such as Jefferson were appalled by Genet's conduct, and the Cabinet issued a formal request for his recall in August 1793.[16]

---

[13] See Elkins and McKitrick, *Age of Federalism,* 79–89, 133–63, 195–257, 315; and Robert C. Tucker and David Hendrickson, *Empire of Liberty: The Statecraft of Thomas Jefferson* (New York: Oxford University Press, 1990), chaps. 2–5.

[14] As U.S. minister to France, Jefferson helped draft the Declaration of the Rights of Man and described the French Revolution as "the first chapter of the history of European liberty." John Marshall declared that human liberty depended "in a great measure on the success of the French Revolution," and even Hamilton later remarked that the French had "sullied a cause once glorious and that might have been triumphant." Quoted in Michael Hunt, *Ideology in American Foreign Policy* (New Haven: Yale University Press, 1987), 98; and Elkins and McKitrick, *Age of Federalism,* 310–11, 360; and also see Dumas Malone, *Jefferson and the Ordeal of Liberty* (Boston: Little, Brown, 1962), 48.

[15] See Malone, *Jefferson and the Ordeal of Liberty,* esp. 68–75; Deconde, *Entangling Alliance,* 87–91; 186–97; and Charles Marion Thomas, *American Neutrality in 1793: A Study in Cabinet Government* (New York: AMS Press, 1967), chap. 1.

[16] See DeConde, *Entangling Alliance,* 284–85; Harry Ammon, *The Genet Mission* (New York: W. W. Norton, 1973), 141–45; and Eugene R. Sheridan, "The Recall of Edmond Charles Genet," *Diplomatic History* 18, no. 4 (1994).

These events accelerated the polarization between Federalists and Republicans. Jefferson and his associates saw U.S. neutrality as de facto support for England and suspected the Federalists of seeking to establish a monarchy.[17] Hamilton and the Federalists were alarmed by the Republicans' pro-French sympathies, the surge of popular support for France, and Genet's overt attempts to encourage and exploit these sentiments. Thus, while Republicans brooded over "Anglomane" plans to subvert the Constitution and establish a monarchy, Federalists feared a Republican plot to embroil the United States in a war with England and establish a "popular democracy" in league with France.[18]

Ironically, the decision to remain neutral did not prevent Anglo-American relations from approaching war the following year. The central issue was a conflict over maritime policy, the catalyst being the English Order-in-Council of November 6, 1793, imposing a blockade over the French West Indies. The Royal Navy's policy of halting U.S. vessels in order to impress former English citizens intensified anti-British feeling, and confrontations between English and U.S. forces along the northwestern frontier further complicated Anglo-American relations.[19] Although London relaxed the November order in January, sympathy for France increased, and many Americans now believed that a war with England was both likely and desirable.[20] Tensions rose higher when fears of a U.S. attack led English officials in Canada to

---

[17] In May 1793, Jefferson described his domestic opponents as "zealous apostles of English despotism" and France's enemies as "the confederacy of princes against liberty." After resigning as secretary of state, he warned a friend, "There are in the U.S. some characters of opposite principles . . . all of them hostile to France and looking to England as the staff of their hope." Such men, he asserted, saw the Constitution "only as a stepping stone to monarchy." Quoted in DeConde, *Entangling Alliance*, 56; and Elkins and McKitrick, *Age of Federalism*, 317.

[18] Hamilton regarded the Republicans as "deeply infected with those horrid principles of Jacobinism, which, proceeding from one excess to another, have made France a theater of blood." He also suggested that their zeal for France was "intended by every art of misrepresentation and deception to be made the instruments first of controlling, finally of overturning the Government of the Union." The Federalists blamed Genet for the growth of "Democratic Societies" during this period, which they mistakenly regarded as products of French subversion. Quoted in Buel, *Securing the Revolution*, 69; and Elkins and McKitrick, *Age of Federalism*, 360, 456; and also see Robert R. Palmer, *The Age of the Democratic Revolution: A Political History of Europe and America, 1760–1800* (Princeton: Princeton University Press, 1959–64), 2:529–31.

[19] In the spring of 1794, Governor George Clinton of New York reported that the British governor of Canada, Lord Dorchester, had told a gathering of Indian tribes that war was likely within a year. See Ritcheson, *Aftermath of Revolution*, chap. 13; and Jerald Combs, *The Jay Treaty: Political Battleground of the Founding Fathers* (Berkeley: University of California Press, 1970), 121–22.

[20] The American minister in London, Edward Pinckney, was so certain that war was imminent that he requested permission to move his family to France. See Deconde, *Entangling Alliance*, 99 n. 93, and 130–31; and Ritcheson, *Aftermath of Revolution*, 304–306.

send troops to the Maumee rapids in March 1794, a step that placed the two nations on the verge of war.[21]

The Federalists still believed that war with England would be a disaster for the United States, and President George Washington dispatched John Jay to London in a final effort to reach a negotiated settlement. The so-called Jay Treaty resolved most of the disputed issues (though not the question of impressment), but the Cabinet kept the terms of the treaty secret until the Senate had ratified it, in order to deflect Republican criticism. Despite its limitations, the treaty preserved peace between the United States and Great Britain and led to a final British withdrawal from U.S. territory.[22] The agreement also opened the way for the rapid expansion of U.S. commerce, particularly in the Atlantic carrying trade, and the U.S. economy entered a period of extraordinary growth.[23]

The Federalists gained a second diplomatic triumph with an agreement with Spain known as Pinckney's Treaty. Spain had allied itself with France in 1795, and the Jay Treaty had fueled Spanish fears of an Anglo-American assault on their North American possessions. Spain was thus more willing to make concessions, and the treaty established a border with Spanish Florida along the thirty-first parallel and gave U.S. settlers the right to deposit goods for shipment from New Orleans. The Federalists also persuaded the Indians along the northwestern frontier to cede most of Ohio and parts of Indiana through the Treaty of Greenville in August 1795. Together with the withdrawal of British forces obtained via the Jay Treaty, this agreement heralded a major shift in the balance of power in the Northwest and greatly facilitated U.S. expansion there.[24]

Finally, the Federalist period also witnessed a new crisis in relations between the French and Americans, which culminated in the so-called Quasi-War of 1797–1800. The neutrality proclamation and Genet's inept diplomacy had already strained Franco-American relations, and a misguided French at-

[21] According to Charles Ritcheson, this step "brought war so close . . . that the preservation of peace involved acts of almost miraculous self-restraint on both sides." See *Aftermath of Revolution*, 310–13.

[22] See Combs, *Jay Treaty*; Samuel Flagg Bemis, *Jay's Treaty: A Study in Commerce and Diplomacy* (New Haven: Yale University Press, 1962); and Varg, *Foreign Policies of the Founding Fathers*, chap. 6. It is easy to imagine a different outcome to the Anglo-American confrontation. At the Battle of Fallen Timbers in August 1794, for example, the U.S. forces gained a decisive victory when the commander of a nearby British fort refused to allow the fleeing Indians to enter his stockade. Elkins and McKitrick suggest that "the spark of war might have been struck then and there," and Ritcheson concludes that "quite obviously an armed clash between British and American troops was avoided by a hairsbreadth." Elkins and McKitrick, *Age of Federalism*, 438–39; and Ritcheson, *Aftermath of Revolution*, 320.

[23] See Douglas C. North, *The Economic Growth of the United States, 1790–1860* (New York: W. W. Norton, 1966), 25, 30, 53; and Horsman, *Diplomacy of the New Republic*, 63–64.

[24] See Bemis, *Pinckney's Treaty*; and Reginald Horsman, *Expansion and American Indian Policy, 1783–1812* (Norman: University of Oklahoma Press, 1992), esp. 98–102.

tempt to aid the Republicans in the election of 1796 had reinforced U.S. suspicions and helped the Federalists retain power. Jacobin excesses had undermined U.S. sympathies for France, while the French government saw the Jay Treaty as yet another betrayal of the Franco-American alliance. In March 1797, the French Directory declared that neutral vessels carrying British goods would be subject to seizure, a step that directly threatened U.S. maritime interests. President John Adams sent a diplomatic mission to France to negotiate a settlement, but the foreign minister, Charles Talleyrand, refused to see them and sent three agents (known to posterity as X, Y, and Z), to arrange a bribe of $250,000 for himself and a loan of $12 million for the French government as preconditions for beginning negotiations. The U.S. commissioners rejected the terms and the mission accomplished nothing, but news of Talleyrand's actions ignited a storm of protest in the United States, where demands grew for a declaration of war. Congress authorized the construction of twelve new warships and initiated plans to increase the regular army as well. Some Federalist leaders tried to use the crisis to discredit the Republican cause, while others entertained hopes of an Anglo-American campaign against the French and Spanish possessions in the Western Hemisphere.[25]

These measures were justified by fears of French subversion or invasion, magnified by the internal struggle between Federalists and Republicans. Prominent Federalists continued to fear a Republican uprising on behalf of France, while Jefferson and the Republicans saw the Federalists as closet monarchists who were betraying the sacred principles of the revolution.[26] The fear of French subversion also led to the passage of the controversial Alien and Sedition laws in the summer of 1798. Although less severe than similar laws in Europe, these measures included a ban on the publication of "false, scandalous, and malicious writing . . . against the government" and marked a noteworthy departure from the initial revolutionary commitment to liberty and free speech.[27]

---

[25] On these events, see Elkins and McKitrick, *Age of Federalism,* 645; William Stinchcombe, *The XYZ Affair* (Westport, Conn.: Greenwood Press, 1980); Alexander DeConde, *The Quasi-War: The Politics and Diplomacy of the Undeclared War with France, 1797–1801* (New York: Scribner's, 1966), chap. 2; and Gilbert Lycan, *Alexander Hamilton and American Foreign Policy: A Design for Greatness* (Norman: University of Oklahoma Press, 1970), 381–90.

[26] Thus Hamilton wrote Washington in May 1798, "It is more and more evident that the powerful faction which has for years opposed the government, is determined to go every length with France. . . . They are ready to *new-model* our Constitution under the *influence* or *coercion* of France, and . . . in substance . . . to make this country a province of France." For his part, Jefferson accused the Federalists of seeking "to keep up the inflammation of the public mind" and argued that "it was the irresistible influence and popularity of General Washington played off by the cunning of Hamilton, which turned the government over to anti-republican hands." Quoted in Lycan, *Hamilton,* 360–63; and see also Elkins and McKitrick, *Age of Federalism,* 583–84.

[27] Federalist fears of France were not without some basis, as the Directory did have ambitions in the Western Hemisphere and the French negotiators had told their U.S. counterparts,

Despite the widespread belief that war with France was inevitable, a combination of Republican opposition, military weakness, and divisions within Federalist ranks prevented a further escalation of the conflict. Adams was committed to defending U.S. maritime rights and preserving its commercial ties with England, but he recognized that public support for war was lacking and he preferred to place the onus for war on France.[28] Thus, the conflict was limited to an undeclared naval war, and a rapid increase in U.S. naval power quickly ended the French threat to U.S. shipping. Talleyrand offered to resume negotiations, Adams sent a new mission to France, and the Convention of Mortefontaine in September 1800 ended the Quasi-War by abrogating the moribund alliance and restoring most-favored commercial relations.[29] It also marked the Federalists' last diplomatic achievement, as splits within the party and a personal rivalry between Adams and Hamilton enabled Jefferson and the Republicans to capture the presidency in 1801.

*The Era of Republican Expansion, 1801–1812.* Where the Federalists believed that U.S. weakness required a willingness to compromise with more powerful states (such as England), Jefferson's party was convinced that the United States could achieve its aims independently. And where the Federalists sought a strong central state and a more powerful military establishment, the Republicans saw a strong military as a threat to liberty and believed that the lure of U.S. commerce would allow the country to preserve its interests without recourse to war.[30]

At the same time, Jefferson was committed to a program of national expansion. He regarded the acquisition of additional territory as essential to the United States' retaining its agrarian character, and the creation of "sister republics" throughout North America would also prevent the European

---

"With the French party in America, . . . [we would be able] to throw the blame that will attend the rupture of negotiations on [you] . . . and you may assure yourselves that this will be done." As Buel notes, however, "Talleyrand and his agents could not have done more to undermine the Republican position than if they had been in the Federalists' pay." Quoted in Buel, *Securing the Revolution*, 163, and also see 172–74.

[28] In July, Congress defeated a motion to permit the seizure of armed and unarmed French vessels by a vote of 52 to 31, which DeConde describes as "in a sense, the closest the House came to taking a test vote on full-scale war." A motion permitting the seizure of armed vessels and the commissioning of privateers passed on July 9. *Quasi-War*, 106–108.

[29] On the naval aspects of the Quasi-War, see Elkins and McKitrick, *Age of Federalism*, 644–54. The Convention of Mortefontaine is reprinted in DeConde, *Quasi-War*, 351–72.

[30] According to Tucker and Hendrickson, "Rather than adjusting to `the general policy of Nations,' Jefferson and Madison sought to overturn it." *Empire of Liberty*, 18–21, 35, 39–43. On Jefferson's attitudes toward the use of force, see Reginald C. Stuart, *The Half-Way Pacifist: Thomas Jefferson's View of War* (Toronto: University of Toronto Press, 1978).

powers from threatening the new republic directly or contaminating it with aristocratic ideals.[31]

Jefferson's foremost accomplishment as president was the acquisition of the Louisiana Territory in 1803. Both the Directory and Napoleon had contemplated reestablishing an empire in North America, and France obtained the retrocession of Louisiana from Spain with the secret Treaty of San Ildefonso in October 1800. Jefferson responded by accelerating the acquisition of Indian lands east of the Mississippi River and by threatening to align with England in the event that France reoccupied New Orleans.[32] When Spain restricted U.S. use of the port of New Orleans, Jefferson sent James Monroe to Paris to purchase New Orleans and the Floridas. The Peace of Amiens was unraveling by the time Monroe arrived, and Napoleon now offered to sell the entire Louisiana Territory to the United States. The negotiations were completed in April 1803. Jefferson relaxed his earlier views on the limits of executive power and forced the treaty through the Senate rather than submit it for public approval via a constitutional amendment. It was an unmistakable triumph: the United States gained control over the mouth of the Mississippi and roughly doubled its total territory.[33]

Jefferson's expansionism turned next to the Spanish territories in Florida. Based on a dubious reading of previous agreements, the United States laid claim to the region between New Orleans and the Perdido River, but the claims collapsed when France backed the Spanish position.[34] Jefferson tried to convince Spain to abandon the region, through a "campaign of persuasion, bribery, and threat," but his hopes that Spain would follow the French lead and abandon North America proved overly optimistic and the Floridas were still in Spanish hands when he left office in 1808.[35]

---

[31] See Tucker and Hendrickson, *Empire of Liberty*, 29–31, 96–98, 158–62; and Horsman, *Diplomacy of the New Republic*, 12–13.

[32] In a letter to the U.S. minister in France (intended for French eyes as well), Jefferson wrote, "There is on the globe one single spot, the possessor of which is our natural and habitual enemy. It is New Orleans." He added, "The day that France takes possession of New Orleans . . . from that day on we must marry ourselves to the British fleet and nation." Even if intended solely as a warning, it was a remarkable statement for a confirmed Anglophobe and Francophile. Quotations from Dumas Malone, *Jefferson the President: First Term, 1801–1805* (Boston: Little, Brown, 1970), 254–57; and Tucker and Hendrickson, *Empire of Liberty*, 98.

[33] See Alexander DeConde, *This Affair of Louisiana* (New York: Scribner's, 1976), 180–86; Tucker and Hendrickson, *Empire of Liberty*, 122–35, 163–71; and Malone, *Jefferson the President: First Term*, chaps. 15–16.

[34] See Tucker and Hendrickson, *Empire of Liberty*, 137–41.

[35] The quotation is from Stuart, *Halfway Pacifist*, 40; and see also Tucker and Hendrickson, *Empire of Liberty*, 139–41; DeConde, *This Affair of Louisiana*, 215–40; Malone, *Jefferson the President: First Term*, 343–47, and *Jefferson the President: Second Term, 1805–1809* (Boston: Little, Brown, 1974), 45–55, 62–77, 91–94.

The central problem of Jefferson's second term, however, was a renewed maritime conflict with England. Prior to 1805, England had permitted U.S. vessels to transport goods from the French West Indies to France provided they first stopped in a U.S. port (a procedure known as the "broken voyage"). As the war with France intensified, however, many Britons began to see this policy as an unwarranted boon to the French war effort and a threat to English commerce. English appeals courts declared these cargoes liable to seizure in 1805; the Royal Navy's policy of stopping U.S. merchant vessels in order to impress British subjects caused further U.S. resentment; and efforts to resolve the dispute by negotiation were unsuccessful. Anglo-American relations deteriorated further in June 1807, when an English warship fired upon and boarded the USS *Chesapeake* and removed four seamen, triggering a storm of popular protest and renewed calls for war.[36]

Yet Jefferson's own aversion to the use of force and the Republicans' longstanding belief in the coercive power of U.S. commerce soon dampened the momentum for war. Instead, Jefferson decided to employ "peaceable coercion" in the form of an economic embargo. In February 1808 Congress authorized the enforcement of the Non-Importation Act against selected English goods and approved Jefferson's request for an Embargo Act restricting all U.S. trade. This decision reflected Jefferson's desire to protect U.S. vessels by keeping them in port, as well as his tendency to play for time before resorting to violence and his idealistic belief that the new American republic could teach the corrupt European monarchies a lesson about peaceful alternatives to war.[37]

Unfortunately, Jefferson had underestimated English resolve and exaggerated U.S. leverage, and the embargo turned out to be both a poor instrument of coercion and a disaster for U.S. commerce. The resulting depression exacerbated divisions between commercial and agrarian interests in the United States and squandered much of the popularity Jefferson had won during his first term.

The crisis of 1807–1808 laid the foundation for the formal outbreak of war in 1812. The issues in dispute had not changed significantly; although Jefferson repealed the embargo just before leaving office, trade with England and France was restricted by a new Non-Intercourse Act, and efforts to lift the ban reinforced each side's perceptions of hostility. In 1810, Congress authorized the president to bar U.S. commerce with the opponents of any state that formally acknowledged U.S. maritime rights. Napoleon promised to re-

---

[36] As Jefferson remarked following the *Chesapeake* affair, "The British have often enough, God knows, given us cause of war before. . . . But now they have touched a chord which vibrates in every heart." Quoted in Malone, *Jefferson the President: Second Term*, 425–26; and see Bradford Perkins, *Prologue to War: England and the United States, 1805–1812* (Berkeley: University of California Press, 1963), 2–31, 77–95.

[37] See Tucker and Hendricksen, *Empire of Liberty*, 204–209.

scind French restrictions on American commerce provided England lifted its own ban on U.S. trade with France, and even though this pledge was meaningless so long as the Royal Navy prohibited commerce between the United States and France, Jefferson's successor, James Madison, swallowed the bait and agreed to reimpose a ban on U.S. trade with England in 1811.[38]

Under rising Anglo-American tensions, England had already resumed covert support to the Indian tribes along the northwestern frontier. Madison and the Republicans became convinced that war was necessary to protect the frontier and defend U.S. maritime rights, and they thought an invasion of Canada would force Britain to alter its maritime policy and would eliminate British influence from North America once and for all. Prominent Republicans were extremely optimistic, based on exaggerated estimates of U.S. military prowess and the belief that the Canadian population would greet them as liberators. The governor of New York predicted that "one-half of the militia of Canada would join our standard," and Representative John Randolph of Virginia anticipated a "holiday campaign . . . with no expense of blood, or treasure, on our part—Canada is to conquer itself—she is to be subdued by the principles of fraternity."[39] Despite strong Federalist opposition, Congress approved Madison's war message by a vote of 79 to 49, and Madison signed the war bill on June 18, 1812. Nearly thirty years after gaining independence, the United States had entered its first real war.

### Is the American Revolution an Exception?

At the most general level, the American case demonstrates the value of a systemic perspective. U.S. diplomacy was not simply the product of ideological preferences and domestic pressures; it was also shaped by the state of relations among the other great powers and the policies that they adopted. French support for the colonies during the War of Independence was a by-product of the Anglo-French rivalry in Europe, and the wars of the French Revolution formed the backdrop for many of the problems U.S. leaders faced after 1787. France, England, Spain, and the Barbary states all took advantage of U.S. weakness after the American Revolution, and the United States was able to evade or defeat these threats largely because the other great powers were at such odds with each other. Thus, this case confirms

---

[38] See Perkins, *Prologue to War*, 239–53; and J. C. A. Stagg, *Mr. Madison's War: Politics, Diplomacy, and Warfare in the Early American Republic, 1783–1830* (Princeton: Princeton University Press, 1983), 28–29, 54–57.

[39] Jefferson echoed the prevailing Republican optimism by saying that "the acquisition of Canada . . . will be a mere matter of marching," and Henry Clay of Kentucky declared that "the militia of Kentucky are alone competent to place Montreal and Upper Canada at our feet." Quoted in Donald R. Hickey, *The War of 1812: A Forgotten Conflict* (Urbana: University of Illinois Press, 1989), 73; and Stagg, *Mr. Madison's War*, 5 n. 8.

that one cannot understand the foreign policy of a revolutionary state by looking solely at its internal characteristics or ideological underpinnings.

Another similarity was the Founding Fathers' belief that the creation of the republic was an event of universal significance. This vision was sometimes used to justify support for sympathetic revolutions elsewhere (as in Hamilton's dreams of fomenting democratic revolutions in Latin America or Jefferson's vision of an "Empire of Liberty" in the Western Hemisphere), but attempts to carry out these ambitions were limited by U.S. weakness, the belief that the American experience was unique and would be difficult to duplicate, and the fear that trying to export the revolution would compromise American "virtue," generate excessive military requirements, and tarnish the republican experiment.[40]

Like other revolutionary elites, U.S. leaders were also prone to a combination of insecurity and overconfidence. On the one hand, they viewed the republic as fragile and worried that the new nation would succumb to a combination of foreign subversion and internal division. These fears intensified the bitter struggle between Federalists and Republicans, as each faction feared that the other intended to betray the republic to an alien ideal. Such behavior is characteristic of revolutionary regimes, where founding principles are seen as sacred but are still being translated into concrete policies and where political competition is not yet bounded by traditions, norms, and institutions.[41] Insecurity also lay at the root of U.S. expansionism, as Jefferson believed that foreign control of the Mississippi Valley and the Floridas would pose a permanent threat to the new nation.

On the other hand, U.S. leaders were optimistic about America's long-term potential and "confident of America's importance in the world . . . and of its future greatness."[42] This hopeful vision could be used to justify a policy of either accommodation or confrontation, however; Hamilton argued against war with England in 1795 by invoking both America's present weakness and its glowing long-range prospects, while Jefferson and Madison saw American commerce as a powerful diplomatic weapon and advocated an aggressive commercial policy against England.[43] Like other revolutionary states, in short, the United States was repeatedly torn between concern for its immediate survival and a remarkable confidence in its ability to chart its own course.

---

[40] As a result, until 1812 U.S. leaders did not succumb to the same bellicosity displayed by other revolutionary states. Elkins and McKitrick, *Age of Federalism,* 313.

[41] See Elkins and McKitrick, *Age of Federalism,* 78, 270.

[42] See Horsman, *Diplomacy of the New Republic,* 4–6; and Hutson, *John Adams,* 6–10.

[43] As Hamilton put it, "few nations can have stronger inducements than the United States to cultivate peace." Quoted in Lycan, *Hamilton,* 216; and see also Combs, *Jay Treaty,* 118–19; and Elkins and McKitrick, *Age of Federalism,* 434.

U.S. relations with other countries were also subject to spirals of misperception and hostility, most obviously with revolutionary France. The revolutionaries in France initially regarded the United States as a inspiration, and many U.S. leaders saw the fall of the French monarchy as a vindication of their own experience and a crucial advance in the struggle for liberty. These perceptions obscured the many differences between the two nations' experiences, however, and disillusionment was swift. Genet's tenure as France's minister to the United States was a disaster because of his erroneous belief that a direct appeal to the American people would enable him to reverse the Federalists' policy of neutrality, and his successors' efforts to aid the Republicans in the 1795 election backfired just as badly. The XYZ negotiations in 1797 revealed equally profound misconceptions on France's part, as exaggerated beliefs in the strength of the "French party" in the United States led Talleyrand to provoke a quarrel that neither country wanted.

Domestic divisions within the United States contributed to these problems by preventing foreign powers from anticipating U.S. responses correctly. Genet's blunders are understandable in light of the enthusiastic welcome he received upon his arrival; ironically, the sympathies he had aroused made his activities seem even more dangerous to the Federalists and fueled their desire to restrain him. Similarly, although the Republicans condemned English maritime policy in 1794 and 1805, the Federalists emphasized the need to avoid a direct confrontation for which the United States was poorly prepared. In these circumstances, it is not surprising that Britain could not foresee how the United States would react, while the fear that their internal rivals were in cahoots with the foreign adversary encouraged both Federalists and Republicans to respond more vigorously than circumstances warranted.[44]

Finally, this case highlights the trade-offs and tensions between revolutionary ideals and external constraints. The idealism of the Founding Fathers was evident in their aversion to traditional diplomacy and their disdain for protocol, in their desire to avoid "entangling alliances" and their opposition to a permanent military establishment, and in their faith that commercial policy would be a powerful diplomatic weapon and their fear of "foreign corruption." Yet despite these deeply rooted convictions, the foreign policy behavior of the new republic did not differ dramatically from that of other powers. U.S. leaders were keenly concerned with enhancing

---

[44] These same divisions may have encouraged spiraling but discouraged war. Because the Federalists would not support war with England while the Republicans were opposed to war with France, it was difficult for the nation as a whole to go to war with either one. The War of 1812 supports this conjecture: the Federalists still opposed the decision for war, but the Republicans now controlled both the legislative and executive branches and did not need the Federalists' approval.

their security; they also favored the preservation of a balance of power and were willing to modify their revolutionary ideals in the face of external pressure.[45] The demands of the War of Independence led to the alliance with France in 1778 (which directly contradicted the principles of the Model Treaty), and external pressures eventually convinced the new nation to abandon the Articles of Confederation in favor of a federal system that could stand up more effectively to foreign pressure. The need for economic recovery encouraged Hamilton and the Federalists to seek a rapprochement with England via the Jay Treaty, and the naval threat from France inspired a rapid military buildup in 1797–98. Even Jefferson, whose idealism and Anglophobia were especially pronounced, was quick to use U.S. naval power against the Barbary pirates and was willing to contemplate an alliance with England in order to check French ambitions in the Mississippi Valley.[46] Jefferson also recognized the strategic benefits of removing the European presence in North America, and he was willing to relax his Republican convictions in order to achieve this goal.[47] Like other revolutionary states, in short, in its early diplomacy the United States displayed both a commitment to strongly held ideals and a willingess to abandon them in the name of national security.

The similarities just noted are striking, if only because Americans today are not inclined to see any resemblance between the Founding Fathers and such figures as Robespierre, Lenin, and Khomeini. Yet the differences between the American Revolution and the other cases we have examined are equally important, beginning with the relative mildness of the revolutionary process itself. The American Revolution resembles an elite "revolution from above" in certain respects, in that most of its leaders, who were drawn from the prerevolutionary elite, did not set out to overturn the established social order. Although their actions had revolutionary effects and gave rise to the creation of a novel set of political and social institutions, the process was also a remarkably deliberate and carefully reasoned

---

[45] The realist component of early U.S. foreign policy is presented most revealingly in Hutson, *John Adams*, "Early American Foreign Policy," and "Intellectual Foundations"; and Gerald Stourzh, *Benjamin Franklin and American Foreign Policy* (Chicago: University of Chicago Press, 1954).

[46] Jefferson at one point maintained that United States "should practice neither commerce nor navigation, but stand with respect to Europe precisely on the footing of China." But he added that this was "theory only, and a theory which the servants of America were not at liberty to follow." See Combs, *Jay Treaty*, 74; and Tucker and Hendrickson, *Empire of Liberty*, 30–31.

[47] Jefferson's pragmatism is also revealed by his decision to ratify the Louisiana Purchase via congressional approval rather than via a constitutional amendment. As Dumas Malone suggests, Jefferson "was generally more realistic when in office than when in opposition, less doctrinaire; and his situation with respect to the treaty and its promises can best be described by saying that he was caught in a chain of inexorable circumstances." *Jefferson the President, First Term*, 318–20, 332; and see Kaplan, *Colonies into Nation*, 149.

[283]

affair.[48] There were sharp political quarrels, and occasional uprisings such as the Shays's and Whiskey rebellions, but these events pale in comparison to the Jacobin Terror, the Vendée rebellion, the Russian Civil War, or the internal struggles in the Islamic Republic of Iran. The divisions between Federalists and Republican did not end in the expulsion or extermination of one side by the other but in a peaceful transfer of power in 1801. And because the internal struggle was less severe, the perceived threat of outside interference was less ominous as well.[49]

A second difference was the ideology of the revolution. The American revolutionaries did not see the capture of state power as the means to impose a far-reaching reconstruction of society. On the contrary, they were deeply suspicious of state power and devoted to the preservation of liberty, which they conceived as freedom from arbitrary government authority.[50] Thus, where the French, Russian, and Iranian revolutions produced strong state bureaucracies designed to facilitate social change at home and mobilize the nation for war, the American state was constrained by the profound opposition to a large military establishment and by a system of checks and balances that formed its principal defense against arbitrary executive power and the tyranny of democratic majorities.[51]

This discussion brings us to the central question: Why didn't the American Revolution lead to war? The revolution created a radically different vision of society and government and disrupted the balance of power in North America. The new nation was internally divided and suspicious of foreign powers, and it faced serious diplomatic challenges from several quarters. Yet with the partial exceptions of the Quasi-War with France, the naval war with the Barbary states, and its frontier skirmishes with the indigenous Indian tribes, the United States did not go to war until 1812. The explanation for this apparent anomaly rests on four main factors.

First, unlike that of most of the other revolutions examined in this study, the ideology of the American Revolution discouraged active efforts to export its principles. Where the Jacobins, Bolsheviks, and Iranian clerics used

[48] See Gordon S. Wood, *The Creation of the American Republic, 1776–1787* (Chapel Hill: University of North Carolina Press, 1969), 3–10.

[49] See John Shy, "Force, Order, and Democracy in the American Revolution," in Greene, *American Revolution,* 76–77.

[50] See Bernard Bailyn, *The Ideological Origins of the American Revolution* (Cambridge: Harvard University Press, Belknap Press, 1967), 35–43, 55–93, 319; Wood, *Creation of the American Republic,* 18–28, 61–65, 608–609; and Buel, *Securing the Revolution.*

[51] According to Lois Schwoerer, "the anti-standing army bias . . . became a basic assumption of almost every political leader" in America. *"No Standing Armies!": The Anti-Army Ideology in Seventeenth Century England* (Baltimore: John Hopkins University Press, 1974), 195; and Carp, "Problem of National Defense," 20–24.

control of the state to promote social change at home and abroad, the Founding Fathers saw state power as a danger and refused to grant it unchecked authority. By inhibiting efforts to build a strong state (and especially a strong military establishment), their ideology strictly limited the ability of U.S. leaders to conduct an activist diplomacy. In addition, many U.S. leaders sought to limit their involvement with other states so as not to contaminate the republican experiment, and even men as politically opposed as Jefferson and Hamilton agreed that the United States should serve as an example while refraining from active efforts to spread its principles abroad. The United States would be a model for other societies but would not try to remake them in its own image.[52]

The absence of war was also due to the new country's paradoxical combination of weakness and invulnerability. On the one hand, the United States was too weak to pose a serious threat to the other great powers, so those states could take a more relaxed view of events across the ocean. Indeed, neither England nor France placed a high priority on relations with the United States during the 1790s, preoccupied as they were with domestic events and the expanding war in Europe.[53] At the same time, its vast size, sparse population, and poorly developed communications made the new nation extremely difficult to conquer (as the English experience in the War of Independence had demonstrated).[54] Thus, foreign powers had little reason to confront the United States (except at sea) but ample incentive to avoid a major military commitment in North America. These same considerations dampened U.S. concerns: although U.S. leaders were worried about subversion and disloyalty and occasionally indulged in unfounded

[52] As John Quincy Adams put it in 1821: "Wherever the standard of freedom and independence has been or shall be unfurled, there will [America's] heart . . . be. But she goes not abroad in search of monsters to destroy. She is the well wisher to the freedom and independence of all. She is the champion and vindicator only of her own." Quoted in Armstrong, *Revolution and World Order*, 52; and see also DeConde, *Entangling Alliance*, 6–7; Tucker and Hendrickson, *Empire of Liberty*, 240–43, 252–54; and Hutson, "Early American Diplomacy," 49–50.

[53] During the XYZ affair, Talleyrand remarked that the United States was of nor more "consequence to [the Directory] nor ought it to be treated with greater respect than Geneva or Genoa," and Director Jean-François Reubell devoted only three lines of a thirty-four page report on French diplomacy to the United States and referred to John Adams as "President of Congress." British officials were similarly inclined. According to Jerald Combs, Prime Minister Pitt "tended to ignore American problems" and left them in the hands of his subordinates. According to DeConde, "in the 1790s the United States was relatively so insignificant . . . that in any struggle in which the major maritime powers took a real interest it could be little more than a pawn." See Combs, *Jay Treaty*, 87; DeConde, *Entangling Alliance*, 503; Elkins and McKitrick, *Age of Federalism*, 401–403, 506–507, 570, and 874–76 n. 131; and Stinchcombe, *XYZ Affair*, 35.

[54] See Shy, "Force, Order, and Democracy," and Jonathan R. Dull, "Two Republics in a Hostile World," in Greene, *American Revolution*, 78, 158.

[285]

fears of invasion, their relative invulnerability discouraged a precipitous re-sort to force. Thus, Hamilton argued against war in 1794 by saying that "to subvert by force republican liberty in this country, nothing short of entire conquest would suffice," and the attempt "would be absolutely ruinous to the undertakers."[55]

Third, U.S. efforts to avoid war were greatly aided by its geographic sep-aration from Europe. Distance reduced the threat that it might pose to Eu-ropean interests and raised the costs of European involvement in North America. This effect was perhaps most evident in Napoleon's decision to abandon his plans to occupy New Orleans and his willingness to sell the Louisiana Territory, but the same factor made it easier for Britain to cede dominance of the continent to its former colonies. Although fears of foreign invasion did arise from time to time, they were generally fleeting.

Lastly, the revolution in France (and the subsequent outbreak of war in Europe) was a stroke of good fortune for the United States, although it cre-ated a number of problems as well. On the one hand, the European con-flict discouraged England, France, and Spain from taking direct action against the new republic, helped U.S. leaders obtain the Jay and Pinckney treaties, and led directly to the Louisiana Purchase. On the other hand, the war in Europe repeatedly threatened to drag the U.S. in, as it finally did in 1812. On balance, however, rivalries elsewhere were an asset for the United States. They aided the expansion of U.S. commerce and gave other states an incentive to stay on good terms with it. Given the relative weak-ness of the United States during its first three decades, this was no small advantage.

The American Revolution bears more than a passing resemblance to the cases examined in chapters 3–5. Foreign responses to the revolution were heavily influenced by a concern for the balance of power; the Founding Fathers attributed to the revolution a universal significance, and they saw themselves as both vulnerable in the short term and destined to control a continent over time. Like other revolutionary leaders, they were suspi-cious of foreign powers and obsessed with security, and a combination of internal divisions and misperceptions helped trigger hostile spirals with France and England. These disputes brought the United States close to war on several occasions and might have led to open warfare in any of them. At a minimum, therefore, the American Revolution supports the claim that revolutions intensify security competition and increase the like-lihood of war.

---

[55] Quoted in Lycan, *Hamilton*, 216. Madison expressed a similar view ten years earlier, say-ing, "No European nation can ever send against us such a regular army as we need fear." Quoted in Combs, *Jay Treaty*, 73.

Unlike revolutionary France, Russia, or Iran, however, the United States did not cross the line for nearly three decades. This anomaly is explained by the limited aims of the Founding Fathers and by the size, weakness, and geographic isolation of the new nation, which combined to make the large-scale use of force either impossible or unappealing. Had the new nation bordered on the other great powers, the danger of war would have been far greater. Although this case demonstrates that revolutions do not *necessarily* lead to war, it is largely consistent with the theory.

## THE MEXICAN REVOLUTION

Like the American Revolution, the revolution in Mexico at first appears to challenge many of the central arguments of this book. The revolution was prolonged and violent, with far-reaching effects on Mexico itself, but its international effects were relatively mild. In particular, although other states' interests were affected by the revolution, they did not see it as a major threat, and it did not lead to war. Thus, the Mexican case presents a partial contrast to the French, Russian, and Iranian revolutions.

Upon closer examination, however, the Mexican Revolution does not seem quite so different. Although all-out war did not occur, U.S. troops did intervene in 1914 and 1916 and the border between the two states was the site of repeated raids and armed clashes.[56] These events brought the two states close to war in 1916, after which U.S.-Mexican relations remained troubled for nearly two decades. Most importantly, relations between the revolutionary government and several other states exhibited many of the same sources of conflict that were present in the French, Russian, and Iranian cases. Thus, this case supports the claim that revolutions heighten security competion and increase the risk of war.

### The Diplomacy of the Mexican Revolution

The Mexican Revolution began in November 1910, when a group of liberal reformers led by Francisco Madero issued a proclamation calling for the overthrow of Porfirio Diaz, the de facto dictator who had governed Mexico for nearly thirty-five years.[57] This initiative sparked a series of rural rebellions

---

[56] In 1920, a U.S. Senate subcommittee estimated that 550 Americans had been killed in Mexico between 1911 and 1920, while U.S. armed forces had killed 541 Mexicans on Mexican soil. Robert Freeman Smith, *The United States and Revolutionary Nationalism in Mexico, 1916–1932* (Chicago: University of Chicago Press, 1972), 176–77.

[57] On Madero and the onset of the revolution, see Stanley Ross, *Francisco Madero: Apostle of Mexican Democracy* (New York: Columbia University Press, 1955); Charles C. Cumberland, *Mexican Revolution: Genesis under Madero* (Austin: University of Texas Press, 1952); and Alan Knight, *The Mexican Revolution* (Cambridge: Cambridge University Press, 1986), vol. 1.

that overwhelmed the federal army and forced Diaz into exile in April 1911. Madero became president in November, but he was unable to overcome conservative resistance and unwilling to satisfy the demands of the rural rebels. His popularity declined, the rural rebellions resumed, and Madero was ousted and killed in a counterrevolutionary coup in February 1913.

Madero was replaced by Victoriano Huerta, a conservative general who tried to restore the Porfirian system. Pressures for change were too far advanced, however, and Huerta was soon challenged by the so-called Constitutionalist movement, a diverse coalition that united moderate reformers such as Venustiano Carranza (its self-designated "first chief") with rural populists such as Francisco "Pancho" Villa and Emiliano Zapata. Huerta eventually faced opposition from the United States as well, as President Woodrow Wilson viewed him as an illegitimate usurper and withheld U.S. recognition. When diplomatic pressure failed to persuade Huerta to hold elections and establish a legitimate constitutional order, Wilson stepped up his own efforts to bring the dictator down. He lifted the U.S. embargo on weapons shipments to Mexico in February 1914 (allowing the Constitutionalists to obtain arms more easily) and ordered the U.S. Marines to occupy the port of Vera Cruz in April. The latter decision triggered unexpected opposition in Mexico and the United States alike, and brought a sharp letter of protest from Carranza.[58]

Huerta's resignation in July caused a brief burst of optimism, but the Constitutionalist coalition had already begun to unravel and a civil war between the main revolutionary factions was underway by the fall.[59] U.S. officials favored Villa at first, believing that he would win quickly and would be easier to deal with than Carranza, and hoped that a rapid end to the fighting would eliminate the need for U.S. involvement.[60] As the fighting intensified and Carranza gained the upper hand, however, Wilson and his aides began to worry about the safety of foreign nationals and property and acknowledged that intervention might be necessary.[61] Relations with Car-

[58] See Arthur S. Link, *Woodrow Wilson and the Progressive Era, 1910–1917* (New York: Harper and Row, 1954), 125 n. 41.

[59] On the origins of the civil war, see Charles C. Cumberland, *Mexican Revolution: The Constitutionalist Years* (Austin: University of Texas Press, 1972), chap. 6; Robert E. Quirk, *Mexican Revolution, 1914–1915: The Convention at Aguascalientes* (Bloomington: Indiana University Press, 1960); and Knight, *Mexican Revolution*, vol. 2, chap. 2.

[60] Whereas Carranza had opposed the occupation of Vera Cruz and rejected U.S. mediation, Villa endorsed the Vera Cruz intervention and went to some lengths to court U.S. officials. See Arthur S. Link, *Wilson: The Struggle for Neutrality, 1914–1915* (Princeton: Princeton University Press, 1960), 251–52, 258–59; and Clarence C. Clendenen, *The United States and Pancho Villa: A Study in Unconventional Diplomacy* (Ithaca: Cornell University Press, 1961), 53–55, 75–76, 120–21, 128–40.

[61] Wilson at first hoped to stay out of Mexico and told a crowd in Indianapolis in January, "It is none of my business, and it is none of your business how long [the Mexican people] take in determining [their form of government]. . . . The country is theirs. . . . And so far as my influence

ranza had been strained since Vera Cruz, and reports from confidential agents in Mexico convinced Wilson that Carranza lacked the stature or ability to unify the country.[62] U.S. officials now began to press for the formation of a coalition government in Mexico, in part because this solution would allow Washington to play the rival factions off against each other.[63] In June, Wilson issued a formal note calling for the contending factions "to act together . . . for the relief and redemption of their country," and he warned that the United States might be forced to intervene "in order to help Mexico save herself." Villa accepted Wilson's proposal but Carranza rejected it, declaring, "History furnishes no example in any age or any country of civil war terminating by the union of the contending parties. One or the other must triumph."[64] Wilson invited representatives from the contending factions to a conference of Latin American states in August and offered the unworkable suggestion that both Villa and Carranza retire in favor of some alternative leader. The conference accomplished nothing, and a number of U.S. officials began to support the idea of a counterrevolutionary coup by a group of conservative Mexican exiles.[65] Wilson was increasingly preoccupied by events in Europe and concerned about German intrigues in Mexico, however, and he soon reversed course and extended de facto recognition to Carranza in October.[66]

Recognition brought a brief honeymoon between the United States and Carranza, but lingering suspicions and misunderstandings took the two

---

goes, while I am President nobody shall interfere with them." By March, however, Wilson admitted to Secretary of State Lansing, "I do not yet allow myself to think of intervention as more than a remote *possibility* . . . [but] the possibility is worth preparing for." Arthur Link notes, "The stronger Carranza grew, the stronger seemed to become the determination of the President and his advisors not to recognize [him]." See Link, *Struggle for Neutrality*, 459, 464, 468.

[62] In August 1915, Lansing remarked, "I doubt very much as to [Carranza's] personality being strong enough or one that would be able to restore peace in Mexico." Quoted in P. Edward Haley, *Revolution and Intervention: The Diplomacy of Taft and Wilson with Mexico, 1910–1917* (Cambridge, Mass.: MIT Press, 1970), 174.

[63] Lansing wrote in July, "We do not wish the Carranza faction to be the only one to deal with in Mexico. Carranza seems so impossible that an appearance, at least, of opposition to him will give us the opportunity to invite a compromise of factions. I think, therefore, it is politic for the time to allow Villa to obtain sufficient financial resources to remain in arms until a compromise can be effected." Quoted in Quirk, *Mexican Revolution*, 285; and see also Friedrich Katz, *The Secret War in Mexico: Europe, the United States, and the Mexican Revolution* (Chicago: University of Chicago Press, 1981), 300; Haley, *Revolution and Intervention*, 174; and Link, *Struggle for Neutrality*, 487.

[64] Carranza's rejection led Wilson to declare, "I think I have never known of a man more impossible to deal with on human principles than this man Carranza." For these quotations see Link, *Struggle for Neutrality*, 476–77, 481; and Haley, *Revolution and Intervention*, 165.

[65] See Katz, *Secret War*, 303–305; and Link, *Struggle for Neutrality*, 471–76.

[66] Wilson's decision-making is recounted in Link, *Struggle for Neutrality*, 488–91. On the role of Germany in U.S. calculations, see Katz, *Secret War*, 301–302, and "Pancho Villa and the Attack on Columbus, New Mexico," *American Historical Review* 83, no. 1 (1978), 108.

countries to the brink of war the following year. The catalyst was Villa, who was now convinced that Carranza had sold out to the United States. In a last-ditch attempt to revive his fortunes, Villa launched a series of attacks on U.S. citizens and property, beginning with the murder of seventeen U.S. mining engineers in January 1916 and culminating in a raid on Columbus, New Mexico in March.[67] The border region had been torn by a number of violent raids and intrigues during the previous year, and Wilson now dispatched a "Punitive Expedition" under General John J. Pershing to apprehend Villa or destroy his forces.[68]

As Villa had hoped, the U.S. decision to intervene ended the rapprochement with Carranza and partly restored his own prestige. Wilson believed (incorrectly) that Carranza had approved the U.S. expedition, and though the Mexican leader's initial response was measured, he could not afford to be viewed as a U.S. lackey and his opposition soon stiffened. Tensions grew worse when talks between U.S. and Mexican military representatives failed to produce an agreement, U.S. troops clashed with a group of Mexican civilians in the village of Parral in April, and Mexican bandits attacked Glen Springs, Texas in May. Wilson promptly mobilized 150,000 U.S. militiamen along the border. The U.S. Army began preparing plans for a full-scale invasion, and another skirmish between U.S. and Mexican forces at Carrizal on June 21 convinced several U.S. officials that war was imminent.[69]

Both Carranza and Wilson were committed to avoiding war, however, and the crisis eased when the two leaders agreed to form a "joint commission" to discuss the various points of dispute. Wilson offered to withdraw the Punitive Expedition in exchange for Mexican adherence to a series of one-sided conditions regarding border security, the protection of foreign lives and property, religious tolerance, and other domestic issues. No Mexi-

[67] See Katz, "Pancho Villa and the Raid on Columbus," and *Secret War,* 305–310; and James A. Sandos, "Pancho Villa and American Security: Woodrow Wilson's Mexican Diplomacy Reconsidered," *Journal of Latin American Studies* 13, no. 2 (1981).

[68] Some of the instability along the border arose from the "Plan of San Diego," an obscure group of Mexican radicals who hoped to spark a revolt in the southwestern United States by building networks among the Mexican-American communities in southern Texas and sponsoring a number of cross-border raids. See Charles H. Harris III and Louis R. Sadler, "The Plan of San Diego and the Mexican–United States War Crisis of 1916: A Reexamination," *Hispanic-American Historical Review* 58, no. 3 (1978); James A. Sandos, "The Plan of San Diego: War and Diplomacy on the Texas Border, 1915–1916," *Arizona and the West* 14, no. 1 (1972); and Charles C. Cumberland, "Border Raids in the Lower Rio Grande Valley—1915," *Southwestern Historical Quarterly* 57, no. 3 (1954).

[69] General Hugh L. Scott told Wilson that "there will be no way to stave off war, and we should at once seize all the border towns . . . and shove the Mexicans into the desert." Similarly, Colonel House wrote Wilson, "I have been praying that we could get out of the Mexican difficulty without war, but it looks now as if it were inevitable." Quoted in Haley, *Revolution and Intervention,* 203, 214.

can leader could have accepted these terms, however, and Carranza would not even discuss them until the Punitive Expedition was gone.[70]

His stubbornness was rewarded in January 1917 when Wilson decided to withdraw the expedition unilaterally. Although war had been averted, the Punitive Expedition left an enduring residue of suspicion and resentment. Carranza still faced continued opposition from Villa, Zapata, and several other rebel groups, and he was understandably resentful of U.S. and British support for Manuel Peláez, an independent landlord and rebel leader whose troops controlled the main oil fields, as well as the growing number of economic and commercial restrictions imposed on Mexico.[71] U.S.-Mexican relations were strained further by article 27 of the new Mexican Constitution, which appeared to threaten the position of foreign investors in Mexico, particularly in the oil and mining industries.[72] Yet despite these tensions (as well as opposition from U.S. business interests), Wilson decided to extend full diplomatic recognition to Carranza in August 1917, primarily to keep U.S.-Mexican relations quiet as war with Germany approached.

Carranza's stubborn defense of Mexican independence enhanced his popularity temporarily, but persistent economic problems and protracted internal opposition continued to plague his presidency. After World War I, his efforts to assert control over Mexico's raw materials led to new tensions with the United States, when a coalition of U.S. corporations, Republican congressmen, and administration officials (notably Secretary of State Lansing, Ambassador Henry Fletcher, and State Department official Boaz Long) launched a campaign of intimidation that brought the United States close to war with Mexico in the fall of 1919. In addition to the goal of protecting U.S. investments in Mexico, this effort reflected the U.S. desire to prevent the spread of economic nationalism in Latin America. Lansing at one point threatened direct intervention in an attempt to persuade Carranza to moderate his policies, but even he hoped to avoid the use of force. Moreover, although advocates of intervention mounted an extensive public relations effort to portray the Carranza regime as hostile and "Bolshevistic," public support for intervention remained weak. Wilson remained unconvinced that such a course was necessary, and Lansing's various maneuvers merely

[70] Among other things, the United States demanded that Mexico provide "full and adequate protection to the lives and property of citizens of the United States," and it reserved "the right to re-enter Mexico and to afford such protection by its military forces in the event of the Mexican government failing to do so." See Haley, *Revolution and Intervention*, 235–36.

[71] The United States imposed export controls on Mexico that limited U.S.-Mexican trade and made it difficult for Carranza to obtain arms, and also restricted Mexican access to loans from U.S. banks. See Katz, *Secret War*, 515–16.

[72] Article 27 declared that all subsoil deposits were the property of the Mexican nation and that concessions could only be granted by the national government. Foreigners were forbidden to acquire property in Mexico unless they registered as Mexican for purposes of ownership and gave up the right to seek aid from foreign governments.

accelerated his own departure from office. Carranza and the oil companies eventually compromised on the most important points of contention, and the crisis was over by early 1920.[73]

Carranza's fatal mistake came later in the year, when he tried to prevent a popular general, Alvaro Obregon, from entering the presidential contest. The Mexican Army defected to Obregon's side, and Carranza was killed while attempting to flee to Vera Cruz. Obregon was elected president in September 1920, and although he also faced several internal challenges during his presidency, he became the first Mexican president to serve a full term since Diaz. Obregon also achieved a guarded rapprochement with the United States and helped set the stage for the final consolidation of the revolution under President Lazaro Cardenas.

### Is the Mexican Revolution an Exception?

Does the Mexican Revolution support the theory proposed in this book? The answer is a qualified yes. As expected, the collapse of central authority in Mexico encouraged foreign powers to intervene either to improve their own positions or to prevent other states from doing so. This tendency was most pronounced in the case of Great Britain, whose economic interests in Mexico were second only to those of the United States. Britain recognized the Huerta government in 1913 despite strong U.S. opposition, a step that a number of British officials saw as a way to protect British interests in Mexico and to undermine the U.S. position throughout Latin America.[74] The British retreated when events in Europe made it more important to maintain good relations with the United States, but British officials continued to interfere in Mexico throughout the revolutionary period.[75] British activities in Mexico were driven both by the need to protect their oil supplies and the desire to prevent either a Mexican-German rapprochement or a unilateral

---

[73] See Smith, *United States and Revolutionary Nationalism*, chaps. 6 and 7, esp. 158; and Mark T. Gilderhus, *Diplomacy and Revolution: U.S.-Mexican Relations under Wilson and Carranza* (Tucson: University of Arizona Press, 1977), chap. 6.

[74] The clearest exponent of this view was Sir Lionel Carden, who became British minister to Mexico in October 1913. Carden recommended that Britain formally declare its opposition to U.S. policy and predicted that "by adopting such a line . . . we should leave ourselves free to afford effective protection to the great interests we have at stake which are being constantly imperiled by the . . . interested action of the United States; and we should regain the influence we used to have in Latin America and with it a considerable part of the trade which we have lost and are still losing." Quoted in Katz, *Secret War*, 176. See also Arthur S. Link, *Wilson: The New Freedom* (Princeton: Princeton University Press, 1956), 365–77; and Peter Calvert, *The Mexican Revolution, 1910–1914: The Diplomacy of Anglo-American Conflict* (Cambridge: Cambridge University Press, 1968), pt. 2.

[75] The British also discovered that the quality of the oil from their holdings in Mexico was too low to meet their naval requirements, forcing them to rely on U.S. companies and discouraging further confrontations with the United States.

U.S. invasion that would jeopardize the British position in Mexico completely.[76]

U.S. policy toward the Mexican Revolution was driven by a similar desire to protect its own position and prevent other countries from improving theirs. Wilson's repeated attempts to guide the revolution stemmed in part from his belief that "European imperialism" was responsible for the instability that afflicted "backward" countries such as Mexico, and he consistently opposed measures that might enhance European influence.[77] Wilson opposed Huerta in part because he believed that foreign (i.e., British) support was keeping Huerta in power, and he denounced interference by "foreign capitalists" in a major speech in October 1913.[78] U.S. officials favored the creation of a coalition government because it would maximize U.S. leverage, and the decision to extend de facto recognition to Carranza in October 1915 was largely a response to the fear of German influence.[79] The possibility of a German-Mexican rapprochement also influenced the decision to intervene in 1916, and Carranza's occasional efforts to use Germany as a counterweight to the United States remained a major concern for U.S. policy makers until the end of World War I.

These fears were not entirely misplaced, as Germany also tried to exploit the turmoil in Mexico to further its own interests. The Germans' policy in Mexico initially aimed at protecting their investments and preserving good relations with the United States; to this end, they tried unsuccessfully to mediate between Huerta and the United States and proposed joint intervention to restore order in 1913. After Huerta's ouster and the outbreak of World War I, however, Germany began to see the revolution primarily as a means of hindering U.S. support for Britain and France.[80] Germany deflected Carranza's initial inquiries about an alliance (to avoid provoking the United States), but when the onset of unrestricted submarine warfare made conflict with the United States virtually inevitable, Germany tried to entice Car-

[76] "In the years 1917–18 the British were attempting to fight a three-front war in Mexico against Germany, the United States, and the Mexican nationalists." Katz, *Secret War,* 464.

[77] See Katz, *Secret War,* 191–93, 222–23, 493–96.

[78] The U.S. ambassador in London also warned a group of British businessmen that the United States "will warmly welcome your investments in all parts of the Americas on the condition that these investments do not give you control of the country in question." Quoted in Katz, *Secret War,* 180; and see also Gilderhus, *Diplomacy and Revolution,* 8–9; Haley, *Revolution and Intervention,* 108–110; and Link, *New Freedom,* 320.

[79] As Lansing put it, "Germany does not wish to have one faction dominant in Mexico, *therefore, we must recognize one.* . . . Our possible relations with Germany must be our first consideration, and all our intercourse with Mexico must be regulated accordingly." See Link, *Woodrow Wilson and the Progressive Era,* 134 n. 59; and Gilderhus, *Diplomacy and Revolution,* 30–31.

[80] German state secretary Gottlieb von Jagow remarked in May, "It would be very desirable that America be drawn into a war and be distracted from Europe, where it tends to be pro-English." Quoted in Katz, "Pancho Villa and the Attack on Columbus," 126.

ranza into attacking the United States by offering to help Mexico regain Texas, New Mexico, and Arizona.[81] Like Britain and the United States, in short, German policy illustrates how intervention in a revolution can be motivated by the desire to improve a state's position vis-à-vis other powers.

The Mexican case also illustrates revolutionary states' tendency to spiral with foreign powers, as was most apparent in Mexico's relations with the United States. Although leaders in both countries sought to avoid a serious conflict, a combination of legitimate differences and unfortunate misunderstandings nearly drove the two states to war in 1916 and continued to afflict U.S.-Mexican relations for many years thereafter. Tensions between the two were due partly to incompatible objectives (Wilson wanted to foster a liberal capitalist order in Mexico that would protect foreign property rights, while Carranza and his followers sought to defend Mexican autonomy and consolidate their hold on power) and partly to more immediate conflicts of interest (such as the safety of U.S. citizens, the security of the border region, and Mexican efforts to tax U.S. properties). These concrete disputes were exacerbated by each side's propensity to exaggerate the other's hostility and to ignore how threatening its own conduct might appear. Because U.S. officials disavowed any aggressive aims and genuinely believed that their actions were in Mexico's best interest, they took Carranza's refusals to accept U.S. guidance as a sign of deep-seated hostility.[82] U.S. officials were upset when Carranza rejected an offer of U.S. support in 1913 and condemned the intervention at Vera Cruz in 1914, and his unwillingness to compromise led Wilson to conclude that "nothing can be done with or through the First Chief."[83] By 1917, Wilson was referring to Carranza as a "pedantic ass" and complaining that "all that [he] has said and done shows his intense resent-

---

[81] This gambit backfired when Carranza declined the offer and British intelligence intercepted and released a secret German message describing their efforts. See Katz, *Secret War*, chaps. 9–10; and Barbara Tuchman, *The Zimmermann Telegram* (New York: Macmillan, 1966).

[82] In 1913, Wilson declared, "We are actuated by no other motives than the betterment of the conditions of our unfortunate neighbor, and by the sincere desire to advance the cause of human liberty." Quoted in Link, *New Freedom*, 394, and see also 386–87. Two years later, Wilson admitted, "What makes Mexico suspicious of us is that she does not believe as yet that we want to serve her. She believes that we want to possess her, and she has justification for the belief in the way in which some of our fellow citizens have tried to exploit her. . . . [But] I will try to serve all America, . . . by trying to serve Mexico herself." Quoted in Haley, *Revolution and Intervention*, 224. The U.S. belief that its actions were benevolent is also revealed in House's comment to Wilson: "Heaven knows, you have done all a man could to help the people there, and the fact that they are not able to follow your kindly lead, is no fault of yours." Quoted in Lloyd C. Gardner, *Safe for Democracy: The Anglo-American Response to Revolution, 1913–1923* (New York: Oxford University Press, 1984), 66.

[83] Quoted in Haley, *Revolution and Intervention*, 180. The image of Mexican intransigence was reinforced by Carranza's decision to close the port of Progeso (cutting off the U.S. supply of sisal), his opposition to the Punitive Expedition, his refusal to discuss internal matters in the Joint Commission, his occasional attempts to use Germany as a counterweight to U.S. and British pressure, and his stubborn defense of the Constitution of 1917.

ment of this Administration."[84] For their part, the Mexican revolutionaries saw U.S. interference as a direct threat to the goal of establishing Mexican sovereignty and independence, and they failed to appreciate either Wilson's altruistic motives or his reluctance to use force.

These suspicions were compounded by another familiar feature of revolutionary situations: namely, the difficulty of obtaining reliable information or forecasting the future course of the revolution itself. Wilson tried to alleviate this problem by dispatching a series of special agents to gather information, but most of them proved to be woefully unreliable.[85] In 1913, for example, Wilson's hostility to Huerta was reinforced when special agent John Lind reported, erroneously, that British oil interests were controlling British policy and that foreign support was keeping Huerta in power, and the subsequent decision to seize Vera Cruz was based on Lind's similarly misguided assertion that the Mexicans would not oppose a U.S. landing.[86] Other U.S. attempts to predict the course of the revolution were equally unreliable; Secretary of State Bryan stated in September 1913, "We have nearly reached the end of our trouble," and he offered an equally optimistic (and inaccurate) forecast after Huerta's departure the following year.[87] U.S. leaders misread the course of the civil war as well, at first expecting Villa to win quickly and discounting Carranza's chances until the latter's triumph was nearly complete.[88] Once again, this error was partially based on inaccurate

[84] Quoted in Gilderhus, *Diplomacy and Revolution*, 64. Frustration at Mexican unwillingness to accept U.S. help was a recurring theme among U.S. officials. House remarked, "If the Mexicans understood that our motives were unselfish, she should not object to our helping adjust her unruly household," and the chief U.S. representative on the Joint Commission wrote Wilson that the Mexicans "certainly are discouraging people to try to help." Quoted in Knight, *Mexican Revolution*, 2:153; and Arthur S. Link, *Wilson: Campaigns for Progressivism and Peace, 1916–1917* (Princeton: Princeton University Press, 1965), 53–54.

[85] According to one author, "Wilson's judgment in selecting diplomatic agents was, for the most part, notoriously poor." Frederick Calhoun, *Power and Principle: Armed Intervention in Wilsonian Foreign Policy* (Kent: Kent State University Press, 1986), 35.

[86] Lind predicted that U.S. intervention could "be accomplished without the military loss of an American," but the landing left 19 U.S. soldiers dead and 71 wounded, while the Mexicans suffered 126 killed and 195 wounded. Quoted in Haley, *Revolution and Intervention*, 130; also see Link, *New Freedom*, 400. Larry Hill argues that Lind's analysis "had little basis in fact," and Alan Knight describes Lind's reporting as "garbled, ill-informed, and naive, displaying a crude racism and a paranoid suspicion of Britain." See Larry D. Hill, *Emissaries to a Revolution: Woodrow Wilson's Special Agents in Mexico* (Baton Rouge: Louisiana State University Press, 1973), 99–102; Knight, *Mexican Revolution*, 2:139, 150–53; and Calvert, *Mexican Revolution*, 233–34.

[87] In December 1914, Bryan wrote Wilson, "The situation seems to be clearing up in Mexico. Villa and Zapata are working in harmony and interim president Gutierrez seems to be about to assume authority over most of the country." Wilson's assessment was more measured, but even he believed "we have certainly cleared the stage and made a beginning." Link, *Struggle for Neutrality*, 232, 260, and *New Freedom*, 363.

[88] Villa's efforts to cultivate U.S. support convinced Wilson that he "certainly seems capable of good things." In August 1914, House described Villas as "the only man of force now in

testimony from U.S. agents in Mexico, who painted a rosy portrait of Villa and an unflattering one of the first chief.[89] U.S. ignorance is also evident in Wilson's repeated attempts to arrange a compromise peace, which rested on the naive hope that Carranza would be willing to share power (or to withdraw entirely) even though his armies held the upper hand. Uncertainty also exacerbated tensions during the Punitive Expedition, especially after the skirmishes at Parral and Carrizal. In the latter case, however, the rapid acquisition of more accurate information reduced pressure for U.S. retaliation and helped both sides back away from the brink.[90]

Similar problems contributed to a spiral between Great Britain and Mexico in 1917–18. Britain was worried about Carranza's efforts to use Germany as a counterweight to the Allies, especially after intercepting German diplomatic communications that conveyed an exaggerated impression of German influence. These reports helped convince Great Britain to attempt to overthrow the Carranza government; by contrast, because the United States had better sources of information by this point (and was not relying on intercepted German messages), it held a far more sanguine view of German influence and merely wanted to keep Mexico calm.[91]

Again we arrive at the final issue: Why did the Mexican Revolution not lead to war? There are at least four interrelated reasons.

First, the revolution in Mexico was only modestly threatening, owing to the enormous asymmetry of power between the United States and Mexico. Even if the revolution created greater uncertainty about the precise balance of power, leaders on both sides knew that Mexico was not a major military threat to the United States. Because Mexico was so much weaker, the Mexi-

---

sight in Mexico," noting further that Carranza was "not equal to the situation." Quoted in Link, *Struggle for Neutrality*, 239–41. According to Edward Haley, "lacking reliable information about the military capacities of the Constitutionalists, [Wilson] discounted [their] victories [over Villa]. Rather than reports of Constitutionalist progress, the President received countless despatches describing widespread starvation and suffering in Mexico." *Revolution and Intervention*, 158–60.

[89] In November 1914, a State Department official reported, "General Villa is the only individual who can put the country on a peaceful footing," and predicted that "one good fight will settle the question and Carranza will find himself with scant forces and will have to flee the country." Another special agent, Duval West, confirmed this assessment after visiting Villa, Zapata, and Carranza in the spring of 1915, and his negative report on Carranza convinced Wilson that the first chief was not the man to bring order to Mexico. See Link, *Struggle for Neutrality*, 258–59, 459–61, 469–71; and Haley, *Revolution and Intervention*, 158–61.

[90] When news of the clash at Carrizal reached Washington, Wilson's first belief was that "the break seems to have come in Mexico; and all my patience seems to have gone for nothing." He prepared a message to Congress requesting authorization to occupy northern Mexico, but public opinion was strongly opposed to war, and a report that U.S. troops had started the fighting convinced Wilson to make another attempt to avoid escalation. See Haley, *Revolution and Intervention*, 210–23; Katz, *Secret War*, 310–11.

[91] See Katz, *Secret War*, 485–95.

cans knew all-out war would be foolhardy and U.S. leaders knew they could afford to act with forebearance. Thus, Wilson justified his policy of "watchful waiting" in 1913 by saying, "We can afford to exercise the self-restraint of a really great nation, which realizes its own strength and scorns to misuse it," and he offered a similar appraisal the following year.[92]

Second, the "ideology" of the Mexican revolutionary movements did not menace other states in the same way as French republicanism, Soviet Marxism, or Khomeini's version of Islamic fundamentalism. Instead, U.S. leaders were sympathetic to the basic ideals of the revolution (despite their reservations about specific issues), and Wilson's various interventions were intended to guide the revolution but not to reverse it.[93] And in contrast to the other revolutions we have examined, in Mexico the revolutionaries did not develop a universalist ideology and did not see themselves as a model for other societies.[94] The danger of contagion was further reduced because the central goals of the revolution—the establishment of a liberal constitutional order and far-reaching agrarian reform—were simply not relevant north of the border. Apart from the minor threat posed by banditry and border raiding, therefore, there was no danger that the revolution would spread and thus little incentive for preventive war.

A partial exception to this argument was the U.S. concern that Mexican efforts to assert control over foreign investments might establish a dangerous precedent for other developing countries. Especially after World War I, some U.S. officials seem to have believed that the Mexican government was fomenting unrest in the United States and was in cahoots with the Bolsheviks and the International Workers of the World movement. Yet this danger was never great enough to justify intervention, because Carranza's revolutionary nationalism was not directed against private property per se and did not pose a serious threat to U.S. business interests. Indeed, some U.S. businessmen recognized that intervention might harm rather than protect U.S. assets in Mexico.[95]

Third, U.S. leaders were aware that an invasion would not be easy or cheap; indeed, Wilson's diplomatic efforts were clearly inspired by his de-

---

[92] In March 1914, Wilson told a reporter that "a country of the size and power of the United States can afford to wait just as long as it pleases. Nobody doubts its power, and nobody doubts that Mr. Huerta is eventually to retire." Quoted in Haley, *Revolution and Intervention*, 100, 130.

[93] On the broad ideological compatibility of the United States and Mexico, see Alan Knight, *U.S.-Mexican Relations, 1910–1940* (San Diego: Center for U.S.-Mexican Studies, University of California, San Diego, 1987), 5–10.

[94] On this point see Knight, *Mexican Revolution*, 2:297; and also Eric Wolf, *Peasant Wars of the Twentieth Century* (New York: Harper, 1969), 25–26. The ideological background to the revolution is summarized in James D. Cockcroft, *Intellectual Precursors of the Mexican Revolution, 1900–1913* (Austin: University of Texas Press, 1968).

[95] See Smith, *United States and Revolutionary Nationalism*, 158–59, 174–75.

sire to avoid having to do more. Wilson had agreed to occupy Vera Cruz in 1914 because he believed (incorrectly) that the Mexicans would not resist, but the experience had been chastening. U.S. military leaders estimated that an all-out intervention in Mexico would require roughly five hundred thousand men, and given the deep divisions that persisted throughout the country, merely sending an expedition to Mexico City would not have restored order. Instead, a prolonged and costly occupation would have been necessary, on a much larger scale than the earlier U.S. occupations of Cuba or Nicaragua. Thus, the awareness that there was no offensive advantage vis-à-vis Mexico reinforced Wilson's already strong desire to avoid war.

The most important barrier to a North American war, however, was the outbreak of World War I. Wilson and his advisors recognized that large-scale involvement in Mexico would limit their ability to influence events in Europe, which they regarded as far more important. As Wilson told his private secretary in 1916: "It begins to look as if war with Germany is inevitable. If it should come . . . I do not wish America's energies and forces divided for we will need every ounce of reserve we have to lick Germany."[96] This consideration also explains why Germany was eager to promote a U.S.-Mexican conflict; as Lansing put it in 1915, "Germany desires to keep up the turmoil in Mexico until the United States is forced to intervene; *therefore, we must not intervene.*"[97] This concern increased as the U.S. entry into the world war approached and helped persuade Wilson to withdraw the Punitive Expedition. House told the new U.S. ambassador, Henry Fletcher, "to do everything possible to avoid a break with Carranza," and Fletcher later recalled that "during the war my job was to keep Mexico quiet, and it was done."[98]

Thus, the absence of war was due to the relatively low level of threat created by the revolution, as well as to the fact that events elsewhere posed an even greater danger.[99] Like the United States during the wars of the French Revolution, the Mexican revolutionaries were fortunate that a war in Europe encouraged its potential opponents to act with restraint. U.S.-Mexican

---

[96] See Joseph Tumulty, *Woodrow Wilson As I Know Him* (Garden City, N.Y.: Garden City Publishing, 1927), 159.

[97] Quoted in Link, *Wilson and the Progressive Era,* 134 n. 59. Lansing later told a friend that concern for Germany "was a decided factor in our Mexican policy, I might say, a *controlling* factor." According to Boaz Long, "but for the European war, the Mexican situation would have been one of the foremost foreign issues of our time." Quoted in Smith, *United States and Revolutionary Nationalism,* 68–69.

[98] Quoted in Smith, *United States and Revolutionary Nationalism,* 93; and see Katz, *Secret War,* 313.

[99] Similar conditions facilitated Cardenas's consolidation of the revolution in the 1930s, especially his nationalization of the Mexican oil industry in 1938. The United States would have opposed this step more strongly had the rise of Nazi Germany and the growing tensions in Europe not encouraged efforts to solidify ties with anti-Fascist leaders such as Cardenas.

relations deteriorated again after the armistice (and unlike in 1916, the United States now possessed a sizeable army), but Wilson's attention was still focused primarily on European affairs and he remained firmly set against intervention for the remainder of his term.

Overall, this case is best seen as a near miss. Although war did not occur, the risk of war was very high on more than one occasion, and for many of the reasons identified by the theory. The Mexican instance also confirms that intervening in a revolution is a difficult and unpredictable business; despite its more or less benevolent intentions and the absence of intense ideological conflict, U.S. efforts to guide the course of events in Mexico were unsuccessful at best and counterproductive at worst.

## THE TURKISH REVOLUTION

Beginning in 1919, the Nationalist movement led by Mustafa Kemal transformed the core of the former Ottoman Empire from the center of multinational Muslim dynasty into a secular Turkish state. Bernard Lewis describes this development as "one of the major revolutions of modern times," and it eventually enabled the Turks to escape the punitive conditions imposed at the end of World War I and to reemerge as an accepted member of the European system.[100]

Like the American and Mexican cases, the revolution in Turkey did not result in significant interstate violence. Although some familiar sources of conflict were present, their effects were relatively weak and short-lived. The revolution was accompanied by a major war with Greece, but this conflict was a *cause* of the revolution rather than an effect. The revolution also led to a protracted confrontation with Great Britain, and nearly to open warfare at one point, but a direct clash was avoided and Turkey soon established itself as a status quo power within the European order.

The comparatively mild repercussions of the Turkish Revolution were due in part to the origins and character of the revolutionary movement and its limited international objectives. This was not a mass revolution-from-below, guided or exploited by a revolutionary vanguard party; rather, it was an elite revolution-from-above conducted by dissident members of the old regime.[101] In constructing their new state, the leaders of the revolution explicitly rejected a pan-Turanian or pan-Islamic agenda in favor of a program based on modernization and the promotion of Turkish nationalism within Anatolia proper. Thus, unlike most revolutionary states, Turkey did not pose a signif-

[100] See his *Emergence of Modern Turkey* (London: Oxford University Press, 1968), 1.
[101] See Ellen Kay Trimberger, *Revolution from Above: Military Bureaucrats and Development in Japan, Turkey, Egypt, and Peru* (New Brunswick, N.J.: Transaction Books, 1978).

icant threat to its immediate neighbors once its borders were reestablished after World War I. The Turks also benefited from favorable international conditions, which gave the new regime ample room for maneuver and aided its efforts to secure foreign recognition and diplomatic support.

### The Revolutionary Process

The Ottoman Empire had been in decline since the seventeenth century, steadily losing territory and influence to its European neighbors.[102] In 1908, the so-called Young Turk movement forced the sultan to recall Parliament and invited Western advisors to conduct military and economic reforms, but its initiatives failed to halt the empire's decline. Austria-Hungary annexed Bosnia-Herzegovina in 1908, the Albanians revolted the following year, and the empire lost 83 percent of its European territory and 69 percent of its European population in the Balkan wars of 1912–1913.[103]

The decision to join the Central Powers in November 1914 was the Ottoman Empire's final, fatal mistake.[104] By 1915, the Entente had agreed to partition the empire in the event of victory, with Russia receiving control of the Turkish Straits and Britain and France dividing the Arab portions of the empire into separate spheres of influence. Italy was promised the Dodecanese Islands, Libya, and portions of Anatolia, and Greece was eventually brought into the war with similar promises.[105]

Although the Ottoman forces fought well on some fronts and obtained a large portion of Russian territory at Brest-Litovsk, the German collapse ended any chance of victory and the sultanate negotiated an armistice with the Entente on October 30, 1918. Based on the stated war aims of the Entente and Woodrow Wilson's pledge to preserve Turkish sovereignty, the Turks expected fairly lenient treatment at the hands of the Allies. To their surprise,

---

[102] A map delineating the Ottoman Empire's territorial losses is in Stanford J. Shaw and Ezel Kural Shaw, *History of the Ottoman Empire and Modern Turkey* (Cambridge: Cambridge University Press, 1977), 2:xxiv.

[103] The Young Turk movement was accompanied by a protracted debate of the Ottoman ideal of a decentralized, multinational empire, the concept of a new state based on Turkish nationalism, and proposals to reconstitute the empire along pan-Islamic lines. See Roderic Davison, *Turkey* (Englewood Cliffs, N.J.: Prentice-Hall, 1968), 110–12; Lewis, *Emergence of Modern Turkey*, 351–52; Shaw and Shaw, *Ottoman Empire and Modern Turkey*, 2:301–305. On the Balkan wars, see E. C. Helmreich, *The Diplomacy of the Balkan Wars* (Cambridge: Harvard University Press, 1938).

[104] The decision to enter the war reflected both the pan-Turkic ambitions of some Turkish leaders (most notably Enver Pasha) and the belief that the war was an ideal opportunity to attack Russia. Shaw and Shaw, *Ottoman Empire and Modern Turkey*, 2:310–11.

[105] For the texts of the various agreements, see J. C. Hurewitz, *Diplomacy in the Near and Middle East* (1956; reprint, New York: Octagon Books, 1972), 2:7–25. On the Greek decision to enter the war, see A. A. Pallis, *Greece's Anatolian Adventure—and After* (London: Methuen, 1937), esp. 18.

however, the end of the war unleashed the victors' acquisitive ambitions, accompanied by intense disputes over the size and distribution of the spoils. Istanbul was occupied and placed under military administration. French troops moved into Cilicia and eastern Thrace, Greece seized western Thrace, and British forces occupied Mosul, the Dardanelles, Samsun, and several other strategic points.[106] The newly independent Armenian state expanded into eastern Anatolia, and its claims for portions of former Ottoman territory received a favorable hearing at the Paris Peace Conference. Greece and Italy also presented extensive claims for Turkish territory at the conference and began to back up their demands with military force. Italy landed troops on the southern coast of Anatolia in April 1919, and Britain, France, and the United States helped Greek forces occupy Smyrna (Izmir) in May.[107]

The Greek decision to occupy Smyrna was a manifestation of its long-standing desire to reunify the Greek peoples of the former Byzantine Empire. The Entente supported this step in order to forestall an Italian occupation of the same area, partly because British prime minister David Lloyd George was sympathetic to the Greeks and saw this move as a way of enhancing British influence in an important strategic area. As the Greek forces moved into the surrounding countryside, however, armed resistance groups began to form among the local population.[108] The sultanate was incapable or unwilling to resist the Greek assault on Turkish sovereignty, and the stage was set for a challenge to the sultan's authority.

Allied occupation and pressure from the emerging Armenian state had already sparked resistance movements in eastern Anatolia, but it was the Greek occupation of Smyrna that was most responsible for inspiring the Nationalist movement in Turkey.[109] As the resistance grew, a group of nationalist officers led by Mustafa Kemal, inspector-general of the Ninth Army in Samsun, began to unite the resistance into a coherent movement. Kemal resigned his commission and formed a Representative Committee to guide the new organization, and this group issued a proclamation in June declaring

---

[106] See Hurewitz, *Diplomacy in the Near and Middle East*, 2:36–37; Salahi Ramsdan Sonyel, *Turkish Diplomacy, 1918–1923: Mustafa Kemal and the Turkish National Movement* (Beverly Hills, Calif: Sage Publishing, 1975), 2–3; and M. Phillips Price, *A History of Turkey from Empire to Republic* (London: Allen and Unwin, 1956), 96.

[107] Greece asked for all of Thrace, the Aegean islands, and a substantial portion of western Asia Minor, while Italy wanted the Dodacanese Islands and similar portions of Anatolia in accordance with the Tripartite Agreement of 1917. See Harry N. Howard, *The Partition of Turkey: A Diplomatic History, 1913–1923* (Norman: University of Oklahoma Press, 1931), 222–23.

[108] The population of Smyrna was predominantly Greek, but the surrounding territory was mainly Turkish.

[109] See Howard, *Partition of Turkey*, 257. Harry J. Psomiades argues that although many Turks accepted the Allied occupation as a necessary evil, "it was the Greek occupation which was an affront which no patriotic Turk could endure." *The Eastern Question: The Last Phase: A Study in Greek-Turkish Diplomacy* (Thessalonica: Institute for Balkan Studies, 1968), esp. 31.

that "national independence [was] in danger" because the sultanate was "unable to carry out its responsibilities."[110] Kemal consolidated additional support at a congress of the so-called Society for the Defense of the Rights of Eastern Anatolia in July, and a new National Congress consisting of three delegates from each province then confirmed these resolutions in September.

The Nationalists dominated elections for the Chamber of Deputies in November, and Kemal informed the Entente that the sultan's emissaries at the Paris Peace Conference no longer represented the will of the nation. The new parliament met in Istanbul in January 1920 and proclaimed a new National Pact that reaffirmed the resolutions of the earlier congresses and demanded "complete independence and liberty."[111]

### International Consequences

These developments threatened the Entente's plans for extensive spheres of influence in Anatolia and jeopardized British hopes of controlling the Turkish Straits. In response, British troops occupied the Turkish areas of Istanbul in March 1920 in order to arrest and deport the Nationalist deputies. Most of the Nationalists managed to escape, however, and Kemal organized a Grand National Assembly in Ankara outside the reach of the Allied forces. Declaring that the sultan was a prisoner who was unable to exercise his authority, the Assembly and Representative Committee proclaimed themselves the true government of a new Turkish state.

Meanwhile, the Entente had completed its negotiations for the distribution of Ottoman territories and submitted the Treaty of Sèvres to the sultan in May. To forestall a Nationalist attack on Istanbul, the Supreme Allied Council approved a Greek proposal for an offensive against the Nationalist forces. The attack was successful and the Greek forces had occupied substantial portions of Anatolia and Thrace by midsummer. When the sultan accepted the peace treaty in August, the triumph of Allied ambitions over Turkish weakness seemed complete.[112] Yet a combination of astute diplo-

---

[110] Quoted in Elaine Diana Smith, *Turkey: Origins of the Kemalist Movement and the Government of the Grand National Assembly, 1919–1923* (Washington, D.C.: Judd and Detweiler, 1959), 12–13. Mustafa Kemal was one of the Ottoman Empire's most accomplished commanders. He was connected with the Young Turk movement but had fallen out with its leaders before World War I and did not play a political role during the war.

[111] See Roderic Davison, "Turkish Diplomacy from Mudros to Lausanne," in *The Diplomats, 1919–1939*, ed. Gordon Craig and Felix Gilbert (Princeton: Princeton University Press, 1953), 178–79; and Hurewitz, *Diplomacy in the Near and Middle East*, 2:74–75.

[112] The Treaty of Sèvres opened the Dardanelles to international shipping, established Kurdish autonomy, gave Greece de facto control over Smyrna and the surrounding region, forced Turkey to recognize Armenian independence and made the rest of the former empire either independent or placed under British, French, or Italian control. See Hurewitz, *Diplomacy in the Near and Middle East*, 2:81–89; and Howard, *Partition of Turkey*, 242–49.

macy and the Nationalists' growing military power gradually restored the Turkish position, overthrew the sultanate, and turned the Treaty of Sèvres into an irrelevant anachronism.[113]

The Nationalists began by seeking an alliance with Soviet Russia. Soviet Russia had extended diplomatic feelers to Kemal in 1919, and though progress was delayed by their competition in Transcaucasia, the two governments signed a formal friendship treaty in March 1921 and Moscow began providing arms and financial assistance.[114]

The Nationalists were equally successful in their efforts to divide the Entente and isolate the Greeks. Relations among the Allies were already strained by conflicting imperial interests, contentious discussions at the peace conference, and growing public opposition to costly military commitments, and the Nationalists exploited these tensions with considerable skill. The Turks also benefited when a Greek plebiscite removed Prime Minister Elftherios Venizelos and restored the deposed King Constantine, undermining French and Italian support for the Greek cause and forcing the Greeks to rely solely on Great Britain. Allied fears of the growing Soviet-Turkish rapprochement led them to propose a formal revision of the Sèvres agreement. The resulting London conference in February 1921 enhanced the status and prestige of the Nationalists. Kemal refused to send a delegation until the Nationalists received a direct invitation, and the decision to let the Nationalist representative, Bekir Sami, speak on behalf of the Istanbul and Ankara governments underscored the Nationalists' dominant position still further. Britain still refused to end its support for the Greeks, but France and Italy now broke ranks and agreed to withdraw from Anatolia in exchange for economic concessions. Although Kemal later declared that Sami had exceeded his authority and repudiated the agreements, the London conference had exposed the rifts within the Entente and revealed that the Treaty of Sèvres was not cast in stone.[115]

Turkey's improved military position aided its attempts at fostering divisions within the Entente. The Greek advance had been halted in January 1921, and the Nationalists defeated a second Greek offensive in April. When a third offensive was thwarted in July, British support began to waver, and the Supreme Allied Council now declared that it would remain neutral in the Greco-Turkish conflict. The breakthrough came with an agreement with

---

[113] For an account of Kemal's diplomatic and military strategy, see George W. Gawryeh, "Kemal Atatürk's Politico-Military Strategy in the Turkish War of Independence, 1918–1922: From Guerrilla Warfare to the Decisive Battle," *Journal of Strategic Studies* 11, no. 3 (1988).

[114] See Davison, "Turkish Diplomacy," 186–91; and Jane Degras, ed., *Soviet Documents on Foreign Policy* (London: Oxford University Press, 1951–52), 1:237–42.

[115] The background and results of the London conference of 1921 are discussed in Davison, "Turkish Diplomacy," 188–90; Sonyel, *Turkish Diplomacy*, 95–105; Howard, *Partition of Turkey*, 260–61.

France. The French government regarded the Treaty of Sèvres as excessively favorable to Britain, and its forces in Cilicia were facing increasingly effective resistance from the Nationalist forces. Negotiations began in earnest in June 1921, and the final treaty was completed in October, whereby France agreed to withdraw from Cilicia in exchange for temporary control over the disputed district of Alexandretta. The French also agreed to recognize the Turkish National Pact, in effect abandoning the Treaty of Sèvres.[116] Italy was next. The Italian government, which viewed the Treaty of Sèvres with even less enthusiasm than France, had begun withdrawing its troops from Adalia in June 1921. A formal rapprochement with the Nationalists was delayed by political shifts in Italy, and subsequent negotiations in the fall of 1921 foundered on Turkey's refusal to grant economic concessions, but it was clear that Italy had given up any hope of making territorial gains at Turkey's expense.[117]

These improvements in Turkey's relations with the West threatened its ties with the Soviet Union and forced Kemal to walk a fine line. The Nationalists assured Soviet foreign minister Chicherin that the *détente* with France would not undermine the Soviet-Turkish friendship treaty, and they signed a formal treaty guaranteeing their eastern frontier with Russia, Georgia, Armenia, and Azerbaijan in October 1921. A visit by a Soviet military mission to Ankara in December arranged for additional military aid and was followed by a friendship treaty between Turkey and the Ukrainian Soviet Socialist Republic in January 1922. A Soviet ambassador took up residence in Ankara, and the Soviet mission soon became the largest foreign delegation there.[118]

The cessation of hostilities with France and Italy and the guarantee of Turkey's eastern border allowed Kemal to turn his attention back to the Greeks. Britain and France tried to arrange a negotiated settlement, but the Nationalists refused to modify the terms of the National Pact and continued their preparations for an all-out offensive. The attack was finally launched in August 1922, the Greek forces were routed, and the remnants of the Greek Army had withdrawn by the end of the month.[119]

---

[116] According to Kemal, the agreement with France "proved to the whole world that the treaty [of Sèvres] was merely a rag." Quoted in Sonyel, *Turkish Diplomacy,* 135–38; and see Hurewitz, *Diplomacy in the Near and Middle East,* 2:97–99.

[117] Italy reportedly provided Kemal's forces with additional military equipment during this period, although the precise sources and magnitude of the support is hard to determine. See David Lloyd George, *The Truth about the Peace Treaties* (London: Victor Gollancz, 1938) 2:1349; Harold Nicolson, *Curzon: The Last Phase, 1919–1925: A Study in Postwar Diplomacy* (Boston: Houghton Mifflin, 1934), 264; and Pallis, *Greece's Anatolian Adventure,* 135.

[118] See Davison, "Turkish Diplomacy," 194; and Degras, *Soviet Documents,* 1:263–69.

[119] See Shaw and Shaw, *Ottoman Empire and Modern Turkey,* 2:362–63; Sonyel, *Turkish Diplomacy,* 171–73; Davison, "Turkish Diplomacy," 197; Howard, *Partition of Turkey,* 267–68.

This campaign caused a final crisis with Great Britain, briefly bringing the two sides to the brink of war in September 1922. The Nationalists sought the complete withdrawal of foreign troops from Turkish territory, including the removal of the remaining Greek forces in eastern Thrace. Lloyd George was still committed to the Greek cause, however, and the British government was worried that a further Turkish advance would jeopardize freedom of navigation in the Turkish Straits. As the Greeks withdrew, therefore, Great Britain reinforced its positions in the neutral zone established by the Treaty of Sèvres and the Cabinet ordered the British commander, Lieutenant-General Charles ("Tim") Harington, to oppose any attempt to force the straits. The French and Italian commanders sent small contingents in response to Harington's request for a show of Allied solidarity, but both states subsequently withdrew their forces after Lloyd George and Winston Churchill dispatched a bellicose message to the Dominions requesting support to defend the neutral zones. The rift was soon patched, and a joint proposal for armistice negotiations was dispatched to the Turks on September 23, but it was clear that neither France nor Italy would go to war over this issue. Support within England and the rest of the British Empire was doubtful as well, leaving Lloyd George virtually alone in his willingness to confront the Turks.[120] Egged on by the Soviets and by hard-liners within the Nationalist movement, elements of Kemal's forces entered the neutral zone and eventually stood face-to-face with the outnumbered British garrison at Chanak.

Lloyd George was still determined to resist, however, and the British Cabinet issued an ultimatum on September 29 demanding that the Turkish forces pull back from Chanak or be fired upon. Convinced that such an ultimatum would merely provoke the Turks and make it more difficult to reach a negotiated solution, Harington and the British high commissioner, Horace Rumbold, chose to ignore the Cabinet's order. This decision prevented an immediate clash and gave time for cooler heads to prevail. Negotiations between military representatives began on October 3, and a compromise was finally reached on the eleventh, just seventy-five minutes before the British troops were to have opened fire on the Turkish positions.[121] The Nationalists agreed to remain outside the neutral zones at Istanbul, Gallipoli, and Ismit pending a final peace settlement, while the Allies pledged that Greece would withdraw from eastern Thrace up to the Maritsa River.[122]

---

[120] See Peter Rowland, *Lloyd George* (London: Barrie and Jenkins, 1975), 578.

[121] See Stephen F. Evans, *The Slow Rapprochement: Britain and Turkey in the Age of Kemal Atatürk, 1919–1938* (Beverley, Eng.: Eothen Press, 1982), 63; and Briton Cooper Busch, *Mudros to Lausanne: Britain's Frontier in West Asia, 1918–1923* (Albany: State University of New York Press, 1976), 351–55.

[122] On these events, see Evans, *Slow Rapprochement*, chap. 5; David Walder, *The Chanak Affair* (London: Hutchinson, 1969); Busch, *Mudros to Lausanne*, 340–58; Sonyel, *Turkish Diplomacy*, 173–76; Howard, *Partition of Turkey*, 269–73; Nicolson, *Curzon*, 274–75; Laurence Evans, *United States Policy and the Partition of Turkey, 1914–1924* (Baltimore: Johns Hopkins Univer-

The armistice set the stage for the Lausanne Conference in 1923, which formally dismantled the Treaty of Sèvres and placed Turkey's relations with the West on a new basis. The Nationalists' primacy was now unchallenged, and when the Allies tried to invite representatives from the Istanbul and Ankara regimes, the Assembly simply abolished the sultanate and placed the office of the caliphate under its authority. After two separate rounds of negotiations, a final agreement was reached in July. With the exception of a clause granting Britain control over Mosul, Turkey's new borders corresponded almost perfectly to the principles of the National Pact.[123] The Entente accepted the borders established by the Treaty of Kars, and the restoration of eastern Thrace gave Turkey a foothold in Europe as well. The treaty abolished the foreign capitulations established during the Ottoman period (meaning that foreign residents and companies would now be subject to Turkish law) and opened the Turkish Straits to international shipping under the control of an international commission. The parties also agreed to conduct a compulsory population exchange between Turkish nationals of the Greek Orthodox religion and Greek nationals of the Muslim religion. The exchange agreement eliminated the main source of Greco-Turkish rivalry and paved the way for a major rapprochement at the end of the decade.[124]

The Lausanne Conference also signaled Turkey's reemergence as a member of the international community. Elections for a new National Assembly were held in August 1923, the new Republic of Turkey was officially proclaimed in October with Mustafa Kemal (Atatürk) as its first president, and the capital was moved from Istanbul to Ankara. With their triumph now complete, Kemal and his followers launched the extensive program of westernization that created the modern Turkish state.[125]

### Is the Turkish Revolution an Exception?

The Turkish Revolution differs in a number of ways from the other cases examined in this book, but many familiar features are present as well.

sity Press, 1965), 378–86; Davidson, "Turkish Diplomacy," 197–99; and Kenneth O. Morgan, *Consensus and Disunity: The Lloyd George Coalition Government, 1918–1922* (Oxford: Clarendon Press, 1979), 319–23.

[123] The text of the treaty is reprinted in Hurewitz, *Diplomacy in the Near and Middle East*, 2:119–127.

[124] See Psomiades, *Eastern Question*, chap. 7; and Dimitri Pentzopoulos, *The Balkan Exchange of Minorities and Its Impact on Greece* (Paris: Mouton, 1962).

[125] Turkish diplomacy at Lausanne is described in Davison, "Turkish Diplomacy," 199–208; Sonyel, *Turkish Diplomacy*, 185–229; Edward Reginald Vere-Hodge, *Turkish Foreign Policy, 1918–1948* (Ambilly-Annemasse: Imprimerie Franco-Suisse, 1950), 38–50; Howard, *Partition of Turkey*, chap. 9; and Evans, *U.S. Policy and Turkey*, chap. 14. For an account emphasizing Curzon's success in weaning Turkey away from Russia, see Nicolson, *Curzon*, chaps. 10–11.

Turkey's fragility in the aftermath of World War I led Britain, France, Italy, Greece, and Russia to seek territorial acquisitions at the Turks' expense, and their conflicting ambitions gave rise to serious disagreements once the war was over. The revolution was not responsible for this power vacuum, however, as Turkey's weakness was a direct result of its decision to align with the Central Powers and their subsequent defeat in 1918. Instead, the Nationalist revolution was itself a response to the sultan's inability to defend Anatolia. Thus, although Turkey's vulnerability made it the object of intense foreign competition and encouraged direct military intervention, this was not directly attributable to the revolution.

Once the revolution was underway, however, both sides quickly concluded that the other was hostile and potentially threatening. The Nationalist movement arose from Turkish opposition to foreign (especially Greek) intervention, and Kemal remained suspicious of the Entente for quite some time.[126] Similarly, Britain and France saw the Kemalist movement as a threat to their postwar ambitions in the Near East, leading them to occupy Istanbul in March 1920 and to endorse the Greek offensive later that summer.

In addition to the obvious conflicts of interest—the Allies wished to partition Turkey while the Nationalists sought to reestablish Turkish sovereignty—Allied hostility was increased by several unfortunate misperceptions, particularly by the British. Lloyd George's belief that the Kemalist movement was a linear descendant of the Young Turks' Committee on Union and Progress (CUP) reinforced his pro-Greek sympathies, and the suspicion that Kemal harbored the same pan-Turkic tendencies displayed by earlier Turkish nationalists made the Nationalists seem even more threatening.[127] Lloyd George regarded the Turks as an "unspeakable" race that had "forfeited their title to rule majorities of other peoples," and he once referred to Kemal as "no better than a carpet seller in a bazaar." Stephen Evans reports that British officials placed the Nationalists "side by side with the CUP and the Bolsheviks," a view that nicely reveals British ignorance about the true character of the Nationalist movement. In particular, British leaders seem to have been unaware that Kemal had broken with Enver Pasha and the CUP in 1914, had explicitly rejected a pan-Turkic agenda, and had repeatedly expressed his desire for harmonious relations with the West.[128]

---

[126] In 1921, he told his followers, "I am not sure of the good faith of England, who wants to play us a trick." Quoted in Sonyel, *Turkish Diplomacy*, 95.

[127] The CUP had played a central role in the Ottoman decision to ally with the Central Powers, and CUP leaders such as Enver Pasha were strongly committed to a pan-Turkic foreign policy.

[128] See Evans, *Slow Rapprochement*, 64–65; Morgan, *Consensus and Disunity*, 319; and Busch, *Mudros to Lausanne*, 171–72. On the rivalry between Kemal and Enver Pasha, see Salahi R. Sonyel, "Mustafa Kemal and Enver in Conflict, 1918–1922," *Middle Eastern Studies* 25, no. 4 (1989).

Not surprisingly, these suspicions encouraged intransigence on both sides. Several unfortunate incidents reinforced perceptions of hostility, including the execution of a British subject on charges of espionage (which the British high commissioner in Istanbul saw as sign of the Nationalists' "uncompromising hostility towards His Majesty's government"), a Nationalist raid on the British ship *Palitana*, and Britain's open support for the Greeks.[129] These events sustained the Nationalists' desire for the complete removal of all foreign troops and help explain why Lloyd George sought to oppose the Turkish advance on Istanbul in 1922.[130]

The Nationalists' opponents also seem to have consistently underestimated Kemal's popularity and the military prowess of his troops while exaggerating their own capacity to impose a solution by force. This was most evident in the case of Greece and its British patron; although a number of British, French, and Greek officials argued that Kemal would be difficult to defeat, Prime Minister Venizelos assured the Allies that the Greeks "would be able to clear up the whole of the neighborhood between Smyrna and the Dardanelles in the course of fifteen days."[131] The Greeks' initial successes boosted this overconfidence and silenced opposition but failed to overcome the Nationalist resistance and left the Greek forces badly overextended. Nonetheless, Venizelos's successor as prime minister described Kemal's forces as a "rabble worthy of little or no consideration" and promised that a new offensive would "scatter the Kemalist forces and . . . impose the will of the powers" within three months.[132]

As usual, these problems were exacerbated by uncertainty and misinformation. In June 1919, for example, the British foreign office representative stated that he "knew nothing of Mustapha Kemal," and another Allied report declared that "the whole movement appears to have had little success and for the most part not much interest is taken." Other British agents reported that the Nationalist Congress at Erzerum had been a failure, and as noted earlier, top British officials were convinced that Kemal was either a Bolshevik or a follower of the CUP or else was under the control of the offi-

[129] The remarks were made by High Commissioner Horace Rumbold; quoted in Sonyel, *Turkish Diplomacy*, 115.

[130] Lloyd George later blamed the failure of his policy in part on lack of information. Describing the initial emergence of Mustafa Kemal, he wrote that "no information had been received as to his activities in Asia Minor in reorganizing the shattered and depleted armies of Turkey. Our military intelligence had never been more thoroughly unintelligent." *Truth about the Peace Treaties*, 2:1285.

[131] See Howard, *Partition of Turkey*, 259. On the ill-advised nature of the Greek advance, see Pallis, *Greece's Anatolian Adventure*, 54–58, 102–105.

[132] The Greek government opposed any modification of the Sèvres agreement at the London conference in February 1921, and the deputy chief of staff told the delegates that a renewed Greek advance would proceed "up to Ankara *as a first stage.*" Quoted in Sonyel, *Turkish Diplomacy*, 96 (emphasis added); and Busch, *Mudros to Lausanne*, 239–40.

cial government in Istanbul. Moreover, the lack of official contacts forced Kemal to rely on unofficial channels, allowing these misconceptions to survive intact.[133]

Thus, although the Nationalist revolution in Turkey did not lead directly to war, it does provide partial support for my main propositions. Foreign powers did seek to exploit the vacuum resulting from the Ottoman collapse, and the revolutionary movement was seen as threatening to their interests and objectives. The level of threat was exaggerated, however, and opposing states overstated their ability to defeat the revolutionary movement by force. These misperceptions and miscalculations stemmed in part from a lack of information and inadequate channels of communication (although the impact of this factor varied). Finally, although all-out war was avoided, Britain and Turkey did come close in 1922 and could easily have stumbled into a serious clash. In short, the Turkish case is a partial exception at best: although war did not occur, the pressures for war that did arise are consistent with the theory.

Why were Turkey and the great powers able to avoid war, and why were the Turks able to integrate themselves into the existing order with far less difficulty than other revolutionary states?

First, the Turkish Revolution owed much of its moderate impact to its character as an elite revolution. Its leaders were for the most part prominent members of the old regime, and they were willing and able to seize power because the sultanate had been discredited by defeat and because they retained the loyalty of key institutions (especially the army). In addition, the Nationalists did not have to wage an extended struggle against internal opponents, because the sultan lacked the capacity to resist and was increasingly dependent on foreign support. As a result, the Nationalist movement did not develop an elaborate ideology of social revolution in order to mobilize supporters and to justify its rule. The principle of national independence was sufficient, especially after the Greek invasion galvanized Turkish resistance. Although pan-Turkic and pan-Islamic programs were actively debated during the Young Turk period, Kemal explicitly rejected these more ambitious programs in favor of the limited goal of independence based on Turkish nationalism. Thus, the Nationalist program was limited to restoring national sovereignty within a specific geographic area, exporting the revolution was precluded by definition, and the revolution posed no ideological threat to its neighbors.[134] Thus, whereas the Jacobins, the Bolsheviks, and the Iranian

---

[133] "This lack of diplomatic contact only reinforced the [British] High Commission's false assumptions concerning the Nationalists, and had the effect of keeping the two sides apart." Stephen Evans, *Slow Rapprochement*, 65; and see Busch, *Mudros to Lausanne*, 169–72.

[134] Armenia is a partial exception in this regard, because it had established itself on territories that the Nationalists regarded as part of the Turkish homeland. See Shaw and Shaw, *Ottoman Empire and Modern Turkey*, 2:376.

clerics saw their opponents as intrinsically evil and endorsed revolutionary transformations at home and abroad, Kemal and his followers sought a rapid reconciliation with the West in order to concentrate on modernization.[135]

Second, like Mexico in 1916 and the United States after 1787, the revolutionary Turks profited from favorable international conditions. The Central Powers had been defeated and disarmed. The Entente was exhausted and war-weary. Russia was weakened and distracted by its own revolution. Great Britain tried to use the Greeks as surrogates but was unwilling to escalate when this expedient failed, giving Kemal and the Nationalists the time they needed to consolidate their position. The revolution in Russia and the antipathy between Moscow and the West was a valuable asset for the Turks as well. In addition to obtaining modest amounts of financial and military assistance from the Bolsheviks, Kemal was able to play off the two sides, with considerable success. As in the French and Russian cases, in short, divisions among the other great powers prevented joint action to arrest or reverse the revolution.

The Turkish case reveals many familiar dynamics of revolutionary situations, but in a muted and less dangerous form. The preferences and goals of the Nationalists differed from those of the old regime and threatened the interests of several foreign powers. These states found it difficult to formulate an effective response to the revolutionary movement because they overestimated its hostility and underestimated its capabilities, giving rise to exaggerated perceptions of threat and making the use of force somewhat more attractive. These states revised their estimates over time, however, and eventually reestablished more or less cordial relations.

## THE CHINESE REVOLUTION

As my theory would predict, the revolution in China contributed to the emerging security competition between the United States and the Soviet Union and played a major role in bringing the Cold War to Asia. The new regime went to war in Korea less than a year after gaining power, and the origins of its involvement bear a striking resemblance to those of the wars that followed the French, Russian, and Iranian revolutions.

The foreign policy of the People's Republic of China (PRC) also highlights the tension between revolutionary objectives and systemic constraints. Although the Chinese Communist Party (CCP) openly endorsed the goal of

[135] Kemal warned in a 1923 speech: "The successes which our army has gained up to now cannot be regarded as having achieved the real salvation of our country. . . . Let us not be puffed up with military victories. Let us rather prepare for the new victories in science and economics." Quoted in Lewis, *Emergence of Modern Turkey*, 255–56.

world revolution and saw its victory as a model for other developing countries, Chinese foreign policy tended to be cautious and defensive, focused more on preserving Chinese security than on promoting revolution. On the whole, therefore, the Chinese Revolution provides strong support for the main argument of this book.

### Maoist Revolutionary Ideology

Maoist political thought closely resembles the ideal type of revolutionary ideology described in chapter 2.[136] During its long struggle against both the Guomindang (GMD) and Japan, the CCP developed a body of revolutionary doctrine designed to inspire prolonged sacrifices and provide tactical guidance to the Communist cadres. As a Marxist-Leninist, CCP leader Mao Tse-tung viewed politics as inherently competitive and regarded opponents—especially the imperialist powers—as hostile.[137] The Maoist worldview was also intrinsically optimistic: although enemies might appear stronger, they were actually "paper tigers." "In appearance [they] are terrifying but in reality they are not so powerful." As a result, victory was inevitable provided the cadres did not lose heart.[138] Like Lenin, Mao tempered this optimism with a sense of realism, stressing the need to analyze political and strategic problems systematically and warning against both rightist deviations (passivity and fear of struggle) and leftist deviations (overconfident recklessness). In his words, the CCP should "despise the enemy strategically while taking full account of him tactically," meaning that although victory was inevitable, achieving it required prolonged effort, careful preparation, and tactical flexibility.[139] Maoist ideology combined nationalist

[136] In addition to Mao's writings, this summary of Maoist ideology is based on Stuart Schram, *The Thought of Mao Tse-tung* (Cambridge: Cambridge University Press, 1989); Peter Van Ness, *Revolution and Chinese Foreign Policy: Peking's Support for Wars of National Liberation* (Berkeley: University of California Press, 1970), chap. 2; J. D. Armstrong, *Revolutionary Diplomacy: Chinese Foreign Policy and the United Front Doctrine* (Berkeley: University of California Press, 1977); chaps. 1–2; Edward L. Katzenbach and Gene Z. Hanrahan, "The Revolutionary Strategy of Mao Tse-tung," *Political Science Quarterly* 70, no. 3 (1955); and Tang Tsou and Morton H. Halperin, "Mao Tse-tung's Revolutionary Strategy and Peking's International Behavior," *American Political Science Review* 59, no. 1 (1965).

[137] Likening imperialism to a "wild beast," Mao told his followers not to show "the slightest timidity." In his words: "Either kill the tiger or be eaten by him—one or the other." He also warned that "when we say 'imperialism is ferocious,' we mean that its nature will never change, the imperialists will never lay down their butcher knives, they will never become Buddhas, till their doom." *Selected Works of Mao Tse-tung* (Peking: Foreign Languages Press, 1961–65), 4:416, 428.

[138] See Mao, *Selected Works*, 1:117–18, 2:132–36; 4:100–101; and Van Ness, *Revolution and Chinese Foreign Policy*, 40–41.

[139] See John Shy and Thomas Collier, "Revolutionary War," in *Makers of Modern Strategy: From Machiavelli to the Nuclear Age*, ed. Peter Paret (Princeton: Princeton University Press, 1986), esp. 842–43; Richard H. Solomon, *Mao's Revolution and the Chinese Political Culture*

and universalistic themes: the removal of foreign (i.e., imperialist) influence from China was a central goal of the revolution, but the struggle in China was merely one part of the worldwide transition to socialism.[140] Mao also stressed the importance of identifying the "principal contradiction"—defined as the main threat at any given time—and endorsed Lenin's strategy of the "united front," which permitted temporary alliances with non-Communist groups against the most dangerous adversary, combined with preparations to undermine one's present allies when the opportunity arose.[111]

## The Chinese Revolution and the Balance of Threats

*The Balance of Power.* As in the French, Russian, and Iranian cases, other states saw the revolution in China as a potential threat to the balance of power and as an opportunity to improve their own positions. Such perceptions were not entirely new, as China had been the object of great-power competition since the nineteenth century, and the collapse of the Manchu dynasty in 1911 had intensified foreign involvement in China's domestic affairs. The Soviet Union, Japan, Great Britain, and the United States continued to compete for influence during the interwar period, and Japanese expansionism in China was a crucial underlying cause of World War II in the Pacific.

The GMD became the main Asian ally of the United States during the war, although relations between Washington and Chongqing were strained by Chiang Kai-shek's (Jiang Jieshi's) constant requests for assistance and U.S. irritation at his preoccupation with fighting the CCP instead of the Japanese.[142] The United States also sent a small military mission to CCP headquarters in 1944, but support for Mao's forces never approached the level of aid provided to Chiang.[143] Nonetheless, U.S. president Franklin Roosevelt was convinced that U.S.-Soviet cooperation would continue after

(Berkeley: University of California Press, 1971), 179–89; Tsou and Halperin, "Mao Tse-tung's Revolutionary Strategy"; and Mao, *Selected Works*, 4:181–82.

[140] See Mao, *Selected Works*, 2:342–47. After the Sino-Soviet split, Chinese commentators emphasized that "world revolution relies on the thought of Mao Tse-tung. . . . [It] belongs not only to China but also has its international implications." Quoted in Tsou and Halperin, "Mao Tse-tung's Revolutionary Strategy," 82.

[141] See Mao, *Selected Works*, 2:441–49; Armstrong, *Revolutionary Diplomacy*, chap. 2; and Lyman P. Van Slyke, *Enemies and Friends: The United Front Doctrine in Chinese Communist History* (Stanford: Stanford University Press, 1967).

[142] See Barbara Tuchman, *Stillwell and the American Experience in China, 1911–1945* (New York: Macmillan, 1971); Herbert Feis, *The China Tangle: The American Effort in China from Pearl Harbor to the Marshall Mission* (Princeton: Princeton University Press), 74–77, 151–54, 187–99; and Tang Tsou, *America's Failure in China, 1941–1950* (Chicago: University of Chicago Press, 1963), chap. 4.

[143] See David D. Barrett, *Dixie Mission: The United States Army Observer Group in Yenan, 1944* (Berkeley, Calif.: Center for Chinese Studies, 1970).

the war and envisioned a peaceful resolution of the CCP-GMD conflict that would grant the "so-called communists" a legitimate (albeit minority) position in a postwar Chinese government.[144]

As World War II came to an end, however, U.S. officials became increasingly concerned that Communist control of Manchuria would lead to an adverse shift in the balance of power in Asia.[145] Truman and his advisors therefore favored the emergence of a strong and unified China that would help prevent Soviet expansion in the Far East, and Truman sent General George C. Marshall to China in December 1945 in a last-ditch attempt to broker a settlement between the rival Chinese factions. Although Marshall's efforts were initially promising, he was unable to overcome the mutual suspicions between the GMD and CCP, and a full-scale civil war was underway by the spring of 1946. In the meantime, the United States continued to send military aid to Chiang's forces and helped transport GMD units to northern China in an attempt to limit Communist influence there.[146]

As U.S.-Soviet relations deteriorated and the CCP gained the upper hand, U.S. officials became even more concerned about the impact of a Communist victory on the global balance of power. Although U.S. officials disagreed over the magnitude of the threat, by 1949 there was a widespread belief that a Communist victory in China would constitute a major gain for the Soviet Union.[147] Truman and Acheson faced growing domestic criticism for having "lost China" after the CCP victory, and though the administration still refused to commit itself to defend Taiwan (where the remnants of the GMD had fled), U.S. policy in the Far East increasingly sought to contain Communist expansion and "drive a wedge" between the Soviet Union and the PRC.[148]

---

[144] See Odd Arne Westad, *Cold War and Revolution: Soviet-American Rivalry and the Origins of the Chinese Civil War* (New York: Columbia University Press, 1993), 24–27.

[145] At the end of 1945, U.S. officials feared that Communist control of Manchuria "would . . . place under the control of the Soviet Union the greatest agglomeration of power in the history of the world." Six months later, a State Department memorandum warned, "Our exclusion from China would probably result . . . in an expansion of Soviet influence over the manpower, raw materials, and industrial power of Manchuria and China. The U.S. and the world might then be faced . . . with a Soviet power analogous to that of the Japanese in 1941, but with the difference that the Soviets could be perhaps overwhelmingly strong in Europe and the Middle East as well." Quoted in Melvyn Leffler, *A Preponderance of Power: National Security, the Truman Administration, and the Cold War* (Stanford: Stanford University Press, 1992), 127–28; and Steven I. Levine, "A New Look at American Mediation in the Chinese Civil War: The Marshall Mission and Manchuria," *Diplomatic History* 3, no. 4 (1979), 354.

[146] See Westad, *Cold War and Revolution,* 143–159, and Forrest C. Pogue, *George C. Marshall,* vol. 4: *Statesman, 1945–1959* (New York: Viking, 1987), 54–143.

[147] See Leffler, *Preponderance of Power,* 246–49. In May 1950, Assistant Secretary of State Dean Rusk concluded that the loss of China "marked a shift in the balance of power in favor of Soviet Russia." Quoted in Rosemary Foot, *The Wrong War: American Policy and the Dimensions of the Korean Conflict, 1950–1953* (Ithaca: Cornell University Press, 1985), 52.

[148] On U.S. policy in the Far East, see John Lewis Gaddis, *The Long Peace: Inquiries into the History of the Cold War* (New York: Oxford University Press, 1987), chaps. 4 and 6; Warren I.

Soviet responses to the revolution in China reveal a similar preoccupation with the balance of power. Stalin's diplomacy in the Far East was aimed at securing specific territorial gains for the USSR and preventing either large-scale U.S. intervention or the emergence of a pro-Western Chinese government.[149] The Soviet Union had already obtained favorable territorial concessions in China at the Yalta summit, and Soviet troops had occupied Manchuria at the end of the war and carried off a substantial quantity of industrial equipment. Soviet support for the CCP was quite limited during this period, however, and Stalin sought to preserve his gains by signing a friendship treaty with the GMD in 1945. Aid to the CCP rose substantially during the Chinese Civil War, but the Soviets refused to commit themselves to defend the CCP in the event that the United States intervened, and Stalin advised Mao to compromise with the GMD in order to further reduce the danger of a U.S. occupation.[150] Like his U.S. counterparts, in short, Stalin was primarily interested in preventing events in China from causing an adverse shift in the regional balance of power. And though U.S. officials believed that Communist ideology created a strong bond between the Soviet Union and the CCP, Marxist solidarity had relatively little effect on Soviet calculations.[151]

*Perceptions of Intent.* The deterioration of Sino-American relations also illustrates the tendency for revolutions to trigger spirals of exaggerated hostility. Of course, given the CCP's worldview and the onset of the U.S.-Soviet Cold War, the United States and the PRC were unlikely to establish a close relationship. Yet Mao had predicted that the "international united front" of capitalist and socialist states would remain intact after

---

Cohen, "Acheson, His Advisers, and China, 1949–50," and Waldo Heinrichs, "American China Policy and the Cold War in Asia: A New Look," in *Uncertain Years: Chinese-American Relations 1947–1950,* ed. Dorothy Borg and Waldo Heinrichs (New York: Columbia University Press, 1980); Harry Harding and Yuan Ming, eds., *Sino-American Relations, 1945–1955: A Joint Reassessment of a Critical Decade* (Wilmington, Del.: Scholarly Resources, 1989); Nancy Bernkopf Tucker, *Patterns in the Dust: Chinese-American Relations and the Recognition Controversy, 1949–1950* (New York: Columbia University Press, 1983); and David Allan Mayers, *Cracking the Monolith: U.S. Policy Against the Sino-Soviet Alliance, 1949–1955* (Baton Rouge: Louisiana State University Press, 1986).

[149] See Sergei N. Goncharov, John W. Lewis, and Xue Litai, *Uncertain Partners: Stalin, Mao, and the Korean War* (Stanford: Stanford University Press, 1994), chap. 1; and Westad, *Cold War and Revolution,* 118–21.

[150] See Goncharov, Lewis, and Xue, *Uncertain Partners,* 7, 25–26, 52–53.

[151] See Westad, *Cold War and Revolution,* chap. 2. Useful accounts of Soviet relations with the rival Chinese factions include Goncharov, Lewis, and Xue, *Uncertain Partners;* Steven I. Levine, "Soviet-American Rivalry in Manchuria and the Cold War," in *Dimensions of China's Foreign Relations,* ed. Hsueh Chun-tu (New York: Praeger, 1977); and Robert Slusser, "Soviet Policy in the Far East, 1945–1950," in *The Origins of the Cold War in Asia,* ed. Yonosuke Nagai and Akira Iriye (New York: Columbia University Press, 1977).

World War II, and several CCP leaders hoped to minimize dependence on the Soviet Union by maintaining cordial relations with the United States as well. As Zhou En-lai told Marshall in 1946: "Of course we will lean to one side. But how far depends on you."[152] CCP officials repeatedly expressed their desire for diplomatic relations with all countries (including the United States), and the CCP made several overtures to U.S. officials in 1949.[153] Similarly, key U.S. officials did not think Sino-American hostility was inevitable (despite the widespread notion that the CCP was under Moscow's tutelage), and Secretary of State Dean Acheson apparently intended to pursue better relations with Beijing "when the dust had settled." Indeed, despite his basic belief in U.S. hostility, even Mao assumed that recognition would be granted eventually and active U.S. opposition would be limited.[154]

Unfortunately, a combination of real conflicts of interest and repeated misperceptions magnified each side's suspicions.[155] The idea that capitalist states were inherently aggressive was deeply rooted in Mao's worldview, and with the onset of Soviet-American rivalry he revised his earlier belief in postwar cooperation. Mao now concluded that war between the "two camps" was inevitable, and he predicted that U.S. imperialists would begin by trying to subjugate the "vast intermediate zone" (which included China). Thus, Mao's ideological image of imperialist behavior and his specific

[152] Quoted in Tucker, *Patterns in the Dust*, 45. After the arrival of the Dixie mission in 1944, Zhou En-lai told an aide that "with this channel established, future contacts will not be difficult. . . . The prospects for future cooperation are boundless." Mao declared in 1945 that the wartime cooperation between capitalist and socialist states would continue indefinitely, because the Soviet Union was strong enough to deter a challenge and because "progressive forces" in the capitalist world would constrain the reactionary elements. Quoted in Westad, *Cold War and Revolution*, 61–69, and Steven I. Goldstein, "Chinese Communist Policy towards the United States," in Borg and Heinrichs, *Uncertain Years*, 238–45.

[153] Mao authorized Huang Hua to begin informal talks with U.S. ambassador J. Leighton Stuart in June, and another CCP official, Yao Yilin, began a similar initiative with Edmund Clubb, the U.S. consul-general in Beijing. U.S. military attaché David Barrett also received a conciliatory message, allegedly from Zhou himself, but Stuart was ordered not to meet with Hua and nothing came of these initiatives. See Michael Hunt, "Mao Tse-tung and the Issue of Accommodation with the United States," in Borg and Heinrichs, *Uncertain Years*, 207–209; and Tucker, *Patterns in the Dust*, 47–48, 57. For a skeptical appraisal of these initiatives, see Goldstein, "Chinese Communist Policy," 274–78.

[154] At the same time, the United States also began a series of initiatives—including covert actions—aimed at undermining the Communist forces in China. See Gordon H. Chang, *Friends and Enemies: The United States, China, and the Soviet Union* (Stanford: Stanford University Press, 1990), 16; and Thomas J. Christensen, "A Lost Chance for What? Mao, Truman, and the Failure to Avoid Escalation in the Korean War," paper presented at the annual meeting of the Association for Asian Studies (Boston, March 24–27, 1994), 7–9.

[155] Summarizing the results of a 1986 conference between Chinese and American scholars, Harry Harding notes that the participants agreed that "each side also made decisions in the late 1940s that magnified the mistrust and skepticism of the other." See Harding and Yuan, *Sino-American Relations*, xxi–xxii.

analysis of postwar international circumstances strongly inclined him to interpret U.S. actions in a negative light.[156]

U.S. policy in the Far East did nothing to allay Mao's suspicions. The central problem was U.S. support for the GMD; although U.S. officials saw their earlier efforts to mediate between the CCP and GMD as evenhanded, U.S. policy makers had tried to minimize CCP influence and had consistently favored Chiang.[157] Not surprisingly, Mao concluded that the United States could not be trusted and referred to Marshall's mediation effort as "a smoke screen for strengthening Chiang Kai-shek in every way."[158] Although Acheson and his advisors eventually concluded that a Communist victory was inevitable and further U.S. assistance would be counterproductive, pressure from pro-GMD congressmen and his own unwillingness to see China "go Red" prevented Truman from suspending U.S. aid to the GMD. The CCP also accused the United States of helping sink the cruiser *Chongqing* when its crew tried to defect to the Communists in March 1949, and CCP leaders saw additional evidence of U.S. hostility in Ambassador Leighton Stuart's refusal to meet with Mao, the continued presence of American troops on Chinese soil, the U.S. effort to rebuild Japan, and the growing support in Washington for Taiwanese independence.[159] The CCP also accused the United States of supporting counterrevolutionary activities in China (correctly, as it turned out), a suspicion reinforced by Acheson's ill-advised statement that "ultimately the profound civilization and democratic individualism of China will reassert themselves and she will throw off the foreign yoke."[160]

---

[156] On the theory of the "intermediate zone" and Mao's suspicions of the United States, see *Selected Works*, 4:99; Goldstein, "Chinese Communist Policy," 238–42, and "Sino-American Relations," 125–26.

[157] Roosevelt saw Chiang as "the only man . . . who could hold China's people together"; Truman declared, "My policy is to support Chiang K.C.," and Marshall agreed that if a settlement in China proved elusive, "it would still be necessary . . . to back the Nationalist Government of the Republic of China—through the Generalissimo." U.S. Marine and Air Force units helped the GMD reoccupy several strategic areas at the end of World War II, and Lend-Lease shipments to the GMD increased after the Japanese surrender. Quotations from Westad, *Cold War and Revolution*, 100–102, 133; Tao Wenzhao, "Hurley's Mission to China and the Formation of U.S. Policy to Support Chiang Kai-Shek against the Communist Party"; and William Stueck, "The Marshall and Wedemeyer Missions: A Quadrilateral Perspective," in Harding and Yuan, *Sino-American Relations*, 78–81, 84–87.

[158] See Mao, *Selected Works*, 4:109. He later remarked, "[Since] it was the first time we had dealt with the U.S. imperialists, . . . we were taken in. Now with the experience we won't be cheated again." Quoted in Shu Guang Zhang, *Deterrence and Strategic Culture: Chinese-American Confrontations, 1949–1958* (Ithaca: Cornell University Press, 1992), 18–19.

[159] See William W. Stueck, *The Road to Confrontation: American Policy towards China and Korea, 1947–1950* (Chapel Hill: University of North Carolina Press, 1981), 52–54; Shu Guang, *Deterrence and Strategic Culture*, 18–26; Chang, *Friends and Enemies*, 12–41; and Christensen, "Lost Chance for What?" 9.

[160] This statement appears in Acheson's letter of transmittal to the official State Department "White Paper" on events in China. Acheson added that the United States should "encourage all developments in China which . . . work towards this end." See *The China White Paper, Au-*

The Chinese Communists had ample grounds for concern, but their perceptions of threat rested on a significant misreading of U.S. intentions. U.S. officials were convinced that the CCP was under Soviet influence and would have to be contained, but the Truman administration had no plans for direct intervention. It placed a higher priority on other regions, and sought to curtail aid to the GMD in order to avoid pushing China even closer to Moscow.[161] U.S. officials had already conceded northern China and Manchuria to the CCP by 1948, and the decision to continue a small aid program to the GMD in 1948 was partly a concession to Republican hard-liners in Congress and partly an effort to bolster the GMD position in southern and central China.[162] Predictably, Mao and his associates saw this decision as a sign of continued U.S. hostility and regarded bellicose statements by pro-GMD congressmen as authoritative expressions of U.S. policy. Similarly, the lingering American military presence in China was largely a legacy of World War II, and though U.S. forces did aid the GMD on several occasions, these troops were hardly the advance wave of a counterrevolutionary invasion. U.S. efforts to rebuild Japan and to keep Taiwan free from CCP control were directed against the Soviet Union rather than China and were not part of a campaign to control the "intermediate zone"; on the contrary, the United States favored decolonization except where it seemed likely to produce a Communist government. Finally, Acheson's statement that China would eventually "throw off the foreign yoke" was an attempt to deflect right-wing pressure for greater aid to the GMD and not a proclamation of counterrevolutionary ambitions, though it is hardly surprising that Mao interpreted it as he did. In short, although the CCP was correct to regard the United States as hostile, they overstated the U.S. commitment to overthrowing the regime and exaggerated the threat that U.S. opposition represented.[163]

As one would expect, Chinese responses reinforced U.S. fears and moved U.S. leaders to take more extensive measures of their own. Relations with

---

*gust 1949* (Stanford: Stanford University Press, 1967), xvi. The report was intended to prove that the GMD's defeat was due to its own mistakes rather than a lack of U.S. support, but Mao saw its documentation of U.S. involvement in China as further proof of U.S. hostility. See *Selected Works*, 4:425–59.

[161] Early in 1950, the National Security Council and Joint Chiefs of Staff concluded that "the strategic importance of Formosa [Taiwan] does not justify overt military action," and Truman told a press conference, "The United States government will not provide military aid or advice to Chinese forces on Taiwan." Quoted in Goncharov, Lewis, and Xue, *Uncertain Partners*, 98.

[162] See Gaddis, *Long Peace*, 75; Stueck, *Road to Confrontation*, 52–56; and Leffler, *Preponderance of Power*, 248–49.

[163] Some CCP accusations were simply wrong; for example, CCP leaders reportedly believed that the U.S. and Great Britain were helping the GMD blockade several Chinese ports in July 1949. Christensen, "Lost Chance for What?" 9–10.

the CCP had been strained by clashes between CCP units and U.S. Marines in late 1945 and the detention of a group of U.S. diplomats in Shenyang (Mukden) in November 1948, but Acheson had downplayed such incidents as part of the normal disorder accompanying a revolution. In June 1949, however, Mao announced that the threat from U.S. imperialism gave China no choice but to "lean to one side," and China and the Soviet Union signed a treaty of alliance in January 1950.[164] This development, which discredited the earlier hope that Chinese nationalism would be a stronger force than Communist solidarity, strengthened the case for a heightened U.S. commitment in the region.[165] The Communist victory in China also spawned growing fears of revolutionary contagion throughout Asia; according to the CIA, "the urgent question of 1950 [was] whether Soviet-oriented, China-based communism can continue to identify itself with nationalism, exploit economic privations and anti-Western sentiment, and sweep into power by one means or another elsewhere in Asia."[166]

To be sure, it is unlikely that the United States and revolutionary China would have become close allies in the absence of these misperceptions. Mao faced a basic strategic dilemma: given his belief that the PRC needed Soviet aid and protection, it was essential that he convince Stalin that China would be a reliable ally. Although Mao and other CCP leaders wanted recognition from (and trade with) the United States and its allies, overt efforts to achieve this goal would only have fed Stalin's suspicions and jeopardized the alliance. By the same logic, Chinese efforts to reassure Moscow merely reinforced U.S. fears and impeded recognition. Thus, the deterioration of Sino-American relations was partly due to the logic of bipolarity, which forced Mao to choose between the two camps.[167]

At the same time, there was more than structural forces at play. Both sides inflated the other's hostility and let slip an opportunity to forge a less acrimonious relationship. In treating the CCP solely as a Soviet puppet, the United States missed a chance to minimize Soviet influence in Asia. By viewing the United States as a rapacious imperialist power, the PRC was forced to rely more heavily on the Soviet Union and was denied potentially beneficial trade relations. Thus, even if close relations were not a realistic

[164] See Tucker, *Patterns in the Dust*, 44; Mao, *Selected Works*, 4:411–24; and Goncharov, Lewis, and Xue, *Uncertain Partners*, chap. 3.

[165] Pressure to bring Taiwan within the U.S. security umbrella increased throughout spring, and the commander of U.S. forces in the Far East, General Douglas MacArthur, warned that "the strategic interests of the United States will be in serious jeopardy if [Taiwan] is allowed to be dominated by a power hostile to the United States." See Goncharov, Lewis, and Xue, *Uncertain Partners*, 156; Gaddis, *Long Peace*, 80–87; and Stueck, *Road to Confrontation*, 146–50.

[166] Quoted in Leffler, *Preponderance of Power*, 337–38; and see also Shu Guang, *Deterrence and Strategic Culture*, 45, 117.

[167] See Goncharov, Lewis, and Xue, *Uncertain Partners*, 102.

possibility in the aftermath of the revolution, the exaggerated suspicions that had emerged by 1950 had very real costs.[168]

The Korean War

The same dynamics that fueled the Sino-American spiral helped bring the two states into the Korean War, and this unexpected clash offers another example of the effects of revolutions on perceptions of hostility and on optimism about the use of force.[169] The conflict also hardened each state's image of the other and helped keep Sino-American relations in a deep freeze for nearly two decades.

*Mutual Misperceptions.* Prior to the North Korean attack, U.S. policy makers believed that Communist military expansion in Asia was unlikely. The invasion seemed to discredit this view completely, and Truman rushed U.S. troops to South Korea under the auspices of the United Nations and sent the U.S. Seventh Fleet to the Taiwan Straits in order to deter an assault on Taiwan.[170] American intervention soon turned the tide and the UN forces crossed the thirty-eighth parallel in October and headed north to eliminate the Communist government and reunify the country.

The rapid UN advance raised Chinese perceptions of threat to new heights and prompted extensive military preparations.[171] Truman's decision to interpose the Seventh Fleet between Taiwan and the mainland forced Mao to abandon his dream of unifying China under Communist auspices, and Mao now saw U.S. involvement in Korea as "the first step in the whole U.S. Asian scheme of aggression." Even if the United States did not attack China immediately, Mao was convinced that Korea would be the staging ground for an

[168] Steven Goldstein likens the Sino-American relationship to a Greek tragedy: "the result of an interactive process in which the leaders of two nations were so severely limited in their perceived policy options that they were unable to explore meaningfully the possible bases of accommodation or respond to open gestures by the other side." "Sino-American Relations, 1948–1950: Lost Chance or No Chance?" in Harding and Yuan, *Sino-American Relations,* 120–21.

[169] It is worth noting that the North Korean decision to invade (and the Soviet decision to support them) rested on North Korean leader Kim Il Sung's erroneous belief that an attack would spark a massive uprising by Communist sympathizers in the south. Thus, the Korean War was caused in part by the (misguided) belief that the "revolution" in the north would be easy to export, consistent with my theory. See Goncharov, Lewis, and Xue, *Uncertain Partners,* 135, 141–44.

[170] On January 5, 1950, Truman had declared that "the United States Government will not pursue a course which will lead to involvement in the civil conflict in China [and] . . . will not provide military aid or advice to Chinese forces on [Taiwan]." Text in Roderick MacFarquahar, ed., *Sino-American Relations, 1949–1971* (New York: Praeger, 1972), 70.

[171] See Goncharov, Lewis, and Xue, *Uncertain Partners,* 174; Jonathan D. Pollock, "The Korean War and Sino-American Relations," in Harding and Yuan, *Sino-American Relations,* 215–17; and Shu Guang, *Deterrence and Strategic Culture,* 90–91.

inevitable imperialist invasion. This threat would force the PRC to maintain large, costly defenses along the Sino-Korean border, and Chinese officials expressed the fear that the reunification of Korea would encourage "reactionary forces" and "make other states shift sides towards the American imperialists."[172] U.S. policy thus threatened Mao's entire revolutionary strategy, and he concluded that it was necessary to demonstrate China's ability to thwart a U.S. attack. Despite the obvious costs and risks, therefore, Mao decided that China's long-term security required it to enter the war.[173]

Sadly, this decision was based on a fundamental misreading of U.S. objectives. U.S. leaders had no intention of invading China and tried to reassure the PRC that the United Nations armies were not a threat.[174] Unfortunately, because U.S. leaders had reversed their earlier pledge not to protect Taiwan and U.S. spokesmen had previously declared that the UN forces would not cross the thirty-eighth parallel, Chinese officials discounted these assurances and remained convinced that the occupation of Korea was the beginning of a coordinated imperialist assault.[175]

[172] As Mao put it, "If we do not send troops [to Korea], the reactionaries at home and abroad would be swollen with arrogance." See Goncharov, Lewis, and Xue, *Uncertain Partners*, 181; Thomas J. Christensen, "Threats, Assurances, and the Last Chance for Peace," *International Security* 17, no. 1 (1992), esp. 136; Zhang, *Deterrence and Strategic Culture*, 96–97; and Pollock, "Korean War and Sino-American Relations," 221–22; and Michael H. Hunt, "Beijing and the Korean Crisis," *Political Science Quarterly* 107, no. 3 (1992).

[173] As the Chinese press proclaimed in November, "Only if we resist can American imperialists be taught a lesson, and can the issues of Korea, liberation, and the independence of other areas be settled on the basis of justice and the will of the people." Quoted in Shu Guang, *Deterrence and Strategic Culture*, 106–107. According to Jonathan Pollock, "internationalist obligations may have served as a principal justification for Chinese actions, but long-term security was uppermost in Mao's calculations." See his "Korean War and Sino-American Relations," 221.

[174] U.S. policy makers considered retaliating against Chinese territory in the event of Chinese intervention but did not intend to attack if the PRC stayed out. See Foot, *Wrong War*, 82–83. The U.S. did drop propaganda leaflets and parachuted GMD agents into the mainland during this period. Although these efforts were neither extensive nor effective, they undoubtedly reinforced Beijing's perceptions of threat. See William M. Leary, *Perilous Missions: Civil Air Transport and CIA Covert Operations in Asia* (University: University of Alabama Press, 1984), 127–43.

[175] Zhou En-lai later recalled, "We saw through [the American] tricks. . . . Nehru told me that the [UN forces] would stop 40 miles short of the Yalu River. . . . Obviously, this was the second time [for them] to fool us. If we did nothing, the . . . enemy would surely continue its advance and would devise a second scheme [against China]." In November, a *Peoples' Daily* editorial warned, "The mouthpieces of the American imperialists are still spreading the smokescreen of guaranteeing that MacArthur's troops . . . will not push beyond the border of Korea. However, *in light of the experience afforded by history*, such [a] statement is in fact a prediction that U.S. aggressors will push beyond the border of Korea." Quoted in Goncharov, Lewis, and Litai, *Uncertain Partners*, 193–94; and Melvin Gurtov and Byong-Moo Hwang, *China under Threat: The Politics of Strategy and Diplomacy* (Baltimore: Johns Hopkins University Press, 1980), 57 (emphasis added). See also Zhai Zhihai and Hao Yufan, "China's Decision to Enter the Korean War: History Revisited," *China Quarterly* 121 (1990); Christensen, "Threats, Assurances," 136; and Foot, *Wrong War*, 68.

The leaders of the PRC were also confident that the risks of war could be controlled and that they would eventually emerge victorious. Despite obvious disadvantages in weaponry and resources, the advocates of intervention argued that the Chinese "volunteers" would enjoy numerical superiority, shorter supply lines, and better morale (because they were fighting for a just cause), and they anticipated a rapid victory over the UN forces. Chinese officials downplayed the significance of U.S. atomic weapons by arguing that such strikes would be costly but not definitive, and suggested that in the worst case, the PRC could always return to the strategy of "protracted war" that had defeated Japan.[176] Thus, China's decision for war reflected the by-now familiar combination of insecurity and overconfidence. On the one hand, intervention in Korea was necessary because the external threat was severe, but on the other hand, intervention would be successful because China's military forces enjoyed important strategic advantages.[177]

U.S. decision making in Korea reveals equally impressive misjudgments.[178] Although the invasion was an independent North Korean initiative (albeit one taken with the knowledge and approval of the Soviet and Chinese leadership), the Truman administration viewed it as a clear case of Soviet aggression and responded accordingly.[179] At the same time, U.S. leaders believed that the Soviet Union would not risk a world war over Korea and that the PRC would follow Moscow's orders. As a result, they assumed that China would not intervene and ignored Chinese warnings stating that Beijing regarded the advance to the Yalu as an extremely seri-

---

[176] Marshal Peng Dehuai argued in favor of intervention by saying, "If China is devastated in war, it only means that the Liberation War will last a few years longer." Quoted in Chen Xiaoliu, "Chinese Policy towards the U.S., 1949–1955," in Harding and Yuan, *Sino-American Relations*, 191. Shu Guang Zhang quotes a CCP Politburo estimate that "the war can be limited to Korea and our objective is by all means attainable" and concludes "Chinese leaders were confident that their large-scale counteroffensive would not lead to either a military stalemate or a general war with the United States." *Deterrence and Strategic Culture*, 107.

[177] See Gurtov and Hwang, *China under Threat*, 59–62; and Zhai and Hao, "China's Decision," 107–108.

[178] One authoritative review essay argues that "recent scholarship concurs that American policymakers grievously misread Soviet and Chinese intentions with regard to Korea" and concludes that the Truman administration "made a monumental miscalculation of Chinese Communist intentions and capabilities as . . . MacArthur marched to the Yalu." Robert J. MacMahon, "The Cold War in Asia: Toward a New Synthesis," *Diplomatic History* 12, no. 3 (1988), 316–17.

[179] The definitive analysis of the civil origins of the Korean War is Bruce Cumings, *The Origins of the Korean War*, 2 vols. (Princeton: Princeton University Press, 1981–91); the best analysis of the knowledge and calculations of North Korea, China, and the Soviet Union is Goncharov, Lewis, and Xue, *Uncertain Partners*, chap. 5; and see also Allen Whiting, *China Crosses the Yalu: The Decision to Enter the Korean War* (New York: Macmillan, 1960).

ous threat.[180] The lack of reliable diplomatic channels forced Zhou En-lai to communicate his warnings via the Indian ambassador, K. M. Panikkar, but as U.S. officials did not regard Panikkar as a reliable source, Acheson concluded that Zhou's warning was "not an authoritative statement of policy."[181] U.S. decision makers also dismissed Chinese capabilities, arguing that China's internal problems would discourage it from taking action and the Red Army would not be a serious obstacle.[182] According to General Douglas MacArthur, commander of U.S. forces in the Far East, "Only 50/60,000 Chinese troops could be gotten across the Yalu. . . . If the Chinese tried to get down to Pyongyang, there would be the *greatest slaughter*."[183] Thus, both sides saw the other as dangerous but defeatable and held their collision courses. Instead of the easy victories that each expected, however, the conflict ended in an inconclusive stalemate after two more bloody years of war.

*Exiles, Information, and Instability.* Several familiar features of postrevolutionary confrontations were present in this case. First, as suggested earlier, U.S. responses were partly shaped by the influence of GMD exiles and their sympathizers (e.g, the "China lobby"), whose efforts sharpened U.S. perceptions of Chinese hostility and prolonged U.S. support for the GMD, in turn reinforcing Beijing's own sense of insecurity. Second, the lack of reliable information permitted each side's misperceptions to flourish unchecked. The CCP exaggerated U.S. hostility in part because it did not understand the U.S. political system, while the U.S. misread China's intentions and capabilities because it regarded its past actions as having been friendly and could not understand that the CCP held a very different view.[184] The limited contacts between the CCP and the U.S. government

---

[180] Thus, Acheson later asserted, "No possible shred of evidence could have existed in the minds of the Chinese Communist authorities about the [peaceful] intentions of the United Nations." Quoted in Richard Ned Lebow, *Between Peace and War: The Nature of International Crisis* (Baltimore: Johns Hopkins University Press, 1981), 205–16.

[181] See Chen Xiaoliu, "China's Policy towards the U.S.," 189 n. 1.

[182] See Shu Guang, *Deterrence and Strategic Culture*, 101–15. U.S. officials underrated Chinese capabilities in part because they saw it as an illegitimate Soviet puppet. Truman believed that the PRC regime was "Russian and nothing else," Marshall referred to the Chinese and Russian Communists as "co-religionists," and Dean Rusk believed that Mao's regime was a "colonial Russian government . . . it is not Chinese." Quoted in Michael Schaller, *The United States and China in the 20th Century* (New York: Oxford University Press, 1979), 125; and Leffler, *Preponderance of Power*, 400.

[183] Quoted in Shu Guang, *Deterrence and Strategic Culture*, 104 (emphasis in original). U.S. leaders downplayed the danger of Chinese intervention because they also believed that the CCP was preoccupied with domestic problems, that its army was unfit for conventional warfare, and that, as Acheson put it, it would be "sheer madness" for China to send troops to Korea when its real threat lay on the border with the Soviet Union. Foot, *Wrong War*, 81.

[184] This contrast is apparent in Mao's harsh reaction to the rosy vision of past U.S. involvement in China presented in the State Department White Paper. As he put it, "The 'international responsibilities' of the United States and its 'traditional policy of friendship' for China are nothing but intervention against China." See Mao, *Selected Works*, 4:435.

prior to 1946 only made matters worse, and contacts declined even more as relations eroded.[185] The impact of uncertainty is also apparent in the ambivalence that afflicted U.S. policy throughout this period; because no one could be sure what Mao and the CCP would do, U.S. policy vacillated between "letting the dust settle" and continuing their support for the GMD. Unfortunately, the CCP tended to see inconsistent U.S. behavior not as a sign of confusion or a response to changing circumstances but as evidence of U.S. duplicity. Neither side possessed adequate information about the other's preferences, capabilities, or political constraints, and so both were prone to malign interpretations of the other's actions.[186]

In short, the immediate international consequences of the Chinese Revolution support the central arguments of this book. The revolution caused a potentially significant shift in the balance of power and encouraged U.S. efforts to contain further Communist expansion. This policy led to increased support for the GMD and a corresponding decline in U.S. relations with the CCP, and each side's subsequent actions proceeded to reinforce the other's worst fears. The conflict came to a head in Korea, after the PRC concluded that war was both unavoidable and winnable and the United States discounted Chinese warnings and denigrated Chinese military capabilities. Like other postrevolutionary wars, the Sino-American struggle in Korea turned out to be longer and bloodier than either side expected. And it might have been bloodier still, as U.S. policy makers considered escalating the war on several occasions and would probably have done so had the Communist negotiators rejected the final UN armistice proposal in June 1953.[187]

*Realism and Radicalism: Chinese Foreign Policy, 1953–1960*

The subsequent course of Chinese foreign relations illustrates the tension between ideological objectives and the need for security in an anarchic world. Although ideology and domestic politics clearly influenced Chinese foreign-policy decision making, external factors (especially Chinese perceptions of the balance of threats) were usually more important.

The struggle in Korea convinced Mao that China could best defend itself by standing up to U.S. imperialism, and he tried to compel the United States to end its support for the GMD by shelling the GMD-held islands of Que-

---

[185] Acheson later admitted, "While we had regular diplomatic relations with the National Government and . . . voluminous reports from our representatives in their territories, our direct contact with the Communists was limited in the main to the mediation efforts of General Hurley and General Marshall." *China White Paper,* xiv.

[186] See Shu Guang, *Deterrence and Strategic Culture,* 276–77; and Hunt, "Mao Tse-tung and Accommodation with the United States," 226–33.

[187] See Foot, *Wrong War,* 230, and *A Substitute for Victory: The Politics of Peacemaking at the Korean Armistice Talks* (Ithaca: Cornell University Press, 1990).

moy and Matsu in 1954 and again in 1958. In response, the United States signed a defense agreement with Taiwan in 1954 and threatened to retaliate (including possibly using nuclear weapons) if China tried to occupy the off-shore islands or Taiwan.[188]

These confrontations strengthened the U.S. image of the PRC as a reckless revolutionary power that was even more aggressive and dangerous than the Soviet Union.[189] The United States rebuffed several Chinese attempts to improve relations in the mid-1950s (although the two states did begin bilateral discussions at the ambassadorial level in 1955), and Secretary of State John Foster Dulles described Sino-American relations as a "state of semi-warfare" in 1957.[190] China's enthusiastic endorsement of "wars of national liberation" and Mao's seemingly cavalier views on nuclear weapons reinforced the American impression of China as an especially bellicose and irrational foe, and these concerns increased further when China detonated its own nuclear device in 1964.[191] Indeed, the Kennedy administration was sufficiently concerned to explore the possibility of a joint U.S.-Soviet preemptive strike against Chinese nuclear facilities.[192] U.S. fears of Chinese-backed subversion also underlay the Americans' growing involvement in Vietnam, and the violence and xenophobia unleashed during the Cultural Revolution in China merely confirmed the image of the PRC as an irrational and unpredictable adversary.[193]

This impression was at best a caricature and at worst extremely misleading. Although its leaders were willing to implement far-reaching and ill-conceived *domestic* programs such as the Great Leap Forward, China's foreign policy was acutely sensitive to external constraints and its use of

[188] See Shu Guang, *Deterrence and Strategic Culture*, chaps. 6–8; Gurtov and Hwang, *China under Threat*, chap. 3; Jan Kalicki, *The Pattern of Sino-American Crises: Political-Military Interactions in the 1950s* (Cambridge: Cambridge University Press, 1975), chaps. 3, 6, 8; and Allen S. Whiting, "New Light on Mao: Quemoy 1958, Mao's Miscalculations," *China Quarterly* 62 (1975).

[189] Foot, *Wrong War*, 27–28.

[190] Quoted in Shu Guang, *Deterrence and Strategic Culture*, 239.

[191] For Mao's statements about nuclear weapons, see Alice Langley Hsieh, *Comunist China's Strategy in the Nuclear Era* (Englewood Cliffs, N.J.: Prentice-Hall, 1962), 1, 52, 132; and Stuart Schram, *Mao Tse-tung* (Harmondsworth: Penguin, 1966), 291. On China's nuclear program, see John Wilson Lewis and Xue Litai, *China Builds the Bomb* (Stanford: Stanford University Press, 1988); and Avery Goldstein, "Understanding Nuclear Proliferation: Theoretical Explanation and China's National Experience," *Security Studies* 2, nos. 3–4 (1993).

[192] See Chang, *Friends and Enemies*, chap. 8.

[193] In 1966, Assistant Secretary of State William P. Bundy referred to the PRC as "a government whose leadership is devoted to the promotion of communism by violent revolution," and Secretary of State Dean Rusk told a congressional hearing that "a country whose behavior is as violent, irascible, unyielding, and hostile as that of Communist China is led by leaders whose view of the world and of life itself is unreal." See Franz Schurmann and Orville Schell, eds., *The China Reader*, vol. 3: *Communist China* (New York: Vintage, 1967), 378–79, 508.

force was cautious and restrained.[194] Mao was willing to raise tensions in the Taiwan Straits in order to convince the United States that the PRC could not be intimidated, but he went to some lengths to limit the risks and stayed well clear of the brink.[195] With the exception of Korea and Vietnam (where Chinese strategic interests were directly involved), Beijing's support for "wars with national liberation" was more rhetorical than real, and Mao stressed that foreign revolutionaries must rely on their own efforts.[196] Similarly, Mao's seemingly provocative statements about nuclear weapons were intended primarily to bolster Chinese morale and to convince the United States that China could not be cowed by nuclear threats; significantly, Mao's private remarks were quite prudent, and his public statements became more moderate as China's nuclear capability increased.[197]

China's overriding concern for security was also evident in its sensitivity to shifts in the global balance of power and its willingness to ignore ideological principles in responding to them.[198] During the 1950s, the PRC saw the United States as its principal threat and chose to "lean to one side" with the Soviet Union. By the end of the decade, dissatisfaction with Soviet support led Mao to adopt a neutral position between the two superpowers, while China expanded its ties with Western Europe and Japan and tried to unite the Third World in an "international united front." The latter effort did not attract many adherents, however, and the onset of the Cultural Revolution in 1966 initiated a brief period of self-imposed isolation.[199]

---

[194] See Allen S. Whiting, "The Use of Force in Foreign Policy by the Peoples' Republic of China," *Annals of the American Academy of Political and Social Science* 402 (1972), 55–66, and *The Chinese Calculus of Deterrence: India and Indochina* (Ann Arbor: University of Michigan Press, 1975).

[195] During the 1954 crisis, Mao prohibited "offensive actions against foreign warships and airplanes," and the Central Military Commission told Chinese troops that they could retaliate to a U.S. attack only "if this involves no grave risks." When the GMD evacuated the offshore island of Dachen in February 1955, the Central Military Commission denied a local commander's request to occupy the island for fear that it would entangle them with U.S. forces. Mao acted cautiously in 1958 as well, rejecting a proposed air strike on Quemoy in August and ordering his artillery not to fire on U.S. ships. See Shu Guang, *Deterrence and Strategic Culture*, 198, 219, 236–37; and Chang, *Friends and Enemies*, 72.

[196] See Van Ness, *Revolution and Chinese Foreign Policy*, 72.

[197] In 1965, Mao claimed that his calling the atomic bomb a "paper tiger" was "just a figure of speech." He suggested that a nuclear war "would be a catastrophe for the whole world" and stated, "If one must fight one should confine oneself to conventional weapons." See Schurmann and Schell, *China Reader*, 364–65. See also Avery Goldstein, "Robust and Affordable Security: Some Lesson from the Second-Ranking Powers During the Cold War," *Journal of Strategic Studies* 15, no. 4 (1992), 492–96, 500–503; and Lewis and Xue, *China Builds the Bomb*, 34, 215–18, and app. A.

[198] According to A. Doak Barnett, "when security interests have been at stake, Chinese Communist leaders have generally . . . given them priority over other interests, including ideological and economic ones." *China and the Major Powers in East Asia* (Washington, D.C.: Brookings Institution, 1977), 254–55.

[199] See Harry Harding, "China's Changing Roles in the Contemporary World," in Harding, *China's Foreign Relations*, 186–87; and Armstrong, *Revolutionary Diplomacy*, 77–90.

By the late 1960s, the growth of Soviet military power in the Far East and a series of border clashes between Soviet and Chinese troops convinced Mao that the main threat was "Soviet hegemonism."[200] Just as the PRC had once "leaned to one side" to balance the perceived threat from the United States, it now turned to the United States to balance the threat from the Soviet Union. The rapprochement became overt after President Richard Nixon's 1972 visit to Beijing, and given the aura of suspicion that had surrounded Sino-American relations since the late 1940s, it would be hard to find a more vivid example of unsentimental realpolitik. Moreover, this shift occurred in period when ideology was especially important in shaping policy *within* China. Thus, although the Sino-Soviet alliance can be seen as the result of either balancing or ideological solidarity, the Sino-American rapprochement represented strictly the former.[201]

China's willingness to subordinate ideological principles to its security interests was evident in other relationships as well. Despite their public commitment to "Asian solidarity" and "peaceful coexistence," recurring border disputes and mutual suspicions led to a major deterioration of Sino-Indian relations in the late 1950s. The two states eventually fought a brief border war in 1962, and China's forces acted both cautiously and defensively in repelling the Indian challenge. India's subsequent tilt toward the Soviet Union was matched by a de facto alliance between China and Pakistan, despite the latter's nonsocialist character and its close ties to the United States.[202] Similarly, the U.S. withdrawal from Indochina in the early 1970s allowed the long-suppressed rivalry between China and Vietnam to reemerge; Vietnam strengthened its alliance with the Soviet Union while China backed the Khmer Rouge in Cambodia, and China and Vietnam eventually fought a brief but intense border war following the Vietnamese invasion of Cambodia in 1979.

In addition to providing evidence of China's willingness to sacrifice principles to the requirements of balance-of-power politics, these developments can be viewed as part of the gradual process of learning and adaptation. Although the United States and China continued to exaggerate each other's hostility after the Korean War, they avoided a direct clash in subsequent crises in part because each had learned that such a war would be costly.[203]

---

[200] See Thomas W. Robinson, "The Sino-Soviet Border Conflict," in Stephen S. Kaplan, *Diplomacy of Power: Soviet Armed Forces as a Political Instrument* (Washington, D.C.: Brookings Institution, 1981).

[201] I am indebted to Avery Goldstein for this insight.

[202] See Anwar H. Syed, *China and Pakistan: Diplomacy of an Entente Cordiale* (Amherst: University of Massachusetts Press, 1974), chap. 4; and Ya'acov Vertzberger, *The Enduring Entente: Sino-Pakistani Relations, 1960–1980*, Washington Papers no. 95 (New York: Praeger, 1983), 15–24.

[203] China reportedly suffered over 260,000 dead in Korea, while the United States lost around 47,000. Awareness of what another clash might cost helped keep the United States out of Indochina in the 1950s, and the fear of Chinese intervention constrained U.S. behavior during the height of its subsequent involvement there.

Over time, the PRC gradually evolved from a radical state to a reformist state to a conservative state, and although the CCP remains in power as of this writing, its policies bear little resemblance to the ideals of Marx or Mao, and its foreign policy aims are largely indistinguishable from the goals of other great powers.

The Chinese Revolution fostered intense perceptions of threat with other major powers, based on the shared belief that the other was inherently aggressive and that the threat could be reduced or eliminated through the use of force. Over time, however, the impact of these early views faded and the new regime and its neighbors gained a more accurate understanding of their respective interests and capabilities. Despite its revolutionary origins, revolutionary China generally behaved in a restrained and prudent manner after the Korean War. My theory thus receives further support.

Although the comparison is hardly novel, the similarities between the Chinese and Russian experiences are worth noting. Both regimes came to power after a world war, a situation that helped shape their early perceptions and gave them a "breathing space" in which to consolidate their power. Both fought and won a civil war, faced pressure from hostile imperialist powers, and exaggerated their opponents' willingness to attack them directly. Having fought wars shortly after gaining power (though China's involvement in Korea was far more costly than Russia's war with Poland), both states gradually overcame their initial isolation and reemerged as accepted (albeit suspect) players on the world stage. Finally, although both China and Russia were willing to compromise their ideological principles in order to preserve their security, neither abandoned these ideals completely, and they continued to interpret world events through the distorting prisms of a revolutionary worldview. This tendency helps explain why other states kept them at arm's length even when there were obvious incentives to forge a closer relationship.

## CONCLUSION

Each of the revolutions examined in this chapter increased the intensity of security competition, and each of these states came close to war on one or more occasions. The conflicts arose for reasons that are consistent with the mechanisms identified in chapter 2 and bear more than a passing resemblance to the dynamics observed in the French, Russian, and Iranian cases.

First, foreign reactions to each of these revolutions were heavily influenced by the potential impact on the balance of power. To France, the American Revolution was an opportunity to weaken Britain; several foreign states saw the turmoil in Mexico as both a threat to their existing interests and a chance to improve their positions at others' expense; Great Britain and Greece considered the revolution in Turkey a "window of opportunity" in the Near East; and the Chinese revolution was viewed as a major gain for the Soviet Union. In each case, foreign powers sought to take advantage of the power vacuum produced by the revolution, and their efforts led to conflict with the new regime, other foreign powers, or both.

Second, after the revolution each of these states experienced spirals of hostility with other states that brought them to the brink of war at least once. The revolutionary state and other powers tended to suspect each other's intentions, and each new regime was jealous of its sovereignty and obsessed with issues of security. Although each of these states did face real security threats after the revolution, the threats were usually exaggerated and, at times, wholly illusory. This paranoia was most pronounced in the case of China, but misunderstandings and exaggerations marred Anglo-Turkish relations during the Nationalists' bid for power, exacerbated U.S. relations with Britain and France in the 1790s, and disturbed revolutionary Mexico's relations with the United States as well. As expected, lack of information and poor channels of communication generally made these problems worse.

These states also exhibited the expected combination of vulnerability and optimism, although the intensity varied greatly. U.S. leaders were deeply fearful of foreign interference yet confident that their new nation would eventually control the entire continent, and their long-term optimism discouraged the use of force on several occasions. The Nationalists in Turkey and the Constitutionalists in Mexico were equally opposed to foreign interference and willing to use force to prevent it, yet each ultimately preferred to negotiate rather than fight; moreover, foreign intervention was clearly discouraged by an awareness of what such a campaign might entail. Thus, the predicted mixture of fear and overconfidence was muted in these three cases. It was clearly present in China, however, and helps explain Mao's decision to intervene in Korea in 1950. Intervention risked U.S. retaliation and jeopardized the reconstruction of his war-torn country, but Mao was convinced that the threat was too great to ignore and that his army could accomplish its mission at an acceptable cost.

Given the presence of these familiar sources of conflict, it is not surprising that each of these states came close to war. Yet as we have seen, the American, Mexican, and Turkish revolutions did not go over the brink. The explanation lies in the strong condition of *defense* dominance that accompanied each; unlike in the four other cases examined in this book, both the internal character and external circumstances of the American, Mexican, and Turkish revolutions made the use of force less attractive. Although conflicts and crises did occur, both sides ultimately concluded that going to war would not be worth the cost and risk.

This condition of defense dominance was attributable to three main factors. First, the American, Mexican, and Turkish revolutions were all comparatively moderate, relative to our other cases. In particular, none was based on a explicitly universalist ideology (the Founding Fathers being at best ambivalent about the ability of other societies to replicate the U.S. experience), and none of these states did much to export their principles to other countries. This greatly reduced the potential threat they posed and reduced the need for other states to take countermeasures to contain them. Another consequence was to allow each of these states to reenter the existing system of states more rapidly than postrevolutionary France, Russia, Iran, or China could do.

Second, each of these three states was both large and relatively weak—especially in comparison with the other great powers—making a war by miscalculation less likely. U.S. weakness helped limit pressures for war in the 1790s, as both Washington and Adams ultimately chose to negotiate with their foreign adversaries rather than risk a war for which they were clearly unprepared. Similarly, early in this century Mexican and U.S. leaders both understood that Mexico was by far the weaker of the two (and thus not much of a threat), though its sheer size would have made it difficult to occupy and subdue. As a result, both sides had ample reason to act with forebearance. The Turks were willing to fight the Greeks, Armenians, or Georgians (the latter two being even weaker than they), but Kemal recognized that a war with the Entente would be counterproductive and possibly fatal. By contrast, the combination of China's vast population, Soviet support, and the proximity of Korea made it possible for Mao to contemplate the overt use of force, especially as he believed that the United States was preparing to attack as soon as it established its position in the Far East.

Third, these three revolutionary states were favored by geographic isolation and fortuitous timing. The United States lay an ocean away from the other great powers, and its potential opponents were preoccupied by events closer to home. Mexico enjoyed similar advantages; although the outbreak of World War I encouraged a certain amount of foreign meddling, the war in Europe distracted its potential opponents and played a key role in dissuading the United States from more active interference. The Turks profited from the revolution in Russia and the war-weariness afflicting the other European powers, which discouraged Western intervention and allowed the Turks to set the two sides against each other. Had the timing of these revolutions been different, it is easy to imagine a less favorable outcome.

Finally, the cases examined in this chapter suggest a reciprocal connection between revolution and war. Revolutionary change will make war more likely, but the onset of war will shape the revolutionary process itself. In France, the outbreak of war in 1792 radicalized the revolution and led to the founding of the republic. Foreign intervention encouraged the Bolsheviks to take more extreme measures, and the outbreak of war with Iraq strengthened the radical elements in Iran as well. By contrast, the American, Mexican, and Turkish revolutions had more moderate outcomes in part because these states managed to avoid war until the revolution was essentially complete.

The American, Mexican, Turkish, and Chinese revolutions enhance our confidence in the propositions developed elsewhere in this book. That confidence is increased by the diversity of the cases and by the fact that even the apparent exceptions demonstrate that revolutions create strong pressures for war. In the next and final chapter, I consider whether more recent events fit this pattern as well and summarize the lessons that national leaders might draw from these results.

# [7]

## *Conclusion*

"Revolutions . . . occurred and will always occur so long as human nature remains the same."

—Thucydides

"In a revolution, as in a novel, the most difficult part to invent is the end."
—Alexis de Tocqueville

This book has explored some of the ways that revolutions affect international politics, focusing primarily on the relationship between revolution and war. I argued that revolutions alter the balance of threats between states, leading to more intense security competition and a heightened probability of war. I tested and refined this argument by examining three major revolutions in detail—those of France, Russia, and Iran—as well as four additional cases where the fit between theory and reality was less obvious.

Four tasks remain. The first is to summarize and compare the results of the seven case studies, in order to highlight the principal theoretical conclusions we may infer from these events. The second is to identify the policy implications of these results: when a revolution occurs, what precautions should other states take? What actions should they avoid? The third is to sketch what the theory tells us about the recent collapse of the Soviet empire and its effects on the likelihood of war. The final task is to consider the long-term relevance of this study: is mass revolution a fading phenomenon, or are the problems caused by past revolutions likely to occur in the future?

### REVOLUTION, SECURITY COMPETITION, AND WAR

The cases examined in this book confirm that revolutions increase the intensity of security competition between states and raise the probability of war. Although war did not occur in every case, each regime came close to war soon after gaining power and each revolution fostered greater security competition among the other major powers. The occurrence of revolution was hardly the only source of competition and conflict, but in each case the level of tension was higher than it would have been without the revolution.

In the French case, the collapse of the old regime caused competition between Austria, Prussia, and Russia to rise, triggered a spiral that placed France and Austria on a collision course, and brought the rivalry with England to the point of open warfare in 1793. Although war might have occurred even if the revolution had been averted, the internal turmoil in France was directly responsible for the war that did break out and for its rapid expansion.

Similarly, although the collapse of the Romanov dynasty temporarily lowered the level of conflict by taking Russia out of World War I, the establishment of Soviet Russia ultimately increased it. The revolution encouraged other states to compete over the lands of former tsarist empire and brought to power a regime that supported the violent overthrow of other states. The tsarist regime would never have acted as Soviet Russia did, and the other great powers would never have seen it as a subversive force. Again, it is safe to infer that the revolution was directly responsible for much of the enmity and insecurity that characterized relations between Soviet Russia and most other powers.

This pattern is even more apparent in the Iranian case. The revolution alarmed Iran's Arab neighbors, led directly to a protracted war with Iraq, and transformed U.S.-Iranian relations from close alliance to bitter rivalry. Relations with most other countries deteriorated as well, leaving the Islamic Republic largely isolated. Although the shah's ambitions had alarmed his neighbors on occasion, they never provoked the level of international enmity that the Islamic Republic has. Thus, Iran's present position is simply incomprehensible outside the context of the revolution.

The same effects were present in the other four cases, albeit to varying degrees. The United States experienced repeated conflicts with both its former British rulers and its putative French ally, coming close to war with each on one or more occasions. The revolution in Mexico exacerbated the competition for influence between the United States, Britain, and Germany, led the United States to intervene in 1914 and again in 1916, and continued to mar relations between Mexico and the United States until the late 1930s. The Nationalist revolution in Turkey challenged European ambitions in the Near East, brought the new regime to the brink of war with Great Britain in 1922, and eventually forced the Entente to withdraw its troops and abandon the Treaty of Sèvres. Needless to say, it is hard to imagine the Ottoman sultan achieving like results. Finally, the Communist triumph in China ended decades of foreign interference, moved Beijing firmly into the socialist camp, and placed the new regime on the path to war in Korea. Once again, it is unlikely that Chiang Kai-shek and the GMD would have acted the same way or provoked similar responses.

Hypothetical scenarios can never be tested, of course, but the possibility that these states would have experienced equally high levels of conflict in the absence of revolution seems remote. Although other causes of conflict were undoubtedly present, these cases show that revolutions have *independent* causal effects on the level of security competition and the probability of war.

### Balance-of-Threat Theory

Why do revolutions make competition and war more likely? As described in detail in chapter 2, balance-of-threat theory suggests that revolutions cause security competition by altering the perceived level of threat between the revolutionary state and its main adversaries, on one hand, and by encouraging both sides to believe that the use of force can overcome the threat at an acceptable cost, on the other.

The evidence strongly supports this general argument. The crises or wars that followed each of the revolutions examined here resulted from a combination of opportunism and insecurity, based on misjudgments about the balance of power, overly malign perceptions of intent, and (in the worst cases) exaggerated beliefs about the likelihood of contagion or counterrevolution. Compounding the problem were uncertainty and misinformation, which reinforced each side's prior beliefs and made peaceful settlements more elusive.

*The Balance of Power.* In the French, Russian, and Iranian cases, the revolution's effect on the balance of power was a central cause of war. Yet the impact of a revolution on the balance of power does not cause war by itself. In particular, these effects cannot explain why some states try to exploit the opportunities while others remain aloof, nor can they account for aggressive behavior on the part of the revolutionary state. For example, although Prussia saw French weakness after 1789 as a chance for expansion, most European states welcomed the erosion of French power and did not use force to exploit it. Instead, the war began when, reacting to Austria's efforts to intimidate the French, the Girondins convinced the Assembly to declare war in April 1792. Similarly, Iran's weakness after the revolution does not fully explain why Iraq saw a military attack as desirable or necessary; the apparent collapse of Iranian power might just as easily been considered an opportunity for Iraq to turn its attention to other problems.[1] The four cases examined in chapter 6 reinforce this conclusion: although the American, Mexican, Turkish, and Chinese revolutions created significant power vacu-

---

[1] Furthermore, focusing on power alone cannot explain why Iraq decided to go to war but Iran's other neighbors (the Soviet Union, Turkey, Afghanistan) did not.

ums and fostered greater security competition between other powers, only China was subsequently involved in war. If the belief that a revolution has weakened its victim is part of the link between revolution and war, it is hardly the whole story.

*Perceptions of Intent.* Each of these revolutions produced sharp departures from the foreign policies of the old regime, in turn creating sharp conflicts of interest with other states. Furthermore, both the revolutionary state and the other great powers tended to exaggerate one another's hostility and aggressiveness. One of the most characteristic features of postrevolutionary foreign policy, this tendency is also one of the most pernicious.

These cases also confirm that spirals of suspicion can arise from several distinct sources. The most obvious source is ideology: if the worldview of a revolutionary movement stipulates that certain regimes are inherently hostile, the new regime is likely to interpret the behavior of foreign powers in the worst possible light. A second source is domestic politics. As the French and Iranian cases suggest, factions within a revolutionary movement may dramatize foreign dangers in order to consolidate their own positions. Spiraling may also be fueled by testimony from émigrés or foreign revolutionaries, whose desire for support gives them an obvious incentive to foster conflicts between the revolutionary state and other powers. This tactic played a modest role in several of these cases; French émigrés echoed European fears of the revolution in France, Russian exiles stiffened Allied resistance against normalizing relations with the Bolshevik regime, and Iranian exiles (including the shah) contributed to the deterioration of Iranian foreign relations. The activities of the "China lobby" and the misleading testimony provided by some U.S. diplomats after the American Revolution further illustrates this danger.

*Offense, Defense, and the Export of Revolution.* The cases examined in this study also confirm that revolutions cause war by affecting perceptions of the offense-defense balance, conceived in both military and political terms. In the French, Russian, Iranian, and Chinese cases, decisions to go to war were encouraged by a combination of fear and overconfidence, usually based on each side's calculations of the likelihood that the revolution will spread or be reversed. Expecting that their example would be contagious, the revolutionary state was more confident, less willing to compromise, and prone to support revolutionary efforts abroad. At the same time, the general belief that the revolution might also be easily reversed made exporting the revolution seem necessary to the revolutionary state and helped convince its adversaries that they could eliminate the threat with little effort.

Ironically, history suggests that both these beliefs are usually misguided. Although each of these revolutions was accompanied by evidence of discontent in other societies, none of them spawned successful imitators during the decade after the seizure of power, and efforts to spread the revolution via propaganda or contagion only angered and alarmed other states. The Girondins' predictions of a universal crusade for liberty were disappointed; "Bolshevik" uprisings in Finland, Hungary, and Bavaria collapsed quickly, the Polish proletariat welcomed the Red Army with bayonets instead of flowers; and Soviet attempts to spark Communist revolutions in the Near East and China all failed. Efforts to export the Iranian Revolution have been equally abortive thus far, despite the universalist pretensions of Khomeini's Shiism and Iran's support for fundamentalist groups throughout the Muslim world. We should not be surprised at these results, however, because would-be propagators of revolution face several significant obstacles.

First, although a revolution often comes as a surprise to virtually everyone (including the revolutionaries themselves), it also provides a timely warning to others. As a result, potential targets will be less prone to the mistakes that let the old regime be toppled. Thus, the French example alerted the other European powers to keep a close watch on potential "Jacobins" and to make a number of modest reforms. These measures were universally successful except in areas conquered by French troops. Similarly, states facing a Bolshevik challenge acted vigorously to suppress potential uprisings after 1917, just as the Persian Gulf states suppressed, coopted, or expelled anyone suspected of spreading Iran's revolutionary message. Louis XVI in Paris, Nicholas II in St. Petersburg, and Mohammad Reza Pahlavi in Tehran may have dithered their way to their own destruction, but their contemporaries in other countries seem to have learned from their mistakes.

Second, potential victims of a spreading revolution also learn to balance against this frightening possibility. The growing danger from revolutionary France led to the formation of a large (if unruly) coalition by the summer of 1793, and the Entente maintained a common front against Bolshevism until the mid-1920s. In the same way, the threat from Iran prompted greater cooperation between Iraq, Saudi Arabia, Kuwait, and the United States.[2]

Third, the failure of revolutions to spread underscores the advantages that incumbent regimes ordinarily enjoy. Even states with severe internal problems usually retain some shreds of legitimacy, as well as a substantial asymmetry of power over their internal rivals. Moreover, the combination of favorable circumstances and coincidences that make the first revolution possible are unlikely to occur elsewhere in precisely the same fashion. Thus, pro-French radicals in England were quickly overcome by prompt government action, the German Communists proved to be no match for the Reichs-

---

[2] By contrast, because foreign powers were not especially worried that the U.S., Mexican, or Turkish revolutions would spread, they did not band together in strong opposing coalitions.

wehr in 1919, 1921, and 1923, and the Shiites in Iraq were crushed when their leaders tried to duplicate the Iranian experience. Given the barriers to a revolution's spreading beyond a single state's borders, the real mystery is why anybody believes that it will.[3]

The evidence also suggests that reversing a revolution is nearly as difficult as spreading one. Revolutionary regimes survive because they are usually adept at mobilizing military power; whatever their other failings, revolutionary movements are especially good at persuading people to run grave risks and make large sacrifices for the sake of an ideal.[4] Foreign interference can facilitate this task by providing the legitimacy that a revolutionary regime needs, and a foreign threat can make it easier for leaders to eliminate rivals in the name of "national unity."

When foreign powers do not possess reliable sources of information and do not discount the testimony of émigrés sufficiently, they are likely to end up backing far-fetched counterrevolutionary schemes that hold little chance of success—as illustrated by English support for the Quiberon expedition in 1795, British and French aid to the White armies in the Russian Civil War, Iraq's support for various Iranian exile groups in Baghdad, and covert U.S. efforts to support anti-Communist groups in China. Supporting counterrevolutionary forces may be a cost-effective means of pressuring a revolutionary regime, but it is unlikely to remove it from power and will almost certainly fuel its perceptions of threat.

These obstacles do not mean that counterrevolutionary efforts never succeed, but success will be more difficult than other states expect. Foreign intervention did reverse the Dutch revolt of 1787 and the Polish "revolt" of 1791, to cite but two examples, and both superpowers intervened to reverse unwanted upheavals in their own spheres of interest throughout the Cold War.[5] These examples suggest that outside intervention can work when

---

[3] Exceptions arise when the new regime is able to defeat and occupy its adversaries and impose its system upon their populations by force. Thus, France's "sister republics" and the Soviet empire in Eastern Europe resulted from military expansion rather than the spread of revolutionary ideals. Examples of "spontaneous" Communist revolutions include those in the People's Republic of China, North Korea, Vietnam, Cuba, Ethiopia, Angola, and Nicaragua, but these "triumphs" occurred decades after the 1917 revolution.

[4] See Theda Skocpol, "Revolutions and Mass Military Mobilization," *World Politics* 40, no. 2 (1988); and Ted Robert Gurr, "War, Revolution, and the Growth of the Coercive State," *Comparative Political Studies* 21, no. 1 (1988).

[5] The Soviet Union intervened in East Germany in 1953, in Hungary in 1956, and in Czechoslovakia in 1968. The Polish Army declared martial law (with Soviet support) in 1980, and the Red Army invaded Afghanistan in 1980 in an attempt to prop up a faltering Marxist regime there. The United States helped topple the Mossadegh regime in Iran in 1953 and the Arbenz regime in Guatemala in 1954 and played a subordinate role in removing the Allende regime in Chile in 1968. In 1983, a U.S. invasion ousted the New Jewel Movement in Grenada, and the U.S-backed *contras* forced the Sandinista government in Nicaragua to agree to new elections (in which they were voted out of office) after a protracted and bloody civil war.

there is a large disparity in power between the two states involved. Even in such cases, however, the effort often turns out to be greater than the intervening power anticipated.

In short, the perceptions of a mutual offensive advantage that accompany most revolutions are especially dangerous, because the combination of insecurity and overconfidence that leads to the use of force is usually ill-founded. In fact, revolutions are hard to export *and* difficult to reverse, and in most cases, both sides are more secure than they think and would be better off remaining at peace.

The tendency for revolutions to foster perceptions of offense dominance is not universal, and the absence of this factor is the main reason why the American, Turkish, and Mexican revolutions did not lead to war. These revolutions altered the balance of power and generated both real conflicts of interest and spirals of suspicion. Yet in each case, key leaders were aware that the revolution was unlikely to spread and that war would be expensive. As a result, both sides ultimately refrained from the large-scale use of force.

*Uncertainty and Misinformation.* If revolutions are both hard to export and difficult to reverse, then why do states worry about either possibility? Our cases provide part of the answer: it will be extremely difficult for states to gauge their situation accurately after a revolution, because relations between revolutionary states and other powers will be afflicted by very high levels of uncertainty and misinformation. The problem arises from several different aspects of the revolutionary process, so it will usually be difficult to overcome.

For example, it is hardly surprising that both sides have trouble estimating the balance of military power, because the military capacity of the new state will rest on novel institutions whose effects can only be discovered through battlefield experience. Foreign powers will usually have good reasons to discount a revolutionary state's capabilities, if only because the armed forces of the old regime usually deteriorate in the short term. Yet in almost every case examined here, the revolutionary regime managed to use new myths, symbols, and institutions to create an unexpectedly formidable military machine.[6]

The political consequences of a revolution are even harder to calculate in advance, because the political appeal of a revolutionary model is virtually impossible to gauge with confidence. Neither the revolutionaries nor their foreign opponents know if the revolution will attract adherents abroad or if foreign intervention will spark a counterrevolutionary upheaval. Faced

---

[6] The United States and Mexico are partial exceptions to this claim, because neither revolution faced a large-scale foreign invasion. The rapid mobilization of U.S. naval power during the Quasi-War and the Constitutionalists' unexpected success in the civil war against Villa are consistent with this argument, however.

[337]

with this uncertainty, elites on both sides will tend to rely on ideology and recent experience and to assume that the initial revolutionary success was a harbinger of things to come. Even relatively modest signs of a sympathetic response elsewhere will be taken as evidence of a rising revolutionary tide, and testimony from foreign revolutionaries or counterrevolutionary exiles can reinforce these erroneous expectations.

Both sides overstate the likelihood of counterrevolution for much the same reason. The danger of an "aristocratic conspiracy" terrified the French from 1789 onward; the Bolsheviks feared their hold on power might lapse at any moment; the Islamic Republic has waged a brutal campaign against former opponents as well. These fears reflect the intrinsic difficulty of accurately gauging the loyalty of the population at large. Although signs of dissent will always be present, neither the ruling authorities nor outside powers can know how strong the opposition really is.

To make matters worse, revolutions impede the acquisition of the information that might help correct these erroneous impressions. The revolutionary states in France, Russia, and Iran were cut off from normal diplomatic contacts, intensifying their perceptions of threat and making subsequent efforts to reach a modus vivendi more difficult. Indeed, a striking feature of most of these cases is the extent to which states were forced to conduct diplomacy through unofficial agents whose expertise and reliability usually left much to be desired.

Lastly, with all the uncertainty, other states will have trouble deciding how to respond to a revolution, and foreign powers will be hard-pressed to agree on a common course of action.[7] If the power of a revolutionary state is unclear, the danger of contagion uncertain, and the prospects for counterrevolution unknown, it will be difficult to obtain a consensus for intervention or abstention, and the other states will be more likely to respond in a haphazard and poorly coordinated manner. This problem arose in several of our cases: the European powers were often divided over how to respond to the revolution in France; the Entente could not adopt a unified policy toward the Bolshevik or Turkish revolutions; Britain and the United States disagreed over the proper approach to take toward the revolutionary governments in Mexico and China; and there was little consensus on how to respond to Iran's revolution until its army had crossed into Iraqi soil. The result, unfortunately, may have been the worst of both worlds: other states did enough to antagonize the new regimes but not enough to eliminate them.

[7] I identify some other reasons for this tendency in my chapter, "Collective Security and Revolutionary Change: Promoting Peace in the Former Soviet Empire," in *Collective Security after the Cold War*, ed. George W. Downs (Ann Arbor: University of Michigan Press, 1993).

*Realism and Revolution*

The cases examined in this book both confirm the basic explanatory power of realism and suggest which strands of realist thought are most useful. In particular, realism is most powerful when it goes beyond a narrow focus on the gross distribution of power and instead examines the balance of *threats*. Although the balance of power is hardly irrelevant, the behavior of states is also affected by how national leaders assess the intentions of other states and how they perceive the relative advantage to offense or defense. The offense-defense balance is not merely a function of geography or military doctrine, however, but may also be affected by the potential appeal of particular *ideas* (such as a new revolutionary ideology). Realism gains even more explanatory power by incorporating the possibility that states will misread these factors, and as we have seen repeatedly, such misperceptions are especially common after revolutions.[8] Beliefs about the possibility of revolutionary contagion—which ultimately rest on beliefs about the persuasive power of revolutionary ideas—have been critical in shaping perceptions of the offense-defense balance and help explain why some revolutions led to war and others did not. In short, by incorporating domestic politics and ideas into the anarchic setting depicted by realism, we obtain a more complete picture of the forces that shape state behavior.

This argument points to another insight: realism may tell us more about international behavior in postrevolutionary periods than in more "normal" periods. Some realists depict international politics as a relentless struggle for survival where security is extremely scarce and states must constantly strive for any advantage.[9] Proponents of this perspective are likely to view revolutionary states as exceptions to realist logic, because their foreign policy objectives are heavily affected by ideology and their leaders are presumed to be less familiar with the subtleties of international diplomacy. Yet in the three main cases examined here, each side saw the other as an imminent and intense threat and discounted the possibility of a lasting peace. In other words, relations between these revolutionary states and other powers were virtually identical to the relationships depicted by the more extreme versions of realism. The key point, however, is that the level of conflict is not

[8] Stephen Van Evera refers to this as "Type IV Realism." It differs from other strands of realist theory by focusing on what Van Evera calls the "fine-grained structure of power" and by explicating the factors that shape how states perceive that structure. *Causes of War*, vol. 1: *The Structure of Power and the Roots of War* (Ithaca: Cornell University Press, forthcoming), chap. 1. On the impact of ideas on the offense-defense balance, see George Quester, *Offense and Defense in the International System* (New York: Wiley, 1977), 67.

[9] This view is most clearly expressed in the writings of John J. Mearsheimer: "Back to the Future: Instability in Europe after the Cold War," *International Security* 15, no. 1 (1990); and "The False Promise of International Institutions," *International Security* 19, no. 3 (1994–95).

merely due to the state of anarchy and a particular distribution of capabilities (as a neorealist such as John Mearsheimer would have it) but is also heavily influenced by perceptions of intent and beliefs about the likelihood that the revolution will spread or be reversed.

With the passage of time, however, each side will acquire a more accurate estimate of the true threat that it faces. The security dilemma between them will ease and each will adopt a less vigilant posture. The relentless competition depicted by some realists will abate, and prospects for cooperation will probably increase. By restricting themselves to examining the gross distribution of power, however, neorealists cannot explain why the level of conflict varies even though the distribution of power is constant. This shortcoming is another reason to prefer balance-of-threat theory to the overly spare world of neorealist balance-of-power theory.

Finally, the neorealist claim that revolutionary states will be "socialized" to the system seems to be only partly correct. Although external pressures did lead all of these regimes to alter their behavior in significant ways, their tendency to cling to counterproductive strategies despite substantial costs was equally striking—especially in the Soviet, Chinese, and Iranian cases, where a commitment to avowedly revolutionary objectives kept these regimes isolated and beleaguered far longer than was necessary. One may speculate that such a tendency will be most severe when, first, the ideology in question is particularly extreme, and second, it has been formally institutionalized within a hegemonic ruling party. Thus, the American, Mexican, and Turkish revolutionary leaders adapted quickly because they began with more moderate ideas, and the French were able to abandon the more utopian visions of the Girondins and Montagnards because those had not been enshrined in a formal party ideology and were not central to the legitimacy of the postrevolutionary state.

### Critical Theory, Identity, and Revolutionary Change

The cases examined here also shed light on the relative merits of critical-theory as an approach to international politics. Critical theory emphasizes the role of language and social processes in shaping actors' goals, identities, and collective self-understandings.[10] From this perspective, the international system is not an independent structure arising from the interactions of preexisting states; rather, it is the product of concrete social practices that reflect the purposes and perceptions of the actors themselves.

Revolutions are crucial cases for critical theorists, because in them state identities are rapidly and radically transformed through changes in the dis-

---

[10] For important examples of critical theory approaches to international politics, see the references above in chap. 1, n. 10.

cursive practices of a community.[11] A revolution transformed Britain's North American colonies into a "new republic"; the absolutist regime of Louis XVI reemerged as the French *nation*; the tsarist empire was recast as the world's first "workers' and peasants' state," the multinational Ottoman Empire became the secular Republic of Turkey, and the Peacock Throne of the Pahlavis was replaced by Khomeini's Islamic Republic. Because critical theory regards the identities of social actors as powerful determinants of behavior, the behavior of revolutionary states would be expected to differ dramatically from the conduct of the old regime and from the practices of other states in the system. And since in this view the identity of a revolutionary state is closely linked to its ideology, foreign policy behavior should conform closely to its ideological principles. Thus, where realism predicts that the constraining effects of anarchy will force revolutionary states to moderate or abandon their more radical objectives, critical theory anticipates both dramatic and enduring change, even in the face of strong external pressures.

Do our seven cases support this view? On the one hand, the evidence does support a limited version of the argument: in each case, the revolutionary elite saw the seizure of power as a decisive break with the past and adopted policies that departed sharply from those of the old regime. In this sense, therefore, one can say that the change in "identity" produced by the revolution was associated with a change in behavior. But this is a very limited claim, roughly akin to arguing that actors with different preferences are likely to pursue different goals. One hardly needs critical theory to make that case.

On the other hand, the cases in this book offer little support for the more ambitious claim that shifts in discursive practices and collective understandings could produce a far-reaching transformation in the international system.[12] Although each of these revolutions featured dramatic changes in discourse and each regime made idealistic claims about its own conduct, their utopian visions soon gave way to the familiar principles of realpolitik. Irrespective of their ideological pretensions, each of these states fought wars, formed alliances, made diplomatic compromises, signed treaties of commerce, and in general conformed to most (if not all) norms of international conduct, while continuing to espouse revolutionary doctrines of one sort or another. Indeed, it is striking how readily these states abandoned many of their initial objectives under pressure: the French repudiated the

---

[11] Thus, Keith Michael Baker defines a revolution as a "transformation of the discursive practice of a community, a moment in which social relations are reconstituted and the discourse defining the political relations between individuals and groups is radically recast." *Inventing the French Revolution* (Cambridge: Cambridge University Press, 1990), 18.

[12] For examples of this sort of claim, see Rey Koslowski and Friedrich Kratochwil, "Understanding Changes in International Politics: The Soviet Empire's Demise and the International System," and Richard Ned Lebow, "The Long Peace, the End of the Cold War, and the Failure of Realism," both in *International Organization* 48, no. 2 (1994).

Decree on Liberty, the Bolsheviks sought trade and investment from the international class enemy, and even revolutionary Iran was willing to deal with the "Great Satan" in order to wage war against Iraq. In short, these states were willing to do virtually anything that a "normal" state would do, which suggests that systemic pressures had at least as great an impact as their revolutionary identities or ideological underpinnings.

In response, critical theorists might argue that this book offers an unfair test of their perspective, because it focuses primarily on the short- to medium-term effects of a revolution and does not examine the indirect and long-term impact of revolutions on attitudes, norms, and ideas. And if isolated revolutionary states are forced to adjust their behavior to the constraints of the existing international system, it is still possible that a critical mass of like-minded states would have transformative effects resembling the Westphalian transition between the feudal period and the modern state system. One could also argue that even deradicalized revolutions affect prevailing notions of international legitimacy and gradually alter the ends that individuals and states deem worthy of pursuit and the means they regard as legitimate.

These are valid points, and this book should not be regarded as offering a definitive challenge to the critical theory approach to international politics. What it does show, however, is that such an approach does not tell us very much about relations between revolutionary states and other powers in the immediate aftermath of the seizure of power. If the question of the long-term transformation of the international systems remains open, these cases suggest that the modified realism of balance-of-threat theory offers a more useful way to think about the practical difficulties that ordinarily follow a revolution.

## IMPLICATIONS FOR POLICY

The evidence assembled here confirms that foreign leaders have ample reason to be worried when a revolution occurs, but it also suggests that the usual prescriptions for dealing with such an event are not very helpful. In particular, neither appeasement nor intervention is an especially promising approach. Appeasement is often recommended as a way to avoid spiraling and promote good relations over time, but this advice ignores the fact that revolutionary states do commit acts of aggression, and convincing them to stop may require the threat or use of force. The case for overt intervention is usually even weaker. Advocates of intervention believe that diplomatic, economic, or military pressure will exert a positive effect on the revolutionary process, either by helping one faction consolidate its power or by convincing the revolutionary government to adopt policies that are consistent with foreign interests. But as we have seen, intervention is very often counterproductive. Emperor Leopold's attempts to manipulate French domestic politics in 1791–92 further undermined Louis's position, and Woodrow Wilson's efforts to shape the revolutionary process in Mexico alienated the various revolutionary factions and reinforced the latent anti-Americanism of the Mexican government. Foreign attempts to guide the course of events in Russia, Iran, and China were equally unsuccessful: foreign powers lacked sufficient leverage or adequate information (or both), and their activities were regarded with suspicion in each case.

Advocates of intervention will usually argue that the revolutionary state is both extremely dangerous and highly vulnerable, justifying active efforts to overthrow it. But as we have seen, this combination of fear and optimism is usually misplaced.[13] Revolutions are usually hard to export—reducing the need to remove the new regime—and intervention will reinforce the revolutionaries' own perceptions of threat and push the regime in a more radical direction. Revolutions are also more difficult to reverse than outside powers generally expect, and because war is so unpredictable, intervention may actually facilitate the spread of revolution, thereby causing the very process it was intended to prevent.[14]

A policy of containment is the best approach toward most revolutions, especially for great powers facing a relatively weak revolutionary state. Such a strategy would aim to prevent the spread of revolution and deter expansionist policies by bolstering potential targets and punishing the revolutionary state for overt acts of aggression, but its practitioners would otherwise eschew the use of force and would not attempt to overthrow the new regime. Foreign powers would also remain open to the idea of establishing normal relations when possible. Containment is not easy and may require patience, however, because revolutionary states usually interpret the behavior of other states in an extremely biased fashion. For this reason, foreign powers should communicate the rationale behind their responses as clearly as possible, taking pains to avoid appearing duplicitous or inconsistent. They should also avoid premature or overly enthusiastic efforts to embrace a suspicious revo-

---

[13] A possible exception to this stricture are cases—such as the U.S. invasion of Grenada in 1982—where the revolutionary state is so small and inconsequential that intervention is virtually certain to succeed. Under these conditions, however, the need to act will be even less compelling.

[14] There is a paradox here: the greater the *perceived* danger from a revolution, the more likely other states are to take action to contain or eliminate the threat, thereby diminishing the chance that the danger will be realized. In other words, the fear of revolution is a self-defeating prophecy: a revolution may fail to spread precisely because others are so worried that it will. But vigilance alone does not ensure success; indeed, efforts to overthrow a revolutionary regime may unwittingly facilitate revolutionary expansion, as they did in the French case and (to a lesser extent) the Iran-Iraq war. As a result, potential victims should focus their efforts on containing the revolution instead of trying to overturn it.

lutionary state, as such well-intentioned efforts are likely to be seen as self-interested attempts to manipulate the new regime. A policy of "benevolent neglect" may be most appropriate in such circumstances, allowing the new regime to set the pace for the resumption of more extensive relations.

How would such an approach have fared in the past? A policy of containment would have prevented war in 1792 and averted the various interventions in Soviet Russia in 1918–21. Containment proved to be an effective long-term response to the Bolshevik Revolution, and Iraq would have been far better off had it refrained from attacking Iran in 1980 and concentrated on building barriers to Iranian expansion in league with the other gulf states. Sino-American relations would almost certainly have been less acrimonious if the two states could have avoided a direct clash in Korea, and the absence of war after the American, Turkish, and Mexican revolutions undoubtedly facilitated their rapid reemergence as accepted members of international society.

Finally, the misperceptions found in virtually all of these cases highlight the importance of obtaining accurate information in postrevolutionary situations, as well as the difficulty of doing so. For example, foreign powers need to know if they are dealing with a mass revolution from below, inspired and directed by a universalist ideology, or an elite revolution with more limited aims. Therefore, they should devote much effort to maintaining reliable channels of communication with the new regime, even in the face of considerable hostility or resistance. National leaders should also recognize that much of the information they obtain will be biased, especially when it comes from members of the old regime. Among other things, foreign governments should go to great lengths to avoid breaking relations so they retain some capacity to monitor events and communicate with the new leaders.

## THE REVOLUTIONS OF 1989–1992 AND THE PROSPECTS FOR PEACE

What does balance-of-threat theory tell us about the international implications of the revolutionary transformation of the former Soviet empire?

Let us begin by making an obvious distinction: the rapid collapse of the Communist governments in Eastern Europe demonstrates that contagion can occur, under certain circumstances. This exception to our rule is not as damning as it first appears, however, for two reasons. First, the regimes that were overturned by the "velvet revolutions" were artificial creations to begin with, and the catalyst for their overthrow was the recognition that Moscow was no longer willing to enforce orthodoxy within the Warsaw Pact.[15] Second, the contagion observed in Eastern Europe did not arise from

[15] Gorbachev's reforms in effect lowered the expected cost of resistance to the existing Communist governments, thereby facilitating collective mobilization against them.

a revolutionary state's efforts to export its own universalist principles; rather, the revolutions were essentially nationalist revolts *against* the universalist hegemony of the Communist Party of the Soviet Union. Thus, where nationalism is ordinarily an obstacle to contagion, it facilitated the spread of revolution in this particular case. This nationalism, together with the unusual features of well-established social networks and relatively high levels of communication, made possible a rapid and nearly bloodless transformation.[16]

As for its international implications, happily, the revolutions in the former Soviet empire are unlikely to spark intense security competition among the great powers, and certainly not to the degree observed after earlier revolutions. Like other revolutions, the collapse of the Soviet Union has caused a major shift in the global balance of power and led to the creation of a series of new regimes whose principles and objectives are dramatically different from those of their predecessors. Yet the other great powers have not tried to exploit or reverse these developments through the use of military power. The United States did take advantage of Russian weakness to obtain favorable concessions on arms control and several other issues; Germany seized this opportunity to reunite; the various constituent republics took the occasion to obtain their independence; and a number of foreign powers have begun to compete for economic advantage in the former Soviet bloc.[17] In a sense, therefore, other states did see the Soviet collapse as a chance to enhance their own positions. Unlike the other revolutions considered in this book, however, the collapse of Communism has not led to increased security competition either among the other great powers or between the new regimes and the outside world.

From the perspective of balance-of-threat theory, there are at least five reasons why the international consequences of the revolutions of 1989 have been comparatively benign. First, the collapse of the Soviet empire was not the result of a mass revolution. For the most part, it did not involve replacing the old elite with new leaders drawn from a different group or class. Instead, the upheaval began with a "revolution" in the minds of key members of the Soviet elite, many of whom still (or again) hold influential positions in the new order. Like the Nationalist revolution in Turkey, in short, the collapse of the Soviet Union began as an elite revolution intended to transform

---

[16] For an intriguing theoretical analysis of these dynamics, see Susanne Lohmann, "The Dynamics of Informational Cascades: The Monday Demonstrations in East Leipzig, 1989–91," *World Politics* 47, no. 1 (1994). On the question whether these events were "true" revolutions, see Charles Tilly, *European Revolutions, 1492–1992* (Oxford: Basil Blackwell, 1993), 233–35.

[17] By linking economic concessions to nuclear weapons policy, the United States was able to persuade Belarus, Kazakhstan, and Ukraine to give up the weapons they had inherited when the Soviet Union broke up.

both the internal workings of the state and its relations with the outside world.[18] As discussed in chapters 2 and 6, elite revolutions tend to be less dangerous than mass revolutions, in part because the ideologies that inform them rarely pose a direct threat to other states.

The second reason, which follows from the first, is that the revolution in the former Soviet Union and its satellites was conducted by elites who sought to abandon the *existing* revolutionary legacy of Marxism-Leninism in favor of the political and economic models that had proven so successful in the West. In other words, the events of 1989–92 were a revolution *against* a revolutionary state. Instead of bringing to power a movement whose founding principles were at odds with political institutions prevailing in the other great powers, the revolutions of 1989–92 created a set of states whose principles and intentions are for the most part compatible with the existing order. Though specific conflicts of interest do exist, the potential for spiraling is significantly reduced by the absence of a Manichean ideology that portrays others as intrinsically evil or aggressive. It is hardly surprising, then, that the level of conflict is low between the new regimes and the outside world.

Third, relations between Russia and the rest of the world continue to be governed by a strong condition of defense dominance, which further reduces the level of security competition. In addition to the presence of nuclear weapons on each side (which creates a powerful defensive advantage through deterrence and dampens the impact of shifts in the balance of power), the absence of significant ideological conflict enhances security by eliminating the fear of contagion or counterrevolution. Unlike in previous revolutions, neither side need fear that its rule will be undermined by the spread of potentially corrosive ideas.

Fourth, access to information about events in Eastern Europe has been much more extensive than in the cases examined in this book. Rapid changes inevitably introduce greater uncertainty, but foreign powers have maintained their diplomatic connections, and the collapse of the secretive Soviet regime has actually facilitated the ability of other states to monitor events there. Thus, the danger of miscalculation is probably lower than in past revolutions.

Finally, the dissolution of the Soviet empire occurred in extremely favorable international circumstances. If competition among the other great powers is especially intense when a revolution occurs (as it was in the 1790s and

---

[18] The predominant role of former members of the Communist elite is documented in Karen Dawisha and Bruce Parrott, *Russia and the New Nations of Eurasia: The Politics of Upheaval* (Cambridge: Cambridge University Press, 1994), app. B. On the "new thinking" that inspired these reforms, see Thomas Risse-Kappen, "Ideas Do Not Float Freely: Transnational Coalitions, Domestic Structures, and the End of the Cold War," *International Organization* 48, no. 2 (1994).

in 1917, for example), they will be strongly inclined to seek gains for themselves and to deny potential gains to others. By the time the Soviet Union disintegrated, however, most of the other great powers had been close political and military allies for nearly four decades. Because these states did not regard each other as potential security threats, the normal concern with relative position was muted. Instead of debating whether or not to intervene—as great powers did after every revolution we have examined—the Western powers have tried to support the new regimes by providing aid and advice. In addition, because the Cold War inhibited the development of extensive economic or political ties between East and West, foreign powers did not have major interests in the Soviet Union (unlike Britain and France in 1917 Russia or the United States in Iran, for example) and could take a more detached view of events there.

For all of these reasons, therefore, postrevolutionary relations between the former Soviet Union and the other major powers have been unusually tranquil. Circumstances continue to evolve rapidly, however, and relations could easily deteriorate if Russian elites become convinced that the West either is responsible for their plight or is taking excessive advantage of it.[19] This danger suggests that Western diplomacy must strike a balance between acknowledging the legitimate interests of the new Eurasian states (especially Russia) and turning a blind eye to internal abuses or resurgent expansionism. To date, however, the international consequences of the revolutions of 1989–92 have been uncharacteristically benign.

Unfortunately, relations *within* the former Soviet Union have been more conflictive, and for reasons that are consistent with balance-of-threat theory. First, the collapse of the USSR created an unstable and uncertain balance of power among the constituent republics (or between competing ethnic or national groups within them). As illustrated by the recent wars—between Armenia and Azerbaijan and between Russia and the breakaway province of Chechnya—uncertainties about the true balance of power can encourage both sides in such a dispute to go to war confident of success.[20]

---

[19] At the December 1994 summit of the Conference on Security and Cooperation in Europe, for example, Russian president Boris Yeltsin charged the West with "sowing the seeds of mistrust" and complained of excessive U.S. influence, saying that "it is a dangerous illusion to suppose that the destinies of continents . . . can somehow be managed from some single capital." "Yeltsin Says NATO Is Trying to Split Continent Again," *New York Times*, December 6, 1994, A1, A4.

[20] Although Azerbaijan had reason to believe it was stronger (its gross national product was roughly 60 percent bigger than Armenia's and its population and armed forces more than twice as large), the Armenians turned out to be far more capable on the battlefield. See *The Military Balance 1993–94* (London: International Institute of Strategic Studies, 1993). Similarly, the Chechens were extremely confident that they could defy Russian pressure despite the enormous odds against them, and their resistance was unexpectedly effective.

Second, just as revolutionary states usually adopt policies that differ from those of the old regime, the newly independent republics of the former Soviet Union are now free to pursue interests that were forgotten, suppressed, or irrelevant under Soviet domination. Thus, Ukraine has sought to regain control of Crimea; Armenia and Azerbaijan have fought over ethnic enclaves within their respective territories; and a number of ethnic and national groups have advanced claims for independence from their respective republics. Disputes over how to divide the assets of the former USSR have been frequent as well, and the Soviet legacy of interdependence has complicated matters by making each government's situation dependent on policies adopted elsewhere.[21] In short, where Western perceptions of Russian intentions have improved since the collapse of Communism, a number of former Soviet republics now view each other with considerable suspicion.

Third, because the newly independent republics face the same problems of legitimacy and order that revolutionary states often confront, the temptation to mobilize support by invoking nationalism has been difficult to resist. Unfortunately, such efforts often involve playing up both real and imagined grievances against others, and because different groups within the former Soviet Union are now free to teach their own versions of history, the danger has increased that past quarrels will fuel future conflicts.[22] Needless to say, these are ideal conditions for spiraling. When conflicts of interest arise, each side will be more likely to see its own actions as entirely justified while viewing the actions of others as unwarranted aggression.

These problems will be compounded by the intermingling of ethnic or national groups within and across existing political boundaries, which creates the possibility that isolated ethnic minorities will see themselves as vulnerable to persecution by majorities who regard them as potentially disloyal "fifth columns."[23] When national or ethnic groups are scattered within different political units, one community may worry that a nationalist resurgence in another republic could trigger a sympathetic response from conationals within its own borders. Thus, nationalist ideologies can create fears of contagion similar to those produced by a transnational revolutionary ideology.

A final source of conflict is Russia's growing effort to reassert its influence within the "near abroad," either to protect ethnic Russian populations, to re-

---

[21] See Dawisha and Parrott, *Russia and the New States of Eurasia*, 197–98.

[22] On this general phenomenon, see Van Evera, *Causes of War*, vol. 2: *National Misperceptions and the Roots of War* (Ithaca: Cornell University Press, forthcoming), chap. 11; and E. H. Dance, *History the Betrayer: A Study in Bias* (London: Hutchinson, 1960).

[23] See Barry Posen, "The Security Dilemma and Ethnic Conflict," *Survival* 35, no. 1 (1993); and Stephen Van Evera, "Managing the Eastern Crisis: Preventing War in the Former Soviet Empire," *Security Studies* 1, no. 1 (1992); and "Hypotheses on Nationalism and War," *International Security* 18, no. 4 (1994).

tain access to valuable resources, or to stabilize the situation along its lengthy border.[24] Increased Russian influence might deter or dampen violence in those areas in the long run, but its immediate impact has been to alarm its neighbors and to reawaken Western concerns. Relations within the former Soviet Union and relations with other powers are thus inextricably linked, and it will be much more difficult for Russia to maintain amicable relations with the rest of the world if the level of conflict within its former empire is on the rise.

In sum, relations among the newly independent states of Eurasia are characterized by uncertain balances of power, serious conflicts of interest, exaggerated perceptions of hostility, and fears of nationalist contagion. Not surprisingly, therefore, relations within the former Soviet Union have been (and are likely to remain) much less tranquil than relations between Russia and the other major powers.

Thus, balance-of-threat theory does shed light on the likely consquences of the Soviet collapse and helps identify where the probable axes of conflict will be found. These events also underscore the value of a systemic approach, as the absence of great-power conflict in their aftermath is not due solely to the character of the new regimes: it is also due to the benign international context in which the collapse of the Soviet empire took place and the fact the the "revolutions" of 1989–92 brought these regimes into greater ideological conformity with the West. Therefore, the events of 1989–92 reinforce a central contention of this entire book: one cannot understand the international implications of revolutionary change by looking solely at the revolutionary state; one must also consider the configurations of power and interest in the system as a whole.

THE FUTURE OF REVOLUTION

For some writers, the grand ideological struggles that have rent modern society for nearly four centuries are now fading away, to be replaced by more limited (and for the most part, peaceful) disputes over national interests and an increasingly tranquil world order. This perspective sees mass revolution as inextricably linked to the process of modernization—to the spread of market forces and the transition from hierarchical forms of government to political orders based on equality, mass participation, and individual rights. With the collapse of Communism and the apparent triumph of modern liberal capitalism, so the argument runs, the great ideological

[24] See Alexei G. Arbatov, "Russian Foreign Policy Priorities for the 1990s," in *Russian Security after the Cold War: Seven Views from Moscow,* ed. Teresa Pelton Johnson and Steven E. Miller (Cambridge, Mass.: Center for Science and International Affairs, 1994), 13–20; and Vladimir P. Lukin, "Our Security Predicament," *Foreign Policy* 88 (fall 1992).

struggles of the past are behind us and humankind has reached the "end of history."[25] If this view is correct, then my theory explains a phenomenon that may not trouble us any longer. It might be correct but irrelevant, and the lessons drawn from this study of little enduring value.

Because revolutions are so dangerous and destructive, we might prefer a world in which Marx's "locomotive of history" no longer ran. Unfortunately, there are good reasons to question this optimistic expectation.

First, even if mass revolution were strictly a modern phenomenon, the process of modernization is not yet complete. A mass revolution may be unlikely in any of the advanced industrial powers, but it remains a possibility in many other parts of the world. The Iranian Revolution occurred less than two decades ago (a rather short period by historical standards), and it takes little imagination to see revolutionary potential in places such as Egypt, India, Pakistan, China, parts of Latin America, and much of sub-Saharan Africa. The collapse of Communism may have discredited Marxism, but other alternatives—ranging from liberalism to radical nationalism to religious fundamentalism—are available to take its place.

Second, the belief that the current hegemony of liberal capitalism will bring an end to ideological conflicts and eliminate the allure of revolutionary transformation overlooks several matters: the possibility of unintended consequences, the alienating effects of liberal capitalism itself, and the human capacity to create new and appealing visions of a preferable social order. As Kenneth Jowitt persuasively argues, all social orders alienate some of their members, and the amoral, acquisitive individualism of liberal capitalist society will create space for new ideologies emphasizing transcendant moral values and communitarian ideals. Instead of ideological homogeneity, therefore, Jowitt predicts that the end of the Cold War will foster a period of ideological ferment in which new ideologies arise to challenge the hegemony of liberal-capitalist individualism.[26]

Thus, the liberal-capitalist order may not always be seen as universally or eternally preferable, and it is too soon to dismiss the possibility that present discontents will foster the emergence of new dissident ideologies. Indeed, these possibilities are already evident in the rise of religious fundamentalism (whose underlying principles challenge liberalism's notions of tolerance), the growing pressure for cultural diversity (where lib-

---

[25] Exponents of this view include Francis Fukuyama, *The End of History and the Last Man* (New York: Basic Books, 1992); Theodore S. Hamerow, *From the Finland Station: The Graying of Revolution in the Twentieth Century* (New York: Basic Books, 1990); and John Mueller, *Retreat from Doomsday: The Obsolescence of Major War* (New York: Basic Books, 1989); and *Quiet Cataclysm: Reflections on the Recent Transformation of World Politics* (New York: HarperCollins, 1995).

[26] See Kenneth Jowitt, *New World Disorder: The Leninist Extinction* (Berkeley: University of California Press, 1991).

eralism's emphasis on *individual* rights confronts claims for the *collective* rights of particular groups), and the emergence of the Greens, the militia movement in America, or neo-fascism in Europe. My point is not that any of these movements will spawn the next great revolutionary ideology, but simply that new challengers will emerge, maybe sooner than we think. If their adherents achieve political power in some existing state—especially if through violent means—the dynamics I have identified are likely to come into play. Indeed, the scope and speed of mass communications could make it easier for dissident social movements to spread their principles across existing borders and amplify the normal fear of contagion. Instead of a relatively stable world of well-ordered national states, in short, we may be entering a period of renewed ideological ferment and increased transnational turbulence.[27]

If this argument is correct, then we are unlikely to enjoy the tranquility of a world in which violent revolution is a thing of the past. Armed with a better understanding of the connection between revolution and war, however, we may still avoid some of the tragic results of earlier revolutions. That hope is both the purpose and the paradox of social science: by gaining a better grasp of the causal forces that shape social phenomena, we may be able to manipulate them so as to render our own theories invalid. Given the regrettable international consequences that accompany most revolutions, that would be a small price to pay.

[27] See Sidney Tarrow, *Power in Movement: Social Movements, Collective Action, and Politics* (Cambridge: Cambridge University Press, 1994), 193–98. Tarrow also suggests that the impact of these movements may "first be ferocious, uncontrolled, and widely diffused, but later ephemeral."

[351]

# Index

Abadan, 241
Abercrombie, Ralph, 116n
accommodation, 2, 204, 342; American revolu-
    tion and, 281; by England of Soviet Union,
    176, 178; Iranian revolution and, 256, 259;
    Mexican revolution and, 296; Russian civil
    war and, 158–60, 163–64, 203–4, 207
Acheson, Dean, 35, 313, 315–18, 322
Adams, John, 271n, 276–77, 285n, 329
Adams, John Quincy, 285n
Afghanistan. *See* Soviet Union
Africa, sub-Saharan, 350
Aland Islands, 167
Albania, 300
Algeria, Islamic Salvation Front in, 247, 248n.
    *See also* Iranian revolution
Algiers accord, 238
Allende, Salvador, 336n
Alsace, 56, 60, 63, 69, 120
Amal, 249
Amanullah, Emir, 180–81
American Independence, War of, 269–71, 280,
    283; France and, 47, 53
American revolution, 13n, 16, 269–87, 310, 327,
    330, 337n, 344; Barbary states and, 280, 284;
    comparison with other revolutions, 283, 287;
    Continental Congress of, 270; England and,
    270–72, 280, 327–28, 332; Founding Fathers
    and, 270, 271n, 281–83, 285–86; France and,
    270–71, 280, 327–28, 332; Indian tribes and,
    271, 284; Latin America and, 281; Model
    Treaty and, 270, 283; Spain and, 270–71, 280.
    *See also* American Independence, War of;
    United States
Amiens, 117
Amiens, Peace of, 278
al-Amin, Sayyid Ibrahim, 245

Amur, 152
Anatolia, 299–303, 307
Anglo-French convention, 150
Anglo-Persian treaty (1919), 179–80
Anglo-Russian Convention of 1907, 179
Anglo-Soviet trade agreement (1921), 175–79,
    188, 195, 204
Angola, 336n
Ankara, 306
Antoinette, Marie, 58, 96
Arbenz, Jacobo, 35, 336n
Archangel, 134, 136–37, 141, 146
Armenia, 166, 182, 301, 304, 329, 347–48
Armstrong, David, 7
Articles of Confederation, 271–72, 283
Artois, comte d', 54, 58, 61n, 64. *See also* Louis
    XVIII
al-Assad, Hafez, 249
Auckland, Lord. *See* William Eden
Austria: mobilization of forces (1792), 72; for-
    mal convention with Prussia (1791), 63, 65;
    and War of the First Coalition, 72, 74–75,
    77–78, 80, 82, 89–91, 96–97, 101, 104–8; and
    War of the Second Coalition, 110–11, 113–14,
    117. *See also specific revolutions*
Austria-Hungary, 154, 300
Austrian Netherlands, 71, 74–75, 80, 119
Austro-Prussian alliance, 70, 73, 120
Avignon, 56, 60, 70
Azerbaijan, 166, 180, 182, 304, 347–48
Aziz, Tariq, 239

Baath regime, 237–39, 261
Babeuf, François-Noel (Gracchus), 109n
Baden, 89
Bahonar, Muhammed, 217
Bahrain, 244, 261

*Index*